Constraining the Court

Law and Society Series
W. Wesley Pue, Founding Editor

We pay tribute to the late Wes Pue, under whose broad vision, extraordinary leadership, and unwavering commitment to socio-legal studies our Law and Society Series was established and rose to prominence.

The Law and Society Series explores law as a socially embedded phenomenon. It is premised on the understanding that the conventional division of law from society creates false dichotomies in thinking, scholarship, educational practice, and social life. Books in the series treat law and society as mutually constitutive and seek to bridge scholarship emerging from interdisciplinary engagement of law with disciplines such as politics, social theory, history, political economy, and gender studies.

Recent books in the series:

Mandi Gray, *Suing for Silence: Sexual Violence and Defamation Law* (2024)
Azar Masoumi, *Refugees Are (Not) Welcome Here: The Paradox of Protection in Canada* (2023)
Jonathan Swainger, *The Notorious Georges: Crime and Community in British Columbia's Northern Interior, 1909–25* (2023)
Emilie Biland, translated by Annelies Fryberger and Miranda Richmond Mouillot, *Family Law in Action: Divorce and Inequality in Quebec and France* (2023)
Kate Puddister and Emmett Macfarlane, eds., *Constitutional Crossroads: Reflections on Charter Rights, Reconciliation, and Change* (2022)
Derek Silva and Liam Kennedy, eds., *Power Played: A Critical Criminology of Sport* (2022)
Erez Aloni and Régine Tremblay, eds., *House Rules: Changing Families, Evolving Norms, and the Role of the Law* (2022)
Florence Ashley, *Banning Transgender Conversion Practices: A Legal and Policy Analysis* (2022)
Dia Dabby, *Religious Diversity in Canadian Public Schools: Rethinking the Role of Law* (2022)
Kim Stanton, *Reconciling Truths: Reimagining Public Inquiries in Canada* (2021)

For a complete list of the titles in the series, see the UBC Press website, www.ubcpress.ca.

Constraining the Court

Judicial Power and Policy Implementation
in the Charter Era

James B. Kelly

UBCPress · Vancouver

© UBC Press 2024

All rights reserved. No part of this publication may be reproduced, stored in a retrieval system, or transmitted, in any form or by any means, without prior written permission of the publisher, or, in Canada, in the case of photocopying or other reprographic copying, a licence from Access Copyright, www.accesscopyright.ca.

Printed in Canada on FSC-certified ancient-forest-free paper (100% post-consumer recycled) that is processed chlorine- and acid-free.

UBC Press is a Benetech Global Certified Accessible™ publisher. The epub version of this book meets stringent accessibility standards, ensuring it is available to people with diverse needs.

Library and Archives Canada Cataloguing in Publication

Title: Constraining the court: judicial power and policy implementation in the Charter era / James B. Kelly.
Names: Kelly, James B. (James Bernard), author.
Series: Law and society series (Vancouver, B.C.)
Description: Series statement: Law and society series | Includes bibliographical references and index.
Identifiers: Canadiana (print) 20240316223 | Canadiana (ebook) 20240316290 | ISBN 9780774870474 (hardcover) | ISBN 9780774870481 (softcover) | ISBN 9780774870504 (EPUB) | ISBN 9780774870498 (PDF)
Subjects: LCSH: Judicial power – Canada – Cases. | LCSH: Judicial review – Canada – Cases. | LCSH: Political questions and judicial power – Canada – Cases. | LCSH: Federal government – Canada. | LCSH: Canada. Supreme Court. | LCSH: Canada. Canadian Charter of Rights and Freedoms. | LCSH: Canada – Social policy.
Classification: LCC KE4775 .K45 2024 | DDC 347.71/012 – dc23

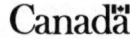

UBC Press gratefully acknowledges the financial support for our publishing program of the Government of Canada, the Canada Council for the Arts, and the British Columbia Arts Council.

This book has been published with the help of a grant from the Canadian Federation for the Humanities and Social Sciences, through the Scholarly Book Awards, using funds provided by the Social Sciences and Humanities Research Council of Canada.

UBC Press is situated on the traditional, ancestral, and unceded territory of the xʷməθkʷəy̓əm (Musqueam) people. This land has always been a place of learning for the xʷməθkʷəy̓əm, who have passed on their culture, history, and traditions for millennia, from one generation to the next.

UBC Press
The University of British Columbia
www.ubcpress.ca

This book is dedicated to
Michèle, Fiona, Liam, Suzanne, and Oona

Contents

List of Figures and Tables / ix

Acknowledgments / xi

List of Abbreviations / xiv

Introduction: Constraining the Court / 3

1 Judicial Power and Policy Implementation in the Charter Era / 20

2 Quebec and the *Canadian Charter of Rights and Freedoms: Une province pas comme les autres* / 50

3 Minority Language Education Rights and the *Charter of the French Language: Plus ça change, plus c'est la même chose* / 74

4 Bridging Schools and the "Major Part Requirement": Designing and Implementing the 2010 *Charter of the French Language* / 102

5 Quebec's "Sign Law" and Freedom of Expression: *Ford, Devine,* and the Bourassa Government's Response / 142

6 Supervised Consumption Sites and the *Respect for Communities Act*: How the Harper Government Outflanked the McLachlin Court / 170

7 The Opioid Crisis and Canadian Federalism: Supervised Consumption to Overdose Prevention Sites / 206

8 Physician-assisted Suicide to Medical Assistance in Dying: When *Carter* Met Federalism / 248

Conclusion: Legislative Disagreements and Policy Implementation in the Charter Era / 293

Appendix: Remedial Activism, 1982–2022 (Statutes, Ministerial Discretion, and Administrative Decisions) / 302

Notes / 312

Bibliography / 369

Index / 405

Figures and Tables

Figures

3.1 Anglophone interprovincial migration, 1971–2016 / 92
3.2 School enrollment trends in Quebec as a baseline / 93
3.3 Attendance in English schools by language group in Quebec, 1971–2018 / 94
3.4 School enrollments in Quebec by language of instruction, 1971–2022 / 95
3.5 Interprovincial migration and immigration to Quebec, 1971–2018 / 96
3.6 Certificates of eligibility issued under section 73 of the *Charter of the French Language*, 1977–2013 / 98
4.1 Two approaches to section 73 and the MPR / 109
4.2 Categories of unsubsidized private schools in Quebec, 2010–22 / 127
4.3 Certificates of eligibility and Bill 115: 2010 *Charter of the French Language*, 2010–16 / 138
6.1 Preamble to Bill C-2, *Respect for Communities Act* / 192
8.1 MAiD deaths in Canada, 2016–21 / 286
8.2 MAiD deaths by setting, 2019–21 / 287

Tables

1.1 Judicial remedies by the Supreme Court of Canada, 1982–2022 / 35
1.2 Legislative disagreements, issue salience, and implementation context / 44
2.1 Statutory invalidation by decision type, 1982–2022 / 52
2.2 Quebec statutes and administrative decisions invalidated, 1982–2022 / 58
2.3 The *Charter of the French Language* and the *Canadian Charter* / 70
3.1 A comparison of the Quebec clause (1977 and 1984) and the Canada clause / 82
3.2 Quebec's response to *Protestant School Boards*, [1984] 2 SCR 66 / 90
4.1 The Charest government's responses to *Solski* and *Nguyen* / 116
4.2 Division 1: Schooling: weighted scores for attendance at Type A, B, and C English-language institutions / 124
4.3 Division 2: Consistent, true commitment: Changes or inconsistencies in terms of the language of instruction during the schooling invoked in support of the eligibility request / 129
4.4 Division 2: Continued commitment, changes, or inconsistencies in siblings' school attendance / 130
4.5 Viable Type A English language institutions, 2020–21: Class size and tuition fees / 133
5.1 Responding to *Ford* and *Devine:* 1988 *Charter of the French Language* and the Notwithstanding Clause / 154
5.2 Five years after *Ford* and *Devine:* A comparison of Bill 178, *Charter of the French Language* 1988 and Bill 86, *Charter of the French Language* 1993 / 160
7.1 Key legislative changes: From Bill C-2, *Respect for Communities Act* (Harper) to Bill C-37, *Act to Amend the CDSA* (Trudeau) / 222
7.2 Supervised consumption sites review: UCP's terms of reference / 237

Acknowledgments

This project was funded by the Social Sciences and Research Council of Canada (SSHRC), and I would like to thank the SSHRC for their continued support. Randy Schmidt at UBC Press was, once again, a wonderful editor, and I want to thank him for his support on this project and the previous two. This manuscript benefited from a careful reading by the anonymous reviewers. Thanks for your helpful suggestions and constructive feedback. I really appreciate it. Thanks also to Melissa Pitts, Megan Brand, and the Publications Board at UBC Press for their support. Copyediting was performed by Stacy Belden, and I want to also extend my appreciation to you for improving the text. Several research assistants contributed to this project – Dónal Gill, Samira Manfon, and Jordano Nudo – and deserve thanks. Like my other books, the ideas were first presented as lectures at Concordia University, and I want to thank the students in my undergraduate and graduate courses on judicial politics for their attention and feedback. Near the end of the writing process, I taught an intensive course at Bar-Ilan University in Ramat Gan, Israel, in May 2022, where I presented the manuscript in its entirely as a visiting professor at the Faculty of Law. I would like to thank the students in the Bar-Ilan seminar for their feedback as well as my dear friend, and faculty sponsor at Bar-Ilan University, Ittai Bar-Siman-Tov.

Richard J. Schultz read the entire manuscript and provided valuable feedback, both on and off the golf course. Thanks for your mentorship and friendship the past thirty years. Special thanks to my wife Michèle, and our children Fiona and Liam. Michèle and the kids are the happiest that this book is finished, no longer having to listen to me go on and on about sign laws, English language instruction in Quebec, supervised consumption sites, medical assistance in dying, the *Canadian Charter of Rights and Freedoms* (*Canadian Charter*), and the Supreme Court of Canada.[1] Thanks also to our dog, Oona, who kept me company while I wrote this book in the basement and always seemed interested when I read the manuscript out loud.

Commercial Expression and a Space Ranger
My interest in the question of the policy impact of judicial decisions began in a toy store in the Ville LaSalle district of Montreal in 2012. When my children were small, my mother, who was living in Ontario, sent them a Sheriff Woody doll from the character in *Toy Story* voiced by Tom Hanks. If they pulled a string on his back, Woody said their favourite expressions from *Toy Story*. I went to buy them Buzz Lightyear in Montreal so that Tim Allen, who voiced the character, could say their favourite catchphrases when a button was pushed on his jet pack. All of the Sheriff Woodys and Buzz Lightyears were packaged exclusively in French and said their catchphrases only in French. Although my children are fluently bilingual and educated in the French system, they just wanted to hear Buzz Lightyear say "To infinity ... and beyond!" and not "Vers l'infini ... et au-delà!"[2] I asked the clerk whether there was a feature on Buzz Lightyear where I could reset his memory settings and change his language from French to English. This, I explained to the clerk, happened in *Toy Story 3* when Woody and Andy's toys accidentally changed Buzz's language setting to Spanish. I had, without a doubt, crossed the parental Rubicon.

The clerk explained that under section 54 of Bill 101, *Charter of the French Language*, they could not sell a Buzz Lightyear with a "non-French vocabulary."[3] Whether this was an accurate understanding of the *Charter of the French Language*, I do not know, but I could only find Buzz L'Éclair and Shérif Woody in Montreal, and so my mom sent Buzz Lightyear from Ontario. As an academic, I figured that as trademarked products of Disney, Woody and Buzz would be protected under *Ford v Quebec* and the *Irwin Toy* decisions, as their speech was commercial expression.[4] I do not mean that Woody and Buzz have freedom of expression – each time my children pulled Woody's string or pushed the button on Buzz's jet pack, it was compelled expression (and potentially conscripted evidence under section 24(2) if Sheriff Woody questioned Buzz in disregard to his Charter right against self-incrimination!). But as licensed products of the Walt Disney Company, surely their "non-French vocabulary" constituted commercial expression protected under section 2(b) of the *Canadian Charter*? As the Supreme Court of Canada noted in *Ford* and *Devine*, compelled commercial expression was incompatible with freedom of expression and did not constitute a reasonable limitation under section 1 of the *Canadian Charter* or the Quebec *Charter of Human Rights and Freedoms*.[5] This episode about prohibitions on toys with "non-French vocabularies" led me to the core issue considered in this study – the policy impact of judicial decisions or, more accurately, the conditions under which judicial decisions have limited policy impact and lack fulsome implementation. And this is where this book's journey began – in a toy store in Montreal, acting out a scene from *Toy Story 3* between Woody, Andy's toys, and Buzz Lightyear, in Spanish – *Salir de la etapa derecho*.[6]

Abbreviations

ATQ	Administrative Tribunal of Quebec
BNA Act	*British North America Act*
CAQ	Coalition Avenir Québec
CBSA	Canadian Border Services Agency
CCP	Court Challenges Program
CDSA	*Controlled Drugs and Substances Act*
CEGEP	Collège d'enseignement général et professionnel (General and Vocational College)
CHA	*Canada Health Act*
COPE	Coalition of Progressive Electors
COVID-19	2019 coronavirus
CTS	consumption and treatment services
DTES	Downtown Eastside of Vancouver
EAC	Expert Advisory Committee
HESA	Standing Committee on Health
IRPA	Individual Rights Protection Act
JUST	Standing Committee on Justice and Human Rights
LCJC	Standing Senate Committee on Legal and Constitutional Affairs

MAiD	medical assistance in dying
MP	member of parliament
MPR	major part requirement
Non-RFND	non-reasonable foreseeability of natural death (MAiD)
NDP	New Democratic Party
NPA	non-partisan association
OPS	overdose prevention sites
PC	Progressive Conservative
PHS	Portland Hotel Society
PDAM	Special Joint Committee on Physician-Assisted Dying
RFND	reasonable foreseeability of natural death (MAiD)
RPA	regime politics approach
SCS	supervised consumption sites
SECU	Standing Committee on Public Safety and National Security
TAC	therapeutic abortion committee
UCP	United Conservative Part of Alberta
VANDU	Vancouver Area Network of Drug Users
VCHA	Vancouver Coastal Health Authority
VPD	Vancouver Police Department

Constraining the Court

Introduction
Constraining the Court

Activist judicial decisions have force. They have profile. And they command the constitutional moment when the highest court invalidates a statute. But do they always have policy impact? These are the core issues considered in this study that considers the interplay between judicial review, judicial invalidation, substantive public policy, and legislative disagreements in the Charter era.[1] I attempt to understand judicial impact and policy implementation by asking the following questions. Do Parliament and the provincial and territorial legislatures fully implement the Supreme Court of Canada's rulings? How much discretion do governments retain when framing their responses? Has judicial power and policy impact in the Charter era been overstated? What role does federalism play in the implementation puzzle that confronts a judicial decision? Is the notwithstanding clause the only way to confront the Court when a government disagrees with the Supreme Court of Canada? And, finally, perhaps Charter dialogue theory is not such a good theory after all?[2]

This book is a study of the framing and implementation of public policy in the wake of statutory invalidation involving significant issues of public policy – Bill 101, *Charter of the French Language,* supervised consumption sites, abortion, and medical assistance in dying.[3] It seeks to understand what happens after a statute is declared unconstitutional by the Supreme Court of Canada as incompatible with the *Canadian Charter of Rights and Freedoms (Canadian Charter)* and, in the case of Quebec, the Quebec *Charter of Human*

*Rights and Freedoms (Quebec Charter).*⁴ While it considers the nature of a judicial ruling, and the remedy employed under section 24(1) of the *Canadian Charter*, it focuses on tasks that are the domain of Parliament, the provincial legislatures, and the territorial assemblies: designing legislation in response to judicial invalidation and implementing legislative responses by public and private actors within a federal system. As such, it contributes to an emerging body of political science scholarship that looks beyond legal mobilization and judicial invalidation and seeks to understand the policy impact of judicial decisions.⁵ It is a book about the governments and societies of Canadian federalism and their responses to judicial invalidation in a post-Charter policy environment.⁶

As I argue throughout this book, the preoccupation with the judicial function within legal scholarship has overshadowed a consideration that is of critical importance to the study of judicial politics in Canada – how governments react to judicial invalidation in their core areas of responsibility. While the Court's importance cannot be denied, the policy impacts of its decisions can be – and have been – overstated. A judicial decision does not determine a policy outcome. Whether Charter dialogue causes or influences the legislative response to judicial invalidation is open to dispute. While the Court can articulate the broad constitutional parameters that an issue of public policy operates within, as will be shown, once an issue of policy salience re-enters the political arena for legislative redesign, the Court is at the mercy of those actors charged with implementing its ruling.⁷

A complex set of factors exist that determine whether an activist judicial decision that invalidates a statute has – or does not have – policy impact. Simply put, the Supreme Court of Canada is an "implementer-dependent" institution, reliant on Parliament and the provincial and territorial assemblies to introduce legislative responses when the Court declares statutory provisions unconstitutional.⁸ Much can happen from invalidation to implementation in the Canadian federation, and the strongest judicial nullification and the most forceful judicial opinion can be tempered by the design and implementation phases of the legislative process. Judicial policy impact is shaped by federalism,⁹ the limited reach of a negative rights instrument, of which the *Canadian Charter* principally is, and the mix of public and private actors that respond to the new legislative environment that emerges in response to judicial invalidation. And because of federalism, complex implementation chains made up of public and private actors must implement any judicial decision that involves a salient issue of public policy. All of these factors confront – and may contain – judicial policy impact in important areas of public policy, as this book will demonstrate.

Notable examples of judicial power abound, particularly in regard to the Supreme Court of Canada and the Conservative government led by Stephen Harper,[10] though this is true of all governments since the patriation of the Constitution in 1982.[11] From the unsuccessful attempt at Senate reform,[12] to the Court declaring that Justice Marc Nadon's appointment as one of Quebec's three representatives on the Supreme Court of Canada was invalid,[13] and, finally, to the ill-fated effort to establish a national securities regulator, the Court blocked constitutional issues of critical importance to the Harper government.[14] The former Conservative government also experienced important setbacks via the *Canadian Charter*. From the Court's invalidation of *Criminal Code* provisions regulating prostitution in *Bedford*,[15] to granting Insite the legal ability to continue (at the time) as North America's only supervised consumption facility,[16] the Supreme Court of Canada regularly upended the Conservative government's law-and-order agenda.[17]

There is no doubt that the Court issued a powerful rebuke in the context of Insite and *PHS Community Services Society* when Chief Justice Beverley McLachlin chastised the Harper government, noting that "Insite saves lives. Its benefits have been proven. There has been no discernible negative impact on the public safety and health objectives of Canada during its eight years of operation."[18] This unprecedented reprimand continued when the chief justice granted an immediate, but temporary, exemption to Insite under section 56 of the *Controlled Drugs and Substances Act (CDSA)*: "There is therefore nothing to be gained (and much to be risked) in sending the matter back to the Minister for reconsideration."[19] The Court also established five broad criteria that the minister of health must employ when reviewing future applications for supervised consumption sites. These were strong, forceful statements – and actions – by the Supreme Court of Canada against an incumbent government.

What does this discussion of supervised consumption sites suggest about the Supreme Court of Canada in the Charter era? It shows the importance of legal mobilization and judicial review as instruments of agenda setting. Further, it demonstrates the ability of the Supreme Court of Canada to assume the statutory powers provided to the minister of health under section 56 of the *CDSA*. It also illustrates how the Court can structure, and perhaps determine, a legislative response when issuing policy instructions to Parliament through an expansive interpretation of section 24(1), one of two remedy clauses available to courts of "competent jurisdiction" under the *Canadian Charter*.[20] And, for the purposes of this book, it leaves the impression that Canada possesses the most powerful Supreme Court in the Commonwealth tradition[21] and, perhaps, in the world.[22]

This book challenges this narrative surrounding judicial power in the Charter era. The Supreme Court of Canada is powerful. There is no denying this. An institution that participates in the salient issues of public policy considered in this book, such as Quebec's *Charter of the French Language*, supervised consumption sites, abortion, and medical assistance in dying, is not without power or influence. Charter review provides the Supreme Court of Canada with the unique ability to engage in agenda setting. And it also allows the Court to strongly suggest legislative amendments that it considers necessary to ensure constitutionality in the future.[23] It also provides, as Christopher Manfredi demonstrated in the context of feminist legal mobilization,[24] and what Christopher Manfredi and Antonia Maioni observed in the context of health-care judicialization,[25] the momentum to sustain strategic litigation for groups that seek public policy outcomes via the judicial arena.[26]

Christopher Manfredi is correct that many significant invalidations during the Harper years involved statutes passed by previous governments, and there are no discernible differences in the record of invalidation experienced by the Harper government in comparison to all governments in the Charter era.[27] However, there is no denying that liberalizing access to prostitution, allowing for supervised consumption sites, and removing the legal restrictions on medical assistance in dying (MAiD) in *Carter v Canada*,[28] were unpopular with the Conservative government led by Stephen Harper.[29] How did the Harper government respond to these forceful judicial decisions? Did it accept the decisions and follow the Court's suggested policy frameworks? Or did it, like federal and provincial governments before and after it, actively pursue legislative strategies to contain the policy impact of judicial decisions in salient areas of public policy?

The forceful governmental responses introduced in light of these decisions – from the cumbersome application process for new supervised consumption sites contained in the *Respect for Communities Act*,[30] to the controversial response to *Bedford* and the regulation of sex work in the *Protection of Communities and Exploited Persons Act*,[31] to punting the issue of MAiD to an expert committee less than a year before the 2015 election[32] – suggest that the Conservative government rejected the Supreme Court of Canada's participation. In regard to MAiD, it is plausible to conclude that, if the Harper government had been re-elected in 2015, it would have amended the *Criminal Code* in a similar fashion to that of *PHS Community Services Society*, skating the boundary between compliance and non-compliance by creating a cumbersome administrative process that severally limited, if not denied, access to medical assistance for competent adults suffering grievous and irremediable conditions that wished to end their suffering. Indeed, it may have enacted a response like the one passed by the Trudeau government in 2016, Bill C-14, *Act on Medical Assistance in Dying* (2016 *Act on MAiD*), where a key provision was invalidated by the Superior Court of Quebec in October 2019.[33]

The above discussion, particularly the novel remedies employed by the Supreme Court of Canada under section 24(1) of the *Canadian Charter*, have led political scientists such as F.L. Morton and Rainer Knopff to conclude that the Supreme Court of Canada "now functions more like a *de facto* third chamber of the legislature than a court."[34] This sentiment was also expressed by Christopher Manfredi in his detailed study of the Supreme Court and liberal constitutionalism in the Charter era.[35] While I acknowledge the significant contributions made by these critics of the Supreme Court of Canada, their conclusions are open to dispute for a very specific reason. The Supreme Court of Canada, to invoke Dennis Baker's aptly named book, is not quite supreme.[36] The assumptions surrounding judicial power and the Charter focus largely on the functions available to the Supreme Court under the *Canadian Charter*, which are judicial review, judicial invalidation, and judicial remedy via section 24(1). These are, undoubtedly, the rawest manifestations of judicial power. But are they sufficient to evaluate Canadian constitutionalism, the power of the Supreme Court of Canada, and the policy resilience of our executive-dominated Parliament and provincial legislatures in the Charter era?

Governments across the party spectrum have given into the temptation to initiate forceful legislative responses when they disagree with the Supreme Court of Canada. This occurs when the policy stakes are high for an incumbent government, whether or not they passed the statute in question. There are no partisan differences when significant acts of Parliament or a legislature have been found wanting for their relationship to the *Canadian Charter* by the Supreme Court of Canada. Liberal governments have been as willing as Conservatives to contain judicial policy impact, as I found in an earlier study with Matthew Hennigar.[37] This dynamic also holds true at the provincial level. In the case of Quebec, the Parti Québécois, and the Parti libéral du Québec have been consistent in their responses to judicial invalidation of the *Charter of the French Language* despite the federalist-sovereigntist divide.

And, more recently, a more aggressive response to judicial power has emerged in Quebec under the Coalition Avenir Québec government, with a preemptive use of the notwithstanding clause to protect core policies from judicial remedy under section 24(1) of the *Canadian Charter*. Provincial and territorial governments have also decided whether to provide supervised consumption sites, despite the *Insite* decision, and whether to provide access to abortion as a medical service, despite *Morgentaler*.[38] The mere fact that governments retain the discretion of how to respond, and whether to provide access to a public service that informed a constitutional case, lays bare the implementation challenges facing any decision by the Supreme Court of Canada that invalidates a statute as inconsistent with the *Canadian Charter*.

Although the Liberal government led by Justin Trudeau has a propensity to voice both its respect for the Supreme Court of Canada and the *Canadian Charter*, it deviated from the clear instructions of the Supreme Court in its first handling of a Charter-required legislative response. By way of illustration, the Trudeau government's opening narrative was that it considered the Harper government's approach to the *Canadian Charter*, the Supreme Court of Canada, and, in particular, the treatment of McLachlin CJ to be wanting. In the mandate letter issued to Jody Wilson-Raybould, his first minister of justice, the prime minister signalled that his government would strike a more respectful tone and posture:

> I expect you to ensure that our initiatives respect the Constitution of Canada, court decisions, and are keeping with our proudest legal traditions. You are expected to ensure that the rights of Canadians are protected, that our work demonstrates the greatest possible need to respecting the Charter of Rights and Freedoms, and that our government seeks to fulfil policy goals with the least interference with the rights and privacy of Canadians as possible.[39]

In the lead up to the Trudeau government's first constitutional test, MAiD, this public commitment to the *Canadian Charter* and greater respect toward the Supreme Court of Canada was reinforced by then house leader Dominic LeBlanc. Normally, an issue such as MAiD would be considered a conscience issue, the party whip would be removed, and parliamentarians would be provided with the rarest opportunity in our parliamentary system – a free vote on a matter before the House of Commons. At first, LeBlanc informed the Liberal caucus that MAiD would be a whipped vote.[40] This was in keeping with the 2015 election manifesto that provided for free votes unless an issue involved the Liberal manifesto, a traditional matter of confidence, or "those that address our shared values and the protections guaranteed by the *Charter of Rights and Freedoms*."[41] In addition, because the Supreme Court of Canada had determined that MAiD was to be accessible for competent adults suffering a "grievous and irremediable medical condition that causes enduring and intolerable suffering,"[42] the house leader decided against a free vote on this issue of confidence because "at the end of the day, the Supreme Court has defined a right around the issue of assisted dying, and we will always be voting to uphold Charter rights."[43]

How did a commitment to the *Canadian Charter* and a respect for court rulings play out in the Trudeau government's handling of its first, and, to date, most significant, attempt to govern with the Charter in the context of a judicial invalidation? The mandate letter to the minister of justice, the 2015 election platform, and public statements by the house leader were meant to convey the idea that questionable legislative responses, such as the Harper government's *Respect for Communities Act* pertaining to supervised consumption sites, were a thing of the past. The Trudeau government acted like governments before it when faced with a compelling issue of public policy that was judicialized – it skated the boundary between compliance and non-compliance. The 2016 *Act on MAiD* departed from the Supreme Court of Canada's decision in a number of important respects, and a fulsome treatment is presented in Chapter 8.[44] The most significant was that individuals suffering from grievous and irremediable medical conditions must also satisfy the reasonably foreseeable of natural death requirement (RFND). As the Supreme Court of Canada's eligibility requirement did not specify the presence of a terminal illness, the RFND standard is a clear example of non-compliance with a core aspect of the *Carter* decision.

This RFND provision was so controversial, and considered to be inconsistent with the spirit of the *Carter* decision as well as being potentially unconstitutional, that the Senate refused to pass Bill C-14 in its original form,[45] returning it to the House of Commons with the end-of-life requirement removed.[46] Although the Trudeau government accepted several amendments approved by the Senate, it reinstated the RFND requirement before returning Bill C-14 to the Senate. Unsure whether it could thwart the will of the House of Commons once it was reasserted, the Senate acquiesced and approved Bill C-14 and the end-of-life requirement in June 2016. Carissima Mathen, among others, questioned whether Bill C-14 complied with *Carter* and satisfied the right to MAiD, as outlined by the Supreme Court of Canada: "Whether the government intends to frustrate the spirit of the *Carter* decision is a close question the answer to which must await the outcome of future litigation. But it is clear that the government elected to take a narrow approach which may prove to be constitutionally suspect."[47] The answer to this question was provided in October 2019 by Justice Christine Baudouin of the Quebec Superior Court. In *Truchon c Procureur général du Canada*, Baudouin J ruled that section 241.2(2)(d) of *Criminal Code*, an amendment included in the 2016 *Act on MAiD*, and Article 26(3) of Quebec's Bill 52, *Act Respecting End-of-Life Care*, were unconstitutional,[48] as they violated section 7 (right to life, liberty, and security of the person) and section 15 (equality rights) and were not considered a reasonable limit under section 1 of the *Canadian Charter*.[49] The decision was suspended for six months, and both the Trudeau and Legault governments chose not to appeal the decision.[50]

The apparent about-face on the issue of MAiD by the Trudeau government may be viewed as evidence that our governments ultimately comply with the Supreme Court of Canada and that judicial policy impact is a fact of life in the Charter era. Delayed compliance is compliance nonetheless and will provide fodder for the proponents of dialogue theory, such as Kent Roach,[51] and lend credence to Mark Tushnet's characterization of the *Canadian Charter* as exhibiting the tendencies of "strong-form" judicial review.[52] These may come to be the lessons of the Trudeau government's second attempt to comply with *Carter v Canada*. It does not, however, take away from the fact that the governments of Canadian federalism decide how to respond to judicial invalidation, when to respond, and whether to provide the public service that informed the constitutional challenge. We should not assume that compliance by Parliament and the legislatures, dominated by their respective cabinets,[53] is the default when the courts invalidate signature government policies or strike at the heart of federal and provincial legislative sovereignty. Moreover, we should not discount the importance of federalism and that the invalidation of a federal statute, as in the cases of *Morgentaler, PHS Community Services Society*, and *Carter*, places few, if any, constitutional obligations on the provincial governments to provide access to a medical service decriminalized through judicial invalidation.

Objectives and Scope

This book has a set number of objectives and a limited scope. First, it aims to demonstrate the conditions under which a government can limit the impact of judicial invalidation through the legislative design and implementation phases of public policy. Here, I explore the legislative agreement/

disagreement dichotomy and how a government's reaction to a judicial decision can determine whether a judicial decision will have observable policy impact. While this book prioritizes legislative disagreements – instances in which a government does not accept the policy direction of a court decision and seeks to minimize judicial impact through a legislative response – I do consider how important legislative agreement is for the ultimate implementation of a judicial decision.

To illustrate concrete examples of legislative disagreement and how they can limit judicial policy impact, this book considers judicial invalidation of the *Charter of the French Language* involving the "sign-law" provisions and restrictions on English public education, the issue of supervised consumption sites, and Bill C-14, 2016 *Act on MAiD*, and Bill C-7, *Act on Medical Assistance in Dying* (2021 *Act on MAiD*), the Trudeau government's first and second legislative responses to MAiD and the *Carter/Truchon* decisions.[54] MAiD also demonstrates the importance of legislative agreement and how provincial and territorial acceptance of this issue has resulted in widespread accessibility of this medical service by competent adults suffering grievous and irremediable medical conditions. Without provincial and territorial buy-in, or what I call legislative agreement, access to MAiD may have experienced the same accessibility issues that abortion services and supervised consumption sites have faced in many provinces and territories.

The second objective is to suggest that the impact of judicial review, despite the invalidation of a statute, may be rather modest because of the overriding trait of the *Canadian Charter* as principally, though not entirely, a negative rights instrument. Positive rights, such as the language rights provisions of the *Canadian Charter* (sections 16–23), require governments to provide a constitutionally mandated service. Under sections 16–22, the federal government and New Brunswick are required to accord French and English equal status, to allow the public to communicate with these governments in either official language, and to provide services in either official language (sections 16–22). Similarly, section 23 requires the provision of minority language education services by provincial governments to official language minority communities where numbers warrant. But these positive rights constitute a small part of judicial review involving the Canadian Charter of Rights, which has largely focused on the negative rights provisions such as section 7. In contrast, a negative rights instrument does not compel government action. It prohibits government interference. While the scope of judicial review may be broad in Canada, its reach is limited by a largely negative rights instrument that rarely places a positive constitutional obligation on governments to provide access to a public service.

The third objective is to consider the importance of federalism for understanding judicial impact and policy implementation. As this book demonstrates, the Supreme Court of Canada, as an "implementer-dependent" institution, relies on Parliament, the provincial legislatures, and the territorial assemblies to implement its rulings when salient issues of public policy are invalidated as being inconsistent with the *Canadian Charter*. Some policy issues chosen for investigation, such as the sign-law provisions and English language eligibility criteria of the *Charter of the French Language*, conform to the water-tight view of federalism and have simply required a legislative response from the National Assembly of Quebec. Others, such as supervised consumption sites and MAiD, function as a shared responsibility between the two orders of government and the devolved territorial assemblies in Canada. For instance, the federal government regulates these areas through the *Controlled Drugs and Substances Act* (supervised consumption sites) and the *Criminal Code* (MAiD).[55] However, the provinces and territories have responsibility for these health services. Thus, I seek to investigate the functioning of Canadian federalism and how complex implementation chains that comprise public and private actors in certain areas of public policy directly condition judicial policy impact.

In terms of scope, this book does not analyze all examples of judicial invalidation in the Charter era. Instead, I focus on a subset of cases that represent significant policy issues where constitutional invalidation creates the possibility of judicial policy impact. I refer to this subset as "salient issues" of public policy that result in a policy disagreement between courts and legislatures in the Charter era. As I argue below, not every judicial invalidation in the Charter era has involved a compelling issue of public policy, and, thus, we can generally expect legislative compliance when the policy stakes are low or a government's interest is marginal. It is the conditions that facilitate non-compliance or "strong-form" legislative responses to "strong-form" judicial review that is the focus of this book. Two factors are highlighted as they can limit, deflect, and blunt the policy impact of judicial review. These factors are the popularity of a judicial decision or its congruence with the policy preferences of the incumbent government[56] and the implementation context conditioned by federalism. In regard to the first consideration, is the judicial decision invalidating a statute popular with an incumbent government? Or, more correctly, is the decision unpopular with the very government that is required to implement the Court's ruling? Thus, I prioritize legislative disagreement as a necessary precondition for governments that seek to limit judicial policy impact.

The second consideration is the implementation context and the importance of federalism – is it straightforward, only requiring a legislative response by one order of government or is it complex, requiring Parliament to amend a statute such as the *Criminal Code* and dependent on (but not constitutionally required) that the provinces or territories provide access to a public service? As this book demonstrates, the implementation context becomes rather byzantine when a diversity of responses occurs at the provincial and territorial levels, which, in turn, is further complicated by a nexus of public and private actors with design and implementation responsibilities.[57] How federalism and devolution complicates judicial impact via the implementation context is an important consideration that I explore in this book. Federalism and devolution matter, plain and simple, to any understanding of judicial policy impact. This is evident when considering the difficulty in many provinces and territories in accessing abortion as a medical service or gaining access to supervised consumption sites, despite judicial victories in *Morgentaler* or *PHS Community Services Society*.

In *Worcester v Georgia*, the US Supreme Court, led by Chief Justice John Marshall, declared Georgia's criminal statute prohibiting non-native Americans from being on Native American lands without a state license unconstitutional. The celebrated quote by President Andrew Jackson, "John Marshall has made his decision; now let him enforce it,"[58] illustrates the implementation challenges that a judicial decision faces when it is opposed by an incumbent government. We can easily imagine former Prime Minister Stephen Harper making a similar remark about McLachlin CJ's decisions in *PHS Community Services Society* and that of "The Court" in *Carter* or, for that matter, former Quebec Premier Jean Charest in regard to the *Solski* and *Nguyen* decisions that invalidated sections of the *Charter of the French Language*. Several marquee legislative responses by the Harper, Trudeau, and Charest governments are Jacksonian in nature as they echo the sentiment of non-compliance. This highlights the strategic disadvantage of the Supreme Court of Canada in Charter politics, particularly when legislatures must implement judicial rulings.

One of the limitations of the judicial politics literature in Canada is the assumption that, short of invoking the notwithstanding clause, the decisions of the Supreme Court of Canada are final and adhered to. What does this mean from a public policy perspective? Does it require parliamentary acceptance of the policy implications of the decision? Clearly, the judicial decision is final, but the policy response is fluid and, given the right set of circumstances, may ultimately depart from the judicial decision. In his analysis of legislative responses to statutory invalidation by the Supreme Court of Canada, Emmett Macfarlane found, similar to earlier studies by Manfredi and Kelly,[59] that parliamentary compliance is the dominant characteristic of amendments passed in relation to statutory nullification.[60] We should not make too much of this finding, however. Not every statute declared unconstitutional by the Supreme Court of Canada involves a compelling issue of public policy, nor one in which an incumbent government is motivated to legislate against judicial nullification and reassert its jurisdictional autonomy.

The policy significance of a nullification is important, as F.L. Morton noted when he asked: "How many procedural nullifications of the federal Criminal Code does it take to equal nullification of Quebec's language-education policy?"[61] The reality is, as Manfredi, Kelly, and Macfarlane identify, that the governments of Canadian federalism generally accept judicial interpretation of statutes and do not challenge judicial nullification. Why? Because the vast majority do not involve salient issues of public policy in which an incumbent government has a strong policy attachment or political investment. This confirms Peter Russell's early prediction that Charter review would focus largely on criminal policy and not involve the core (and contested) areas of social policy via equality rights.[62]

The Importance of Legislative Disagreement

The issues chosen for analysis in this book represent important legislative disagreements in which governments are motivated to offset the policy implications of judicial nullification. Two of the issues – MAiD and supervised consumption injection sites – are complex policy issues that intertwine the constitutional responsibilities of the two orders of government as well as the devolved responsibilities of the territorial assemblies. Their complex implementation frameworks can mitigate the policy impact of judicial decisions, declaring provisions of the *Criminal Code* as well as the use of ministerial discretion in the *Controlled Drugs and Substances Act* unconstitutional. Several issues considered do conform to the division of powers and are of critical importance to incumbent governments, regardless of whether they enacted the statute invalidated by the Supreme Court.[63]

For instance, support for the *Charter of the French Language* transcends the party-political divide in Quebec, and all governments – federalist and sovereigntist – have condemned the invalidation of key provisions by the Supreme Court of Canada since 1982. Similarly, the Harper government did not enact the *Criminal Code* provisions prohibiting physician-assisted death that were invalidated in *Carter*, nor did it enact those provisions regulating prostitution that were invalidated in *Bedford*. However, it was invested in the issue of criminal policy reform[64] and reacted strongly against the policy direction established by the Court. As well, it was the government of Pierre Trudeau that enacted the *Criminal Code* provision regulating abortion that was invalidated by the Supreme Court during the Progressive Conservative government led by Brian Mulroney. Once motivated against judicial invalidation, the governments of Canadian federalism have demonstrated an impressive resilience, toughness, and a determination to avoid the short game by eschewing the notwithstanding clause, though this has changed with recent uses of the notwithstanding clause by provincial governments. Instead, governments have played the long game and defended their core policy priorities when legislating in response to judicial invalidation, which has not been fully appreciated in the Charter era.

The authority with which the Supreme Court of Canada speaks strongly influences whether the ministry retains some discretion when responding to judicial determinations of unconstitutionality. For instance, policy issues that divide the Court and produce narrow majority decisions, such as five-to-four judgments, can create the conditions for a legislative response that departs from the majority opinion. Indeed, a legislative response that reflects the minority opinion may survive future constitutional review when the composition of the Court changes in favour of the minority opinion. Thus, majority opinions provide some policy discretion to governments when designing statutory amendments to address judicial determinations of unconstitutionality.[65] As Mathen noted in the context of close majority decisions in cases dealing with sexual assault, "one possible lesson of *O'Connor* and *Mills* is that divided decisions allow the legislature to respond to the Court without precisely following a majority opinion."[66] In contrast, unanimous opinions by a highest appellant court, such as the Supreme Court of Canada, convey a different message for parliamentary actors – that the decision is final, authoritative, and without ambiguity and that future policy must conform to the constitutional boundaries established by the Court.[67]

In addition to policy salience and importance to an incumbent government, I have selected judicial decisions that, on the surface, appear to provide little or no room for a discretionary legislative response. Thus, I test the ability of the governments of Canadian federalism to offset judicial nullification, without invoking the notwithstanding clause, by analyzing the most difficult set of cases. The decisions considered see the Court speak with one voice,[68] releasing unanimous decisions authored by a single justice,[69] written by the chief justice on behalf of the Court[70] or unanimous opinions released in the name of "The Court."[71] As well, several of these unanimous judgments see the Court employ the remedy of judicial amendment under section 24(1) of the *Canadian Charter*, further narrowing the possibility of legislative disagreement, short of invoking the notwithstanding clause, if it in fact applies.[72] The challenge for this book, therefore, is to explain how the executive can bend "strong-form" judicial review and advance their policy priorities, regardless of the authoritative nature in which the Court has declared statutes unconstitutional in critical areas of public policy.

Outline of This Book

As this study of judicial power in the Charter era focuses on the framing of public policy, the parliamentary responses to judicial nullification, and the implementation gap that federalism presents, the individual chapters that centre on issues of public policy (Chapters 2–8) will follow a basic pattern. Each begins with a discussion of the public policy that was challenged successfully before the Supreme Court of Canada, followed by an analysis of the critical elements of the Court's decision – the reasons why a statute, or provisions of a statute, is determined to be a violation of the *Canadian Charter*, the remedy employed under section 24(1) by the Court, the political reaction to the decision by the incumbent government, the legislative response passed, and, finally, the implementation context of the public policy in question once it has returned to the day-to-day workings of public administration. This methodological pattern relies on the textual analysis of judicial decisions, qualitative assessments of parliamentary debates involving legislative responses, and public statements made by incumbent governments when responding to judicial power that manifests as statutory invalidation of their policies or policies passed by previous governments that the current government is committed to protecting in the aftermath of judicial nullification.

Chapter 1 presents an overview of key theories associated with the judicialization of politics literature, both in Canada and abroad. After surveying these theories, the chapter concludes that none are particularly suited to understand judicial policy impact in a federation of Canada's complexity. Although these alternative theories focus on important questions, such as the impact of the Charter on Canadian constitutionalism, judicial power and the *Canadian Charter*, legal mobilization, changes to the policy process within government, and the institutional dialogue between courts and legislatures, many of these approaches make a series of questionable assumptions – first, that the Supreme Court of Canada has policy impact because it rules on important questions of public policy and, related to this, that governments follow judicial policy directions when responding to judicial invalidation.

While the latter assumption is generally correct, as governments largely comply with judicial remedies under section 24(1), the principal assumption equating judicial review with direct policy impact is open to dispute because of the particular relationship that exists between courts and legislatures in the Charter era. Here, I am not referring to the "Charter dialogue" between courts and legislatures, which is the most popular understanding of this inter-institutional relationship. Instead, an understanding of courts as "implementer-dependent institutions" is advanced and how this can constrain judicial policy impact, particularly when the implementation context of the Canadian federation is factored in. Thus, the chapter focuses on important legislative disagreements between courts and legislatures in an effort to understand judicial policy impact,[73] when these disagreements produce strong legislative responses that operate within a complex implementation chain that is the result of Canadian federalism.

Chapters 2–5 consider Quebec and the *Canadian Charter* and focuses on judicial invalidation of statutes passed by the National Assembly of Quebec as inconsistent with the *Canadian Charter* or the *Quebec Charter*. Chapter 2 argues that Quebec is *une province pas comme les autres* (a province unlike the others) in regard to judicial review and the *Canadian Charter*. Indeed, Quebec has experienced the highest number of statutes ruled inconsistent with rights and freedoms, save the Parliament of Canada, seen the Supreme Court of Canada adopt an authoritative approach toward the National Assembly, and issued landmark invalidations of the *Charter of the French Language* in the name of "The Court." Quebec's Charter "distinctiveness" is furthered by its complicated history with the 1982 constitutional settlement, as there is a belief that Bill 101 was explicitly targeted by Pierre Elliott Trudeau for constitutional remedy during the constitutional politics surrounding patriation. This set of circumstances has conditioned the National Assembly of Quebec in its dealings with the Supreme Court and is why this jurisdiction is most likely to challenge judicial invalidation on Charter grounds.

In Chapters 3 and 4, the judicialization of the language of instruction provision of the *Charter of the French Language* is considered. Focusing on the landmark decisions of *Protestant School Boards* (Chapter 3) and *Solski* and *Nguyen* (Chapter 4), I consider how successive governments in Quebec amended the *Charter of the French Language* in response to judicial findings of unconstitutionality.[74] The overarching theme of the chapters involving section 73 of the *Charter of the French Language* is the Québécois expression *"plus ça change, plus c'est la même chose"* ("the more things change, the more they stay the same"). I argue that Quebec has generally protected its policy autonomy involving language of instruction, despite losing critical Charter cases, through the design and implementation of successive statutory responses to the Supreme Court of Canada. In these chapters, the actions of private actors as agents of implementation are explored to understand how strong-form decisions like *Protestant School Boards, Solski,* and *Nguyen* can produce limited policy impact. One of the ironies of the Charter era is that, despite having the right to public instruction for the anglophone community constitutionalized and reaffirmed through judicial review, anglophone parents are sending their children to either the French public system or the private system in growing numbers. As a result, English public instruction in Quebec is on the decline, despite strong-form judicial review. Similar to the fate of the sign-law invalidations, the private choices of the rights bearer have a direct impact on the implementation of a judicial decision.

Chapter 5 considers the invalidation of the sign-law provisions of Bill 101 and Quebec's response through two statutory amendments: Bill 178, *Charter of the French Language* 1988, and Bill 86, *Charter of the French Language* 1993.[75] This chapter considers the importance of commercial actors as agents of implementation. While the 'sign law' regulates public signs, these public signs are the private property of commercial actors that have significant discretion under the *Charter of the French Language* regarding public signage. While Quebec cannot require the exclusive use of French on public signs, as it did before *Ford* and *Devine*, neither the Court's decisions nor the Quebec government's amendments to the *Charter of the French Language* require languages other than French on public signs. Surprisingly, most public signs in Quebec remain French only more than thirty years after *Ford* and *Devine*. This suggests that the impact of strong-form decisions can be mitigated by the implementation context and shows how policy actors operate within a legislative framework, even one that has become judicialized.

Chapters 6–8 involve the implementation gap that Linda White identified in federations that engage in the judicialization of politics, as it considers the nullification of statutes, such as the *Criminal Code,* that regulate provincial health-care policy.[76] Chapters 6–7 consider the issue of supervised consumption sites and the legislative responses of two consecutive federal governments that addressed the 2011 *PHS Community Services Society* decision: Bill C-2 by the Harper government in 2015 and Bill C-37 by the Trudeau government in 2017.[77] In Chapter 8, another issue that straddled the Harper and Trudeau governments is considered – MAiD, in which the Supreme Court of Canada reversed its earlier precedent in *Rodriguez* and removed the *Criminal Code* restriction on assisted death.[78] Although the Harper government did not legislate on this issue, as *Carter* was released in early 2015 and the Harper government was defeated in October 2015, its approach to the issue, like *PHS Community Services Society*, indicated that the Harper Conservatives disagreed with the Court's ruling.

In response to Insite and supervised consumption sites, the Harper Conservatives never approved a new facility and took over four years to pass the legislation, just before the 2015 election. A similar delaying tactic occurred in *Carter*, when the Conservative government established a panel that reported after the 2015 election, once it had been removed from office. However, the 2015 Conservative platform indicated that, if re-elected, the Harper Conservatives would have introduced a response that, perhaps, would have limited the impact of the Court's decision by providing a legal protection for physicians that refused to participate: "This is an extremely sensitive issue and there are many considerations, including the protection of freedom of conscience, that must be part of the discussion."[79] Chapter 8 analyzes the legislative responses introduced by the Trudeau government – the 2016 *Act on MAiD* and the 2021 *Act on MAiD*[80] – as well as the rules introduced by the Royal College of Physicians in every province or their territorial equivalents. The legislative approach to the 2016 *Act on MAiD*, with the establishment of the Special Joint Committee on Physician-Assisted Dying, may be the finest example of rights-based scrutiny in the Charter era, despite notable departures from the Court's decision in *Carter* and the rules introduced by the Royal Colleges of Physicians.

The conclusion provides a summary of the book's main findings and the challenges that judicial policy impact faces once the question of implementation is considered as well as the test that federalism poses to any salient issue of public policy. To be clear, I do not dispute that the Supreme Court of Canada has become a powerful institution since the introduction of the *Canadian Charter* in 1982. What this book attempts to demonstrate is the conditions under which Parliament, the provincial assemblies, and the territorial legislatures may confront – and constrain – judicial power when legislative disagreements manifest in significant issues of public policy within the Canadian federal and devolved context.

Judicial Power and Policy Implementation in the Charter Era   1

An important scholarly debate in Canada has come to understand judicial power and the *Canadian Charter of Rights and Freedoms (Canadian Charter)*.[1] This debate has produced important findings on the counter-majoritarian difficulty that the Charter poses for Canadian constitutionalism, what Christopher Manfredi referred to as the paradox of liberal constitutionalism.[2] It has also explained the reasons why bills of rights are adopted in advanced liberal democracies,[3] the form that judicialization takes,[4] the conditions that facilitate the judicialization of politics,[5] approaches to legal mobilization,[6] altered litigation strategies,[7] and how the legislative process has changed within government.[8] What the *Canadian Charter* debate has not yet fully explored is the policy impact of judicial decisions.[9] In many ways, the early debate assumed that the Supreme Court of Canada had policy influence because it ruled on important policy issues under the Charter and that these decisions would be faithfully implemented by the responsible legislature.

As I stated in the opening chapter, there is no denying that the Supreme Court of Canada is a powerful institution. It would be folly to suggest otherwise. What is less clear is whether powerful judicial decisions have a clear and unfettered policy impact. This is particularly important when the policy stakes are high and governments are opposed to the direction suggested by the Supreme Court of Canada. Courts can have policy impact. And they may not have any policy impact at all if judicial decisions produce sustained legislative disagreements that structure a legislative response.

Furthermore, if a complex implementation chain is present in a judicialized area of public policy, this can further diminish judicial impact, particularly in a federation such as Canada's.

The purpose of this chapter is to understand judicial impact and to map out when judicial decisions do not fundamentally change policy direction, despite the Court issuing powerful rebukes of government action. In addition, the chapter argues that the dialogue metaphor, while generating an interesting debate on its merits for addressing the counter-majoritarian difficulty, is not particularly useful for understanding judicial policy impact, and it may be time to abandon the metaphor altogether, as Aileen Kavanagh has suggested.[10] Reduced to its core, dialogue theory is the ability of a government to respond to judicial invalidation in the Charter era,[11] as Peter Hogg and Allison Bushell concluded: "Where a judicial decision is open to legislative reversal, modification, or avoidance, then it is meaningful to regard the relationship between the Court and the competent legislative body as a dialogue."[12]

There are several problems with this approach, least of which is that any legislative response, be it formal rejection of the Court's decision via the notwithstanding clause or full compliance with the Court's remedy under section 24(1), is viewed as evidence of dialogue.[13] There is a deeper conceptual problem with the suggested dialogue between courts and legislatures. It is simply not accurate to view Parliament or the legislatures as the centre of policy-making, as legal scholars do, given the executive-dominated nature of our parliamentary system.[14] What dialogue theory does not do is evaluate the nature of the legislative response and whether the Court's decision has policy influence because it is adhered to by the responsible government or does not have any impact because a government seeks to contain and negate the Court's policy preferences. It is not enough to say, as dialogue theory purports, that the counter-majoritarian difficulty has been avoided because a legislature responds to a judicial decision.[15]

How should the judicial-legislature relationship be understood once we are free from the lure and limitations of dialogue? Relying on the work of Matthew Hall,[16] and echoing back to Alexander Hamilton in *Federalist no. 78*,[17] I argue that the Supreme Court of Canada is best understood as an "implementer-dependent" institution when it invalidates statutes and requires a legislative response on the part of Parliament, a provincial or territorial assembly, or all three when a collaborative response is needed. Manfredi, in his earlier work, alluded to this implementation dilemma for courts and their remedial powers under section 24(1):

> While courts may have numerous remedial alternatives available to them, they can only impose those remedies through coercive orders whose implementation depends on institutions over which they have little control. The manner in which a legislature or administrative agency complies (or fails to comply) with an order can significantly affect its impact. All of these factors reduce the flexibility of adjudication as a policy-making tool.[18]

The role of the courts in a judicialized policy process is that of agenda setting, whereby judicial review identifies issues of public policy for parliamentary attention. However, because the courts cannot implement their rulings, with few exceptions, they are dependent on the political executives in the remaining aspects of the policy process: designing legislative responses in light of judicial agenda setting and implementing these responses, either on their own or in partnership with other governments or private actors, such as medical practitioners, in the case of abortion, medical assistance in dying, and supervised consumption sites.

In this chapter, I argue that two variables directly affect judicial policy impact in this implementer-dependent context: first, the popularity of a judicial ruling and evidence of legislative disagreement and, second, the implementation context. Either variable can significantly reduce judicial impact in the post-agenda setting phase. By the popularity of a judicial decision, I am referring to its acceptance by either the government with statutory responsibility for an invalidated statute or any of the governments or actors in the implementation chain once the statutory framework is enacted into law. If any of these actors disagrees with judicial policy preferences, judicial impact is compromised, particularly if a government legislates in opposition to the judicial decision or invokes the notwithstanding clause in section 33 of the *Canadian Charter*. However, the popularity of a judicial decision and its importance is intensified in Canada because of a diverse implementation context, as a breakdown in the implementation chain reduces judicial impact. Although federalism is premised on divided jurisdictional responsibilities, many of the issues judicialized under the *Canadian Charter*, such as healthcare policy (abortion, medical assistance in dying, supervised consumption sites, and so on), are shared responsibilities, from an implementation perspective, between the two orders of governments and the devolved assemblies – one to legislate (Parliament) and two levels to provide access (provincial and territorial legislatures). As Linda White discussed in light of narrow legislative compliance in regard to equality rights decisions, there is an implementation gap in the Canadian federation when responsibility is divided: "In the case of divided sovereignty, the challenge is not to ensure compliance but rather cooperation."[19]

Federalism as a constraint on judicial impact can arise under a diverse set of scenarios. If the implementation of a policy response rests with one government, as Bill 101, *Charter of the French Language* does with Quebec, then legislative disagreement can fundamentally reshape and redirect judicial impact.[20] As well, if statutory responsibility rests with one order of government, but the public good must be provided by the other order of government, judicial impact can be seriously compromised and even negated. In short, federalism matters, as this chapter will argue in the context of judicial impact in the Charter era. We simply have overlooked it until recently, focusing on macro questions such as the judicial activism debate and the associated questions of judicial power and the response to this debate – Charter dialogue – first as a metaphor and then as a theory of judicial-legislature relationships.

Given that there are existing theories regarding the judicialization of politics – in Canada and abroad – the first section of this chapter surveys these alternative approaches and explains why they are not suited to a consideration of judicial policy impact. The second section unpacks the two variables that can deny judicial impact beyond agenda setting – the popularity of the decision, with a particular focus on legislative disagreement, and the implementation context within the Canadian federation. This chapter considers legislative disagreement in an executive-dominated Westminster parliamentary democracy with a federal and devolved constitutional structure and how these factors significantly affect the impact of judicial decisions.

Theoretical Approaches to Judicial Politics

Stephen Gardbaum and Mark Tushnet have written important works on the institutional approaches to bills of rights in advanced democracies such as Canada, the United Kingdom, and New Zealand. For Gardbaum, these countries advance a new approach to the protection of rights, which he dubbed the "Commonwealth model of constitutionalism" because of their attachment to Westminster parliamentary democracy and their efforts to ensure that these principles are not eroded by adopting rights-based judicial review.[21] What Gardbaum and Tushnet made clear, however, was that a tremendous institutional variation existed between these Westminster systems, best illustrated by Tushnet's "strong-form" versus "weak-form" categorization that allocated the distinct countries along a spectrum of judicial review. According to Tushnet, the United States exemplifies "strong-form" judicial review for the following reason: while judicial decisions can be reversed, the processes for their reversal are cumbersome, which ensures that decisions by the US Supreme Court endure in the long term. For instance, judicial decisions can be reversed through constitutional amendment or changes in the personnel of the Court that revisit, and reverse, earlier precedents.[22]

The fundamental difference between the two systems is summarized by Tushnet as follows: "Strong-form systems allow the political branches to revise judicial interpretations in the longish run, weak-form ones in the short run."[23] For Tushnet, the inclusion of the notwithstanding clause in the *Canadian Charter* is evidence of the potential for weak judicial review as legislatures can reverse judicial decisions in the short term.[24] He also concludes that Canada is the "strongest" of the weak-form systems, as the *Canadian Charter* is a constitutional document and courts of competent jurisdiction have full remedial authority under section 24(1). These are the strong-form features of Canadian judicialization, which are tempered by the inclusion of the notwithstanding clause, leading Tushnet to conclude that Canada falls just outside of strong-form review. One of the questionable suggestions made by Tushnet is that weak-form systems are unstable and, in the case of Canada, will collapse into judicial supremacy and strong-form review. This is said to occur through political deference to the Supreme Court of Canada and the general reluctance of governments to use the notwithstanding clause.

As I argued with Matthew Hennigar, the central difficulty with Tushnet's conclusion about the *Canadian Charter* is the over-reliance on section 33 in his argument as well as the position that parliamentarians will be reluctant to challenge the Court's decision to nullify their statutes.[25] We suggested, like Kent Roach and Janet Hiebert,[26] that Tushnet failed to appreciate the ability of parliamentary systems, because of the concentration of power within the ministry, to produce strong legislative responses to judicial invalidation in the short term through simple statutory amendment, as the ministry did in regard to the issue of sexual assault in the *Seaboyer-Darrach* and *O'Connor-Mills* dialogic sagas.[27] We labelled this process as "notwithstanding-by-stealth" to indicate legislative reversal without recourse to the notwithstanding clause, though we simply meant that the Cabinet retains the design and implementation functions and can employ them rather rapidly when motivated, regardless of the authority in which the Court renders a Charter decision.[28]

Kavanagh clearly summarized the problem with Tushnet's framework when she asked "what's so weak about 'weak-form review,'" suggesting that he overplayed the formal constitutional design features of the model and undervalued how these systems actually function.[29] She makes a similar criticism of Gardbaum's defence of the "Commonwealth model" and his justification that it allows parliamentary actors to retain the "final word" in the rights-based dialogue between courts and legislatures. Along with Hiebert, I questioned whether dialogic mechanisms produced the engagement of human rights once a bill was introduced into Parliament. We suggested that strong-form government, and not strong-form judicial review, was the most important institutional variable that determined whether legislation complied with rights-based obligations.[30] As our study demonstrated, the functioning of parliamentary democracy, and the dominance of the ministry within both the legislative process and assembly, allowed the ministry to advance its policy agenda without significant input from either the opposition benches or the government backbench.[31] This study on New Zealand and the United Kingdom highlighted the central importance of understanding judicial impact in relation to legislative responses, though it did not consider the critical role of federalism given the unitary structures of these two parliaments.

The Canadian Contributions: Charter Revolutions and Dialogic Constitutionalism

The debate surrounding judicial activism and the response to it in the form of dialogue theory represent the Canadian contribution to judicial politics. In *Governing with the Charter*, I provided an extensive review of the initial academic debate surrounding judicial review in Canada[32] and will simply highlight several of the prominent theories, such as the "court party thesis" by F.L. Morton and Rainer Knopff, and "dialogue theory" by Hogg and Bushell.[33] In addition to the work of Morton and Knopff is that of Manfredi, who explored the paradox of liberal constitutionalism when the boundaries of judicial review are subject to the discretionary choices made by judicial actors. Dialogue theory quickly became an important understanding of the institutional relationships between courts and legislatures and greatly influenced the debates in other Westminster systems that adopted bills of rights, such as the United Kingdom[34] and New Zealand,[35] or were contemplating the adoption of bills of rights, such as Australia.[36]

In *The Charter Revolution and the Court Party*, Morton and Knopff develop the "court party thesis" to explain the fundamental differences between judicial review under the 1960 *Canadian Bill of Rights* (Bill of Rights), and the

1982 *Canadian Charter*.³⁷ For Morton and Knopff, with the exception of their status as the Bill of Rights is statutory whereas the *Canadian Charter* is constitutional, the degree of judicial activism since 1982 cannot be explained by any fundamental textual differences: "Despite a few textual innovations in the Charter, Canadians did not go to bed on April 17, 1982 with a substantially new set of rights and freedoms."³⁸ The differences in rates of invalidation and judicial activism, according to Morton and Knopff, are largely explained by the Court succumbing "to the seduction of power" that the *Canadian Charter* provided after 1982.³⁹ What makes the "Charter revolution" possible, however, was not simply judicial activism but also a broad-based, progressive support structure that embraces judicial review as an instrument of policy change: what Charles Epp referred to as the "legal mobilization support structure" in his comparative study of Canada, India, the United States, and the United Kingdom.⁴⁰ This constellation of actors is called the "court party" by Morton and Knopff, is drawn from the political left, and advances a post-material policy agenda in the judicial arena.⁴¹

What sustains the court party, and, thus, its use of the judicial arena, is "state connectedness" and funding under the Court Challenges Program established by the Trudeau Liberals in 1977⁴² as well as a "jurocracy" that supports a progressive agenda set by the Supreme Court of Canada through its Charter decisions.⁴³ Rights advocacy structures such as human rights tribunals are part of the jurocracy as well as Canadian legal academics that engage in "rights advocacy scholarship," who, in turn, educate and provide future law clerks to the Supreme Court of Canada. In an interesting summation of this development, Morton and Knopff refer to the Supreme Court as the "vanguard of the intelligentsia," suggesting a crypto-Marxist movement in which the Court's role is to ensure that the Charter proletariat achieves the necessary consciousness to sustain the Charter revolution.⁴⁴

Morton and Knopff's engaging work is a notable study of legal mobilization during the Charter era by actors that Marc Galanter referred to as "repeat players" in his seminal article on this phenomena.⁴⁵ So is Manfredi's study on the Legal Education Action Fund, which is the best Canadian study of interest groups that pursue sustained and successful legal mobilization.⁴⁶ Morton and Knopff draw strong conclusions regarding legal mobilization under the *Canadian Charter*, suggesting that it is "deeply and fundamentally undemocratic."⁴⁷ However, while their study considers the implementation of judicial decisions, they largely conclude that the policy direction set by the Supreme Court of Canada is adhered to and produces a direct, though negative, policy impact.

Regime Politics Approach and the Harper Conservatives

This approach to the judicialization of politics is associated with Robert Dahl's defence of judicial nullification, in which Dahl suggested that the US Supreme Court was never far out of line with the views of the dominant governing coalition.[48] In this respect, Dahl was responding to the counter-majoritarian critique by Alexander Bickel that outlined the anti-democratic nature of judicial review.[49] Advanced by Cornell Clayton and Mitchell Pickerill, the regime politics approach (RPA) agrees with Dahl's basic claim that the Supreme Court is generally supportive of the policy direction of the dominant governing coalition. However, RPA does not accept that the Supreme Court is passive, as envisioned by Dahl, but is active in advancing, defending, extending, and according legitimacy to the policy choices of the dominant governing coalition.[50]

Emmett Macfarlane has used the RPA to understand the contentious relationship between the Harper Conservatives and the Supreme Court of Canada in two areas: reference cases involving constitutional reform, such as senate reform, and the *Canadian Charter*. Although Macfarlane is not proposing the RPA as a meta theory to understand Canadian judicial politics, he suggests that it can explain the Harper Conservatives as an outlier since "the 2006 federal election signalled an electoral shift to a government hostile to the Charter project and judicial review generally."[51] Consistent with regime politics approach, the "Harper government's attempt to disrupt the dominant regime was ultimately stymied by the Court."[52] Thus, the dominant governing coalition in Canada, before and during the Harper era, was a "bipartisan pro-Charter regime in favour of the Court's role and supportive of judicial power."[53] Darrell Bricker and John Ibbitson refer to this group as the "Laurentian Consensus," which is "dominated by elites from the Toronto, Montreal, and Ottawa region (the Laurentian elites), who advance a particular conception of Canadian political identity."[54] While Macfarlane uses the RPA, he recognizes that important institutional differences exist between the American and Canadian political systems that must be considered: first, that it is easier to identify the dominant governing coalition in Canada because of the concentration of power in a parliamentary system and, second, that Canadian prime ministers have not used partisanship (or agreement with the "Laurentian Consensus") as a criteria for appointment to the Supreme Court of Canada.

Despite the use of the RPA by Macfarlane, I do not believe it can be, or should be, applied in the Canadian context. Roach noted that "the judicial activism debate that has emerged in Canada since the *Charter* is an unfortunate example of a branch-plant mentality that ignores the differences between the *Charter* and American *Bill of Rights*."[55] In Macfarlane's defence, he acknowledges important institutional differences and does account for how the RPA manifests differently in Canada. That being said, the institutional differences are too great, the construction of power too different, and the RPA comes to founder on the Canadian Shield. At the core of the RPA is bipartisanship, as understood in the American congressional system, and the need to construct a dominant governing coalition on salient policy issues on a case-by-case basis. This is the result of a divided government in the United States, where Congress and the executive may be under the control of different parties, as well as the situation within Congress, where the House and Senate may be controlled by different political parties, as it is under the 117th Congress. The fundamental problem with the RPA in Canada is the following: parliamentary systems that produce strong majority government, with disciplined cohesive parliamentary parties, do not need to be part of a dominant governing coalition, nor do they coalesce around such a construct. Thus, public policy is not transactional, and the party leadership is not required to negotiate between parliamentary factions.

On its own, the ministry is dominant within the House of Commons, and, thus, Parliament, and within the party caucus. The characterization of a "bipartisan pro-Charter regime" by Macfarlane is somewhat problematic as bipartisanship in regime politics has a much different construction because of its origin in the United States. For instance, Macfarlane is using it to suggest that the Liberal Party of Canada and the former Progressive Conservative Party, led by Brian Mulroney, represent bipartisan support for the Charter project: in effect, this is the dominant governing coalition of regime politics during the Charter era. This is not, however, how regime politics views bipartisanship in the context of the dominant governing coalition – this is inter-party agreement on the *Canadian Charter* and the Supreme Court's role and not bipartisanship as it is understood in the context of the design and passage of legislation in the American system of divided government.

There is a more basic problem with the RPA in Canada – it requires us to accept that, despite the Harper Conservatives dominating Parliament during minority and majority governments, it was not part of the dominant governing coalition and was simply an outlier during its ten years at the centre of government. It was dominant without being part of the dominant governing coalition. If this is true, then the dominant governing coalition seems out of place in a parliamentary system. What matters in a parliamentary system, such as Canada, is the party that forms the ministry, which chairs

Cabinet, and which staffs the Prime Minister's Office. As such, the institutional differences and power dynamic in a parliamentary system are too different, thus rendering the RPA a questionable way to understand the judicialization of politics in Canada.

Charter Dialogue Revisited

In their seminal article, Hogg and Bushell suggested in their subtitle that "Perhaps the Charter of Rights Isn't Such a Bad Thing after All" as the vast majority of nullifications resulted in a statutory response by the competent legislative body, which they suggested occurred in nearly two-thirds of nullifications by the Supreme Court of Canada.[56] For Hogg and Bushell, judicial nullification initiated a dialogue between the courts and legislatures, with a judicial decision outlining the constitutional boundaries that public policy must operate within and Parliament and the provincial legislatures being free to design statutory amendments that comply with the Constitution, as interpreted by the Court.[57] As a defence of judicial review, it appears to create a path between parliamentary supremacy and judicial supremacy, which largely explains why dialogic constitutionalism became an appealing framework for Westminster parliamentary democracies that contemplated bills of rights after 1982.[58] Indeed, dialogue theory suggests that the benefits of judicial review can be harnessed by parliamentary systems without the costs typically associated with "strong-form" review in systems such as the United States, which involve judicial supremacy and the dominant role of the courts in fundamental policy debates.[59]

I was, for a brief period, a proponent of Charter dialogue theory.[60] Since that time, however, I have talked myself out of this position.[61] A number of criticisms have been made against dialogue theory from across the political spectrum and the academy, and, for the purposes of brevity, I will focus on the substantive criticisms made by the Canadian academic community, though similar criticisms are made by the broader academy.[62] One of the main criticisms of Charter dialogue theory is that a judicial decision rarely allows a legislature to fashion an independent response, which is captured by Grant Huscroft's observation that "a government that wishes to pass replacement legislation must revisit an issue that had been regarded as settled. The price of doing so may be high – so high, in fact, that as a practical matter it cannot be paid."[63] This was based upon Huscroft's assessment of Parliament's response to the invalidation of the *Tobacco Product Control Act* in *RJR-MacDonald*, which closely mirrored the policy framework suggested by the majority opinion authored by Justice Beverley McLachlin.[64] As well,

Carissima Mathen is skeptical about Charter dialogue as a theory and whether it demonstrates the endurance of weak-form review in Canada, noting that "the fact that the legislature can respond – by changing the law or enacting a new one – does not diminish the courts' powers."[65]

There is, I think, a more compelling reason to stop talking about Charter dialogue as a framework to understand judicial politics, at least regarding Canada. As Andrew Petter observed, the fact that governments can, and do, respond to the Supreme Court of Canada, is not particularity surprising.[66] It is the use of dialogue by Hogg, Thornton, and Wright that is problematic, as they move between dialogue as an interactive exchange between courts and legislatures, to dialogue as judicial finality on the meaning of rights and freedoms. On the one hand, Hogg, Thornton, and Wright defend the *Canadian Charter* as consistent with weak-form judicial review until the point, however, that a legislative response (a "second look case") is reviewed by the Court, in which case any continuing statutory disagreement must be resolved in the Court's favour as "final authority to interpret the Charter rests properly with the judiciary."[67] Qualifying this claim, Hogg, Thornton, and Wright state that judicial supremacy over the interpretation of the *Canadian Charter* does not mean judicial supremacy over policy outcomes,[68] suggesting that Charter review and public policy are distinct processes with different institutional authority.

This claim would be acceptable if judicial supremacy was confined to the interpretation of rights and freedoms and not to section 1 of the *Canadian Charter* – the reasonable limits clause – which is a policy test as it asks the following questions about the public policy found to violate a protected right or freedom. Are the policy objectives "pressing and substantial"? Are the limitations on rights the "least restrictive" in the circumstances? Is there a rational connection between the policy objective and the means chosen? Do the societal benefits of the policy outweigh the costs to the rights holder? It is unclear why institutional supremacy, regarding this part of the Charter, rests properly with the judiciary, as Hogg, Thornton, and Wright suggest, or how they can be separated if final interpretive authority must rest with the Court. More importantly, legislative disagreement does not appear to fall within the operationalization of dialogue during "second look cases" because of the normative claim involving the Supreme Court of Canada having final interpretive authority.

In claiming judicial supremacy over the *Canadian Charter* and its interpretation, Hogg, Thornton, and Wright were not separating the judicial (rights construction) from the political (policy construction via section 1) but were extending it over the whole Charter. Presumably, this would also extend to section 33, where its use, perhaps, could be subjected to judicial review, as was argued by Lorraine Weinrib during the controversy surrounding the Ford government's decision to override the lower court in Bill 31.[69] In the end, Charter dialogue, for its proponents, is about judicial supremacy, strong-form judicial review, and parliamentary deference to courts as policy makers, despite their protestations to the contrary. Instead of mitigating the "counter-majoritarian difficulty," as it intended to do, dialogue theory muddies the institutional roles of courts and legislatures and cannot help us understand policy impact. And, for an understanding of judicial policy impact in the Charter era, it is a "bridge too far" or a quagmire, depending on your metaphorical preference.

The Supreme Court as an "Implementer-dependent" Institution
The preceding discussion has argued that, while valuable, much of the judicialization of politics literature does not consider the impact of judicial decisions on compelling issues of public policy. Either the literature explains why bills of rights are adopted or the form that bills of rights take. When it does consider judicial impact, it is an analysis of the effect of judicial review on the constitutional system, or what Alexander Bickel referred to as the "counter-majoritarian difficulty."[70] These are important questions, but they cannot answer the fundamental question explored in this book regarding judicial impact and salient issues of public policy.

In the Canadian debate, the "court party" thesis and "dialogic constitutionalism" do consider judicial impact but repeat the mistakes first identified by Alan Cairns in his seminal article on the Judicial Committee of the Privy Council. In this article, Cairns squarely addressed the limitation with early scholarship as it had a singular focus on judicial decisions as the principal variable to account for the evolution of Canadian federalism:

> It is impossible to believe that a few elderly men in London deciding two or three constitutional cases a year precipitated, sustained, and caused the development of Canada in a federalist direction the country would otherwise not have taken. It is evident that on occasion the provinces found an ally in the Privy Council, and that on balance they were aided in their struggles with the federal government. To attribute more than this to the Privy Council strains credulity. Courts are not self-starting institutions. They are called into play by groups and individuals seeking objectives which can be furthered by judicial support. A comprehensive

explanation of judicial decisions, therefore, must include the actors who employed the courts for their own purposes.[71]

Both the "court party" thesis and "dialogic constitutionalism" equate judicial review with policy impact and, in this sense, place too much emphasis on the Supreme Court of Canada and repeat the mistakes of early scholarship. This comes without a proper consideration of the role of the legislative state. Moreover, they overlook the ability of the ministry to overcome judicial review through a legislative response that disagrees with the Supreme Court. Further, the approaches minimize that a negative rights instrument, such as the *Canadian Charter*, is an impediment to judicial impact. And, finally, such approaches overlook the complex implementation chains facing issues of public policy judicialized under the *Canadian Charter*, particularly when a judicial decision requires coordination and cooperation among the two orders of government as well as the devolved assemblies.

Like Gerald Rosenberg's work that explored the practical limitations of policy change via the judicialization of politics,[72] this book focuses on the implementation challenges that confront any activist judicial decision by the Supreme Court of Canada, particularly when it centres on a substantive issue of public policy. In the American context, the implementation challenge is also explored in the work of Bradley Canon and Charles Johnson who noted the paradox of implementation and how institutional dependence by supreme courts can check judicial policy impact: "Courts must work with existing implementation groups – they cannot fire unenthusiastic implementors and hire new ones. To compound the problem, the groups that immediately implement the policies are frequently parties to the decision. If the implementing group loses its case, then it must immediately execute a decision which it fought against for months or even years."[73]

In the Canadian context, Manfredi's early work was conscious of the implementation paradox under section 24(1) of the *Canadian Charter* and how the Supreme Court of Canada's heavy reliance on Parliament and the legislatures blunted this judicial instrument and, presumably, directly affected judicial policy impact.[74] An important contribution made by Rosenberg, Canon, and Johnson, as well as Manfredi and Hall, is to reintroduce the important insight made by Hamilton in *Federalist no. 78* – that the judiciary can be the "least dangerous" branch, particularly when its decisions are reliant on other actors for their implementation.[75] Indeed, Hall echoes *Federalist no. 78* when he labels supreme courts as "implementer-dependent" institutions as they are reliant on lower courts and non-judicial actors, such as Congress or Parliament, to implement judicial rulings.[76] Hall classifies judicial decisions implemented by lower courts as vertical issues and those implemented by non-judicial actors such as the ministry as lateral issues. Briefly put, a vertical issue is a final appellant court decision that establishes judicial rules implemented by lower courts, such as the rules governing trial procedures or the admissibility of evidence. A lateral issue arises when a final appellant court reviews the constitutionality of a statute and declares it unconstitutional, and this judicial determination necessitates some response from the political actor with responsibility for the statute in question. The Canadian manifestation of a lateral issue is the "Charter dialogue" debate that has considered the significance of legislative responses to judicial invalidation of statutes by the Supreme Court of Canada.[77]

Hall's position is that the popularity of a judicial decision, combined with the nature of the issue (vertical versus lateral) and the institution required to implement the decision (lower courts versus legislative bodies), determine the conditions under which a supreme court may or may not be powerful. For instance, a supreme court can generally expect a vertical issue, regardless of the popularity of the decision, to be largely implemented by lower courts, given the judicial hierarchy and the fact that lower courts are bound to follow judicial precedents established by the Supreme Court.[78] Similarly, a popular lateral ruling will be implemented since public opinion supporting the decision restricts the ability of legislative bodies to engage in "court-curbing" strategies.[79] However, according to Hall, an unpopular lateral judicial ruling provides the potential for legislative reversal as the parliamentary body required to implement the decision may use popular disagreement with the decision to fashion a legislative response that limits the policy impact of the judicial review.

A Court of "Competent Jurisdiction": Section 24(1) and Judicial Remedies

Leaving aside the classification scheme, a more pressing issue is Hall's reaffirmation of Hamilton in *Federalist no. 78* as well as Rosenberg's position that final appellant courts cannot implement their rulings and must rely exclusively on lower courts or political institutions such as the Cabinet. Given that the *Canadian Charter* includes a remedy clause under section 24(1), the assumption that a final appellant court is an implementer-dependent institution does not fully apply in the Canadian context.[80] This judicial remedy clause allows a court of "competent jurisdiction" to fashion a remedy that "the court considers appropriate and just in the circumstances." In response, the Supreme Court of Canada has established three-broad remedies for courts of competent jurisdictions,[81] largely in relation to acts of Parliament, the provincial legislatures, and the territorial assemblies: immediate statutory invalidation; suspended declarations of unconstitutionality; and, finally, judicial amendment of legislation.[82]

The first two remedies are clear illustrations of the Supreme Court of Canada as an implementer-dependent institution, as immediate and suspended invalidity leave it to the ministry to decide how, and if, to respond to a judicial determination of statutory incompatibility with the *Canadian Charter*. According to its proponents, they would also constitute evidence of Charter dialogue theory as they generally result in a legislative response and demonstrate the central premise of this defence of judicial review: that the Supreme Court rarely has the final word when it declares that acts of Parliament or the legislatures are unconstitutional.[83] While it has been debated whether a judicial ruling, in fact, can facilitate a legislative response that addresses the counter-majoritarian critique of judicial review, as Charter dialogue theory claims,[84] the first two remedies under section 24(1) do allow for the possibility of judicial policy impact being checked. This is for a very specific reason so that the Court's remedy and policy direction can be reviewed and amended by parliamentary actors.

The remedy labelled as a "judicial amendment" defies the notion that final appellant courts are "implementer-dependent" institutions and, more importantly, that, in the context of Canada, the Supreme Court, as Roach contends, may not have "been careful to craft gentle, patient, and flexible remedies that do not dictate to government the exact steps to be taken to remedy a constitutional violation."[85] The characterization of judicial deference by Kent Roach is correct in terms of immediate and suspended invalidity but less so when the Court has engaged in other forms of remedial activism. To provide some context, the Supreme Court of Canada has issued 3,250 decisions between 1982 and 2022, and 640 of them (or nearly 20 percent) involve the *Canadian Charter*. The breakdown of the decisions involving the *Canadian Charter* is the following: 278 statutes and regulations (44 percent); 355 conduct cases, such as those involving the police (55 percent); and seven cases involving administrative or ministerial discretion (11 percent) such as supervised consumption sites in *Canada v PHS Community Services Society*.[86] In terms of remedial activism and section 24(1) of the *Canadian Charter* (n = 101), the breakdown is as follows: 94 statutes have been nullified as inconsistent with the *Canadian Charter,* one statute has been found to be inconsistent with the Quebec *Charter of Human Rights and Freedoms,*[87] and six instances of administrative or ministerial discretion have been found to violate the *Canadian Charter.*

Appendix 1 outlines this subset of remedial activism (101 cases), and Table 1.1 indicates the general remedy used by the Court under section 24(1): immediate invalidation (fifty cases); suspended invalidity (twenty-seven cases); and judicial amendment (twenty-four cases). Roach is generally correct that the Supreme Court of Canada has adopted "gentle, patient, and flexible remedies" as this has occurred in seventy-seven cases (76 percent) in which it has fashioned remedies under section 24(1). However, in the remaining cases, the Court has acted "more like a *de facto* third chamber of the legislature than a court."[88] In a significant dimension of remedial activism (twenty-four cases), once having found legislation to be unconstitutional or that ministerial discretion has been exercised inconsistently with the *Canadian Charter,* the Court itself has remedied these findings of unconstitutionality. Indeed, leading dialogue theorists, such as Hogg, Thornton, and Wright, have suggested that the judicial amendment of statutes works against Charter dialogue as it generally precludes a legislative response.[89] In addition, there is a clear jurisdictional divide in the use of this remedy, sixteen out of twenty-four cases (68 percent) of judicial amendment by the Court have involved statutes under the authority of the Parliament of Canada.

The most common approach to judicial amendment by the Supreme Court of Canada has been to "read down" statutes to establish their compatibility

Table 1.1 Judicial remedies by the Supreme Court of Canada, 1982–2022

Government	Invalidation	Suspended	Amended	Total
Canada	36	13	16	65
Quebec	8	2	2	12
British Columbia	2	4	1	7
Ontario	1	3	1	5
Alberta	2	1	1	4
Prince Edward Island	1	1	0	2
Saskatchewan	0	1	1	2
Nova Scotia	0	1	1	2
Manitoba	0	0	1	1
New Brunswick	0	1	0	1
Total	*50*	*27*	*24*	*101*
Federal	36	13	16	65
Provincial	14	14	8	36

with the *Canadian Charter*, which the Court has used in nearly two-thirds of cases or fifteen of twenty-four cases. Generally speaking, this judicial technique sees the Court sever a section or a phrase to ensure the constitutionality of an offending statute such as the *Criminal Code*.[90] For instance, after determining that the definition of "constructive murder" in section 21(2) of the *Criminal Code* was unconstitutional in *R. v Logan*, the Court severed the phrase "ought to have known" to ensure the continued application of this *Criminal Code* provision.[91]

A more controversial approach, however, is the practice of "reading-in" where the Court changes the intention of legislation by updating statutory definitions or stretches statutory applications to remedy constitutional limitations identified by the Court. In *Vriend v Alberta*, the Supreme Court of Canada determined that Alberta's human rights code, the *Individual Rights Protection Act (IRPA)*, was a violation of section 15(1) by virtue of its under-inclusion as it did not extend protection to gays and lesbians.[92] To remedy this constitutional violation, the Court read sexual orientation into several sections and stretched the *IRPA* to cover a ground for protection recognized by the court in *Egan v Canada*.[93] Thus, *Vriend* was remedied by the Court's expansion of equality rights to include sexual orientation in *Egan*.

Less prevalent remedies have involved the use of ministerial discretion, where the Supreme Court of Canada has established constitutional parameters for its exercise. For instance, in *PHS Community Services Society*, the Court read in five criteria that must be used by the minister of health when evaluating applications for supervised consumption sites under section 56 of the *Controlled Drugs and Substances Act (CDSA)*.[94] As well, in *Solski (Tutor of) v Quebec (Attorney General)*, the Court determined that the quantitative approach to the "major part requirement" for assessing eligibility for English public education under the *Charter of the French Language* was incompatible with section 23 of the *Canadian Charter*.[95] To remedy this constitutional defect, the Court read in a four-part qualitative test for assessing eligibility for this public service.[96] In other cases, the Court set aside ministerial directives and reinstated the decisions of other public bodies, as it did in *Arsenault-Cameron v Prince Edward Island* regarding minority language education services.[97]

Curbing Judicial Impact: Issue Salience, Unpopularity, and Federalism
The Supreme Court of Canada, by virtue of statutory review and section 24(1) of the *Canadian Charter*, is an implementer of its decisions. And it is also dependent on governments to implement its rulings. In addition, these parliamentary actors may be dependent on private actors to implement the

statutory frameworks they create in response to judicial invalidation, such as medical and nurse practitioners. Moreover, professional organizations such as the provincial colleges of physicians and surgeons, and their territorial equivalents, have responsibility for the professional standards governing medical services regulated by the federal *Criminal Code* or equivalent statutes.

Despite certain reservations with Hall's framework, which was developed to understand judicial power in the context of the US Supreme Court, it may be better suited to understand the Supreme Court of Canada and salient issues of public policy in the Canadian federation. This is for two reasons. First, the functioning of an executive-dominated parliamentary system, whereby the House of Commons is frequently controlled by a one-party majority government, may be a more hospitable environment for legislative disagreements that limit judicial impact through strong legislative responses challenging judicial remedies and policy directions. Second, as Linda White observed in the context of federalism and the implementation of equality rights decisions in Canada, "federalism complicates matters by involving two levels of government: one to acknowledge the legality of the action; and the other to ensure access to the services."[98] This is particularly relevant in the Charter era, as high-profile invalidations of the federal *Criminal Code* or the *CDSA* regulate activities under provincial control, such as abortion, medical assistance in dying, and supervised consumption sites.

My study focuses only on what Hall describes as lateral issues – policy decisions implemented by political actors – as I consider key areas of public policy invalidated by the Supreme Court of Canada that represent the core responsibilities of the governments of Canadian federalism at the nexus of law and politics during the Charter era. I do not consider judicial impact in vertical issues – judicial rules that are largely implemented by lower courts. The highest court in any jurisdiction has clear impact in vertical issues because of a hierarchal "implementer-dependent" context, but this relationship is not the focus of this study, which is about courts and legislatures in the Canadian federation. Unlike Hall, I consider any issue with a statutory basis to be a lateral issue and, moving forward, will simply refer to these issues as involving statutory review where the focus is on the statutes, regulations, and ministerial discretion. Judicial decisions declaring such instruments or actions unconstitutional require a response, either acceptance of the decision or, as Parliament failed to do on two occasions in response to *Morgentaler*, an inability to amend legislation.[99] Alternatively, Parliament and the legislatures can question, challenge, and, perhaps, reject the policy framework established via remedial activism under section 24(1) of the *Canadian Charter*.

As I will demonstrate, there are several factors that determine the conditions under which the Supreme Court of Canada, despite remedial activism under section 24(1) of the *Canadian Charter*, may not influence legislative outcomes in salient areas of public policy. For instance, does the responsible parliamentary actor agree with the Court's determination that a statute is constitutionality suspect? Second, does the judicial decision impose a constitutional obligation to provide access to a service (a positive right) or does the decision articulate a negative right, where the Court mandates limits on government interference with personal autonomy? As Macfarlane demonstrates in the context of health-care policy, the Supreme Court has generally framed constitutional challenges in *Morgentaler, Carter,* and *PHS Community Services Society* as negative rights cases and has declined to place any policy obligations on provincial governments.[100] As many judicial decisions in the Charter era regulate what governments may not do (negative rights), as opposed to what they must do (positive rights), this creates the conditions for limited policy impact via remedial activism under section 24(1) of the *Canadian Charter*.[101] The third factor considers whether the parliamentary body with statutory responsibility accepts the remedy imposed by the Supreme Court of Canada. And, finally, what is the institutional context of implementing a legislative response to a judicial determination of unconstitutionality?

Is the policy context relatively straightforward, conforming to the division of powers, thus requiring only one order of government to frame a response to the Supreme Court of Canada's ruling? Is the policy context complicated, requiring coordinate action by both orders of government to realize the full impact of remedial activism under section 24(1) of the *Canadian Charter*? In relation to an issue that requires coordinate action, is there a consistent approach by the provincial and territorial legislatures – do some comply, while others engage in non-compliance that mitigates the impact of remedial activism by the Supreme Court of Canada? How does "checkerboard" federalism and asymmetrical access to services given constitutional parameters by the Supreme Court of Canada factor into our analysis of judicial power in the Charter era? In short, how do institutional context, federalism, and the reaction of the actor(s) with statutory responsibility affect the implementation of judicial decisions in salient areas of public policy?[102]

Legislatures and Disagreement: Popularity in an Executive-Dominated Parliamentary System

In *The Nature of Supreme Court Power,* Hall contends that the popularity of a judicial decision determines whether Congress or a legislature accepts a ruling involving a lateral issue, suggesting that "elected officials may be unwilling or unable to resist the Court when it is supported by strong public opinion."[103] In contrast, an unpopular ruling provides the possibility for non-compliance, as Congress may pursue its own policy preferences if a consensus forms against a judicial ruling.[104] Much of Hall's consideration of popularity is derived from public opinion surveys, which he uses to determine whether a popular basis exists for a judicial decision to be opposed and judicial power can be constrained.[105]

In a two-party congressional system based on the separation of powers, such as the United States, popular support may be a useful indicator whether Congress, or a state legislature, can oppose a judicial decision. For instance, in a system of divided government, supporters of a judicial decision can mobilize and target either chamber of Congress, or, failing this, the executive branch can safeguard the intended policy impact of a judicial decision. Even an unpopular judicial decision may be more difficult to reverse in the American context, given that backers of the decision can target the House of Representatives, the Senate, or the executive branch in support of the decision, thus complicating or even preventing a legislative response that seeks to limit the policy impact of a judicial decision. Congressional responsiveness to public opinion is stronger, perhaps, in the United States, with mid-term elections every two years that limit the distance that political actors can move away from public opinion on salient issues of public policy.

Again, the Canadian case requires a different approach to the issue of popular support as the latitude to strike a policy response may be greater in Canada. This may occur not because public opinion is less important but, rather, because it is channelled very differently and operates under a different set of constitutional principles, with a different threshold in a multi-party parliamentary system. Turning first to the constitutional principles of significance, the fusion of power in a parliamentary system creates fewer points for popular opinion to constrain legislative action. Indeed, the presence of disciplined parties within a multi-party setting,[106] and the dominance of the ministry within the legislature,[107] provides a policy latitude that does not exist in the two-party American compound republic. For instance, there have been twelve federal elections during the Charter era, and the party forming government has averaged 39.1 percent of the vote in each election.[108] Controlling for majority governments (seven elections) increases the plurality slightly to 41.85 percent support, though the last two majority governments, led by Stephen Harper and Justin Trudeau, have secured control of the House of Commons by securing less than 40 percent of the vote. The appointed

Senate has not historically constrained the ministry in any meaningful way, though this may be changing as a result of the reforms introduced by Justin Trudeau, first as Liberal Party leader and subsequently as prime minister. Even greater autonomy is exercised by provincial ministries that operate within comparatively small unicameral legislative assemblies.[109] The Canadian case is thus distinct from that of the American as the ability of popular opinion to influence legislative opinion is much reduced.

In his assessment of the United Kingdom's *Human Rights Act 1998* and whether it has constrained the ministry, K.D. Ewing provided a pessimistic view, suggesting that the *Human Rights Act*'s ineffectiveness is "the problem of centralized power and executive dominance, and the ability of governments with the support of the House of Commons to do pretty much what they want."[110] This assessment does not fully hold in Canada as judicial review is much stronger and the remedies available to Canadian courts are not permitted in the United Kingdom.[111] However, it does suggest that the structure of parliamentary systems, particularly ones such as the Canadian and the British, where the threshold for majority government is based on a declining plurality of the vote, requires a different approach to public opinion as a constraint on legislative action. Moreover, the recurring presence of one-party minority governments in Canada since 2004 has not undermined the ability of the government to achieve its legislative agenda. What is of greater importance in a parliamentary system, therefore, is whether an incumbent government agrees with a judicial decision invalidating a statute under its legislative and constitutional authority. George Tsebelis refers to this as "policy congruence" in parliamentary systems,[112] and I simply refer to it as the popularity of a judicial decision within an incumbent government. Clearly, public opinion influences legislative perception of a judicial decision, but it is not paramount in a parliamentary system such as Canada's.

Federalism and the Implementation Gap

In her study of equality rights and implementation, White analyzed policy areas where responsibility was functionally divided between the federal and provincial/territorially governments: abortion and reproductive choice and the issue of same-sex marriage. In particular, the federal government determines the legality of these issues, and the provincial and territorial governments have responsibility for providing access to the services legally regulated by the federal government. White refers to this as an "implementation gap" that "requires a second and (sometimes reluctant) autonomous player to act in order to ensure implementation" where the second government's "distance from the original legislative action can create a gap in response, or even outright defiance of the judicial ruling."[113] This is an important observation. However, it is not limited to equality rights but is also an implementation "dilemma" across the entirety of judicial review under the *Canadian Charter*. Indeed, it is a seminal factor that strongly determines whether judicial review can produce policy change or whether governments can bend the judicial decision through the implementation prism to better reflect their policy preferences and priorities.[114]

In one of the first analyses of the *Canadian Charter* and federalism, Cairns voiced concern that judicial review would have a centralizing effect on Canadian federalism and undermine the sovereignty of the provinces in their areas of responsibility.[115] The "centralization thesis" was an important element of the academic debate surrounding the *Canadian Charter* during its first two decades. The consensus position was that judicial interpretation of a national charter of rights by the Supreme Court of Canada would have serious negative implications for the principle of policy diversity and provincial autonomy.[116] What this important critique discounted, however, was the ability of federalism to be safeguarded, either by the courts demonstrating sensitivity to this principle in its Charter jurisprudence[117] or by governments redesigning the policy process within the bureaucracy to safeguard against judicial invalidation and, thus, preserve the constitutionality of statutes in core areas of responsibility.[118] Added to this is the implementation context of Canadian federalism that allows for a range of responses to judicial activism that may negate, or significantly constrain, the impact of judicial review: a development referred to as "safeguarding federalism" in the American context, whereby state legislatures protect their jurisdictional authority by determining how, and whether, to participate in policy exercises led by the national government.[119]

Morton was skeptical that the provinces could protect their constitutional authority and suggested that, in the context of the *Canadian Charter* and federalism, "provinces can win a Charter 'battle' but still lose the policy 'war.'"[120] As I will demonstrate, governments can lose the Charter "battle" but win the policy "war" since they, and they alone, control the design and implementation of legislative responses to statutory nullification. Several of the prominent areas of public policy considered in this book, such as abortion, medical assistance in dying, and supervised consumption sites, allow the provincial and territorial governments to decide whether to participate in national policy frameworks governed by the *Criminal Code* or other federal statutes such as the *CDSA*.

This demonstrates the importance of White's observation that "when reviewing major legislation or definitive rulings, it is important to scrutinize not only the outcomes of the decisions but also the implications regarding the legislative authority of the federal parliament vis-à-vis provincial legislatures."[121] In particular, judicial invalidation of federal statutes such as the *Criminal Code* and the *CDSA* may not necessarily result in greater access to these public services, as it requires legislative responses on behalf of both orders of government: Parliament, in amending the legislation declared unconstitutional by the Court, and the provinces and territories, which must decide whether to provide access to these services. This is further complicated when the provinces and territories diverge in their responses to the implementation gap. As the Court rarely mandates the provision of public services, the impact of judicial review is conditioned by the scope of the remedy, federalism, and policy choices of the provincial and territorial governments.

To illustrate, the *Morgentaler* decision saw the Supreme Court of Canada invalidate the legal framework governing access to therapeutic abortion as a violation of the security of the person protected by section 7 of the *Canadian Charter*. According to a majority of the Supreme Court, section 251(4) of the *Criminal Code* was unconstitutional because the procedural framework governing abortion, whereby a woman was required to have the approval of a therapeutic abortion committee, resulted in unnecessary delays that undermined both the physical and mental security of women seeking this medical procedure. While the Court did not rule on a right to abortion, it ruled that the regulation of abortion under the *Criminal Code* violated section 7. In particular, the Court took exception to the cumbersome process for approving legal abortion under the *Criminal Code* and noted that, in certain provincial jurisdictions, there were significant accessibility issues at public institutions. For the Supreme Court, the *Criminal Code* required women to decide between two stark choices regarding unwanted pregnancy: approval by a therapeutic abortion committee, where issues of accessibility and delay required women to carry an unwanted foetus longer than what was necessary, posing a risk to their physical and mental health, or to seek a private and illegal abortion that subjected them and the performing physician to legal jeopardy and potential imprisonment.[122]

What was the policy impact of this activist decision? Did it result in greater access to abortion services once the Supreme Court invalidated the *Criminal Code*'s provisions governing legal abortions? As Joanna Erdman observed, "the decriminalization of abortion thus ensured neither its availability nor accessibility as an integrated and publicly funded health service."[123] At first glance, the Supreme Court appeared to engage in "strong-form" judicial review in the context of the criminalization of abortion services outside of public institutions, as it invalidated the *Criminal Code* restriction.[124] In turn, Parliament failed to enact a legislative response on two attempts, and, thus, the Supreme Court's decision endures as the constitutional statement on the legal provision of abortion services in Canada. However, as an implementer-dependent institution, the Supreme Court of Canada needed more than Parliament's acceptance of *Morgentaler* via legislative failure. What was necessary, though not required as part of the *Morgentaler* decision, was for the provinces and territories to address delays by increasing the availability of abortion as a public service in facilities approved by the provincial and territorial ministers of health. As Rachael Johnstone's book suggests, the provinces and territories adopted a varied response.[125] Some increased access to publicly available abortion services, others increased the procedural restrictions on this medical service, while others simply refused to allow public institutions to provide abortion services.[126] Federalism, or, more correctly, the implementation context in a federation such as Canada's, conditions the policy impact of judicial invalidation.

Legislative Disagreements and Issue Salience

In Table 1.2, the salient issues of public policy discussed in this book are outlined, with a particular focus on the jurisdictional structure and implementation context of legislative disagreements under the *Canadian Charter*. The next chapters consider when the governments of Canadian federalism fight for policy autonomy in the context of judicialization and how judicial impact is mitigated through the jurisdictional structure (watertight or coordinated) and implementation chains (watertight or coordinated and voluntary) once judicial invalidation serves a discursive function as agenda setting. The characteristic of "watertight" is used to describe an issue of public policy that conforms to the division of powers, and only one government is required to legislate and to implement a public policy response. In contrast, "coordinated and voluntary" is used if a policy issue requires coordination by the two orders of government and the devolved assemblies – a legislative response by one government, usually Parliament regarding the *Criminal Code* or another criminal justice statute, and the provision of a service by the provincial and territorial governments. This scenario generally arises in health-care policy and the regulation of moral issues, such as abortion, supervised consumption sites, and medical assistance in dying. These issues

Table 1.2 Legislative disagreements, issue salience, and implementation context

Chapter	Issue	Statute/Regulation	Judgment	Right	Implementation context
Chapter 3 *A.G. (Que.) v Quebec Protestant School Boards*, (1984)	Language of instruction **Salience:** High	*Charter of the French Language (CFL)*	**Unanimous:** (The Court) **Remedy:** Invalidation	**Positive:** section 23 (minority language education rights)	**Jurisdictional structure: Watertight** – National Assembly of Quebec has sole responsibility for the *CFL*. **Implementation chain: Watertight** – National Assembly of Quebec is sole implementation actor. **Veto player(s): Single** – National Assembly is both <u>designer</u> and <u>implementer</u> of legislative response.
Chapter 4 *Solski (Tutor of) v Quebec (Attorney General)*, (2005) *Nguyen v Quebec (Education, Recreation and Sports)*, (2009)	Language of instruction **Salience:** High	*CFL*	**Unanimous:** *Solski* (The Court); *Nguyen* (LeBel) **Remedy:** *Solski* (Judicial amendment); *Nguyen:* (Suspended declaration)	**Positive:** section 23 (minority language education rights)	**Jurisdictional structure: Watertight** – National Assembly of Quebec has sole responsibility for the *CFL*. **Implementation chain: Watertight** – National Assembly of Quebec is sole implementation actor. **Veto Player(s): Single** – National Assembly is both <u>designer</u> and <u>implementer</u> of legislative response.
Chapter 5 *Ford v Quebec (Attorney General)*, (1988) *Devine v Quebec (Attorney General)*, (1988)	French-only public signs **Salience:** High	*CFL* *Regulation Respecting the Language of Commerce and Business*	**Unanimous:** (The Court) **Remedy:** Invalidation	**Negative:** section 2(b) (freedom of expression)	**Jurisdictional structure: Watertight** – National Assembly of Quebec has sole responsibility for the *CFL*. **Implementation chain: Watertight** – National Assembly of Quebec is sole implementation actor. **Veto Player(s): Single** – National Assembly is both <u>designer</u> and <u>implementer</u> of legislative response.

Chapters 6–7 *Canada (Attorney General) v PHS Community Services Society*, (2011)	Supervised consumption sites **Salience:** High	*Controlled Drugs and Substances Act* (CDSA)	**Unanimous:** (chief justice) **Remedy:** 1. Court issued temporary exemption to Insite 2. Court created five-part guidelines for ministerial discretion under section 56	**Negative:** Section 7 (right to life, liberty, and security of the person)	**Jurisdictional structure:** Coordinated – Parliament has statutory responsibility for the *CDSA*; provinces have responsibility for the provision and access to the health service. **Implementation chain:** Coordinated and voluntary – provinces are not required to provide service (negative rights). **Veto player(s):** Multiple – Parliament as sole designer of legislative response; provinces as coordinate and voluntary providers of services.
Chapter 8 *Carter v Canada (Attorney General)*, (2015)	Medical assistance in dying **Salience:** High	*Criminal Code* (CC)	**Unanimous:** (The Court) **Remedy:** Suspended declaration	**Negative:** Section 7 (right to life, liberty, and security of the person)	**Jurisdictional structure:** Coordinated – Parliament has statutory responsibility for the *CC*; provinces have responsibility for the provision and access to the health service. **Implementation chain:** Coordinated and voluntary – provinces are not required to provide service (negative rights). **Veto player(s):** Multiple – Parliament as sole designer of legislative response; provinces as coordinate and voluntary providers of services.

are also described as "voluntary" because the provincial governments are under no constitutional or legal requirement to provide services regulated by a federal statute. Indeed, this is the negative rights dilemma that confronts judicial policy impact in salient issues of public policy in the Charter era.[127]

Several important characteristics emerge from this comparison of legislative disagreements. Whether an issue of public policy conforms to the "watertight compartment" approach to federalism or "coordinated and voluntary" appears to make only modest differences regarding legislative disagreement and stunted judicial impact. Successive Quebec governments have overcome judicial invalidation of the *Charter of the French Language* through statutory amendment and regulatory changes. As the *Constitution Act, 1867* provides Quebec with sole responsibility for this jurisdictional issue, the ministry has been able to overcome strong-form judicial review of the *Charter of the French Language*.[128] Indeed, the watertight model allows the Quebec government to act as a veto player that consigns judicial impact to agenda setting, as the Court's judgments have resulted in several amendments to the *Charter of the French Language* in response to judicial invalidation. However, these amendments have not favoured judicial preferences regarding language of instruction but have seen Quebec reassert its legislative sovereignty and policy preferences that mitigate judicial impact.

The only notable difference in jurisdictional structure is the possibility of a legislative agreement and disagreement co-existing that does allow for some judicial impact in areas of public policy. This has arisen in the context of the legalization (in Parliament) of health-care policy (provincial/territorial responsibility). Indeed, the issue of supervised consumption sites demonstrates how this agreement/disagreement co-existence among the provinces and territories can moderate judicial policy impact. The initial response to the *PHS Community Services Society* decision by the Harper government clearly exhibited legislative disagreement, as the *Respect for Communities Act* created a cumbersome process designed to prevent the submission of new applications for additional facilities.[129] In this respect, the Harper government acted as a veto player, using its jurisdictional responsibility for the *CDSA* to marginalize any judicial impact outside of the Insite facility in Vancouver. However, the Trudeau government that succeeded the Conservatives was in broad agreement with the Supreme Court of Canada and its support for supervised consumption sites. It rescinded the *Respect for Communities Act*, replaced it with amendments to the *CDSA*, and streamlined the application criteria to conform to those suggested by the Court in *PHS Community Services Society*.

While this legislative agreement created the possibility of judicial impact in regard to supervised consumption sites, it still requires coordinated and complementary action on the part of the service providers – the ten provincial and three territorial governments. Provincial and territorial health facilities must submit applications, and these applications must be supported by provincial and territorial departments of health. However, provincial and territorial departments of health are under no constitutional obligation to support supervised consumption sites or to permit their operation. Currently, supervised consumption sites are available in five provinces (Alberta, British Columbia, Ontario, Quebec, and Saskatchewan), as these are the only jurisdictions to have applied under the terms established by the *CDSA* and Bill C-37, *Act to Amend the Controlled Drugs and Substances Act*.[130] The Supreme Court of Canada has had a policy impact because the Trudeau government has accepted the five guidelines established by the Court in *PHS Community Services Society* and removed the administrative obstacles constructed by the Harper Conservatives under the *Respect for Communities Act*.

The Court has also had a policy impact because several provincial jurisdictions agree with supervised consumption sites as a component of healthcare treatment and voluntarily agreed to establish facilities under the terms of the *CDSA*. Thus, legislative agreement and voluntary actions cannot be minimized as factors that facilitate judicial impact. Conversely, judicial impact has been offset by a majority of the provinces and territories that have yet to apply for an exemption to operate supervised consumption sites under section 56 of the *CDSA*. While the remaining provinces do represent a significant proportion of the Canadian population, nevertheless, it illustrates how important the implementation chain is to an understanding of judicial policy impact, particularly when an issue of public policy requires coordinate, independent, and voluntary action in the Canadian federation.

Conclusion

Understanding judicial impact in salient areas of public policy is an important, yet understudied, endeavour in the Charter era. My argument – that judicial impact has been misunderstood and largely assumed in salient areas of public policy – is not meant to convey that existing theories of judicial review or the judicialization of politics are without value. Quite the contrary. They are simply better suited to answering the first-generation questions of this scholarly endeavour, such as why bills of rights are adopted, the form that bills of rights take, and the institutional implications of judicial review for constitutional theory, better known as the "counter-majoritarian" difficulty.

They are also well suited to the second-generation questions that consider the broader institutional response to judicialization, whether it involves legal mobilization, the "court party" thesis in Canada, or changes to the machinery of government and the attempt to govern with the *Canadian Charter* under the guidance of the Department of Justice and its provincial counterparts.

Dialogue as a framework is viewed as a compelling response to the third generation of Charter inquiry – the public policy impact of judicial review. For the defenders of dialogue, judicial impact is real, comprehensive, and largely beneficial for Canadian democracy and public policy. This understanding of judicial impact concludes that Charter dialogue improves public policy in the following way: by identifying Charter values overlooked by Parliament and the legislatures. In turn, this requires a court to invalidate such legislation as constitutionally suspect; judicial invalidation allows for a statutory "second look" by the competent legislature, which largely, though not always, amends a statute to ensure its continued legal application. In short, according to its defenders, Charter dialogue answers the "countermajoritarian" difficulty as courts rarely have the final word on issues of public policy. And Charter dialogue is suggested to have a positive impact on public policy as judicial invalidation requires a rights-based response by the legislature with statutory authority. Rights talk, therefore, is the principal outcome of judicial review, and this impacts how public policy is framed, designed, and implemented by the governments of Canadian federalism.

For a period, this dialogic approach was viewed as a compelling answer to the third-generation questions that consumed the scholarship. As I have argued in this chapter, the fundamental problem with dialogue theory is that it focuses on the act of responding and not on the substance of a legislative response. If every legislative response, or nearly every one, is dialogue, then what does dialogue say about courts and legislatures in the Charter era? In this respect, the dialogic framework overlooks a central feature of the institutional relationship at the core of its understanding of judicial impact – that the Supreme Court of Canada is, in the context of a legislative response and remedial activism under section 24(1) of the *Canadian Charter*, an "implementer-dependent" institution reliant on the cabinets at both orders of government. Once this is understood, it allows for the introduction of variables that explain the actual impact of judicial review on public policy outcomes. It also requires a more modest view of judicial reach and rediscovery of the continued centrality of the ministry, particularly when federal, provincial, and territorial cabinets disagree with judicial policy incursions.

To understand judicial impact, I have introduced two variables when a salient issue of public policy is invalidated by the Supreme Court of Canada: first, legislative disagreement and how it can be the beginning of the end for judicial impact. This is not to suggest that legislative disagreement is the default response by governments to judicial invalidation. In fact, governments generally comply with judicial invalidation. Why then focus on legislative disagreement if the assembled cabinets largely accept judicial impact in public policy? For a very simple reason – legislative disagreement is likely to arise in compelling or salient issues of public policy and presents the ideal test of judicial impact. Although the notwithstanding clause is an instrument of legislative disagreement, it does not feature prominently in this book. Instead, the focus is on the more common aspect of disagreement – statutory amendments that seek to mitigate judicial impact. The second variable is the implementation chain and how a legislative response in a federal system, particularly when it requires coordinated and voluntary action, can mitigate the impact of the most forceful judicial decision.

Two complementary themes frame the remaining chapters: first, that federalism and devolution matters for an understanding of judicial impact in the Charter era and, second, that legislative disagreements are the best way to understand judicial impact. Indeed, if the ministry disagrees with judicial decisions, but simply accepts judicial policy directions and legislates accordingly, then judicial impact is real, evident, and confirmed. Perhaps, then, Charter dialogue theory is right after all. However, if judicial disagreement produces legislative responses that mitigate judicial review, then our assumptions about judicial impact must be rethought and dialogue reframed as a metaphor and not as a theory. I suspect that these two considerations will not dissuade dialogue theorists about fidelity to their understanding of the *Canadian Charter*. Nor will the critics of judicial power be deterred that, as an "implementer-dependent" institution operating within a complex federation, the Supreme Court of Canada is not as powerful as they claim.

In the remainder of this book, I explore the significance of the legislative disagreement/agreement dichotomy that manifests as statutory amendments, and the implementation chains that exist in salient issues of public policy judicialized in the Charter era. A consideration of these variables begins in the next four chapters that focus on Quebec, the *Charter of the French Language*, and the successful resistance to judicial invalidation and policy impact in *la belle province* by all the successors to the Lévesque government.

Quebec and the *Canadian Charter of Rights and Freedoms*
Une province pas comme les autres

2

The Canadian jurisdiction best placed to understand judicial impact and policy implementation in the Charter era is Quebec. There are several reasons why this book begins with a consideration of Quebec and the *Canadian Charter of Rights and Freedoms (Canadian Charter).*[1] Simply put, the minority language education provisions of section 23 of the *Canadian Charter* were drafted with an explicit constitutional purpose – to invalidate the statutory restrictions placed on English language educational services within the *Charter of the French Language*, the defining act of the Lévesque government introduced as Bill 101 in 1977.[2] Section 23 is a unique constitutional provision with a clear political purpose. No other provision of the *Canadian Charter* identifies an area of public policy for judicial review, targets an area of jurisdictional responsibility solely assigned to the provinces under the *Constitution Act, 1867*,[3] and was drafted with a clear remedial intention regarding Quebec and the *Charter of the French Language*.[4] Quebec is an ideal case to understand the nature of judicial power in the Charter era. It is also the hardest case to demonstrate the central argument of this book concerning judicial policy-making for three reasons: first, the explicit political intention of the constitutional *Canadian Charter* to remedy the statutory *Charter of the French Language;* second, the predominance of unanimous judicial decisions invalidating Quebec statutes that, seemingly, limit the discretion available to the Quebec government when responding to the Court; and, third, the inability of Quebec to invoke the notwithstanding clause to override judicial invalidation of the *Charter of the French Language* when section 23 of the *Canadian Charter* is engaged.

The explicit political purpose of the *Canadian Charter*,[5] as it relates to the *Charter of the French Language*, was acknowledged by the Supreme Court of Canada in *Protestant School Boards*, where it reviewed for the first time the relationship between the *Charter of the French Language* and the *Canadian Charter*.[6] In a judgment delivered in the name of "The Court," the justices were clear on the political purpose of section 23: "By incorporating into the structure of s. 23 of the *Charter* the unique set of criteria in s. 73 of *Bill 101*, the framers of the Constitution identified the type of regime they wished to correct and on which they would base the remedy prescribed."[7] Section 23 of the *Canadian Charter* allows at a minimum for an empirical testing of whether the intention of constitutional design by the Trudeau Liberals has, in fact, determined public policy outcomes in access to public English instruction in Quebec since 1982.

This chapter begins with an empirical overview of the *Canadian Charter* and its distinctive application to Quebec and those legislative areas under the exclusive authority of the National Assembly. Key trends used as evidence of constitutional design leading to judicial empowerment and a loss of policy autonomy for Quebec are highlighted. The chapter then shifts to a discussion of the constitutional politics surrounding patriation of the *British North America Act, 1867 (BNA Act)*, its renaming as the *Constitution Act, 1867*, and the implementation of the *Constitution Act, 1982*, of which the *Canadian Charter* is the most significant part.[8] Given that the unpopularity of a judicial decision is a necessary precondition whether political actors attempt to limit the policy impact of judicial review, Quebec's initial reaction to the *Canadian Charter* between 1982 and 1985 is instructive.

A Province Unlike the Others

The 101 judgments where the Supreme Court of Canada engaged in remedial activism under section 24(1) of the *Canadian Charter* between 1982 and 2022 are outlined in Table 2.1. Invalidated Quebec statutes exhibit several features that suggest it is *une province pas comme les autres* (a province unlike the others). First, in comparison to the other provinces, Quebec has experienced the highest number of statutes declared unconstitutional (n = 12), which is equal to the number of combined invalidations of British Columbia (n = 7) and Ontario (n = 5).[9] The Court has also spoken authoritatively when invalidating Quebec statutes. Judicial decisions can take one of three forms: a divided court where constitutionality is decided by majority decision; a

Table 2.1 Statutory invalidation by decision type, 1982–2022

Government	"The Court"	Unanimous	Majority	Total
Canada	3	33	29	65
Quebec	5	5	2	12
British Columbia	0	5	2	7
Ontario	0	1	4	5
Alberta	0	1	3	4
Prince Edward Island	0	2	0	2
Saskatchewan	0	1	1	2
Nova Scotia	0	1	1	2
Manitoba	0	1	0	1
New Brunswick	0	0	1	1
Total	8	50	43	101
Federal	3	33	29	65
Provincial	5	17	14	36

united court delivering a unanimous decision authored by a single justice or a series of concurring opinions; and, finally, an authoritative body that renders a unanimous decision in the name of "The Court." The type of decision is important as it indicates whether any discretion is available when framing a legislative response, with narrow majority decisions providing interpretive flexibility, and unanimous decisions as well as those by "The Court" appearing to foreclose any departure from a judicial decision.[10]

Overall, the Supreme Court of Canada has favoured a united approach to Charter review, rendering unanimous decisions in fifty of the 101 cases (nearly 49 percent) and eight cases in the name of "The Court" (nearly 8 percent), resulting in 58 percent of its decisions being unanimous and authoritative. Regarding Quebec, the Court has issued unanimous judgments in five of the twelve cases concerning statutes declared unconstitutional (nearly 42 percent). An identical number of statutes invalided have been authoritative decisions issued in the name of the "The Court," bringing the total number of invalidations by a united court to ten cases, which is over 83 percent for Quebec.

There is also a qualitative difference that suggests Quebec invalidations are substantively weightier than those of Parliament and the other provinces: half of Quebec statutes invalidated involve two iconic measures passed by the National Assembly – the *Charter of the French Language* (n = 5) and the *Referendum Act* (n = 1).[11] Although the Parliament of Canada has seen more statutes invalidated by the Court, a large majority involve criminal justice policy, which has led F.L. Morton to ask: "How many procedural nullifications of the federal Criminal Code does it take to equal the nullification of Quebec's language-education policy?"[12] While this statement does require some moderation, as recent invalidations of the *Criminal Code* and related statutes have involved substantive issues such as physician-assisted dying and the use of ministerial discretion regarding supervised consumption sites, the basic premise does hold after Morton's assertion nearly twenty-five years ago.[13] Thus, Quebec demonstrates the conditions for judicial policy impact identified in the introductory chapter as salient areas of public policy have been judicialized by virtue of the *Canadian Charter*. The potential for judicial power led Québécois academics to conclude that "the Charter has destroyed whole sections of the language regime gradually adopted by the province over the years."[14] Much of this concern centres on the *Canadian Charter* as a nation-building instrument[15] and the imposition of national standards in provincial areas of jurisdiction via judicial review.[16] And, in the case of Quebec, the 1982 settlement was, according to Eugénie Brouillet, a significant loss of control for Quebec in the areas of language and culture.[17]

If the invalidation of iconic Quebec statutes provides for the possibility of judicial policy impact, the legislative responses by the Quebec National Assembly also display the conditions under which judicial power can be confronted, redirected, and constrained. As many Supreme Court invalidations involve the *Charter of the French Language,* which has, at least among Quebec's political and intellectual class, a quasi-constitutional status,[18] judicial invalidation of the *Charter of the French Language* has not been well received. The National Assembly's sharp disapproval of decisions such as *Protestant School Boards, Ford, Devine, Libman, Solski,* and *Nguyen* transcends the party-political/federalist-sovereigntist divide.[19] This satisfies an essential criterion for understanding judicial policy impact, and its limitations, in the Charter era. It also creates the essential condition for confronting judicial review by the Cabinet once an issue returns to the National Assembly for reflection, amendment, and implementation.

The implementation context is important as it explains how Quebec has been able to neutralize the judicialization of salient areas of public policy within its jurisdictional authority. While the concerns raised by Québécois academics that Charter review would undermine federalism and Quebec's jurisdictional autonomy are valid,[20] they overstate the ability of agenda setting, which is the direct outcome of judicial invalidation, to dictate the design and implementation phases of public policy.[21] The Quebec government, and it alone, decides how to respond to judicial invalidation of statutes within its sovereign authority, given the executive-dominated nature of our parliamentary system. Given that the Court's invalidations of key provisions of the *Charter of the French Language* have not been well received, and the Court is dependent on the National Assembly to implement unpopular rulings, these legislative responses take on added importance. As the next chapters show, successive Quebec governments have adopted an approach that may be described as constitutional "sleight of hand" – while appearing to comply by incorporating judicial language into the legislative responses, the Quebec Cabinet has offset judicialization through statutory amendment and regulatory changes. The policy outcome is an illustration of the Québécois expression *"plus ça change, plus c'est la même chose"* ("the more things change, the more they stay the same"). In this respect, constitutional design and framers' intent have not significantly altered the policy objectives of the *Charter of the French Language*, which have been advanced by all Quebec governments since 1977.[22]

An additional factor that explains the general resilience of the statutory *Charter of the French Language*, despite judicial invalidation, is unique to Quebec: the failure to support the final constitutional package in November 1981, in part because of Quebec's fierce opposition to the judicialization of language and education policy during the patriation debate.[23] It is not surprising that successive Quebec governments have introduced legislative responses designed to frustrate the *Canadian Charter*'s application to Quebec involving language and education policy, given that the 1982 constitutional settlement has less legitimacy among Quebec's political class, compared to the rest of Canada,[24] as it is associated with the "night of the long knives" and Quebec's isolation within the 1982 settlement.[25] This policy of resistance is best captured by René Lévesque's statement on the *Canadian Charter*, "to make it as complicated, legitimately, and as difficult as we can for some aspects of that bloody Charter to be applied to Québec."[26] With refreshing candour, Lévesque articulated the general approach to the *Canadian Charter* that has been advanced, without exception, by his federalist, sovereigntist, and now nationalist successors as Quebec premier.[27]

That Bloody Charter

Quebec's opposition to the patriation project, and, in particular, the application of the *Canadian Charter* to language and education policy,[28] centred on the implication that judicial review posed for the *Charter of the French Language*. Henri Brun noted the anti-federal characteristics of the Supreme Court of Canada, including the absence of a provincial consultative mechanism in regard to the appointment to the Court and the fact that the *Canadian Charter* is imposed in provincial areas of jurisdiction, making the Court the "ultimate decision-maker of the validity of law, both Quebec and federal."[29] For Brouillet and many Québécois intellectuals, the *Canadian Charter* would lead to the "nationalization" of the *Charter of the French Language* via the Supreme Court of Canada – a process suggested to occur when the *Charter of the French Language* is evaluated against a national statement on Canadian values, which ignores the particular circumstance of Quebec that necessitated the politicization of language policy starting in the 1960s.[30]

Opposition to the *Canadian Charter* and unilateral patriation manifested in several actions that were initiated by the Lévesque government and largely supported by the Quebec Liberal Party. In November 1980, the Parti Québécois introduced and passed a motion, supported by thirty-three of the forty-one Liberal members of the National Assembly, condemning the Trudeau government's decision to proceed unilaterally to patriate the *BNA Act*. This motion was followed by the submission of reference questions to the Quebec Court of Appeal regarding the constitutionality of unilateral patriation,[31] which were unsuccessfully appealed to the Supreme Court of Canada.[32] Finally, once patriation occurred without the consent of Quebec, an act was passed in June 1982 that repealed all statutes previously passed by the National Assembly as well as their immediate reintroduction, with a provision indicating that the act operated notwithstanding sections 2 and 7–15 of the *Canadian Charter*, as required by section 33 of the *Canadian Charter*.[33] Until it was abandoned by the Bourassa government following the defeat of the Parti Québécois in 1985, pre-emptive use of the notwithstanding clause was a standard legislative technique in Quebec.[34]

Except for the blanket use of the notwithstanding clause, which was upheld by the Supreme Court of Canada in the 1988 *Ford v Quebec* decision, Quebec's opposition to the patriation project was not validated by judicial review.[35] For instance, neither the Quebec Court of Appeal nor the Supreme Court of Canada overturned the Trudeau government's strategy of unilateral patriation.[36] As well, neither court found that a constitutional convention existed that required the Parliament of Canada to obtain Quebec's consent before Parliament could send a resolution to Westminster seeking to patriate the *BNA Act*.[37] These defeats were important, as Peter Russell argued, since judicial support for Quebec's position in either reference would have undermined the legality and legitimacy of the constitutional settlement agreed to by the Trudeau government and the nine English-speaking premiers in November 1980.[38]

Despite these judicial defeats, they foreshadow the general response by successive Quebec governments, largely supported by a cross-party consensus in the National Assembly, that provisions of the *Canadian Charter* targeting Quebec's language and educational policies would, themselves, be challenged by aggressive legislative responses designed to negate the policy impact of judicial review. Legislative non-compliance by Quebec in salient areas of public policy has taken many forms. The most public manifestation is that of the Lévesque government and its blanket use of section 33 between 1982 and 1985.[39] Similarly, Robert Bourassa's use of the notwithstanding clause in response to the invalidation of the "sign-law" provision of the *Charter of the French Language* in *Ford* and *Devine* (Bill 178, *Charter of the French Language* [1988 *Charter of the French Language*]), and the pre-emptive use of the notwithstanding clauses in the *Canadian Charter* and the Quebec *Charter of Human Rights and Freedoms (Quebec Charter)* by the Legault government in regard to Bill 21, *Act Respecting the Laicity of the State,* and Bill 96, *Act Respecting French,* would also be included in this approach to legislative non-compliance.[40] Indeed, the uses of section 33 in respect to the *Act Respecting the Laicity of the State,* the *Act Respecting French,* and the 1988 *Charter of the French Language* allowed the offending laws to operate notwithstanding clear breaches of the *Canadian Charter* as well as the *Quebec Charter.*

The use of the notwithstanding clause is the most public manifestation of legislative non-compliance. It is also the least used approach. The more common response is what has been referred to as constitutional "sleight of hand" whereby an amendment approved by the National Assembly has the appearance, but not the form, of legislative acceptance of a judicial decision. As Chapters 3–5 demonstrate, this strategy generally involves a complex legislative response that incorporates language from a judicial decision invalidating a statutory provision (compliance) with additional amendments that negate the incorporation of judicial language into the new legislative scheme (non-compliance). The legislative responses to the *Solski* and *Nguyen* decisions – Bill 115, *An Act Following upon the Court Decision on the Language of Instruction* in 2010 – demonstrates the importance of understanding how a legislature responds to judicial invalidation in a salient issue of public policy.[41] The ultimate outcome is non-compliance as it succeeds in re-establishing the policy approach favoured by the Quebec government despite a negative judicial ruling. This illustrates the limitations of judicial policy impact when the courts are dependent on political institutions to implement judicial rulings in a public policy context.

Quebec and the *Canadian Charter*

The twelve cases in which the Supreme Court of Canada has nullified Quebec statutes, regulations, or ministerial and administrative decisions between 1982 and 2022 are outlined in Table 2.2. In this period, the Court reviewed a total of 278 federal and provincial statutes and seven instances of ministerial discretion in cases such as *PHS Community Services Society* for a total of 285 cases involving statutory and ministerial authority. The overall rate of judicial invalidation was 35 percent (101 out of 285 cases), with a similar rate for federal and provincial statutes. In comparison, eighteen Quebec statutes were reviewed in this time period, with an invalidation rate nearly double the federal and provincial average at 67 percent (twelve out of eighteen cases).[42]

This table also lists the amendments passed by the National Assembly, categorizes them based on issue salience, and determines whether the legislative response is an example of compliance or non-compliance. The distinction between a salient or a minor issue is important as the likelihood of non-compliance significantly increases when the Court invalidates an important area of public policy. In the case of Quebec, this would involve the *Charter of the French Language*. There are two reasons why the invalidation of a salient policy issue creates the conditions for non-compliance: first, the judicial decision will most likely be unpopular with the responsible legislative assembly, given its public policy importance; second, the Court must rely on a legislative body, which is generally opposed to its decision, to implement its judicial ruling in the form of a statutory or regulatory amendment. These two conditions – unpopularity and implementation context – provide a legislative body with the ability, if so inclined, to limit the impact of judicial review to agenda setting.

Turning to the legislative response, Quebec governments have been even-handed, with an equal number classified as compliance and non-compliance (n = 6). This raises an important question – does legislative compliance suggest that, over time, Quebec has come to accept the application of the *Canadian Charter* to fundamentally important statutes such as the *Charter of the French Language*? Perhaps, but not once issue salience is considered. The fact that the Quebec government has complied with a significant number of statutory invalidations is not surprising (n = 6), and we should expect governments to comply with judicial rulings, particularly when the issue involves routine or minor issues of public policy. As the introductory chapter argued, most examples of judicial invalidation do not involve issues at the heart of governance and do not invalidate the core priorities of the government of

Table 2.2 Quebec statutes and administrative decisions invalidated, 1982–2022

Case	Focus	Judgment	Issue salience	Legislative response
A.G. (Que.) v Quebec Protestant School Boards, (1984)	**Statute:** CFL, s. 73 CCRF, s. 23	**Unanimous:** (The Court) **Remedy:** Invalidation	**High:** restrictions on access to English public education to Quebec residents, parents, or siblings, educated in English in Quebec	**Non-compliance:** *CFL* 1984 (Bill 57); *CFL* 1993 (Bill 86); *CFL* 2002 (Bill 104)
Ford v Quebec (Attorney General), (1988)	**Statute:** CFL, ss. 52, 57, 58, 59, 60, 61, 69, 214	**Unanimous:** (The Court) **Remedy:** Invalidation	**High:** languages other than French prohibited on public signs	**Partial Compliance:** *CFL* 1988 (Bill 178) **Non-compliance:** *CFL* 1993 (Bill 86); *Regulation Respecting the Language of Commerce and Business Charter of the French Language*; *Regulation Defining the Scope of the Expression "Markedly Predominant" for the Purposes of the Charter of the French Language*
Devine v Quebec (Attorney General), (1988)	**Regulation:** *Regulation respecting the language of commerce and business* CCRF, s. 23			
Corporation professionnelle des médecins du Quebec v Thibault, (1988)	**Statute:** *Summary Convictions Act*, s. 75 CCRF, s. 11	**Unanimous:** 1 (Lamer J) **Remedy:** Invalidation	**Low:** a right to appeal from an acquittal by way of trial de novo	**Compliance:** *Code of Penal Procedure*
Libman v Quebec (Attorney General), (1997)	**Statute:** *Referendum Act*, ss. 402, 403, 404, 406, para. 3, 413, 414, 416, 417, Appendix 2 CCRF, s. 2(b)	**Unanimous:** (The Court) **Remedy:** Invalidation	**High:** spending restriction on third parties during referendum campaigns	**Compliance:** *Act to Amend the Elections Act, the Referendum Act, and other Legislative Provisions* 1998 (Bill 450)

Case	Type	Vote	Severity & Description	Outcome
Solski (Tutor of) v Quebec (Attorney General), (2005)	**Ministerial discretion:** CFL, s. 73(2) CCRF, s. 23	**Unanimous:** (The Court) **Remedy:** Judicial amendment	**High:** ministerial directive regarding "major part requirement" criteria for access to English public education solely based on time spent in English system	**Non-compliance:** CFL 2010 (Bill 115); Regulation Respecting the Criteria and Weighting Used to Consider Instruction in English Received in a Private Educational Institution Not Accredited for the Purposes of Subsidies
Chaoulli v Quebec (Attorney General), (2005)	**Statute:** Health Insurance Act, s. 15 Hospital Insurance Act, s. 11 PQCHRF, s. 1	**Majority:** (4:3) 3 judgments **Remedy:** Suspended decision (6 months)	**High:** prohibition on the purchase of private medical insurance	**Non-compliance:** Health Services and Social Services and Other Legislative Provisions 2006 (Bill 33)
Multani v Commission scolaire Marguerite-Bourgeoys, (2006)	**Administrative decision:** wearing of kirpan CCRF, s. 2(a)	**Unanimous:** (3 concurring) **Remedy:** Invalidation	**High:** school board prohibits the wearing of a religious symbol, the kirpan, on school grounds	**Compliance:** The wearing of religious symbols permitted
Nguyen v Quebec (Education, Recreation and Sports), (2009)	**Statute:** CFL, s. 72, paras. 2 and 3 CCRF, s. 23	**Unanimous: 1** (LeBel J) **Remedy:** Suspended decision (1 year)	**High:** periods of attendance at un-subsidized English-language private schools and instruction in English received pursuant to special authorization disregarded when determining whether child eligible to receive English instruction	**Non-compliance:** CFL 2010 (Bill 115); Act Respecting Private Education 2010 (Bill 115); Regulation Respecting the Criteria and Weighting Used to Consider Instruction in English Received in a Private Educational Institution Not Accredited for the Purposes of Subsidies

Case	Focus	Judgment	Issue salience	Legislative response
Loyola High School v Quebec (Attorney General), (2015)	**Ministerial discretion:** *Regulation Respecting the Application of the Act Respecting Private Education*, s. 22 CCRF, s. 2(a)	Unanimous: (2 concurring) **Remedy:** Judicial amendment	**Low:** Minister refused to grant private Catholic institution an exemption to teach a provincially mandated ethics course	**Compliance:** *Act Respecting Private Education 2010* (Bill 115) – updated to April 1, 2019; *Regulation Respecting the Application of the Act Respecting Private Education*
Conférence des juges de paix magistrats du Québec v Quebec (Attorney General), (2016)	**Statute:** *Act to Amend the Courts of Justice Act and Other Legislative Provisions as Regards the Status of Justices of the Peace*, ss. 27, 30, 33	Unanimous: 1 (Karakatsanis, Wagner, and Cote JJ) **Remedy:** Invalidation	**Low:** Judicial remuneration	**Compliance:** *Act to Implement Certain Recommendations of the 20 August 2018 Report of the Committee on the Remuneration of Judges and Justices of the Peace for 2016–2019* (Bill 20)
Quebec (Attorney General) v Alliance du personnel professionnel et technique de la santé et des services sociaux, (2018)	**Statute:** *Pay Equity Act*, ss. 76.3, 76.5, 103.1, para. 2 CCRF, s.15(1)	Majority: (6:3) 2 judgments **Remedy:** Invalidation	**Low:** calculation of pay equity formula and approach to auditing	**Compliance:** *Act to Amend the Pay Equity Act Mainly to Improve the Pay Equity Audit Process* (Bill 10)

Notes: CCRF – *Canadian Charter of Rights and Freedoms*; CFL – *Charter of the French Language*; PQCHRC – *Quebec Charter of Human Rights and Freedoms* the day or long-standing policies that transcend the party-political divide. This is one of the fatal flaws of dialogue theory as it does not consider issue salience and views a robust number of legislative responses as evidence of the vitality of democratic engagement with the judiciary.[43] As Andrew Petter caustically remarked, "when all is said and done, the dialogue thesis advanced by the authors appears to boil down to the unremarkable insight that legislatures have the capacity to modify legislation following adverse Charter rulings by the courts."[44] Indeed, it is unsurprising that governments respond to judicial invalidation. What matters is how they respond to judicial invalidation, whether a legislature accepts a judicial decision, and whether a legislature seeks to override judicial invalidation, either through statutory amendment or section 33 of the *Canadian Charter*.[45]

Invalidated Quebec statutes are distinct in several respects. As Morton and Guy Laforest separately observed in 1995, which holds true today, invalidated Quebec statutes or ministerial decisions tend to involve substantive issues of public policy, which sets this province apart from the other provinces and, to a lesser extent, the Parliament of Canada.[46] Many Quebec statutes invalided cannot be considered routine, mundane, or unexciting areas of public policy. Indeed, they are woven into the state building project associated with Quebec's Quiet Revolution and reside at the core of Quebec's complicated constitutional odyssey with its partners in the Canadian federation. The second notable difference is the nature of the legislative response when judicial invalidation involves substantive issues of public policy. In regard to issue salience and legislative compliance, Quebec has generally accepted judicial participation when it has involved relatively minor areas of public policy but rejects it when a policy issue is of sufficient importance to an incumbent government or when a judicial decision generates cross-party opposition to the Court's decision, as occurred in successive invalidations of the *Charter of the French Language*.[47] While the National Assembly may be divided on how to respond to the court's rulings,[48] the National Assembly has generally been united in opposition to judicial invalidation of the *Charter of the French Language*.

The National Assembly introduced legislative amendments that complied with the Supreme Court's ruling in *Thibault* when it rescinded the *Summary Convictions Act* that allowed an acquittal to be appealed through a new trial and replaced it with the *Code of Civil Procedure* that did not include such a procedure.[49] In response to *Conférence des juges de paix magistrats du Québec v Quebec (Attorney General)*, the 2016 decision that invalidated the *Courts of Justice Act* because it did not properly compensate justices of the peace, the

National Assembly fully complied with this decision and passed Bill 20, *An Act to Implement Certain Recommendations of the 20 August 2018 Report of the Committee on the Remuneration of Judges and Justices of the peace for 2016–2019*, which streamlined their compensation to ensure parity with other members of the judicial profession.[50] Similarly, in *Quebec (Attorney General) v Alliance du personnel professionnel et technique de la santé et des services sociaux*, the Court invalidated provisions of Quebec's *Pay Equity Act* that concerned the auditing procedures underlying the pay equity formula as a violation of equality rights.[51] The National Assembly fully complied with this ruling when it introduced Bill 10, *An Act to Amend the Pay Equity Act Mainly to Improve the Pay Equity Audit Process*.[52] Finally, the minister of education fully complied with the Court's ruling in *Loyola High School*,[53] a case involving freedom of religion that centred on the minister's refusal to grant a private Catholic school an exemption from teaching a provincially mandated ethics course.[54] In response to the Court's decision, the minister of education provided Loyola High School with an exemption under section 22 of the regulations pertaining to Bill 115, *Act Respecting Private Education*.[55] The minister of education approved an alternative course that would be taught from the Catholic perspective but in a way that was determined by the Ministry of Education to be consistent with the objectives of Quebec's Ethics and Religious Culture Program.

While the general pattern has been to engage in non-compliance, on two occasions, the National Assembly has fully complied with judicial invalidation of a statute with high issue salience.[56] While *Libman* and *Multani* are exceptions, legislative compliance can be explained by the relative narrowness of the judicial decisions and, in the case of *Libman*, the simplicity of the legislative amendment required to re-establish the constitutionality of the *Referendum Act* as well as the affected provisions in the *Election Act*.[57] In *Libman v Quebec*, the Supreme Court of Canada invalidated the spending restrictions under section 404 of the *Referendum Act* that restricted third parties or individuals not affiliated with the "Non" or "Oui" committees, as required by the law, to a total expenditure of six hundred dollars.[58] In a decision delivered by "The Court," a united bench concluded that the spending restrictions violated freedom of expression, arguing that the spending restrictions were too low to be considered a reasonable limitation on a fundamental freedom such as section 2(b). In its judgment, the Court suggested that increasing the spending limit to one thousand dollars for third parties, as recommended by the Lortie Commission, would constitute a reasonable limit of freedom of expression under section 1 of the *Canadian*

Charter.[59] Bill 450, passed by the National Assembly in 1998, fully complied with the Court's decision and accepted the suggested policy recommendation, increasing the spending restriction to one thousand dollars for third parties in general election and referendum campaigns.[60]

One would be hard pressed to characterize any of these cases as encompassing fundamental questions of public policy, approaches rooted in the preservation of Quebec's language and culture, or part of Canada and Quebec's complicated constitutional odyssey.[61] And, as I contend, this explains why various Quebec governments fully complied and quickly introduced legislative amendments to address the constitutional issues raised by the Court in these six instances. The limited importance of these legislative responses questions the value of dialogue theory as an understanding of judicial power, as it is unsurprising that legislatures accept judicial participation when the policy stakes are so low. In this respect, I echo Matthew Hennigar's suggestion that "it seems prudent to avoid the metaphor entirely"[62] and would add the following justification – applying Peter Hogg and Allison Bushell's approach to dialogue – which is simply "[w]here a judicial decision striking down a law on Charter grounds can be reversed, modified, or avoided by a new law,"[63] would be incorrectly interpreted as Quebec and the Supreme Court of Canada engaged in this democratic exchange in every instance of judicial invalidation, as demonstrated in Table 2.2.

This would lead to the questionable and, frankly, wrong conclusion that Quebec has accepted the judicialization of language and education policy because of a robust Charter dialogue between Quebec and the Supreme Court of Canada. The National Assembly, albeit executive dominated, has vigorously responded to judicial invalidation in salient issues of public policy not as a participant committed to constitutional dialogue that, along with the Supreme Court, engages in inter-institutional dialogue to establish the constitutionality of legislation considering the *Canadian Charter*. Instead, Quebec has had a steadfast purpose – to limit the impact of judicial policy-making on its sovereign areas of jurisdiction, particularly when judicial review involves language and education policy. Whereas dialogue theory suggests complementary interactions to advance constitutionalism, the legislative responses introduced by Quebec are largely, if not exclusively, about re-establishing sovereign legislative authority over language and education policy.

In my estimation, this is the central flaw of dialogue theory, both normatively and empirically, as it has a singular focus on process (the passage of a legislative amendment), without any consideration of the intent of the legislative response (possibly to defy the Supreme Court of Canada). There is a fundamental difference between dialogue and defiance that manifests as legislative non-compliance. Kent Roach referred to such interactions as "in your face legislative responses," which accurately captures Quebec's approach to judicial invalidation of the *Charter of the French Language*.⁶⁴ If, at the end of the day, Charter dialogue is as prevalent in Quebec as the raw numbers suggest because any legislative response is included within the definition of dialogue,⁶⁵ is devoid of any evaluation of issue salience and motivation, and fails to understand that, in regard to language and education policy, the Quebec government acts with the singular purpose of overcoming judicial policy intrusions, then perhaps Charter dialogue is not such a good thing after all.

Maîtres Chez Nous: The Politicization of Language

The ushering in of the Quiet Revolution is best captured by the 1960 election slogan of the Quebec Liberal Party led by Jean Lesage – *"Il faut que ça change"* (things have to change) – and the 1962 slogan *"maîtres chez nous"* (masters in our own home). One of the significant outcomes of the Quiet Revolution was the politicization of language that emerged at the end of the 1960s, both in Quebec and in Canada. Indeed, the issue of Quebec – its place within Canada and whether the francophone *chez nous* (our home) was Canada or simply Quebec – were the core political questions that motivated both Pierre Trudeau as prime minister of Canada (1968–79, 1980–84) and René Lévesque, first as a cabinet minister (1960–66) in the government of Quebec premier Jean Lesage and, after his departure from the Quebec Liberal Party in 1968, as Parti Québécois premier (1976–85). For instance, Trudeau introduced the *Official Languages Act* in 1969 that established Canada as an officially bilingual country where citizens were guaranteed federal government services in either French or English, the two official languages.⁶⁶ In contrast, Lévesque introduced the *Charter of the French Language* in 1977, which built upon Bill 22, the *Official Language Act*, which was introduced by the previous Liberal government of Robert Bourassa in 1974: Bills 22 and 101 declared French as the official language of Quebec in government, business, and labour relations.⁶⁷ On the issue of language of instruction in public schools, Bill 101 was a significant departure from previous legislative attempts to navigate this sensitive issue in Quebec.

The *Charter of the French Language* passed by the Lévesque government contained only two notable differences from its immediate predecessor, the *Official Language Act*.⁶⁸ These differences would prove to be significant departures once the *Canadian Charter* was entrenched and judicial review of Bill 101 was permitted under the Charter's minority language education provisions. The first notable difference between the *Charter of the French Language* and the *Official Language Act* involved public signs and commercial expression. Under section 35 of the *Official Language Act*, "public signs must be drawn up in French or in both French and another language, except within certain limits provided by regulation."[69] The *Charter of the French Language* would significantly restrict the use of languages other than French. Although section 58 of the *Charter of the French Language* contained a number of narrow exceptions, the law generally prohibited languages other than French, as "signs and posters and commercial advertising shall be solely in the official language."[70] In this respect, the *Charter of the French Language* largely abandoned bilingualism that characterized the *Official Language Act* in regard to public signs and commercial expression and was therefore at odds with Pierre Trudeau's conception of Canada as a bilingual federation of two official language communities.[71] For Camille Laurin, who introduced *Charter of the French Language* as minister of state for cultural development, "Quebec is a French-language society. There will therefore be no question of a bilingual Quebec."[72]

The second and most significant difference involved language of instruction in public schools. While the *Official Language Act* provided for a small degree of freedom of choice in public education, section 73 of the *Charter of the French Language* effectively ended this approach to public instruction, subject to several limited exceptions. Under section 73, instruction in English was restricted to the following children, when requested by their father and mother:

(a) a child whose father or mother received his or her elementary instruction in English, in Québec;
(b) a child whose father or mother domiciled in Québec before 26 August 1977, received his or her elementary instruction in English outside Québec;
(c) a child, who in his last year of school in Québec before 26 August 1977, was lawfully receiving his instruction in English, in a public kindergarten class or in an elementary or secondary school;
(d) the younger brothers and sisters of a child described in paragraph c.[73]

The *Charter of the French Language* had two objectives regarding education policy: first, to prevent the integration of the allophone community into the anglophone community through parental choice in public education and, second, to narrow accessibility to English education to simply Quebec anglophones. In particular, the children of anglophones emigrating from other provinces after August 26, 1977, would be ineligible for English education under section 73(b) of the *Charter of the French Language*, regardless of their parents having been educated in English outside of Quebec.

Pierre Elliott Trudeau and the *Charter of the French Language*
The Trudeau government opposed elements of the *Charter of the French Language* and had several provisions within the *BNA Act* at the ready to confront the Lévesque government over its language and education policy. The Trudeau government could delay the passage of the *Charter of the French Language* by instructing Quebec's lieutenant governor to withhold royal assent by reserving it for consideration by the Trudeau Cabinet (section 55), as permitted by section 90 of the *BNA Act*, which extended the powers of the governor general (sections 55–57) to the lieutenant governors.[74] Under the power of disallowance (section 56), the Trudeau Cabinet could veto the *Charter of the French Language* within one year of its passage by the National Assembly of Quebec, as William Lyon Mackenzie King's government had done in relation to legislation passed by Alberta's Social Credit government in 1937.[75] However, any direct engagement would come at a significant political cost to national unity,[76] given that the Lévesque government was required, under the Parti Québécois's Constitution, to hold a referendum on Quebec's political future during its first mandate.

In addition to these constitutional instruments, the possibility of judicialization and legal mobilization existed, though in a much more limited form before the patriation of the Constitution in 1982. Under section 52 of the *Supreme Court Act*, the federal Cabinet can submit reference questions to the Supreme Court of Canada, and the Trudeau government had the ability to submit a series of references on the constitutionality of the *Charter of the French Language* once it had been granted royal assent by Quebec's lieutenant governor.[77] Again, similar to the powers of reservation and disallowance, the reference procedure and judicialization by the Trudeau government would represent a clumsy response in the context of the "national question" and the forthcoming referendum on Quebec's constitutional future.

Beyond the political risk associated with direct judicialization, the Trudeau government faced a more practical and stark reality: few provisions of the *BNA Act* could be used to frame a reference with a modicum of success, particularly those provisions of the *Charter of the French Language* involving language of instruction and the restrictions on public signs. For instance, only three potential challenges existed before 1982: a federalism challenge that the *Charter of the French Language* was *ultra vires* Quebec's responsibility under section 92 of the *BNA Act;* a section 93 challenge that the *Charter of the French Language* negatively affected denominational school rights of the protestant minority in Quebec; and, finally, a section 133 challenge against the *Charter of the French Language*'s declaration of French as the official language of Quebec. The last challenge would centre on the notion that the *Charter of the French Language* was inconsistent with the constitutional guarantee that parliamentary and court proceedings may be conducted in either English or French in the Parliament of Canada and the National Assembly, as permitted under section 133 of the *BNA Act*.[78]

The first two constitutional challenges were non-starters. As the *Charter of the French Language* is clearly within the jurisdictional responsibilities assigned to Quebec under section 92 of the *BNA Act*, the Parti Québécois's signature legislation was (and is) immune from judicial review on federalism grounds, as the Court noted in *Devine:* "That the overall object of the *Charter of the French Language* is the enhancement of the French Language in Quebec does not make the challenged provisions any less an intended regulation of an aspect of commerce within the province. As such, they fall within provincial jurisdiction under the Constitution Act, 1867."[79] Further, the *Charter of the French Language* does not impact denominational school rights, and any recourse to remedial legislation by the Trudeau Cabinet under section 93(4) would be viewed as politically motivated and without constitutional merit. The only possible constitutional challenge against the *Charter of the French Language*, therefore, involved section 133.[80] However, instead of submitting a reference directly to the Supreme Court of Canada, the Trudeau government outsourced it with the creation of the Court Challenges Program (CCP) in 1978. Housed within the Social Action Branch at the Secretary of State of Canada, the CCP provided funding to language groups that pursued legal mobilization and litigation against language policies such as the *Charter of the French Language*.[81]

Given that sections 7–13 of the *Charter of the French Language* declared French as the official language of the legislature and court proceedings, groups and individuals that would unite to create Alliance Quebec as an English language lobby group in 1982[82] launched a successful constitutional challenge funded under the CCP.[83] In *Blaikie*, a unanimous decision in 1979 by "The Court" declared the challenged provisions of the *Charter of the French Language ultra vires* the National Assembly, and unconstitutional in light of section 133. The challenged provisions were a legislative attempt to interfere with a constitutional guarantee, and the Court ruled that Quebec could not diminish a constitutional provision such as section 133 by virtue of the *Charter of the French Language*.[84] This would be the only successful legal mobilization against the *Charter of the French Language* before 1982, and it clearly demonstrates the limited ability of judicialization as a political strategy in this period of Canadian mega-constitutional politics. In the end, both the sign-law provisions and the restrictions on access to English public instruction remained in place because any constitutional challenge against these provisions of the *Charter of the French Language* would be unsuccessful.

The CCP's significance is apparent once the *Canadian Charter* was part of the *Constitution Act, 1982*. And this would be for a very important reason: unlike the *BNA Act*, which was renamed the *Constitution Act, 1867*, the *Canadian Charter* contained several sections with real potential to invalidate broad swaths of the *Charter of the French Language*. According to Morton,

> the Charter has thus allowed the federal government to achieve indirectly what it could not have achieved directly. Indeed, combining the Charter with the CCP and SOS [Secretary of State] funding was something of a political master stroke. By removing the greatest disincentive in using litigation as a tactic, the funding guaranteed that Charter challenges would occur and also provided Ottawa with political cover.[85]

The constitutional instrument that posed the greatest threat to the *Charter of the French Language* would prove to be section 23, the minority language education provisions. It is, perhaps, the most unique section of the *Canadian Charter* and the one with the clearest political intention on the part of the Trudeau Liberals to remedy a provincial law that it found distasteful.

Much of the *Canadian Charter* involves negative rights, which provide protection against state interference but do not place any substantive policy obligations on a government. Section 23 departs from this general characteristic, as the Court acknowledged in *Mahe v Alberta*: "Section 23 confers upon a group a right which places positive obligations on government to alter or develop major institutional structures."[86] Further, a minority language community is only entitled to education services "where numbers warrant," as outlined in section 23(3)(b), and the Court has employed a sliding-scale approach where the level of services is determined by the demographics of a local language minority community.[87] At one end of the spectrum, the maximum level of "management and control" provided is the establishment of an independent school board and at the lower end is representation on a school board, where the linguistic minority is provided "with exclusive authority to make decisions relating to minority language instruction and facilities."[88]

Section 23 is a declaratory provision that allows for judicial determination of education services "where numbers warrant" for an official language minority. But it is much more. It is, in combination with section 24(1) of the *Canadian Charter*, a dual remedy power, as it allows a court of competent jurisdiction to impose a policy requirement on a provincial government under section 23(3) that is also considered "appropriate and just in the circumstances" under section 24(1). Finally, its uniqueness is accentuated by the fact that judicially imposed policy requirements under section 23, and remedies applied under section 24(1), cannot be negated by the *Canadian Charter's* notwithstanding clause. Quebec's opposition to the *Canadian Charter*, and, in particular, section 23, was rooted in these distinctive features. Although the Parti Québécois could not agree, in principle, to the patriation of the Constitution in 1982, as its political program was independence/sovereignty association, it was opposed to the *Canadian Charter* on substantive grounds, recognizing the danger that the *Charter of the French Language* faced.

The provisions regulating language of instruction under the *Charter of the French Language* and the *Canadian Charter* are outlined in Table 2.3 and clearly demonstrate that section 23 was designed with a clear remedial intention regarding the *Charter of the French Language* and section 73. For instance, the original version of the *Charter of the French Language* enacted in 1977 made narrow exceptions to section 72's declaration that "instruction in the kindergarten classes and in the elementary and secondary schools shall be in French." A child whose parents or siblings were educated in English in Quebec (section 73(a)), a child whose parents were living in Quebec when the *Charter of the French Language* was proclaimed (August 26, 1977) and educated in English outside of Quebec (section 73(b)), a child lawfully receiving instruction in English in their last year of school before the proclamation of the *Charter of the French Language* (section 73(c)), and, finally, the siblings of a child lawfully receiving English instruction under section 73(c) were eligible for English instruction. Section 72 specified that restrictions on English instruction applied to institutions "declared to be of public interest or recognized for purposes of grants in virtue of the Act respecting private education." In short, the *Charter of the French Language* declared that language of instruction was a public benefit granted by the state and extended

Table 2.3 The Charter of the French Language and the Canadian Charter

Charter of the French Language 1977 (Bill 101)	Canadian Charter of Rights and Freedoms 1982	Charter of the French Language 1984 (Bill 57)
Language of instruction	Language of instruction	Language of instruction
72. Instruction in the kindergarten classes and in the elementary and secondary schools shall be in French, except where this chapter allows otherwise.	23. (1) Citizens of Canada	72. Instruction in the kindergarten classes and in the elementary and secondary schools shall be in French, except where this chapter allows otherwise.
This rule obtains in school bodies within the meaning of the Schedule and also applies to subsidized instruction provided by institutions declared to be of public interest or recognized for purposes of grants in virtue of the Act respecting private education (chapter E-9).	(a) whose first language learned and still understood is that of the English or French linguistic minority population of the province in which they reside, or*	This rule obtains in school bodies within the meaning of the Schedule and also applies to subsidized instruction provided by institutions declared to be of public interest or recognized for purposes of grants in virtue of the Act respecting private education (chapter E-9).
73. In derogation of section 72, the following children, at the request of their father and mother, may receive their instruction in English:	(b) who have received their primary school instruction in Canada in English or French and reside in a province where the language in which they received that instruction is the language of the English or French linguistic minority population of the province,	73. In derogation of section 72, the following children, at the request of their father and mother, may receive their instruction in English:
(1) a child whose father or mother received his or her elementary instruction in English, in Québec;	have the right to have their children receive primary and secondary school instruction in that language in that province.	(1) a child whose father or mother received elementary instruction in English in Québec, *provided that that instruction constitutes the major part of the elementary instruction he or she received in Québec;*

(b) a child whose father or mother domiciled in Québec on 26 August 1977, received his or her elementary instruction in English outside Québec;

Continuity of language instruction

(2) Citizens of Canada of whom any child has received or is receiving primary or secondary school instruction in English or French in Canada, have the right to have all their children receive primary and secondary school instruction in the same language.

Application where numbers warrant

(3) The right of citizens of Canada under subsections (1) and (2) to have their children receive primary and secondary school instruction in the language of the English or French linguistic minority population of a province

  (a) applies wherever in the province the number of children of citizens who have such a right is sufficient to warrant the provision to them out of public funds of minority language instruction; and

  (b) includes, where the number of those children so warrants, the right to have them receive that instruction in minority language educational facilities provided out of public funds.

(2) a child who, in his last year of school in Québec before 26 August 1977, was lawfully receiving his instruction in English, in a public kindergarten class or in an elementary or secondary school;

(b) a child whose father or mother is, on 26 August 1977, domiciled in Québec and has received elementary instruction in English outside Québec, *provided that that instruction constitutes the major part of the elementary instruction he or she received outside Québec;*

(2) a child who, in his last year of school in Québec before 26 August 1977, was lawfully receiving his instruction in English, in a public kindergarten class or in an elementary or secondary school;

Notes: The "major part requirement" added in the 1984 *Charter of the French Language* is indicated in *italics*.

* Section 23(1)(a) does not currently apply to Quebec as it has yet to be adopted by the National Assembly of Quebec or Government of Quebec.

the restrictions to all elementary and secondary public institutions as well as private institutions receiving a public subsidy. This limited English instruction to Quebec's historical anglophone community and to the children of those residing in Quebec that were educated in English outside of Quebec before the *Charter of the French Language*'s proclamation.[89]

The *Canadian Charter*'s minority language education provisions challenged several of the defining characteristics of the *Charter of the French Language* that regulated language of instruction. First, language of instruction was elevated from a public service provided at the discretion of the National Assembly to a constitutional guarantee that placed a constitutional duty on the provincial and territorial legislatures regarding their official language minority communities. Second, it redefined Canadian citizenship to include a right to public instruction for official language communities. Third, section 23 placed a constitutional obligation on provincial and territorial governments to provide, out of public funds, educational services to their minority language communities "where numbers warrant" such a provision. Finally, and in combination with section 24(1) of the *Canadian Charter*, section 23 provided for judicial remedy of provincial educational policies that derogated from these constitutional rights granted to Canadian citizens and the constitutional duties placed on provincial and territorial governments.

Conclusion: Master Strokes and Magnificent Obsessions

From a drafting perspective, Morton is correct that the *Canadian Charter* represents a "master stroke" by the Trudeau government regarding the *Charter of the French Language*. By introducing a supreme law charter of rights with a clear remedial intention, the Trudeau government appeared to put the *Charter of the French Language* in constitutional checkmate. Once Trudeau's "magnificent obsession" was achieved with the patriation of the Constitution in 1982,[90] the *Charter of the French Language* was ripe for constitutional invalidation. The early months of the *Canadian Charter* were not favourable to Quebec, as one of the first constitutional challenges under the *Canadian Charter* was launched against the language of instruction provisions of the *Charter of the French Language*. In *Quebec Association of Protestant School Boards v Attorney General of Quebec*, the Quebec Superior Court found that section 73 of the *Charter of the French Language* was inconsistent with the *Canadian Charter*'s minority language education provisions.[91] This decision would be delivered on September 8, 1982, only five months after the enactment of the *Canadian Charter*. Further, this decision would be upheld on appeal to the Quebec Court of Appeal on June 9, 1983.[92] Given these decisive rulings on the constitutional incompatibility of section 73 of the *Charter of the French Language*, how did the Lévesque government respond? Did it amend section 73 to comply with the rulings and replicate the language of instruction found in section 23 of the *Canadian Charter*, the minority language education provision?

The Lévesque government did the opposite. In 1984, it doubled down and amended the *Charter of the French Language* to reaffirm that language of instruction services were only available to the children or siblings of individuals educated in English in Quebec before the introduction of the *Charter of the French Language* in 1977. Quebec, therefore, firmly rejected the rights-based citizenship approach within section 23 and Trudeau's pan-Canadian approach (see Table 2.3). The 1984 amendment also anticipated a potential drafting flaw in section 73 – the length of instruction required to quality for English language of instruction was not specified.[93] This gave rise to the major part requirement (indicated in *italics* in Table 2.3) that would, itself, become a future constitutional challenge in *Solski*. Indeed, the Lévesque government anticipated that the open-ended nature of the residency requirement under the 1977 version of the *Charter of the French Language* could be exploited to the detriment of the policy objectives of language of instruction as it related to Quebec's allophone population, streamlining Quebec's growing immigrant population into the French language educational system. That Quebec weathered this constitutional and judicial storm is remarkable. How successive Quebec governments faced a perfect storm of constitutional design and judicial review against the *Charter of the French Language* is the focus of the next three chapters.

Minority Language Education Rights and the *Charter of the French Language* 3
Plus ça change, plus c'est la même chose

Chapter 1 introduced the concept of the "implementation chain" and how the legislative responses introduced by the various cabinets in Canada, as well as the actions of private actors, can change the inflection point of a judicial decision. This chapter pushes it further and considers the interplay between section 23 of the *Canadian Charter of Rights and Freedoms (Canadian Charter)*, which requires provincial and territorial governments to provide educational services to Canadian citizens that are members of an official language minority community, and section 73 of Bill 101, *Charter of the French Language*, which specifies who can access English language instruction in Quebec.[1] These two provisions are at odds and are the best example of a legislative disagreement in the Charter era, as section 23 was drafted with the intention of remedying section 73 of the *Charter of the French Language*. Moreover, this policy disagreement has played out over three landmark decisions by the Supreme Court of Canada[2] and a series of responses by Quebec governments to the invalidation of section 73,[3] one of the language-of-instruction provisions in the *Charter of the French Language*. It is therefore an ideal test case whether constitutional design and judicial remedial activism can shape legislative outcomes.

This chapter and the next are different in several respects from the others in this book. Unlike the rest of the *Canadian Charter*, which is a negative rights instrument, regulating what government cannot do, section 23 of the Charter is a positive right that places a constitutional obligation on provincial and territorial governments to provide minority language education services "where numbers warrant" to Canadian citizens within their jurisdiction. This is a difference of importance as the remedial nature of section 23 can facilitate judicial policy impact. Additionally, unlike other rights and freedoms in the *Canadian Charter* that are universal and available to "everyone" in Canada (fundamental freedoms, legal rights, and equality rights) or to "every citizen" (democratic rights and mobility rights), section 23 is a group right that belongs to a specific category of Canadian citizen. In the case of Quebec, it is the anglophone community.[4] Finally, section 23 involves a jurisdictional responsibility solely under provincial control, and the devolved responsibilities of the territorial governments, and subjects it to national standards involving official language minority communities. This is particularly significant in Quebec, given that the educational system is organized along linguistic lines,[5] with nine English school boards and sixty French school boards.

The linguistic organization of school boards in Quebec presents a unique opportunity to evaluate the policy impact of judicial decisions involving section 23. There is a rich amount of empirical evidence to evaluate the policy impact of section 23 decisions by the Supreme Court of Canada and how it has – or has not – affected the nine English school boards in Quebec. For instance, Quebec residents that want to send their children to English public instruction must first apply for a "certificate of eligibility" issued by the ministry of education, and yearly statistics on the numbers issued under section 73 are available. This allows for evidence-based conclusions to be drawn about the impact of judicial review under section 23 of the *Canadian Charter* and not simply academic speculation. Further, the linguistic profile of Quebec, patterns of immigration, and interprovincial migration rates all have a direct impact on the vitality of the anglophone community in Quebec. And because the provision of minority language educational services is provided "where numbers warrant," the demographic strength of the anglophone community is particularly relevant for the robustness – or frailty – of the nine English school boards.

Section 23 has a clear and identifiable rights beneficiary in Quebec – namely, the anglophone community. Because of this, in addition to evaluating the legislative responses of successive Quebec governments, the following questions will be considered. Is the anglophone community a growing or declining component of Quebec society? What are the enrollment trends in the nine English public school boards in Quebec? How many requests for "certificates of eligibility" for English public instruction are made each year under section 73 of the *Charter of the French Language*? Do anglophones overwhelmingly send their children to the English public system? And, finally, are anglophones deciding to educate their children in French, despite section 23 of the *Canadian Charter*? Why are these questions relevant for a consideration of judicial policy impact? For one, they reinforce the importance of the implementation chain and how the responses by public actors (the Quebec government) and private actors (the anglophone community) can change the trajectory of a judicial decision. And they reiterate that the implementation of a judicial decision rests on actors and actions beyond the control of a court.

The Québécois expression *"plus ça change, plus c'est la même chose"* (the more things change, the more they stay the same) is apt for understanding the legislative and regulatory changes by successive Quebec governments regarding the judicial invalidation of section 73 of the *Charter of the French Language*. There are several factors that work in tandem to produce this outcome: the legislative choices of successive Quebec governments, the personal choices of the anglophone community regarding school attendance, and the vitality of the anglophone community and its institutions. Despite the invalidation of section 73 that restricted English language instruction to Quebec's historic anglophone community (*Protestant School Boards*), the rewriting of section 73 of the *Charter of the French Language* to mirror section 23 of the *Canadian Charter* (1993 *Charter of the French Language*), the invalidation of the ministerial approach to the "major part requirement" (MPR) under section 73 (*Solski*), and the invalidation of the legislative prohibition on unsubsidized private schools as a way to satisfy the MPR (*Nguyen*), access to public English instruction in Quebec remains firmly under the control of the Quebec government.[6] This outcome is partially explained by the passage of cross-purpose legislative and regulatory changes that constrain judicial policy impact. For instance, the typical response to judicial invalidation of section 73 by successive Quebec governments has been to incorporate the language of a judicial decision while simultaneously carving out exceptions to the Court's decisions in *Protestant School Boards, Solski,* and *Nguyen*. By working at cross-purposes, these legislative and regulatory changes have preserved the policy autonomy of the Quebec government and advanced the objectives of the language of instruction provisions of the *Charter of the French Language*.

The relative strength of these decisions, where "The Court" issued rulings in *Protestant School Boards* and *Solski* and Justice Louis LeBel delivered the decision on behalf of a unanimous bench in *Nguyen*, did not prevent various

Quebec governments from passing strong, forceful, and autonomous legislative responses. It is important to emphasize, again, that these responses occurred in the context of a clear constitutional intention on the part of the Trudeau Liberals to invalidate the language of instruction provisions of the *Charter of the French Language* and the exclusion of section 23 of the *Canadian Charter* from the override provisions of section 33. The judicialization of language and education policy has not undermined the autonomy, or maneuverability, of the Quebec government.[7] Quite the contrary. While the "centralization thesis" remains a dominant understanding of judicial review and its impact on the *Charter of the French Language*,[8] it is not an accurate one,[9] as Frédéric Bérard shows in his recent analysis of this question.[10]

The legislative and regulatory changes introduced by successive Quebec governments have a direct bearing on which Quebec residents will be issued "certificates of eligibility" to attend English language public instruction. One of the implementation challenges that judicial impact faces under section 23 of the *Canadian Charter* is rooted in the changing character of the anglophone community – it is a declining linguistic group that is increasingly sending its children to the French school system, despite having a constitutional right to attend English language instruction. The reality in Quebec is that an upward trend exists for private school attendance, fewer requests are being made for "certificates of eligibility" for English language instruction, and downward pressure is being exerted on the English school system and student enrollments. In this chapter and the next, I elaborate on this three-part explanation for limited impact of judicial decisions involving section 73 of the *Charter of the French Language*, focusing on legislative changes, the changing character of the anglophone community, and the educational choices of this community.[11] This chapter considers the first section 23 decision by the Supreme Court of Canada in 1984, *Protestant School Boards*, and the amendments to the *Charter of the French Language* introduced by the Bourassa government in 1993.

Language of Instruction: The Quebec and Canada Clauses
Section 73 of the *Charter of the French Language* is referred to as the "Quebec clause" regarding language of instruction, whereas section 23 of the *Canadian Charter* and its pan-Canadian application is referred to as the "Canada clause." The *Charter of the French Language* provides for a set of language-of-instruction guarantees and exemptions for those temporarily in Quebec due to work (section 85) or experiencing learning difficulties best addressed in the English language system (section 81). For instance, the 1977 version of section 73(a)

restricted English language instruction to the children of individuals educated in English in Quebec; those domiciled in Quebec as of August 26, 1977, and educated in English outside of Quebec (section 73(b)); a child in school during the academic year ending August 26, 1977 (section 73(c)); and the siblings of those permitted English language instruction under section 73(c). In effect, language of instruction would be a public good provided to Quebec's historic anglophone community, and freedom of choice would effectively end for Quebec's growing allophone population, which, with few exceptions, would be streamlined into the French language system.[12] As the *Charter of the French Language* is solely within provincial jurisdiction, and immune from judicial review on federalism grounds, limiting language and education guarantees to Quebec's anglophone minority is permitted by sections 92 and 93 of the *Constitution Act, 1867*.[13]

The concept of minority language guarantees outside of Quebec began as a political commitment during the eighteenth Annual Premiers' Conference in 1978: "The Premiers agree that they will make their best efforts to provide instruction in education in English and French where numbers warrant."[14] This language guarantee sharpened during a meeting of the premiers in Montreal six months later, where "[e]ach child of the French-speaking or English-speaking minority is entitled to an education in his or her language in the primary or secondary schools in each province where numbers warrant."[15] There are a number of important features of the provincial approach to language of instruction that need to be emphasized. First, the premiers advanced a legislative approach to minority language education guarantees that preserved provincial jurisdictional sovereignty under section 92 of the *British North America Act, 1867 (BNA Act)*.[16] Second, the premiers did not support the judicialization of language and education services for matters that fell within their jurisdiction, nor did they support a judicial remedial power in relation to language and education guarantees. During the period in which the minister of justice circulated the draft Charters to his provincial counterparts, the premiers released their own document outlining what they would accept in an entrenched *Canadian Charter* on August 28, 1980. As there was no consensus, the provincial proposal did not include support for language and education rights enforced in a constitutional charter of rights and freedoms.[17]

Conscious of provincial opposition to the *Canadian Charter* project, an initial draft of language rights presented to the provincial attorney generals and ministers of justice, written on July 4, 1980, drew heavily on the premiers' communique of February 23, 1980. While this draft Charter contained rights in regard to language of instruction (section 16), the provinces retained the discretion under section 16(2) to "enact provisions for determining whether the number of children of citizens of Canada who are members of an English-speaking or French-speaking minority population in an area of the province warrant the provision out of public funds of minority language education facilities in that area."[18] Although this draft Charter contained a judicial remedy clause (section 19), it is unclear how it would apply to section 16(2) as this provision reaffirmed provincial sovereignty over the provision of minority language education services. For instance, the draft Charter combined contradictory constitutional principles as it recognized parliamentary sovereignty in section 16(2) as well as constitutional supremacy in section 18 and required the courts to reconcile this contradiction in section 19. This muddling of constitutional principles would be reaffirmed during a subsequent meeting of the Continuing Committee of Ministers on the Constitution on August 26, 1980,[19] and at the First Ministers' Conference on September 8–12, 1980.

The draft circulated during the First Ministers' Conference reproduced the language regarding provincial control over the criteria for the provision of minority language instruction in section 22(2).[20] Further, it appeared to weaken the judicial remedy power in regard to minority language education rights as the reasonable limitations clause included a broad reference to the principles of parliamentary supremacy.[21] For instance, as the provinces retained discretion over the provision of this service, if a court of competent jurisdiction found a language rights violation, the justification standard of reasonable limits that are "generally accepted in a free and democratic society with a parliamentary system of government" suggested judicial deference to parliamentary choices. This approach to reasonable limits would rarely, if ever, see a court conclude that a rights violation was unreasonable, as many witnesses before the Special Joint Committee on the Constitution of Canada testified. It was the precise wording of section 1 – the reasonable limits clause – and its reference to parliamentary democracy that generated intense criticism during the public hearings held by the Special Joint Committee. This criticism saw Jean Chrétien, the minister of justice, propose a new reasonable limits clause that addressed the concerns raised before the parliamentary committee by associated interest groups and officials.[22]

The First Ministers' Conference in September 1980 failed to secure provincial agreement on patriating the *BNA Act*, and on October 6, 1980, Pierre Trudeau announced that his government would seek to unilaterally patriate the Constitution without provincial consent.[23] For the most part, the strategy of unilateral patriation did not change the content of the draft Charter, which had been discussed in detail with the provincial premiers and ministers of justice. The draft resolution presented by the minister of justice on October 6, 1980, was a modest document, and a slight improvement in terms of rights protection, on the 1960 *Canadian Bill of Rights*.[24] However, once freed from the constraints of federal-provincial negotiations and relocated to the Special Joint Committee on the Constitution of Canada, the draft Charter was transformed into a much stronger instrument of rights protection, as many of the textual concessions to gain provincial consent were removed.[25]

There was one notable difference in the resolution presented to Parliament on October 6, 1980 – the language-of-instruction protections were substantively altered, foreshadowing the judicialization of language policy that emerged after the entrenchment of the *Canadian Charter* in April 1982. For the first time, these protections were removed from the "Language Rights" section of the *Canadian Charter* and presented as a stand-alone "Minority Language Education Rights" provision. More substantively, the reference to provincial legislatures devising the criteria for determining when sufficient numbers warranted the provision of minority language instruction was removed in section 24(2). This occurred without provincial consultation or agreement.[26]

This represented a significant loss of jurisdictional control of educational policy for provincial governments as the criteria would now be created by judicial interpretation. Further, judicial creation of the criteria for minority language instruction would be augmented by judicial remedy of rights violations (section 25), though the reference to "parliamentary system of government" remained in the wording of section 1 of the *Canadian Charter*. This suggested that, perhaps, the judicialization of language of instruction would be tempered by judicial deference to the choices of provincial legislatures in the provision of minority language instruction provided. However, this concession would be short-lived as the reference to "parliamentary system of government" would be replaced with "a free and democratic society" on January 12, 1981, and the standard of "generally accepted," written October 6, 1980, would be increased to "demonstrably justified" on January 12, 1981, to satisfy the requirement of a reasonable limitation on a right or freedom.[27] The final document would contain all of these changes, and minority language education rights would become section 23 of the *Canadian Charter* when proclaimed into law in April 1982.[28]

It did not take long for the government of Quebec to initiate what would become the first legislative disagreement in the Charter era. In response to the federal-provincial agreement reached in November 1981 without the consent of Quebec, Premier René Lévesque made the following statement to the National Assembly:

> It is therefore clear that we absolutely cannot accept this new constitution created in a night of double dealing. First of all, because it would force us to accept a significant limitation to the exclusive powers of the Assemblée Nationale with respect to the language of instruction in our schools. I have said it before and I repeat: No self-respecting Quebec government could ever abandon the smallest fraction of this absolutely fundamental right to protect the only French island in the English-speaking sea of the North American continent.[29]

This was followed by the minister responsible for the *Charter of the French Language*, Camille Laurin, publishing an eight-page declaration on May 5, 1982, reiterating the *Charter of the French Language*'s continued application despite the entrenchment of the *Canadian Charter* one month previously:

> In my capacity as Minister of Education and Minister responsible for the application of the *Charte de la langue française*, I wish to reaffirm, clearly, calmly, but firmly, that Bill 101 will continue to apply as written in all its parts, in all aspects and throughout the whole of Quebec ... This is why the linguistic policy will be maintained fully and reaffirmed constantly. Also, and in spite of the strong possibility of illegal action and unilateral constitutional measures by the federal power which weigh upon our collective future, the Government of Quebec today solemnly declares that all provisions of the *Charte de la langue française* are confirmed and would seem to be even more necessary and pressing than ever. This means, in particular, that the sections in Chapter VIII on the language of instruction will continue to apply fully.[30]

Within five months of the enactment of the *Constitution Act, 1982*, the language of instruction provision of the *Charter of the French Language* would be invalidated by the Superior Court of Quebec on September 8, 1982,[31] and then by the Quebec Court of Appeal on June 9, 1983.[32]

Quebec's response to the passage of the *Canadian Charter* and section 23 is the first example of legislation disagreement in the Charter era, as the National Assembly would pass the Bill 57, *Charter of the French Language* (1984 *Charter of the French Language*) on February 1, 1984, in the context of

Table 3.1 A comparison of the Quebec clause (1977 and 1984) and the Canada clause

Charter of the French Language, 1977 (Bill 101)	Canadian Charter, 1982	Charter of the French Language, 1984 (Bill 57)
73. In derogation of section 72, the following children, at the request of their father and mother, may receive their instruction in English:	23.(1) *Citizens of Canada* whose first language learned and still understood is that of the English or French linguistic minority population of the province in which they reside, or who have received their primary school instruction in Canada in English or French and reside in a province where the language in which they received that instruction is the language of the English or French linguistic minority population of the province, have the right to have their children receive their primary and secondary school instruction in that language in that province.	73. In derogation of section 72, the following children, at the request of their father and mother, *may receive their instruction in English*:
(1) a child whose father or mother *received his or her elementary instruction in English, in Québec*;		(1) a child whose father or mother received *elementary instruction in English in Québec, provided that that instruction constitutes the major part of the elementary instruction he or she received in Québec*;
(b) a child whose father or mother domiciled in Québec on 26 August 1977, *received his or her elementary instruction in English outside Québec*;	Continuity of language instruction	(b) a child whose father or mother is, on 26 August 1977, domiciled in *Québec and has received elementary instruction in English outside Québec*, *provided that that instruction constitutes the major part of the elementary instruction he or she received outside Québec*;
(2) a child who, in his last year of school in Québec before 26 August 1977, was lawfully receiving his instruction in English, in a public kindergarten class or in an elementary or secondary school;	(2) *Citizens of Canada of whom any child has received or is receiving primary or secondary school instruction in English or French in Canada*, have the right to have all their children receive primary and secondary school instruction in the same language.	(2) a child who, in his last year of school in Québec before 26 August 1977, was lawfully receiving his instruction in English, in a public kindergarten class or in an elementary or secondary school;

Application where numbers warrant

(3) The right of citizens of Canada under subsections (1) and (2) to have their children receive primary and secondary school instruction in the language of the English or French linguistic minority population of a province

applies wherever in the province the number of children of citizens who have such a right is sufficient to warrant the provision to them out of public funds of minority language instruction; and

includes, where the number of those children so warrants, the right to have them receive that instruction in minority language educational facilities provided out of public funds.

Note: Key differences between the 1977 and 1984 *Charter of the French Language* (Bill 101 and Bill 57) and section 23 of the *Canadian Charter* are indicated in the use of italics. The "major part requirement" is indicated in bold.

judicial determination that section 73, the language of instruction provisions in the *Charter of the French Language* was incompatible with section 23 of the *Canadian Charter*.[33] As Table 3.1 demonstrates, the National Assembly refused to accept the authority of the *Canadian Charter* over the statutory 1984 *Charter of the French Language*. For instance, section 73 of the 1984 *Charter of the French Language* reaffirmed that access to the language of instruction was limited to the children or siblings of individuals educated in English in Quebec, the children of individuals who resided in Quebec on August 26, 1977, and educated in English outside of Quebec, children lawfully receiving their education in English in Quebec before August 26, 1977, and, finally, the siblings of such children who lawfully received English in Quebec before August 26, 1977 (key provisions in italics). The 1984 *Charter of the French Language* would also redefine access to section 23 through the MPR (in bold). Thus, Quebec rejected the pan-Canadian application of minority language and education rights to Canadian citizens that constituted official language communities in each province.

In an assessment of judicial review of the *Charter of the French Language*, Emmanuelle Richez argues that "Bill 57 accepted the Canada clause but imposed two limitations on it."[34] Richez argues that the 1984 *Charter of the French Language* legalized the practice whereby Quebec "had consistently issued certificates of exemption allowing Canadians who had received their education in English outside of Quebec to send their to publicly funded English schools, thereby informally enforcing the Canada clause."[35] The second concession to the Canada clause in the 1984 *Charter of the French Language* was "the requirement that to qualify for exemption, parents must have received their English instruction in a province that offered instruction to Francophones that was similar to the minority-language instruction offered to Anglophones in Quebec."[36] Despite this scholarly contribution, I do not agree with Richez's assessment of the 1984 *Charter of the French Language*, though I do recognize that it can be considered a pre-emptive response to a court decision. First, the 1984 *Charter of the French Language* did not comply with the language of the Canada clause and its application to Canadian citizens. It reiterated that section 73 of the 1977 *Charter of the French Language*, the Quebec clause, applies to Quebec residents, though there is a concession for those educated in English outside of Quebec. Second, the Canada clause does not require a reciprocal provision of educational services by provincial governments to access minority language education services. It is a right of Canadian citizens to have their children or siblings educated in the official language where numbers warrant the provision for minority language communities. It is not, as section 73 required in the 1984 *Charter of the French Language*, when other provincial governments provide equivalent minority language educational services to that of Quebec.

There are several points of departure between the minority language education provision in section 23 of the *Canadian Charter* and section 73 of the *Charter of the French Language Charter* that are worth emphasizing, particularly since the Lévesque government amended the *Charter of the French Language* after the *Canadian Charter*'s entrenchment and considering two judicial invalidations of the language of instruction provisions of the *Charter of the French Language*. As the *Canadian Charter* is a constitutional document, whereas the *Charter of the French Language* is simply a statutory instrument, Laurin's position that section 73 would continue to fully apply was simply not a realistic assessment of the relationship between the Canada clause and the Quebec clause. The second notable feature is the guarantee provided as well as the application of the guarantee. For instance, section 23 is unequivocal that access to minority language education instruction is a right of Canadian citizens – "*Citizens of Canada ... have the right to have their children receive their primary and secondary school instruction in that language in that province*," subject to the 'where numbers warrant' criteria (emphasis added). In contrast, section 73 remained limited to residents of Quebec and largely, though not exclusively, to those educated in English in Quebec. It is also a much more discretionary guarantee as the language lacks the robustness of section 23 as it only provides for the possibility of access to English language instruction: "In derogation of section 72, the following children, at the request of their father and mother, *may receive their instruction in English*" (emphasis added). The inclusion of the qualification "*may receive*" is critical as it suggests that language of instruction is conditional and subject to review and approval. For instance, under section 75 of the *Charter of the French Language*, the certificate of eligibility required to attend English instruction stated that "the Minister of Education may empower such persons as he may designate to verify and decide on children's eligibility for instruction in English."[37] Thus, language of instruction under section 73 is simply a public good bestowed by the state that may, or may not, be granted, depending on whether the minister's designate grants a certificate of eligibility, subject to administrative criteria and review.

The most significant difference between the 1977 and 1984 *Charter of the French Language* is the inclusion of the (MPR), highlighted in bold (see Table 3.1). However, the MPR was introduced after the constitutional challenge against section 73 was launched, which culminated in the 1984 *Protestant*

School Boards decision. The appeal heard by the Supreme Court of Canada, therefore, simply involved the provision in the 1977 *Charter of the French Language* and not the changes introduced by the 1984 *Charter of the French Language* considering lower court judicial invalidation. It would not be until *Solski* in 2005 that the MPR would be subject to judicial review under section 23 of the *Canadian Charter*.[38] According to Richez, the MPR widened access to English instruction:

> Prior to this amendment, the governmental admissibility bureau had interpreted the Quebec clause as guaranteeing access to English schools only for children whose parents had received the "totality" of their primary instruction in English in Quebec, whereas the appeal commission had applied the "major part" requirement. The Quebec government decided to resolve the conflict in favour of the Anglophone community, which wished to increase eligibility for English schooling.[39]

This may very well have been the outcome of the 1984 *Charter of the French Language* and the MPR addition to section 73. However, it does not take away from the incompatibilities between the 1984 amendment to section 73 and section 23 of the *Canadian Charter*. Neither does it signal an alignment between the Quebec and Canada clauses nor Quebec's acceptance that the *Charter of the French Language* is subordinate to the *Canadian Charter*. Finally, if the 1984 *Charter of the French Language* did broaden access to English instruction, this was not the result of the judicialization of politics but, rather, the decision of the Quebec government to do so.

According to Richez, "the Quebec government understood that the Quebec clause would not withstand a constitutional challenge." This led Richez to conclude that "[s]ince the enactment of the *Charter*, Quebec's National Assembly has been increasingly unsuccessful at counteracting the effects of the Court's jurisprudence on *Bill 101* in order to promote and protect the French language in Quebec."[40] There is an alternative understanding of this constitutional reality – that Quebec governments across the political spectrum understood something more profound about the legalization of language politics – that a robust "legislative counter-attack" is more than sufficient to safeguard the *Charter of the French Language*, despite the inability to wield the notwithstanding clause to counter judicial invalidation in regard to section 23 of the *Canadian Charter*.[41] Judicial impact has never reached the tipping point suggested by Richez and others, either in regard to the "sign law," as Chapter 5 demonstrates, or the language of instruction, as this chapter shows. This is a combination of several developments: legislative disagreements manifesting as amendments to the *Charter of the French Language* that work at cross-purposes; important demographic changes involving the anglophone community since 1971, and, finally, the decision by anglophone parents as to which school system – English or French – their children will attend.

The Supreme Court of Canada and the Quebec clause

Although Pierre Trudeau rejected the constitutional recognition of Quebec as a distinct society in both the Meech Lake and Charlottetown accords, he did accept an asymmetrical application of section 23 to Quebec, as it is the only province in which section 23(1)(a) does not apply until it has been authorized by either the National Assembly or the Quebec government.[42] As this has yet to occur, section 23 has a more limited application in Quebec, and the province has a special status under this part of the *Canadian Charter*. The right to minority language education in the *Canadian Charter* outlines several conditions that must be met before the child of a Canadian citizen is entitled to its provision out of public funds: first, a parent must have received their primary or secondary school instruction in English or French in Canada or a sibling has "received or is receiving" their education in English or French in Canada; second, the public provision is provided "where numbers warrant." As a result, section 23 does not specify the length of residency in English or French instruction or the type of educational institution (public or private) providing instruction to satisfy section 23. It simply requires that Canadian citizens have "received or [are] receiving" language instruction in either official language to ensure that their children or siblings have access to minority language education services.

It is perhaps fitting that the second *Canadian Charter* decision by the Supreme Court of Canada involved section 23 and its relationship to the *Charter of the French Language*.[43] The constitutional challenge to section 73 of the *Charter of the French Language* was launched by Quebec's anglophone community and funded under the Court Challenges Program. In *Protestant School Boards*, the Supreme Court of Canada sided with the anglophone community and declared section 73 of the *Charter of the French Language* unconstitutional because of its incompatibility with section 23 of the *Canadian Charter*. The government of Quebec readily admitted that aspects of the *Charter of the French Language* violated section 23 of the *Canadian Charter* but contended that the limitations were reasonable because of the important legislative objectives pursued. In making this argument, the

Attorney General of Quebec relied upon more restrictive language policies in multi-linguistic societies, such as Belgium and Switzerland. As these nations had adopted stricter language polices subsequently upheld by the Swiss and European courts, Quebec reasoned that this policy would be upheld through section 1 of the *Canadian Charter*.[44] While the Supreme Court was sensitive to the policy objectives underlying the *Charter of the French Language*, the Court determined that denying educational instruction to the children of Canadian citizens educated in English outside of Quebec was not reasonable but, rather, a total limitation of section 23(1)(b):

> If, because of the *Charter*, s. 73 could not be validly adopted today, it is clearly rendered of no force or effect by the *Charter* and this for the same reason, namely the direct conflict between s 73 of *Bill 101* and s 23 of the *Charter*. The provisions of s 73 of *Bill 101* collide directly with those of s 23 of the *Charter*, and are not limits which can be legitimized by s 1 of the *Charter*. Such limits cannot be exceptions to the rights and freedoms guaranteed by the *Charter* nor amount to amendments of the *Charter*.[45]

In reaching this decision delivered by the "The Court" and relying on a consideration rarely used by the Supreme Court of Canada – framers' intent – this unanimous judgment considered the political intention of this *Canadian Charter* provision[46] and concluded that it was drafted with the explicit intention of invalidating section 73 and remedying the limited provision of minority language educational instruction at the provincial level:

> This set of constitutional provisions was not enacted by the framers in a vacuum. When it was adopted, the framers knew, and clearly had in mind the regimes governing the Anglophone and Francophone linguistic minorities in various provinces in Canada so far as the language of instruction was concerned ... Rightly or wrongly – and it is not for the courts to decide – the framers of the Constitution manifestly regarded as inadequate some – and perhaps all – of the regimes in force at the time the *Charter* was enacted, and their intention was to remedy the perceived defects of these regimes by uniform corrective measures, namely those contained in s. 23 of the *Charter*, which were at the same time given the status of a constitutional guarantee.[47]

The Court also stated what provincial governments could not do regarding section 23: "In our opinion, a legislature cannot by an ordinary statute validly set aside the means chosen by the framers and affect this classification. Still less can it remake the classification and redefine the classes."[48] The Court was clear that provincial governments could not legislatively modify section 23 of the *Canadian Charter* as this would be tantamount to a constitutional amendment without adherence to the amendment process adopted in 1982.[49] In regard to Quebec, "s. 73 of *Bill 101* directly alters the effect of s. 23 of the *Charter* for Quebec, without following the procedure laid down for amending the Constitution."[50] For these reasons, section 73 could not be considered a reasonable limitation on section 23 of the *Canadian Charter* as "such limits cannot be exceptions to the rights and freedoms guaranteed by the *Charter* nor amount to amendments of the *Charter*."[51]

The first section 23 ruling by the Supreme Court of Canada suggests that the Trudeau government's intentions were realized – section 73 was invalidated, and the National Assembly was cautioned that it could not amend the *Charter of the French Language* to conflict with section 23 of the *Canadian Charter*. Subsequent amendments to section 73 demonstrate the instability of judicial review, as *Protestant School Boards* represents the high-water mark of judicial activism involving the *Charter of the French Language*. In subsequent amendments to the *Charter of the French Language*, Liberal and Péquiste governments did exactly what the Court ruled they could not do – through ordinary statutes, they remade the classification, redefined the classes, and effectively amended the application of section 23 of the *Canadian Charter* to the *Charter of the French Language*.

Bill 86, *Act to Amend the Charter of the French Language*, 1993
The passage of Bill 86, *Act to Amend the Charter of the French Language* in 1993 (1993 *Charter of the French Language*) by the Bourassa government addressed two invalidations of the 1977 *Charter of the French Language* by the Supreme Court of Canada: the invalidation of the "sign-law" provisions in *Ford* and *Devine* and the invalidation of section 73 and the language of instruction provision in *Protestant School Boards*.[52] The 1993 amendment to section 73 incorporated language directly from section 23 of the *Canadian Charter* and broadly complied with *Protestant School Boards*. Table 3.2 indicates those elements of section 23 that were incorporated into the 1993 *Charter of the French Language*. The 1993 amendment accepted the pan-Canadian application of minority language education rights as it now extended language of instruction to Canadian citizens educated in English in Canada. The pan-Canadian dimension of section 73 understandably led Quebec academics to conclude that the 1993 *Charter of the French Language* signified the triumph

Table 3.2 Quebec's response to *Protestant School Boards*, [1984] 2 SCR 66

Canadian Charter of Rights and Freedoms	Charter of the French Language 1993 (Bill 86)
23. (1) *Citizens of Canada* (b) *who have received their primary school instruction in Canada in English or French and reside in a province where the language in which they received that instruction is the language of the English or French linguistic minority population of the province, have the right to have their children receive primary and secondary school instruction in that language in that province.* Continuity of language instruction (2) *Citizens of Canada of whom any child has received or is receiving primary or secondary school instruction in English or French in Canada, have the right to have all their children receive primary and secondary school instruction in the same language.* Application where numbers warrant (3) The right of citizens of Canada under subsections (1) and (2) to have their children receive primary and secondary school instruction in the language of the English or French linguistic minority population of a province (a) applies wherever in the province the number of children of citizens who have such a right is sufficient to warrant the provision to them out of public funds of minority language instruction; and (b) includes, where the number of those children so warrants, the right to have them receive that instruction in minority language educational facilities provided out of public funds.	73. The following children, at the request of one of their parents, *may receive instruction in English:* a child whose father or mother is a Canadian citizen and received elementary instruction in English in Canada, **provided that that instruction constitutes the major part of the elementary instruction he or she received in Canada;** (2) *a child whose father or mother is a Canadian citizen and who has received or is receiving elementary or secondary instruction in English in Canada, and the brothers and sisters of that child,* **provided that that instruction constitutes the major part of the elementary or secondary instruction received by the child in Canada;** (3) a child whose father and mother are not Canadian citizens, but whose father or mother received elementary instruction in English in Québec, **provided that that instruction constitutes the major part of the elementary instruction he or she received in Québec;** (4) a child who, in his last year in school in Québec before 26 August 1977, was receiving instruction in English in a public kindergarten class or in an elementary or secondary school, and the brothers and sisters of that child; (5) a child whose father or mother was residing in Québec on 26 August 1977 and had received elementary instruction in English outside Québec, **provided that that instruction constitutes the major part of the elementary instruction he or she received outside Québec.**

Note: Key changes and differences between the 1993 *Charter of the French Language* (Bill 86) and section 23 of the *Canadian Charter* are indicated in the use of italics. The "major part requirement" is indicated in bold.

of the Canada clause over the Quebec clause as section 73 adopted core language found in the section 23 guarantee.[53] For instance, section 73(a) was amended from *"a child whose father or mother received his or her elementary instruction in English, in Quebec"* (emphasis added) to *"a child whose father or mother is a Canadian citizen and received elementary instruction in English in Canada"* (emphasis added) under section 73.1 of the 1993 *Charter of the French Language*. A similar provision regarding eligibility through a sibling was included as section 73.2 in this same Charter.

Despite the incorporation of language that replicates section 23 of the *Canadian Charter*, key provisions of section 73 continued to jar with section 23, as language from the 1977 and 1984 versions of the *Charter of the French Language* were reproduced in the 1993 *Charter of the French Language*. In *Protestant School Boards*, the Court was clear that Canadian citizens, as a right, have access to minority language instruction where numbers warrant. Additionally, section 23 stated that Canadian citizens satisfying the requirements of this constitutional provision *"have the right to have their children receive primary and secondary school instruction in that language in that province"* (emphasis added). In sharp contrast, the 1993 *Charter of the French Language* reiterated that section 73 only provided for the possibility of minority language instruction by maintaining the phrase *"may receive instruction in English"* (emphasis added). This clearly conveyed that section 23 would be conditional on the issuing of a certificate of eligibility by administrative review under section 75 of the *Charter of the French Language* and not a right of Canadian citizens that were members of Quebec's anglophone community. Further, the 1993 *Charter of the French Language* retained the MPR to evaluate whether Canadian citizens qualified for English instruction in Quebec. Given that *Protestant School Boards* guaranteed the rights of Canadian citizens to minority language education services, either through their parent or siblings, the MPR requirement was clearly directed against Quebec's growing allophone community, whose members, overwhelmingly, were not educated in English in Canada and unlikely to satisfy this requirement under section 73.

The pan-Canadian reconfiguration of section 73 must be evaluated not in the abstract but, rather, in regard to its effect on access to English language instruction for the anglophone and allophone communities. Given that *Protestant School Boards* only benefited Canadian citizens moving to Quebec who had been educated in English in Canada, interprovincial migration is key to whether the Court's decision produced any negative policy impact for the *Charter of the French Language* and section 73. As Figure 3.1 demonstrates,

Figure 3.1 Anglophone Interprovincial Migration, 1971–2016

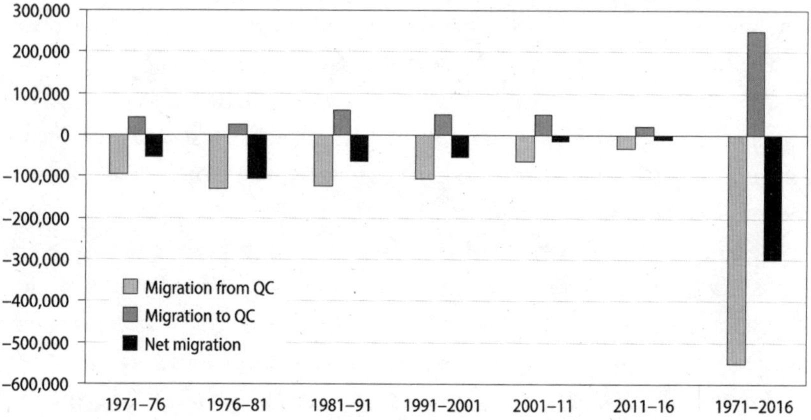

Source: Statistics Canada, "Interprovincial Migration between Quebec and Other Provinces and Territories for the Population with English as a Mother Tongue, 1971 to 2016."

there has been a net outflow of anglophones from Quebec in each decade since the politicization of language that began with the passage of Bill 63, *An Act to Promote the French Language in Québec* in 1969.[54] Nearly a third of the outflow of anglophones occurred in the critical period between the election of the Parti Québécois in 1976, the passage of the *Charter of the French Language* in 1977, and the 1980 referendum on sovereignty association. This is particularly significant in terms of section 23 of the *Canadian Charter*. While *Protestant School Boards* guarantees access, and the 1993 amendments to the *Charter of the French Language* grants language of instruction services, both are regarding a declining linguistic community. This demonstrates the importance of the implementation context and whether it requires a government to introduce legislation complying with a judicial decision or, in the context of English language instruction, the demographics of the community that benefits from a judicial decision.

A further reason to question the impact of *Protestant School Board* is the sharp enrollment decline of the English school system in Quebec (see Figure 3.2). Using 1971 as the baseline, which roughly corresponds to the initial impact of the *Act to Promote the French Language in Québec*, there has been a steep downward enrollment trend. Despite *Protestant School Boards* and the alignment between section 23 and section 73 in the 1993 *Charter of the French Language*, enrollment in English schools in the 2021–22 academic

Figure 3.2 School enrollment trends in Quebec, 1971 as a baseline

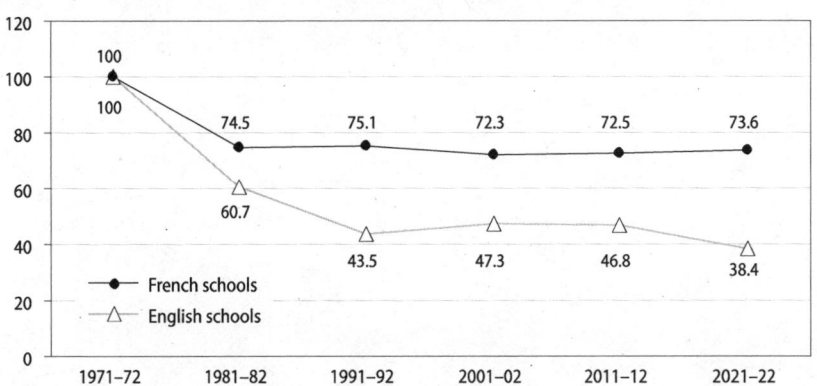

Source: Richard Y. Bourhis, "Evaluating the Impact of Bill 101 on the English-speaking Communities of Quebec," *Language Problems and Language Planning* 43, 2 (2019): 217. This is adapted to include the 2021–22 numbers derived from Institut de la statistique du Québec, *Effectif scolaire de la formation générale des jeunes, selons diverses variables, années scolaires 2005–2006 à 2021–2022* (Quebec City: Government of Quebec, 2022).

year represent 38.4 percent of the enrollment a generation ago in the 1971–72 academic year. In terms of numbers of students (see Figure 3.4), a total of 256,251 were enrolled in English schools in Quebec in 1971–72, with a current enrolment in 2021–22 of only 98,865.[55] As Richard Bourhis suggests, the decline in English school enrollments is the result of anglophone migration out of Quebec, initially in response to the passage of the *Charter of the French Language*. It is also the result of the growing number of anglophone parents that send their children to the French system, despite their children being eligible for English language instruction under section 73 of the *Charter of the French Language*.[56] This demonstrates the particular circumstances of section 23 of the *Canadian Charter* as a positive right as it requires the rights holder to choose minority language instruction services. With anglophones, the choice is increasingly French language instruction.

With the passage of the *Charter of the French Language*, it was inevitable that a decline in the number of students enrolled in English schools would occur, as section 73 was designed to ensure that allophones would largely, though not completely, be streamlined into the French school system. As outlined in Figure 3.3, a large majority of allophones (85.4 percent) chose English language instruction when permitted to under the *Act to Promote the French Language in Québec*. The net impact of Bill 22, *Official Language Act*, and the 1977 *French Language Charter* in the period ending 1981–82 was

Figure 3.3 Attendance in English schools by language group in Quebec, 1971–2018

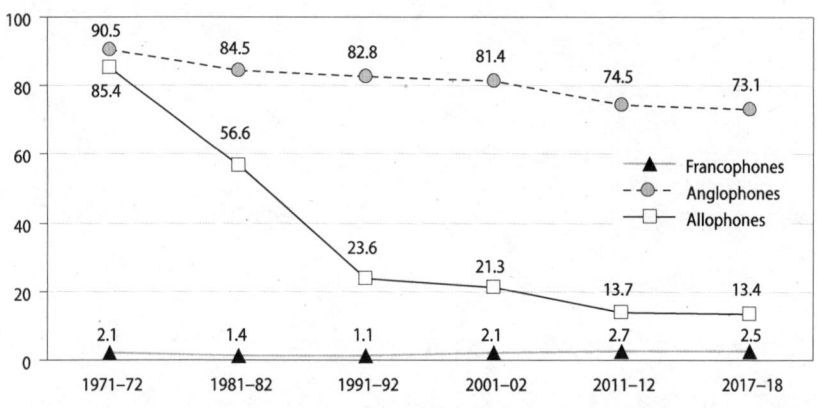

Source: Richard Y. Bourhis, "Evaluating the Impact of Bill 101 on the English-speaking Communities of Quebec," *Language Problems and Language Planning* 43, 2 (2019): 218.

a further drop in allophone access to English language instruction (56.6 percent), which was not addressed in the subsequent periods, despite the judicial victory in *Protestant School Boards*, and the 1993 *Charter of the French Language* aligning with key parts of section 23 of the *Canadian Charter*.[57] Indeed, only 13.4 percent of allophones attended English schools in 2017–18, which is approximately the mirror image of school attendance in 1971–72, when only 14.6 percent of allophones attended French language schools. More importantly, a lower percentage of anglophones attended English schools in 2017–18 (73.1 percent) than in 1971–72 (90.5 percent), despite the entrenchment of minority language education rights in 1982, the judicial victory in *Protestant School Boards,* and the broadening of section 73 to include a pan-Canadian dimension.

The policy objectives of the *Charter of the French Language* have been achieved in regard to the allophone community, despite the judicialization of politics. And, more importantly, the attendance at English schools has not increased despite a reconfiguration of section 73 to include a pan-Canadian orientation considering *Protestant School Boards.* Anglophones are declining as a community in Quebec, and when this declining community chooses language of instruction, it is increasingly choosing to send its children to French schools. As a landmark ruling, the Supreme Court of Canada confirmed the remedial intention of section 23 of the *Canadian Charter* for the *Charter of the French Language*. This early example of judicial activism

Figure 3.4 School enrollments in Quebec by language of instruction, 1971–2022

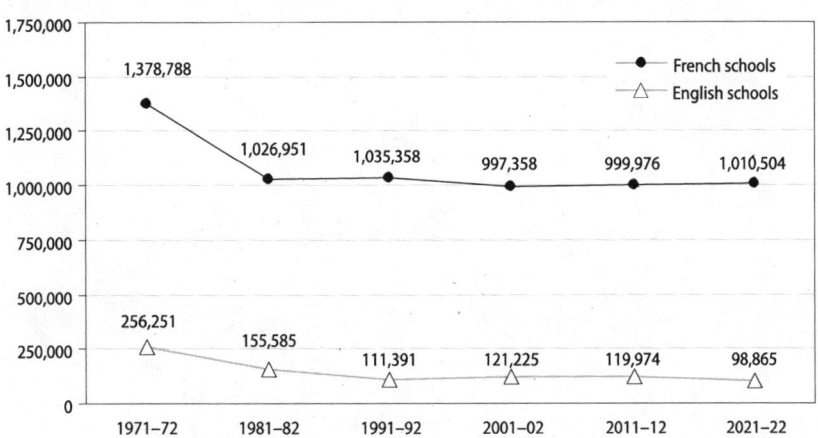

Source: Richard Y. Bourhis, "Evaluating the Impact of Bill 101 on the English-speaking Communities of Quebec," *Language Problems and Language Planning* 43, 2 (2019): 217. This is adapted to include the 2021–22 numbers derived from the Institut de la statistique du Québec, *Effectif scolaire de la formation général des jeunes, selons diverses variables, années scolaires 2005–2006 à 2021–2022* (Quebec City: Government of Quebec, 2022).

demonstrates, for Guy Laforest, the "federal deficit" produced by the judicialization of politics[58] and, for André Burelle, the ability of the Canadian government to interfere in Quebec's control over language and education policy.[59] While school enrollments in the English system would have been lower in the absence of *Protestant School Boards*, a decelerated decline should not be equated with a loss of control over the direction of education policy in Quebec. In short, none of the empirical data support the dire predictions about the judicialization of politics,[60] and its effect on the language of instruction provisions of the *Charter of the French Language*.[61]

There is one trend to highlight as the decline in English school enrollment was addressed for a brief period. As indicated in Figure 3.4, there was an increase in English school enrollment from 1991–92 to 2001–02 for a net gain of 9,834 students in the English system. This period generally corresponds to a time frame in which the changes to section 73 in the 1993 *Charter of the French Language* were in force, backed by the *Protestant School Boards* decision. This leads to the following question: what accounts for the temporary increase in English school enrollment in Quebec? There are two potential explanations. First, it could be the result of the judicialization of politics and

Figure 3.5 Interprovincial migration and immigration to Quebec, 1971–2018

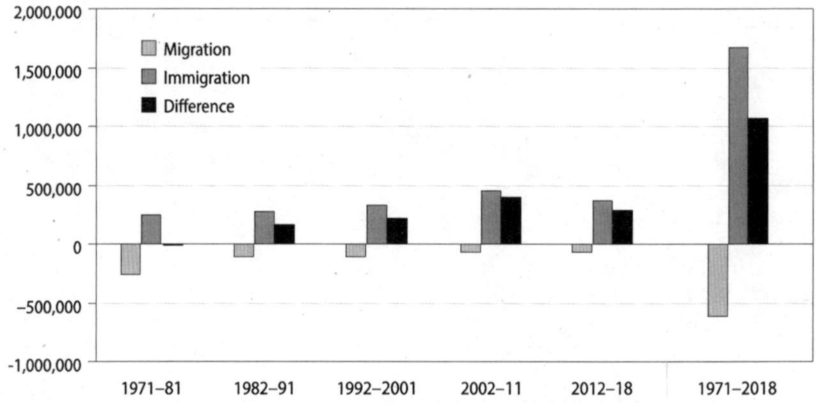

Source: Statistics Canada, Immigrants to Canada, by Province or Territory," Table 17-10-0011-01.

Protestant School Boards, or, second, it could be the result of the legislative choices of the Quebec government and how it operationalized the MPR, particularly the criteria adopted to assess eligibility requests under section 75 of the *Charter of the French Language*.

Turning to the judicialization of politics explanation, *Protestant School Boards* only benefited Canadian citizens who migrated to Quebec and were educated in English in Canada that satisfied the MPR under section 73. The migration patterns identified in Figure 3.1 demonstrate that the growth in English schools in Quebec is not the result of *Protestant School Boards* as anglophone migration was negative between 1991–2001 (–53,700) as 104,400 anglophones migrated from Quebec and only 50,700 migrated to Quebec in this period. The immigration and migration patterns outlined in Figure 3.5 are significant as Quebec has experienced a net loss of Canadian citizens to other provinces since at least 1971. The brief upturn in English school enrollments (1991–2002) can only be the result of immigration to Quebec – individuals, incidentally, that do not qualify for English instruction under either the *Canadian Charter* or the *Charter of the French Language*. As indicated in Figure 3.5, the population growth in Quebec since 1971 is the result of immigration and not interprovincial migration of section 23 rights bearers enrolling their children in English public schools.

The answer is more complex than immigration and is also explained by the distinct nature of the Quebec educational system and how it interfaces with the *Charter of the French Language* and acts a gateway to language of instruction. Similar to other jurisdictions, Quebec has a public and private school system. However, a subset of schools within the private system are designated as "unsubsidized private schools." These schools do not accept the yearly subsidy of $4,500 per student by the Quebec government,[62] and, as unsubsidized private schools, they are not regulated by the *Charter of the French Language*. In this respect, there are two categories of private schools in Quebec: those operating within (subsidized) and those operating outside (unsubsidized) the *Charter of the French Language*. If a parent is willing to send their child to a fully private English school – an unsubsidized private school – they do not require a certificate of eligibility to attend. In this respect, unsubsidized private schools do constitute a limited form of freedom of choice if francophone and allophone parents can afford this costly educational pathway.

Because of the per student subsidy, Quebec has the highest proportion of students enrolled in private schools in North America, with 346 institutions and a total enrollment of 129,188 students in the 2018–19 academic year.[63] In terms of school systems, only the French system in Quebec has more students enrolled than are in private schools, with the English public system a distant third. Given that private schools have grown in overall enrollments, whereas the French and English public systems have declined (see Figure 3.3), the growth in English public instruction centres on the relationship between unsubsidized private schools as a gateway to certificates of eligibly under section 73.2 of the *Charter of the French Language*.

Section 73 does provide for a total of five derogations to section 72 of the *Charter of the French Language* (see Table 3.1), and a sixth once unsubsidized private schools are factored into the analysis. A total of 658,676 certificates of eligibility have been issued for English language instruction under the *Charter of the French Language* between 1977 and 2013.[64] However, two derogations are no longer viable routes to satisfy the eligibility requirements (sections 73.4, 73.5), and a third (section 73.3) applies to resident non-citizens. In particular, section 73.4 guarantees English instruction for children who were attending English schools at the time of the *Charter of the French Language*'s passage on August 26, 1977, and section 73.5 provided for English instruction for children whose parents resided in Quebec at the time of the *Charter of the French Language*'s passage and were educated in English outside of Quebec. These are "grandfather" provisions designed to fade over time. While sections 73.4 and 74.5 account for 46 percent (303,396/658,676) of all certificates of eligibility issued under section 73, 98 percent (296,696/303,396)

Figure 3.6 Certificates of eligibility issued under section 73 of the *Charter of the French Language*, 1977–2013

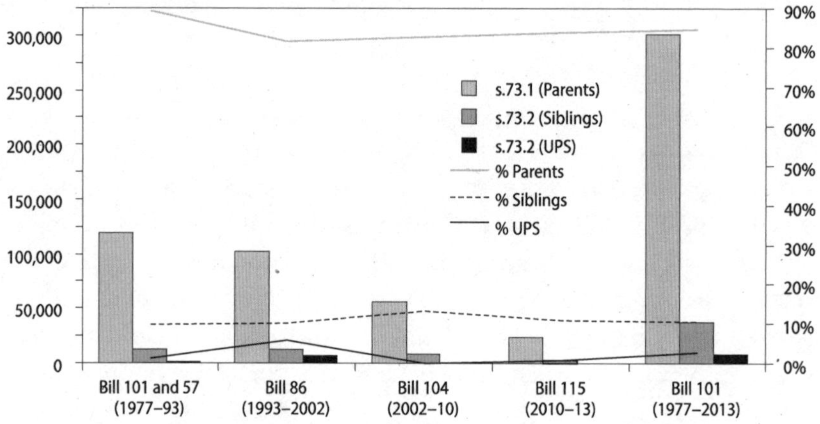

Source: Ministère de l'éducation, du loisir et du sport, Indicateurs linguistiques – Secteur de l'éducation, 2013.

were issued before 1989. Finally, section 73.3 provides for certificates of eligibility for the children of Quebec residents (non-citizens) educated in English in Quebec that satisfy the MPR (7,484/303,396). These certificates of eligibility (310,880) are not considered in Figure 3.6.

Of the remaining certificates of eligibility issued under section 73 of the *Charter of the French Language* (347,796), more than 97 percent were issued under section 73.1 (301,065) and section 73.2 (37,650), and less than 3 percent via attendance at unsubsidized schools (9,081). As Figure 3.6 reveals, there was a sharp increase in the use of unsubsidized private schools after the passage of the 1993 *Charter of the French Language* to meet the MPR, suggesting that the amendments introduced in response to *Protestant School Boards* account for the expansion of this eligibility route and the upward trend in English school enrollment. For instance, the number of certificates issued under this route – section 73.2 (unsubsidized private schools) – increased from 1 percent (1,349/133,241) under the 1977 *Charter of the French Language* and 1984 *Charter of the French Language* (1977–93) to more than 6 percent (7,499/122,872) under the 1993 *Charter of the French Language* (1993–2002). More importantly, nearly 83 percent (7,499/9,081) of all certificates of eligibility issued after attending unsubsidized schools occurred under the 1993 *Charter of the French Language*.

The first two pathways – section 73.1 (parents) and section 73.2 (siblings) of the *Charter of the French Language* – do not explain the brief increase in English school enrollment, given the migration patterns outlined in Figure 3.4. Certificates of eligibility issued after satisfying the MPR through attendance at an unsubsidized private school is the only realistic way that allophones immigrating to Quebec can gain access to English language instruction. Section 23 is a right of Canadian citizens educated in English in Canada to have their children educated in English in Quebec. For first generation immigrants, section 23 is beyond reach as the language of instruction, even if it were English, would have occurred outside of Canada. As a result, this provision works in tandem with section 73 of the *Charter of the French Language* as it streamlines the vast majority of new immigrants into the French language system in Quebec. This leaves attendance at unsubsidized private English schools – section 73.2 (unsubsidized private schools) – as the only viable explanation for the increase between 1991 and 2002.

What accounts for the increase in "bridging" or "gateway" schools as a way to satisfy the MPR for Quebec residents not permitted to attend English public schools under section 73?[65] This is particularly important given the timeline and the increase in the use of unsubsidized private schools in the period immediately after the passage of Bill 86 (*Charter of the French Language* 1993). The judicialization of politics does not explain this development for a very simple reason. The constitutionality of the MPR was not considered in *Protestant School Board* as this case involved the 1977 *Charter of the French Language* and not the 1984 version, which added this requirement to section 73 of the *Charter of the French Language* through the 1984 *Charter of the French Language*. More critically, the MPR would not be reviewed by the Supreme Court of Canada until 2005, nearly twenty years after its inclusion in the 1984 *Charter of the French Language*.

Conclusion

Pierre Elliott Trudeau tendered his resignation to Governor General Jeanne Sauvé on June 30, 1984, at which time John Turner was invited to form a ministry and serve as the seventeenth prime minister of Canada. Less than one month later, on July 26, 1984, the Supreme Court of Canada dismissed the Quebec government's appeal in *Protestant School Boards*. By doing so, "The Court" upheld the lower court rulings that section 73 of the *Charter of the French Language* was a violation of section 23 of the *Canadian Charter* and, thus, unconstitutional. Stephen Clarkson and Christina McCall's biography of Pierre Elliott Trudeau begins with the wonderful line: "He haunts us still."[66] For René Lévesque, who opposed the judicialization of language and education policy, the *Protestant School Boards* decision forewarned the undeniable constitutional nightmare for the *Charter of the French Language* that the Parti Québécois, and its successor governments, would face because of "that bloody Charter."[67]

There is no doubt that *Protestant School Boards* represents a strong judicial rebuke of the *Charter of the French Language* through its reliance on framers' intent, as the Court laid out why Pierre Elliott Trudeau constitutionalized minority language education rights – to override the statutory *Charter of the French Language*. Despite judicial invalidation, and the clear textual impact that section 23 had on the subsequent revisions of section 73 of the *Charter of the French Language*, important questions remain. How much policy impact did an activist judicial decision have on the vitality of the English public school system in Quebec? Did *Protestant School Boards* correct the downward trend of attendance at English public instruction given that section 23 is a positive right and the Quebec government has a constitutional duty to provide minority language educational services to an official language community? Does *Protestant School Boards* validate the "centralization thesis" and its claim that provincial sovereignty and federal diversity would be deeply compromised by the *Canadian Charter* and the Supreme Court of Canada's application of national standards in provincial areas of jurisdiction?

These are important question, but they cannot be answered by reading a judicial decision, no matter how activist it is or how authoritatively the Supreme Court of Canada rendered its decision. To have policy impact, a judicial decision must be implemented. In the case of section 73, both the Lévesque and Bourassa governments disagreed with the Supreme Court of Canada when they revised the *Charter of the French Language*, as Lévesque did by passing the 1984 *Charter of the French Language*, and Bourassa when his government responded to *Protestant School Boards* as well as *Ford v Quebec*, when it passed the 1993 *Charter of the French Language*. The most significant part of their legislative responses to the *Canadian Charter* (Lévesque) and to *Protestant School Boards* (Bourassa) was the inclusion of the MPR to satisfy English language eligibility under section 73 of the *Charter of the French Language*. As I argued in this chapter, the inclusion of the MPR was a legislative response designed to negate, or, at a minimum, severally constrain, the permissive approach by the Court in *Protestant School Boards* to section 23 of the *Canadian Charter*.

Two empirical trends work in tandem that question whether Quebec's control over language and education policy were undermined by *Protestant School Boards* or the remaining section 23 cases that are discussed in the next chapter. First, any Charter victory involving section 23 in Quebec only benefits a community in decline, as interprovincial migration rates in Figure 3.5 demonstrate. This decline has also been intensified by the personal choices of Quebec's anglophones, who are sending their children to private schools or to the French public system in increasing numbers, despite the constitutional right to English public instruction. Declining enrollments in the English public system question how much of a policy defeat *Protestant School Boards* was for the Quebec government once the MPR, and the legislative changes to it, further reduced accessibility to English public instruction under section 73 of the *Charter of the French Language*.

For a brief period, there was an increase in English public instruction enrollments, as the MPR did result in the section 73 requirements being met for members of Quebec's allophone community. This is the second trend that questions whether *Protestant School Boards* undermined Quebec's ability to determine eligibility criteria under section 73. For critics of the *Canadian Charter* and the judicialization of language and education policy, the increase in student enrollments in English public instruction speaks an inconvenient truth. It was not the result of remedial activism by the Supreme Court of Canada. It was the result of the minister of education, and their designate under section 75 of the *Charter of the French Language,* accepting attendance at unsubsidized private schools by allophones as satisfying the MPR. This was not judicially required but the sovereign decision of the Quebec government. In short, federalism explains the brief change in the trajectory of English public school enrollments. And federalism and provincial sovereignty also explains how Quebec addressed this perceived public policy problem when it revised the ministerial approach to the MPR and introduced an absolute prohibition on the use of unsubsidized private schools for the section 73 eligibility. These issues would return to the judicial arena in *Solski* and *Nguyen,* producing activist decisions where the Court once again determined that Quebec had undermined section 23 of the *Canadian Charter*. These activist decisions, as well as the activist legislative responses by the Quebec government, are considered in the next chapter.

Bridging Schools and the "Major Part Requirement"
Designing and Implementing the 2010 *Charter of the French Language*

4

One of the first legislative responses to the *Canadian Charter of Rights and Freedoms (Canadian Charter)* by the Lévesque government was Bill 57, *Charter of the French Language* (1984 *Charter of the French Language*), which amended section 73 to include the "major part requirement" (MPR) for assessing eligibility for English language public instruction.[1] Originally limited to elementary instruction in Quebec, section 73 of the *Charter of the French Language* would be amended once again in 1993 to broaden the MPR to a consideration of elementary and secondary education that occurred in Canada.[2] The constitutionality of the MPR and section 73 of the 1993 *Charter of the French Language*, as well as the ministerial directive on how to operationalize this requirement, were reviewed by the Supreme Court of Canada in *Solski (Tutor of) v Quebec (Attorney General)*.[3] Section 73 would be amended again in 2002 when Bill 104, *Charter of the French Language* (2002 *Charter of the French Language*) prohibited the use of unsubsidized private schools to satisfy the MPR.[4] This prohibiting of bridging schools or *"écoles passerelles"* was considered by the Court in *Nguyen v Quebec (Education, Recreation and Sports)*.[5] In *Solski* and *Nguyen*, the Supreme Court of Canada issued momentous decisions within a three-and-a-half-year period, in which the ministerial directive on the the MPR (*Solski*) and the legislative prohibition that prevented attendance at unsubsidized private schools from satisfying the MPR under section 73 (*Nguyen*) were declared unconstitutional. In the case of *Solski*, an authoritative decision was released by "The Court," and, for *Nguyen*, a unanimous decision was authored for the Court by Justice Louis LeBel. Moreoever, the Court would determine that two legislative responses by successive Quebec governments – the 1993 and 2002 versions of the *Charter of the French Language* – remained constitutionally suspect. In this respect, section 23 of the *Canadian Charter* and the "Canada clause" for minority language education eligibility appeared, once again, to trump the statutory "Quebec clause" within section 73 of the *Charter of the French Language*.

A consistent feature of the judicialization of the *Charter of the French Language*, regardless of which party has sat on the government benches in the National Assembly, is a sustained and intense disagreement with the Canadian government over the rules governing access to English public school instruction. That successive Quebec governments have sought to minimize judicial invalidation of the *Charter of the French Language* through statutory amendment of the same Charter is, perhaps, the clearest manifestation of this legislative disagreement. In this chapter, I consider the legislative response passed by the Charest government in the aftermath of *Solski* and *Nguyen*, Bill 115, which saw the passage of the *Act Following upon the Court Decision on the Language of Instruction* (2010 *Charter of the French Language*) and the *Act Respecting Private Education* in 2010.[6] The regulatory changes introduced to assess the MPR when attendance occurs at unsubsidized private schools are also considered.[7] While the Court was forceful in the *Solski* and *Nguyen* decisions, the Charest government was equally forceful in its legislative response.

As I argue in this chapter, the legislative and regulatory responses to *Solski* and *Nguyen* have largely limited judicial impact and neutralized judicial invalidation of the *Charter of the French Language*. In short, Quebec has retained sovereign control over education policy, despite the judicialization of this provincial responsibility under section 23 of the Charter and landmark judicial invalidations of the *Charter of the French Language*. In fact, the response introduced by the Charest government in regard to section 73 of the *Charter of the French Language* is far more draconian than the one invalidated by the Supreme Court of Canada in *Solski* and *Nguyen*. Additionally, the classification of unsubsidized private schools for the purposes of the MPR has significantly reduced the viability of this educational pathway for satisfying section 73's eligibility criteria, despite the Court's validation of these institutions in *Nguyen*.

This chapter begins with a discussion of the motivation behind the 2002 *Charter of the French Language* and why Quebec became increasingly concerned with the use of bridging schools to satisfy the eligibility requirements of section 73 for English public education. After a consideration of the *Solski* and *Nguyen* decisions, it analyzes the four-part response introduced by the Charest government in 2010. What Bill 115 and the regulatory changes introduced in 2010 demonstrate is how sustained legislative disagreement and an implementation context, in which Quebec was the sole initiator of legislative responses when the Court had invalidated parts of the *Charter of the French Language*, can contain judicial policy impact and confine it to agenda setting.

2002 *Charter of the French Language* and the Ministerial Directive
Recognizing the implications of unsubsidized private schools as a pathway to English language public instruction, the Quebec government simply closed this loophole in 2002. Under the 2002 *Charter of the French Language*, the Parti Québécois government of Bernard Landry amended section 73 to prohibit the use of unsubsidized private schools to satisfy the MPR.[8] The Landry government viewed unsubsidized private schools as "bridging" schools or *écoles passerelles* that allowed a circumvention of the *Charter of the French Language* by the allophone community, whereby brief attendance at unsubsidized private institutions would be the route to satisfy the MPR of section 73.[9] The term "bridging" or "gateway" school was used to depict an educational institution that provides a pathway into English public instruction independent of the eligibility requirements of the *Charter of the French Language*.[10] Under this practice, once one child was briefly educated in English at a private institution, allophone parents could apply for a certificate of eligibility for English public instruction for their remaining children, arguing that the MPR had been met under section 73.2 of the *Charter of the French Language*.

According to the Attorney General of Quebec, more than twenty-one hundred students attended "bridging" schools in the 2001–02 academic year without having certificates of eligibility, and this figure increased to four thousand students in the 2007–08 academic year.[11] Until the passage of Bill 104 in 2002, the administrative practice in Quebec was to accept attendance at an unsubsidized private school when assessing eligibility requests under section 73.2 of the *Charter of the French Language*.[12] The practice simply required at least one year of attendance before reviewing an eligibility request.[13] After the passage of the 2002 *Charter of the French Language*, attendance at unsubsidized private schools would no longer be a valid pathway to satisfy the MPR.

The impact of the prohibition was immediate as the number of certificates of eligibility issued after attendance at unsubsidized private schools declined from a high of 6.1 percent (7,499/122,872) under the 1993 *Charter of the French Language* to zero under the 2002 *Charter of the French Language* (2002–10) (see Figure 3.6).[14] In addition to these important restrictions on the use of unsubsidized private schools, the minister of education issued a directive to his designate under section 75 of the *Charter of the French Language*, outlining how the MPR would now be operationalized in assessing requests for certificates of eligibility:

> The Minister has interpreted the "major part" requirement in a disjunctive and strictly mathematical manner. The Minister will consider either the child's primary school attendance or the child's secondary school attendance, but will not consider them cumulatively (appellant's record, vol. III at pp. 400–35). Further, the Minister will determine eligibility solely on the basis of the number of months spent in each language. Other factors, including the availability of linguistic programs and the presence of learning disabilities or other difficulties, which are developed below, are not considered.[15]

The ministerial directive is particularly significant as it reduced any discretion the minister's designate had under section 75 when reviewing eligibility requests for English instruction. In addition, section 83.4 of the *Charter of the French Language* provides that any decision by the minister's designate can be appealed to the Administrative Tribunal of Quebec (ATQ) within sixty days of the decision.[16] However, as the ATQ had also adopted the ministerial directive for assessing the MPR, this further reduced the possibility of certificates of eligibility being issued upon appeal.

Quebec's response to a perceived public policy problem in the form of Bill 104 and the ministerial directive – the circumvention of the *Charter of the French Language* through unsubsidized private schools by allophones – was consistent with the division of powers and provincial control over education. And, more importantly, because the MPR had yet to be tested under the *Canadian Charter*, the 1993 modification to the *Charter of the French Language* was constitutional in so far as the courts had yet to rule on its relationship to section 23 of the *Canadian Charter*.[17] This issue would return to the judicial arena in 2005 when the MPR and the ministerial directive were challenged in *Solski* and, again in 2009, when the prohibition on unsubsidized private schools was considered by the Supreme Court of Canada in *Nguyen*. Both cases were launched by members of the francophone and allophone communities that had enrolled their children in unsubsidized private schools for brief periods and were denied certificates of eligibility for English instruction under the 2002 *Charter of the French Language* and the ministerial directive.

Solski and the MPR

The *Solski* decision was the result of three families (Solski, Casimir, and Lacroix) that were denied certificates of eligibility after administrative reviews and appeals determined that they did not satisfy the MPR under section 73(2) of the *Charter of the French Language*. The Solski and Lacroix families abandoned their appeal after the trial proceedings, and their rights claim was not adjudicated by the Supreme Court of Canada, despite featuring prominently in the naming of the decision. Regarding the Casimir family that migrated from Ottawa to Montreal, the children had been educated in a French immersion program where 50 percent of instruction took place in both official languages.[18] For the Lacroix family, the oldest child completed two years in private French instruction in Quebec before attending an unsubsidized private school that provided 60 percent of instruction in English. Based on the ministerial directive and the requirement that the MPR be assessed in a "strictly mathematical manner," neither family were determined to have satisfied the eligibility requirement of section 73.[19] Upon appeal to the ATQ, the denials of the certificates of eligibility were upheld for both families.

The Supreme Court of Canada considered two constitutional issues in *Solski* and reached two different conclusions, finding the statutory provision of the MPR constitutional but the ministerial directive unconstitutional. Invoking federalism as a justification for the MPR, the Court relied on its judgment in *Arsenault-Cameron*[20] and ruled that "each province has a legitimate interest in the provision and regulation of minority language education."[21] As a result, the amendments to section 73(2) introduced by Bill 86, *Charter of the French Language* (1993 *Charter of the French Language*) were consistent with the *Canadian Charter* and were within provincial jurisdiction.[22] However, the Court upheld the appeal in part and ruled that the ministerial directive was inconsistent with the purpose of the minority language education provision. Relying on *Arsenault-Cameron*, the Court reiterated in *Solski* that "[a]lthough the Minister is responsible for making education policy, his discretion is subordinate to the *Charter*."[23] Though the Court said two different things, the differences were negligible for the continued application of the MPR, as directed by the minister of education, and it did not matter whether one aspect was constitutional and the other unconstitutional.

In its ruling, the Supreme Court of Canada concluded that the Casmiri and Lacroix families had satisfied the MPR, based on a qualitative reading, and were eligible for English language instruction under section 73(2) of the *Charter of the French Language*.[24] The Court ruled that a purely quantitative approach violated the purpose of section 23(2), as only a significant part and not the majority of a child's education needed to be in English to qualify for minority language education in Quebec.[25] While recognizing that provinces retain the discretion to determine eligibility for minority language education, the criteria must be consistent with the purpose of section 23. To address this constitutional defect, the Court engaged in an activist remedy and issued a qualitative directive to guide future assessments of the MPR.

Despite upholding the constitutionality of the MPR as a statutory provision, the Supreme Court issued a strong rebuke of the ministerial construction of this eligibility requirement. For instance, the ministerial directive indicated that the assessment would be based on either a child's primary or secondary school attendance "but will not consider them cumulatively."[26] In *Solski*, the Supreme Court rejected this and revised it to require a cumulative assessment of the time spent in an educational setting:

> Based on the proper interpretation of s. 23(2), which we will set out in detail below, we are of the view that in order to comply with this constitutional provision, the *CFL*'s "major part" requirement must involve a qualitative rather than a strict quantitative assessment of the child's educational experience through which it is determined if a significant part, though not necessarily the majority, of his or her instruction, considered cumulatively, was in the minority language.[27]

And in a strong rebuke of ministerial discretion, the Supreme Court of Canada read into the directive the very considerations that the minister of education had instructed his designate not to consider when reviewing edibility requests under section 73 of the *Charter of the French Language*: "Other factors, including the availability of linguistic programs and the presence of learning disabilities or other difficulties, which are developed below, are not considered."[28] In *Solski*, the Court reasoned that "a strict mathematical approach lacks flexibility and may even exclude a child from education vital to maintaining his or her connection with the minority community and culture."[29] Instead, "all the circumstances of the child must be considered including the time spent in each program, at what stage of education the choice of language of instruction was made, what programs are or were available, and whether learning disabilities or other difficulties exist."[30]

There are several important aspects of the Supreme Court's remedy to highlight as Quebec's legislative response to *Solski* and *Nguyen* – the 2010 *Charter of the French Language* – did introduce a comprehensive set of amendments and regulations governing the MPR as well as the issue of unsubsidized private schools.[31] In regard to a qualitative approach to the MPR, the Court was clear that "although it is not a conclusive factor, it is nonetheless important to consider the time spent in the minority language program, cumulatively, at the primary and secondary levels."[32] While the Supreme Court of Canada cautioned against a quantitative approach to section 73 of the *Charter of the French Language*, it did establish the requirement that parents demonstrate a commitment to the educational pathway: "It cannot be enough, in light of the objectives of s. 23, for a child to be registered for a few weeks or a few months in a given program to conclude that he or she qualifies for admission, with his or her siblings, in the minority language programs of Quebec."[33] More importantly, the Court was clear that section 23(2) of the *Canadian Charter* "does not specify a minimum amount of time a child must spend in a minority language education program" and, further, "nor does it require that the time spent in the minority language education program be greater than the time spent in the majority language education program."[34]

As "The Court" employed the most activist remedy at its disposal – reading in a qualitative assessment for the MPR – this is a clear example of a strong-form decision as the Court amended the ministerial directive, and the Quebec government was prevented from introducing a legislative response, which would have occurred if the Court simply invalidated those parts of section 73 that referred to the MPR. Perhaps more importantly, by expanding the criteria away from a strict mathematical interpretation, the impact of judicial policy-making, presumably, would see an increase in the number of certificates of eligibility issued by the Quebec government.

As Figure 4.1 demonstrates, the *Solski* decision did not change the downward trend line for certificates of eligibility issued under sections 73(1), 73(2), 73(3), and 73(5) of the 1993 *Charter of the French Language*, though there is a slight upward trend in 2008–09.[35] As a point of comparison, data for the five years preceding the *Solski* judgment are provided (quantitative MPR) and the data for the MPR post-*Solski* (qualitative MPR). The data ends at 2009–10 as the Court issued its ruling in *Nguyen* in 2009, and the approach to both the MPR and the issue of unsubsidized private schools was revised by the

Figure 4.1 Two approaches to section 73 and the MPR

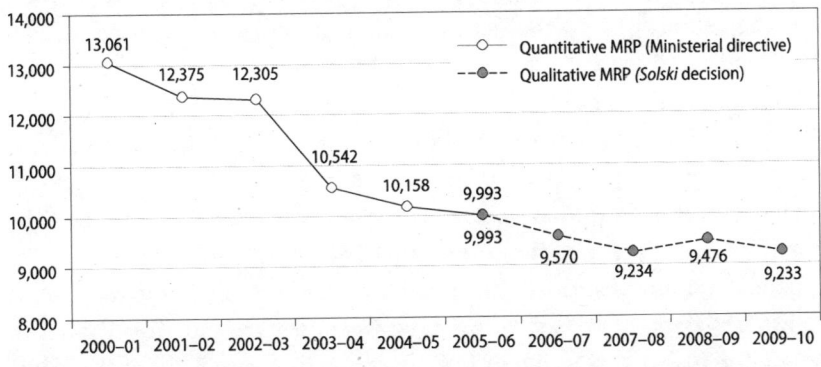

Source: Ministère de l'éducation, du loisir et du sport, Indicateurs linguistiques – Secteur de l'éducation, 2013.

Quebec government in the 2010 *Charter of the French Language*. In the five-year period that preceded *Solski*, a total of 58,441 certificates of eligibility were issued for a yearly average of 11,689. In the same period after *Solski*, a total of 47,506 certificates were issued, and the yearly average declines to 9,501. This represents a 19 percent decline in certificates of eligibility. Extending the comparison to the twelve-year period in which the 1993 *Charter of the French Language* and the ministerial directive were in force (1993–94–2004–05), a total of 149,357 certificates of eligibility were issued for a yearly average of 12,447. The decline is even more precipitous in the post-*Solski* era, as it represents a 25 percent decline in comparison to the twelve-year average under the 1993 *Charter of the French Language* (9,501 versus 12,447).

What are we to make of this downward trend? For one, it reinforces the central premise of this book that courts are, for the most part, implementer-dependent institutions when their statutory decisions wade into salient areas of public policy. And in the context of a positive right, it shows that the executive is not the sole implementer of a judicial decision or that legislative disagreements are what change the policy trajectory of a judicial decision. At its barest, the post-*Solski* period shows that the implementation of judicial decisions rests on a range of considerations. In the context of minority language education rights, these include the demographic trends of the community that benefits from a judicial decision and, more importantly, whether these rights beneficiaries choose to access a judicially regulated public service. There is no evidence that Quebec's ministry of education ignored the qualitative assessment established by the Supreme Court of Canada after *Solski*.

Like any administrative test, the Court's framework is malleable, and a qualitative assessment can come to function in a "strictly mathematical manner" depending on how the qualitative elements are weighted in the overall assessment. This point will be returned to once Quebec's legislative and regulatory responses to *Solski* and *Nguyen* – Bill 115 – are considered.

What this downward trend indicates, however, is an inconvenient truth for dialogue theorists as well as critics of the 1982 constitutional settlement in Quebec. It suggests that the dialogue that matters may not be that of the Court, the legislature, or the executive but, rather, the one within the anglophone community and whether it accesses English public instruction. In short, did anglophones apply for – and were they granted – certificates of eligibility in growing numbers using a qualitative assessment of the MPR? The empirical evidence suggests the answer to this question is said with a resounding "*non*." For critics of the 1982 constitutional settlement, unfortunately, this dialogue is increasingly articulated in Québécois, with increasing numbers of anglophones attending the French school system, despite the Court's remedial activism and the constitutional protections provided to this community under section 23 of the *Canadian Charter*. And because of Quebec's stringent approach to unsubsidized private schools, both before and after Bill 115, fewer allophones are accessing this pathway to satisfy the MPR. The combined effect of these factors is a downward pressure on English school enrollments and a sharp blunting of judicial impact via section 23 remedial activism.

Unsubsidized Private Schools and the 2002 *Charter of the French Language*

Although the Supreme Court of Canada would raise the issue of the 2002 *Charter of the French Language*'s ban on the use of unsubsidized private schools in the *Solski* decision, it would not rule on the constitutionality of the 2002 *Charter of the French Language* until *Nguyen* in 2009.[36] The 2002 *Charter of the French Language* added paragraphs 2 and 3 to section 73, and the key parts are provided in *italics*:

> However, instruction in English received in Québec in a private educational institution not accredited for the purposes of subsidies by the child for whom the request is made, or by a brother or sister of the child, *shall be disregarded*. The same applies to instruction in English received in Québec in such an institution after 1 October 2002 by the father or mother of the child.

Instruction in English received pursuant to a special authorization under section 81, 85 or 85.1 *shall also be disregarded*.[37]

Two separate challenges involving section 23 of the *Canadian Charter* were considered in *Nguyen*, and both originated from Quebec's allophone community. The first involved the prohibition on attendance at unsubsidized private schools as satisfying the MPR under paragraph 2 of section 73. It was launched by the Nguyen family and represented 131 families that were denied certificates of eligibility by the minister's designate under paragraph 2.[38] Each family had attended unsubsidized private schools for short periods of time before applying for a certificate of eligibility for their children to attend English public schools. As the Court noted in *Nguyen*, the Quebec government had accepted periods of attendance at unsubsidized private schools to satisfy the MPR, and, until 2002, "no concern was shown in the *CFL* for unsubsidized private schools."[39] The second challenge involved the Bindra family where the eldest child had been granted a ministerial dispensation on humanitarian grounds to attend English public instruction under section 85.1. Afterwards, the family applied for a certificate of eligibility for the remaining child but was denied based on the prohibition outlined in paragraph 3 of section 73.[40] Upon appeal to the ATQ, the decisions of the minister's designate involving both cases were upheld.

In a unanimous judgment written by Justice Louis LeBel, the Supreme Court of Canada declared paragraphs 2 and 3 of section 73 to be an infringement of section 23 of the *Canadian Charter*. More importantly, the Court did not consider that either constituted a reasonable limitation under section 1 of the *Canadian Charter*. Unlike *Solski*, where the Court read the MPR to be constitutional through a qualitative interpretation, the remedy in *Nguyen* was to suspend the constitutional invalidation of the 2002 *Charter of the French Language* for one year.[41] In terms of the constitutional issues and the 2002 *Charter of the French Language*, LeBel J noted the following incompatibilities between section 73, the prohibition on unsubsidized private schools, and section 23 of the *Canadian Charter*: "Finally, in the very words of s 23(2) – which refers to instruction that the child has received or is receiving for the purpose of determining whether the child has a right to receive instruction in the minority language – no distinction is made between instruction that is public and instruction that is private, whether subsidized or unsubsidized."[42] Although LeBel J did not refer to *Protestant School Boards*, his reasoning is reminiscent of the first section 23 decision in which "The Court" identified a fundamental problem between section 73 and the

Canadian Charter's minority language education provision: "In our opinion, a legislature cannot by ordinary statute validly set aside the means chosen by the framers and affect this classification. Still less can it remake the classification and redefine the classes."[43]

For the Court, the main difficulty with paragraphs 2 and 3 of section 73 and the 2002 *Charter of the French Language* was the inability to engage in a global assessment of an applicant's educational pathway caused by the total prohibition on unsubsidized private schools or attendance at English schools by virtue of a ministerial dispensation under section 81, 85, or 85.1:

> The inability to assess a child's educational pathway in its entirety in determining the extent of his or her educational language rights has the effect of truncating the child's reality by creating a fictitious educational pathway that cannot serve as a basis for a proper application of the constitutional guarantees. In *Solski*, this Court stated that the child's entire educational pathway must be taken into account in order to determine whether it meets the requirements of s 23(2) of the *Canadian Charter*. If an entire portion of the educational pathway is omitted from the analysis because of the nature or origin of the instruction received, it is impossible to conduct the global analysis of the child's situation and educational pathway required by *Solski*.[44]

Although LeBel J found a constitutional violation between the 2002 *Charter of the French Language* and section 23 of the *Canadian Charter*, the Court accepted that "bridging" schools posed a serious challenge to section 73 of the *Charter of the French Language*:

> The "bridging" schools appear in some instances to be institutions created for the sole purpose of artificially qualifying children for admission to the publicly funded English-language school system. When schools are established primarily to bring about the transfer of ineligible students to the publicly funded English-language system, and the instruction they give in fact serves that end, it cannot be said that the resulting educational pathway is genuine. However, it is necessary to review the situation of each institution, as well as the nature of its clientele and the conduct of individual clients. As delicate as this task may be, this is the only approach that will make it possible to comply with the framers' objectives while averting, especially in Quebec, a return to the principle of freedom of

choice of the language of instruction that the framers did not intend to impose (*Gosselin*, at paras. 2, 30 and 31).[45]

In this respect, the Court established an important distinction between an unsubsidized private school (a genuine educational pathway) and a "bridging" school (an instrument to circumvent section 73). For the purposes of the MPR, attendance at an unsubsidized private school could not be prohibited, but attendance at a "bridging" school could be.

In its section 1 analysis, the Supreme Court of Canada accepted that Quebec had pursued a "pressing and substantial" legislative objective, thus satisfying the first branch of the *Oakes* test for evaluating reasonable limitations on a protected right and freedom "in view of the unique linguistic and cultural situation of the province of Quebec."[46] However, the Court found that the legislative measures "are excessive in relation to the objectives being pursued, and do not meet the standard of minimal impairment."[47] In regard to the use of unsubsidized private schools, the Court surveyed statistics provided by the ministry of education that showed that attendance at these institutions had remained relatively low but were increasing in recent years. For instance, twenty-one hundred students had enrolled in unsubsidized private schools without certificates of eligibility in the 2001–02 academic year, and this had increased to four thousand by 2008–09. This represented about 1.5 percent of the students eligible for instruction in English,[48] and the Court considered the complete prohibition on these institutions as "overly drastic" given that attendance at unsubsidized private schools without a certificate of eligibility, though increasing, was still very low: "What is happening is not a de facto return to freedom of choice with disruptive changes to the categories of rights holders. The legislature could have adopted different solutions that would involve a more limited impairment of the guaranteed rights and could more readily be reconciled with the concrete contextual approach recommended in *Solski*."[49]

LeBel J also found that the denial of a certificate of eligibility to the youngest Bindra child was an unreasonable limitation given the limited number of ministerial dispensations issued under sections 81, 85, and 85.1. More importantly, while the minister of education retained full discretion concerning whether to issue a special dispensation, once an authorization was granted, the minister could not "deny any rights flowing from the authorizations in question that are guaranteed by the *Canadian Charter*."[50] Finally, paragraph 3 interfered with section 23(2) of the *Canadian Charter* and its objective to preserve family unity in educational experience as the provisions added by the 2002 *Charter of the French Language* "are likely to make it impossible for children of a family to receive instruction in the same school system."[51]

In regard to the specific requests for certificates of eligibility, the Supreme Court ordered the files of the 131 families that participated in the *Nguyen* appeal returned to the Ministry of Education and "reviewed in light of the criteria established in *Solski* and in this judgment." The Court was unsure whether sufficient information existed to evaluate their requests and reasoned that a subsequent administrative review was the appropriate course of action. For the Bindra family, the Court ordered the Ministry of Education to immediately issue a certificate of eligibility for the remaining child. With the invalidation of paragraph 3 of section 73, the MPR had been satisfied, and the second child was entitled to a certificate of eligibility based on the *Canadian Charter*'s objective of ensuring family unity in the educational system.[52] In finding the 2002 *Charter of the French Language* unconstitutional, the Court sympathized with Quebec's concern with unregulated "bridging" schools, as LeBel J noted that "the bridging schools could become a mechanism for almost automatically circumventing the *CFL*'s provisions on minority language education rights, creating new categories of rights holders under the *Canadian Charter* and, indirectly, restoring the freedom to choose the language of instruction in Quebec."[53]

Although the declaration of unconstitutionality was suspended for one year, LeBel J provided guidance for the Quebec government to achieve its policy objectives consistent with the *Canadian Charter*. First, the Court accepted the dubious nature of "bridging" schools that "raises doubts regarding the genuineness of many educational pathways, and regarding the objectives underlying the establishment of certain institutions."[54] Thus, the Court required Quebec to refine its approach to unsubsidized private schools. While it would not condone the prohibition of all unsubsidized private schools, as Quebec had done, the Court would accept the prohibition on "bridging" schools, particularly those established with the intention of circumventing the *Charter of the French Language*: "When schools are established primarily to bring about the transfer of ineligible students to the publicly funded English-language system, and the instruction they give in fact serves that end, it cannot be said that the resulting educational pathway is genuine."[55] In addition, the Court did not consider attendance periods of six months to one year as sufficient to satisfy the purpose of section 23(2) of the *Canadian*

Charter or the MPR under section 73 of the *Charter of the French Language*. And, finally, the Court recommended that Quebec engage in a comprehensive review of all unsubsidized private schools, consistent with the *Solski* principles, which "would relate to the duration of the relevant pathway, the nature and history of the institution and the type of instruction given there."[56]

The Charest Government and the Charters: A Play in Four Parts

The Charest government introduced a comprehensive response to *Nguyen* that also addressed the *Solski* ruling. It consisted of an act passed by the National Assembly (Bill 115) that amended two statutes (the 2010 *Charter of the French Language* and the *Act Respecting Private Education*), a set of regulations concerning the *Charter of the French Language*,[57] the classification of all unsubsidized private schools by the Ministry of Education for the purposes of assessing the MPR,[58] and a prohibition on "bridging" schools. Although the main response to *Solski* and *Nguyen* was Bill 115, it was first introduced as Bill 103, *An Act to Amend the Charter of the French Language and Other Amendments* on June 2, 2010.[59] It was reviewed by the Committee on Education and Culture on September 8–28 of the same year and approved in principle by the National Assembly on October 6. Bill 103 would be withdrawn and reintroduced in a modified version as Bill 115 on October 18 and passed the next day after closure was invoked.[60] Unlike Bill 104, which was unanimously passed, Bill 115 was approved on a party-political vote, with only the Liberal government voting in favour of the bill (sixty-one to fifty-four). The four-part response by the Charest government is outlined in Table 4.1.

Did the Supreme Court provide the Charest government with a pathway to navigate the judicialization of politics away from the *Charter of the French Language*? The answer depends on whether you are a dialogue theorist (absolutely) or a critic of the 1982 constitutional settlement in Quebec (*absolument pas!*). Neither answer is particularly compelling, though there is undoubtedly support for both positions to be found in the Charest government's response. On the issue of "bridging" schools, the *Charter of the French Language* (section 78.2) and the *Act Respecting Private Education* (section 12) were amended to empower the minister of education to prohibit their establishment. Thus, Quebec accepted the Court's distinction between genuine educational pathways (unsubsidized private schools) and those that sought to circumvent section 73 ("bridging" schools).

The most consequential changes to the *Charter of the French Language* involved section 73 as it was heavily amended in response to *Solski* and

Table 4.1 The Charest government's response to *Solski* and *Nguyen*

Constitutional challenge	Legislative, regulatory, and administrative responses (n = 4)
Charter of the French Language 1993 and 2002 (Bill 86 and 104)	#1 Charter of the French Language 2010 (Bill 115)
73. The following children, at the request of one of their parents, may receive instruction in English:	73. The following children, at the request of one of their parents, may receive instruction in English:
(1) a child whose father or mother is a Canadian citizen and received elementary instruction in English in Canada, provided that that instruction constitutes the major part of the elementary instruction he or she received in Canada;	a child whose father or mother is a Canadian citizen and received elementary instruction in English in Canada, provided that that instruction constitutes the major part of the elementary instruction he or she received in Canada;
(2) a child whose father or mother is a Canadian citizen and who has received or is receiving elementary or secondary instruction in English in Canada, and the brothers and sisters of that child, provided that that instruction constitutes the major part of the elementary or secondary instruction received by the child in Canada;	(2) a child whose father or mother is a Canadian citizen and who has received or is receiving elementary or secondary instruction in English in Canada, and the brothers and sisters of that child, provided that that instruction constitutes the major part of the elementary or secondary instruction received by the child in Canada;
	(3) *repealed*
	(4) *repealed*
	(5) *repealed*
	Paras. 2 and 3 repealed
	73.1. The Government may determine by regulation the analytical framework that a person designated under section 75 must use in assessing the major part of the instruction received, invoked in support of an eligibility request under section 73. The analytical framework may, among other things, establish rules, assessment criteria, a weighting system, a cut-off or a passing score and interpretive principles.

(3) a child whose father and mother are not Canadian citizens, but whose father or mother received elementary instruction in English in Québec, provided that that instruction constitutes the major part of the elementary instruction he or she received in Québec;

(4) a child who, in his last year in school in Québec before 26 August 1977, was receiving instruction in English in a public kindergarten class or in an elementary or secondary school, and the brothers and sisters of that child;

(5) a child whose father or mother was residing in Québec on 26 August 1977 and had received elementary instruction in English outside Québec, provided that that instruction constitutes the major part of the elementary instruction he or she received outside Québec.

The regulation may specify the cases and conditions in which a child is presumed or deemed to have satisfied the requirement of having received the major part of his instruction in English within the meaning of section 73.

...

78.2. No person may set up or operate a private educational institution or change how instruction is organized, priced or dispensed in order to circumvent section 72 or other provisions of this chapter governing eligibility to receive instruction in English.

It is prohibited, in particular, to operate a private educational institution principally for the purpose of making children eligible for instruction in English who would otherwise not be admitted to a school of an English school board or to a private English-language educational institution accredited for the purposes of subsidies under the Act respecting private education (chapter E-9.1).

#2 *Act Respecting Private Education 2010 (Bill 115)*

12. The Minister shall issue, after consulting the Commission consultative de l'enseignement privé, for a particular institution and for particular educational services or categories of educational services, a permit to any person

...

(3) who has not been convicted of or pleaded guilty to, or whose chief executive officer has not been convicted of or pleaded guilty to an offence under this Act or section 78.1 or 78.2 of the Charter of the French language (chapter C-11), or a criminal offence committed in relation to the operation of an educational institution in the three years preceding the application;

...

Constitutional challenge	Legislative, regulatory, and administrative responses (n = 4)
Paras. 2 and 3 However, instruction in English received in Québec in a private educational institution not accredited for the purposes of subsidies by the child for whom the request is made, or by a brother or sister of the child, shall be disregarded. The same applies to instruction in English received in Québec in such an institution after 1 October 2002 by the father or mother of the child. (para. 2) Instruction in English received pursuant to a special authorization under section 81, 85 or 85.1 shall also be disregarded. (para. 3)	However, the Minister may refuse to issue a permit if, during the three years preceding the application, a permit held by the applicant was revoked. Moreover, the Minister may refuse to issue a permit if, in the Minister's opinion, doing so could allow the circumvention of section 72 of the Charter of the French language or of other provisions of that Act governing eligibility for instruction in English. The Minister may also, with a view to preventing such a result, subject a permit to any condition the Minister judges necessary. #3 *Regulation respecting the criteria and weighting used to consider instruction in English received in a private educational institution not accredited for the purposes of subsidies* The regulation can be accessed [at https://www.legisquebec.gouv.qc.ca/en/document/cr/C-11,%20r.%6202.1]. #4 *Ministre de l'Éducation de de l'Enseignement supérieur* Classification of all unsubsidized private schools in Quebec: Catégories des établissements privés non subventionnés (EPNS)

Nguyen. The most significant was to repeal paragraphs 2 and 3, which had been added by the 2002 *Charter of the French Language* as the total prohibition on unsubsidized private schools was unconstitutional after *Nguyen*. More critically, section 73 came to fully align with section 23 of the *Canadian Charter*, suggesting a modern-day conquest of the Quebec clause by the Canada clause. For instance, section 73 was reduced to two derogations and provided English language instruction to the children or siblings of Canadian citizens educated in English in Canada (see Table 3.1). This provision no longer resembled the one enacted by the Lévesque government in 1977, where section 73 was limited to Quebec's anglophone community, or that of the subsequent Péquiste and Liberal governments, which may have complied with decisions by the Supreme Court of Canada but retained distinct provisions such as section 73(3), (4), and (5) that differentiated it from section 23 of the *Canadian Charter*.

In a final concession to the judicialization of politics, the Charest government accepted that the ministerial directive regarding the MPR as a quantitative assessment was, according to the Supreme Court of Canada in *Solski*, incompatible with the purposes of section 23(2) of the *Canadian Charter*. In response, the *Charter of the French Language* was amended to include section 73.1, which provided that a broader assessment of the MPR would be enacted through regulations. While 73.1 did not refer specifically to the assessment criteria outlined by the Court in *Solski* – the time spent in an educational program, the stage it was chosen, the availability of programs, and the presence of learning disabilities – it did signal an intention to break from a "strictly mathematical approach" and an acceptance that an educational pathway must be assessed with additional criteria.

If the analysis were to end at the four-part response by the Charest government, a strong case could be made for dialogue theory or, for that matter, those arguing that the judicialization of politics had severally compromised Quebec's language and education policy. I would then have lost in challenging both the dominant understandings of the judicialization of politics and its impact on the *Charter of the French Language*. For instance, the complex response conforms to the process of dialogue as the Charest government introduced a set of measures within the one-year suspended declaration of unconstitutionality regarding *Nguyen*, which largely complied with the Court's decision, as well as *Solski*. Section 73 was amended, and the Charest government engaged in a rights-based dialogue that, from the Court's perspective, ultimately placed the *Charter of the French Language* on firmer constitutional footage. This is what its proponents meant by Charter dialogue.

I have no doubt that dialogue theorists such as Peter Hogg, Allison Bushell Thornton, and Wade Knight or Kent Roach would have any reservations in pointing to this as an outstanding example of Charter dialogue in action.[61]

Nor do I have any hesitation that critics of the judicialization of language politics such as Guy Laforest, Henri Brun, Jose Woerhling, Alain G. Gagnon, or Eugénie Brouillet would conclude that the Charest government capitulated to the Trudeau vision of the *Canadian Charter* as a symbol of national unity, guaranteeing a pan-Canadian application of language and education rights.[62] Such an argument would proceed as follows. The Quebec clause became the mirror image of the Canada clause, the ministerial directive was replaced with section 73.1 that committed Quebec to the *Solski* principle, and the Charest government followed the Court's directive to classify unsubsidized private schools for the purposes of section 73. It is easy to see how a damning assessment of the Charest government could be reached in regard to the Liberal government's response to the *Solski* and *Nguyen* decisions.[63]

Like many things, where you stand – and where you stop – largely determine how you see things. It is folly to stop at a judicial decision, as the Supreme Court of Canada generally renders strong rebukes of governments when it invalidates legislation as being incompatible with the *Canadian Charter*. This is the height of judicial power but not necessarily any indication of policy impact, and the analysis must progress to an understanding of the legislative response. This too may be the wrong stopping point, particularly when a positive right is at issue. The anglophone community is accessing English public instruction in declining numbers, questioning the impact of the Court's remedial activism. Without increased requests for certificates of eligibility, none of the Court's section 23 decisions affecting section 73 of the *Charter of the French Language* can be implemented on a scale that undermines the objectives of this formative statute or undermines the sovereign authority of Quebec over its distinct language and education policy. All the trend lines suggest an implementation challenge facing the Court's remedial activism regarding the *Charter of the French Language*. As such, legislative disagreements and apathy by the rights bearers can significantly limit the policy impact of a judicial decision.

The Charest government's response to *Solski* and *Nguyen* introduces a new variable to consider when evaluating judicial impact – regulations authorized in legislation. An implementation paradox emerges – or what the opening pages of Chapter 3 referred to as a constitutional "sleight of hand" – whereby elements of a legislative response comply with a judicial decision, but additional statutory provisions or the accompanying regulatory framework inhibit the implementation of a judicial decision. Judicial policy impact is offset, and a legislative disagreement emerges through this set of amendments and regulations that work at cross purposes. The most significant part of the legislative response, and the one where legislative disagreement with *Solski* and *Nguyen* manifests, is not Bill 115. It is in the remaining aspects of the Charest government's response to the Court's language of instruction decisions.

To be sure, there were judicial openings in the *Nguyen* decision that saw the Quebec government introduce more drastic restrictions on access to English public instruction, despite lifting the ban on unsubsidized private schools. For instance, LeBel J's assertion that attendance for periods less than a year would not satisfy either the MPR in section 73 or the purposes of section 23(2) of the *Canadian Charter* is particularly noteworthy and provided Quebec with a legislative opening on the issue of unsubsidized private schools. The administrative practice in Quebec before the 2002 *Charter of the French Language* was to accept one-year attendance at an unsubsidized private school as sufficient for the purposes of the MPR. After the 2010 *Charter of the French Language*, the Quebec government would require a minimum attendance of three years, although this could be as much as seven to eleven years, depending on the classification of a particular unsubsidized private school as well as the educational pathway of all family members. While the Court would not accept a complete prohibition after *Nguyen*, LeBel J's statement on minimum residency provided a legislative opportunity that the Charest government seized on when it interpreted this in its regulatory and administrative response. The 2010 *Charter of the French Language* complies with *Solski* and *Nguyen*. But the remainder of the Charest government's response questions its overall compatibility with the Court's interpretation of section 23 of the *Canadian Charter*.[64]

What then to make of this mixture of compatibility and legislative disagreement within a four-part response? Simply stated, it refutes the narrative surrounding the judicialization of language politics in Quebec.[65] The classification scheme for unsubsidized private schools introduced by the regulatory framework, as well as the test adopted for ascertaining the MPR, effectively returned Quebec, for all intents and purposes, to a "strictly mathematical approach" to the MPR. By introducing a complex regulatory labyrinth for satisfying the MPR, and seven classifications of unsubsidized private schools (Types A, B3, B2, B1, C3, C2, C1) with varying time frames to satisfy the residency requirements,[66] the Charest government effectively restricted this route to English public instruction to a handful of unsubsidized private institutions along "The Boulevard" in Westmount (Type A). For those outside Montreal, "The Boulevard" refers to a leafy residential area in Upper Westmount, where the Molson, Bronfman, and Saputo families reside. It is second only to West Vancouver in terms of residential wealth.

The shortest route to qualify for English public instruction after attendance at unsubsidized private schools is through historic anglophone institutions along "The Boulevard" – St. Georges, The Study, and Miss Edgar's and Miss Cramp's Schools – as well as Selwyn House on the "Flats" in Westmount and Lower Canada College in the Notre-Dame-de-Grâce area adjacent to Westmount. The Study and Miss Edgar's and Miss Cramp's Schools are all-girls institutions. The Westmount institutions are within one kilometre of each other, and Lower Canada College is just over three kilometres to the west. While other unsubsidized private schools do exist, none are realistic pathways to English public instruction, despite the Quebec government accepting them as institutions that can satisfy the MPR. As previously suggested, where you stop and where you stand determine how you see things. In the context of unsubsidized private schools as a pathway to English public instruction, it also depends on where you live or where you can afford to send your kids to school.

This is not to suggest that these schools are restricted to residents of Westmount or Notre-Dame-de-Grâce. Instead, as private institutions with significant tuition fees and limited space, only the privileged few can genuinely access what the Supreme Court of Canada referred to in *Solski* as representing a "genuine commitment to a minority language educational experience."[67] In short, the Charest government introduced significant disincentives, both financial and geographical, that may not have prohibited unsubsidized private schools, as the 2002 *Charter of the French Language* had done, but came as close to doing so as constitutionally permissible for the vast majority of institutions. In this respect, a more draconian approach to unsubsidized private schools and the MPR emerged for francophones and allophones. This ultimately questions the constitutional "victories" in *Solski* and *Nguyen*, particularly from an implementation and access perspective.

The Major Part Requirement after 2010: A "Bridging" School Too Far?

In response to section 73.1, the Charest government published an extensive set of regulations that operationalized the MPR and provided criteria to categorize unsubsidized private schools to satisfy section 73 of the *Charter of the French Language*. To be issued a certificate of eligibility after attending an unsubsidized private school, an applicant must achieve a passing score of fifteen, which is weighted under three divisions in Schedule 1: Division 1: "Schooling"; Division 2: "Consistent, true commitment"; and Division 3: "Specific situation and overall education." Once a file is assessed under all three divisions, and a weighted score of fifteen is attained, a certificate of eligibility to attend English public instruction is issued by the minister's designate under section 75 of the *Charter of the French Language*, provided an applicant provides proof of Canadian citizenship and filiation.

Division 1 provides a weighted score for each year that an applicant attends a Type A, B, or C institution. Although the weighted score is heavily tied to years of attendance, it categorizes unsubsidized private schools based on other factors: "Among other elements, the following are considered: the different type of educational institutions attended and the characteristics of their enrolments that illustrate their relationship with the Québec anglophone minority, as well as any special educational projects or programs of study the institution offers to meet the needs of certain groups of students."[68] For instance, the score in Division 1 does provide for a weighted score (0 to +5) for those attending schools with a "special mission or purpose," which the regulation defines as schools where most of the "enrollments are students requiring special services because of a physical or mental handicap, behavioural problems, social maladjustments, learning difficulties or other similar problems."[69] In this respect, it does comply with the *Solski* principle that, among other things, an eligibility assessment considers "what programs are or were available, and whether learning disabilities or other difficulties exist."[70] However, in another respect, the approach to Division 1 does not comply with *Solski* as the Court was clear that individuals do not require a connection with the anglophone community to be eligible for minority language educational services: "It must indeed be noted here again that children qualified under s. 23 are not required to have a working knowledge of the minority language, or to be members of a cultural group that identifies with the minority language."[71]

For simplicity, the weighted scores for yearly attendance and the criteria used to classify unsubsidized private schools as Type A, B, and C are provided in Table 4.2. Generally speaking, at least 60 percent of the students enrolled in Type A institutions have a certificate of eligibility or special authorization to receive English instruction, and at least 70 percent of the students pursue higher education at the same institution. Type B is neither a Type A or C institution, and Type C are bilingual or multilingual institutions where less than 60 percent of students enrolled have a certificate of eligibility or special

Table 4.2 Division 1: Schooling: weighted scores for attendance at Type A, B, and C English language institutions

Type A: English language institution					
Years	Level	Weight	Years	Level	Weight
1	elementary and secondary	+2	3	elementary and secondary	+15
2	elementary	+6	6	elementary	+20
2	elementary and secondary	+6	4	secondary	+25
2	secondary	+8	6 to 9	elementary and secondary	+30
3 or 4	elementary	+15	10 or 11	elementary and secondary	+35

Notes:

Type A English language institution: a private educational institution to which one of the following situations applies:

(1) 60 percent or more of the students enrolled in the first three years of elementary or secondary school have a certificate of eligibility or a special authorization to receive instruction in English under the *Charter of the French Language* or

(2) the institution provides elementary- and secondary-level instruction and satisfies the following two criteria:

 (a) 70 percent or more of the students at the elementary level go on to attend the institution throughout their secondary studies and

 (b) 70 percent or more of the hours of instruction are provided in English at both the elementary and secondary levels, the proportion of English instruction having been determined by the institution concerned and certified by a member of the professional order of accountants authorized by law to audit books and accounts.

Type B and C: English language institution						
Years	Level	B3	B2	B1	C3	C2 . C1
2 to 3	elementary or secondary or both	+5	+4	+3	+4	+3 +2
4 to 6	elementary or secondary or both	+13	+10	+8	+9	+7 +5
7 to 11	elementary or secondary	+21	+16	+13	+14	+11 +8

Notes:

Type B English language institution: a private educational institution that is not a Type A or Type C institution:

B3: 41–59 percent of the enrollments hold a certificate of eligibility or a special authorization to receive instruction in English;

B2: 26–40 percent of the enrollments hold a certificate of eligibility or a special authorization to receive instruction in English; and

B1: 0–25 percent of the enrollments hold a certificate of eligibility or a special authorization to receive instruction in English.

Type C English language institution: a private educational institution that is specially dedicated to providing bilingual or multilingual learning to students in the context of an immersion or other program and less than 60 percent of whose students have a certificate of eligibility or special authorization to receive instruction in English under the *Charter of the French Language:*

C3: 41–59 percent of the enrollments hold a certificate of eligibility or a special authorization to receive instruction in English;

C2: 26–40 percent of the enrollments hold a certificate of eligibility or a special authorization to receive instruction in English; and

C1: 0–25 percent of the enrollments hold a certificate of eligibility or a special authorization to receive instruction in English.

Source: Regulation Respecting the Criteria and Weighting Used to Consider Instruction in English Received in a Private Educational Institution Not Accredited for the Purposes of Subsidies, RRQ 2010, C-11, 2.1.

---

authorization for English language instruction. There are also subcategories within Type B (B1, B2, B3) and Type C (C1, C2, C3) institutions, and points are weighted according to the type of English language institution attended. The number of years of attendance to achieve a score of +15 based on Division 1 is provided in *italics*.

There are several important aspects of Table 4.2 to highlight. The first is that the weighted score favours institutions with a higher percentage of students enrolled with a certificate of eligibility and an established pathway throughout all levels of the private English educational system. For instance, the weighted yearly score favours Type A institutions that require periods of attendance of three to four years to achieve a score of +15. Second, while certain Type B institutions can achieve a weighted score of +15 (B3, B2), they require a much longer residency period ranging between seven and eleven years at the elementary and secondary levels. Finally, while Type C institutions are not prohibited, they are classified as bilingual or multilingual institutions. These institutions cannot achieve a weighted score of +15, regardless of years of attendance, as the highest weighted score that can be awarded under Division 1 is +14 at a Type C3 institution.

Table 4.2 suggests, therefore, that only Types A, B3, and B2 institutions are realistic pathways to satisfy the MPR under section 73.1 of the *Charter of the French Language*. This is more apparent than real. In Quebec, high school ends at Grade 11, and two years of *Collège d'enseignement général et professionnel* (CEGEP), which is a college system that acts as a bridge between high school and university, follow. The *Charter of the French Language* does not currently apply to CEGEPs or universities, and francophones and allophones are therefore permitted to attend Quebec's twelve English language CEGEPs and three English language universities (Bishop's, Concordia, and McGill). However, with the passage of Bill 96, *An Act Respecting French, the Official and Common Language of Québec*,[72] the current Coalition Avenir Québec government has introduced new requirements and restrictions on English CEGEPs, beginning in 2024: the total enrollment in English CEGEPs cannot exceed 17.5 percent of the enrollment in French CEGEPs; priority will be given to those applicants that possess a certificate of eligibility for English public instruction; at least three courses at the CEGEP level must be in French; and, to graduate, attendees at English CEGEPs must pass a French proficiency test. The dilemma for Type B3 and B2 unsubsidized private schools is the following – it may require an entire school career to attain a weighted score of +15 under Division 1. Graduating from these Type B private schools earns enough points to attend English public high school. It is therefore appropriate to speak of unsubsidized private schools that are a viable pathway to satisfying the MPR (Type A) and those that are not (Type B and Type C).

There is another significant aspect of the classification of unsubsidized private schools – the list is malleable as the classifications can change, depending on whether a school is categorized as a Type A, B, or C institution, based on the criteria applied by the Ministry of Education. Each year, the Ministry of Education reviews all recognized unsubsidized private schools, and as Figure 4.2 reveals, there have been significant changes in the yearly categorization of unsubsidized private schools. For instance, in 2010–11, a total of fifteen out of fifty-eight Type A institutions were recognized,[73] which represented roughly 26 percent of all unsubsidized private schools. By 2021–22, this declined to seven out of fifty-nine institutions,[74] or just over 11 percent of unsubsidized private schools recognized for the purposes of the MPR under section 73.1 of the *Charter of the French Language*. To be sure, this is the result of some schools being reclassified as Type B schools, such as Académie Kells, which represented seven of fifteen schools, or nearly half of the Type A institutions in 2010–11. In addition, some schools have refused the per student subsidy by the Quebec government at the elementary level (Selwyn House) or all levels of education (The Priory). As a result, they are exempt from the *Charter of the French Language*, and attendance at these institutions cannot be used for the purposes of satisfying the MPR. Regardless of the reasons, the number of Type A institutions has narrowed significantly since 2012–13 and are now located principally within Upper Westmount in the 2021–22 school year.

Figure 4.2 Categories of unsubsidized private schools in Quebec, 2010–22

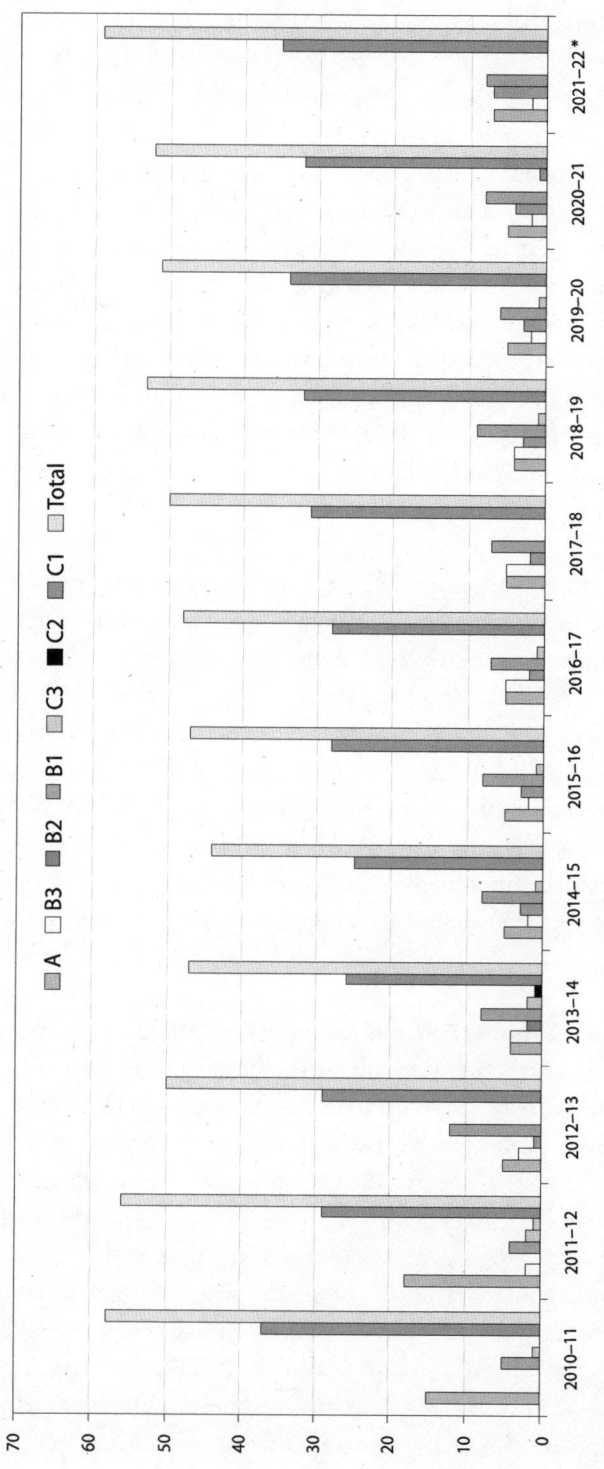

Note: * Type A institutions will decline by at least two institutions in 2022–23 as Selwyn House is no longer accepting the per student subsidy for private schools. As a result, it will no longer be considered an unsubsidized private school that can satisfy the MPR.

Source: Figure 4.2 is a compilation of the data provided at Ministère de l'éducation de l'énseignement supérieur, "Types des établissements privés non subventionnés (EPNS)," http://www.education.gouv.qc.ca/references/tx-solrtyperecherchepublicationtx-solrpublicationnouveaute/resultats-de-la-recherche/detail/article/categories-des-etablissements-prives-non-subventionnes/.

Once a weighted score is assessed under Division 1: "Schooling," the distinct educational pathway of the applicant is assessed. Under Division 2: "Consistent, true commitment," the regulations deduct points if an applicant has spent any time at a French language institution. As outlined in Table 4.3, a set of penalties are assessed for each year spent in the French language system. This penalty, presumably, is based on the principle that attendance in the French language system does not demonstrate a "consistent, true commitment" to minority language educational instruction. This approach is fundamentally at odds with the *Solski* decision, which declared that the commitment to a particular educational pathway or language of instruction system may not occur until later in one's educational pathway. In discussing why a strict mathematical approach to the MPR is inconsistent with section 23 of the *Canadian Charter*, "The Court" was unequivocal that Quebec's approach before *Solski* was too rigid:

> The strict mathematical approach lacks flexibility and may even exclude a child from education vital to maintaining his or her connection with the minority community and culture. For example, a child who has completed grades 1, 2 and 3 in French and grades 4, 5 and 6 in English may have formed a sufficient link with the minority language community, but would not qualify under s 73(2). It might also be that the language learned in the last three years may provide a better marker than that learned in the first three years. Too many relevant factors are ignored. In short, the strict approach mandated by the Minister of Education fails to deal fairly with many persons who must be qualified under a purposive interpretation of s 23(2) of the *Canadian Charter*.[75]

A similar constitutional concern can be raised regarding the penalties assigned for individuals that first attend French language instruction. An even stricter "mathematical approach" exists under section 73.1 of the *Charter of the French Language* that may exclude a child from accessing minority language education if the commitment is made after their education begins.

The weighted score of +15 points is also a function of the educational pathways of each family member in the school system. For instance, as outlined in Table 4.4, points are added for each year that one or more siblings attend a Type A institution, and points are deducted for each year that one or more siblings attend a French language institution. This reinforces the idea that the regulations heavily favour attendance at Type A institutions as

Table 4.3 Division 2: Consistent, true commitment: Changes or inconsistencies in terms of the language of instruction during the schooling invoked in support of the eligibility request. Score adjustment for attendance at French language institutions

Length of interruption or change in language of institution or school	Level*	Weight
1 year	elementary	–3
2 years	elementary	–3 per year
3 or more years	elementary	–5 per year for each additional year after the first 2 years
1 year	secondary	–5
2 years	secondary	–5 per year
3 or more years	secondary	–8 per year for each additional year after the first 2 years

Note:
* Enrollment in a French language institution is not considered if motivated by the availability of special services needed because of a physical or mental disability, behavioural problems, social maladjustments, learning difficulties, or other similar problems. Similarly, the period of enrollment in a French language institution is to be disregarded if ascribable to the student's participation in a special program of studies with limited access or availability, such as sports study or music study programs.
Source: *Regulation Respecting the Criteria and Weighting Used to Consider Instruction in English Received in a Private Educational Institution Not Accredited for the Purposes of Subsidies*, RRQ 2010, C-11, 2.1.

only these institutions are a realistic pathway to satisfying the MPR and its reformulation under section 73.1 of the *Charter of the French Language*.

Divisions 1 and 2 are not fit for constitutional purpose as the weighted score is heavily determined by time spent in each educational system, and other factors for assessing the MPR are, at best, at the periphery or, worse, irrelevant. For instance, the easiest way to attain a score of +15 is to send a child to a Type A institution for three years at the beginning of their educational pathway. Any deviation from this pathway, whether it is the child in question or one or more siblings attending a French school, significantly increases the amount of time required at a Type A institution. For instance, if a child attended three years of French language instruction (–11) before joining a Type A institution, they would have to complete six to nine years of elementary and secondary schooling (+30) to achieve a weighted score of +19 (+30 – 11 = +19). At this point, with a student on the verge of high school graduation, would a family switch their child into English language public instruction for their final two years? Probably not, which is what the weighted score of +15 is most likely premised on, as it is a difficult threshold to cross.

Table 4.4 Division 2: Continued commitment, changes, or inconsistencies in siblings' school attendance. Score adjustments for changes or inconsistencies in siblings' school attendance

Sibling	Type A: English language institution	Weight
1 or more	Siblings attended a type A English language institution at the elementary or secondary level for a total of 1 year of instruction	+2
1 or more	Siblings attended a type A English language institution at the elementary or secondary level for a total of 2 years of instruction	+5
1 or more	Siblings attended a type A English language institution at the elementary or secondary level for a total of 3 or 4 years of instruction	+8
1 or more	Siblings attended a type A English language institution at the elementary or secondary level for a total of 5 or 8 years of instruction	+15
1 or more	Siblings attended a type A English language institution at the elementary or secondary level for a total of 9 or more years	+20
	French language institution	
1 or more	Siblings attended a French-language (–2) institution* at the elementary or secondary level for a total of 1 year of instruction	–2
1 or more	Siblings attended a French-language (–5) institution* at the elementary or secondary level for a total of 2 years of instruction	–5
1 or more	Siblings attended a French-language (–15) institution* at the elementary or secondary level for a total of 3 or 4 years of instruction	–15
1 or more	Siblings attended a French-language (–20) institution* at the elementary or secondary level for a total of 5 or 8 years of instruction	–20
1 or more	Siblings attended a French-language (–30) institution* at the elementary or secondary level for a total of 9 or more years of instruction	–30

Notes:
* Enrollment in a French language institution is not considered if motivated by the availability of special services needed because of a physical or mental disability, behavioural problems, social maladjustments, learning difficulties, or other similar problems. Similarly, the period of enrollment in a French language institution is to be disregarded if ascribable to the student's participation in a special program of studies with limited access or availability, such as sports study or music study programs.

Source: *Regulation Respecting the Criteria and Weighting Used to Consider Instruction in English Received in a Private Educational Institution Not Accredited for the Purposes of Subsidies*, RRQ 2010, C-11, 2.1.

What is further problematic is that any attendance by older siblings in the French system complicates the attainment of a certificate of eligibility for a younger child that attends a Type A institution. If there is an age gap of three years, and an older sibling attends French school, the child seeking a certificate of eligibility through attendance at a Type A institution would begin their educational pathway with a deficit of –15 points. After three years of attendance at a Type A institution, they would receive +15 points. However, an older sibling would have spent six years in the French system at this point, which is assessed a large penalty (–20), and the child attending a Type A institution would have a weighted score of –5. As devised, any points deficit caused by an older sibling attending the French educational system quickly becomes insurmountable, particularly when an age difference of more than three years exists for siblings attending different school systems in Quebec.

As outlined in Table 4.2, the highest number of points than can be allocated by attendance at a Type A institution is +35 (ten or eleven years of instruction). However, if one or more siblings completes at least nine years of French instruction, this costs –30 points, for a net +5 points, which is 10 points short of the required score of +15. A clear lesson emerges from the weighted approach to Division 1 and Division 2 – all family members must attend a Type A institution as this is the only viable educational pathway to a certificate of eligibility through attendance at an unsubsidized private school. Attendance at the remaining institutions – Type B and Type C – are exercises in weighted futility. Further, if you plan to have more than one child, and the older child or children attend the French language system, you cannot exceed a two-year age difference between your children. Anything more and the child attending English language instruction in a Type A institution cannot overcome the points deficit accrued by their siblings attending the French language system. The weighted system is devised to significantly reduce the number of certificates of eligibility that will be issued through attendance at unsubsidized private schools. Indeed, this sentiment was expressed by Michelle Courchesne, the Charest government's minister of education, who stated: "I won't deny that the objective is to have as few as possible (approved)."[76] Similarly, the Quebec English School Board Association reached a similar conclusion when appearing before the parliamentary committee reviewing Bill 103: "We repeat, not a single new student is likely to be registered in an English public school as a result."[77]

While fifty-nine unsubsidized private schools were recognized for the purposes of the MPR in 2021–22, only Type A institutions are realistic pathways, and the rest – Type B and Type C – are fictitious educational pathways as +15 weighted points are nearly impossible to achieve (B2, B3) or cannot be achieved based on years of attendance (B1, C3, C2, C1). Most are still viewed by the Quebec government as a "bridging" school, so to speak. Although seven institutions were classified as Type A institutions in 2021–22, the practical list is actually much smaller. OneSchool Global in Baie-d'Urfe is closely associated with the Plymouth Brethren Church, and the student body is limited to its Christian congregation.[78] Two schools in Westmount are all-girls schools (The Study, Miss Edgar's and Miss Cramp's), and The Study only accepts the per student subsidy at Grade 6. As a result, years of attendance at the elementary level at The Study cannot be used for ascertaining the MPR under section 73.

Assuming that families sending a child to Type A institutions are motivated to earn the required points (+15) after three years of attendance (kindergarten to Grade 2), there are only four Type A institutions that are viable pathways to satisfy section 73 of the *Charter of the French Language*. Two institutions are located in Upper Westmount and are 750 metres apart (St. Georges, and Miss Edgar's and Miss Cramp's), one is on the "Flats" in Westmount (Selwyn House), the last is in Notre-Dame-de-Grâce (Lower Canada College), the district adjacent to Westmount. As they are not boarding schools, there is a clear accessibility issue for families that do not live within a commutable distance of these neighbourhoods on the Island of Montreal.

Unlike the 2002 *Charter of the French Language*, which prohibited all unsubsidized private schools from satisfying the MPR, the classification system associated with the 2010 *Charter of the French Language* effectively prohibits all but four, and the rest are treated no differently than they were before the 2002 *Charter of the French Language*. This approach, incidentally, was found to be unconstitutional in *Nguyen*. The constitutionality of the Charest government's response, therefore, rests on whether a byzantine regulatory system that, for the purposes of the MPR, narrows accessibility to three elite anglophone institutions clustered in a part of Montreal that is west of Boulevard Saint-Laurent ultimately complies with the Court's 2005 and 2009 decisions involving language of instruction.

The accessibility implications of this regulatory classification system are captured in Table 4.5, which provides the total enrollments for these institutions as well as their tuition levels in 2020–21. Selwyn House is not considered

Table 4.5 Viable Type A English language institutions, 2020–21: class size and tuition fees

	Institution	Kindergarten	Grade 1	Grade 2	Grade 3	Grade 4	Grade 5	Grade 6
Enrollment levels	Lower Canada College	36	36	38	38	40	42	42
	Miss Edgar's and Miss Cramp's*	20	20	20	20	24	24	30
	St. Georges	24	24	26	30	32	32	32
	The Study*	–	–	–	–	–	–	20
	Total enrollment	80	80	84	88	96	100	124
Tuition fees	Lower Canada College	$18,070	$22,154	$22,154	$23,127	$23,127	$23,479	$23,479
	Miss Edgar's and Miss Cramp's*	$19,525	$22,800	$22,800	$22,800	$22,800	$22,800	$23,000
	St. Georges	$19,125	$22,605	$22,766	$22,928	$23,035	$23,144	$23,360
	The Study*	–	–	–	–	–	–	$25,810
	Average	$18,907	$22,520	$22,574	$22,912	$22,994	$23,141	$23,912

Note: * All-girls school.
Source: Our Kids: The Trusted Source – 20 Years," https://www.ourkids.net/school/.

as it stopped accepting the private school subsidy for Quebec in 2022–23 and is no longer be subject to section 73 of the *Charter of the French Language*. Focusing on the remaining schools, a total enrollment of just over eighty spaces exists for these three Type A institutions during the first three years of elementary education (kindergarten to Grade 2). More importantly, the average total cost for three years of attendance (kindergarten to Grade 2) is $64,000. One of the criticisms levelled against the Charest government's response from then Parti Québécois leader Pauline Marois, as well as from nationalist groups such as Société St-Jean Baptiste, was that it allowed francophones and allophones to buy the right to English language instruction through Type A institutions.[79] This suggests that freedom of choice is simply a Type A institution away. This represents a pithy political criticism of the Charest government as it downplays the reality of the regulations and the complexity associated with satisfying the MPR under the 2010 *Charter of the French Language*. Nor does it fairly convey accessibility issues and how difficult it is to secure a space, even if a family can afford these private institutions.

All Quebeckers – francophones, allophones, and anglophones – since the inception of the *Charter of the French Language* in 1977 have been permitted to send their children to English private institutions, provided they can afford it. Whether language groups that are not permitted under section 73 to attend English public instruction can buy this right is not as simple as the criticism presented by the official opposition and nationalist groups in 2010. From a practical perspective, there are simply too few spaces in these Type A institutions to suggest that the changes introduced in 2010 represent a return to freedom of choice in language of instruction. As well, the regulations have built-in measures that limit the number of francophones and allophones that can attend these Type A institutions. In particular, Type A institutions are unsubsidized private schools where at least 60 percent of the students have certificates of eligibility or special authorization to attend an English institution. Using this measure, the three institutions in Table 4.5 could only allocate roughly thirty-two of their total yearly spaces (kindergarten to Grade 2) to retain their Type A classification. Whether retaining this designation motivates enrollment decisions by these schools, it does demonstrate, nonetheless, the hollowness of the "money-for-rights" arguments directed against the Charest government and its response to the language-of-instruction decisions by the Supreme Court of Canada. It may actually be "money for nothing" as the regulations produce dire straits for families seeking a certificate of eligibility.

While it does allow a small number of francophones and allophones to access public English instruction for their child after attending Type A institutions, this is less a case of "buying a right" than a risky investment with a low rate of return. This will become apparent once the final consideration in the weighted score, Division 3: "Specific situation and overall education," is discussed. However, before explaining why attending a Type A institution is a risky investment for francophones and allophones seeking a certificate of eligibility, it does raise a more practical question – if you can afford to send your children to schools with an average tuition of $21,000 per year and a three-year expense of $64,000, are you really seeking their transfer to the English public system? I would venture not. Before the 2002 *Charter of the French Language* prohibited the use of unsubsidized private schools, the Office québécois de la langue française estimated that over twenty-one hundred students enrolled in English language unsubsidized private schools did not have certificates of eligibility in the 2001–02 school year.[80] Even after the prohibition was enacted under the 2002 *Charter of the French Language*, this number increased to four thousand in the 2007–08 school year, suggesting that unsubsidized private schools may not have been used to circumvent the *Charter of the French Language*. For instance, sending your child to an unsubsidized private school between 2002 and 2010, knowing full well that the time spent could not be used to satisfy the MPR (2002 *Charter of the French Language*), may simply have indicated a desire by francophones and allophones to educate their children in English, which is only possible in the private system.

For those francophones and allophones enrolling their children in Type A institutions for the purposes of a certificate of eligibility, Division 3: "Specific situation and overall education," poses a tremendous risk for attaining the weighted score of +15, even after three years of attendance and a minimum cost of just over $64,000. Under the regulations supporting the 2010 *Charter of the French Language*, Division 3 requires the minister's designate under section 75 of the *Charter of the French Language* to assess a score (+8 to −8) based on the following considerations: "related or distinct contextual elements that allow a more in-depth assessment, with respect to the child's personal family situation, of the authenticity of the commitment made."[81] The minister's designate, presumably through an in-person interview, will question francophone and allophone families as to the reasons why their children were enrolled in private English institutions as a way to ascertain the authenticity of their commitment to the anglophone community and institutions. This *gardien de porte* aspect of Division 3 becomes apparent once section 4 of the regulations is considered and how it is to be assessed in light of the weighted score (+8 to −8) for satisfying the MPR:

> 4. When interpreting and applying Schedule 1, in particular Division 3, it is important, among other things, to make a distinction between cases that demonstrate a genuine commitment to an English-language education, and cases where attendance at a private educational institution described in the first paragraph of section 2 could simply denote a desire to create an artificial educational pathway in order to circumvent the Charter of the French language.[82]

At present, there is no ministerial directive to assess the major part "authenticity" requirement by the minister's designate. And, if there were, it would most likely run afoul of the purposes of section 23(2) of the *Canadian Charter*, as laid out by the Court in the *Solski* decision.

Division 3 has come under criticism, most notably from the Quebec ombudsperson, who raised concerns during the legislative hearings on Bill 103 regarding the large scope for administrative interpretation as "the very broad weighting of certain criteria in the bill leaves too much scope for interpretation."[83] As well, the lawyer representing the 131 families in *Nguyen*, Brent Tyler, stated that the regulations are inconsistent with the spirit of *Nguyen*, particularly Division 2, and the penalties for siblings attending French schools: "Those 15 points can be subtracted from, depending on where the brothers and sisters went to school, depending on where the parents went to school – and a whole series of factors that are completely irrelevant to the situation of the child."[84] In regard to Division 3 and the minister's designate's discretion (+8 to −8), Tyler remarked: "So conceivably, you could have a child that did all their elementary instruction in English at a private non subsidized school, and they still wouldn't get a certificate."[85] This is why the 2010 *Charter of the French Language* is a risky investment and does not provide the straightforward ability to purchase a right to English public instruction for francophones and allophones. Given that Type A institutions, as elite anglophone private institutions with a deep history in the community, are not the traditional educational route for francophones and allophones,[86] it is difficult to see anything other than a loss of points under Division 3, and a weighted score that falls short of +15, once all the divisions of Schedule 1 are assessed.

There is a more fundamental problem with Division 3 and why it is ripe for constitutional invalidation. Previously, the Quebec government considered "bridging" schools to be an artificial pathway used to circumvent the *Charter of the French Language*. To address this issue, the 2002 *Charter of the French Language* banned all unsubsidized private institutions. And, in *Nguyen*, while the Court accepted that "bridging" schools did represent an artificial pathway and Quebec had a legitimate interest to prevent such abuse, this was not the case for all unsubsidized private schools. This is the constitutional challenge that Division 3 faces – artificial educational institutions have been banned in the 2010 *Charter of the French Language* (section 78.2) and the 2010 *Act Respecting Private Education* (section 12), which is consistent with *Nguyen*. But regulating the artificial educational *intentions* of francophones and allophones who attend long-standing anglophone private institutions is a constitutional step too far that would most likely fail the rational connection branch of section 1 of the *Canadian Charter*. More practically, how does the minister's designate assess an intention to circumvent the *Charter of the French Language* whereby allophones and francophones create an artificial educational pathway? The only metric to understand this intention, it seems, is allophones and francophones attending Type A institutions – the very institutions approved for the purposes of the MPR by the Quebec government. Is there a viable route to a certificate of eligibility for francophones and allophones under the 2010 *Charter of the French Language* created by this regulatory pantomime? The answer is probably not, which, as we know, was the intention of the 2010 *Charter of the French Language*, as the minister of education publicly acknowledged.

The impact of the 2010 *Charter of the French Language* on certificates of eligibility issued through attendance at unsubsidized private schools is presented in Figure 4.3. The data are incomplete as the Ministry of Education no longer releases detailed information regarding section 73, as was past practice.[87] However, the data are sufficient to understand the impact of the 2010 *Charter of the French Language* on certificates of eligibility issued through attendance at unsubsidized private schools. Before the 2002 *Charter of the French Language*, a total of 7,499 certificates of eligibility were issued through one-year attendance at unsubsidized private schools between 1993 and 2002.[88] This is a yearly average of 833 certificates of eligibility issued in the period of the 1993 *Charter of the French Language*, which ended with the passage of the 2002 *Charter of the French Language* until it was invalidated by the Court in the 2009 *Nguyen* decision. Since the passage of the 2010 *Charter of the French Language* and the regulations pertaining to the MPR, only 233 certificates of eligibility have been issued through attendance at unsubsidized private schools from 2010 to 2013 or a yearly average of seventy-eight certificates of

Figure 4.3 Certificates of eligibility and Bill 115, *Charter of the French Language,* 2010–16

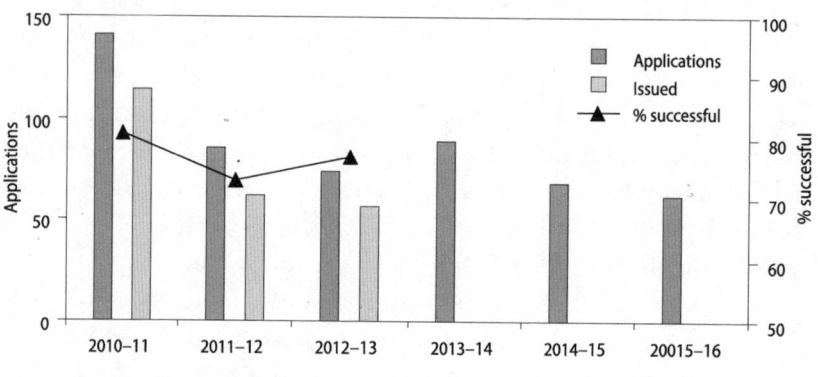

Source: Ministère de l'éducation, du loisir et du sport, Indicateurs linguistiques – Secteur de l'éducation, 2013.

eligibility. Further, the number of applications for certificates of eligibility through attendance at private English schools is also quite low, with a total of 519 applications submitted to the Ministry of Education from 2010 to 2016 for a yearly average of eighty-seven.

At several points in this chapter and the last, I have returned to the most compelling statement made by the Supreme Court of Canada in *Protestant School Boards* in which the Court laid out the relationship between a supreme law instrument such as the *Canadian Charter* and a statutory instrument such as the *Charter of the French Language:* "In our opinion, a legislature cannot by ordinary statute validly set aside the means chosen by the framers and affect this classification. Still less can it remake the classification and redefine the classes."[89] Unfortunately, this is exactly what the Quebec government, regardless of political affiliation, has done in response to every invalidation of the *Charter of the French Language.* It has remade the classifications and redefined the classes of Canadian citizens who are eligible for English language instruction in Quebec. Bill 115 and the 2010 *Charter of the French Language,* therefore, are just the latest example of how legislative disagreements, and the Court's reliance on the very actors that disagree with the Court to implement its ruling, may ultimately change the policy trajectory of a judicial decision.

Conclusion

The most recent report of the Office québécois de la langue française notes that the number of children eligible for English language instruction in 2019 was at its lowest level in thirty years.⁹⁰ What does this suggest about judicial victories and policy outcomes? If anything, the judicial and legislative saga of the language of instruction provision of the *Charter of the French Language* is a cautionary tale about policy impact and its relationship to a judicial decision. Without the invalidation of section 73 in *Protestant School Board*, the ministerial directive in *Solski*, or the prohibition on unsubsidized private schools in *Nguyen*, the language of instruction provisions of the *Charter of the French Language* would have simply applied to Quebec's historic anglophone community, as the 1977 version of the *Charter of the French Language* intended. In this respect, judicial review did require the Quebec government to align section 73 with section 23 of the *Canadian Charter*, as it now incorporates a pan-Canadian approach to minority language education rights. These are important changes and the direct result of judicial invalidation of section 73 as incompatible with the minority language education provision of the *Canadian Charter*.

Whether a judicial decision is important and whether it has sustained policy impact are two separate issues. Evaluated on their own, judicial victories in *Protestant School Boards, Solski,* and *Nguyen* suggest profound policy implications for the language of instruction provision of the *Charter of the French Language*. But judicial decisions should not be evaluated in isolation but in relation to the legislative changes introduced and the degree to which a judicial decision is implemented by public and private actors. As I have argued in this chapter and the last, judicial impact is dependent on a number of variables outside the control of the Supreme Court of Canada. For one, the decisions of the courts are implemented by political actors that may disagree with the direction of a judicial decision and seek to blunt the impact of judicial review. In the case of Quebec and section 73 of the *Charter of the French Language*, the legislative responses of successive Quebec governments were motivated to limit access to English public instruction by creating new eligibility criteria for the allophone community. The addition of the MPR (1984 *Charter of the French Language*), the ministerial operationalization of this eligibility requirement, the prohibition on unsubsidized private schools (2002 *Charter of the French Language*), the weighted approach to the qualitative MPR (2010 *Charter of the French Language*), and the supporting regulations all demonstrate the significance of legislative disagreement and how cross-purpose legislative and regulatory measures can change the trajectory of a judicial decision and temper judicial impact.

Moreover, a judicial decision may inadvertently create a legislative opening that a government exploits to reduce judicial impact. The Supreme Court sanctioned a distinction between "bridging schools" (illegitimate pathways) and unsubsidized private schools (legitimate pathways) and provided the Quebec government with judicial cover to prohibit the former and to categorize the latter. As shown, the creation of seven types of unsubsidized private schools has significant implications for accessibility to institutions to satisfy the MPR, especially for those living outside of Montreal. Lebel J's caution that short periods of attendance at an unsubsidized private school would not be sufficient to demonstrate a "genuine commitment" to an educational pathway was seized upon by the Charest government when it fashioned its four-part response to the *Solski* and *Nguyen* decisions. This created a paradoxical outcome that, despite judicial victories that invalidated section 73, the Quebec government introduced eligibility criteria that are more difficulty to satisfy than the ones that preceded judicial review. The post-*Nguyen* residency requirement is now a minimum of three years at a Type A institution, and the classification scheme has effectively reduced unsubsidized private schools to a small subset of three institutions that can satisfy the MPR. These institutions are expensive with very small enrollments, which has a direct bearing on whether francophones and allophones can satisfy the MPR through these historic anglophone Type A institutions along "the Boulevard" in Westmount.

One criticism of my approach would be to suggest that I have dismissed the importance of the *Canadian Charter*, judicial review, and the remedial character of sections 23 and 24(1). This would be an inaccurate reading of this chapter, the general argument of this book, or my cumulative scholarly work.[91] Each of the decisions considered in this chapter are important judgments rendered by the Supreme Court of Canada that saw the introduction of legislative responses by a host of Quebec governments. Their contribution to the policy process is agenda setting, and, without judicial invalidation, the Quebec government would not have amended the *Charter of the French Language* as often as it has. However, and despite this contribution, my position is that too many works that consider the policy implication of judicial review stop at the judicial decision and fail to consider whether a judicial decision has been implemented and, thus, has actual policy impact. Assessing a judicial decision in the abstract is merely academic speculation that may or may not be borne out. And in the cases considered in this chapter, academic speculation as to the policy implications of *Protestant School Boards, Solski*, and *Nguyen* has been far off the mark.

To explain this, I have sought to understand when a strong-form judicial decision has a "road to Damascus" moment and what accounts for limited or non-existent judicial impact. This chapter prioritized a number of components of the implementation chain surrounding section 23 decisions by the Supreme Court of Canada: first, federalism, and the jurisdictional control of language and education policy by the National Assembly of Quebec, operating under an executive-dominated parliamentary system, and, second, the state of the anglophone community in Quebec as well as the educational choices of this community. Focusing on the anglophone community is apt as it is the main beneficiary of section 23 in Quebec and the Supreme Court's minority language education rights jurisprudence. On their own, the legislative and regulatory responses by successive Quebec governments are probably sufficient to blunt the policy impact of *Protestant School Boards*, *Solski*, and *Nguyen*. However, in combination with the changing linguistic profile of Quebec and the educational choices of the anglophone community, the public and private dimensions of this implementation chain question two bodies of scholarship: the empirical footings of dialogue theory and the normative critique of the judicialization of language politics in Quebec by opponents of the 1982 constitutional settlement.

In 1977, when the Lévesque government passed the *Charter of the French Language* and, in 1982, when the Trudeau government entrenched the *Canadian Charter* and section 23, no one could have foreseen the sharp decline of the anglophone community as a linguistic group in Quebec. Nor could anyone have predicted that, among those anglophones that remained in Quebec, an increasing number would send their children to the French school system within a generation of Bill 101. But these are the developments that have a direct bearing on the policy impact of section 23 decisions and why a judicial decision, on its own, does not shape the direction of Canadian federalism. Before drawing policy conclusions, we must understand how the governments and societies of Canadian federalism respond to a judicial decision and how this can change the trajectory of judicial review. In the case of language of instruction, strong judicial decisions have faced the headwinds of strong legislative responses, strong downward pressure on the anglophone community, and declining enrollments in the English school system. This is why judicial impact has been slight, dialogue is rather muted, and academic criticisms of "that bloody Charter" are off the mark.

Quebec's "Sign Law" and Freedom of Expression
Ford, Devine, and the Bourassa Government's Response

The judicialization of language policy exhibits the two variables that can limit judicial policy impact and relegate it to agenda setting: judicial invalidation of a salient issue of public policy that produces an important legislative disagreement and the implementation context that shapes a legislative response to judicial invalidation. Bill 101, *Charter of the French Language*, is about the legislative disagreements of two capitals, their governments, and how this disagreement manifested in their responses to the policy instruments (and intentions) of the other.[1] For instance, Pierre Elliott Trudeau disagreed with Bill 22, *Official Language Act,* passed by the Bourassa government in 1974, which declared French as the official language of Quebec.[2] And Trudeau also strongly disagreed with those parts of the *Charter of the French Language* that ended freedom of choice in public education.[3] This policy disagreement was constitutionalized by entrenching minority language education rights in section 23 of the *Canadian Charter of Rights and Freedoms (Canadian Charter)* and, to a lesser extent, freedom of expression in section 2(b).[4]

Speaking on the issue of language and education rights in 1977, and Trudeau's desire for their constitutional entrenchment, René Lévesque telegraphed the position of all subsequent Quebec governments: "Québec will never accept that its sovereignty in such a vital matter be replaced by a limited jurisdiction subject to judicial interpretation ... It would be unthinkable that the Supreme Court of Canada, a majority of whose members will always be English-speaking and non-Quebeckers, replace the Québec National Assembly as the final authority in the area of education."[5] By refusing to be a signatory to the 1982 constitutional settlement, Lévesque registered his and future Quebec governments' opposition to the judicialization of a critical area of provincial jurisdiction by the *Canadian Charter*.

This chapter focuses on two landmark rulings, *Ford* and *Devine*, in which the Supreme Court of Canada invalidated provisions of the *Charter of the French Language* that prohibited the uses of languages other than French on public signs and commercial names.[6] Both judgments occurred in a highly charged political atmosphere that focused on the "distinct society" provisions within the Meech Lake Accord, which ultimately failed to become part of the *Constitution Act, 1982*. Given its quasi-constitutional status as a modern instrument of *la survivance*,[7] the invalidation of the *Charter of the French Language* by the Supreme Court of Canada has produced deep and intense legislative disagreements in Quebec. These invalidations have been used as evidence of judicial policy impact and of the strategic advantage that a constitutional instrument such as the *Canadian Charter* wields over a statutory mechanism such as the *Charter of the French Language*. They have also been taken as proof of a sustained constitutional dialogue between Quebec and the Supreme Court of Canada. Judicial invalidation of the *Charter of the French Language* has always seen the Quebec government, regardless of party affiliation, pass amendments to re-establish the continued application of the *Charter of the French Language*. Courts invalidate, legislatures respond, and, according to dialogue theory, revised statutory provisions conform to constitutional standards as a result of this institutional interaction. And, for dialogue theorists, this is the core of their defence of the judicialization of politics and why "the Charter of Rights Isn't Such a Bad Thing after All."[8]

The evidence for judicial policy impact and the sounds of dialogue simply do not hold once the legislative replies are evaluated. In response to every invalidation of the *Charter of the French Language*, the Quebec government has passed amendments that effectively constrain the Court's remedial activism under section 24(1) of the *Canadian Charter*. These legislative responses have the appearance of real and sustained judicial impact as the amendments frequently incorporate language from a judicial decision into a revised version of the *Charter of the French Language*. Can we conclude, therefore, that the Trudeau-Lévesque debate has been answered in favour of a pan-Canadian approach to rights and freedoms and a loss of policy autonomy for the National Assembly?[9] The short answer is that there is clear evidence of judicial influence when an amendment to the *Charter of the*

French Language incorporates the language of a Charter ruling. Quebec has done more, however, than simply copy judicial language into statutory amendments. The standard response to judicial invalidation has seen Quebec engage in constitutional "sleight of hand," whereby compliance – the inclusion of judicial language in a legislative response – is coupled with new statutory provisions and regulations that drown out the Court's voice and, thus, can significantly reduce and, at times, negate judicial impact against the *Charter of the French Language*.

The ability of Quebec to diminish judicial impact through statutory amendment and regulatory change is the result of federalism, the jurisdictional structure of language and education policy, the implementation chain in which a legislative response operates, and the relative strength of the veto player(s) in these areas of public policy. For instance, commercial expression as well as language and education policy conform to the watertight compartment view of federalism. The areas regulated by the *Charter of the French Language* are solely within provincial jurisdictional authority, though now subject to judicial review under the *Canadian Charter*. This conception of federalism also structures the implementation chain as the National Assembly of Quebec is the only legislative body with the constitutional ability to introduce amendments in response to the invalidation of the *Charter of the French Language*. These factors are not enough, on their own, to withstand the judicialization of politics and the targeting of the *Charter of the French Language* by entrenching minority language and education rights or freedom of expression in the *Canadian Charter*. They are, however, more than enough when the Quebec government strongly disagrees with the Court's invalidation of the *Charter of the French Language* and demonstrates a clear intention to reassert its legislative sovereignty. And this is what Quebec has done in regard to every invalidation of the *Charter of the French Language* by the Supreme Court of Canada, starting with the first constitutional invalidation of the *Charter of the French Language* in the 1984 *Protestant School Boards* decision and the language of instruction provisions.[10]

To demonstrate legislative autonomy and policy resistance in the context of judicial invalidation, this chapter first considers the distinct Quebec response to *la question nationale* and how the *Canadian Charter* transformed a legislative disagreement into one with constitutional standing. In short, the *Canadian Charter* entrenched a fundamental policy disagreement between Canada and Quebec that has been played out during successive invalidations of the *Charter of the French Language*. It is the first, deepest, and perhaps most intense, legislative disagreement in the Charter era. The chapter then presents a case study of the "sign-law" provisions that regulate commercial expression and their invalidation as a violation of both the *Canadian Charter*'s and the Quebec *Charter of Human Rights and Freedom*'s (*Quebec Charter*) guarantee of freedom of expression.[11] It focuses on the two responses by the Bourassa government and the current state of the *visage linguistique* (public face) of Quebec more than thirty years after the *Ford* and *Devine* decisions.[12]

The first response was Bill 178, *Charter of the French Language* (1988 *Charter of the French Language*) in which the Bourassa government, among other legislative measures, invoked the notwithstanding clause to override the *Ford* and *Devine* decisions between 1988 and 1993.[13] And the second response was Bill 86, *Charter of the French Language* (1993 *Charter of the French Language*), which the Bourassa government enacted in lieu of extending the notwithstanding clause's invalidation of the sign-law provisions for a second five-year period.[14] The 1993 *Charter of the French Language* also saw the introduction of regulations governing commercial expression after 1993,[15] and the chapter considers the significance of regulatory responses to judicial invalidation as a strategy of non-compliance. This chapter also looks at how the Bourassa government's responses to the sign-law invalidation was implemented and the role of private actors as agents of implementation.

This chapter argues that the 1988 and 1993 *Charter of the French Language*, as well as the supporting regulations, preserve, with some exceptions, the French-only approach to commercial expression in Quebec. The 1993 *Charter of the French Language* still prohibits the use of languages other than French on commercial signs in certain situations, despite the *Ford* and *Devine* decisions. On the Island of Montreal, where the anglophone population is largely concentrated, and especially in the regions where anglophones are sparse, the vast majority of public signs in Quebec remain French only.[16] How can this be, given that *Ford* and *Devine* are strong decisions issued in the name of "The Court" to emphasize the absence of interpretive discretion? The answer is found in the nature of the *Canadian Charter* as a negative rights instrument, in what *Ford* and *Devine* prohibit but do not require, and in the importance of commercial enterprises as agents of implementation.

Under the 1993 *Charter of the French Language*, commercial enterprises have the discretion whether to include languages other than French, provided that French is given "marked predominance" as the Court determined in *Ford* and *Devine*. They are not prohibited from using languages other than French on commercial signs and firm names as they were between 1977 and 1993.[17] Nor are they required to use languages other than French on public signs and firm names after 1993. Commercial enterprises, therefore, decide how to implement Quebec's response to *Ford* and *Devine*. Much of the analysis of judicial review and the Supreme Court of Canada, both critical and supportive, overstates the reach of a negative rights instrument such as the *Canadian Charter*, which is largely about what governments cannot do and not what they must do. These positions also ignore the importance of implementation and the role of private actors in actually determining the reach of judicial decisions and legislative instruments. To question judicial impact is not to dispute the role of the Supreme Court of Canada in our constitutional democracy. It is simply to say that, to have impact, a judicial decision must be complied with and implemented. And this is where our focus should be – not simply on the act of judicial invalidation.

Two Questions, Two Answers, Two Charters

Beginning with the Quiet Revolution, Quebec's answer to *la question nationale* had three main dimensions and a fourth attributed solely to the Parti Québécois and its project of independence, which transformed into sovereignty association. First, the politicization of language policy that began in 1960s with the passage of Bill 63, *An Act to Promote the French Language in Quebec* in 1969,[18] the *Official Language Act* in 1974, and, culminated in the *Charter of the French Language* in 1977. At the core of this development was the view that the preservation of Quebec's language, and, thus, its cultural distinctiveness, required a different approach to the issue of immigration and the dilemma this posed for freedom of choice in language of instruction for minority communities.[19] In particular, the declining birthrate among francophones, the growing allophone community, and clear evidence that, when given the freedom of choice,[20] this minority community preferred English over French language instruction[21] largely explain the removal of freedom of choice in Chapter VIII (Language of Instruction) of the *Charter of the French Language* passed by the Parti Québécois in 1977.[22]

The second dimension was a strict adherence to federalism and the jurisdictional sovereignty provided to Quebec in language and education policy under section 92 of the *British North America Act, 1867*.[23] Indeed, the politicization of language policy and streamlining the growing allophone population into French instruction were constitutional under the division of powers and, as the last two chapters argued, were immune from the judicialization of politics until section 23 of the *Canadian Charter* became part of the constitutional settlement in 1982. Related to this was the conception of Canadian federalism as a compact between two founding peoples – English and French

– where the federal bargain was based on duality and respect for *la survivance*. For Guy Laforest, rightly or wrongly, the 1982 constitutional settlement represents a rejection of the federal bargain struck in 1867 and "the end of duality, in my mind, portends the end of the Québécois' Canadian dream."[24]

The third dimension of Quebec's approach to the "national question" was the gradual emergence in 1981 of the policy of inter-culturalism in response to the Trudeau policy of multiculturalism. According to Alain Gagnon and Raffaele Iacovino, the model of inter-culturalism was viewed within government as a moral compact between Quebec and its immigrant communities operating within the following parameters: "A society in which French is the common language of public life; a democratic society where participation and the contribution of everyone is expected and encouraged; and a pluralist society open to multiple contributions within the limits imposed by the respect for fundamental democratic values, and the necessity of inter-communal exchange."[25] The policy of inter-culturalism is also advanced by the *Charter of the French Language* as, unlike multiculturalism, it is designed to facilitate a collective identity through a common public language.

The final dimension of Quebec's approach to the national question was the political project of the Parti Québécois that began as independence[26] and evolved into sovereignty association that was rejected in the 1980 and 1995 Quebec Referenda. Although this approach is solely the Parti Québécois's, a thread has run through successive approaches to *la question nationale* by Quebec governments since the Quiet Revolution – a fundamental disagreement with the initiatives of the Trudeau Liberals such as the 1969 *Official Languages Act*, the 1971 Canadian Multiculturalism Policy, their elevation to constitutional status with the passage of the *Constitution Act, 1982*, and the attempt to subjugate the distinctive approaches of successive Quebec governments since the 1960s to this vision of the Canadian federation.[27]

In his memoirs, Pierre Elliott Trudeau recounts his profound disagreement with the politicization of language policy in Quebec, particularly the actions of the Bourassa government in 1974:

> If Bourassa had talked about French as the principal language of Quebec, which it is, or the working language, which it even was under the Civil Code, we would have had no objection. But when the provincial government said there will be one official language in Quebec and it will be French – after we had been redoubling our efforts to sell the two

official languages across the land, and after we had managed at Victoria to get the provinces to accept a measure of official bilingualism even at the provincial level – I thought the bill was political stupidity, and I said so in public.[28]

This philosophical disagreement transcends the federalist/separatist feud between Pierre Trudeau and René Lévesque that conditioned the patriation round of constitutional politics between 1960 and 1982. Indeed, it is simplistic to suggest that Lévesque's decision to withhold Quebec's agreement during the November 1981 First Ministers Conference boils down to a separatist premier recognizing that a political project of independence/sovereignty association precluded being a signatory to "reconfederation" in 1982.

Could a federalist premier of Quebec have accepted the 1982 constitutional agreement reached between Pierre Trudeau and the English-speaking premiers?[29] Probably not.[30] In addition to extinguishing Quebec's claim to a historical veto over constitutional change, as one of the two founding peoples of the Canadian federation, the 1982 constitutional settlement did not address the issue of immigration as successive Quebec governments had requested, particularly the desire to constitutionalize the Cullen-Couture agreement between Ottawa and Quebec that provided greater administrative, but not constitutional, control over the selection, resettlement, and integration of new immigrants into Quebec.[31] The opposition to the 1982 constitutional agreement is rooted in a deeper disagreement, and this involves the challenge that the *Canadian Charter* presents to Quebec's answer to *la question nationale* – the *Charter of the French Language* – and, eventually, those parts of the *Charter of the French Language* that advance the project of interculturalism by streamlining new immigrants into French language instruction as well as a common public language through instruments such as the sign-law provisions of the *Charter of the French Language*.

The remainder of this chapter considers the interplay between legislative disagreement, federalism, and the implementation chain that conditioned judicial invalidation of the sign-law provisions by the Supreme Court of Canada. Similar to Frédéric Bérard, my conclusion about the *Canadian Charter* does not accept the myth of judicial empowerment, centralization, and a loss of policy autonomy for Quebec.[32] Quite the contrary. Every new iteration of the *Charter of the French Language* has blunted judicial impact and reasserted Quebec's policy preferences and legislative sovereignty. Indeed, the more the *Charter of the French Language* has changed, the more it has remained the same.

Charter of the French Language and the Sign-Law Provisions

The *Charter of the French Language* declares under section 1 that "French is the official language of Québec" and applies this statutory requirement to all responsibilities that fall within provincial jurisdiction. For instance, French is "the Language of the Legislature and the Courts" (Chapter III), "The Language of Civil Administration" (Chapter IV), "the Language of Semipublic Agencies" (Chapter V), "the Language of Labour Relations" (Chapter VI), "the Language of Commerce and Business" (Chapter VII), and, finally, "the Language of Instruction" (Chapter VIII). Given that the Supreme Court of Canada declared the prohibition on the use of English in the National Assembly *ultra vires* in *Blaikie*, and the fact that the *Charter of the French Language* was amended in 1993 to comply with the *Blaikie* decision, post-Charter challenges have focused exclusively on "the Language of Commerce and Business" (Chapter VII) and "the Language of Public Instruction" (Chapter VIII).[33]

The regulation of commercial expression on signs, posters, and advertising are collectively referred to as the sign-law provisions of the *Charter of the French Language*. Sections 58 and 69 of the *Charter of the French Language* were challenged as a violation of freedom of expression protected under section 2(b) of the *Canadian Charter* and section 3 of the *Quebec Charter*. Section 58 required that "public signs and posters and commercial advertising shall be solely in the official language,"[34] though it did provide the Office de la langue française,[35] an arm's length public agency that enforces the *Charter of the French Language*, with the discretion provided through regulation, to allow bilingual signs or the sole use of languages other than French. In addition, section 69 required that "subject to section 68, only the French version of a firm name may be used in Quebec."[36] Individuals or firms violating the sign-law provisions of the *Charter of the French Language* were subject to fines under sections 205 and 206 that significantly increased with each additional infraction.

Several individuals found in violation of these provisions and fined by the Office de la langue française launched constitutional challenges against the *Charter of the French Language* in February 1984. The five claimants were successful at the Superior Court and the Quebec Court of Appeal, and the judgments were subsequently appealed to the Supreme Court of Canada by the Attorney General of Quebec.[37] On December 15, 1988, the Court dismissed the appeals launched by the Attorney General of Quebec in *Ford* and *Devine* and declared sections 58 and 69 unconstitutional as an unreasonable limitation on freedom of expression protected under both the Canadian and

Quebec Charters. Further, the Court determined that the offending provisions did not represent a reasonable limitation under section 1 of the *Canadian Charter* or section 9.1 of the *Quebec Charter.*

The *Ford* and *Devine* decisions were handed down in 1988 during the three-year ratification period for the Meech Lake Accord (1987–90), which was designed to gain Quebec as a signatory to the *Constitution Act, 1982.* Both decisions, incidentally, were authored by "The Court" and are thus unanimous decisions intended to convey judicial authority,[38] which was perhaps appropriate given the subject matter before the Court and the gravity of invalidating the *Charter of the French Language* during the Meech Lake saga. In *Ford,* the Court invalidated sections 58 and 69 as a violation of freedom of expression because of the close relationship between language, expression, and identity: "Language is so intimately related to the form and content of expression that there cannot be true freedom of expression by means of language if one is prohibited from using the language of one's choice."[39] Further, the Court reasoned that language is "as the preamble of the Charter of the French Language itself indicates, a means by which a people may express its cultural identity."[40]

In *Devine,* the Supreme Court argued that the section 2(b) violation was noteworthy because of the compelled use of French on public signs and firm names and the total prohibition on other languages: "That freedom is infringed not only by a prohibition of the use of one's language of choice but also by a legal requirement compelling one to use a particular language."[41] Commenting on Quebec's position that commercial expression should not be protected by section 2(b)[42] and, thus, that the challenged provisions of the *Charter of the French Language* were non-justiciable, the Court rejected this, arguing that "there is no sound basis on which commercial expression can be excluded from the protection of s 2(b) of the Charter."[43] The Court reasoned in *Ford* that the protection under the *Canadian* and *Quebec Charters* "includes the freedom to express oneself in the language of one's choice."[44] And it concluded: "Although the expression in this case has a commercial element, it should be noted that the focus here is on choice of language and on a law which prohibits the use of a language."[45] According to Richard Moon, "section 2(b) was violated by both the prohibition on other languages and the compulsion to use French."[46]

While the Supreme Court was supportive of the policy rationale of the *Charter of the French Language,* which was to promote and maintain the *visage linguistique* ("linguistic profile") of Quebec, it did not accept that the section 2(b) violation constituted a reasonable limitation under section 1 of the *Canadian Charter*. Finding that sections 58 and 69 advanced pressing and substantial legislative objectives, the Court determined that the provisions failed the minimal impairment requirement of section 1.[47] In its section 1 analysis, the Court took issue with the compelled and exclusive use of French: "Thus, whereas requiring the predominant display of the French language, even its marked predominance, would be proportional to the goal of promoting and maintaining a French 'visage linguistique' in Quebec and therefore justified under the *Quebec Charter* and the *Canadian Charter*, requiring the exclusive use of French has not been so justified."[48] Indeed, the Court did not accept that the compelled use of French was essential to the maintenance and promotion of the French language in Quebec, whereas the marked predominance of French, alongside other languages, would advance this objective and be consistent with the demographic reality of Quebec: "Such measures would ensure that the 'visage linguistique' reflected the demography of Quebec."[49]

The Supreme Court of Canada was authoritative, clear, and prescriptive in its judgment regarding the constitutionality of sections 58 and 69 of the *Charter of the French Language*. Authoritative, in that it released its judgments in the name of "The Court," signalling that the *Ford* and *Devine* decisions must be adhered to by the National Assembly of Quebec and that there was no room for interpretive discretion. Clear, in that it outlined without ambiguity, that the compelled use of French and the prohibition on languages other than French, was a violation of freedom of expression protected by both the *Canadian Charter* and the *Quebec Charter*. And, finally, it was prescriptive as the Court outlined an approach to public signs and commercial expression to which the *Charter of the French Language* must adhere. Indeed, the standard of "marked predominance" was the policy remedy established by the Court to ensure the constitutionality of sections 58 and 69 and not, as in the case of the 1983 *Charter of the French Language*, the compelled and exclusive use of French on public signs.

Bill 178, *Charter of the French Language*

What is perhaps most interesting about the *Ford* and *Devine* judgments is that the approach to commercial expression advanced by the Supreme Court closely mirrored the position adopted by the Quebec Liberal Party in 1985. During the 1985 Quebec election, Robert Bourassa committed a future Liberal government to easing the *Charter of the French Language* and allowing bilingual signs as long as French was given greater visibility.[50] This position was adopted during the June 1986 General Council of the Quebec Liberal

Party, where, as the government of Quebec, the Liberal Party not only reiterated its commitment to protecting the French image of Quebec but also supported the use of bilingual signs as long as French was given greater prominence.[51] In determining that the challenged provisions of the *Charter of the French Language* were an unreasonable limitation on freedom of expression, the Court, therefore, endorsed the policy position of the Quebec Liberal Party as an acceptable legislative response to the invalidation of sections 58 and 69. Although there is no evidence that the Court was influenced by, or aware of, the 1985 policy position, the fact that the Court and the Quebec Liberal Party agreed on the broad parameters of commercial expression suggest that legislative compliance could be expected in response to the 1988 invalidations of the sign-law provisions of the *Charter of the French Language*.

The Bourassa government introduced two legislative responses to *Ford* and *Devine*: Bill 178, *Charter of the French Language* (1988 *Charter of the French Language*), which, for a five-year period, overrode the Court's decisions in these cases by passing a legislative resolution involving section 33 of the *Canadian Charter* – the notwithstanding clause – and the 1993 *Charter of the French Language*, which replaced the 1988 *Charter of the French Language* when the notwithstanding clause expired in 1993.[52] Instead of re-invoking the notwithstanding clause, which the National Assembly of Quebec had the constitutional ability to do, and passing a resolution with broad cross-party support, the Bourassa government introduced the 1993 *Charter of the French Language*. The 1993 *Charter of the French Language* would amend two areas of the 1977 *Charter of the French Language* that had been invalidated by the Supreme Court of Canada: first, with *Protestant School Boards* in 1984 and Chapter VII ("the Language of Commerce and Business") and the provisions invalidated as a violation of freedom of expression in *Ford* and *Devine* and, second, Chapter VIII ("the Language of Public Instruction") in which the Court invalidated section 73 and the provisions governing access to public English instruction in Quebec.

The first legislative response to the invalidation of sections 58 and 69 was the 1988 *Charter of the French Language*, which both complied with, and departed from, the Court's decisions in *Ford* and *Devine*. The amendments passed by the Bourassa government are presented in Table 5.1. Introduced into the National Assembly on December 19 and assented to on December 22, 1988, the 1988 *Charter of the French Language* amended section 58 to create the inside/outside rule for public signs, posters, and advertising. Section 68 was amended to reiterate that only the French version of a firm could be used in Quebec.⁵³ Section 58, the outside rule, established that "public signs and posters and commercial advertising, outside or intended for the public outside, shall be solely in French."⁵⁴ The 1988 *Charter of the French Language*, therefore, disregarded the Court's ruling in *Ford* that the exclusive use of French was inconsistent with section 2(b) of the *Canadian Charter* as well as freedom of expression protected in the *Quebec Charter*. Section 58.1, the inside rule, provided that "inside establishments, public signs and posters and commercial advertising shall be in French,"⁵⁵ but it allowed for the use languages in addition to French "provided they are intended only for the public inside the establishment and that French is marked predominant."⁵⁶ The inside/outside rule compelled the exclusive use of French on public signs, posters, and advertisement but did allow for limited use of languages in addition to French so long as the signs were located inside and French was "marked predominant."

During the debate on the 1988 *Charter of the French Language*, Liberal Premier Robert Bourassa argued that the *Ford* and *Devine* decisions created a tension between collective rights and individual freedoms that the government had to arbitrate in its response to the Supreme Court of Canada. Anywhere else in North America, as Bourassa argued, the arbitration would be in favour of individual rights. Recognizing that the 1988 *Charter of the French Language* was at odds with the Court's ruling in *Ford*, the Bourassa government invoked section 33 of the *Canadian Charter* to protect the 1988 amendments to the 1977 *Charter of the French Language* against judicial invalidation for a period of five years. In addition, section 10 of the 1988 *Charter of the French Language* allowed the amendments to proceed despite their inconsistency with the *Quebec Charter*. In justifying the 1988 *Charter of the French Language*, its departure from *Ford* and *Devine*, and, more importantly, the use of the legislative override in section 33 of the *Canadian Charter*, Bourassa argued that he alone possessed the moral authority to invoke section 33: "I repeat that I am the only head of government in North America who has the moral justification to act in this manner because I am the only leader of a people that is very much a minority on this continent. Who can best and better defend, protect and promote French culture than the Prime Minister of Quebec?"⁵⁷

The 1988 *Charter of the French Language* was introduced and passed in a politically charged atmosphere. Three anglophone members of the Bourassa Cabinet resigned in light of the 1988 *Charter of the French Language* and the use of the notwithstanding clause,⁵⁸ and the 1989 Quebec election saw the Equality Party – an English rights political party that directly benefited from

Table 5.1 Responding to Ford and Devine: 1988 Charter of the French Language and the Notwithstanding Clause

Invalidated provisions	Bill 178, Charter of the French Language 1988
Charter of the French Language 1983 58. *Public signs and posters and commercial advertising shall be solely in the official language.* Notwithstanding the foregoing, in the cases and under the conditions or circumstances prescribed by regulation of the Office de la langue française, public signs and posters and commercial advertising may be both in French and in another language or solely in another language. 68. A firm name may be accompanied by a version in another language for use outside of Quebec. That version may be used together with the French version of the firm name in the inscriptions referred to in section 51, if the products in question are offered both in and outside Quebec. *Charter of the French Language 1986* 69. *Subject to section 68, only the French version of a firm name may be used in Quebec.*	10. The provisions of section 58 and those of the first paragraph of section 68, enacted by sections 1 and 6, respectively, of this Act, shall operate notwithstanding the provisions of paragraph b of section 2 or section 14 of the Constitution Act, 1982 (Schedule B to the Canada Act, chapter 11 in the 1982 volume of the Acts of the parliament of the United Kingdom) and apply despite sections 3 and 10 of the Charter of human rights and freedoms (R. S. Q., chapter C-12). 58. *Public signs and posters and commercial advertising, outside or intended for the public outside, shall be solely in French.* Similarly, *public signs and posters and commercial advertising shall be solely in French.* 1. Inside commercial centres and their access ways, except inside the establishments located there; 2. Inside any public means of transport and its access ways; 3. Inside the establishments of business firms contemplated in section 136; 4. Inside the establishments of business firms employing fewer than fifty but more than 5 persons, where such firms share, with two or more business firms, the use of a trademark, a firm name or an appellation by which they are known to the public. The government may, however, by regulation, prescribe the terms and conditions according to which public signs and posters and public advertising may be both in French and in another language under the conditions set forth in the second paragraph of section 58.1, inside the establishments of business firms contemplated in subparagraphs 3 and 4 of the second paragraph. The government may, in such regulation, establish categories of business firms, prescribe terms and conditions which vary according to the category and reinforce the conditions set forth in the second paragraph of section 58.1.

58.1 Inside establishments, public signs and posters and commercial advertising shall be in French.

They may also be both in French and in another language, provided they are intended only for the public inside the establishments and that French is markedly predominant.

68. *Except as otherwise provided in this section, only the French version of a firm name may be used in Quebec.*

A firm name may be accompanied by a version in another language for use outside of Quebec. That version may be used together with the French version of the firm name in the inscriptions referred to in section 51, if the products in question are offered both in and outside Quebec.

On public signs and posters and in commercial advertising,

1. a firm name may be accompanied with a version in another language, if they are both in French and in another language;
2. a firm name may appear solely in its version in another language, if they are solely in a language other than French.

69. (Repealed)

Note: Similarities between the 1983 and 1988 versions of the *Charter of the French Language* authorizing French-only public signs are provided in italics.

anglophone anger against the 1988 *Charter of the French Language* – elect four members to the National Assembly.[59] During the December news conference when he defended the use of the notwithstanding clause, Bourassa "suggested that invoking the notwithstanding clause was necessary because Meech Lake had not been ratified."[60] For Patrick Monahan, this was used by the critics of the Meech Lake Accord, and the distinct society clause, to argue that "the hidden agenda underlying the accord was the denial of the rights of the anglophone minority."[61] Outside Quebec, Bourassa's use of the notwithstanding clause is considered a decisive event that ultimately derailed the Meech Lake Accord and its recognition of Quebec as a distinct society.[62]

Why then did the Bourassa government use the notwithstanding clause to override *Ford* and *Devine* but not reinvoke it in 1993 when section 33's authorization expired? What had changed that justified this legislative course correction, whereby the Bourassa government amended the sign-law provisions of the 1977 *Charter of the French Language* in 1993, at least to appear to comply with the Court's decisions involving freedom of expression? Perhaps the Bourassa government's responses to *Ford* and *Devine* were simply a sign of the constitutional times. Another example of what André Laurendeau and Léon Dion referred to as the "hurt dignity" of the Quebec people;[63] this time a result of Quebec's Confederation partners failing to ratify what it viewed as its minimum constitutional demands to endorse the *Constitution Act, 1982*. As Jamie Cameron noted, "many years after the Meech Lake and Charlottetown Accords failed, it is difficult to convey the intensity, drama, and tensions of these moments in Canada's history."[64]

As the Meech Lake Accord was introduced as a single resolution, it required unanimous consent by Parliament and the provincial legislature to become an entrenched part of the Canadian Constitution under section 41 of the *Constitution Act, 1982*. Before any province ratified the Meech Lake Accord, Pierre Elliott Trudeau published his op-ed pieces attacking the draft accord in *La Presse* and the *Toronto Star* on May 27, 1987.[65] The final accord was unanimously agreed to on June 2–3, 1987, and Quebec was the first province to ratify the final draft of the Meech Lake Accord on June 23, 1987, which began the three-year time frame for unanimous ratification. This was followed by Saskatchewan on September 23, 1987, and Alberta on December 7, 1987. Even before the *Ford* and *Devine* decisions were released on December 15, 1988, and the 1988 *Charter of the French Language* overrode the decisions by invoking the notwithstanding clause on December 22, 1988, the constitutional ratification process experienced significant setbacks.

First, the Progressive Conservative government of New Brunswick, which had agreed in principle to the Meech Lake Accord, was defeated before the legislature passed a resolution in support of the accord. In the lead up to the 1987 provincial election on October 13, the Liberal Party led by Frank McKenna initially campaigned against the Meech Lake Accord and the distinct society clause.[66] This became of the utmost concern once the Liberals won every seat in the 1987 New Brunswick general election.[67] This setback was followed by the defeat of the NDP government in the 1988 Manitoba general election on April 26, its replacement with a minority Progressive Conservative government, and a revitalized provincial Liberal Party led by Sharon Carstairs, which opposed the Meech Lake Accord and was holding the balance of power.[68] After the passage of the 1988 *Charter of the French Language* and the introduction of the notwithstanding clause overriding *Ford* and *Devine*, Manitoba Premier Gary Filmon withdrew his support for the accord.[69]

The use of the notwithstanding clause occurred in this context – the rejection of Quebec's constitutional demands by enough provinces to prevent its passage under section 41 of the *Constitution Act, 1982*. In this raw political moment, Quebec protected the continued application of a statute of the utmost importance through section 33, though Peter Russell questioned whether the use of the notwithstanding clause was necessary, as the 1988 *Charter of the French Language* "might well have met the rule set down by the Supreme Court in the signs case that a law requiring predominantly (but not exclusively) French signs was a reasonable limit on freedom of expression."[70] I agree with Russell's assessment of the 1988 *Charter of the French Language* but suggest that it would not have survived the political context,[71] which is why the Bourassa government ultimately invoked the notwithstanding clause. The irony is that its successor, the 1993 *Charter of the French Language*, is less consistent with the *Ford* and *Devine* decisions, and, as I will argue, departs markedly from the constitutional standards established in 1988.

Why then did the Bourassa government appear to comply with *Ford* and *Devine* in 1993? One explanation is that, five years after the invalidation of the sign-law provisions and three years after the demise of the Meech Lake Accord, political tensions had cooled, and the Bourassa government recognized that it could legislate within the parameters established by the Supreme Court of Canada. For instance, Robert Sharpe and Kent Roach argue in the context of *Ford* that, "[w]hile the decision struck down the existing law, the Court's section 1 analysis gave Quebec considerable latitude to pursue a vigorous language policy favouring the use of French."[72] There is much merit in this analysis. After the 1989 Quebec general election, the Liberal Party retained its overwhelming majority of seats in the National Assembly (92/125) and would have had the support of the Parti Québécois if the Bourassa government decided to renew the notwithstanding clause's override of *Ford* and *Devine* for another five years. Only the Equality Party would have voted against the continued use of section 33.

There is perhaps a more fundamental reason why the Bourassa government introduced the 1993 *Charter of the French Language* – it recognized the paradox of the sign-law decisions and the implementation challenges that *Ford* and *Devine* faced. Unless commercial interests changed their public signs and firm names to include languages other than French, consistent with the *Ford* standard that French be given "marked predominance," the sign-law provisions would function largely in their pre-invalidation form. This argument will be returned to once the 1993 *Charter of the French Language* is considered and the actual impact on the public face of commercial expression in Quebec is considered.

1993 *Charter of the French Language*

Shortly before the five-year time limit on the notwithstanding clause expired in December 1993, the Bourassa government introduced its second legislative response to *Ford* and *Devine*. Bill 86 was introduced by Claude Ryan, the minister responsible for the *Charter of the French Language* on May 6, 1993, and assented to on June 18, 1993. Because the Bourassa government decided against reinvoking the notwithstanding clause, the 1993 *Charter of the French Language* has been considered to represent legislative compliance with the Court's earlier ruling that languages other than French are permitted on public signs, provided that French is given "marked predominance."[73]

A comparison of the 1988 and 1993 amendments and regulatory changes to the *Charter of the French Language* in light of *Ford* and *Devine* are presented in Table 5.2. There are several changes in 1993 that comply with the Court's rulings permitting the uses of languages other than French on public signs, commercial expression, and firm names. For instance, the outside/inside rule of the 1988 *Charter of the French Language* was repealed, and a new version of section 58 implemented in 1993 with the passage of the 1993 *Charter of the French Language*. The outside rule prohibited the uses of languages other than French on public signs, and commercial expression was inconsistent with the *Ford* and *Devine* decisions but was legally permitted by the use of the notwithstanding clause between 1988 and 1993. The 1993 iteration of section 58 aligned with the Court's decisions as it clearly stated that commercial expression and public signs "must" be in French but "may" be permitted in other languages, provided that French has "marked predominance." As well, "only" the French version of a firm name was permitted under section 68 in the 1988 *Charter of the French Language*, subject to certain exceptions within sections 58 and 68. If there were any doubts as to section 68's constitutionality and the exceptions to the French-only rule for firm names, they too were protected by the use of the notwithstanding clause in the 1988 *Charter of the French Language*. Finally, the Quebec government introduced a series of regulations in support of the 1993 *Charter of the French Language*, the most notable being a clear approach to the standard of "marked predominance," which roughly requires that French be at least twice the size of any other language on a public sign, commercial expression, or firm name.[74]

Despite these instances of full legislative incorporation of the Court's approach to commercial expression in the context of the sign-law provisions of the 1977 *Charter of the French Language*, the 1993 *Charter of the French Language* and the *Regulation Respecting the Language of Commerce and Business* do allow for legislative deviation from *Ford* and *Devine*.[75] Sections 58 contains a qualifying provision (in *italics* in Table 5.2) that allows the Quebec government to decide "by regulation, the places, cases, conditions or circumstances where public signs and posters must be in French only," although it can allow for English-only signs or bilingual signs where French is not given "marked predominance." The point is this – the qualifying paragraph provides the executive with the full discretion whether to comply with Supreme Court of Canada's 1988 decision that invalidated the sign-law provisions of the 1977 *Charter of the French Language*. More importantly, while section 68 appears to comply with the Court as it does allow for the use of bilingual firm names, it too contains a qualifying paragraph (in *italics* in Table 5.2) that allows the executive to derogate from this in accordance with section 58 "and the regulations enacted under that section."[76] As a result, the qualifying paragraph in section 58 that allows for a French-only approach to public signs is extended to firm names as well.

This legislative disagreement crystallizes in the regulations enacted in support of the 1993 iteration of section 58.[77] Division III of the regulation is entitled "Public Signs and Posters and Commercial Advertising" and specifies the conditions when French must be used exclusively and not simply given "marked predominance." For instance, section 15 specifies "a firm's commercial advertising, displayed on billboards, on signs or posters or on

Table 5.2 Five years after Ford and Devine: A comparison of Bill 178, Charter of the French Language 1988 and Bill 86, Charter of the French Language 1993

1988 Charter of the French Language	1993 Charter of the French Language	Regulations
		Regulation defining the scope of the expression "marked predominate" for the purposes of the Charter of the French Language
58. Public signs and posters and commercial advertising, outside or intended for the public outside, shall be solely in French.	58. Public signs and posters and commercial advertising must be in French.	1. In signs and posters of the civil administration, public signs and posters and posted commercial advertising that are both in French and in another language, French is markedly predominant where the text in French has a much greater visual impact than the text in the other language.
Similarly, public signs and posters and commercial advertising shall be solely in French.	They may also be both in French and in another language provided that French is marked predominant.	In assessing the visual impact, a family name, a place name, a trademark or other terms in a language other than French are not considered where their presence is specifically allowed under an exception provided for in the Charter of the French language (chapter C-11) or its regulations.
1. Inside commercial centres and their access ways, except inside the establishments located there;	*However, the Government may determine, by regulation, the places, cases, conditions or circumstances where public signs and posters and commercial advertising must be in French only, where French need not be predominant or where such signs, posters and advertising may be in another language only.*	2. Where texts both in French and in another language appear on the same sign or poster, the text in French is deemed to have a much greater visual impact if the following conditions are met:
2. Inside any public means of transport and its access ways;		
3. Inside the establishments of business firms contemplated in section 136;	68. A firm name may be accompanied with a version in a language other than French provided that, when it is used, the French version appears at least as prominently.	(1) the space allotted to the text in French is at least twice as large as the space allotted to the text in the other language;
4. Inside the establishments of business firms employing fewer than fifty but more than 5 persons, where such firms share, with two or more business firms, the use of a trademark, a firm name or an appellation by which they are known to the public.		
The government may, however, by regulation, prescribe the terms and conditions according to which public signs and posters and public advertising may be both in French and in another language under the conditions set forth in the second paragraph of	*However, in public signs and posters and commercial advertising, the use of a version of a firm name in a language other than French is permitted to the*	

section 58.1, inside the establishments of business firms contemplated in subparagraphs 3 and 4 of the second paragraph.

The government may, in such regulation, establish categories of business firms, prescribe terms and conditions which vary according to the category and reinforce the conditions set forth in the second paragraph of section 58.1.

58.1 Inside establishments, public signs and posters and commercial advertising shall be in French. They may also be both in French and in another language, provided they are intended only for the public inside the establishments and that French is markedly predominant.

68. Except as otherwise provided in this section, only the French version of a firm name may be used in Quebec.

A firm name may be accompanied by a version in another language for use outside of Quebec. That version may be used together with the French version of the firm name in the inscriptions referred to in section 51, if the products in question are offered both in and outside Quebec.

On public signs and posters and in commercial advertising,

1. a firm name may be accompanied with a version in another language, if they are both in French and in another language;

extent that the other language may be used in such posters or in such advertising pursuant to section 58 and the regulations enacted under that section.

In addition, in texts or documents drafted only in a language other than French, a firm name may appear in the other language only.

3. Where texts both in French and in another language appear on separate signs or posters of the same size, the text in French is deemed to have a much greater visual impact if the following conditions are met:

(1) the signs and posters bearing the text in French are at least twice as numerous as those bearing the text in the other language;

(2) the characters used in the text in French are at least twice as large as those used in the text in the other language; and

(3) the other characteristics of the sign or poster do not have the effect of reducing the visual impact of the text in French.

4. Where texts both in French and in another language appear on separate signs or posters of a different size, the text in French is deemed to have a much greater visual impact if the following conditions are met:

(1) the signs and posters bearing the text in French are at least as numerous as those bearing the text in the other language;

1988 *Charter of the French Language*	1993 *Charter of the French Language*	Regulations
2. a firm name may appear solely in its version in another language, if they are solely in a language other than French.		(2) the signs or posters bearing the text in French are at least twice as large as those bearing the text in the other language;
69. (Repealed)		(3) the characters used in the text in French are at least twice as large as those used in the text in the other language; and
		(4) the other characteristics of the signs or posters do not have the effect of reducing the visual impact of the text in French.
		Regulation respecting the language of commerce and business Charter of the French language
		15. A firm's commercial advertising, displayed on billboards, on signs or posters or on any other medium having an area of 16 m^2 or more and visible from any public highway within the meaning of section 4 of the Highway Safety Code (chapter C-24.2), must be exclusively in French unless the advertising is displayed on the very premises of an establishment of the firm.
		16. A firm's commercial advertising on or in any public means of transportation and on or in the accesses thereto, including bus shelters, must be exclusively in French.

Note: The key departure between the 1993 *Charter of the French Language* and *Ford* and *Devine* are indicated by *italics*.

any other medium having an area of 16 m² or more and visible from any public highway within the meaning of section 4 of the Highway Safety Code ... must be exclusively in French unless the advertising is displayed on the very premises of an established firm."[78] Similarly, public signs and commercial advertising on public means of transportation and bus shelters must be exclusively in French.[79]

These legislative and regulatory changes cannot be interpreted as straight compliance that resulted from the Bourassa government's decision not to reintroduce the notwithstanding clause in 1993. Nor can they be viewed as a clear legislative disagreement, which re-invoking the notwithstanding clause for an additional five years would surely have communicated. The statutory and regulatory changes work at cross purposes, complying with, and departing from, the *Ford* and *Devine* decisions at the same time. Even a committed dialogue theorist would struggle to consider the 1988 *Charter of the French Language* as dialogue in action since Quebec's message is easy to discern – the executive will decide under what conditions languages other than French are permitted on public signs, commercial advertising, and firm names. If this is an example of dialogue, it is a poor one that speaks to executive interpretive discretion and not fealty to the Supreme Court of Canada's interpretation of how the sign-law provisions can be reconciled with freedom of expression.

Contemporary Challenges to the 1993 *Charter of the French Language*
Section 58 of the 1993 *Charter of the French Language* was challenged in 1999 when an antique store owned by Simpson and Hoffman in the Eastern Townships displayed a bilingual firm name, "La Lionne et le Morse – The Lyon and the Walrus," where French and English were equal in size.[80] Clearly in violation of section 58 of the *Charter of the French Language* and the accompanying regulations, as French was not "marked predominant," Simpson and Hoffman were fined five hundred dollars under section 205 of the *Charter of the French Language*.[81] Initially successful at the Court of Quebec, where Simpson and Hoffman challenged that section 58 and the requirement of "marked predominant" were an unreasonable violation of freedom of expression, the finding of unconstitutionality was reversed at the Superior Court. Upon appeal, the Quebec Court of Appeal upheld the constitutionality of section 58, arguing that the appellants had failed to demonstrate that the restrictions on languages other than French were no longer necessary in 1999.[82] An application for leave to appeal was filed with the Supreme Court of Canada on December 21, 2001, and the Court dismissed the leave

to appeal without reasons on October 11, 2002.[83] The Supreme Court of Canada, as well as the Quebec Court of Appeal, reached the correct decision, as Simpson and Hoffman were clearly in violation of section 58. More importantly, section 58 is consistent with the constitutional standard established by the Court in *Ford* requiring French to be given "marked predominance" on bilingual signs, which did not occur in the context of the signage for the "Lyon and the Walrus."

The constitutionality of section 58, as well as sections 51 and 52, were once again considered by the Quebec Court of Appeal in 2017 when eleven anglophone businesses in the Montreal area were charged with various breaches of the sign-law provisions of the *Charter of the French Language*. Several businesses were found to be in breach of section 58 and the *Regulation Defining the Scope of the Expression "Markedly Predominant" for the Purposes of the Charter of the French Language* as their signs were exclusively in English, or, when present, French was not given "marked predominance."[84] Others were found to violate section 51 as their merchandise was packaged exclusively in English. Finally, a number of businesses were found in violation of section 52 of the *Charter of the French Language* as their company websites were exclusively in English without any French content.[85] In the 2017 challenge to the *Charter of the French Language*, the appellants argued that the court of appeal should revisit the *Ford* and *Devine* precedents, as the French language was no longer in jeopardy and the factual basis of 1988 decisions could no longer justify the infringement on freedom of expression that resulted from the challenged provisions of the *Charter of the French Language*.[86]

In response, the court of appeal argued that the appellants had not demonstrated that the status of the French language had materially changed, and, therefore, the court of appeal could not revisit the *Ford* and *Devine* precedents.[87] Finally, although the court of appeal acknowledged that the *Ford* and *Devine* decisions did not consider the issue of commercial advertising and the Internet, this form of expression must be used in a manner that conforms with the *Charter of the French Language*: "If the publications on a website aim to conduct or promote business in the territory of Quebec, then they are part of the *"visage linguistique"* of Quebec and thus subject to s 52 C.F.L."[88] In this respect, this judgment was less about the constitutionality of the 1993 *Charter of the French Language* and the 1993 version of section 58 and largely about whether the court of appeal could revisit a precedent established by the Supreme Court of Canada, which it declined to do.

Starting in 2010, the Office québécois de la langue française began to interpret the *Regulation Respecting the Language of Commerce and Business* to require firms with trademarks in English or established outside of Quebec to have a sufficient presence of French on firm names and other forms of commercial expression. This interpretive change was supported by the Attorney General of Quebec and argued to be necessary to ensure compliance with section 58 of the *Charter of the French Language* and section 25 of the regulation. In 2015, the Quebec Court of Appeal ruled on this matter as the actions of the Office québécois de la langue française were challenged by several large multinational corporations that argued their English-only names were permitted under the *Charter of the French Language* and the exceptions provided under section 25 of the regulations for trademarked names.[89] In a unanimous ruling, the Quebec Court of Appeal determined that the companies had functioned within the exceptions provided by section 25 of the regulations and that the Office québécois de la langue française's interpretation of the regulation after 2010 was not appropriate.[90] In response, the Couillard government amended the regulation in 2016 by adding sections 25.1–25.5 to require "a sufficient presence of French" on English trademarked names or firms established outside of Quebec that used English-only names on their displays or other forms of commercial expression.[91] To facilitate this modification to section 58's application, a transitional period of three years was provided for companies to comply with this regulatory change.[92]

The legislative and regulatory changes introduced in response to *Ford* and *Devine* have yet to face a direct or serious constitutional challenge. The lower court proceedings after 1993 have been either weak constitutional cases where commercial signages were in clear violation of the *Charter of the French Language*,[93] or the interpretation of the regulatory requirements involving trademarked firm names by the Office québécois de la langue française were inconsistent with past practices and a clear reading of section 58 and the supporting regulations.[94] While the Supreme Court of Canada no longer permits the prohibition of languages other than French on commercial signs, the regulatory and statutory changes to the *Charter of the French Language* suggest that the Quebec government disagrees with this constitutional position. The amendments to the *Charter of the French Language* and the supporting regulations carve out exceptions to this rule, providing the Quebec government with the ability to prohibit languages other than French on public signs and other forms of commercial expression, albeit in a narrow set of circumstances. Perhaps the Quebec government considers these narrow exceptions as a more precisely tailored infringement that would survive the Court's proportionality analysis under section 1 of the *Canadian Charter*. This is not an unreasonable assumption to make. Even when a senior court ruled against a public actor and its interpretation of the *Charter of the French Language*, as the Quebec Court of Appeal did in the *Best Buy* decision, the Quebec government has simply amended the regulations supporting the *Charter of the French Language* to require corporations to include "a sufficient presence of French" on their trademarked names and public signage.[95]

The Visage Linguistique of Public Signs after *Ford* and *Devine*

It has been more than thirty years since the *Ford* and *Devine* decisions were decided. Enough time has passed to assess the policy impact of the Supreme Court of Canada's invalidation of the French-only provisions of commercial expression in the *Charter of the French Language*. How has the *visage linguistique* of commercial expression changed in Quebec in this period? In 1997 and 2017, the Office québécois de la langue française released studies that evaluated compliance with the sign-law provisions of the *Charter of the French Language* on the Island of Montreal.[96] It has not conducted studies off the Island of Montreal, which is natural given the concentration of anglophones on the Island of Montreal and the greater possibility of bilingual signs in this part of Quebec. As the Office québécois de la langue française is mandated to monitor compliance with the *Charter of the French Language*, these studies are particularly relevant in understanding the impact of *Ford* and *Devine* on the Island of Montreal, particularly in its downtown commercial district and in the West Island where the anglophone population is largely concentrated.

The 1997 report surveyed over seven thousand businesses on the Island of Montreal over three years (1995, 1996, 1997) and reviewed a total of sixty-two thousand commercial messages.[97] For comparative purposes, Montreal is divided into two sectors, East and West, and Boulevard Saint-Laurent is the line of demarcation. Although it no longer holds, Boulevard Saint-Laurent is the traditional dividing line between francophone and anglophone Montreal. For greater clarity, the 1997 survey subdivided Montreal into four sectors: Centre, West, East, and North. The sectors correspond roughly to downtown Montreal (Centre), the "East End" with the highest concentration of francophones (East), the "West Island" with the highest concentration of anglophones (West), and the North, which shares a border with all the other sectors. Sherbrooke Street is the dividing line between the Centre, West, and North zones, Avenue Papineau the dividing line for the East sector, and Avenue Atwater roughly the dividing line between the West and Centre sectors. Finally, the Canadian National Railway lines are the demarcation between the North and West sectors.

On the Island of Montreal, the 1997 report found that nearly 98 percent of store signage contained French in 1997, and nearly 50 percent had the presence of English.[98] The highest presence of French was in the East zone (99.3 percent) and the highest presence of English in the West zone (60.5 percent). Further, nearly 46 percent of stores on the Island of Montreal had French-only signs in 1997, with the highest rates in the East (63.4 percent), North (45.7 percent), and Centre (40.1 percent), with the lowest rate of French-only signs in the West (35.1 percent).[99] In contrast, less than 1 percent of commercial enterprises had English-only signs in 1997.[100] In terms of language used on billboards, the 1997 study found that nearly 85 percent were unilingual French, with a sector variance between East (91.3 percent) and West (79.2 percent), and zone differences as follows: East (91.9 percent), North (85.1 percent), Centre (80.8 percent), and West (78.5 percent).[101] It can be concluded that, within four years of the 1993 *Charter of the French Language*'s passage and the 1993 iteration of section 58 of the *Charter of the French Language* and the supporting regulations, the public face of commercial expression in Montreal remained overwhelmingly French. For instance, there were a significant number of French-only signs, despite the constitutional ability of firms to have languages other than French on public signs after 1993 with the expiration of the notwithstanding clause.

Twenty years later, the public face of commercial expression in Quebec has remained incredibly stable, and, in some respects, there is a higher percentage of French-only public signs and forms of commercial expression on the Island of Montreal. The 2017 study contains a distinction that was not present in 1997: signs with only French words and French signs that have words of an indeterminate nature (surnames, homonyms, words that cannot be assimilated to another language). Both are classified as "French-only" signs by the Office québécois de la langue française, though it does present data for both versions of "French-only" signs and forms of commercial expression. Based on a survey of 3,612 businesses on the Island of Montreal between February and May 2017, the Office québécois de la langue française estimated that 30.5 percent of company names were exclusively in French. When words of an indeterminate nature are added, this figure increases to 77.2 percent of all signs on the Island of Montreal being "French only."[102] For the four zones on the Island of Montreal, the East remains the highest for store fronts with French-only signs (84.4 percent), followed by the Centre (80.5 percent), the North (78.9 percent), and the West (69.1 percent).[103] Finally, among all commercial messages on the Island of Montreal (company names and other forms of commercial messaging), 65 percent were found to be written exclusively in French, with only 7.8 percent of commercial messaging in a bilingual format (French and English). Although the Office québécois de la langue française does not release data for the remaining regions of Quebec, one can conclude that the rate of French-only signs and forms of commercial expression are even higher off the Island of Montreal or at least as high as the East sector, with a linguistic profile of 86 percent francophone, which is similar to Quebec outside of Montreal.

Conclusion

In an analysis of the judicialization of language policy, Eugénie Brouillet argues that "[c]es décisions judiciaire ont ainsi limité la capacité de légiférer du Québec afin d'assurer l'épanouissement de la langue française dans un environnement linguistique singulièrement difficile."[104] None of the evidence, be it the legislative responses in which Quebec carved out exceptions to the *Ford* and *Devine* principles or the actions of commercial interests that have largely retained their French-only signs, support such a position. The public face of commercial expression in Quebec remains overwhelmingly French, and public signs remain largely French-only nearly thirty years after the *Ford* and *Devine* decisions. This is true on the Island of Montreal and more so for Quebec outside of Montreal. How and why is this? Analyzed outside the pressure-cooker political environment of the Meech Lake saga, perhaps *Ford* and *Devine* are not the decisions they were portrayed to be for the *Charter of the French Language*. Given that a major objective of the Quiet Revolution was the francization of business and commerce and that the *Charter of the French Language* works in tandem with this societal and economic project, we should not conclude that the public face of commercial expression in Quebec is so fragile that a Charter decision can undo a policy that stands on many legs.

Despite judicial victories in *Ford* and *Devine*, the public face of commercial expression has not changed in a way suggested by the critics of the 1982 constitutional settlement. Nor has there been, as Chapter 4 demonstrates, a revitalized English public school system resulting from judicial victories.[105] There are fewer English public schools and fewer students enrolled in the English public system than in 1977, the year in which the *Charter of the French Language* was granted royal assent.[106] How to explain this puzzle of judicial victories without an equivalent policy impact? What have the critics of the judicialization of politics, or its supporters, failed to consider when rendering conclusions about judicial review and salient issues of public policy? They have failed to understand, or to factor in, that to have policy impact, a judicial decision must be implemented. More importantly, there are public and private actions that inform an implementation chain: first, the responsible legislature that introduces amendments to legislation determined unconstitutional and, second, how private actors respond to the new legislative framework.

Legislative disagreements that operate in a complex implementation chain can change the trajectory of a judicial decision and confine judicial impact to the agenda-setting phase of the policy process. This chapter, and the argument of this book, reinforces the enduring point made by Alan Cairns that we should not read too much into how a judicial decision, or judicial body, can change the fundamental character of Canadian federalism.[107] In the context of the sign law and section 58, the legislative responses are "built *Ford* tough" because of the complexity of the policy objectives of francization, the instruments to achieve it, and the commitment of successive Quebec governments to preserve it in the face of judicial invalidation.

Supervised Consumption Sites and the *Respect for Communities Act*
How the Harper Government Outflanked the McLachlin Court

6

In *PHS Community Services Society*, the Supreme Court of Canada considered the choice by the Harper government to allow Insite's temporary legal exemption to expire, which, at the time, was North America's only government-sanctioned supervised consumption site.[1] Although the exemption to operate Insite under section 56 of the *Controlled Drugs and Substances Act (CDSA)* expired in 2008, a judicial declaration by the British Columbia Superior Court, as well as by the BC Court of Appeal, allowed Insite to operate during the appeals process, which concluded at the Supreme Court of Canada in 2011.[2] In *PHS Community Services Society*, the unanimous judgment delivered by Chief Justice Beverley McLachlin conveyed a strong rebuke of the Harper government's handling of this public health issue. Moreover, the Court chastised the minister of health for their failure to renew Insite's temporary exemption under the *CDSA*. The Court ordered the minister of health to immediately issue a renewed exemption to Insite and established the broad guidelines that the minister of health must use when evaluating requests for additional supervised consumption facilities under section 56 of the *CDSA*.

The legislative response to *PHS Community Services Society* was passed shortly before the 2015 Canadian election when the Harper government's Bill C-2, *Respect for Communities Act* received royal assent.[3] Unlike the Supreme Court of Canada, which emphasized the health benefits of supervised consumption sites, the *Respect for Communities Act* placed its emphasis on the law-and-order implications of these facilities and whether a local community agreed with a supervised consumption site within its neighbourhood. The *Respect for Communities Act* would be swiftly replaced by the Trudeau government when Jane Philpott, then minister of health, rescinded much of the *Respect for Communities Act* and its focus on the law-and-order implications of these facilities. The Trudeau government had little respect for the *Respect for Communities Act* and passed Bill C-37, *An Act to Amend the Controlled Drugs and Substances Act*, in early 2017.[4] After a temporary relegation under the Harper Conservatives, supervised consumption sites were reinstated as part of Canada's approach to harm reduction by the Trudeau Liberals.

The next two chapters are the first in which the complexity of Canadian federalism and the distinct implementation chains that operate in the provinces and territories have a direct bearing on judicial policy impact.[5] They are also the first to consider the legislative responses by successive federal governments to a decision by the Supreme Court of Canada and the myriad of responses by provincial and territorial governments. It is an ideal test case for the impact of judicial review when courts are implementer-dependent institutions in a complex policy, jurisdictional, and implementation setting. In the context of supervised consumption sites, the federal government has responsibility for criminal policy and administers statutes such as the *Criminal Code*, the *Narcotics Control Act*, and the *CDSA*.[6] The legal ability to open a facility is thus dependent on an exemption from prosecution being issued under section 56 of the *CDSA* by the federal minister of health to a local health facility.

The operation of supervised consumption sites, however, is part of the public health structure that falls under provincial jurisdiction and the devolved responsibilities of the three territories.[7] Provincial and territorial departments of health must be supportive of these institutions and agree to their request for a section 56 exemption by the federal minister of health. The decision-making and implementation chains are complex and suggest why the establishment of supervised consumption sites has not been uniform in Canada, despite *PHS Community Services Society*. In short, federalism and devolved responsibilities matter more, from a delivery perspective, than a negative rights decision by the Supreme Court of Canada. The Harper Conservatives fundamentally disagreed with supervised consumption sites and the decision in *PHS Community Services Society* by the McLachlin court.[8] It registered its disproval with the Court's decision by fashioning an unnecessary, drawn-out, and complex legislative amendment in the form of the *Respect for Communities Act* – a legislative response that ultimately defied a unanimous court and its approach to this issue.

The legislative response was unnecessary because the Supreme Court upheld the constitutionality of the *CDSA* and simply took issue with the use of ministerial discretion by the minister of health. It was drawn out, as the Harper government took nearly four years to pass the *Respect for Communities Act* in 2015. As a majority government, the Harper legislative agenda was not at the mercy of the opposition parties, and this delayed time frame was a conscious decision to prevent new facilities opening through a tortoise-like approach to legislating *PHS Community Services Society*. It was unnecessarily complex as the *Respect for Communities Act* created an application process of singular difficulty that placed an onerous burden on those community organizations seeking to establish a supervised consumption site. And, because the minister of health would only review completed applications for an exemption under section 56 of the *CDSA*, the outcome was predictable – with the exception of Insite, the Harper government never reviewed an application under section 56 of the *CDSA* for the establishment of a new supervised consumption site in Canada.

The policy cycle of this complex intergovernmental problem informs the general structure of this chapter. The first part of this chapter considers the public health crisis in the late 1980s that led community organizations, activists, local governmental officials, as well as the Vancouver Police Department to seek a paradigm-shifting approach to the drug problem afflicting the Downtown Eastside of Vancouver (DTES). Even before supervised consumption sites emerged as a result of coordinated action through multi-level governance in Canada, it was the outcome of community activism that brought the issue to public attention.[9] Policy harmonization between the city of Vancouver, the British Columbian government, and Ottawa would end with the election of the Harper conservatives in 2006. Cooperative federalism on this issue gave way to uncooperative federalism, despite Stephen Harper's initial commitment to "open federalism" during the 2006 election campaign.[10]

The second part of the chapter considers the judicialization of supervised consumption sites that occurred when civil society, along with the Attorney General of British Columbia, challenged the Harper government's failure to extend Insite's ability to function under the *CDSA*. The third and fourth parts evaluate the Harper government's response to *PHS Community Services Society* and focus on the *Respect for Communities Act*. The fate of the *Respect for Communities Act* is considered in Chapter 7, which studies the policy impact of *PHS Community Services Society* after more than ten years, two legislative responses by the Harper and Trudeau governments, and a variety of responses (and counter-responses) by the provincial and territorial governments.

Opening a Policy Window: Community Activism and Insite

By 1993, fatalities from drug use in Vancouver had reached an annual rate of 357 and were the leading cause of death for people aged fifteen to forty-four in British Columbia.[11] Many of these deaths were concentrated within the DTES, one of the most socially deprived neighbourhoods in Canada. As outlined by the Supreme Court of Canada in *PHS Community Services Society*,

> the DTES is home to some of the poorest and most vulnerable people in Canada. Its population includes 4,600 intravenous drug users, which is almost half of the intravenous drug users in the city as a whole. This number belies the size of the DTES. It is in fact a very small area, stretching for a few blocks in each direction from its heart at the intersection of Main and Hastings.[12]

The densely populated nature of the DTES is significant given the issue of needle sharing and the fact that this community had the highest concentration of intravenous drug users in British Columbia. The 2008 Expect Advisory Committee that reported to then Minister of Health Tony Clement made the following statement about the DTES:

> Based upon two surveys of a sample of approximately 1,000 users, the following key user characteristics have been identified: have been injecting drugs for an average of 15 years; majority (51%) inject heroin and 32% cocaine; 87 per cent are infected with Hepatitis C virus (HCV) and 17% with human immunodeficiency virus (HIV); 18% are Aboriginal; 20% are homeless and many more live in single resident rooms; 80% have been incarcerated; 38% are involved in the sex trade; 21% were using methadone; and 59% reported a non-fatal overdose in their lifetime.[13]

To support the DTES community, the Portland Hotel Society (PHS) was formed in 1991. The PHS is a non-profit organization formed to provide advocacy, housing support, and health services for the DTES community. It would be renamed the PHS Community Services Society in 2003 and started what became the Insite safe injection facility in the DTES. More importantly, PHS Community Services Society launched the initial constitutional challenge in 2008 when the Harper government did not extend Insite's exemption under section 56 of the *CDSA*.[14] The initial approach to harm reduction in the DTES focused on needle exchange programs to prevent the spread of infectious diseases, which were launched by the PHS and the Downtown East Site Youth Activities Society in an effort to contain the spread of HIV-AIDS and other blood borne disease.[15]

Due to the steadily rising drug fatalities and the spread of infectious disease, the Attorney General of British Columbia appointed a task force in 1993 led by the chief coroner, J.V. Cain. The Cain report, which was released in September 1994, recommended a paradigmatic shift in British Columbia's approach to drug policy, as it advocated legalization, decriminalization, and harm reduction strategies to address the health and legal consequences of intravenous drug use.[16] A 1996 report by Vancouver's medical health officer, Dr. Liz Whynot, summarized the growing health crisis in the DTES. This report was recounted in the 2008 British Columbia Superior Court decision that first challenged the Harper government's failure to extend Insite an exemption under section 56 of the *CDSA*:

> Injection drug use was leading to an increased incidence and prevalence of symptomatic infectious disease including HIV/AIDS, Hepatitis A, B, and C, and skin and blood-borne infections; frequent drug overdoses resulting in significant morbidity and mortality; increased hospital and emergency service utilization such as treatment for HIV-related disease, septicaemia and endocarditis, increased ambulance responses and emergency room visits in response to drug overdoses; fetal exposure to addictive substances with short-term and long-term consequences; increased pressure on all community-level outreach nursing and medical services; an increased need for community-level hospice palliative care; and worsening consequences for associated conditions such as mental illness.[17]

By 1997, with HIV/AIDS infecting approximately 27 percent of intravenous drug users in the DTES,[18] the Vancouver Area Network of Drug Users (VANDU) was formed. Along with the PHS, VANDU began to advocate for the establishment of a supervised consumption site and greater access to needle exchange programs.[19] In addition to the HIV/AIDS crisis in the DTES, needle sharing resulted in an epidemic in blood-borne diseases such as Hepatitis A, B, and C. Due to pressure from VANDU and the PHS, the chief medical officer for Vancouver, John Blatherwick, declared a public health emergency in the DTES in September 1997.[20] This public health declaration was followed by a report by the provincial health officer, Dr. John Millar, which, among other recommendations, advocated for a harm reduction approach to drug use in British Columbia.[21]

The emerging consensus on harm reduction strategies would strengthen when an important reorganization of health-care policy and delivery took place in British Columbia. Like all other provinces in the 1990s, with the exception of Ontario, British Columbia decentralized the provision of health-care services and the development of health-care policy to eleven regional health boards.[22] In 2001, the regional health boards would be reorganized into five regional health authorities.[23] The Vancouver-Richmond Health Board, which had responsibility for the DTES, launched a study in 1999 that concluded that the approach to the health crisis in the DTES should focus on intravenous drug use, and it began to advocate for the "four-pillars" approach to the drug problem in Vancouver, "which was based on policy models from Western Europe attempting to balance prevention, enforcement, treatment, and harm reduction."[24] The Vancouver-Richmond Health Board would be integrated into the Vancouver Coastal Health Authority (VCHA) in 2001.

The growing health crisis in the DTES saw the signing of the *Vancouver Agreement* between the City of Vancouver, the NDP provincial government, and the Chrétien government in March 2002,[25] which "made addiction a health-care issue for BC and was crucial in laying the groundwork for the city's next policy move on harm reduction."[26] With the signing of the *Vancouver Agreement*, a broad-based consensus existed on addressing this public health emergency, which aligned municipal and provincial policy in British Columbia with the National Drug Strategy, first introduced by the Mulroney government in 1987. The National Drug Strategy, which was the responsibility of the minister of health when established by the Mulroney government, did not include harm reduction. It would come to include harm reduction as one of the four pillars in the approach of the National Drug Strategy when it was updated by the Chrétien government in 1998.[27]

The *Vancouver Agreement* was signed by Mayor Philip Owen of the Non-Partisan Association (NPA), a centre-right party that had dominated municipal politics in the 1980s. As mayor from 1993 to 2002, Philip Owen had originally favoured a "law-and-order" approach to the drug problem in the DTES, consistent with the centre-right orientation of the NPA. In the later years of his mayoralty, he became a supporter of harm reduction strategies, placing him at odds with his municipal party.[28] Mayor Owen tasked the city's drug policy coordinator, Donald MacPherson, with devising the next phase of Vancouver's approach to the drug crisis in early 2000. A draft version of the report, *A Framework for Action: A Four-Pillar Approach to Drug Problems in Vancouver*, was released in November 2000. The final report was released in April 2001.[29] MacPherson's report was consistent with the *Vancouver Agreement*, as it committed Vancouver to the four-pillars approach of prevention, treatment, enforcement, and harm reduction. In addition to these broad-based community discussions, MacPherson worked closely with the Vancouver Police Department (VPD) in developing the report, which endorsed the four-pillar approach. Moreover, the VPD would write to the federal minister of health endorsing the VCHA's application for a safe-injection facility operated by the PHS Community Services Society at Insite in April 2006.[30]

The issue of harm reduction took centre stage during the 2002 municipal election in November, when Larry Campbell, the Coalition of Progressive Electors (COPE) candidate, defeated Jennifer Clarke of the NPA. The election would serve as a referendum on the issue of harm reduction strategies in the DTES. As the former chief coroner of Vancouver, Campbell and COPE ran on a platform that included the establishment of a supervised consumption site within the DTES to address the drug problem and health-related epidemic caused by needle sharing. This policy resonated with Vancouver voters as the DTES and the drug problem were ranked as the most important issue during the 2002 municipal election (25.7 percent), more than double education and social services, the second-placed issue (11 percent).[31]

In early 2003, the VCHA submitted an application to the federal minister of health for an exemption under section 56 of the *CDSA* to operate a supervised consumption site at Insite in the DTES. This application was supported by the BC Liberal government led by Gordon Campbell, a right-of-centre party that defeated the NDP government in 2001. Health Canada approved a three-year pilot project to operate a supervised consumption site in June 2003[32] and provided $1.5 million to support this policy experiment.[33] Insite opened in the DTES in September 2003.[34] As part of the conditions of this three-year pilot project, Health Canada required that Insite be subjected to a full scientific evaluation.[35] The findings were to be submitted to Health Canada and would be instrumental in deciding whether Insite would be granted an additional exemption once the pilot project ended in September 2006. With funding from Health Canada, twenty-two peer-reviewed studies in leading health and medical journals were published in support of Insite during the three-year pilot study.[36]

Is Insite an example of cooperative federalism or its modern manifestation, collaborative federalism?[37] While the governments of Canadian federalism were instrumental in providing the legal (federal) and jurisdictional (provincial) requirements for the establishment of North America's first supervised consumption site in September 2003, Insite has always been more than an example of federalism in action. It was the result of bottom-up community activism that forged a policy consensus that a paradigm shift was necessary to tackle the issues surrounding intravenous drug use in the DTES.[38] Support for Insite was based on a cross-party policy consensus that included the centre-right NPA and left-of-centre COPE in Vancouver, Liberal and NDP governments in British Columbia, and the Chrétien/Martin Liberal government in Ottawa. It was advanced by NDP members of parliament (MPs) such as Libby Davies from Vancouver East (in office from 1997 to 2015) whose constituency included the DTES and who served as a COPE member of Vancouver City Council from 1982 to 1993.[39] It was supported by the VPD and given a clear mandate from voters in the 2002 municipal election.

More than representing a complex problem of multi-level governance, Insite reveals the complex implementation chain necessary for the establishment of a supervised consumption site in September 2003 and, more importantly, the continued operation of this facility in the DTES after September 2006: an organization applying to establish a facility that was supported by the regional health board, the provincial or territorial minister of health, in which the federal minister of health approved an exemption under section 56 of the *CDSA*. It was this policy consensus that allowed Insite to be elevated to a central component of harm reduction policy in Canada, albeit for a three-year trial in the DTES. In short, Insite emerged despite the complexity of the implementation chain and it being a complex problem of multi-level governance in the Canadian federation.

Slamming a Policy Window Shut: Enter the Harper Conservatives

A critical event occurred during Insite's three-year pilot study that shattered the policy consensus on harm reduction and supervised consumption sites: the election of the Harper Conservatives in January 2006. During its first two campaigns in 2004 and 2006, the Conservative Party of Canada's election manifestos indicated that a future Conservative government would pivot criminal justice policy toward a law-and-order agenda.[40] At a campaign event in British Columbia, then Conservative leader Stephen Harper established the party's opposition to harm reduction strategies: "We as a government will not use taxpayers' money to fund drug use."[41]

The election of the Harper minority government in January 2006 was not, at first, fatal for the harm reduction policy consensus, as Insite's exemption under the *CDSA* lasted until September 2006. But a number of events threatened Insite in the DTES after 2006. First, in September 2006, the Canadian Police Association and the Royal Canadian Mounted Police withdrew support for Insite and came out against the establishment of any new supervised consumption sites.[42] Second, despite Health Canada recommending that Insite be provided a three-and-a-half-year extension,[43] the minister of health, Tony Clement, rejected this on September 1 and issued a sixteen-month extension until December 2007. Further, the minister of health called for a moratorium on additional supervised consumption sites and established an Expert Advisory Committee (EAC) to report on "how supervised injection sites affect crime, prevention and treatment."[44] On October 2, 2007, the minister of health extended Insite's sixteen-month extension by an additional six months (until June 30, 2008) because the EAC report was delayed.[45]

The EAC delivered its report on March 31, 2008, and was generally supportive of Insite.[46] Perhaps the most significant change occurred on October 4, 2007, when the Harper Conservatives revamped the National Drug Strategy. Three important changes were implemented: the National Drug Strategy was renamed the National Anti-Drug Strategy to align with the government's law-and-order agenda; responsibility was transferred from the minister of health to the minister of public safety and emergency preparedness; and harm reduction was dropped as the fourth pillar.[47] While the Conservative government argued that harm reduction could be advanced by the first three pillars, supervised consumption sites as a component of the fourth pillar were not part of the National Anti-Drug Strategy.

In response to the unravelling of this policy consensus, two reactions occurred: first, the VCHA submitted an application on behalf of Insite to Health Canada on May 2, 2008, for a renewed exemption under section 56 of the *CDSA;* second, and in anticipation that this request would be rejected – or simply allowed to expire through a non-response by the minister of health – the PHS Community Services Society launched a series of constitutional challenges against the *CDSA* in April 2008. At the BC Superior Court, two constitutional challenges were filed: a federalism challenge, whereby Insite was argued to be exempt from the *CDSA* under the doctrine of inter-jurisdictional immunity,[48] and a Charter challenge that section 4(1) and 5(1) of the *CDSA* were a violation of security of the person protected under section 7 of the *Canadian Charter of Rights and Freedoms (Canadian Charter)*.[49] This rights violation was argued to occur for the medical professionals employed by Insite and the community they served in the DTES.[50] Section 4(1) prohibited the possession of specific narcotics designated by the

CDSA, and section 5(1) prohibited their trafficking except if possession and trafficking were authorized through regulation pursuant to a section 56 exemption.[51] Only the section 7 challenges were successful, and sections 4(1) and 5(1) of the *CDSA* were declared of no force or effect, with a suspended declaration of unconstitutionality. As a result, Insite was granted an additional twelve-month exemption to operate in the DTES under section 56 until June 30, 2009.[52]

Two days after the lower court decision, the minister of health appeared before the Standing Committee on Health on May 29, 2008, and stated the Conservative government's position on harm reduction and safe injection facilities: "In my opinion supervised injection is not medicine; it does not heal the person addicted to drugs. Each and every injection, along with the heroin and cocaine injected, harms the person."[53] For these reasons, the minister of health informed the Standing Committee that he had requested that the minister of justice "appeal Justice Pitfield's decision at the earliest possible opportunity."[54] During his testimony, Tony Clement was adamant that the Conservative government did not intend to shut Insite down, arguing that the federal government did not have the authority to do so. Instead, according to the minister of health, the Conservative government simply wanted to align Insite's mandate with the three pillars advanced by the National Anti-Drug Strategy. Acknowledging that Insite would not be provided an exemption by the current government, the minister of health argued that harm reduction could be advanced by other services provided by Insite:

> First of all, let me state for the record and make it crystal clear that this was never about closing Insite. I don't have the power to close Insite. It was about whether there would continue to be an exemption under the Controlled Drugs and Substances Act.
>
> Insite does other things. They do some referral, not as much as I'd like, but they do it. They do treatment now. They didn't at the beginning, but now they do. They do needle exchange. I have nothing against needle exchange. They distribute condoms. I have nothing against the distribution of condoms. These are all aspects of harm reduction that our government has no complaint about.[55]

The minister of health's assertations regarding Insite are disingenuous. Insite was established for the specific purpose of providing supervised consumption, which can only be provided through an exemption under the *CDSA*. While the minister of health could not close down Insite, as it continued to operate under a judicial exemption during the appeals process and was the jurisdictional responsibility of the provincial governments, the Conservative government left no ambiguity that, given the choice, it would shut down Insite as a supervised consumption site.

The Conservative government's opposition to supervised consumption sites intensified throughout the summer of 2008 and during the period leading up to the 2008 federal election on October 14, in which the Harper Conservatives would be returned to office as a stronger minority government.[56] During the seventeenth International AIDS Conference in Mexico City on August 3-8, Clement was questioned by journalists regarding the Conservative government's opposition to safe injection services. Clement left no uncertainty whether he would use his discretion under the *CDSA* to allow Insite to provide supervised consumption services:

> I've looked at the evidence. I have read every single report. I've read the evidence, and the evidence says – we did a whole review of the evidence – the evidence says, you know the maximum number of people saved by Insite? 1 person a year. I want to do better than 1 person a year. I want to save, I want to save 5,000 people a year. I'm sorry. That's on the wrong track, and I believe that we are doing the right thing. I believe no person, no person is too far gone. No addict is too far gone to give up on them. That is what Insite does. They say its ok to stick a needle in your vein and to die slowly. I don't believe that. And I don't believe Canadians believe that. And I believe in saving these people. And that's why Insite, to me, is an abomination. And you can put that on YouTube.[57]

This line of attack would soon be directed against the medical profession. During his speech at the 2008 Canadian Medical Association Annual Meeting on August 18, the minister of health questioned the ethics of medical professionals who supported safe injection services as part of harm reduction: "Is it ethical for health-care professionals to support the administration of drugs that are of unknown substance, purity, or potency – drugs that cannot otherwise be legally prescribed?"[58] Further, "[t]he supervised injection site undercuts the ethic of medical practice and sets a debilitating practice for all physicians and nurses, both present and future in Canada."[59]

Before the writ was issued on September 7 for the fortieth general election, which took placed on October 14, 2008, the Harper Conservatives appealed the lower court decision that granted Insite a continuing exemption under the *CDSA*. Surprisingly, the issue of supervised consumption sites was not included in the Conservative Party election platform in 2008, despite a heavy emphasis on law and order. The Conservatives generally avoided this issue during the election campaign. When asked to comment on supervised consumption sites, after Insite supporters attempted to disrupt a campaign event in downtown Vancouver shortly before the election,[60] Conservative leader Stephen Harper reiterated his government's approach to harm reduction: "When it comes to drug use, we want to make sure that we expend our resources on treatment and prevention."[61]

On January 15, 2010, the BC Court of Appeal affirmed that Insite could continue to operate as a supervised consumption site but for a novel reason. Unlike the lower court decision, which dismissed the application of the *CDSA* based on the doctrine of inter-jurisdictional immunity, the court of appeal determined that Insite was exempt from the *CDSA* because of this doctrine.[62] Moreover, given that "no error in the conduct of the trial" was found by the majority decision, the judgment "need not comment further on the constitutional issues raised in the appeal and the cross appeal and would dismiss the appeal as moot."[63] This was a far more resounding defeat for the Harper Conservatives than the lower court decision. While the Superior Court may have found that sections 4(1) and 5(1) of the *CDSA* were unconstitutional as a violation of section 7 of the *Canadian Charter*, it affirmed that this federal statute applied to a provincial health facility such as Insite in the DTES.

The court of appeal's decision would, in the interim, re-establish the policy consensus on Insite and supervised consumption sites in British Columbia. It also reconfigured the policy community as the doctrine of inter-jurisdictional immunity removed the Harper Conservatives as a veto player. While the minister of health was adamant during his testimony before the Standing Committee on Health on May 29, 2008, that the Conservative government could not – nor should it desire to – shut Insite down,[64] the court of appeal's decision effectively resuscitated the fourth pillar of the National Drug Policy and transferred the approval of supervised consumption sites to the provinces and territories.

The Supreme Court of Canada and the Harper Conservatives

The Conservative government lost no time in seeking judicial review of the court of appeal's decision on January 15, 2010: within five weeks of its release, the application for leave to appeal was submitted to the Supreme Court of Canada on February 25. The unanimous decision by the Supreme Court of Canada was released on September 30, 2011. Although a defeat for the

Harper Conservatives, the Court's decision was based on what appeared to be narrower grounds than the court of appeal's: sections 4(1) and 5(1) were found to be constitutional, the doctrine of inter-jurisdictional immunity did not apply in this case, and Insite required a section 56 exemption under the *CDSA* to continue to operate as a supervised consumption site.[65] The Harper Conservatives had been reinstated to the harm reduction policy community by the McLachlin court.

According to McLachlin CJ, who authored the unanimous decision, there were three problems with the application of the doctrine of inter-jurisdictional immunity: safe injection services had yet to be recognized, by the jurisprudence, as being within the core provincial responsibility for health care;[66] the "federal role in the domain of health makes it impossible to precisely define what falls in or out of the proposed provincial 'core'";[67] and, finally, the "application of interjurisdictional immunity to a protected core of the provincial health power has the potential to create legal vacuums."[68] Regarding the constitutionality of section 4(1) of the *CDSA*, while it engaged section 7 of the *Canadian Charter*, it was consistent with the principles of fundamental justice because the act conferred on the minister broad discretion to grant exemptions under section 56.[69] Finally, the unanimous decision failed to find any section 7 engagement that occurred via the prohibition on trafficking by section 5(1).[70]

If the *CDSA* was applicable to Insite and constitutional in its construction, it was the application of section 56 of the *CDSA* by the minister of health that the Supreme Court considered unconstitutional: "If there is a *Charter* problem, it lies not in the statute but in the Minister's exercise of the power the statute gives him to grant appropriate exemptions."[71] Stated more bluntly, the construction of the *CDSA* in 1996 by the Chrétien Liberals was constitutional, but its application by the Harper Conservatives was not. Recognizing that neither lower court decision considered the constitutionality of ministerial discretion, the chief justice noted that the "special circumstances of this case" required the Court to assess its use since, "with all exercises of discretion, the Minister's decisions must conform to the *Charter*."[72] On the question of ministerial discretion, the Attorney General of Canada argued that, in fact, the minister of health had not violated section 7 because he had not made a decision in regard to Insite's application for a further extension under section 56 of the *CDSA*.[73]

The Supreme Court of Canada rejected this argument and based its reasoning on the minister of health's appearance before the Standing Committee on Health on May 29, 2008, where he acknowledged that he had received the commissioned report by the EAC and that a formal application had been sent by the VCHA to Health Canada on May 2, 2008, requesting a continued exemption for Insite to operate as a safe injection facility.[74] According to McLachlin CJ, "[t]he only rational conclusion is that the Minister had considered an application for an exemption that was then before him, and had decided not to grant it."[75] Focusing on ministerial discretion, the chief justice argued that the approach by the minister of health engaged the section 7 rights of the community that Insite served and, further, that ministerial discretion was not exercised in accordance with the principles of fundamental justice, being both arbitrary and grossly disproportionate in its use. Although the Court's approach to arbitrariness was not settled, it had established a two-part inquiry when assessing the principles of fundamental justice: first, that the law's objective be identified and, second, that the relationship between state action and the law's objective be determined. As the objective of the *CDSA* was to protect health and public safety, the minister of health's decision to deny a continued exemption under section 56 of the *CDSA* undermined public safety within the DTES, according to the chief justice, as well as the health of individuals that relied on supervised consumption services provided by Insite. For the Court, the minister of health's approach to Insite was thus arbitrary and inconsistent with the principles of fundamental justice.[76]

On the question of gross disproportionality, "which describes state actions or legislative responses to a problem that are so extreme as to be disproportionate to any legitimate government interest,"[77] McLachlin CJ was scathing in her assessment of the Harper Conservative's approach to harm reduction in the DTES: "Insite saves lives. Its benefits have been proven. There has been no discernible negative impact on the public safety and health objectives of Canada during its eight years of operation. The effect of denying the services of Insite to the population it serves is grossly disproportionate to any benefit that Canada might derive from presenting a uniform stance on the possession of narcotics."[78] Because the question of the *CDSA*'s constitutionality, in both lower court decisions, involved its statutory construction and not its application by the minister of health, the Attorney General of Canada did not present an argument justifying ministerial discretion under section 56 of the *CDSA* as a reasonable limit on section 7. If such an argument had been raised under section 1, McLachlin CJ was clear that a reasonable limitations justification would be rejected and the finding of an unconstitutional use of ministerial discretion would stand.[79]

The Judicialization of Ministerial Discretion

For the Harper Conservatives, a narrower finding of unconstitutionality that rested on ministerial discretion was probably irrelevant as the remedy applied by McLachlin CJ under section 24(1) – and the rationale for the particular remedy adopted – left no doubt that the chief justice had issued a robust finding of unconstitutionality against the government's objection to supervised consumption as a component of harm reduction. In deciding which remedy for the section 7 violation of individuals that relied on Insite was "appropriate and just in the circumstances," the chief justice considered three possible approaches. The first was "to issue a declaration that the Minister erred in refusing to grant a further exemption to Insite in May 2008, and return the matter to the Minister to reconsider the matter and make a decision that respects the claimants' Charter *rights*."[80] This was not considered an appropriate remedy as it could lead to a delay in which Insite's application was reviewed by the minister of health and may very well lead to the refusal to grant a renewed exemption under section 56 where "[l]litigation may well break out anew."[81]

Second, the Supreme Court considered whether granting Insite a permanent exemption under section 56 of the *CDSA* should be its remedy under section 24(1). Again, this was not considered appropriate as it would deprive the minister of health of any discretion under section 56, and, more importantly, if the evidence shifted against Insite as a safe injection facility, "the flexibility contemplated by s. 56 of the *CDSA* would be lost."[82] The Court settled on a third remedy that both preserved the discretion of future ministers of health under section 56 of the *CDSA* and provided a stinging rebuke of why it would not send this issue back for ministerial resolution by the minister of health in the incumbent Harper ministry. Although McLachlin CJ ordered the minister of health to immediately issue a one-year exemption for Insite under section 56 of the *CDSA*, this was argued to preserve future ministerial discretion as "this does not fetter the Minister's discretion with respect to future applications for exemptions, whether for other premises, or for Insite."[83] How the chief justice came to justify this particular remedy – removing the use of ministerial discretion by the Harper Conservatives while, at the same time, preserving it for future governments – is perhaps without precedent in the Charter era. Simply put, the chief justice lacked confidence in the current government and its approach to supervised consumption services and did not believe that the minister of health would exercise their discretion under section 56 of the *CDSA* consistent with the *Canadian Charter:* "The Minister is bound to exercise his discretion under

s. 56 in accordance with the *Charter*. On the facts as found here, there can be only one response: to grant the exemption. There is therefore nothing to be gained (and much to be risked) in sending the matter back to the Minister for reconsideration."[84] That the chief justice publicly questioned whether the Harper Conservatives would act constitutionally in response to the decision in *PHS Community Services Society* may be the closest the Court has come to acknowledging that the unpopularity of a judicial decision with an incumbent government can significantly modify the policy impact of a judicial decision. This lack of faith in ministerial discretion, as it relates to the Court's understanding of the *Canadian Charter,* largely explains a robust approach to section 24(1) and judicially determined criteria for exercising ministerial discretion under section 56 of the *CDSA*.

The judicialization of ministerial discretion continued when McLachlin CJ stated that scientific evidence would determine whether a minister could refuse to grant an exemption under section 56 of the *CDSA:* "Where, as here, the evidence indicates that a supervised injection site will decrease the risk of death and disease, and there is little or no evidence that it will have a negative impact on public safety, the Minister should generally grant an exemption."[85] Moreover, the chief justice outlined the criteria that must be factored into any use of ministerial discretion under section 56 of the *CDSA:* "The factors considered in making the decision on an exemption must include evidence, if any, on the impact of such a facility on crime rates, the local conditions indicating a need for such a supervised injection site, the regulatory structure in place to support the facility, the resources available to support its maintenance, and expressions of community support or opposition."[86] These five conditions, according to the chief justice, would ensure that ministerial discretion would be exercised consistent with the *Canadian Charter* and advance the dual purposes of the *CDSA:* public health and public safety.[87]

There is no doubt that this is a strong-form decision and evidence of a fundamental policy disagreement between the Supreme Court and the Harper ministry. Upholding the constitutionality of the *CDSA* while questioning how the minister of health approached the issue of harm reduction constitutes a personal rebuke of an incumbent government by the chief justice of the Supreme Court of Canada. While *PHS Community Services Society* was a robust decision, it was also a narrow one at the same time. As Kent Roach noted, "the Court's decision was remedially aggressive because it made a mandatory order that required Insite to be granted an exemption, but it was also quite narrow because it was limited to the facts of the particular case."[88]

Binding ministerial discretion to the scientific evidence was intended to ensure that the policy consensus on harm reduction in the DTES that preceded the Harper government could withstand the Harper government.

The Supreme Court was clear that the approval of additional supervised consumption facilities, and future renewals of Insite's exemption under section 56 of the *CDSA*, remained the prerogative of the minister of health provided the minister acted consistently with the *Canadian Charter* by following the five judicially established criteria. This is an important caveat and, perhaps, a judicial sleight of hand meant to obscure the force of this public rebuke. The robust approach to the section 24(1) remedy, the establishment of criteria to structure ministerial discretion under section 56 of the *CDSA*, and the fact that the decision was authored by the chief justice for a unanimous bench were meant to convey a clear message to the current and future governments: provided that supervised consumption services continued to advance the dual purpose of the *CDSA*, ministerial discretion should rarely be used to deny an exemption under section 56 for the provision of safe injection services.

Harper's Fables: The Tortoise and (Not) the Hare

Three MPs would serve as minister of health in the Harper government. While Clement was the minister that prompted the judicialization of supervised consumption services by denying Insite an exemption under section 56 of the *CDSA*, it would be his successors, Ministers of Health Leona Aglukkaq (Bill C-65) and Rona Ambrose (Bill C-2), that tabled the *Respect for Communities Act*.[89] Responding to questions by Libby Davies of the NDP whether the Harper ministry would now endorse supervised consumption services as a component of harm reduction because of *PHS Community Services Society*,[90] Aglukkaq reaffirmed the National Anti-drug Strategy and the focus on prevention and treatment: "Our government believes that spending more money on treatment and support to help people get off drugs is the best investment we can make."[91] More pointedly, Liberal MP Hedy Fry asked the minister of health whether the Harper government would respect the Court's decision "and grant further exemptions for cities to replicate Insite's success?"[92] The minister of health indicated that, while the government was disappointed, it would comply with the decision in *PHS Community Services Society*.[93]

Did the Harper government in fact comply? Knopff and his co-authors argue that the *Respect for Communities Act* is an example of legislative compliance through "clarification dialogue." According to this argument, the amendments to the *CDSA* simply clarified the five-part criteria established by the Court in *PHS Community Services Society*: "This lengthy list of required documents could be read to fulfill the Court's requirement for guided discretion. Moreover, many of the documents seem designed to ensure that the same kind of broad public and private consensus that the Court found praiseworthy with respect to Insite exists for safe-injection sites in other communities."[94] This is a plausible interpretation. The response to *PHS Community Services Society*, in which the Harper government amended section 56 of the *CDSA*, was based upon the five-part criteria established by McLachlin CJ to ensure that ministerial discretion was used in accordance with the *Canadian Charter* and the dual purposes of the *CDSA*.

While plausible, this explanation neglects to consider perhaps the most pressing issue about the *Respect for Communities Act* – was it even necessary or required? The answer is the "The Court" upheld the constitutionality of section 56 of the *CDSA* and, unlike the court of appeal, rejected the doctrine of inter-jurisdictional immunity. The *CDSA* was both constitutional and applicable to Insite. There was no need, or a constitutional requirement, to pass the *Respect for Communities Act*. It was ministerial discretion that ran afoul of the *Canadian Charter* and not the statutory construction of the *CDSA*. The history of Insite's post-*Insite* renewal of the section 56 exemption demonstrates that the *Respect for Communities Act* was a political calculation by the Harper Conservatives to mitigate judicial invalidation of its approach to harm reduction beyond Insite in the DTES. The judicially ordered extension of Insite's exemption in 2011 by the chief justice was for one year. Before the *Respect for Communities Act* was passed in 2015, the Harper Conservatives would grant four yearly section 56 exemptions for Insite between 2012 and 2016 based on the criteria established by the Court in *PHS Community Services Society*.[95] The practice of yearly renewals would continue until 2016, when Insite would be granted a four-year exemption by Jane Philpott, the Trudeau government's first minister of health.[96]

In deciding whether the Harper Conservatives complied with the decision in *PHS Community Services Society*, there are two frames of analysis that must be adopted: one involving Insite in the DTES and the second regarding new facilities that would apply for an initial exemption under section 56.1 of the *CDSA* once the *Respect for Communities Act* was passed in 2015. The 2014 renewal of Insite's exemption in the absence of the *Respect for Communities Act* is clear evidence that the Harper Conservatives recognized that, so long as the scientific evidence indicated that Insite advanced the dual purposes of the *CDSA*, it was powerless to prevent the delivery of supervised consumption services in the DTES. Insite in the DTES represented the Harper government's line in the sand, and the *Respect for Communities Act* was the legislative instrument that would ensure that no additional supervised consumption sites would be granted an exemption while it remained in office.[97]

If the Harper government had fully accepted the decision in *PHS Community Services Society* beyond the DTES, there were two more timely options available other than legislating amendments to the *CDSA:* first, a ministerial directive that decisions by the minister of health under section 56 of the *CDSA* for new applications would comply with paragraph 153 of *PHS Community Services Society* and the criteria outlined by McLachlin CJ and, second, a set of regulations passed through order-in-council that operationalized how ministerial discretion under section 56 would be exercised in light of *PHS Community Services Society.* A ministerial directive could be issued within a matter of days, either through a statement by the minister of health to the House of Commons, a press release, or a policy directive by the minister to Health Canada. Regulations through order-in-council could be published in the *Canada Gazette* within a matter of months, given that McLachlin CJ was rather precise as to the five criteria that must be used for a constitutional approach to ministerial discretion. Of the three options available, the Harper Conservatives pursued the one that travelled the longest route. For instance, Bill C-65, *An Act to Amend the Controlled Drugs and Substances Act,* in June 2013 was introduced twenty months after *PHS Community Services Society* was decided on September 30, 2011, and passed as Bill C-2 in June 2015, more than forty-four months after McLachlin CJ ordered the minister of health to reissue a section 56 exemption to Insite.[98]

Why did the Harper Conservatives choose to be the tortoise when it could have been the hare? Why did it take forty-four months to amend section 56 of the *CDSA*, a provision that was upheld as constitutional by the Supreme Court of Canada in the 2011 decision of *PHS Community Services Society*? This is extremely significant given that the Conservatives had majority control of both houses during the forty-first Parliament and could have expedited the passage of the *Respect for Communities Act* well before June 18, 2015.[99] Surely, a government committed to the decision in *PHS Community Services Society* and "clarification dialogue" would want to outline how the minister of health would assess new applications for supervised consumption services much sooner than a mere six weeks before the writ was issued on August 2, 2015, for the forty-second general election on October 19, 2015? Timing is everything. And with respect to the *Respect for Communities Act,* it clarifies the true reason why the Harper government chose the legislative route over more timely ways to clarify the use of ministerial discretion under the *CDSA*. Simply put, the government was opposed to supervised consumption services, opposed to the *PHS Community Services Society* decision, and legislated according to this opposition. This is why I will argue in the next section that, while the *Respect for Communities Act* fit the legislative purpose of the Harper government in relation to supervised consumption services, the legislative response was not fit for its constitutional purpose.

More pointedly, and perhaps the clearest evidence that the Harper government had clarified its opposition to the decision in *PHS Community Services Society*, was the online petition that appeared on the Conservative Party website the day on which the minister of health introduced Bill C-65, *An Act to Amend the Controlled Drugs and Substances Act*, into the House of Commons on June 7, 2013.[100] Authored by Jenni Byrne, the 2011 National Campaign chair, the online petition asked: "Do you want a supervised drug consumption site in your community? These are facilities where drug addicts get to shoot up heroin and other illicit drugs."[101] It lauded the efforts of the Harper government to prevent the expansion of supervised consumption services and castigated the opposition parties that supported safe injection services.[102] If the *Respect for Communities Act* is "clarification dialogue" on the part of the Harper Conservatives, this petition on the Conservative Party of Canada website leaves no doubt as to the purpose of the proposed amendments to section 56 of the *CDSA*.

It is how the Harper Conservatives responded to *PHS Community Services Society* that signalled a fundamental legislative disagreement between it and the Supreme Court of Canada. Instead of contributing to Charter dialogue through clarification legislation, the *Respect for Communities Act* is an example of non-compliance through statutory amendment.[103] Despite the Court's clear displeasure with the Harper government over the issue of supervised consumption sites, whether *PHS Community Services Society* had a policy impact beyond the DTES was largely determined by the Harper Conservatives during their remaining time in office. The Harper government controlled the ebb and flow of the legislative process. And the Harper Conservatives decided to run out the clock that prohibited new supervised consumption sites by implementing a complex application process under the *Respect for Communities Act*. This would become its standard technique of legislative defiance when disagreeing with judicial participation in salient issues of public policy, which was repeated in *Carter v Canada* and the issue of medical assistance in dying, as Chapter 8 discusses.[104]

While a number of feasibility studies were conducted on potential supervised consumption sites in Toronto, Ottawa, Victoria, and Montreal after *PHS Community Services Society*,[105] only applications from the Dr. Peter Centre in Vancouver in February 2014 and Santé Montréal in May 2015 were submitted.[106] However, these applications were not reviewed by Ambrose before the defeat of the Harper government in October 2015.[107] What explains the general absence of new applications from the decision in *PHS Community Services Society* in September 2011 to the defeat of the Harper government in the 2015 federal election? One possibility is that, in the absence of published rules on how the minister of health would use their discretion under section 56 of the *CDSA*, health organizations simply waited for greater clarity with the introduction and the passage of the *Respect for Communities Act* before submitting applications to Health Canada. The second, and the most likely explanation, is that local health organizations did not believe that the Harper government, despite the *PHS Community Services Society* decision, would authorize the establishment of any new supervised consumption sites outside the DTES. Indeed, Bill C-65, tabled in the House of Commons in June 2013, is a "how-to" manual of legislative non-compliance when responding to a strong-form judicial decision such as *PHS Community Services Society*.

Although Toronto Public Health had supported the establishment of supervised consumption sites since 2005 in the Greater Toronto Area, it did not submit an application to Health Canada until the defeat of the Harper government. It was the onerous and unclear requirements under the *Act to Amend the Controlled Drugs and Substances Act* (the RFCA) that accounted for this outcome: "The requirements in the bill are onerous, and there is no indication as to what level of information or support is needed for a successful application. If the bill is passed as currently drafted, health services seeking to implement safe injection will have great difficulty meeting the requirements for a CDSA exemption."[108] Moreover, the medical officer of health recommended that Toronto Public Health make a submission opposing the *Respect for Communities Act* "and to recommend the development of a more feasible CDSA exemption application process."[109]

Bills C-65–C-2: "R-E-S-P-E-C-T. Find Out What It Means to Me"[110]

That the Harper government introduced the *Respect for Communities Act* and modelled the application process after the five-part criteria outlined by McLachlin CJ does not necessarily mean that it created a constitutional approach to ministerial discretion. There are significant points of departure between the reasons provided by the chief justice in *PHS Community Services Society* and the *Respect for Communities Act* passed by the Harper government. This legislative response is best categorized as non-compliance. It is not clarification dialogue. The Harper Conservatives created an application process of singular difficulty in which the minister of health would only review completed applications as required by the *Respect for Communities Act*. Indeed, if this legislative response had been subjected to "clarification dialogue" through a judicial challenge, it would most likely have been found unconstitutional in its statutory construction as arbitrary and grossly disproportionate in relation to the section 7 rights of those individuals seeking supervised consumption services.

The *Respect for Communities Act* contains a lengthy preamble in which the Harper Conservatives outlined their approach to *PHS Community Services Society* and the dual purposes of the *CDSA* (see Figure 6.1). It refers to illicit drugs as "a worldwide problem with significant impacts on Canada" in which the proceeds of crime finance the consumption of illicit drug use by "vulnerable subsets of the Canadian population." While the preamble does refer to the public health and public safety objectives of the *CDSA*, it is largely about protecting the local community in which a supervised consumption facility may be located from the negative public health and safety implications of illicit drug use. This is a notable departure from *PHS Community Services Society*, which focused on supervised consumption services as a valuable component of the public health of vulnerable members of the DTES. The Court ruled in *Insite* that, where "the evidence indicates that a supervised injection site will decrease the risk of death and disease, and there is little or no evidence that it will have a negative impact on public safety, the Minister should generally grant an exemption."[111] The most striking part of the preamble is perhaps the last paragraph. Under the *Respect for Communities Act*, a section 56 exemption "should only be granted in exceptional circumstances and after the applicant has addressed rigorous criteria." The change from the Court's statement – "should generally grant" – to the Conservative's statement – "should only grant in exceptional circumstances" – is not without consequence once the criteria included in a section 56 application are considered.

First introduced as Bill C-65 in June 2013, the *Respect for Communities Act* was reintroduced as Bill C-2 on October 17 following the Speech from the Throne to open the second session of the forty-first Parliament on October 16, 2013. Two issues appeared in the Speech from the Throne that signalled

Figure 6.1 Preamble to Bill C-2, *Respect for Communities Act*

Whereas Parliament recognizes that the objectives of the Controlled Drugs and Substances Act ("the Act") are the protection of public health and the protection of public safety;

Whereas the Act and its regulations have a dual role of prohibiting certain activities associated with harmful substances and allowing access to those substances for legitimate medical, scientific and industrial purposes;

Whereas the diversion of controlled substances and precursors, as those terms are defined in the Act, which are frequently used in the production of illicit drugs, is a worldwide problem with significant impacts on Canada;

Whereas the money that is used to purchase controlled substances that are obtained from illicit sources often originates from criminal activity such as theft, and that money, in turn, often funds organized crime in our communities;

Whereas the substances that are subject to the Act may pose serious risks to the health of individuals and those risks are exacerbated when those substances are unregulated, untested and obtained from illicit sources;

Whereas the negative consequences associated with the use of illicit substances can have significant impacts on vulnerable subsets of the Canadian population;

And whereas an exemption from the application of the Act and its regulations for certain activities in relation to controlled substances that are obtained from illicit sources should only be granted in exceptional circumstances and after the applicant has addressed rigorous criteria;

Now, therefore, Her Majesty, by and with the advice and consent of the Senate and House of Commons of Canada, enacts as follows: ...

---

points of disagreement between the Supreme Court of Canada and the Harper government during its last term in office: the imminent invalidation of the prostitution provisions in *Canada (Attorney General) v Bedford*,[112] which occurred in December 2013, and the commitment to passing the *Respect for Communities Act* "to ensure that parents have a say before a drug injection site opens in their community."[113] Although sponsored by then Minister of Health Rona Ambrose, the press release discussing Bill C-2 contained additional commentary by Steven Blaney, the minister of public safety and emergency preparedness. The Harper government was attempting to portray the *Respect for Communities Act* as being consistent with the *CDSA*'s dual purpose of public health (Ambrose) and public safety (Blaney). This was simply a compatibility mirage. The two ministers emphasized that the *Respect for Communities Act* prioritized the health and public safety of the communities in which potential supervised consumption sites would be located and not, as the Court did in *PHS Community Services Society*, the section 7 rights of marginalized individuals seeking these services.

According to the minister of health, "as outlined in our Government's Speech from the Throne, we are committed to supporting and protecting Canadian families, who work hard to build safe communities in which to raise their children."[114] The theme of the safety of local communities was reiterated by the minister of public safety and emergency preparedness: "Our Government is committed to keeping our streets and communities safe. Substances obtained from illicit sources affect public safety, may fuel organized crime and undermine the health of individuals."[115] The press release also emphasized the importance that the *Respect for Communities Act* placed on public consultations with the local community, as the minister of health stated that "families deserve to be heard before a drug injection site, where illegal drugs will be consumed, is allowed to be built in their neighbourhood." The minister of public safety also shared: "We believe applications to allow illegal drug use in neighbourhoods must be carefully assessed with input by those who will be most affected."[116] Unlike the Supreme Court of Canada, which suggested it was the section 7 rights of intravenous drug users that should be respected, the Harper government challenged this assumption. Respect, for the Harper Conservatives, would be accorded to the local community that may have a supervised consumption site located within their neighbourhood. Indeed, as Aglukkaq argued in the House of Commons when introducing Bill C-65, "that is why the short title of this legislation is the 'respect for communities act.' This consultation will be an essential part of the application process for a supervised consumption site. We need to know what those living, working or going to school near the potential supervised consumption site think of the proposal."[117]

The *Respect for Communities Act* placed statutory requirements on two actors under section 56.1 of the *CDSA:* the health organization submitting an application for an exemption under section 56 and the federal minister of health reviewing the application. In regard to the health organization, the *Respect for Communities Act* outlined a twenty-seven-part application process that first required the inclusion of scientific evidence demonstrating the health benefits of the proposed site (section 56.1(3)(a)). Five letters were required from the following public actors outlining their views on the health and public safety issues surrounding the proposed facility: a letter from the provincial or territorial minister responsible for health matters (section 56.1(3)(b)); the local municipal government outlining support or opposition to the facility (section 56.1(3)(c)); the head of the local police force with responsibility for the location of the proposed supervised consumption site "that outlines his or her opinion on the proposed activities at the site, including any concerns with respect to public safety and security" facility (section 56.1(3)(e));[118] the lead public health official in the province (section 56.1(3)(g)); and a letter from the provincial or territorial minister responsible for public safety (s.56.1(3)(h)). If the municipality or the local police raised concerns about the impact of the proposed facility, the application process required a description of how the concerns of local government (section 56.1(3)(d)) and law enforcement (section 56.1(3)(f)) would be addressed.

The application required descriptions, if available, of how the proposed site would impact public safety (section 56.1(3)(i)), the provision of statistical trends relating to law enforcement in the vicinity of the proposed facility (section 56.1(3)(j)); statistical trends involving the size of the drug community serviced by the proposed facility (section 56.1(3)(k)); and statistical trends regarding infectious diseases (section 56.1(3)(l)) and death rates due to drug overdoses (section 56.1(3)(m)). If available, the application required any official reports in regard to the proposed faculty and any relevant coroner reports (section 56.1(3)(n)). A number of consultations were required, and the application needed to provide summaries of consultations with local nurses and physicians (section 56.1(3)(o)) and, perhaps most importantly, consultations with a "broad range of community groups from the municipality in which the site would be located" (section 56.1(3)(p)).

The application also required a description of the financing of the proposed facility (section 56.1(3)(q)), the provision of drug treatment services (section 56.1(3)(r)), statistic trends pertaining to rates of loitering (section 56.1(3)(s)), discussions of public health emergencies in the vicinity of the proposed site (section 56.1(3)(t)), discussions of how any disruption caused by the proposed facility would be minimized (section 56.1(3)(u)); and descriptions about procedures for handling illicit substances at the proposed facility (section 56.1(3)(v)). The application required the resumes of any key staff members (section 56.1(3)(w)) and police background checks and police reports, both domestic (section 56.1(3)(x)) and international (section 56.1(3)(y)), detailing any "designated drug offence or designated criminal offence" for a period of ten years for any key staff members in the proposed safe injection facility. Finally, the application required "any other information that the Minister considers relevant to the consideration of the application" (section 56.1(3)(z).

Of the twenty-seven components for a section 56 application, the first twenty-six pertained to new facilities and the twenty-seventh to established facilities seeking additional exemptions. For Insite in the DTES, it would have to provide, if available, any evidence pertaining to changes in crime rates (section 56.1(4)(a)) and public health (section 56.1(4)(b)) during its most recent exemption under the *CDSA*. Not all applications would contain all twenty-six or twenty-seven components as eight contained the caveat that the information was only required "if any" documents or evidence were available.[119] If the minister of health determined that insufficient consultation occurred, or that information that was not included was, in fact, available, the application would be considered incomplete and returned to the responsible organization. Once an application was submitted and determined to be in compliance with section 56.1, the minister of health was required to "give notice" to the local community before it was reviewed, at which time "members of the public have 90 days after the day on which the notice is given to provide the Minister with comments" (section 56.1(6)). This represents potentially the twenty-seventh or twenty-eighth component of an application for a section 56 exemption under the *Respect for Communities Act*.

Once the ninety-day community consultation period ended and a potential report was forwarded, the minister of health could begin a review of an application for a section 56 exemption. Under section 56.1(5), the minister of health's decision was governed by two factors: first, that the minister may only grant an exemption in exceptional circumstances and, second, that the decision be informed by a set of overarching principles:

> (5) The Minister may only grant an exemption for a medical purpose under subsection (2) to allow certain activities to take place at a supervised consumption site in exceptional circumstances and after having considered the following principles:
>
> (a) illicit substances may have serious health effects;
> (b) adulterated controlled substances may pose health risks;
> (c) the risks of overdose are inherent to the use of certain illicit substances;
> (d) strict controls are required, given the inherent health risks associated with controlled substances that may alter mental processes;
> (e) organized crime profits from the use of illicit substances; and
> (f) criminal activity often results from the use of illicit substances.[120]

What was missing from the *Respect for Communities Act* was the relative weight that the minister of health would assign to any of the required application components and, more importantly, whether a file would be considered incomplete, and, thus, not reviewable, if any of the application components were missing despite the qualification "if available." And, more importantly, there was no specified time frame in which the minister of health, having received and accepted an application for a section 56 exemption, would reach a decision on a new facility or the renewal of an existing exemption.

At the second reading of Bill C-65, Aglukkaq began by commenting on the instances in which an exemption for the use of illicit materials had been granted under section 56 of the *CDSA*: "Virtually all the exemptions for illegal drugs are for law enforcement, so that they can use these drugs to train police dogs to detect drugs."[121] Moreover, the minister of health defended the bill as meeting the "high bar set by the Supreme Court of Canada for supervised consumption sites and makes sure communities have a say in any decisions made."[122] This would be the consistent argument made by Conservative ministers, parliamentary secretaries, and private members defending the *Respect for Communities Act* – that it was consistent with *PHS Community Services Society* because section 56.1 of the revised *CDSA* was based on the five criteria referred to in paragraph 153 of McLachlin CJ's reasons. Once responsibility for the *Respect for Communities Act* passed to Ambrose, the minister of health was unequivocal that "this bill is a response to a Supreme Court ruling, and it follows that Supreme Court ruling to the letter."[123]

Does the *Respect for Communities Act* comply with the Supreme Court's decision? And, more importantly, does the legislative response constitute Charter dialogue between the Supreme Court and the Harper government? In the second edition of *The Supreme Court on Trial*, Kent Roach clearly considers the legislative response as incompatible with the Court's decision. More importantly, Roach does acknowledge the ability of a government, when it disagrees with the Court, to marginalize judicial policy impact through a legislative response: "The new law discourages applications for exemptions and then encourages the minister of health to never grant them. This is dialogue with a vengeance."[124] Although Roach concludes that "a government that was so opposed to saving the lives of the addicted would not likely grant an exemption even with less extreme legislation,"[125] he does suggest the "result was a more democratic and transparent dialogue than what would have occurred without the Charter."[126] At this point, Roach appears to be endorsing "clarification dialogue" but not in the way envisioned by Rainer Knopff and colleagues.[127] Indeed, Roach suggests that the *Respect for Communities Act* reveals much about the Harper Conservatives and their views of individuals using supervised consumption services.

In *PHS Community Services Society*, McLachlin CJ suggested that when the minister of health considered an application for a section 56 exemption, "he or she will aim to strike the appropriate balance between achieving the public health and public safety goals." And perhaps more importantly, "whereas here, the evidence indicates that a supervised injection site will decrease the risk of death and disease, and there is little or no evidence that it will have a negative impact on public safety, the Minister should generally grant an exemption."[128] The last consideration – that the minister should generally grant an exemption – is critically important as the Court was clear that this was the standard by which an application determined to balance the public safety and public health considerations under the *CDSA* should be granted. While the Supreme Court did establish five considerations to guide the minister of health's decision, including public consultation, it did not view these factors as constituting an unbreakable decision-making chain. In this respect, the Harper Conservatives placed greater emphasis on community consultation and public safety than the Court and much less emphasis on the public health of those individuals seeking supervised consumption services.

During the second reading debate on Bill C-2, the NDP and the Liberal parties criticized the principles that the minister of health must consider when reviewing an application for a section 56 exemption. According to Libby Davies, the *Respect for Communities Act* was designed to allow the Harper Conservatives to both determine when an application was complete, and, if complete, to deny an application based on the guiding principles established in section 56.1(5): "The bill is designed to create a situation where everything will run in the government's favour to not even consider applications, or, if it does, to simply turn them down based on the principles it has outlined."[129] Joyce Murray declared that "Bill C-2 is just the government's latest attempt in a long series of attempts to shut down any effort to open a safe consumption site elsewhere in Canada."[130]

One of the most insightful critiques of the *Respect for Communities Act* was that of NDP MP Megan Leslie at second reading. Of particular concern was that the standard the Court established for the approval of a section 56 exemption – that the minister of health should generally grant an exemption when the health benefits are proven and that should be no discernible impact on public safety – had been significantly departed from in the *Respect for Communities Act*. There were two departures from the Court's decision-making standard in the *Respect for Communities Act* – from the

Court's instance that when a facility demonstrated it advanced the dual purposes of the *CDSA* the minister should generally grant an exemption to the *Respect for Communities Act*'s alternation via section 56.1 that the "minister may, on any terms and conditions the Minister considers necessary" grant a section 56 exemption. Whereas the Court's decision fettered ministerial discretion when the evidence required the granting of a section 56 exemption, the *Respect for Communities Act* did not impose any such requirements on ministerial discretion.[131] And once ministerial discretion was fully reinstated via section 56.1, the *Respect for Communities Act* raised the decision-making threshold from largely a requirement – "should generally grant," according to *PHS Community Services Society* at paragraph 152 – to one in which the minister of health "may" only grant an exemption in "exceptional circumstances" after having reviewed the section 56 application in light of five guiding principles that spoke only to the public safety purpose of the *CDSA* to the neglect of its twin objective, public health.[132]

Location, Location, Location: The Standing Committee on Public Safety and National Security

That the Harper Conservatives aligned the *Respect for Communities Act* with its law-and-order agenda and placed greater emphasis on the public safety purpose of the *CDSA* is best illustrated by the standing committee that received the *Respect for Communities Act*. Soon after *PHS Community Services Society* was decided by the Supreme Court of British Columbia in 2008, Clement appeared before the Standing Committee on Health (HESA) to voice the government's displeasure with the decision and to notify the standing committee that the government intended to appeal the lower court decision.[133] As the *CDSA* is the responsibility of the minister of health, and the "Standing Committee on Health studies issues that relate to Health Canada, including bills and regulations," it was appropriate – and unsurprising – that the minister of health appeared before the standing committee that scrutinizes the activities of Health Canada.[134] Without any justification, the *Respect for Communities Act* was assigned to the Standing Committee on Public Safety and National Security (SECU),[135] which has a criminal justice and public safety mandate: "The Standing Committee on Public Safety and National Security reviews legislation, policies, programs and expenditure plans of government departments and agencies responsible for public safety and national security, policing and law enforcement, corrections and conditional release of federal offenders, emergency management, crime prevention and the protection of Canada's borders."[136] The change from HESA to

SECU was commented on by opposition members, who suggested it was an attempt to frame the issue as principally one of public safety and not the dual purposes outlined in the *CDSA*. As Randall Garrison of the NDP noted, sending the bill to SECU "illustrates to me their intention to distract the public by characterizing safe injection sites as a threat to public safety rather than an important health measure that would save both lives and money."[137]

At SECU, the minister of health reiterated that only applications deemed to be complete would be reviewed for an exemption under section 56.1 of the *CDSA*.[138] Moreover, the minister of public safety and emergency preparedness defended that the *Respect for Communities Act* was sent to SECU: "I did not get into politics to further human misery and contribute to the total disfigurement of neighbourhoods. That is why it is important, in my opinion, that this bill also be viewed as a matter of public safety."[139] At SECU, officials from Health Canada answered opposition questions on the application process envisioned by the *Respect for Communities Act*. At committee, a number of issues were raised by opposition members such as Libby Davies of the NDP: how broad based could the ninety-day consultation period initiated by the minister of health be; was the minister of health required to grant a section 56 exemption if an application conformed to the requirements set out in Bill C-2; and, finally, how did the minister of health weigh the potentially twenty-seven application components when reviewing a file submitted by a health organization. In short, the opposition members questioned whether ministerial discretion was any less discretionary under the *Respect for Communities Act* than it was before the 2011 Supreme Court of Canada decision. Moreover, given that ministerial discretion was largely unfettered, with the expectation that it would be exercised in accordance with the *Canadian Charter*, how could unfettered discretion be tamed by the Charter? If the minister of health determined when a submitted application was complete and, more importantly, how the twenty-seven-part criteria would be weighted in ministerial decision-making, how was this any different from the approach found to be unconstitutional in *PHS Community Services Society*?

In regard to the ninety-day consultation period initiated by the minister of health, Davies asked whether there was a defined area for the consultation or whether the minister of health was free to decide the parameters of the local consultation: "Is it the immediate, local area where the site is being considered? Is there a radius?"[140] In response, an assistant deputy minister from Health Canada noted that, "based on the application that's put in front of him or her at the time and based on the need for such consultation beyond what would have been received in the application, it would be totally at the minister's discretion."[141] Was the minister of health required to approve an application filed in accordance with the *Respect for Communities Act* and reviewed based on the guiding principles? In response to this question posed by Davies, the Health Canada official stated that "there's nothing that says it must be approved or it must be rejected. There's nothing that fetters the discretion."[142] What weight would the minister of health attach to the twenty-seven criteria when reviewing an application for a section 56 exemption, asked Hedy Fry of the Liberal Party. According to the Health Canada official, because the minister of health was required to weigh all the submitted components, "it's not possible to assign a specific weight to any of the 27 factors in and of themselves. The totality will be there before the minister, and he or she, at the time, will decide, based on the totality of information, what the appropriate decision is. Of course a decision is always subject to judicial review."[143]

This is the constitutional paradox that the *Respect for Communities Act* created – if the granting of a section 56 exemption remains at the discretion of the minister of health, despite a 1,639 word amendment (section 56.1) that created a twenty-seven-part application process to ensure it was exercised consistent with the *Canadian Charter*, is it actually possible to legislate the use of ministerial discretion consistent with the Charter, given that the *Respect for Communities Act* does not address unfettered ministerial discretion? The testimony provided by Health Canada officials appears to be that whether the minister of health exercises their discretion consistent with the *Canadian Charter* is ultimately at the discretion of the minister of health, though ultimately subject to judicial review. Constitutional ministerial decision-making at the discretion of the minister of health is how the Harper Conservatives asserted that the circle had been squared and why the government believed the *Respect for Communities Act* was constitutional.

To be sure, there were supporters of the *Respect for Communities Act* that appeared before SECU, drawn principally from law enforcement organizations across the country.[144] These organizations emphasized the inverse relationship between illicit drugs and public safety and lauded the act and its emphasis on the principles of public safety that would be undermined by the establishment of supervised consumption facilities.[145] These defences were not based on the *Respect for Communities Act*'s compatibility with *PHS Community Services Society* or whether the dual purposes of the *CDSA* were adhered to by the act. Stakeholders in the health-care policy sector, as well as the Canadian Bar Association, vigorously opposed the *Respect for Communities Act* as unconstitutional.[146] There were pointed concerns about the application process, its complexity, the lack of transparency surrounding how the minister of health would reach a decision, and the difficulty with completing an application. As David McKeown, from the Toronto Board of Health, noted, "the Toronto board of health considers the requirements in the act to be excessive and quite disproportionate when compared with processes for making decisions about other kinds of health services, and we urge the development of a more appropriate exemption application process."[147] Indeed, the Toronto Board of Health raised a practical criticism of the *Respect for Communities Act* and the consultative process required: "This breadth of consultation is likely to be beyond the capacity of most health service organizations or health systems seeking to implement these services."[148] Moreover, "the proposed bill does not specify what would constitute an acceptable community consultation process, including the range and type of community groups to be consulted."[149]

On the question of police background checks covering a ten-year period for any staff employed by a safe injection facility, the Toronto Board of Health clearly articulated how difficult it would be to include these police checks in a section 56 application and why most applications would be considered incomplete by the minister of health and, thus, returned and not reviewed: "On a practical note, applicants can't really conduct police checks in advance of submitting an exemption, because they're not likely to be recruiting or retaining or hiring staff until they've secured the exemption and are ready to open."[150] This is particularly important, given that police background checks under section 56.1(3)(x) in the *Respect for Communities Act* must be included for an application to be considered complete and reviewable by the minister of health.

There were concerns among opposition committee members that the witnesses chosen by the Conservative majority were not representative of the briefs submitted, which largely opposed the *Respect for Communities Act*.[151] For instance, the Canadian Association of Nurses in HIV/AIDS Care noted that the *Respect for Communities Act* created significant hurdles to the establishment of a safe injection facility and focused exclusively on the public safety objective of the *CDSA*.[152] The Canadian Bar Association concluded that "Bill C-2 would actually subject applicants to such a rigorous application process and so many new considerations as to make it virtually impossible to establish a new safe injection facility, or to continue to operate existing sites."[153] These positions were echoed in briefs submitted by the Canadian

Medical Association,[154] the Canadian Nurses Association,[155] the Canadian Drug Policy Coalition,[156] and the Pivot Legal Society.[157] Indeed, during an appearance by Adrienne Smith for the Pivot Legal Society before SECU, it was suggested that the *Respect for Communities Act* was unconstitutional and would not withstand judicial review because of significant departures from the 2011 decision in *PHS Community Services Society*:

> It answers the requirement that exemptions should generally be granted, which the court directed, with a presumption in the bill that exemptions will be generally withheld. It ignores the requirement that the CDSA is a balancing bill that requires aspects of public health and public safety by framing the question of supervised injection service as a narrow public safety issue, and only in a negative way ... It will invite an extensive and pointless charter challenge and a long series of litigation on a point of law that is already settled, under a legislative framework that is arguably worse than the one the Supreme Court of Canada condemned.[158]

The claim by Ambrose that the *Respect for Communities Act* "follows that Supreme Court ruling to the letter"[159] was heavily criticized by key members of the policy community that advocated for supervised injection sites as a component of harm reduction policy in Canada. Yes, the *Respect for Communities Act* was based on the five conditions established by the McLachlin CJ and, in this respect, did follow the Court's unanimous judgment. But following a decision and complying with it are not one and the same, as most of the briefs submitted to SECU argued.

Sober Second Thought? The Standing Senate Committee on Legal and Constitutional Affairs

Bill C-2 would be passed without amendment by SECU and sent to the Standing Senate Committee on Legal and Constitutional Affairs (LCJC) after it was received by the Senate in March 2015. There is one important difference between the committees that scrutinized the *Respect for Communities Act*: whereas the majority of witnesses called by SECU supported the act (eight of twelve), the majority of the witnesses called by the LCJC (eight of twelve) were opposed to the act.[160] The vast majority of briefs submitted to the LCJC also opposed the *Respect for Communities Act* and simply reiterated the concerns raised in earlier briefs to SECU.[161] In the end, appearances before, and briefs submitted to, the LCJC would make no difference to the content of the *Respect for Communities Act* as it was reported back to the Senate without amendment by the Conservative majority on the LCJC.

The defence of the *Respect for Communities Act* by the minister of health and the minister of public safety and emergency preparedness before the LCJC would see a noticeable shift that emphasized public safety in their appearance before the LCJC. Both ministers linked the *Respect for Communities Act* to the law-and-order legislative initiatives of the Harper government. For instance, Ambrose argued that the purpose of the act was consistent with the National Anti-Drug Strategy:

> Through our government's National Anti-Drug Strategy, we have made significant progress to reduce both the supply of and the demand for these drugs, as well as addressing the crime that's associated with them. If passed, Bill C-2 would ensure that exemptions for activities involving the use of illegal substances at drug injection houses would only be considered once the criteria in the bill have been addressed.[162]

This is a particularly revealing defence of the *Respect for Communities Act*. The National Anti-Drug Strategy removed harm reduction as the fourth pillar in 2007 and required safe injection sites to prioritize the prevention of illicit drug use in order to break the dependency on illicit drugs through treatment and to enforce existing criminal law to disrupt the production and distribution of illicit drugs – in short, not to function as safe injection sites and without the need for section 56 exemptions under the *CDSA*.

The minister of public safety and emergency preparedness began his defence of the *Respect for Communities Act* with a review of the criminal justice initiatives of the Harper government: Bill C-51, *Anti-terrorism Act;* Bill C-32, *Victims Bill of Rights Act;* Bill C-10, *Safe Streets and Communities Act;* the National Crime Prevention Strategy; and mandatory minimum sentences for serious drug offences.[163] Similar to the minister of health, the *Respect for Communities Act* was placed alongside these achievements of the Harper government: "We have strengthened legislation, so that offenders receive sentences that are in line with the seriousness of the crimes they have committed. All those initiatives always have the same shared theme – the safety of Canadians. When it comes to the Respect for Communities Act, we will continue to take measures to ensure the safety of the Canadian public."[164] In addition, Blainey provided a dystopian view of where supervised consumption sites would be located, suggesting that "law-abiding Canadians deserve to know what is happening in their neighbourhoods and they deserve the chance to provide input into decisions that could have an impact on their safety."[165] Despite the implication that supervised consumption sites could be established in tony neighbourhoods such as Westmount in Montreal, Forest Hill in Toronto, or Shaughnessy Heights in Vancouver, and why public consultation was critical, the reality is very different. Supervised consumption facilities are largely located in socially deprived areas where intravenous drug users live on the margins.

Alongside other criminal justice bills,[166] the *Respect for Communities Act* was granted royal assent on June 18, 2015. Did the Harper government comply with the Court's unanimous decision in *PHS Community Services Society*? In the narrowest of senses, one could answer in the affirmative, as the *Respect for Communities Act* was based on the five requirements that the minister of health must consider when evaluating an application for a section 56 exemption. Following the Court's criteria and creating an application process designed to discourage applications, and, if submitted, to create multiple ways that the minister of health can deny a section 56 request, however, place *PHS Community Services Society* and the *Respect for Communities Act* at constitutional odds. It is for these reasons that the Harper government outflanked the McLachlin court and minimized the policy impact of *PHS Community Services Society*.

Conclusion

The Harper Conservatives followed the Supreme Court's criteria in *PHS Community Services Society* only to defy the Court's intention that supervised consumption sites should generally be established if supported by the evidence. They created a statutory framework for ministerial discretion that returned ministerial discretion to where it was before *PHS Community Services Society*. They left the constitutional use of ministerial discretion under the *Respect for Communities Act* at the discretion of the minister of health, subject to judicial review. They returned us to the unconstitutional past while in the constitutional present. Despite a 1,639 word amendment in the form of section 56.1 of the *CDSA*, the approval of supervised consumption sites operated much as it had before the decision in *PHS Community Services Society* and an unprecedented rebuke of the minister of health by the chief justice of the Supreme Court of Canada.[167] And, at the end of the day, the Harper government's minister of health did not review the two applications she received for new supervised consumption sites by the Dr. Peter Centre in Vancouver and Santé Montréal that were submitted after *PHS Community Services Society* but before its defeat at the forty-first general election.

The Conservative government's approach to this issue in the aftermath of *PHS Community Services Society* echoes the famous statement by former President Andrew Jackson in *Worcester v Georgia* – "John Marshall has made his decision; now let him enforce it."[168] Their approach was Jacksonian in that the *Respect for Communities Act* is unambiguous that the impact of *PHS Community Services Society* would be determined by the legislative response and not a judicial decision. Their constitutional truth would only be answered if the *Respect for Communities Act* was, itself, subject to Charter challenge and judicial review. It would be legislative reversal, and not judicial invalidation, that ultimately decided the fate of the *Respect for Communities Act* within two short years. Before it was replaced by the Trudeau government in 2017 with Bill C-37, *Act to Amend the Controlled Drugs and Substances Act*, the *Respect for Communities Act* represented a strong-form legislative response that neutralized a strong-form judicial decision.[169] For over four years, the Harper Conservatives demonstrated how a government can constrain the Court and contain judicial policy impact without invoking the notwithstanding clause – by legislating around the Court while professing to follow the Court.

The Opioid Crisis and Canadian Federalism
Supervised Consumption to Overdose Prevention Sites

7

Although Liberal leader Justin Trudeau signalled support for harm reduction and supervised consumption sites while in opposition, the Liberal platform, "Real Change: A New Plan for a Strong Middle Class," was silent on this issue.[1] It was unclear whether the incoming Liberal government would replace Bill C-2, *Respect for Communities Act* and adjust the application process for section 56 of the *Controlled Drugs and Substances Act (CDSA)*.[2] Nor, for that matter, did the mandate letter issued to Jane Philpott, the minister of health, identify supervised consumption sites as one of the Trudeau government's policy priorities.[3] This was equally true of every mandate letter issued to members of the first Trudeau ministry on November 12, 2015.[4] It would be more than a year after the Trudeau ministry was formed that Philpott introduced legislation to rescind those provisions within the *Respect for Communities Act* involving the use of ministerial discretion under section 56.1 of the *CDSA*. At less than two years, the shelf life of the *Respect for Communities Act* was brief, as it received royal assent in June 2015 before being replaced in May 2017 by Bill C-37, *Act to Amend the Controlled Drugs and Substances Act (Act to Amend the CDSA)*.[5]

Given that harm reduction and supervised consumption sites were not part of the initial Trudeau policy agenda, what explains the fate of the *Respect for Communities Act*? Was it because the Liberal government was inclined to comply with any Supreme Court of Canada decision involving the *Canadian Charter of Rights and Freedoms (Canadian Charter)*,[6] as House Leader Dominic

LeBlanc stated in regard to medical assistance in dying,[7] whereas the Harper Conservatives had a proven penchant for non-compliance and Jacksonian legislative responses?[8] Is there a partisan divide over the question of judicial compliance that separates the two main political parties in Canada? The mandate letter issued to the minister of justice suggests that the Liberal party believed this to be the case as the prime minister's directives were unequivocal that a new path would be chartered regarding the Constitution, the Supreme Court of Canada, and respect for Charter rulings:

> As Minister of Justice and Attorney General of Canada, your overarching goal will be to ensure our legislation meets the highest standards of equity, fairness and respect for the rule of law. I expect you to ensure that our initiatives respect the Constitution of Canada, court decisions, and are in keeping with our proudest legal traditions. You are expected to ensure that the rights of Canadians are protected, that our work demonstrates the greatest possible commitment to respecting the Charter of Rights and Freedoms, and that our government seeks to fulfil our policy goals with the least interference with the rights and privacy of Canadians as possible.[9]

This mandate letter strongly implies that the confrontational stance of the Harper government toward the Supreme Court of Canada would give way to a more compliant Liberal government, particularly when legislating in response to a judicial declaration of unconstitutionality under the *Canadian Charter*.

The fate of the *Respect for Communities Act* raises several questions about judicial policy impact. Did judicial review, albeit based on a 2011 ruling, drive policy change by the Trudeau government in 2017? Did the defeat of the Harper Conservatives allow the Supreme Court of Canada's *PHS Community Services Society* decision to be finally realized and implemented?[10] If the 2011 decision was the driver, does it explain the thirty-eight supervised consumption facilities approved by the Trudeau government once the *Respect for Communities Act* was replaced in 2017?[11] Have we found direct, though delayed, evidence of judicial policy impact and "Charter dialogue" in action? In short, did the transition from Harper to Trudeau matter for harm reduction policy in Canada?

The transition from Harper to Trudeau did matter, at least with respect to the *CDSA*. The dual purposes of the statute were refocused from primarily public security under the Harper Conservatives to public health after 2017.

Although the Trudeau government was slow to signal a change in direction,[12] it came to embrace the unanimous judgment by Chief Justice Beverley McLachlin in *PHS Community Services Society*. In the interim, Philpott reviewed and approved incomplete applications filed in accordance with the *Respect for Communities Act*. And then she jettisoned the Harper-era law with a new legislative framework that streamlined section 56 of the *CDSA* to reflect the essence of the chief justice's reasoning in *PHS Community Services Society*. How could this discretionary approach happen if the Supreme Court of Canada issued a constitutional decision governing the use of ministerial discretion?

In one respect, it shows the ultimate weakness of a constitutional charter of rights that is principally a negative rights instrument. As Kent Roach noted in the context of criminal justice policy,

> the Charter is interpreted and enforced by the courts. The independent courts play a fundamental role in our criminal justice system and I am a proponent of vigorous judicial review that defends the rights of the unpopular. That said, Parliament still plays a dominant role in our criminal justice system. It establishes much of the context for Charter decisions. Even when the Supreme Court makes a Charter ruling, Parliament still retains and often exercises the ability to respond to the ruling with new legislation.[13]

This is equally true of other policy areas judicialized under the *Canadian Charter*. In the case of *PHS Community Services Society*, the Court did not require the establishment of new facilities – it simply required that, if new facilities were to be established, the minister of health must approach their decision-making authority consistent with the *Canadian Charter*. Moreover, during the second year of the Trudeau government, harm reduction was augmented by the use of temporary "urgent public health need sites" or overdose prevention sites (OPS) in the context of the growing opioid crisis in Canada. OPS were permitted by Health Canada in December 2017 when it issued a class exemption to any province or territory that wanted to establish an OPS for a three- to six-month period as a rapid response to the burgeoning opioid crisis.[14] Unlike the Harper government, its successor was supportive of harm reduction via supervised consumption and overdose prevention sites – two federal governments, two federal ministers of health exercising statutory discretion, and two very different outcomes by the Harper and Trudeau governments.

And, in important respects, the transition from Harper to Trudeau did not matter as the establishment of supervised consumption sites and OPS are outside the jurisdictional authority of the federal government. What mattered, once a liberalized approach to harm reduction was implemented by the Trudeau Liberals, was federalism. Or, more precisely, how the governments with constitutional and devolved responsivities for health care – the provincial and territorial governments – reacted to this liberalized legislative approach to the *CDSA*. In the absence of a judicially created obligation to provide supervised consumption services, the provincial and territorial governments decided how to respond. Some jurisdictions applied to Health Canada for a section 56 exemption and were granted authorization to open supervised consumption sites. Others have yet to submit an application for a section 56 exemption under the Trudeau-amended *CDSA*.[15] While the transition from Harper to Trudeau was important in regard to the *CDSA*, the application process, and how the federal minister of health reviews section 56 applications, the transition does not explain the net increase of thirty-eight safe consumption sites that have opened since the 2015 federal election or the dozens of temporary OPS that were rapidly deployed to address the opioid crisis after 2017.

To understand the transformation of harm reduction policy, and supervised consumption services as a component of health policy, requires an appreciation of the implementation context that surrounds this issue.[16] While a clear jurisdictional divide exists, with the criminal regulation of narcotics the responsibility of the federal government, and health care the constitutional authority of the provincial governments, and a devolved responsibility of the three territories, supervised consumption sites and OPS function as a shared responsibility in the Canadian federation.[17] This shared responsibility requires coordinated action between the two orders of government and the devolved assemblies, one to legislate and approve applications for supervised consumption sites (federal government) and two to support the application for a section 56 exemption and the provision of this health service by community organizations (provincial and territorial governments).[18] These criminally regulated health facilities serve as an illustration of what Richard Schultz referred to as the "vice of federalism," whereby the resolution of a policy issue is at the mercy of the division of powers and devolved responsibilities.[19] This is particularly relevant in the context of supervised consumption sites as any government – federal, provincial, or territorial – can disrupt their operation. At the federal level, the Harper and Trudeau governments have demonstrated how a particular approach to the *CDSA* can deny (Harper) or expedite (Trudeau) section 56 applications. This is equally true within the provincial and territorial governments as they retain the discretion over whether to allow a local health authority to submit a section 56 application to Health Canada and whether to use OPS in an emergency context.

This chapter is divided into three sections. The first section explains how supervised consumption sites returned to the policy agenda, first at the provincial and then at the federal level. As I argue, similar to the public health crisis in British Columbia in the early 2000s that saw supervised consumption services emerge as a component of harm reduction, a new public health emergency – the deepening opioid crisis in British Columbia at the beginning of the Trudeau government's time in office – saw supervised consumption sites augmented by OPS re-emerge as a component of harm reduction policy in late 2016. This health crisis, and not a judicial decision, represents the policy driver that saw the provinces, starting with British Columbia, lobby the Trudeau government to revisit and ultimately replace the Harper-era *Respect for Communities Act*. The second section analyzes the key legislative and policy changes introduced by the Trudeau government that created the possibility for more supervised consumption sites provided by the provincial and territorial governments and the use of OPS in the context of the opioid crisis.

The final section analyzes how the provincial and territorial governments responded to a new federal approach to supervised consumption and harm reduction.[20] The approaches have varied. Five provinces account for all thirty-nine facilities that provide supervised consumption services in Canada.[21] Changes in provincial governments have seen changes in the support for supervised consumption sites in provinces such as Alberta, where the Notley government's support gave way to a more cautious approach by the United Conservative Party first led by Jason Kenney.[22] A somewhat different outcome transpired in Ontario when the Wynne government was replaced by the Ford government in 2018.[23] This is not surprising as it is federalism and the electoral system – and not judicial review – that has been the driver of this policy issue, both before and after the 2011 decision in *PHS Community Services Society*.

The issue of supervised consumption facilities has come full circle. It began as an exercise in community activism to address a public health crisis in British Columbia, transitioned into a "complex intergovernmental problem" of multi-level governance,[24] punctuated with a high-profile judicial decision, followed by legislative resistance and then inertia by the Harper

Conservatives, "evidence-based policy" during the "sunny ways" phase of the Trudeau Liberals,[25] only to return as a "complex intergovernmental problem" of multi-level governance in response to provincial and community efforts in 2016 to address the opioid crisis in British Columbia. While the Court's decision was instructive, the life cycle of this policy issue once again reinforces Alan Cairn's caution about placing too much emphasis on a judicial decision,[26] particularly in the context of the evolution and development of Canadian federalism.[27]

The Opioid Crisis in Canada: Federalism as the Policy Driver

The passage of the *Respect for Communities Act* in June 2015 coincided with a new public health crisis – the presence of deadly fentanyl and carfentanyl in illicit drugs that were smuggled into Canada largely from China.[28] According to the Vancouver Police Department, "fentanyl is a less costly synthetic opioid being used by drug traffickers to boost their profits, and as a cheaper alternative to heroin. Fentanyl has been detected in all illicit drugs now, with the exception of marijuana."[29] Fentanyl is prescribed by medical practitioners for those suffering terminal pain and is also used as an anaesthetic. It is incredibly potent, being one hundred times more powerful than morphine and fifty times more potent than heroin.[30] Carfentanyl is ten thousand times stronger than morphine and one hundred times stronger than fentanyl.[31] Fentanyl and carfentanyl smuggled into Canada are produced in clandestine labs in China, where these opioids are unregulated. As the Vancouver Police Department noted, "large amounts of fentanyl are produced and purchased by drug traffickers. It is mixed with a number of illicit street drugs to increase the high and expand profits or sold alone as a cheaper alternative to heroin."[32] The immense danger that fentanyl-laced illicit drug consumption poses is clear: as little as two milligrams, or a few grains of sand, is a lethal dose of fentanyl.[33] For carfentanyl, a lethal dose is twenty micrograms.[34] Most fentanyl-related deaths occur when fentanyl, used as a potent anaesthetic, "turns off the receptors that make you breath" and death occurs when an individual stops breathing in their fentanyl-induced sleep.[35]

Fentanyl- and carfentanyl-laced narcotics are lethal because "illicit drug users are unaware if the heroin they are about to consume is laced with fentanyl. When they inject their standard dose of heroin, they may inadvertently consume a lethal amount of fentanyl."[36] Between January 2016 and March 2021, 22,828 opioid-related deaths occurred in Canada, with the vast majority occurring in British Columbia, Alberta, Ontario, and Quebec.[37] In regard to British Columbia, the opioid crisis was declared a public health emergency by the public health officer under the *Public Health Act* in April 2016 after a significant increase in opioid-related deaths.[38] In response to the burgeoning opioid crisis, Health Canada removed naloxone from the Prescribed Drug List by reclassifying it in March 2016 from Schedule I (only available in a hospital setting authorized by prescription) to Schedule II (non-prescription available over the counter in pharmacies).[39] Health Canada also provided authorization for provincial colleges of pharmacists to determine the classification of naloxone for emergency use. Naloxone is a lifesaving drug that temporarily reverses the effects of opioid overdose for approximately thirty to seventy-five minutes,[40] at which point professional medical attention is required to prevent a fatality.[41]

Also in March 2016, the BC College of Pharmacists amended the *BC Drugs Schedule Regulations* to allow non-prescription naloxone to be available over the counter in pharmacies.[42] While these decisions were important, they did not generally increase access to naloxone as it is an intramuscular injection that requires specialized training for its administration.[43] To address this, Health Canada issued an interim order on July 2016 that approved for sale in Canada a nasal spray version available in the United States, Narcan nasal spray.[44] This interim order would be replaced with the permanent approval of a Canadian version of a naloxone Nasal spray (Narcan) in June 2017.[45] To ensure greater accessibility of Narcan, the BC College of Pharmacists changed the emergency status of naloxone from Schedule II to unscheduled in September 2016.[46] This life-saving and user-friendly product was now readily available as anyone could purchase Narcan, if permitted by their provincial or territorial college of pharmacists, through the emergency unclassified designation for naloxone.

The BC government amended two acts – the *Health Professionals Act* and the *Emergencies Health Services Act* – on October 13, 2016, which allowed first responders such as paramedics, firefighters, and the police as well as healthcare professionals, social workers, and private citizens to administer naloxone in any setting.[47] All of these policy changes occurred not as a result of *PHS Community Services Society* acting as a policy driver but, rather, as examples of policy change occurring within the context of what has been labelled a "complex intergovernmental problem" – issues such as the opioid crisis, climate change, and the COVID-19 pandemic that cannot be addressed by a single level of government, issues that require high levels of coordination between these governments, and policy problems that "challenge the existing norms and venues of intergovernmental relations."[48]

Although the Trudeau government was a willing partner in addressing the opioid crisis through a collaborative approach with British Columbia and other provinces experiencing the ravages of fentanyl, it struck a cautious posture in deciding whether to repeal sections of the *Respect for Communities Act*. One of the first acts of the Trudeau government was to approve the application for a section 56 exemption submitted by the Dr. Peter Centre in the Downtown Eastside of Vancouver (DTES).[49] This application had been submitted to former Minister of Health Rona Ambrose in February 2014,[50] but a decision was not rendered before the 2015 federal election and the defeat of the Harper government. The approval of the Dr. Peter Centre doubled the number of supervised consumption sites operating in the DTES – and in Canada – by January 2016. In March, Health Canada approved three applications to establish supervised consumption sites in Montreal, increasing the total number to five and establishing the first facilities outside of the DTES.[51]

Perhaps more importantly, Philpott visited Insite in the DTES in late January 2016, which none of her Conservative predecessors had done. This would be followed by the minister of health granting Insite its longest exemption under section 56 of the *CDSA*, when Health Canada approved a four-year extension in March 2016.[52] In recognition of the growing opioid crisis, the minister of health announced in late July that an opioid summit would take place in November with the federal, provincial, and territorial governments as well as with the broader policy community.[53] Finally, the Trudeau government reversed the Harper government's ban on the use of prescription heroin as part of the special access program at Health Canada, which permits medical professionals to prescribe medical-quality heroin for severe substance abusers.[54]

While these were important collaborative changes, as the Trudeau government demonstrated that the restrictive application criteria in the *Respect for Communities Act* could result in the approval of a section 56 exemption under the *CDSA*, the minister of health indicated that the Trudeau government did not intend to revisit this Harper-era law.[55] Perhaps, as Philpott noted, the Liberal government expected to receive more applications under the *Respect for Communities Act* as the change in government was more significant than a legislative change.[56] There is some truth to this, as Chapter 6 showed that the approval of a section 56 exemption remains at the discretion of the minister of health, which could either be used to rebuff (Harper) or support (Trudeau) additional supervised consumption sites. The change in government, however, did not address the fundamental flaw in the *Respect for Communities Act* – namely, that the section 56 application process was cumbersome, if not impossible, for local health authorities to complete, which significantly reduced the number of applications that a favourably disposed minister of health would receive.

We know that the Trudeau government eventually jettisoned the *Respect for Communities Act* in 2017, bringing in changes to the *CDSA* that eased the section 56 application requirements for supervised consumption sites as well as introducing additional measures to address the burgeoning opioid crisis that most impacted British Columbia. What motivated the Trudeau government to shed its reluctance to reform this Harper-era law? Was it the "evidence-based approach" to public policy that the Liberal Party first trumpeted while in opposition? Was it the minister of justice's mandate letter that required the government to revisit its litigation strategy and to strike a new course in relation to the *Canadian Charter* and parliamentary compliance with court rulings? Maybe. But maybe is not good enough when explaining policy impact or changes in direction to address a complex intergovernmental problem such as illicit drug use and the ensuing public health crises.

The same type of actors that pressured a former Liberal government for the establishment of Insite in the DTES in 2003 – community activists, the city of Vancouver, public health organization, and the province of British Columbia – reformed as a result of the opioid crisis and directed their pressure toward a new Liberal government led by Justin Trudeau. This bottom-up, community-led explanation,[57] and not a top-down response to judicial review, provides the better analytical frame to understand the fate of the *Respect for Communities Act* and the issue of supervised consumption sites under the Trudeau government. At the national level, it was NDP members of parliament (MPs) from Vancouver, such as Don Davies, Jenny Kwan, and Murray Rankin, who first called on the Trudeau government to revisit this Harper-era law and address the difficulties in the application process.[58] It was a coalition of nine actors that co-signed a letter from the mayor of Vancouver to the minister of health in August 2016, including the provincial Minister of Health Terry Lake, the chief medical officer of Vancouver Coastal Health, the provincial health officer, and the Pivot Legal Society, which urged Philpott to reconsider her "position and begin steps to repeal the Respect for Communities Act, so that people who need access to medical treatment can get it as soon as possible."[59] And it was a unanimous motion proposed by NDP MP Don Davies and accepted by the Standing Committee on Health to study the opioid crisis on September 22, 2016[60] that resulted in a report submitted to Parliament on December 12, 2016.[61]

Immediately after the Standing Committee on Health unanimously agreed to study the opioid crisis, the minister of health announced, for the first time, that the Trudeau government would consider changes to the *Respect for Communities Act*,[62] though it stopped short of calling for its repeal in mid-November.[63] The Standing Committee on Health released an interim report on November 18 that made a number of important recommendations that were included in the final report: that harm reduction be reinstated as a pillar of Canada's drug strategy (Recommendation 4) and that the *Respect for Communities Act* be either repealed or significantly amended "where it creates barriers to communities in establishment safe consumptions sites" (Recommendation 8).[64]

Events on the ground would force the hands of the Trudeau government and the government of British Columbia. Unsanctioned "pop-up" supervised consumptions sites were established by community activists frustrated by the *Respect for Communities Act* in cities such as Surrey in November 2019.[65] They were also frustrated by Ottawa's failure to act on the BC minister of health's request to declare the opioid crisis a national emergency. This was followed by the establishment of the Overdose Prevention Society in Vancouver, which created a new unsanctioned pop-up to deal with the opioid crisis – the OPS, which was described as "low-threshold supervised injection facilities" that operated in the absence (defiance?) of a section 56 exemption under the *CDSA*.[66]

This pattern of community-driven activism in late 2015 is a throwback to the events that preceded the establishment of Insite in the DTES in 2003 – the creation of the Vancouver Area Network of Drug Users, which began a needle exchange program; the construction of an unsanctioned safe consumption site at a hair salon by the Portland Hotel Society at what is now Insite in 2002;[67] and the eventual granting of a section 56 exemption by the Chrétien government in 2003 due to pressure by the city of Vancouver and the provincial government. This is not to suggest that the Trudeau government failed to recognize the consequences of the opioid crisis or the need for policy innovation. However, as a newly elected majority government, it did appear to be reacting to events and other governments in the federation, particularly British Columbia. In July 2016, the Clark government in British Columbia established the Joint Task Force on Overdose Response, a group of stakeholders tasked with policy innovation.[68] One such recommendation involved publicly sanctioning the use of OPS as a deterrent to the spread of unsanctioned pop-up tent services such as those offered by the Overdose Prevention Society in Vancouver.[69]

On December 9, Terry Lake, the provincial minister of health, issued a ministerial order under the *Emergency Health Services Act* and the *Health Authorities Act* permitting the provincial health officer to authorize the opening of emergency overdose prevention services by the regional health boards.[70] This resulted in the immediate opening of more than twenty OPS in British Columbia within a matter of days.[71] According to the provincial minister of health, legal advice indicated that an OPS did not require an exemption under section 56 of the *CDSA* issued by the federal minister of health. Based on this advice, the services provided at an OPS were considered distinct from those of a supervised consumption site and simply required approval by the provincial minister of health.[72] Health Canada defines a supervised consumption site as

> a safe, clean space for people to bring their own drugs to use, in the presence of trained staff. This prevents accidental overdoses and reduces the spread of infectious diseases, such as HIV. Supervised consumption sites may offer a range of evidence-based harm reduction services, such as drug checking. The sites also provide access to important health and social services, including substance use treatment for those who are ready.[73]

A section 56 exemption is necessary to ensure that staff are exempt from criminal prosecution due to the potential administration of illicit substances prohibited by the *CDSA*.

OPS, in contrast, "are uniquely positioned as low-barrier points of introduction to health and/or social services for people with substance use issues" that "provide various levels of services, including overdose prevention education and take-home Naloxone training and distribution." They also provide many services found in a supervised consumption site as "[s]ome sites may also distribute harm reduction supplies (such as sterile needles, filters, cookers, condoms, etc.), offer safe disposal options, and facilitate referrals to mental health and substance use services. Currently, each British Columbia overdose prevention site offers drug-checking services."[74] The main difference appears to be that supervised consumption sites allow substance abusers to inject or ingest illicit substances under medical supervision or with assistance, whereas overdose consumption sites provide naloxone and drug-checking services for the presence of fentanyl and other dangerous synthetic opioids by medical professionals. In both instances, substances prohibited by the *CDSA* are either consumed or tested in provincially supported facilities.

The differences, in all honesty, are more apparent than real as they are considered to be "emergency" supervised consumption sites by their supporters that can be established while awaiting approval for a section 56 exemption.[75] Lake acknowledged the legal uncertainty of overdose prevention sites in relation to the *CDSA*: "Are we skirting federal law? You could make that argument, I guess, but we weren't prepared to wait for changes to save lives ... These are, I hope, temporary measures until we get approval for supervised consumption sites in all areas of the province. You have to do what you need to do to keep people alive."[76] If they are distinct from supervised consumption sites, it begs the question why OPS were not opened by the BC provincial government during the Harper years as a way to combat the public health crises in the DTES. Perhaps they are not that different, and the only distinction that matters is that the Trudeau Liberals were willing to accept (or overlook) OPS as a necessary response to the "complex intergovernmental problem" posed by the opioid crisis, whereas the Harper Conservatives surely would not have condoned OPS operating outside of the *CDSA*. This legal ambiguity would persist for a year, from December 2016 to December 2017, when Health Canada provided emergency class exemptions (three to six months) to provinces and territories that wanted to establish a temporary "urgent public health need site" in regard to the opioid crisis.[77] Health Canada proactively extended the class exemption for OPS until September 21, 2021, due to COVID-19, and many of these "temporary" facilities operated for nearly five years until their approval as supervised consumptions sites under the *CDSA*.[78]

A number of events collided in December 2016 that signalled that a fundamental change toward supervised consumption sites and harm reduction was forthcoming. On December 8, 2016, the Standing Committee on Health adopted the *Report and Recommendations on the Opioid Crisis in Canada* with its thirty-eight recommendations, and this report was presented to the House of Commons on December 12. The Trudeau government responded positively to this report and formally endorsed, among other recommendations, that harm reduction be reinstated and that the Harper-era approach to section 56 exemptions under the *CDSA* be revisited.[79] On the same day that the House of Commons received the standing committee's report, the minister of health introduced two important changes. First, the Harper-era National Anti-Drug Strategy, which transferred this responsibility from the minister of health to the minister of public security and emergency preparedness and removed harm reduction as the fourth pillar was replaced with the Canadian Drugs and Substances Strategy. The change occurred, according to the Trudeau government's press release, because the National Anti-Drug Strategy "did not reflect this government's approach."[80] This resulted in the reinstatement of harm reduction as the fourth pillar of the Canadian Drugs and Substances Strategy, and responsibility reverted to the minister of health.[81]

By this simple action, nearly ten years of viewing supervised consumption sites through the prism of criminal justice policy ended. The Harper interregnum gave way to the policy framework that both preceded and succeeded it. And, in recognition that the *Respect for Communities Act* had created a burdensome application, the minister of health tabled the *Act to Amend the CDSA*.[82] The main objective of the *Act the Amend the CDSA* was to simplify the application process for section 56 exemptions for the purposes of approving supervised consumption sites.[83] Although supervised consumption sites and harm reduction were not part of the health minister's mandate letter, within thirteen months, these issues would, along with medical assistance in dying, figure prominently in Philpott's brief tenure as minister of health. Indeed, Bill C-37 is the only bill that Philpott introduced into Parliament as minister of health (on December 12, 2016), which was granted royal assent (on May 18, 2017) before her appointment as the inaugural minister of Indigenous services on August 28, 2017.

The introduction of the *Act to Amend the CDSA*, and the reinstatement of harm reduction as the fourth pillar, signalled a return to a cooperative approach to supervised consumption sites by the Trudeau government and its provincial and territorial counterparts. But the decision in *PHS Community Services Society* was not the policy driver that saw the Trudeau government remove parts of the *Respect for Communities Act* that suppressed section 56 applications. Instead, what drove this policy issue after 2015 was the same trigger that led to the opening of Insite in 2003 – a public health emergency, caused this time by the opioid crisis, which saw an expansion in the number of supervised consumption sites and the use of overdose prevention sites – first by provincial authorization and then by federal approval.[84] To be clear, the legislative changes introduced by the Trudeau government are important. But they were not required in light of the decision in *PHS Community Services Society*. The fundamental problem with the Supreme Court of Canada's remedy in this case, and what the Harper government exploited, was the assumption that a constitutional use of ministerial discretion could be operationalized in regard to section 56 of the *CDSA*.

Rescinding the *Respect for Communities Act*

Bill C-37 was introduced into Parliament on December 12, 2016, and was shaped by two contexts. First, the policy context wrought by the opioid crisis, in which the federal government, eight provincial and territorial governments, and a range of public health and community organizations issued a joint statement in November 2016 calling for immediate steps to address this public health emergency.[85] During the second reading debate, Philpott noted that the "legislation is introduced in the context where Canada is facing a national public health crisis related to opioids, characterized by ever-increasing rates of harm, overdose, and death."[86] The second context was legislative in which the *Respect for Communities Act*, by apparent design, created an arduous application process that suppressed section 56 applications and their review by the minister of health. Nor did the act place a statutory requirement on the minister of health to reach a decision on an application submitted in conformity with the *Respect for Communities Act*. Further, the minister of health was not required to provide a reasoned decision if a section 56 application was refused. As discussed in Chapter 6, two applications were submitted under the *Respect for Communities Act* to then Minister of Health Rona Ambrose, but it is unclear whether these applications were even reviewed as a decision was not forthcoming before the 2015 federal election.

At second reading, the minister of health noted that supervised consumption sites were an important component to tackle the public health aspects of the opioid crisis, but the minister informed Parliament that the *Respect for Communities Act* "introduced unnecessary onerous requirements that must be met by communities before the Minister of Health could even respond to the request for an exemption."[87] The main impact of the Harper-era legislation, according to the minister of health, was to deter and delay section 56 applications as the process required a multi-year time frame for completion by community organizations, departmental review, and potential ministerial approval. Commenting on the approval of three supervised consumption sites in Montreal in 2017, the minister of health identified the main problem with the *Respect for Communities Act:* "The time frame to approve these sites was unacceptable. It took a year and a half, and that was due to the onerous 26 criteria that existed under the previous legislation."[88] The Harper-era law, given that it was designed to discourage and delay applications, marginalized harm reduction as a strategy to address the immediate public health emergency posed by the opioid crisis.

The amendments proposed in the *Act to Amend the CDSA* were directed to addressing systemic delays in section 56 applications created by the *Respect for Communities Act* and to empower the Canadian Border Services Agency (CBSA) to reduce the smuggling of opioids into Canada from China. In this respect, it attempted to balance the dual purposes of the *CDSA* – public health and public safety – which were clearly reflected in the *Act to Amend the CDSA*, as both the *CDSA* and the *Customs Act* were amended in light of the opioid crisis.[89] Before the *Act to Amend the CDSA*, the CBSA was prevented from opening international mail and packages weighing thirty grams or less, even if border agents had reasonable grounds to suspect that such items contained substances prohibited or regulated by the *CDSA*.[90] If the CBSA had reasonable grounds to suspect a package or letter weighing thirty grams or less, it was required to receive written permission from the sender to open the item. If permission was denied, the package was simply returned to the sender without any legal consequence.

The background materials on the *Act to Amend the CDSA* note that "this exception allowed illegal importers of dangerous substances, such as pure fentanyl, to ship many separate small envelopes, weighing 30 g or less, knowing some would get through and that there were no legal consequences for the importer if some packages were detained."[91] Once pure fentanyl enters Canada through international mail, it is combined with other illicit substances and repurposed with the use of pill presses. This restriction on packages weighing thirty grams or less was removed by the *Act to Amend the CDSA* in an effort to stem the importation of opioids in small, but deadly, quantities from China. Moreover, to disrupt the reprocessing of pure fentanyl smuggled into Canada, the *Act to Amend the CDSA* also prohibited the "unregistered importation of designated devices that may be used in the illicit manufacture of controlled substances, such as pill presses and encapsulators."[92]

The main differences between the *Respect for Communities Act* and the *Act to Amend the CDSA* are presented in Table 7.1. Direct evidence of judicial impact can be found in the legislative response introduced as the *Act to Amend the CDSA* by the Trudeau government. The minister of health was clear that the amendments proposed as section 56.1 of the *CDSA* were explicitly based on *PHS Community Services Society*, particularly the reduction of the application criteria from twenty-six under the Harper-era law to the five outlined by the Court in this decision. It has been suggested that the five conditions outlined by the McLachlin CJ were merely clarified by the Harper government as twenty-six requirements,[93] which totalled fifty for new applications and fifty-three for renewals once the sub-provisions are included. Whether that is true, the relationship between the *Act to Amend the CDSA* and *PHS Community Services Society* is without ambiguity, as the minister of health asserted that "in fact, the criteria in the proposed legislation are exactly those written in paragraph 153 of the Supreme Court decision."[94] The section 56.1 application requirements were reduced in the following way:

> 56.1(2) An application for an exemption under subsection (1) shall include information, submitted in the form and manner determined by the Minister, regarding the intended public health benefits of the site and information, if any, related to
>
> (a) the impact of the site on crime rates;
> (b) the local conditions indicating a need for the site;
> (c) the administrative structure in place to support the site;
> (d) the resources available to support the maintenance of the site; and
> (e) expressions of community support or opposition.[95]

As the minister of health noted during her appearance before the Senate Standing Committee on Legal and Constitutionals Affairs, the purpose of section 56.1 was to simplify the application process and to allow the provision of a timely and public decision for communities that wanted supervised consumption sites.[96] One way that the *Act to Amend the CDSA* facilitated this was by reducing the five letters from key actors required by the *Respect for Communities Act*, to a single letter from the provincial or territorial minister with responsibility for supervised consumption sites.[97] Although letters from the local police force and the local government actor were no longer required, the minister of health noted that public consultation would remain as part of the *Act to Amend the CDSA*, and the views of these actors may inform the assessment of public consultation that remained within section 56.1 of the *CDSA*.[98]

Other cumbersome requirements of the *Respect for Communities Act* were eliminated. The requirement whereby all personnel employed in a potential supervised consumption site required a ten-year police background check (section 56(3)(w)) was reduced to simply key personnel.[99] Given that peer review by former substance abusers is a component of harm reduction strategies at safe consumption sites, police background checks of former substance abusers, and the likelihood that such individuals would fail a police background check, appears designed to complicate the submission of a successful section 56 application. Further, the requirements under the *Respect*

Table 7.1 Key legislative changes: From Bill C-2, *Respect for Communities Act* (Harper) to Bill C-37, *Act to Amend the CDSA* (Trudeau)

Criteria	*Respect for Communities Act* (Harper)	*Act to Amend the CDSA* (Trudeau)
Application criteria	Legislation lists twenty-six criteria to be addressed in an application for an exemption to establish a supervised consumption site.	Legislation would list the five factors outlined by the Supreme Court of Canada in its 2011 decision regarding Insite.
Review of applications	The minister cannot consider an application until it is complete.	Legislation would clarify that the minister could begin to review the application before all information has been submitted.
Renewal of exemptions	When renewing an exemption, applicants must address the twenty-six criteria as well as two additional criteria.	Applicants would only be required to indicate any changes in information since their last exemption was granted.
Guiding principles	The minister should consider six principles when assessing supervised consumption site applications.	The principles would be removed, recognizing that when properly established and maintained, supervised consumption sites save lives.
Additional public consultations	The minister of health can choose to post a notice to seek comments from the public for ninety days on a specific application.	The minister could still choose to post a notice, but there would be more flexibility on timing (could be posted for up to ninety days).
Transparency	There is no requirement for the minister to be transparent about decisions on exemptions.	The minister would be required to make public any decision on an application, including the reasons for a decision to deny an application.
Exemptions	Exemptions to conduct research with illicit substances are not permitted.	Exemptions to conduct research with illicit substances are permitted.

Source: Government of Canada, "Backgrounder: Streamlining Applications for Supervised Consumption Sites," https://www.canada.ca/en/health-canada/news/2016/12/streamlining-applications-supervised-consumption-sites.html.

for Communities Act that an application demonstrate that supervised consumption sites are effective and have a health benefit were removed by the *Act to Amend the CDSA*. According to the minister of health, this requirement was deleted because "evidence shows that, when properly established and maintained, supervised consumption sites in communities that want them and need them will save lives and improve health without increasing drug use or crime rates."[100] This view was reinforced in the preamble to the *Act to Amend the CDSA*, whereby the starting point was that the health benefit of safe consumption sites were proven – and did not need to be proven, as was the case under the Harper-era *Respect for Communities Act*: "Whereas harm reduction is an important component of a comprehensive, compassionate and evidence-based drug policy that complements prevention, treatment and enforcement measures."[101]

Unlike the *Respect for Communities Act*, in which the minister of health would only review a section 56 application once completed (section 56(3)), the *Act to Amend the CDSA* allows the minister of health to review applications in progress. Moreover, to support local community organizations in the submission of a section 56.1 application, the Office of Controlled Substances at Health Canada is authorized to provide feedback on draft applications.[102] It also created a guidance document that explains the various application components and their requirements for community organizations.[103] As Chapter 6 demonstrated, the *Respect for Communities Act* included a complex number of requirements for the completion of a section 56 application (section 56(3)– (4)) as well as six guiding principles that the minister of health must use to evaluate applications submitted in accordance with section 56 of the *CDSA:*

> 56(5) The Minister may only grant an exemption for a medical purpose under subsection (2) to allow certain activities to take place at a supervised consumption site in exceptional circumstances and after having considered the following principles:
>
> (*a*) illicit substances may have serious health effects;
> (*b*) adulterated controlled substances may pose health risks;
> (*c*) the risks of overdose are inherent to the use of certain illicit substances;
> (*d*) strict controls are required, given the inherent health risks associated with controlled substances that may alter mental processes;

(e) organized crime profits from the use of illicit substances; and
(f) criminal activity often results from the use of illicit substances.[104]

In the *Respect for Communities Act*, the minister of health was only permitted to grant exemptions in "exceptional circumstances" after having considered the six guiding principles outlined in section 56(5). This flies in the face of the constitutional requirements established by a unanimous court in *PHS Community Services Society*, where McLachlin CJ determined that when "the evidence indicates that a supervised injection site will decrease the risk of death and disease, and there is little or no evidence that it will have a negative impact on public safety, the Minister should generally grant an exemption."[105]

Both the requirement that an exemption would only be granted in exceptional circumstances and the six guiding principles of ministerial decision-making were removed by the *Act to Amend the CDSA*. The background materials to this act noted that the principles were removed because of a different starting point in the legislation and the recognition that "when properly established and maintained, supervised consumption sites save lives."[106] And in an effort to increase the transparency with ministerial discretion, unlike the *Respect for Communities Act*, which did not require the minister of health to reach a decision on a completed application or release a reasoned decision when rejecting a section 56 application, the *Act to Amend the CDSA* required the minister of health to publish any decision on a section 56.1 exemption and to provide a reasoned decision.[107] Finally, and what would prove to be a major departure from the *Respect for Communities Act*, supervised consumption sites seeking a renewal are now required to simply provide "any changes in information since their last exemption was granted."[108] In contrast, the *Respect for Communities Act* required the submission of a completely new application for health organizations seeking a renewal on a section 56 exemption.

In a rare move, and contrary to party policy, the NDP tabled a motion at first reading to fast-track Bill C-37 to the Senate.[109] This is a legislative procedure that requires unanimous consent by the house and, if approved, would have seen the bill proceed directly to the Senate, bypassing second reading, committee scrutiny, and third reading in the House of Commons. The NDP's motion was sponsored by Don Davies, of Vancouver Kingsway, and, although it failed due to opposition by the Conservative Party, it was motivated to address the opioid crisis in British Columbia by relaxing the application requirements for a section 56.1 exemption under the *CDSA*. With cross-party support in the House of Commons, and only the Conservative Party opposed, the progression of Bill C-37 to the Senate was never in doubt. Nor was its passage by the Senate, as the combined Senate Liberal Caucus (n = 18) and the Independent Senate Group (n = 35) constituted a majority in the upper chamber.[110] As studies have shown, the Independent Senate Group has overwhelmingly supported government bills during the Trudeau ministry,[111] and Jean-François Godbout has asked whether the non-partisan Senate has become a "crypto-liberal Senate."[112] After a debate that largely focused on the procedural limitations of the *Respect for Communities Act* and the desire to address systemic delay in the approval of supervised consumption sites, Bill C-37 proceeded to the Senate on a third reading vote of 215 to eighty, with only the Conservative Party voting against the bill. In the Senate, Bill C-37 was passed by a "recorded division," which occurs when at least one senator indicates opposition to a bill. Although a recorded division does not reveal the votes of individual senators, given that Bill C-37 was supported by, at a minimum, the Independent Senate Group and the Senate Liberal Group, it received strong cross-grouping support in the non-partisan "crypto-liberal" Senate.

In many respects, the *Respect for Communities Act* and the *Act to Amend the CDSA* are mirror opposites, both in the purpose of their amendments, the framing of the issue, their fidelity to the Supreme Court of Canada's decision, and their legislative journeys. How the two governments responded to this judicialized issue of public policy, and the respective time frames of the *Respect for Communities Act* and the *Act to Amend the CDSA*, is instructive. *PHS Community Services Society* was released by the Supreme Court on September 30, 2011.[113] Although the unanimous decision upheld the constitutionality of the *CDSA* and simply took issue with the use of ministerial discretion, the Harper government introduced two legislative responses. The first, Bill C-65, *An Act to Amend the Controlled Drugs and Substances Act*, was introduced nearly two years after *PHS Community Services Society* and only completed first reading on June 6, 2013 before the first session of the forty-first Parliament was prorogued on September 13, 2013.[114] Bill C-65 would be reintroduced as Bill C-2 on October 17, 2013, one day after the second session of the forty-first Parliament began. The Harper government's response to the Supreme Court of Canada's decision received royal assent on June 18, 2015, with a time frame from introduction to royal assessment at more than twenty-four months. In contrast, the Trudeau government introduced Bill C-37 on December 12, 2016, and royal assent was granted five months later on May 18, 2017.

Why are the legislative time frames of these respective bills instructive? As Chapter 6 argued, there were simpler, and timelier, responses to *PHS Community Services Society* available to the Harper government. A ministerial directive or regulations pertaining to section 56 of the *CDSA* were options, and they would not have required the nearly four years that it took to pass the *Respect for Communities Act*: a twenty-one-month delay in introducing Bill C-65 (September 2011 to June 2013), and the two-year period from the introduction of Bill C-65 to Bill C-2's royal assent (June 2013 to June 2015). By legislating, the Harper government revealed an essential component of judicial policy impact – that the Supreme Court of Canada, in the context of statutory interpretation or the uses of ministerial discretion, is an implementer-dependent institution. Indeed, the Harper government demonstrated how opposition to a judicial decision can negate judicial policy impact or, at a minimum, bring judicial impact to a standstill through a drawn-out legislative response. Perhaps the Supreme Court of Canada learned the lesson of legislative delay when it crafted its section 24(1) remedy in *Canada (Attorney General) v Bedford*,[115] which involved three *Criminal Code* provisions regarding prostitution, and *Carter v Canada (Attorney General)*, which involved the *Criminal Code* restriction on physician-assisted death.[116] Both decisions were released while the Harper government was in office and saw the Court suspend the declarations of unconstitutionality in *Bedford* and *Carter* for twelve months. Maybe the Court wanted to avoid a repeat of *PHS Community Services Society*, and, in these cases, it specified the time frame in which Parliament must legislate to avoid the invalidation of the *Criminal Code* provisions and the full force of judicial remedy.

The Trudeau government demonstrates the conditions under which the Supreme Court of Canada can have policy impact, at least in regard to legislation introduced in response to a judicial decision. The main condition of policy impact being that an incumbent government supports the Court's decision and legislates accordingly or at least does not oppose it. In her study of equality rights and same-sex marriage, Linda White demonstrated the implementation gap that occurs when one order of government determines the legality of action (federal) and one order provides access to the service (provincial/territorial): "Because a federal system of government provides for two loci of authority and thus two levels of government acting on behalf of the people, legislative compliance with the wishes of the people as interpreted by the Supreme Court becomes difficult to ensure, even if one level of government is agreeable."[117] What the *Respect for Communities Act* shows is that an implementation gap occurs when an incumbent government legislates in opposition to a judicial decision.[118] Similarly, the *Act to Amend the CDSA* shows how the implementation chain can be progressed by a government that legislates according to a judicial decision, though this does not ensure implementation for the reasons suggested by White in regard to a federation such as Canada's.

And *Respect for Communities Act* and the *Act to Amend the CDSA* share an affinity. They are simply one piece in the implementation puzzle that decriminalized harm reduction services operate within. While rescinding the *Respect for Communities Act* removed a hinderance that thwarted the establishment of supervised consumption sites, the federal government lacks the constitutional or devolved authority to establish these facilities, except in relation to Indigenous peoples under section 91(24) of the *Constitution Act, 1867*, and inmates within federal penitentiaries.[119] While an additional thirty-eight facilities commenced operations since the Trudeau government, this is the wrong way to look at this public policy outcome. The better angle, I believe, is to emphasize that the provincial governments of British Columbia, Alberta, Saskatchewan, Ontario, and Quebec supported the submission of thirty-eight applications to the federal minister of health. Without providing both jurisdictional and financial support for these institutions, the federal minister of health would have no applications to review. This is a truer depiction of the process that establishes these facilities, which is far more complex than the review of a section 56 application by the federal minister of health.

As of July 2023, five provincial and all three territorial jurisdictions have yet to submit a section 56 application to Health Canada, though the confidence and supply agreement between the Yukon Liberal minority government and Yukon NDP calls for a facility in Whitehorse.[120] How should a policy change implemented by a minority of the jurisdictions in Canada be interpreted? One would be that it provides evidence for limited judicial impact. This is not my interpretation of uneven access to this health service after the Harper interregnum. This view creates an expectation – an unrealistic one – that a negative rights decision by the Supreme Court of Canada can compel the provision of a public service by the provincial and territorial governments. As Colleen Flood, Carolyn Tuohy, and Mark Stabile noted in the context of Medicare, "the role of the courts in determining the boundaries of Medicare is often overstated in the media and/or assumed to be much more significant than is actually the case."[121] Federalism and devolution, for the provinces and territories respectively, explain this policy diversity and the jurisdictional differences. Within this explanation are the electoral process, the defeat of governments that support this component of harm reduction policy, their replacement with governments opposed (or vice versa), as well as the ongoing debate over public policy endemic in any parliamentary democracy. To place too much emphasis on a judicial decision is to misunderstand the policy process, even one where an issue has been judicialized. The chapter now turns to the last piece of this judicialized puzzle, those governments with the jurisdictional and devolutionary authority for harm reduction services.

Provincial and Territorial Responses to, and Responsibility for, Supervised Consumption Sites

Four provinces account for all but one of the thirty-nine supervised consumption sites currently operating in Canada, and most are at fixed locations (n = 38) within downtown urban centres.[122] As studies have shown in relation to access to services developed within a judicialized environment, such as abortion,[123] considerable variation exists between and within jurisdictions. Given that thirteen jurisdictions have constitutional or devolved responsibility for health care in Canada, it is unsurprising that a diverse response to the *Act to Amend the CDSA* has occurred. As the Supreme Court of Canada noted in *Auton* in regard to the *Canada Health Act*, "the CHA [*Canada Health Act*] is a framework by which provinces must abide if they are to receive federal funding for health care. The framework rests on the principle of universal provision of insured benefits and comprehensiveness of coverage for insured core services, largely those provided by physicians and hospitals. Insurance of non-core services is left to provincial discretion."[124] Supervised consumption sites are "non-core services," and this explains why a minority of jurisdictions authorize them as a component of harm reduction policy. The provinces and territories have the discretion, despite *PHS Community Services Society*, whether to fund and allow the establishment of these non-core health services. This is explained by two factors. First, the limited nature of the remedy in *PHS Community Services Society* in which the Court ordered the Harper government to reissue a section 56 exemption for Insite in the DTES but did not create a constitutional requirement to establish additional facilities. And, second, the fact that supervised consumptions sites fall outside of the funding mechanism and universality provision of the *Canada Health Act* due to their "non-core service" designation. Presently, the most easterly location is downtown Montreal and the most northerly one is Grande Prairie, Alberta. This will surely change with the likely approval of Quebec City's section 56.1 application that is currently at the review stage and if the Yukon government honours its confidence and supply agreement with the Yukon NDP and establishes the proposed site in Whitehorse.[125]

In addition to the existing thirty-nine facilities, there are nine open applications at the review stage at Health Canada. As the health ministers in the Trudeau ministry have only approved, and never rejected, a section 56.1 application, the number of supervised consumption sites operating in Canada will rise to at least forty-eight during the current Parliament.[126] The regional imbalance will continue, however, as none of the applications have been submitted by jurisdictions that do not have a supervised consumption site. All provinces and territories have harm reduction strategies, but not all of them include supervised consumption sites as a component.[127] Again, this is permitted under federalism for the provinces and devolved authority for the territories. The Court is thus dependent on actors in the federation to implement its decision if they so choose. The provinces and territories are not required to provide supervised consumption sites nor to submit section 56.1 applications to the federal minister of health. Thus, the "implementation gap" that was identified by White exists in regard to supervised consumption sites largely because of the federal/devolved principle in Canada and the non-core designation for supervised consumption sites.[128]

Although five jurisdictions permit supervised consumption sites, the remainder of this chapter will focus on two that established facilities under the *Act to Amend the CDSA* (Ontario and Alberta). The reason for this narrowed focus is the following. As the momentum for supervised consumption sites began in British Columbia, little is to be gained from a discussion after the Harper era in this province – British Columbia has simply continued its approach and established four facilities in addition to Insite in the DTES of Vancouver. There are now a total of five facilities within the province, and two open applications in Kelowna and Nanaimo, which are at the review stage at Health Canada. Similarly, the city of Montreal unsuccessfully pressured the Harper government to approve supervised consumption sites.[129] Four facilities now operate in Montreal since the election of the Trudeau government.[130] If the four open applications in Quebec City, Gatineau, Montreal, and Chicoutimi are approved, Quebec will have at least eight facilities by the end of the current Parliament.

Manitoba has yet to establish a supervised consumption site or submit a section 56.1 application to Health Canada. The former Pallister government commissioned a report on their establishment, which ultimately recommended against these facilities.¹³¹ There was some controversy over this report and whether the initial support for supervised consumption sites in the draft report was removed due to government pressure.¹³² Moreover, Pallister's successor as leader of the Progressive Conservative Party and premier, Heather Stefanson, has maintained this approach to harm reduction policy. In the remaining provinces and territories, with the exception of Yukon, there has yet to be a public debate within the provincial legislature or territorial assembly on this issue. These jurisdictions have harm reduction strategies such as needle distribution and free access to naloxone. However, incorporating supervised consumption sites within their harm reduction strategies has not been discussed in any meaningful way, and none of the departments of health have begun consultations on this issue.

Why Ontario and Alberta? In the case of Ontario and Alberta, the issue of supervised consumption sites featured prominently during provincial election campaigns in 2018 and 2019 respectively. The governments that established supervised consumption sites under the *Act to Amend the CDSA* – Kathleen Wynne in Ontario and Rachel Notley in Alberta – were defeated by parties that campaigned against this aspect of harm reduction. While the Ford government, with some modifications, largely continues the approach of its predecessor, the Kenney/Smith government has not.¹³³ Alberta, more so than Ontario, illustrates several issues surrounding judicialization and policy impact: how judicial power can be blunted by a negative rights ruling; why courts must be viewed as implementer-dependent institutions, even when delivering a positive rights decision such as section 23 of the *Canadian Charter* as Chapters 3 and 4 demonstrate; how federalism and devolution can result in an implementation gap, particularly when a policy issue exceeds the "water-tight compartment" view of federalism and requires "coordinated and independent" action by federal, provincial, and territorial governments. And, most importantly, that a declaration of unconstitutionality does not necessarily limit policy autonomy or see the centralization of Canadian federalism via Charter review.¹³⁴

Ford Nation and Harm Reduction

Despite the 2012 Toronto and Ottawa Supervised Consumption Assessment Study (TOSCA) recommendation that three supervised consumption sites be established in Toronto and two in Ottawa,¹³⁵ and the Toronto Health Board urging the provincial government to establish a pilot project in downtown Toronto in 2013,[136] the McGuinty and Wynne Liberal governments were reticent about this issue.[137] Perhaps this was grounded in the *realpolitik* of the Harper era and the recognition that, without federal support, supervised consumption sites were a non-starter. This was understood by then Ontario minister of health, Deb Matthews, whose spokesperson laid bare the practical reality facing this component of harm reduction during the Harper years: "Given that the federal government's approval would be a prerequisite, we have no plans to move forward with supervised injection sites."[138]

Under the leadership of Wynne, the Liberal Party would shake-off its lukewarm approach[139] and endorse supervised consumption sites as a component of harm reduction.[140] Key actors in Ontario reconsidered supervised consumption sites in light of the opioid crisis. In Toronto, Mayor John Tory became a supporter in 2016[141] after Toronto City Council received a formal recommendation by the Toronto Health Board calling for the establishment of three facilities.[142] Toronto City Council endorsed this recommendation by a vote of thirty-six to three on July 14, 2016.[143] In Ottawa, Mayor Jim Watson revisited his initial opposition[144] and supported these health facilities by early 2017.[145] For the provincial government, it was the release of the opioid strategy by Eric Hoskins, the minister of health and long-term care, that saw a full endorsement of supervised consumption sites in Ontario.[146] This was reflected in the 2017 provincial budget, which allocated funding for the establishment of three facilities in Toronto and one in Ottawa and the establishment of "a provincial review panel to consider future applications for SIS on a case-by-case basis."[147]

In an eighteen-month period, from the minister of health and long-term care's endorsement of supervised consumption sites in January 2017 to the 2018 provincial election in June that saw the Wynne government defeated, a total of eighteen supervised consumption sites were operating in Ontario. In the lead up to the provincial election, Progressive Conservative (PC) leader Doug Ford stated that he was "dead against" supervised consumption sites and advocated for greater addiction treatment in Ontario.[148] Within a month, the PC leader tempered this statement and said that a future PC government would "consult with experts" over the future of Ontario's eighteen supervised consumption sites.[149]

One of the first acts of the Ford government in July 2018 was to freeze the number of sites in Ontario and to conduct a review of the existing facilities.[150] The review findings were released in October 2022. The main recommendation was to repurpose supervised consumption sites as consumption and treatment services (CTS) as a new delivery model for harm reduction in Ontario: "The new delivery model would not only be equipped to reverse overdoses, it would also include an enhanced and necessary focus on connecting people who use drugs to primary care, treatment and rehabilitation, and other health and social services."[151] Under this new delivery model, the existing sites were required to apply to the ministry of health and long-term care for provincial operating permission, despite holding valid section 56.1 exemptions under the *CDSA*.

This policy shift appears to be significant and a setback for supervised consumption services in Ontario. Two facilities in Toronto and one in Ottawa lost their funding, and the province capped the number of potential supervised consumption sites at twenty-one, though it indicated that it would revisit this number as needed.[152] These changes are more apparent than real, despite critical commentary that suggested a Harper-esque approach by "Ford Nation" to the *CDSA*.[153] Many of the requirements in the application process are modelled on the section 56.1 application and permit facilities to include similar components from the *CDSA* application as part of the Ontario submission.[154] While Ontario does require additional components, they largely encompass directing clients to services outlined in the CTS delivery model, such as "onsite or defined pathways to addiction treatment" and "onsite or defined pathways to wrap-around services including: primary care, mental care, housing and/or other social supports."[155] The most rigorous requirement, and the one that might explain the initial reduction from eighteen to fifteen facilities in early 2019, is the "proximity" consideration. For instance, the *Application Guide* notes that the CTS should be at least six hundred metres from each other and should not be located close to "licensed childcare centres, parks, and schools (including post-secondary institutions)."[156] If a CTS is located in close proximity to these institutions (100–200 metres), the application must demonstrate "evidence of support by local stakeholders, including residents."[157] However, as the *Application Guide* makes clear, "community consultation is a requirement of the federal *CDSA* exemption application and does not have to be carried out separately for the Ontario program application, provided the consultation meets the provincial requirements."[158]

What has been the overall impact of Ford Nation on its predecessor's approach to supervised consumption sites? Does it represent a sharp break and ideological affinity with the Harper government's *Respect for Communities Act*? Or does it suggest fidelity to the latter half of Ontario's provincial motto – "Loyal She Began, Thus She Remains"?[159] While Ford indicated a future PC government would break with the Wynne government's approach, this rhetoric, despite a funding freeze and program review, has given way to fidelity to his predecessor's approach to harm reduction, with some slight modifications. While the initial review saw the reduction of CTS from eighteen to fifteen, this proved to be a short-lived state of affairs. As of July 2023, there are twenty-four CTS facilities operating in Ontario.[160] There are currently four open applications at Health Canada. Pragmatism, and not ideology, characterizes the approach of the Ford government, with at least twenty-eight facilities, or a net gain of ten, operating since the 2018 provincial election. Ford did not begin as a loyal adherent to the Wynne government's approach, but his government is committed to repurposed supervised consumption sites. This stands in stark contrast to the Alberta experience, where ideology – and a policy approach set during the Harper years – now defines the provincial government's response to harm reduction.

"There and Back Again": From the Harper Cabinet to the Alberta Premiership

Alberta's Notley government first made a commitment to supervised consumption sites during the 2017 Speech from the Throne.[161] In response to this policy signal, a total of seven section 56.1 applications were submitted to Health Canada by local health organizations. Six applications were approved in 2017 and a seventh in 2018.[162] During the remainder of its mandate, which ended on April 30, 2019, the Notley ministry supported efforts to establish two more supervised consumption sites: a mobile site to operate in Calgary's Forest Lawn neighbourhood in the city's southeast and a fixed location in Medicine Hat.[163] If the Notley government had been re-elected after the thirtieth general election on April 16, 2019, it would have supported the establishment of at least nine supervised consumption sites in Alberta. If so, Alberta would have been second only to Ontario in the number of provincially supported sites approved since the Trudeau government amended the *CDSA* and section 56.1.

With the formation of the United Conservative Party (UCP) under the leadership of Jason Kenney in October 2017, the policy consensus on supervised consumption sites began to unravel. As I will argue, the approach to supervised consumption sites during the Harper years, of which Kenney was the senior minister from Alberta, became the policy approach of the UCP and, following the 2019 election, that of the UCP government led by Kenney. For the *Respect for Communities Act*, it was "there and back again" once

Kenney travelled from the Harper ministry in Ottawa to the premier's office in Edmonton.[164] Although Kenney was replaced as premier in October 2022 by Danielle Smith, the UCP government continues his approach to supervised consumption sites.

During a visit to Lethbridge in March 2018, then opposition leader Kenney stated that the UCP did not support the use of supervised consumption sites, and he committed a future UCP government to review their continued existence. Using language that was reminiscent of the Harper government, Kenney recycled the normatively laden adjective of "addict" to describe drug users and "injecting poison" in reference to the use of synthetic opioids.[165] Recall that, during a media scrum at the seventeenth International Aids Conference in Mexico City on August 3–8, 2008, then federal minister of health, Tony Clement, voiced the Harper government's position on supervised consumption sites using similar language: "No addict is too far gone to give up on them. That is what Insite does. They say its ok to stick a needle in your vein and to die slowly ... And that's why Insite, to me, is an abomination."[166]

Ten years later, Kenney would reiterate the Harper government's view of supervised consumption sites and drug users in lengthy Facebook and Twitter postings after his March 2018 visit to Lethbridge: "We absolutely need to show compassion for those suffering with addiction, and we need to help them get off drugs. But helping addicts inject poison into their bodies is not a long-term solution to the problem."[167] As a former federal minister of citizenship, immigration, and multiculturalism, Kenney argued that the opioid crisis was a failure of the border security policies of the Trudeau government in respect to China:

> Why isn't the federal government massively increasing resources for the Canadian Border Services to interdict these poisons? Why isn't our federal government demanding that the Chinese government crackdown on these factories? Why aren't we giving the police adequate resources to chase down those who are dealing these drugs on our streets in our communities? Where were the resources in this week's federal budget?[168]

Kenney concluded that supervised consumption was a failed policy and that a revised approach to addiction was required:

> For over a decade, we have been told that we just need to ensure that addicts do drugs "safely." In that time, do you think the crisis of addiction has been getting better or worse? Nearly every day we hear heart wrenching

stories about families devastated by drug use. Enabling someone to commit slow motion suicide – to throw their life away – is not compassion. We need to crack down on the criminals that are bringing poison into our communities. And we need to invest in actual treatment programs to get addicts off drugs – not spend money to help them consume drugs.[169]

This approach to supervised consumption sites would be formalized in the UCP's 2019 election platform, in which it stated: "We will take a sensible, targeted, and compassionate approach to the issue of safe consumption sites."[170]

The 2019 platform contained a four-part commitment to supervised consumption sites. The platform required a UPC government to "only endorse supervised consumption sites if there had been extensive consultations with affected communities, including residents and business owners, and if there is a robust evidence-based analysis of the socio-economic impact of a potential drug consumption site."[171] Additionally, OPS would only be authorized "if they have clear plans to provide treatment services," and, if elected, the UCP would conduct a "socio-economic analysis of the impact of existing drug consumption sites."[172] Similar to the *Respect for Communities Act*, the UCP would ensure that key stakeholders – the local community, local police, and local government – played a role in the potential relocation of safe consumption sites approved by the Notley government.[173] In short, those provisions of the *Respect for Communities Act* removed by the *Act to Amend the CDSA* – formal consultation and support from the local community, local police, and local government actors – were to be reinstated by a UCP government.

After forming a majority government in 2019,[174] the UCP government quickly moved on the commitments made during the general election. On June 1, 2019, a funding freeze was announced for new supervised consumption sites,[175] thus reversing the Notley government's support for additional sites. Freezing the number of safe consumption sites at seven effectively blocked the submission of section 56.1 applications to Health Canada for the proposed mobile facility in Calgary and a fixed location site in Medicine Hat. Neither site has submitted a section 56.1 application to Health Canada since the Kenney government's funding freeze. This led to a heated exchange in the Legislative Assembly between Premier Kenney and NDP leader Rachel Notley, in which the leader of the opposition stated: "Once again it appears this government is putting misinformed ideology over science. Indeed, the Premier himself has said that he thinks these sites only allow people to inject poison into their bodies."[176]

In response, the premier stated that he was merely acting on the promises made during the election campaign. More importantly, he castigated the former government, suggesting that the Notley ministry ignored local interest in the approval and location of supervised consumption facilities in Edmonton.[177] Kenney's comments were in reference to a legal challenge launched by Edmonton's Chinatown and Area Business Association in November 2017, seeking the immediate closure of three supervised consumption sites.[178] In court filings, the association claimed that it was not properly consulted by the Notley government and requested that the federal minister of health reconsider the section 56.1 exemptions. This legal challenge was unsuccessful in federal court, as Justice Richard Mosley determined "the federal Ministry of Health met its duties to the Chinatown business association."[179]

In August 2019, the Kenney government released the terms of the supervised consumption site review, which outlined three objectives: "minimize the adverse social and economic impacts of existing supervised consumption sites (SCS) on local neighbourhoods; help inform decisions around the establishment of future SCS and reduce the potential for negative social and economic impacts; help inform a provincial policy that outlines required criteria for provincial funding of SCS."[180] Table 7.2 provides the precise issues that the expert panel were permitted to consider and what were strictly prohibited. The terms of reference initiated by the Kenney government prioritized public security and economic impact and ignored the public health benefits of supervised consumption sites. This is, in many ways, a repeat of the Harper government's approach to the *Respect for Communities Act*, which prioritized public security and downplayed the public health purpose of the *CDSA*.

The report, entitled *Impact: A Socio-economic Review of Supervised Consumption Sites in Alberta*, was released in March 2020.[181] It contains a mixed methods approach, which relied on a series of town hall meetings (n = 8), key stakeholder meetings (n = 50), and online surveys and submissions by individuals (n = 16,831) and businesses (n = 440).[182] It is highly critical of the socio-economic impact of supervised consumption sites and suggests that crime rates, social disorder, and needle debris have significantly increased in the areas in close proximity to a fixed location supervised consumption site. Property values and local businesses, according to the report, were also negatively impacted by the presence of a supervised consumption site.[183] The report is particularly critical of what it considers a "one-pillar stool" approach

Table 7.2 Supervised consumption sites review: UCP's terms of reference

What is in scope	What is out of scope
Crime rates	The merits of supervised consumption sites as a harm reduction tool
Needle debris	The utility of these services in each community
Complaints of social disorder	Establishing supervised consumption services outside of the current or proposed sites
Residential property values	Provincial funding for supervised consumption services
Emergency medical services calls	Other social issues such as housing or homelessness
Business impacts (bottom lines, trends, closures)	
Data collection	
Referrals to treatment providers	
Overdose reversals	
Proposals for solutions to address impact of the sites	

Note: Scope: the above are examples of topics the committee will cover and are not an exhaustive list. The committee may choose other topic areas for their discussions
Source: Adapted from Alberta, Backgrounder: Supervised consumption sites review, https://www.alberta.ca/system/files/custom_downloaded_images/supervised-consumption-services-backgrounder.pdf (October 23, 2023)

to harm reduction by the former Notley government to the neglect of other aspects of Canada's drug strategy.[184]

A number of key recommendations were made by the review committee: existing and future supervised consumption sites were to be subject to provincial regulation; provincial licensing requirements were to be instituted for supervised consumption sites; harm reduction should be placed within "recovery-orientated" system of care that de-emphasized supervised consumption sites; drug users must show proper identification to be admitted to a supervised consumption site; supervised consumption sites keep records of those using its facilities; supervised consumption sites "should be directed and supervised by physicians with recognized expertise in Addiction Medicine"; and facilities should be subjected to semi-annual audits.[185] The most specific recommendation involved that of the proposed supervised consumption sites in Calgary and Medicine Hat: "Based on consultations and statistical analysis, the Committee is of the view that there is no immediate need for a SCS site in Medicine Hat or the mobile site in Forest Lawn, Calgary."[186]

Given that the UCP had frozen funding for any new supervised consumption sites in June 2019, this recommendation represents the death knell for these facilities while the UCP remains in office.

The reaction to the report and its findings was stark and highly polarized. The report's methodology was attacked by the scientific and policy community, which demanded that the report be withdrawn by the Kenney government.[187] In an open letter, the Canadian Drug Policy Coalition stated: "The findings contained in Alberta's SCS report were produced using unsound research methods and deficient analytical procedures."[188] The Canadian HIV/AIDS Legal Network outlined what these were: "By limiting the review to potential social and economic impacts without looking at the overall health benefits of SCS on people who use drugs, the report is inherently biased and partial."[189] Many of the methodological criticisms were directed at the unrepresentative nature of town hall meetings and online surveys that relied largely on anecdotal evidence. More damaging was the Kenney government's directive that the review committee could not consider the large quantity of peer-reviewed studies on the health benefits of supervised consumption sites. In a peer-reviewed critique of the methodology employed in regard to crime, James Livingston outlined three limitations with the measures used: "(a) improper handling of police service call data, (b) inadequate assessment of public perceptions of crime, and (c) inappropriate reliance on anecdotal accounts of crime."[190] This peer-reviewed study echoed the criticism in the open letters to Kenney by the scientific and policy communities.

The creation of an expert committee to review the impact of safe consumption sites by the UCP is a throwback to how the Harper government confronted the volume of peer-reviewed studies that demonstrated the value of safe consumption sites, both in regard to public health and public safety. Clement, who was then health minister, appointed an Expert Advisory Committee (EAC) in October 2006, which reported in April 2008. Although the report was generally supportive of supervised consumption sites,[191] it stated that "mathematical modelling shows that Insite saves about one death by drug overdose per year."[192] This finding was seized upon by the Harper government to question the value of supervised consumption sites and to dispute the peer-reviewed research that demonstrated the broader value of these facilities. In this respect, the Kenney government followed the Harper play book and laid the groundwork to revisit the approach to harm reduction established by the former Notley government.

The UPC government's response to the report is unsurprising as the minister that received the report, Associate Minister of Health and Addictions

Jason Luan, stated: "I'm deeply troubled with some of the findings of the report ... What we heard was a wake-up call. From increases in social disorder, to discarded needles ... what we see is a system of chaos."[193] Kenney was more pointed in his assessment of supervised consumption sites: "They're now more than injections ... they're just illegal drug sites. I think we see pretty much everywhere a marked increase in crime in the area of those sites and social disorder and negative human consequences."[194] One of the first acts to address this "system of chaos" was the cancellation of the ARCHES fixed location site in Lethbridge in July 2020 and its replacement with a mobile unit in the short term, on the pretext of financial mismanagement.[195] After receiving a complainant about ARCHES, the Kenney government contracted Deloitte to conduct an audit, which reported $1.6 million in unaccounted public funds.[196] This resulted in the immediate closure of ARCHES. However, a police investigation in December 2020 concluded that, in fact, the funds were accounted for. Despite this finding, the Kenney government has yet to permit the fixed location ARCHES facility in Lethbridge to reopen.[197]

Even before the review committee recommended the introduction of a "recovery-orientated approach" to harm reduction, the 2020 Speech from the Throne had committed the Kenney government to this policy direction. For instance, $140 million was committed to a mental health and addictions strategy, with a focus on treatment and recovery. To that end, the Kenney government provided funding for "the creation of at least 4,000 additional treatment spaces."[198] According to Benjamin Perrin, who served as a justice and public safety adviser in the Harper Prime Minister's Office from 2012 to 2013, this shift simply reveals Kenney's long-standing opposition to supervised consumption sites: "Kenney appears to be trying to use increased treatment funding on substance use as political cover for a crackdown on supervised consumption sites. In announcing those funds, Kenney appears to be claiming credit for doing something positive, while taking the opportunity now to act on his long-standing opposition to SCS."[199]

This opposition informed four policy shifts introduced after the supervised consumption site review was made public. First, the *Mental Health Services Protection Act (Mental Health Services Act)* was passed on September 30, 2020, followed by Alberta Health Services revising its policy on psychoactive substance use on November 6, 2020.[200] In April 2021, the *Recovery-oriented Overdose Prevention Services Guide (Prevention Services Guide)* was released, and the *Mental Health Services Protection Regulation* was issued on June 2, 2021.[201] In the interim, the supervised consumption services were prohibited at the Boyle Street Community Services facility in Edmonton, and it closed in April 2021.²⁰² Within two years of forming the government, Kenney and the UCP closed two fixed location sites (in Lethbridge and Edmonton) and blocked the submission of section 56.1 applications for a mobile site in Calgary and a fixed location site in Medicine Hat through a funding freeze on new sites. Given that Alberta had seven sites at the end of the Notley government, which was potentially rising to nine once the Calgary and Medicine Hat applications were submitted to Health Canada,²⁰³ the number of supervised consumption sites was reduced by nearly 50 percent from the possibility of at least nine facilities to just five by April 2021.²⁰⁴

The implementation of the Psychoactive Substance Use Policy by Alberta Health Services fundamentally recalibrated the province's support for supervised consumption sites.²⁰⁵ This policy document removes dozens of references to harm reduction and replaces it with the phrase "recovery-oriented approach."²⁰⁶ This is in keeping with the UCP's commitment in the 2020 Speech from the Throne to a mental health and addiction strategy that focuses on treatment and recovery services.²⁰⁷ Then Minister of Health Tyler Shandro described this approach as a rejection of the "one-pillar approach that focused entirely on harm reduction" by the previous Notley government.²⁰⁸ Instead, the UCP instituted a "recovery orientated system of care" that "is person centered and builds on the strengths and resilience of individuals, families, and communities to achieve a life free of illicit drugs and improved health, wellness, and quality of life for those with or at risk of alcohol and drug problems or mental health issues."²⁰⁹ Recovery, and not harm reduction through supervised consumption, is now the approach of the UCP government.

Each of the policy documents mentioned above, in important respects, bring back key parts of the *Respect for Communities Act* that were removed by the Trudeau government. The fifty-seven requirements under the Harper-era *CDSA* were reduced by the Trudeau government to the five core principles outlined by McLachlin CJ in *PHS Community Services Society*. Despite this simplification of the federal approval process, the Kenney government has returned the regulation of supervised consumption sites in Alberta to the administrative complexity of the *Respect for Communities Act*. Given Kenney's prominent role in the Harper government during the passage of Bill C-2, this is unsurprising. And it reiterates an important point made by F.L. Morton in the context of judicial victories and policy outcomes: "Provinces can win a Charter 'battle' but still lose the policy 'war.'"²¹⁰ Equally so, governments can lose the Charter war and win a policy victory as the Harper Conservatives did in the context of supervised consumption sites and the *Respect for Communities Act*.

But parliamentary democracy and federalism show that victories can be fleeting if the policy direction is not supported by one's successor, as the Trudeau government demonstrated when it rescinded the Harper-era *Respect for Communities Act*. Equally true, the Kenney government tempered Trudeau's reversal of the Harper government's approach to supervised consumption sites in Alberta and, at the moment, has won the policy battle against the Trudeau Liberals. This is because of federalism and the policy instruments that remain the sovereign responsibility of the provinces in a jurisdictional area assigned to them under section 92 of the *Constitution Act, 1867*. A Charter victory in 2011 for Insite has not reduced the policy autonomy of provincial governments in the delivery – or the decision not to deliver – a "non-core" health service.

These factors lay bare the misunderstood relationship between judicial review and policy impact, as I argued more than twenty years ago.[211] In the context of supervised consumption sites in Alberta, a section 56.1 exemption issued by Health Canada is no longer sufficient to provide this harm reduction service. Under section 5 of the *Mental Health Services Act*, a health facility must also be granted a provincial license to operate.[212] This licensing requirement shows how federalism can act as the bulwark against the operation of supervised consumption sites, even those with federal approval, if a provincial government is so inclined. There are two federalism issues at play in Alberta. The first is the creation of a provincial licensing scheme and application process. A facility granted a section 56.1 exemption under the federal *CDSA* cannot operate in Alberta unless it secures a section 5 license under the *Mental Health Services Act*. If, for some reason, Health Canada issued a section 56.1 license to a facility that did not have the support of the provincial government, section 5 of the *Mental Health Services Act* would allow Alberta to override federal authorization.

Although Ontario under the Ford government created an application process for supervised consumption sites, it is not mandatory and only applies to facilities seeking provincial financial support.[213] Alberta, therefore, is unique in having a provincial licensing requirement for supervised consumption sites. And there is a more problematic feature of the interplay between the *CDSA* and the *Mental Health Services Act*. Whereas the practice of the Trudeau government has been to grant section 56.1 exemptions generally for three years for reasons of institutional stability, the UCP's practice has been to grant section 5 licences under the *Mental Health Services Act* for one-year periods. Supervised consumption facilities must submit a new application each year to secure a section 5 license from Alberta Health Services, which requires yearly compliance with the conditions outlined in the *Prevention Services Guide* and the *Mental Health Services Protection Regulation* during the period of federal authorization.

The second federalism dimension is the funding of supervised consumption sites. In the case of Alberta, financial support for new facilities was frozen by the UCP, subject to the release of the socio-economic review of supervised consumption facilities. Although the report acknowledges that these facilities rely almost exclusively on provincial financial support, it states that "operators are not restricted from seeking external funding" and notes that Health Canada "also funds risk mitigation such as needed collection and disposal (e.g., sharps boxes), public awareness/community projects, and training on safe disposal."[214] This statement is somewhat misleading as provincial financial support is essential for these facilities to operate. For instance, the UCP's funding freeze derailed the submission of section 56.1 applications to Health Canada by the proposed mobile site in Calgary and the fixed location in Medicine Hat. To date, neither application has been submitted to Health Canada, which demonstrates the overriding importance of provincial financial support for facilities issued a section 56.1 exemption by Health Canada.

The requirements for a license in the *Mental Health Services Act* are outlined in the *Prevention Services Guide* and the *Mental Health Services Protection Regulation*. This is where Harper-era changes to the *CDSA* reappear in provincial form. Under section 56.3(x) of the *Respect for Communities Act,* all personnel that worked in a facility were required to submit to a ten-year police background check. This was amended by the Trudeau government and now only requires a police-background check for the person in charge of the facility.[215] Recognizing that a dimension of harm reduction is peer counselling by former substance users, which are individuals likely to have criminal records, the Trudeau government removed this potential barrier to the approval of a section 56.1 application. The wide-ranging Harper-era background check requirement has returned in Alberta as the *Mental Health Services Act* obliges facilities to have written guidelines and hiring procedures that "require a criminal records check for each employee who provides services directly to a client."[216] While this condition does contain a number of exceptions, it extends to the vast majority of personnel within a supervised consumption site and, given the UCP's view of illicit drug consumers, is a highly discretionary – and likely – basis to deny a section 5 license.

Additional Harper-era approaches to the *CDSA*, rescinded by the Trudeau government, were reinstated in provincial form by the Kenney government. The *Respect for Communities Act* required the submission of five letters from key public actors as part of a section 56 application,[217] one of which was by the head of the local police force where a facility was to be located. This created five potential veto points for actors that may be opposed to a supervised consumption site. This requirement was reduced by the Trudeau government to a single letter by the provincial/territorial minister with responsibility for supervised consumption sites. As outlined in Alberta's *Prevention Services Guide*, a potential supervised consumption site is required to "include a letter of support from local law enforcement" when applying for provincial funding.[218] Whereas the Trudeau government removed this requirement, the UCP government has reinstated the need for local police support as a condition for provincial funding, which, in reality, represents a requirement that may be used to deny a section 5 license under the *Mental Health Services Act*.

One of the criticisms levelled against the Trudeau government by the Conservative opposition when Bill C-37 progressed through Parliament was that, in comparison to the *Respected for Communities Act*, the *Act to Amend the CDSA* significantly reduced the requirements for community consultation over the location of, and support for, a supervised consumption site.[219] A similar criticism was levelled by the Kenney-led UCP against the Notley government.[220] The UCP government has returned community consultation to the level required by the *Respect for Communities Act* and more. Health facilities submitting a funding application in relation to a section 5 licence under the *Mental Health Services Act* must include a "Good Neighbour Agreement," which is a formal agreement that is negotiated between the facility and "local businesses, community organizations and nearby residents with a minimum 200-metre radius."[221] This requirement calls for "rigorous community consultation and engagement regarding the site" and a yearly engagement with "local government, first responder organizations (local police, fire department, Emergency Medical Services), the local business community and persons with lived experiences."[222] The *Prevention Services Guide* recommends that the "rigorous community consultations" include "parties or organizations within a 500-metre radius that are impacted by day-to-day operations of the site be engaged."[223]

Given that fixed location supervised consumption sites are largely located in downtown urban cores, the five-hundred-metre radius requirement for "rigorous community consultation" in high density areas such as these actually creates a more rigorous approval process than the *Respect for Communities Act*. A Good Neighbour Agreement entails consent from organizations that, under the *Respect for Communities Act*, were required to submit letters as part of a section 56 application but were removed by the Trudeau government. For instance, two of the four organizations in which letters are no longer required under the *Act to Amend the CDSA* but were under the *Respect for Communities Act* – local government and local law enforcement – must be consulted and, in the case of the local police, a funding application must include a letter of support.[224] The level of consultation required by a Good Neighbour Agreement and the opportunity it provides for local organizations to oppose the establishment of a facility, or the renewal of a licence, cannot be minimized under the *Prevention Services Guide*. This requirement is even more significant once the *Mental Health Services Protection Regulation* is considered. Under section 4, "a director may consider the following criteria when issuing or refusing to issue, amend or renew a licence for the provision of supervised consumption service: (a) community support for the service."[225]

Other requirements involve human resource, safety and security, needle debris and distribution, and first responder access policies, all of which must be developed before a section 5 licence can be submitted. Facilities are also required to develop occupational health requirements, clinical practice standards, adverse events protocols, critical incidents protocols, and record creation, maintenance, and retention policies for each person accessing supervised consumption services.[226] For brevity, with one exception (record maintenance), the remaining requirements will not be discussed, as they are simply part and parcel of the application complexity of Alberta's licensing scheme, much as the *Respect for Communities Act* created a process of singular difficulty that largely dissuaded organizations from submitting a section 56.1 application under the *CDSA*. Like the *Respect for Communities Act*, an application under section 5 of the *Mental Health Services Act* can only be reviewed if a completed application is submitted.

Regarding record maintenance, anyone that visits a supervised consumption site must provide their personal health number. The justification for this change is to ensure "clients can be easily referred to a continuum of services within the health care service."[227] In short, personal health numbers are required to facilitate a client's progress through the "recovery-orientated approach" to addiction implemented by the UCP government. This policy was originally set to take effect on September 30, 2021, but was delayed until January 2022 by the UCP government.[228] Like Alberta's licensing scheme, this policy change is fully within provincial authority. Attempts by civil society organizations such as Moms Stop the Harm Society and Lethbridge Overdose Prevention Society have been unsuccessful in securing court injunctions to delay this policy change until the constitutional issues are reviewed by the courts.[229] Justice R. Paul Belzil, of the Court of Queen's Bench, noted that "legislative responsibility for health is shared between the Federal Government and the Provinces with the delivery of health services, falling squarely within provincial jurisdiction."[230] He further noted that "if this Interlocutory Injunction application succeeded, Alberta's ability to formulate addiction policy, pending the outcome of this action, would be severely restricted."[231] At the court of appeal, the injunction was also denied. The unanimous judgment reaffirmed Alberta's ability to advance a "recovery-orientated approach" to addiction strategy but noted that "the government has the mandate to make these decisions and must bear the ultimate responsibility for the decisions it makes."[232]

Regardless of whether personal health numbers, a recovery-oriented approach, or the *Mental Health Services Act* are firmly within provincial jurisdiction, they invariably create barriers to supervised consumption sites and act as impediments for stigmatized individuals attempting to access harm reduction services permitted by the Kenney/Smith UCP government. Most importantly, they may deepen the opioid crisis in Alberta by dissuading drug users from visiting these facilities because of the record-keeping requirement. As a 2016 study by the School of Public Health at the University of Alberta found, only 36 percent of drug users would visit supervised consumption sites if they were required to show their personal health number.[233] This policy, firmly within provincial jurisdiction, may prove to be counterproductive from a public health perspective.

The Kenney government used the Harper play book when confronting a policy issue with which it fundamentally disagreed. Kenney and the UCP opposed the approach to the *CDSA* that was taken by the Trudeau and Notley governments. This policy disagreement is not surprising given the political journey of Jason Kenney – from Ottawa to Edmonton. As the senior minister from Alberta, Kenney helped frame the Harper government's legislative response to *PHS Community Services Society* from 2007 to 2015. As leader of the opposition in Alberta after 2018, Kenny argued against the approach to supervised consumption sites by the Notley government under the Trudeau-amended *CDSA*. And, as premier, he used federalism as a shield to contain (a funding freeze), deconstruct (the socio-economic review), and control (a complex regulatory framework) the footprint of supervised consumption sites in Alberta. Kenny's approach to supervised consumption sites has come full circle, there and back again, from the Harper Cabinet to the premier's office. His respect for the *Respect for Communities Act* now informs Alberta's approach to this issue, despite being replaced by Danielle Smith as UPC leader and premier in October 2022.

Conclusion

Once the Trudeau government amended the *CDSA* to strip away those parts of the *Respect for Communities Act* that frustrated section 56 applications in 2017, the Supreme Court of Canada was rather inconspicuous in this chapter. This absence occurred in a policy area that has been judicialized since 2008 when the Harper government failed to renew Insite's section 56 exemption under the *CDSA*.[234] Moreover, the backdrop to this absence is the opioid crisis in which an expanded approach to harm reduction – from supervised consumption to OPS – frames the public policy narrative. These conditions appear instructive to a greater judicial role in which a judicialized area of public policy grows in issue salience due to changing circumstances.

Why did growing issue salience not see a corresponding increase in judicial policy impact, beyond the 2017 amendments to the *CDSA*? I make this claim despite evidence to the contrary – thirty-nine supervised consumption sites in operation, nine open applications for section 56 exemptions currently under review at Health Canada, and dozens of OPS permitted to open by Health Canada in the fight against the opioid crisis at the provincial and territorial levels. If the Trudeau government approves these open applications, which its track record suggests it will do, the number of supervised consumption sites after the Harper era – interregnum? – will rise from one to forty-eight. Surely these developments constitute evidence of judicialized policy impact? But they do not, and this is because of a somewhat overused adage that will now be employed – correlation does not imply causation. There is causality between *PHS Community Services Society* and the Trudeau government's *Act to Amend the CDSA*. It would be folly to suggest otherwise. But the reality is that a minority of jurisdictions in Canada – five provincial governments – account for all thirty-nine supervised consumption sites currently operating and all the open applications under review at Health Canada. As a result, judicialization cannot be the causation for this thirty-nine-fold increase in supervised consumption sites that will grow to forty-nine by the end of the current Parliament.

Federalism explains this uneven approach or, more precisely, the implementation gap that federalism poses for an area of public policy, judicialized or not. Federalism is the freedom to decide not to establish supervised consumption sites, as five provinces and three territorial governments have demonstrated. And, as the Kenney-led UCP has demonstrated in Alberta, federalism is the freedom to reverse the policy choices of one's predecessor. More poignantly, federalism permits, as Kenney's Alberta shows, the ability to regulate a provincial issue area as premier much as you did as a member of the Harper government when it passed the *Respect for Communities Act*. The provincial and territorial governments, as permitted by federalism and devolved competencies, designate supervised consumption sites as "non-core services" that are provided at their discretion. Now, if they had designated this component of harm reduction as a core service, then perhaps judicialization via the *Canada Health Act* and its requirement of universality would account for the thirty-eight-fold increase in the number of facilities. But this is not where this policy issue is. Because of federalism.

Physician-assisted Suicide to Medical Assistance in Dying
When *Carter* Met Federalism

8

Next to the issues of capital punishment and abortion, ending one's life – with assistance – is perhaps the most difficult moral question with which the Supreme Court of Canada has ever grappled. *Carter v Canada* is particularly striking when compared to the last time the Court considered the issue of physician-assisted suicide, as it was then known, in the 1993 decision *Rodriguez v British Columbia*.[1] *Rodriguez* saw a deeply divided Court render a narrow majority decision (five to four) where the Court under Chief Justice Antonio Lamer narrowly upheld the *Criminal Code* restriction on physician-assisted suicide.[2] This precedent, in which then Justice Beverley McLachlin authored one of the three dissenting opinions that favoured invalidating the *Criminal Code* prohibition, would be reversed by a unanimous Court under McLachlin CJ nearly a quarterly of a century later in the 2015 *Carter* decision.

At first glance, medical assistance in dying (MAiD) appears to be an outlier in this study that considers the conditions under which judicial policy impact can be limited by legislative disagreement between the Supreme Court and the governments of Canadian federalism. Simply put, it seems to demonstrate the ultimate power of judicial review – for several reasons. It is a "second look case" in which the government's 2016 response under Prime Minister Justin Trudeau to *Carter* – Bill C-14, *An Act on Medical Assistance in Dying* (2016 *Act on MAiD*),[3] which departed markedly from the Court's eligibility requirement for component adults that qualified for MAiD – was determined in 2019 by the Superior Court of Quebec in *Truchon c Procureur général du Canada* to be unconstitutional.⁴ In short, legislative disagreement was rather brief as the Trudeau government ultimately accepted the authority of the courts in two important regards: first, by deciding not to appeal the lower court decision in *Truchon* and, second, through statutory amendments in the form of Bill C-7, *An Act on Medical Assistance in Dying* (2021 *Act on MAiD*),⁵ where it fully complied with the Court's eligibility criteria for MAiD. If there is a policy issue that demonstrates judicial impact, then MAiD is surely the gold standard of judicial power ensuring legislative compliance.

Nor would dialogue theorists be silent on what MAiD says about the value of this theory for understanding judicial-legislative relationships in the post-Charter era.⁶ There was an extensive discussion of this issue within and outside Parliament by both the Harper and Trudeau governments. For the Harper government, it established the External Panel on Options for a Legislative Response to *Carter v Canada* (External Panel),⁷ which released its report shortly after the 2015 federal election that resulted in a Liberal majority government.⁸ In addition to the normal committee process, the Trudeau government also employed a rarely used parliamentary configuration when it established the Special Joint Committee on Physician-Assisted Death (PDAM) to advise the executive on its legislative response to *Carter*.⁹ This dialogue would continue with the Supreme Court of Canada when the Trudeau government requested a six-month extension on the *Carter* remedy, which suspended the declaration of unconstitutionality for twelve months. This judicial-executive dialogue resulted in a four-month extension,¹⁰ which culminated with the passage of the 2016 *Act on MAiD*, more than sixteen months after *Carter*.¹¹ Related to this, a strong case can be made, as Dennis Baker, Matthew Hennigar, and Eleni Nicolaides have done, that the Trudeau government's response to *Carter* in the 2016 *Act on MAiD* is an example of coordinated construction whereby Parliament has an equal role to play in determining the boundaries of constitutional reach and the *Canadian Charter of Rights and Freedoms*.¹² Legislative disagreement, according to this view of constitutional construction, is both legitimate and permitted because no single actor has the final say on what the Constitution requires or prohibits.

I do not dispute that these are reasonable understandings of *Carter*, MAiD, and institutional relationships in the post-Charter policy world. To deny the power of the Supreme Court or the extensive dialogue on MAiD is folly, as the book's introduction stated. Despite the authority in which the Court spoke in *Carter*, and the Trudeau government's breakneck retreat from legislative defiance in 2016 to compliance in 2019, there are a number of factors that limit judicial policy impact. The first, as mentioned in previous chapters, is the nature of judicial decisions involving section 7 of the *Canadian Charter*. That *Carter* involves a negative right, by definition, narrows the impact of the Court in this complex policy issue.[13] While the Court may have recognized that competent adults satisfying certain requirements had a right to end their suffering with assistance, and those that counselled or aided were not subject to criminal penalty, it did not require access to this service for competent adults. This represents the second institutional obstacle to policy impact beyond the federal arena. While *Carter* did affect the *Criminal Code*, as it saw the Trudeau government amend it in relation to the 2016 *Act on MAiD* (non-compliance)[14] and the 2021 *Act on MAiD* (full compliance), it was limited, legislatively, to the *Criminal Code* as only a federal statute was deemed unconstitutional by the Court in *Carter*.

To understand policy impact in a federation requires a consideration of the interplay between federal statues, such as the *Criminal Code*, and which order of government is tasked with providing services no longer regulated by a federal statute via judicial review.[15] If it is the federal government with responsibility, then judicial policy impact can be direct. But if the action in question is the responsibility of the provincial or territorial governments, then the invalidation of a federal statute may not necessarily result in judicial policy impact. This leads to the third, and most crucial, explanation for limited judicial policy impact – federalism and the complexity of implementing a policy response to *Carter*.

In the pages that follow, MAiD will be used to illustrate why the legislative disagreement/agreement dichotomy is critical to understanding policy impact, even when it follows a judicial decision of *Carter*'s importance. More importantly, why a negative rights decision cannot ensure policy change or legislative impact in a complex federation such as Canada, particularly when the Supreme Court – and Parliament – are "implementer-dependent" institutions reliant on a supportive policy response by the provincial and territorial governments, as they are in the case of health-care policy. In this respect, MAiD, supervised consumption sites, and abortion rest along an implementation spectrum: widespread implementation in the case of MAiD, uneven policy impact for supervised consumption sites, and even greater accessibility issues for abortion services. What explains this spectrum – ambiguous judicial directives or federalism? As this book has argued, and MAiD confirms, it is federalism and whether the provinces and territories open – or close – the implementation gap that determines policy impact.

What Does *Carter* Explain?

On the surface, *Carter* appears to be a concrete example of judicial policy impact as the invalidation of the *Criminal Code* provisions has seen more than thirty-one thousand Canadians use the MAiD framework to end their suffering between 2016 and 2021.[16] But did these thirty-one thousand Canadians access MAiD because of *Carter* or for reasons beyond *Carter*? That Quebec legislated Bill 52, *An Act Respecting End-of-Life Care*, in 2014, before the 2015 *Carter* decision, illustrates how critical provincial and territorial governments are to the provision of end-of-life medical services.[17]

The success of MAiD is explained by one of the conditions outlined by Matthew Hall for judicial policy impact – when the order of government tasked with implementing a judicial decision agrees with the policy direction of the highest court.[18] Hall referred to this relationship as courts that are "implementer-dependent" institutions, and, in the Canadian context, it was first identified by Christopher Manfredi.[19] The triumph of MAiD, in contrast to the illusive nature of abortion services in Canada, is explained by a policy consensus within the order of government tasked with delivering MAiD. There is no evidence, unlike *Morgentaler*, that provincial or territorial governments disagreed with providing MAiD as a medical service.[20] Indeed, the illusive impact of *Morgentaler* is largely explained by legislative disagreement on the part of several provinces and their failure to provide access to therapeutic abortion services for much of the post-*Morgentaler* era.[21]

Acceptance of the recommendations made by the Provincial-Territorial Expert Advisory Group on Physician-Assisted Dying, before the passage of the 2016 *Act on MAiD*, largely accounts for the implementation of MAiD,[22] although the Supreme Court did engage in agenda setting with the *Carter* decision. In this respect, MAiD fits within the parameters of this study, which largely focus on the importance of the legislative disagreement/agreement dichotomy for understanding judicial policy impact. MAiD is a policy success not because of the actions of the Supreme Court of Canada but, rather, because of the actions of provincial and territorial governments in the absence of judicially imposed constitutional directives. If there had been provincial and territorial resistance to *Carter*, as in the case of *Morgentaler* and abortion services, access to MAiD would have been compromised and judicial policy impact questioned. Agenda setting is important, and, without *Carter*, it is unclear when a policy consensus would have coalesced and produced a profound change such as MAiD.[23] But agenda setting does not lead to policy implementation, despite its importance within the policy cycle. We are where we are because of a policy consensus by the actors who were critical to policy implementation, independent of judicial review.

Neither does dialogue theory serve as a useful understanding of the processes that shaped the 2016 and 2021 *Acts* on *MAiD*. Why is this? Supporters of dialogue-based MAiD point to the fulsome and public debate within PDAM and the Standing Committee on Justice and Human Rights (JUST). This is said to demonstrate a serious attempt by parliamentarians to engage *Carter* and to produce a legislative response that complied with *Carter*. As Thomas Bateman and Matthew LeBlanc note, "the very fact that there is evidence of a robust debate in Parliament about dialogue may cause us to reflect on the notion that Charter values are the preserve of only the courts and the executive."[24] As I suggested in Chapter 1, this is a thin approach to dialogue as a theory since, without legislative impact, dialogue is just words spoken. Clearly, parliamentarians engaged *Carter,* but what ultimately matters in a majority parliamentary setting is whether this non-executive dialogue influenced the substantive direction that Bill C-14 – a government bill – ultimately took.

Consider the fate of the main recommendation made by PDAM to the Trudeau government – that competent adults suffering a grievous and irremediable medical condition should be eligible for MAiD and that it should not require the condition to be terminal.[25] The reaction to Bill C-14 by the co-chair of PDAM, Rob Oliphant, provides a cautionary tale of when dialogue is just words spoken, as this recommendation was rejected by the Trudeau government. Oliphant, a Liberal member of parliament (MP), described the bill as "not good enough" to meet the criteria established by the Court in *Carter*.[26] If any parliamentary committee could facilitate dialogue on *Carter*, it was PDAM, given that the Liberal government did not, unlike JUST, command a majority of its members. While the Liberal-controlled JUST proposed only minor amendments to Bill C-14, it was at the third reading debate in the Senate that a substantive amendment, in line with the recommendation of PDAM, was added to Bill C-14. The Senate removed the phrase "reasonable foreseeability of death"[27] as the upper house was concerned that this addition by the Trudeau government was unconstitutional because it was at odds with the *Carter* decision.[28]

What was the Trudeau government's dialogic response to this amendment passed by the Senate that aligned Bill C-14 with *Carter*? First, the minister of justice and the minister of health, Jody Wilson-Raybould and Jane Philpott, stated that they were "troubled" and "concerned" with this change.[29] In response, the Liberal-controlled House of Commons defeated the amendment and returned Bill C-14 to the Senate, which bowed to the will of the House and passed Bill C-14 as requested by the Trudeau government.[30] The fact that parliamentarians engaged the *Canadian Charter* is significant. What it reveals, however, is that this rights-based dialogue fell on deaf ears, as the Trudeau government largely passed Bill C-14 in the form in which it was introduced into the House by Wilson-Raybould.

There is an important dialogue on Bill C-14 but not the rights-based one that dialogue theorists prioritize. A central theme that emerges from the External Panel, the Provincial-Territorial Expert Advisory Group on Physician-Assisted Dying, and the parliamentary debate on Bill C-14 in PDAM and JUST is the challenge that federalism poses to the realization of MAiD. Responding to the *Carter* decision by amending the *Criminal Code*, while an important step by Parliament, does not ensure that MAiD is available to competent adults suffering a grievous and irremediable medical condition, whether terminal (Parliament) or not (*Carter*). Even before the *Carter* decision, it was changes in professional medical associations, the views of Canadians on end-of-life choices, a provincial and territorial consensus on this issue, and the willingness of medical and nurse practitioners to provide MAiD that made MAiD possible.

From Physician-Assisted Suicide to MAiD

In 1993, the Supreme Court of Canada first considered the constitutionality of the *Criminal Code* restrictions on physician-assisted dying in *Rodriguez*.[31] Sue Rodriguez was suffering from amyotrophic lateral sclerosis (ALS) and wished to end her life before her condition deteriorated to the point that she no longer enjoyed life.[32] Unable to end her suffering without assistance, but prohibited from doing so by section 241(b) of the *Criminal Code*, Rodriguez contended that this provision violated sections 7, 12, and 15 of the *Canadian Charter*. Under section 241(b), anyone that counselled, aided, or abetted a person to commit suicide "whether suicide ensures or not, is guilty of an indictable offence and liable for a term not exceeding fourteen years."[33]

In the majority decision (five to four) authored by Justice John Sopinka, the Supreme Court of Canada dismissed the section 7 and 12 challenges, and, although it assumed the law violated equality rights and would not be saved by section 1, the majority did not make a constitutional ruling on section 15 of the *Canadian Charter*. The most important aspect of the majority and minority judgments involve section 7 of the Charter. For the majority, section 241(b) interfered with section 7 because it "deprives the appellant of autonomy over her person and causes her physical pain and psychological stress in a manner which impinges on the security of her person."[34] Despite this interference, the majority decision found that it was not contrary to the principles of fundamental justice, and, as a result, section 241(b) did not violate section 7. According to Sopinka J, the prohibition on assisted suicide was not arbitrary and, thus, was consistent with the principle of fundamental justice because it advanced the central legislative objective of section 241(b) – "the protection of the vulnerable who might be induced in moments of weakness to committee suicide."[35] Moreover, the Canadian approach to assisted suicide – criminalization – was the consensus approach in comparable western democracies, and none of these courts had found a legal or constitutional right to assisted suicide.[36] Given concerns about the lack of safeguards, the potential for abuse, and the fact that the Canadian Medical Association was against decriminalization, "it cannot be said that the blanket prohibition on assisted suicide is arbitrary or unfair, or that it is not reflective of fundamental values at play in our society."[37]

In contrast, the minority decision by then Justice Beverley McLachlin determined the *Criminal Code* provision to be arbitrary and a violation of the principles of fundamental justice. For McLachlin J, there was a fundamental contradiction within section 241(b) – assisted suicide was a criminal act, whereas attempted suicide was not.[38] While the majority opinion supported this distinction, as the purpose of section 241(b) was to prevent the abuse of vulnerable individuals from being induced into assisted suicide, McLachlin J argued that the effect of this arbitrary distinction was "to prevent people like Sue Rodriguez from exercising the autonomy over their bodies available to other people."[39] Nor did McLachlin J find that the violation of section 7 was a reasonable limit under section 1. If the objective of section 241(b) was to ensure that vulnerable individuals were not pressured into suicide, sufficient safeguards already existed under the *Criminal Code*, and, failing this, safeguards could be created by the courts or by Parliament to protect vulnerable persons.[40] As a result of *Rodriguez*, the criminalization of assisted suicide was narrowly upheld and would remain in force until the *Carter* decision in 2015. While a number of private members bills to decriminalize assisted suicide were introduced after *Rodriguez*,[41] none were passed, and the policy status quo endured until 2015.

Shifting Ground: Toward the Decriminalization of Assisted Suicide
If the justification for the ban on assisted suicide was that western democracies valued life above all and state-sanctioned euthanasia was outside the norm, then section 241(b) was living on borrowed time when the *Carter*

decision was brought forward. Soon after *Rodriguez*, the state of Oregon permitted assisted suicide in 1994 with the passage of the *Death with Dignity Act*.[42] This would be followed by the Netherlands in 2001, Luxemburg in 2008, the states of Washington and Montana in 2008, Vermont in 2013, and, finally, Belgium in 2014.[43] In October 2009, the Collège des médecins du Québec published a paper on euthanasia, and this was followed by the National Assembly creating the Select Committee on Dying with Dignity in December 2009.[44] This committee delivered its report in March 2009 that supported an end-of-life regulatory scheme.[45] In addition, the Royal Society of Canada published a report in 2011 that supported "a permissive yet carefully regulated and monitored system with respect to assisted death."[46] In response to Quebec's Select Committee on Dying with Dignity, Parti Québécois minister Véronique Hivon introduced Bill 52, *An Act Respecting End-of-Life Care*, in June 2013, which would be passed by her Liberal successor, Gaetan Barrette, in June 2014 as a co-authored bill (Hivon and Barrette) to underscore the cross-party consensus on this issue.[47]

The attitudes of Canadians began to shift decisively in favour of assisted death in the years preceding the 2015 *Carter* decision. Polling by Forum reported that 67 percent of Canadians supported physician-assisted suicide for the terminally ill in 2011, and this rose to 74 percent by June 2014.[48] Following *Carter*, support for the Court's decision and assisted suicide rose to 78 percent.[49] The highest support for end-of-life assistance was found in Quebec, where 86 percent of people supported assisted suicide guidelines.[50] These shifts in support saw the initiation of a dialogue between the Canadian Medical Association and its members in June 2014, where a series of town halls with medical professionals were held to gauge views on assisted dying.[51] This would result in an important shift from opposition to assisted suicide to "the right of all physicians, within the bounds of existing legislation, to follow their conscience when deciding whether to provide medical aid in dying."[52] At the political level, the Liberal Party of Canada adopted a resolution in favour of assisted suicide during its 2014 policy convention.[53] By the time of the *Carter* decision, the landscape that saw the Supreme Court under Lamer CJ narrowly uphold the restrictions on physician-assisted death no longer existed in Canada or in comparable western democracies.

A Return to the Judicial Arena: Gloria Taylor and Kay Carter

The factual basis of the landmark case *Carter v Canada* bears striking similarities to its predecessor, *Rodriguez v British Columbia*. In 2009, Gloria Taylor was diagnosed with ALS, and, by 2010, her condition had deteriorated to the point that she was required home support for most aspects of daily living. Taylor considered this "as an assault on her privacy, dignity, and self-esteem" and, soon after, informed her family that she desired a physician-assisted death as the alternative was an "ugly death."[54] Kay Carter was diagnosed with spinal stenosis, "a condition that results in a progressive compression of the spinal cord" in which an individual suffers from chronic pain and has severely limited mobility.[55] Similar to Taylor, Carter was fully dependent on living assistance and also informed her family that she wished a physician-assisted death. Unlike Taylor, Carter's family were able to accompany her to Switzerland, and, in early 2010, she entered a Swiss clinic where a physician-assisted death was administered. The emotional toll and financial cost of travelling to Switzerland resulted in the daughter and son-in-law of Kay Carter – Lee Carter and Hollis Johnson – joining Taylor's constitutional challenge to the *Criminal Code* restrictions on physician-assisted suicide. This case was supported by the BC Civil Liberties Association (BCCLA), which submitted that the *Criminal Code* restrictions violated section 7 and section 15, the equality rights protections.

The constitutional challenge was first heard in the Supreme Court of British Columbia in November 2011, and the decision was delivered by Justice Lynn Smith in June 2012.[56] In her ruling, Smith J argued that, because of a change in factual evidence as well as the evolution of the Court's approach to section 7, the trial court was free to revisit the *Rodriguez* precedent. While agreeing with the *Rodriguez* judgment that the restriction on physician-assisted suicide was a violation life, liberty, and security of the person protected by section 7, the trial judgment determined that the restriction was inconsistent with the principles of fundamental justice and unconstitutional as it was not a reasonable limit by virtue of section 1.[57] The trial court also found that section 241(b) was unconstitutional as an infringement of section 15. This decision would be reversed by the court of appeal in October 2013, in which a majority panel (two to one) determined that lower courts are still bound by the *Rodriguez* precedent. As a result, section 241(b) was consistent with the principles of fundamental justice. Moreover, the trial court finding of a section 15 violation was also overturned, and the constitutionality of section 241(b) of the *Criminal Code* was reaffirmed by the BC Court of Appeal.[58] Leave to appeal to the Supreme Court of Canada was granted to the BCCLA soon after the decision, and the appeal was heard in October 2014.

In a unanimous decision in February 2015, the Supreme Court led by McLachlin CJ ruled overwhelmingly on the side of the trial court in regard to section 7 and whether it was appropriate for a lower court to revisit a constitutional precedent such as *Rodriguez*. Although it is unclear which justice authored *Carter*, as it was authored by "The Court," it is clear that the minority judgment of McLachlin J in *Rodriguez* was now the Court's unanimous position that sections 14 and 241(b) were a clear violation of section 7 and unconstitutional.[59] The main findings of the *Carter* decision are that, in regard to a lower court revisiting a constitutional precedent, the Court noted that "stare decisis is not a straitjacket that condemns law to stasis."[60] Further, the Court held that two conditions justify revisiting a precedent – if a new legal issue is raised or if there is a fundamental change in the evidence or context. Both of these conditions were met for the Court in *Carter*.

For the Supreme Court, there had been a clear shift in the policy context since *Rodriguez* as several western countries had legalized assisted suicide. A new set of social facts distinguished *Carter* from its predecessor case.[61] Perhaps more critical for *Rodriguez* and the constitutionality of section 241(b), the Court's approach to determining whether a restriction on life, liberty, and security of the person was consistent with the principles of fundamental justice had changed significantly since the Court's decision in *Bedford*.[62] While the Court continued to employ the standard of arbitrariness, it was now augmented with two additional considerations elevated to core principles of fundamental justice: whether the restriction suffered from overbreadth and whether the restriction was grossly disproportionate to its objective.[63] In short, a new approach to the principles of fundamental justice ensured that a new set of legal issues were raised in *Carter*, further justifying a lower court decision to overturn *Rodriguez*. If *Rodriguez* is an example of a strong-form decision, as it endured for a generation, its reversal in *Carter* is an example of one way that a strong-form decision can be overturned: when the composition of the Court changes, and a narrow decision no longer has majority support. As the only remaining justice from *Rodriguez*, and author of the leading minority dissent, McLachlin CJ transformed her minority position into the unanimous and anonymous position of *Carter*.

Two constitutional questions were addressed by the Supreme Court in *Carter* in regard to sections 14 and 241(b) of the *Criminal Code:* federalism and jurisdictional autonomy and the *Canadian Charter*. On federalism grounds, the BCCLA argued that the *Criminal Code* restriction was a violation of inter-jurisdictional immunity as the criminal regulation of physician-assisted death was an interference with core provincial responsibility for health care. Similar to the decision in *PHS Community Services Society*, the Court rejected the inter-jurisdictional immunity argument as the BCCLA had failed to demonstrate how the criminal restriction interfered with a core provincial responsibility.⁶⁴ More significantly, the Court affirmed that health-care policy functioned as a concurrent area of jurisdiction and that this "suggests that aspects of physician-assisted dying may be the subject of valid legislation by both levels of government."⁶⁵

Turning to constitutionalism and the *Canadian Charter*, the McLachlin court upheld much of the trial court findings that section 241(b) was a violation of life, liberty, and security of the person and that this engagement was inconsistent with the principles of fundamental justice. Unlike Sopinka J's view in *Rodriguez* that section 7 prioritized the protection of life, the McLachlin court stated that "s. 7 also encompasses life, liberty, and security of the person during the passage to death." Simply put, section 241(b) interfered with choosing the manner and form of one's death. It was the interference with liberty and security of the person that was perhaps most problematic for the Court in *Carter*:

> An individual's response to a grievous and irremediable medical condition is a matter critical to their dignity and autonomy. The law allows people in this situation to request palliative sedation, refuse artificial nutrition and hydration, or request the removal of life-sustaining medical equipment, but denies them the right to request a physician's assistance in dying. This interferes with their ability to make decisions concerning their bodily integrity and medical care and thus trenches on liberty. And, by leaving people like Ms. Taylor to endure intolerable suffering, it impinges on their security of the person.⁶⁶

Although the Court agreed that the interference was not in accordance with the principles of fundamental justice, it rejected the trial court's finding that all three considerations had been breached – section 241(b) was not arbitrary, as the blanket prohibition was designed to protect the vulnerable in moments of weakness,⁶⁷ but it clearly suffered from overbreadth. On this consideration, the Court argued that not all persons suffering from grievous and irremediable medical conditions were vulnerable and in need of protection and that "the blanket prohibition sweeps conduct into its ambit that is unrelated to the law's objective."⁶⁸ Because the law was found to be suffering from overbreadth, the Court declined to comment whether it also suffered from gross disproportionality, as the trial court judgment had.

In its section 1 analysis, the Supreme Court concluded that, while the legislative objectives were pressing and substantial and a rational connection existed between the objective and the legislative instrument chosen, the impairment on the right for adults suffering from a grievous and irremediable medical condition was not a minimal impairment of section 7. The Court rejected the position of the Attorney General of Canada that it was impossible to design a permissive regime for physician-assisted death with sufficient safeguards for competent and consenting adults.[69] Nor did the Court accept that "without an absolute prohibition on assisted dying, Canada will descend the slippery slope into euthanasia and condoned murder."[70]

While the constitutional invalidation of section 241(b) in *Carter* represents a seminal moment in Canadian legal history, as the Court overturned a long-standing precedent and removed the criminal penalty on assisted dying, this negative rights decision was profound because of the remedy and policy prescription offered in *Carter*. As Dave Snow and Kate Puddister noted, *Carter* opened a policy window that had been closed since *Rodriguez*.[71] In its section 24(1) remedy, the Court declared that "s. 241(b) and s. 14 of the *Criminal Code* are void insofar as they prohibit physician-assisted death for a competent adult who (1) clearly consents to a termination of life; and (2) have a grievous and irremediable medical condition (including an illness, disease, or disability) that causes enduring suffering that is intolerable to the individual in the circumstances of his or her condition."[72] The constitutional directive established by the Court was clear – eligibility for physician-assisted death for competent adults satisfying the two outlined conditions does not require a grievous or irremediable medical condition to be terminal or that death is imminent.[73] They simply need to be experiencing intolerable suffering to be eligible for MAiD. More to the point, the authoritative manner in which this decision was released was meant to convey, without ambiguity, that, if Parliament chose to amend the *Criminal Code*, it could not alter the eligibility criteria in paragraph 127 of the *Carter* decision: "It is for Parliament and the provincial legislatures to respond, should they choose, by enacting legislation consistent with the constitutional parameters set out in these reasons."[74]

This is not to say that the Supreme Court of Canada denied Parliament and the provincial legislature some discretion in their legislative and regulatory responses to *Carter*. The Court indicated that, while the eligibility criteria in paragraph 127 must be honoured, "the scope of this declaration is intended to respond to the factual circumstances in this case. We make no pronouncement on other situations where physician-assisted dying may be sought."[75] The factual circumstances involved non-terminal adult patients with grievous and irremediable medical conditions experiencing intolerable suffering that were to be exempt from the restrictions that section 241(b) imposed on assisted suicide.[76] It can be reasonably inferred that, beyond this, Parliament was free to consider whether other medical conditions, and people, may qualify for MAiD. For instance, whether people suffering from mental illness would be eligible for MAiD, whether advance directives could be allowed, and whether mature minors – those under eighteen years of age – may qualify in certain circumstances. These decisions were left to Parliament. In so doing, the Court established the constitutional floor for MAiD eligibility and not the ceiling.[77]

Other degrees of discretion were provided to Parliament, the provinces, and the territorial governments. The Supreme Court noted that the Canadian Medical Association had requested that the conscience rights of physicians be protected by the Court in its decision. While the Court stated that it would not address this issue, it did make the point that "we underline that the Charter rights of patients and physicians will need to be reconciled."[78] This aspect of *Carter* is particularly important as the Court was aware of the limitations of a negative rights decision involving section 7: "In our view, nothing in the declaration of invalidity which we propose to issue would compel physicians to provide assistance in dying. The declaration simply renders the criminal prohibition invalid."[79] Moreover, the Court acknowledged that it was an "implementer-dependent institution," reliant on other actors to implement its ruling: "What follows is in the hands of physicians colleges, Parliament, and the provincial legislatures."[80] And, most importantly, it stated that federalism and the agents of implementation were essential to MAiD's success.

Having found that sections 14 and 241(b) infringed section 7 and an unreasonable limit under section 1, the Court suspended its declaration of unconstitutionality for twelve months.[81] Unless Parliament amended the *Criminal Code* by February 6, 2016, and addressed the constitutional overbreadth of section 241(b), the provision would be rendered "of no force or effect" on that date. At this time, the permissive regime for MAiD outlined in paragraph 127 of the decision would replace the offending provision of the *Criminal Code*. *Carter* and MAiD had been placed squarely on Parliament's legislative agenda, and they represented the last substantive Charter issue that the Harper government faced in the lead up to the 2015 federal election, which would take place on October 19, 2015.

Running Out the Clock: From Harper to Trudeau
Unlike the decision in *PHS Community Services Society*, in which the minister of health registered the Harper government's profound disagreement with

the lower court ruling, the minister of justice was more reserved in response to *Carter:* "This is a sensitive issue for many Canadians, with deeply held beliefs on both sides. We will study the decision and ensure all perspectives on this difficult issue are heard."[82] More importantly, the minister of justice ruled out using the notwithstanding clause.[83] Recognizing the short legislative calendar before the 2015 election, the minister of justice noted that a legislative response to *Carter* was unlikely before Canadians headed to the polls.[84]

The only concrete action taken by the Harper government was to establish the External Panel on July 17, 2015.[85] This three-person panel would submit its report to the Trudeau government after the 2015 election, and the minister of justice and minister of health, Jody Wilson-Raybould and Jane Philpott, received the report on December 15, 2015.[86] Under the original terms of reference, the External Panel was to provide legislative options for Parliament's response to *Carter* and the report by November 15. However, the Trudeau government granted a one-month extension and altered the terms of reference: "Rather than providing legislative options as per your original mandate, we would ask instead you prepare a report summarizing the key results and key findings of your consultations."[87] The final report is simply a summary of the main issues that a legislative response to *Carter* must consider, though there are two noteworthy discussions that emerged: first, the fact that the Court's decision is clear that a terminal illness is not a requirement for MAiD eligibility[88] and, second, that "a safe and thoughtful physician-assisted dying framework with equitable access for eligible Canadians will require substantial cooperation between all Canadian jurisdictions."[89]

Recognizing that a legislative response to *Carter* could not be met by February 6, 2016, the minister of justice sought a six-month extension on the *Carter* remedy.[90] This request was made in mid-November,[91] and the Court considered it on January 11, 2016, and rendered its decision on January 15.[92] Additionally, PDAM was established by Parliament on December 15, 2015, and the ministers of justice and health indicated that the report by the External Panel would be provided to PDAM once the government had reviewed it.[93] In the 2016 decision of *Carter v Canada (Carter II)*, three issues were considered: whether to grant the six-month extension, whether it should apply to Quebec's *Act Respecting End-of-Life Care*, and whether to issue constitutional exemptions for those seeking MAiD in the interim.[94] Unanimity only occurred on the extension request for the *Carter* remedy, and there was majority support (five to four) for the remaining issues.[95] Instead of a six-month extension, the Trudeau government was granted four additional months.[96] The suspended declaration of unconstitutionality now lasted until

June 6, 2016. The other substantive issue involved constitutional exemptions for those seeking MAiD in the interim. Recognizing that this extended period would further delay legal access to MAiD to competent adults permitted by the criteria outlined in paragraph 127 of the 2015 *Carter* decision, the *Carter II* majority instructed those seeking MAiD to apply to provincial superior courts for judicial authorization. As the majority noted, "requiring judicial authorization during that interim period ensures compliance with the rule of law and provides an effective safeguard against potential risks to vulnerable people."[97]

Countdown to *Carter*: PDAM and the 2016 *Act on MAiD*

Having been granted a four-month extension, the legislative response to *Carter* began with PDAM. Over fourteen meetings, the joint committee heard from sixty-one witnesses and reviewed 132 briefs. The committee report was presented to the House of Commons on February 25. Composed of members of the House of Commons and the Senate, it was unique in one important respect. Parliamentary committees are based on party standings, and the Trudeau government would normally have a majority of PDAM's membership as well as the position of the chair.[98] In a departure from this practice, PDAM would see the government neither chair the committee nor have a majority of its members: a Conservative senator and a Liberal MP served as joint chairs, and a Conservative and NDP vice-chairs were appointed from house members. Of the sixteen members, only half would be from the Liberal Party (n = 6) and Senate Liberals (n = 2). In this respect, it was structured much like the Joint Committee on Human Rights in the United Kingdom, tasked with providing the government with non-binding recommendations, where neither party discipline nor partisan division would influence the committee's findings.[99]

In its majority report to the House, PDAM made twenty-one recommendations that focused on eligibility requirements for MAiD, procedural safeguards, and advice on federal-provincial coordination to ensure a uniform approach.[100] The most significant recommendations involved which competent adults should be eligible for MAiD. Noting that the joint committee agreed with the External Panel that *Carter* did not limit MAiD to those suffering a terminal illness,[101] the report recommended that MAiD should be available for adults with terminal and non-terminal illnesses (Recommendation 2). Further, it specified that competent adults suffering from psychiatric conditions should not be excluded from MAiD (Recommendation 3) and that MAiD should be available to individuals facing enduring and intolerable physical and psychological suffering (Recommendation 4). Conservative MPs submitted a dissenting report, suggesting that the absence of sufficient safeguards for vulnerable individuals, and the extension of MAiD to those suffering psychological suffering, went well beyond the *Carter* requirements.[102]

After reviewing PDAM's report, the minister of justice introduced Bill C-14 into the House on April 14, 2016. The bill contained two main dimensions: first, a set of administrative safeguards to ensure that only competent adults could request and be granted this service by medical professionals (section 241.2(3)) and, second, the codification of eligibility criteria for MAiD (section 241.2(1)(2)). Given that the Court left the designing of safeguards to the discretion of the Trudeau government, the process for requesting MAiD was aimed to ensure that only competent adults, free from coercion, could indicate a desire for this medical service. For instance, once a person was determined by a medical or nurse practitioner to be eligible for MAiD under the 2016 *Act on MAiD*'s criteria, they would have to submit a written request, signed by a witness. This would also be verified by two independent witnesses. This verified written request would then be reviewed by a second practitioner to verify eligibility.

Throughout this process, a competent adult requesting MAiD must be informed that their request can be withdrawn at any moment, and at least fifteen days must pass between the request and MAiD being provided by a medical or nurse practitioner. This would be reduced to ten days in the final version of the 2016 *Act on MAiD*. A shorter period was permitted if a practitioner determined that a loss of capacity to provide informed consent was imminent. On the day that MAiD was scheduled to occur, a competent adult must be provided with an opportunity to rescind the written request. And, finally, express consent must be provided immediately prior to the administration of MAiD.[103] The Court in *Carter* agreed with the trial judge that the social science evidence demonstrated that the construction of safeguards was possible. These safeguards would most likely satisfy the McLachlin court as they were carefully designed to protect vulnerable adults. According to Hamish Stewart, while the procedural safeguards may be overly broad and inconsistent with the principles of fundamental justice, they would nonetheless be found reasonable under section 1.[104] The safeguards are also very similar to those suggested by PDAM in its report to the House of Commons.

If there was such a close alignment between these safeguards, the Court, and PDAM, why was the 2016 *Act on MAiD* not a notable example of Charter dialogue, as Bateman and LeBlanc conclude that it is?[105] There is no doubt that there is symmetry between the 2016 *Act on MAiD*'s procedural safeguards, *Carter*, and PDAM's report. But these procedural matters do not constitute the substantive core of the 2016 *Act on MAiD*. The eligibility criteria do. It is here where the Trudeau government showed its lack of commitment to institutional dialogue. Despite the minister of justice's repeated defence of legislating outside the constitutional parameters of *Carter*'s eligibility criteria as consistent with Charter dialogue, the government engaged in non-compliance at the core of the *Carter* decision.[106] And, in this respect, the Trudeau government's defence of the 2016 *Act on MAiD* mirrored the Harper government's repeated assertion that the *Respect for Communities Act* was, itself, consistent with the decision in *PHS Community Services Society*. This appears to be a common pattern among majority governments – the assertion that legislative amendments are constitutional, despite clear departures from constitutional parameters established by the Court.

MAiD Eligibility: When a Legislative Response Is Dialogue's Undoing

To be eligible for MAiD under section 241.2(1), a competent adult must satisfy the following conditions: they are eligible for publicly funded health services in Canada; they are at least eighteen years of age and able to make decisions about their health; they have a grievous and irremediable medical condition; they are able to make a voluntary request for MAiD, free-from-coercion; and, finally, they provide informed consent to the request. On their own, none of the eligibility criteria are at odds with *Carter*. For greater certainty, section 241.2(2) established four mandatory criteria to determine what constitutes a "grievous and irremediable" medical condition:

> (2) A person has a grievous and irremediable medical condition if
> - they have a serious and incurable illness, disease or disability;
> - they are in an advanced state of irreversible decline in capacity;
> - that illness, disease or disability or that state of decline causes them enduring physical or psychological suffering that is intolerable to them and that cannot be relieved under conditions that they consider acceptable; and
> - their natural death has become reasonably foreseeable, taking into account all of their medical circumstances, without a prognosis necessarily having been made as to the specific length of time that they have remaining.[107]

Criteria (a)–(c) are also consistent with the constitutional parameters established in *Carter* as much of the language mirrors that contained within paragraph 127 of the decision. But criterion (d) – that natural death is reasonably foreseeable – is not. This requirement generated an important debate whether the 2016 *Act on MAiD* ultimately complied with *Carter*[108] or was itself an unconstitutional addition by the Trudeau government.[109] This was ultimately decided in 2019 by the Superior Court of Quebec in *Truchon*, when it declared section 241.2(2)(d) unconstitutional as a violation of sections 7 and 15 of the *Canadian Charter*.[110]

As the eligibility criteria are the core of the Trudeau government's response to *Carter*, the discussion of the parliamentary debate on the 2016 *Act on MAiD* will focus on the reasonable foreseeability of natural death (RFND) requirement for MAiD eligibility. The discussion will then shift to the implementation phase of MAiD, as it relies heavily on public (provincial and territorial governments) and private actors (health associations and practitioners). Instead of constituting evidence of dialogue theory, or judicial impact beyond the legislative phase, MAiD's policy impact is better understood as being similar to that of supervised consumption sites – one involving a complex implementation chain where impact is the result of cooperative federalism augmented by the personal choice of medical professionals whether to participate in the delivery of a health service. Or, in the lexicon of this study, when the actors required to implement a judicial decision engage in legislative agreement and give a judicial decision indirect, but observable, policy impact.

Although *Truchon* decided that the RFND requirement was unconstitutional, it is instructive to consider the justification provided by the Trudeau government's minister of justice. The government clearly recognized that it needed to defend this *Carter* departure, releasing a detailed study explaining why the government believed that the 2016 *Act on MAiD* generally complied with *Carter*, with specific attention focused on section 241.2(2)(d).[111] And, in what would become standard practice by the Trudeau government, the release of the first "Charter statement" in regard to a government bill, whereby constitutional validity is set out before the second reading debate on a bill.[112]

Even before the introduction of Bill C-14, a discussion that foreshadowed the RFND criterion took place between members of PDAM and officials from the Department of Justice. When asked by Mark Warawa, a Conservative MP from Langley–Aldergrove, whether a terminal illness was a *Carter* requirement for MAiD, a Department of Justice official responded that the Supreme Court was ambiguous about this issue:

> That is what is not entirely clear. Certainly many commentators have said there's nothing in the Supreme Court's decision that says this is limited to people who are terminally ill. On the other hand, there's nothing in the Supreme Court decision that clearly says this is not limited to people who are terminally ill. Both of these expressions would have taken a very small number of words. Neither of those statements is there, so we cannot say with certainty what the court had in mind.[113]

This was followed by another Department of Justice official that invoked the dialogue metaphor to justify legislative departures from the constitutional standards established by the Court, relying on the *O'Connor* to *Mills* precedent.[114] In *O'Connor,* the Court created a common law test for the judicial disclosure of records held by third parties in sexual assault cases and attempted to balance the right of an accused for a fair trial (full answer and defence) with the privacy rights of the complainant.[115] It was criticized, both within and outside Parliament, as focusing too much on the right of the accused at the expense of the complainant in sexual assault cases. In response, Parliament passed Bill C-46,[116] which departed from the common law disclosure regime created by the majority decision in *O'Connor,* as Bill C-46, *An Act on the Production of Records in Sexual Offence Proceedings,* prioritized the complainant in sexual assault proceedings.[117] Upon judicial review, the Court upheld the *O'Connor* departures in *R. v Mills*[118] and did so by invoking the dialogue metaphor. Before PDAM, the Department of Justice official suggested that a legislative departure from *Carter* was permitted because of the *O'Connor* to *Mills* precedent:

> The bottom line there is that there is some scope within which to manoeuvre. Obviously the committee and Parliament will have to have regard to the principles and broad parameters that the court articulated in *Carter*. At the end of the day, whatever regime Parliament comes up with is going to be assessed against the objective that Parliament was striving to achieve and how rational and proportionate Parliament's solution is as a means of achieving that objective.[119]

The last sentence is particularly revealing. It suggests that the Department of Justice had concluded that the RFND criterion – the only substantive

Carter departure in the soon to be introduced Bill C-14 – violated section 7 of the *Canadian Charter* and would be saved by recourse to section 1, the reasonable limits clause. The suggested constitutionality of this criterion relied heavily on the language of reasonable limits developed in the *Oakes* test, as the Department of Justice official spoke of rational connections and proportionality between the means chosen to achieve the legislative objective.[120]

When defending the inclusion of the natural death requirement, the minister of justice launched a four-part argument: first, that the Supreme Court of Canada failed to define the parameters of a grievous and irremediable medical condition in *Carter*, and, because of this, clarity was necessary to avoid an inconsistent approach by provincial/territorial medical associations; second, the Court would grant Parliament flexibility in its attempt to comply with *Carter*; third, any legislative departure from *Carter* was an illustration of Charter dialogue, which the Court had endorsed in *Mills*; and, finally, that a legislative response "is never as simple as simply cutting and pasting the words from a judgment into a new law."[121] These arguments were made by the minister of justice during parliamentary debates on Bill C-14,[122] her appearance before JUST,[123] as well as before the Standing Senate Committee on Legal and Constitutional Affairs (LCJC).[124]

None of these arguments outlast scrutiny.[125] We know, because of the *Truchon* decision, that the RFND requirement would not be saved by virtue of section 1 of the *Canadian Charter*. We also know that the Trudeau government acknowledged this when it decided not to appeal the lower court ruling. What has not received sufficient attention is how unique the Trudeau government's acquiescence to *Truchon* is, given that it was decided at the Superior Court of Quebec, a judicial body presided over by a single justice. There were two appeal routes that remained available: the Quebec Court of Appeal and the Supreme Court of Canada. *Truchon* and MAiD represent the only salient issue of public policy considered in this book in which the appeals process was not exhausted by the government with legislative authority for the statute in question. That the Trudeau government forewent these appeals suggests that its defence of the 2016 *Act on MAiD* was based more on parliamentary bravado, backed by a majority government, than constitutional certainty.

The first troublesome aspect of the minister of justice's explanation for the *Carter* departure is apparent when compared to the next substantive issue addressed by the Trudeau government – the decision to revisit the Harper government's *Respect for Communities Act* in Bill C-37, *An Act to*

Amend the Controlled Drugs and Substances Act, which was introduced by Philpott, the minister of health, in December 2016, shortly after the passage of Bill C-14 in June.[126] Simply put, Bill C-37 and the application process for supervised consumption sites is an example of the Trudeau government "simply cutting and pasting the words from a court's judgment into a new law." More problematic is the reliance on *Mills* to justify legislative noncompliance and to suggest that the Court would be willing to accept *Carter* departures as evidence of the robust dialogue that produces public policy in the Charter era. The question that the minister of justice and her officials failed to consider is whether *Mills* and *Carter* are equivalents, either in terms of issue salience, the constitutional issue before the Court (procedural versus substantive), the authority in which the Court rendered its decision, and the nature of the legislative departure from a previous judicial ruling.

Mills and *Carter* are not equivalents. *Mills* centres on a procedural matter – how best to disclose records held by third parties in sexual assault cases to the defence that balances the accused's right to a fair trial with the privacy rights of the complainant. While *Carter* does involve a procedural matter – the need to design safeguards to ensure that MAiD would only be administered to competent adults that have freely consented – these safeguards were left entirely to Parliament. At its substantive core, *Carter* involves a profound issue in which the Court was clear about the constitutional parameters that must be adhered to – namely, the eligibility criteria to allow competent adults, with assistance, to exercise personal autonomy and to end their suffering. In this respect, they are not equivalent issues as one is about balancing existing rights (*Mills*) and the other is about the creation of a right for competent adults suffering a grievous and irremediable medical condition that a government has sought to severally restrict.

But, on a more basic level, *Mills* and *Carter* are not equivalents, and the minister of justice and her department erred in suggesting that *Mills* created a precedent for judicial acceptance of legislative departures. As Christopher Manfredi has argued, *Mills* can only be understood in light of *O'Connor* and how it influenced the *Act on the Production of Records in Sexual Offence Proceedings*. While *O'Connor* was a majority decision (five to four), the Court was unanimous that records held by third parties in sexual assault cases must be disclosed to the defence. Where the Court divided was on the process governing disclosure in sexual assault cases. As Manfredi contends, the majority favoured a more liberal approach, whereas the minority favoured a more restrictive approach.[127] Despite sexual assault being a serious issue, *O'Connor* was really about competing judicial approaches to the disclosure of records in judicial proceedings. And, in this respect, the constitutional question facing the Court in *O'Connor* pales in comparison to the one faced in *Carter*.

While the legislative response in *Mills* does depart from the majority decision in *O'Connor*, it does not establish a precedent for judicial acceptance of legislative non-compliance, despite the minister of justice's assertion that it does. As Manfredi clearly demonstrates, the *Act on the Production of Records in Sexual Offence Proceedings* was simply statutory codification of the dissenting opinion in *O'Connor* as an amendment to the *Criminal Code*. While *Mills* was a near unanimous decision (seven to one), with one partial dissent (Lamer CJ), three of the justices that formed the minority in *O'Connor* (Justices Claire L'Heureux-Dubé, Charles Gonthier, and McLachlin) – and what largely informed the disclosure process of records for sexual assault proceedings in the *Act on the Production of Records in Sexual Offence Proceedings* – became the core of the majority opinion in *Mills*, authored by McLachlin and Frank Iacobucci. The *O'Connor* minority would be joined by Iacobucci and Major from the *O'Connor* majority and two additions to the Court since *O'Connor* (Justices Michel Bastarache and Ian Binnie). According to Manfredi, "it is hardly surprising, then, that in *Mills* Justice McLachlin would uphold a policy regime she 'entirely' concurred in *O'Connor*. If any dialogue occurred in *Mills*, it was an internal one among the justices about which *O'Connor* regime would prevail."[128]

What the minister of justice failed to identify is that there are limits to judicial acceptance of legislative non-compliance. That *O'Connor* was a narrow majority decision (five to four) and *Carter* a unanimous decision authored by "The Court" is an important difference that should not be downplayed. Judicial tolerance of legislative departures from a previous decision may be a function of the authority in which a judgment is rendered. In *Mills*, the disclosure regime in the *Act on the Production of Records in Sexual Offence Proceedings* had judicial support within the *O'Connor* minority, and the legislative response co-opted the narrower approach to disclosure by the minority decision that favoured the complainant in sexual assault cases. This act did not represent a drastic alternation in the common law guidelines created by the majority as two members of the *O'Connor* majority accepted the statutory changes reviewed in *Mills* as within the constitutional parameters established by the Court in *O'Connor*.

This is not the case regarding the 2016 *Act on MAiD* and the eligibility criteria established by a unanimous *Carter* bench. The Trudeau government did not alter the eligibility criteria for MAiD at the margins or build upon a minority decision that very nearly was the majority decision when it drafted the 2016 *Act on MAiD*, as a previous Liberal government did in relation to the *Act on the Production of Records in Sexual Offence Proceedings*. It sought to fundamentally narrow the Court's eligibility criteria from all competent adults suffering a grievous and irremediable medical condition to only competent adults whose natural death is reasonably foreseeable. As Joseph Arvay, counsel for Carter argued in regard to the 2016 *Act on MAiD*, "Parliament has essentially carved out from the *Carter* decision a whole and significant group of individuals in our society, and they are the physically disabled whose death is not imminent or reasonably foreseeable."[129] More importantly, the Trudeau government sought to legislate around an authoritative and anonymous judicial opinion and not a narrow five-to-four judgment. In this regard, the minister of justice's assurance of judicial acceptance of the legislative departures in *Carter* because of *Mills* minimizes how different these decisions are and how extensive a legislative departure from *Carter* was being proposed in the 2016 *Act on MAiD*'s eligibility criteria.

This is not to say that the Court, if the 2016 *Act on MAiD*'s invalidation in *Truchon* was to be appealed, would not accept Parliament's attempt to comply with *Carter*. But it depends on what the legislative departure involved – the procedural safeguards or the eligibility criteria. As Arvay argued in his brief before JUST, there can be a dialogue on the procedural safeguards as these were left to the discretion of Parliament. But there cannot be a dialogue on who is eligible for MAiD:

> This is not to say there is no room for a Parliamentary response to *Carter* or a "dialogue" between the Court and Parliament but that response must be more procedural rather than substantive. By which I mean that Parliament might require certain processes such as having two or more doctors and other safeguards *to assess decisional capability* for the defined group but it cannot *redefine the group* in such a way as to deny or exclude the persons that the SCC expressly included as having the right to PAD. Hence, there is no room for Parliament to further restrict let alone justify any further restrictions on the s. 7 rights based on s. 1 of the *Charter*.[130]

In suggesting this, Arvay did acknowledge that it was possible for the Trudeau government to alter the eligibility criteria for MAiD but only in a particular direction. For Arvay, *Carter* established the constitutional floor for MAiD eligibility. While it was possible for the Trudeau government to increase MAiD eligibility for groups that fell outside the *Carter* standard, such as mature minors or those suffering from psychological or mental illness, it could not remove access to those competent adults determined by the Court to be eligible for MAiD in *Carter*.[131] A similar position was advanced by Jocelyn Downie during her appearance before the LCJC[132] and the executive director of the BCCLA.[133]

Although the Canadian Medical Association supported the 2016 *Act on MAiD*, its brief largely focused on the procedural safeguards and not on the eligibility criteria.[134] There was, however, serious opposition to the RFND criterion by notable groups appearing before, or making submission to, JUST on the 2016 *Act on MAiD*. The Canadian Civil Liberties Association, the Canadian Bar Association, the British Columbia Civil Liberties Association, the Barreau du Québec, the College of Family Physicians of Canada, and Dying with Dignity Canada all argued that this requirement was a stark departure from *Carter* and would not be found a reasonable limit under section 1 if challenged in court.[135] These concerns also extended to the Senate and the proceedings of the LCJC. In his questioning of both the minister and the deputy minister of justice, Senator Serge Joyal contended that the RFND criterion was a marked departure from *Carter* and that it would not be considered a reasonable limit under section 1.[136] This position was supported by Peter Hogg during his appearance before the LCJC when he identified the constitutional problem with the RFND criterion:

> I think it's incredible to think that what was intended by the court, when it said to pass legislation consistent with the constitutional parameters of the case, was to exclude a whole category of people who had won the right through three stages of litigation to the Supreme Court of Canada ... I say that the grant of power to Parliament in *Carter* makes clear that they can't turn around and suddenly exclude from the right a group of people who have just been granted the right by the Supreme Court. The court couldn't have intended that, I say.[137]

A common concern among members of LCJC was that the RFND requirement was so inconsistent with the *Carter* decision that the 2016 *Act on MAiD* was unconstitutional.[138]

Both the leader of the Senate Liberals, James Cowan, and the leader of the Conservative caucus in the Senate, Claude Carignan, determined that this criterion violated the constitutional parameters established in *Carter* and was thus unconstitutional.[139] Opposition to this criterion saw the Senate, uncharacteristically, substantively amend Bill C-14 and remove the RFND criterion.¹⁴⁰ This amendment was proposed by Joyal and was defended as essential to ensure that Bill C-14 complied with *Carter*, which its supporters equated with being Charter compliant.¹⁴¹ This amendment was accepted on the floor of the Senate by a vote of sixty-four to twelve, with one abstention.¹⁴² And given that the Senate had amended a bill passed by the House of Commons, Bill C-14 was returned to the House of Commons for reconsideration.

What may have convinced a majority of the Senate that the RFND criterion was unconstitutional, and what motivated the amendment by Joyal, were a series of lower court decisions that cast doubt on the sustainability of the Trudeau government's approach. Many senators that supported the Joyal amendment referred to two lower court judgments that rejected the Attorney General of Canada's position in court that MAiD eligibility was limited to those suffering terminal illness and nearing the end of their natural life. Shortly before third reading of Bill C-14 occurred in the House of Commons on May 31, 2016, and before the Senate began its second reading debate on June 3, 2016, a decision by the Alberta Court of Appeal on May 17, 2016, cast doubts on the constitutionality of the natural death requirement.

At issue in *Canada (Attorney General) v E.F.* was an application for MAiD submitted by a fifty-eight-year-old woman approved by the Alberta Court of Queen's Bench but opposed by the Attorney General of Canada.¹⁴³ In the absence of the 2016 *Act on MAiD*, and as part of the remedy extending the suspended declaration of unconstitutionality for an additional four months, the Court in *Carter II* allowed superior courts to create an interim process for MAiD approval.¹⁴⁴ The Attorney General of Canada opposed E.F.'s application on the grounds that it did not satisfy the *Carter* requirements in two respects: first, her condition was severe but not terminal and, second, she was suffering from a psychiatric condition.¹⁴⁵ In a unanimous decision authored in the name of "The Court," the Alberta Court of Appeal dismissed the Attorney General of Canada's position that MAiD eligibility only applied to competent adults nearing the end of their lives that were suffering grievous and irremediable medical conditions:

> In summary, the declaration of invalidity in *Carter* 2015 does not require that the applicant be terminally ill to qualify for authorization. The decision itself is clear. No words in it suggests otherwise. If the court had wanted it to be thus, they would have said so clearly and unequivocally. They did not. The interpretation urged on us by Canada is not sustainable having regard to the fundamental premise of *Carter* itself as expressed in its opening paragraph, and does not accord with the trial judgment, the

breadth of the record at trial, and the recommended safeguards that were ultimately upheld by the Supreme Court of Canada.[146]

The court of appeal also rejected Canada's argument that competent adults suffering psychiatric illnesses were excluded from MAiD eligibility.[147] As a result, MAiD was approved for a non-terminal competent adult suffering from a long-standing psychiatric illness. Soon after the Alberta Court of Appeal decision, the Ontario Superior Court approved a MAiD application on May 24, 2016, for a ninety-year-old man suffering a series of non-terminal illnesses. Similar to the Alberta decision, the Ontario decision affirmed that neither *Carter* nor *Carter II* required "that a medical condition be terminal or life-threatening."[148]

The minister and deputy minister of justice made two overarching arguments in support of the 2016 *Act on MAiD* and the RFND criterion: first, the term "grievous and irremediable" medical condition was left undefined by the Supreme Court of Canada, and, because the Court did not explicitly prohibit the criterion of natural death, it was fitting for Parliament to operationalize the term and to include the RFND requirement and, second, the 2016 *Act on MAiD* did not have to be *Carter* compliant – it simply had to be Charter compliant.[149] Whereas the senators that supported the Joyal amendment equated *Carter* with the *Canadian Charter*, the minister and deputy minister of justice did not. On this issue, the minister and deputy minister of justice accepted that this *Carter* departure did violate section 7 of the Charter and that "ultimately it will be the question of whether or not this decision for Canada represents a reasonable limit prescribed by law in a free and democratic society."[150]

There are two fundamental problems with this defence of the 2016 *Act on MAiD*. On the question of judicial silence, while the Supreme Court of Canada may not have defined "grievous and irremediable" medical conditions, as much of its ruling was an endorsement of the trial court decision, as the Alberta Court of Appeal noted in *E.F.*, this does not mean that the term was undefined. What the minister and deputy minister of justice failed to discuss was the origin and authorship of this term. In short, it was not a judicial creation at the trial court level. It was the judicial adoption of the definition of MAiD eligibility argued throughout the trial process in British Columbia, and in the appeal heard by the Supreme Court of Canada, by the lead co-counsel for *Carter* – Joseph Arvay. In his brief to JUST and his appearances before the House and Senate committees, Arvay discussed why *Carter*'s counsel framed eligibility around the term "grievous and irremediably ill patient":

> From the very outset, the *Carter* case was brought in order to make physician-assisted dying available to a "grievously and irremediably ill patent." We were very deliberate in our choice of words as they were chosen to ensure that the right to PAD not be limited to those whose illness or disease or disability was "terminal" or any euphemism such as where "*their natural death has become reasonably foreseeable.*"[151]

Arvay's submission states that the Department of Justice "demanded particulars of this term used in the proceedings" and that a definition was provided by Carter's counsel.[152] It also states that "notably absent from this definition is any suggestion that the illness, disease or disability be 'terminal.'"[153]

Moreover, Arvay notes that, while the term "terminal" was used 127 times by the Supreme Court of British Columbia, "the trial court judge declined to use that language in her order."[154] And given that the Supreme Court of Canada in *Carter* fully endorsed the decision of the trial court,[155] and not that of the court of appeal, this casts doubt on the minister and deputy minister of justices' defence of this substantive *Carter* departure. There was neither judicial silence on the meaning of a "grievous and irremediable" medical condition, as contended by the deputy minister of justice,[156] nor an ability for the Trudeau government to include the reasonably foreseeability of death criterion because the Supreme Court of Canada had not explicitly prohibited this term. The only way to justify this substantive departure was to overlook the important role played by Carter's legal counsel in operationalizing this term and the reliance on this definition by the trial court judge. As the Supreme Court of Canada's decision is overwhelmingly an affirmation of the trial court's findings, this defence of the *Carter* departure by the minister of justice and her departmental officials simply does not hold.

Nor does the minister of justice's contention that the RFND requirement may violate section 7 but would be constitutional as a reasonable limit under section 1 of the *Canadian Charter*. In responding to Senator Joyal's reference to the minister of justice's argument that any section 7 violation would be saved via section 1, as Canadians were not yet willing to extend MAiD beyond the terminally ill, Arvay dismissed this suggestion:

> Quite simply because section 1 that the minister is now referring to was fully argued by the government in the *Carter* case. The government in the *Carter* case tried to defend not just the proposed legislation as written but in all of its applications. The court was presented by the government

with the section 1 argument, and it was rejected. To suggest that the bill is constitutional because the minister thinks that there are some people in the public who believe it should only go this far is, in my respectful submission, not legal reasoning and has no merit.[157]

More critically, Arvay rejected the minister of justice's suggestion that, in *Carter*, the Court limited its decision to the facts before it – the particular health challenges facing Gloria Taylor and Kay Carter – and that the 2016 *Act on MAiD*, because it responded to a broader set of facts, could restrict MAiD to those whose natural death is reasonably foreseeable to protect the vulnerable:

> We were very deliberate when we framed the case that it was not going to be about one person. Unlike the Sue Rodriguez case, which was only about one person, we framed the case to make sure that the court heard about the illnesses and disabilities and suffering of people from all across Canada, and elsewhere, because it was our view that the legislation was unconstitutional because of its application not just to one person or two but potentially thousands of Canadians who might face this kind of intolerable suffering.[158]

Although the bill sent to the Senate for review was overwhelmingly supported by the Liberal caucus, Liberal MP David Lametti voted against this bill, arguing that the RFND requirement was inconsistent with *Carter* and the *Canadian Charter*.[159] Lametti's opposition to Bill C-14, while notable at the time as only four Liberal MPs voted against it,[160] would take on added significance when he succeeded Wilson-Raybould as minister of justice on January 14, 2019, and assumed responsibility for the legislative response to *Truchon*, Bill C-7.[161]

The "Other Place" Responds

When the two houses of parliament refer to each other, the phrase the "other place" is used. As the Senate had amended Bill C-14, it returned to the "other place" for a consideration of the proposed changes. In response to the seven amendments passed by the Senate, the Trudeau government accepted several of them when Bill C-14 returned to the House of Commons. The accepted amendments constitute minor technical changes to Bill C-14: palliative care options for patients, the creation of reporting obligations for the minister of health, the creation of an independent review involving advanced requests that must report within two years, and restrictions on the role of beneficiaries in MAiD proceedings.[162]

The most significant amendment was the one proposed by Senator Joyal that removed the RFND requirement for MAiD eligibility. In short, the Senate aligned Bill C-14 with the eligibility criteria provided in paragraph 127 of the *Carter* decision. Moreover, this approach to MAiD eligibility aligned with the one recommended by PDAM[163] and that of the Provincial-Territorial Expert Advisory Group that submitted its report in December 2015 to the eleven jurisdictions that participated.[164] The minister of justice presented a motion to the House outlining how the government intended to respond to the Senate amendments. In parliamentary language, the House sent a message to "other place" outlining which amendments it would accept and which amendments it "respectfully disagrees" with. It was no surprise that the proposed message disagreed with the removal of the RFND requirement for MAiD eligibility.

In rejecting the removal of this eligibility criteria, the minister of justice reiterated the government's view that constitutionality and *Carter* compatibility are not one and the same. Moreover, the Supreme Court of Canada "was clear that it is the role of Parliament to craft a complex, regulatory regime with respect to medical assistance in dying and that such a regime would be given a high degree of deference by the courts."[165] This defence of the 2016 *Act on MAiD* is particularly striking, given that two courts – the Alberta Court of Appeal and the Superior Court of Ontario – had recently refused to accept legal arguments by the Attorney General of Canada that MAiD should be restricted to terminal patients. There is a more fundamental problem with this argument about judicial deference, which the minister of justice once again defended in the context of Charter dialogue between the Court and the Trudeau government.[166] While the Supreme Court of Canada indicated a willingness to accord a degree of deference to government, it was not extended to the entire *Carter* decision but, rather, to the procedural safeguards to protect vulnerable Canadians from involuntary assisted death as well as assisted death without proper and informed consent. It was these measures that were left to the discretion of Parliament and not, as the minister of justice suggested, eligibility criteria designed to protect vulnerable adults in the context of assisted death. According to the minister of justice, broad eligibility criterion, such as the one in Senator Joyal's amendment, which aligned with paragraph 127 of *Carter*, would send the wrong message to vulnerable individuals that it was acceptable to end suffering through death: "This message may encourage some who are in crisis and already considering suicide to act, even privately and without assistance. Procedural safeguards would not help these individuals."[167]

This is not a particularly strong defence as to why *Carter's* eligibility criteria required narrowing or how this narrowing was constitutional. This effectively repurposed the constitutional issue from one of assisted death for those unable to end their suffering to one concerned with the normalization of suicide by those that do not require assistance to end their suffering. The minister of justice was correct that procedural safeguards cannot prevent those able to end their suffering from ending their suffering. But the procedural safeguards that the Court required Parliament to create were to protect vulnerable individuals that required assistance to end their intolerable suffering. As Luc Thériault remarked during the motion presented by the minister of justice regarding the Senate amendments, "she seems to be confusing the concept of being suicidal and assisted suicide ... Does she think that health care professionals would consent to assist someone who is suicidal?"[168]

Justifying a significant reduction of MAiD's eligibility criteria that excluded the disabled to protect the non-disabled, as the minister of justice did, would most likely fail any section 7 analysis. In *Carter*, the Court determined that restrictions on physician-assisted death undermined life, liberty, and security of the person of those unable to end their suffering without assistance. The same outcome would occur if the 2016 *Act on MAiD's* MAiD eligibility criteria were subject to judicial review. Removing eligibility from a whole class of persons granted access to MAiD – non-terminal competent adults suffering from grievous and irremediable medical conditions experiencing intolerable suffering – would most likely fail two components of the principles of fundamental justice (overbreadth and gross disproportionality). As the Court noted in *Bedford*, "overbreadth allows courts to recognize that the law is rationale in some cases, but that it overreaches in its effects in others."[169] This would be the likely judicial finding of the reasonable foreseeability of natural death requirement as it overreaches in its attempt to protect vulnerable adults. And it would also be considered grossly disproportionate to the section 7 rights of competent adults suffering grievous and irremediable medical conditions, as this restriction would continue their intolerable suffering simply to communicate that suicide is not socially acceptable. As the Court noted in *Bedford*, "gross disproportionality under s. 7 of the *Charter* does *not* consider the beneficial effects of the law for society."[170]

The minister of justice believed this restriction on the personal autonomy of a group of competent persons, granted a right to MAiD by the Supreme

Court of Canada in 2015, would now be considered a minimal impairment, merely sixteen months after a unanimous court invalidated a similar restriction. This position was never credibly established by the minister of justice in Parliament, who relied on statements such as: "I have said many times in the House that I am confident this bill is constitutional."[171] If the *Canadian Charter* and *Carter* are not to be equated, as the minister of justice also repeated, saying something should not be equated with demonstrating that it is in fact the case. Additionally, the legislative background on Bill C-14, released by the minister of justice before the third reading debate,[172] did not provide a convincing case that any *Carter* incompatibility in the bill would be a reasonable limit under section 1. The legislative background acknowledges that the eligibility restriction may restrict section 7 and simply provides a rationale for this restriction.[173] This approach to Charter transparency is rather weak and does not make a case for how any limitation would satisfy the distinct parts of the *Oakes* test (legislative objective, proportionality, and minimal impairment).

In the end, however, the minister of justice did not have to present a convincing defence of Bill C-14 as the majority Liberal government had the numbers to reject Senator Joyal's amendment, which the House of Commons did by a vote of 190 to 108.[174] It was sent back to the Senate where the house motion requested "that the Senate do not insist on its amendments 2(a), 2(b), 2(c)(ii), and 2(c)(iii), to which the House of Commons has disagreed."[175] For many senators, because the House had affirmed once again its preference for a more restrictive MAiD eligibility criteria, the unelected Senate must now accept the will of the House.[176] The Senate accepted the House's request and did not insist on removing the RFND requirement of Bill C-14 by a vote of forty-four to twenty-eight. Bill C-14 would be granted royal assent on June 17, 2016, eleven days after *Carter II*'s four-month extension expired.[177]

MAiD and Provincial-Territorial Agreement

Before turning to the role played by provincial and territorial governments, as well as medical and nurse practitioners in the successful implementation of MAiD, an important, yet neglected, discussion did inform part of the parliamentary debate – how this issue depended on provincial-territorial agreement to ensure accessibility to a medical service that the 2016 *Act on MAiD* intended to legalize for certain competent adults. In some ways, the focus on the constitutionality of the eligibility criteria during the passage of Bill C-14 is indicative of a central argument advanced by this book – the undue focus on a judicial decision and the insufficient attention as to how – and whether – a judicial decision is implemented and produces access to the service that inspired the constitutional challenge.

The preamble to the 2016 *Act on MAiD* signalled how critical the provincial and territorial governments were to the implementation of MAiD once the federal government had established the legal framework. Noting that it was important to have a uniform approach, the 2016 *Act on MAiD*'s preamble acknowledged that many critical decisions were left to the provincial and territorial governments.[178] The challenge that federalism posed to the implementation of MAiD was noted by Department of Justice officials before PDAM. Canada would be the only jurisdiction where responsibility for MAiD was divided between two orders of government and the devolved assemblies.[179] The role of federalism was acknowledged by the deputy minister of justice before LCJC when he noted how unique Canada was in a comparative MAiD context.

Although Parliament could establish uniform eligibility criteria and procedural safeguards, it could not ensure uniform access to MAiD because "the different provinces and territories have a role to play with respect to the regulation of medical practitioners and the professional conduct, expectations, standards, norms, and guidelines."[180] Critical decisions that were left to the provinces and territories included which health facilities, if any, would provide MAiD. Would it be at hospitals, private residences, palliative care facilities, residential care facilities, or a combination of all four? Important decisions were also left to provincial colleges of physicians that have responsibility for the regulation of medical practitioners that would administer MAiD. For instance, the issue of conscientious objection to MAiD, and whether medical practitioners opposed to MAiD had a professional responsibility to make an effective referral, were largely left to provincial colleges of physicians and their territorial equivalents.[181]

Like supervised consumption sites, whose delivery is an example of cooperative federalism in those jurisdictions that provide it, the successful implementation of MAiD rested on federal-provincial collaboration. Indeed, Benoît Pelletier, a member of the External Panel established by the Harper government, noted in his testimony before PDAM that, without such collaboration, access to MAiD would be undermined by governments working at cross-purposes.[182] This position was reinforced by the minister of health during her appearance before JUST when she acknowledged how many aspects of MAiD – the regulations governing the conduct of medical and nurse practitioners, questions of conscientious objection, norms, standards, and where MAiD would be administered – were at the discretion of provincial and territorial governments.[183]

In some respects, the ministers of justice and health, as well as departmental officials, acknowledged the limited reach of the *Carter* decision beyond the requirement that MAiD be decriminalized for certain competent adults and those medical professionals that would administer it free from criminal penalty. The preamble to the 2016 *Act on MAiD* designated MAiD as a medically necessary or core service, which was subject to the five principles of the *Canada Health Act (CHA)*.[184] However, the minister of health noted the dilemma that federalism posed to Parliament's designation of MAiD: it was at the discretion of each province to determine which services were medically necessary (core services), and, thus, governed by the *CHA* and the Canada health transfer, and those non-core services that were provided but outside of the *CHA* and the funding mechanism.[185] Provincial control over which health services were medically necessary and those that were non-core services was confirmed by the Supreme Court of Canada in *Auton v British Columbia*, a 2004 decision involving whether provincial failure to fund a medically required service for a form of autism treatment (ABA/IBI therapy) was a violation of section 15(1) of the *Canadian Charter*.[186] In a unanimous decision, Chief Justice McLachlin determined that there was no constitutional requirement to fund a medically required treatment and affirmed provincial discretion over the core versus non-core medical service designation.[187]

The question of withholding federal funding to provinces that did not provide access to MAiD was raised by NDP MP Murray Rankin when officials from the Department of Health appeared before PDAM in January 2016. In short, could the federal spending power be an instrument to ensure MAiD implementation by the provincial and territorial governments? In addition to *Carter* failing to create a constitutional obligation to provide MAiD, the Department of Health indicated the limitations of the federal spending power as an instrument of implementation. Noting that the federal government was very reluctant to dictate "as a condition of federal funding, what forms of care are required to be provided by any individual or by provinces and territories collectively,"[188] the Department of Health official noted a deeper problem with the federal enforcement of a medically necessary service: "Medical necessity, generally speaking, although it's referenced in the *Canada Health Act*, is left to provinces to define. Provinces and territories, as a condition of federal funding through the Canada health transfer, are obligated to provide 'medically necessary' services, but, as I say the act does not define those."[189] Linda White described this issue as the implementation gap that arises in a federation when one order of government has the jurisdictional responsibility for legalizing or decriminalizing an activity and the other order of government has the constitutional responsibility for providing access to the decriminalized service.[190] An implementation gap arises when the order of government responsible for providing a services fails to do so, which can result in the uneven and constrained judicial policy impact.

Although this discussion was overshadowed by the debate surrounding the eligibility criteria, provincial and territorial support is critical for MAiD's implementation. Would access to MAiD be relatively similar at the provincial and territorial level, or would it follow the patchwork approach that characterizes supervised consumption sites and even greater accessibility issues for abortion as a medical service since *Morgentaler* in 1988? That MAiD has not followed a patchwork approach is neither the result of *Carter* nor that of an aggressive use of the federal spending power. The relatively uniform implementation of MAiD was the result of three developments: a collaborative approach by the provincial and territorial governments; general support by the colleges of surgeons and physicians, the regulatory bodies that govern the medical profession; and, finally, the willingness of private actors – medical and nurse practitioners – to provide this decriminalized medical service.

Back to Court: *Lamb, Truchon,* and the 2021 *Act on MAiD*

Before turning to the implementation of MAiD at the provincial and territorial levels, important events occurred that laid bare the minister of justice's repeated assertion that 2016 *Act on MAiD* simply needed to be Charter and not *Carter* compliant. Soon after the passage of Bill C-14, two constitutional challenges to the eligibility criteria were launched: *Lamb v Canada*, which was filed in the Supreme Court of British Columbia on June 27, 2016 and *Truchon c Procureur général du Canada*, which was filed in the Superior Court of Quebec on June 13, 2017.[191] Although *Lamb* would be the first constitutional challenge, the case would be withdrawn in September 2019 after the government of Canada conceded that Julia Lamb, despite suffering a non-terminal illness, met the eligibility criteria for MAiD. Moreover, *Truchon* was delivered one week previously and determined that both the RFND criterion in the 2016 *Act on MAiD* and the end-of-life requirement in Quebec's *Act Respecting End-of-Life Care* were a violation of sections 7 and section 15 (equality rights) of the *Canadian Charter*.[192]

In a repudiation of the Trudeau government's defence of the 2016 *Act on MAiD*, Justice Christine Baudouin in *Truchon* argued that the RFND requirement for non-terminal, non-vulnerable, competent adults simply to advance the objective of suicide prevention presented a cruel choice: "Either to suffer intolerably for an indefinite period of time that can last months or even years, or end their lives, on their own, all to satisfy a general pre-cautionary principle."[193] In finding that the eligibility criteria interfered with personal autonomy protected under section 7 and that it suffered from overbreadth, Baudouin J determined that the Attorney General had failed to demonstrate how the RFND requirement for non-terminal patients represented a minimal impairment on section 7. And, further, given that the individuals in *Truchon* suffered from physical disabilities due to their non-terminal conditions that prevented their ability to end their suffering without assistance, this violated their equality rights that could not be considered a reasonable limit under section 1 of the *Canadian Charter*. Neither the Canadian nor Quebec government appealed *Truchon*. Moreover, Quebec simply accepted judicial invalidation of the end-of-life criterion and chose not to amend the *Act Respecting End-of-Life Care*.

In respect to the Trudeau government's defence of the 2016 *Act on MAiD*, the distinction between *Carter* and the *Canadian Charter* had no bearing on the decision rendered by Baudouin J in *Truchon*. As happened in *Carter*, Baudouin J suspended the decision in *Truchon* and provided both the Canadian and Quebec governments with six months to amend their acts to comply with the *Canadian Charter*. And in another parallel to *Carter*, the Trudeau government requested an additional four-month extension to amend the *Criminal Code* provisions governing MAiD after it was returned to office following the federal election in October 2019. This request was granted by the Superior Court of Quebec. Bill C-7 was introduced by Minister of Justice David Lametti on February 24, 2020, granted royal assent on March 17, 2021,[194] and now contains a two-track approach to MAiD eligibility: first, where death is naturally foreseeable (RFND) and, second, where natural death is not reasonably foreseeable (non-RFND). Both tracks have a set of safeguards to govern MAiD eligibility requests, with Track 1 (RFDN) being a replication of the safeguards in the 2016 *Act on MAiD* with a minor modification[195] and Track 2 (non-RFND) having additional safeguards to those contained within Track 1.

The additional safeguards for non-RFND include the requirement that one of the two independent practitioners that confirm that the eligibility criteria are met "must have expertise in the condition that causes the person's suffering, and if not, must consult another practitioner with that expertise"[196] and that a minimum period of ninety days to assess the MAiD request must occur. This ninety-day period can be reduced if a loss of capacity is imminent and the assessment has been completed.[197] Similar to the RFND safeguards, individuals making non-RFND requests must provide informed consent; must be informed of alternatives; may rescind the written request at any moment; and, immediately before the provision of MAiD, must be provided with a final opportunity to rescind the request and, failing this, must confirm their request to receive MAiD before it can be administered. Finally, the 2021 *Act on MAiD* temporarily excluded from MAiD eligibility those suffering from mental illness for twenty-four months (until March 17, 2023). In the interim, the minister of justice is required to create an expert panel to provide recommendations on eligibility criteria and safeguards for such MAiD requests that would inform any forthcoming amendments to the *Criminal Code*. However, in December 2022, the minister of justice indicated that the government would seek to further delay the exclusion of mental disorders from MAiD eligibility until robust safeguards could be devised.[198]

In the preamble to the 2021 *Act on MAiD,* the Trudeau government acknowledged that it would comply with *Truchon*. No longer would the minister of justice argue that a legislative response simply needed to be Charter and not *Carter/Truchon* compliant. This distinction was never referred to by the Lametti, the minister of justice, who, as a parliamentary secretary, was one of only four Liberal MPs to vote against Bill C-14 because it departed from *Carter*. What explains this about face by the Trudeau government? One explanation may be the party's change from a majority to a minority government following the 2019 election. Any response to *Truchon* could only pass with opposition support, and the NDP and Bloc Québécois had always favoured a more permissive approach to MAiD than the one adopted in the 2016 *Act on MAiD*. A second explanation may be the replacement of Wilson-Raybould with Lametti as minister of justice in January 2019. Following her expulsion from the Liberal caucus on April 2, 2019, and her election as an independent MP following the 2019 election in October, Wilson-Raybould would vote against Bill C-7 and the two-track approach to MAiD eligibility.

There is no denying that the 2021 *Act on MAiD* is an example of judicial impact and the power of judicial review when the Trudeau government's legislative response to *Truchon* is analyzed. But are a loss of majority government and a change in the minister of justice enough to explain the Trudeau government's pivot from defiance – the "Charter not *Carter* compatibility" mantra – to full compliance with a lower court ruling that could have been appealed? Something else is at play that may explain why the Trudeau government no longer felt it had the political capital to continue its opposition to the eligibility criteria outlined by the Court in *Carter*. According to Matthew Hall, the popularity of a judicial decision is a critical factor determining whether a government can potentially work around a judicial decision: a popular decision generally results in legislative compliance, whereas an unpopular judicial decision may allow for legislative defiance.[199] Indeed, one of the reasons that successive Quebec governments – Liberal, Parti Québécois, and Coalition Avenir Québec – have been able to legislate around court decisions involving Bill 101, *Charter of the French Language*, is the general unpopularity of these decisions with francophone voters, which are critical to winning Quebec elections.[200]

In the case of *Carter*, MAiD, and the RFND criterion, we see the opposite dynamic – a Charter decision that grew in popularity and the corresponding unpopularity of the Trudeau government's restrictive approach to MAiD eligibility by the time of the *Truchon* decision. Polling conducted by IPSOS-Reid, on behalf of Dying with Dignity Canada, found that, by 2020, nearly 87 percent of Canadians supported the *Carter* decision,[201] more than 69 percent supported removing the RFND requirement, 76 percent supported extending MAiD to competent adults whose death is not reasonably foreseeable, and 65 percent favoured extending MAiD to mental illness.[202] Perhaps more importantly for the Liberal minority government, which was reliant on the NDP and Bloc Québécois MPs to pass a response to *Truchon*, even greater support was found among NDP and Bloc Québécois voters for removing the RFND requirement and extending MAiD to non-terminal patients.[203]

In the context of *Truchon*, the minority status of the government, and the current minister of justice's position on what form a constitutional response to a judicial decision must take, the conditions for non-compliance, even if it was still supported by the Trudeau government, no longer existed. Yet, as this book has argued, judicial decisions producing legislative impact do not necessarily produce policy impact or ensure access to a service that leads to a successful constitutional challenge. This is because of the complexity induced by federalism, which creates the potential for an implementation gap, as the provinces and territories were under no obligation to provide MAiD, despite the *Carter* and *Truchon* decisions.

Get *Carter* to the Provinces, Territories, and Colleges of Physicians

Unlike abortion and supervised consumption sites, where the implementation gap existed due to some provinces refusing to provide access to these services,[204] this has not been the fate of MAiD. While some religious-based hospitals have refused to administer MAiD, and have transferred patients requesting MAiD to other hospitals, this has been a rare occurrence.[205] A relatively uniform approach to MAiD has occurred in every province and territory, though there are some variations as to how this medical service is administered.[206] The provinces of Alberta, Manitoba, and Saskatchewan use a centralized system for MAiD referrals, whereas the Maritime provinces, British Columbia, and Quebec rely on regional health authorities to facilitate approval of MAiD requests.[207] Ontario uses a hybrid model that combines central coordination with the use of regional health authorities and local hospitals. The territories have less formalized processes established for MAiD approval and administering processes.[208] These are, however, minor variations, and they have not affected access to MAiD as a medical service.

In preparation for the provision of MAiD by medical and nurse practitioners, the provincial and territorial colleges governing these health professionals, and their territorial equivalents, updated their codes of conduct. While the preamble to the 2016 *Act on MAiD* affirmed the principles of freedom of religion and conscience, the *Criminal Code* could not, as a matter of jurisdiction or professional practice, exempt medical and nurse practitioners from providing this medical service, if required by the professional guidelines regulating their conduct. The *Criminal Code* amendments in the *Act on MAiD* were limited to exempting medical and nurse practitioners from criminal prosecution if they participated in the delivery of MAiD. At the provincial level, there has been a uniform approach to the issue of conscientious objection by medical and nurse practitioners as all provinces and territories allow health practitioners to decide whether to participate in MAiD as a medical service. This principle has been affirmed in the guidelines issued by provincial colleges of physicians and surgeons and their territorial equivalents.[209] The principle of conscientious objection has also been affirmed in the regulations issued by provincial colleges of nurses and their territorial equivalents.[210] Only Manitoba has enacted legislation specifying that medical and nurse practitioners are not required to provide MAiD due to conscience objection.[211] While Ontario enacted an omnibus statute regarding MAiD, it simply underlines that medical and nurse practitioners will not be subject to criminal prosecution.[212] The only point of departure among the provinces

Figure 8.1 MAiD deaths in Canada, 2016–21

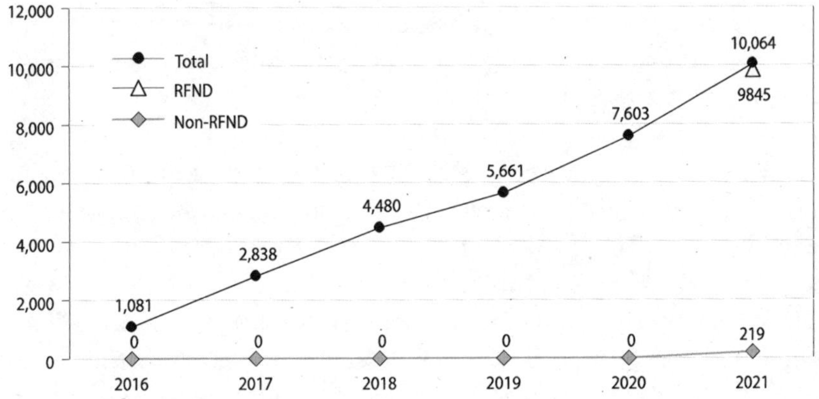

Year	Total	RFND	Non-RFND
2016	1,081		0
2017	2,838		0
2018	4,480		0
2019	5,661		0
2020	7,603		0
2021	10,064	9845	219

and territories is whether medical or nurse practitioners that refuse a MAiD request due to conscience objection are required to provide an effective referral. Except for Manitoba,[213] all provinces and territories require medical and nurse practitioners to provide an effective referral, or its equivalent, due to conscientious objection.

One indicator of the policy impact of *Carter*, and relatively uniform access at the provincial and territorial levels, is the steady increase in deaths due to MAiD between 2016 and 2021.[214] All provinces and territories have experienced a steady year-over-year increase, and a total of 31,664 individuals have accessed MAiD since 2016.[215] Figure 8.1 outlines yearly deaths due to MAiD between 2016 and 2021, which represents a ten-fold increase in this time period. As well, 2021 was the first year in which non-RFDN statistics have been available, and 219 individuals accessed MAiD through this eligibility criteria or just over 2 percent of all MAiD procedures in 2021. A major difference between the *Criminal Code* provisions that regulated abortion and those involving MAiD concerns the location where this medical procedure may take place. Unlike abortion, which specified the location and administrative structure to approve and provide this procedure – a therapeutic abortion committee (TAC) comprised of three medical doctors within an accredited hospital approved by the provincial or territorial minister of health – the *Criminal Code* provisions regulating MAiD do not specify where this medical procedure must be administered. This is important for a variety of reasons. Most importantly, it is left to the discretion of the provincial and

Figure 8.2   MAiD deaths by setting, 2019–21

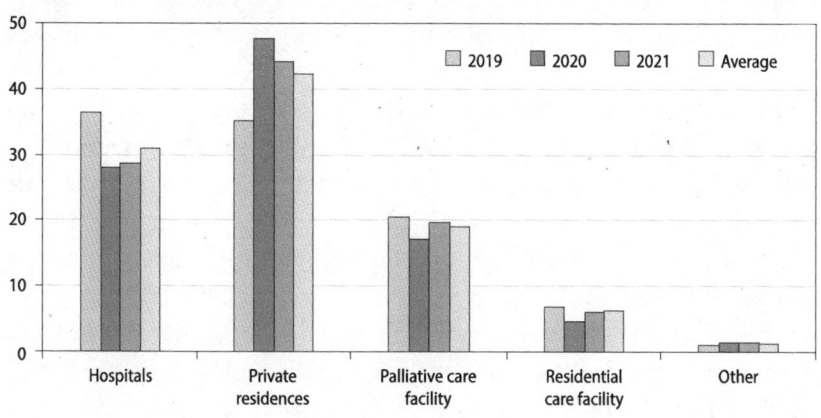

territorial governments where medical and nurse practitioners may administer MAiD. This has serious implications for accessibility to MAiD.

A province or territory that does not support MAiD as a component of health-care policy, or that opposed the *Carter* decision, could significantly limit access by restricting MAiD to hospitals or to certain hospitals. As the location of MAiD services are at the discretion of provincial and territorial governments, a restrictive approach would neither be inconsistent with the 2016 and 2021 *Acts on MAiD*, nor would it be inconsistent with the *Carter* decision. This discretion leaves the real possibility of an implementation gap arising in the context of MAiD, much as it did in the context of abortion and, to a lesser degree, supervised consumption sites. However, the ten-fold increase in the provision of MAiD since 2019, and the steady increase in the provision of this medical service in all provinces and territories, suggest that the governments responsible for MAiD have not created barriers to access. As Figure 8.2 indicates, MAiD's provision is highly accessible. Unlike abortion, where access was controlled through the requirement of a TAC and a panel consisting of three medical doctors within a hospital setting, a more accessible delivery model exists for MAiD. Indeed, the most common location for MAiD is the private residence of the competent adult deemed eligible (42.3 percent), followed by hospitals (31 percent) and palliative care facilities (19.3 percent).

Although there are provincial and territorial variations where MAiD is administered, all jurisdictions in Canada use a variety of settings. And, in some respects, this overcomes the accessibility issues that surrounded abortion, particularly for women living in rural areas who must travel significant distances to have an abortion provided in an accredited hospital and to other provinces if the minister of health has failed to approve the establishment of a therapeutic abortion committee, such as Prince Edward Island for much of the post-*Morgentaler* era. The fact that nearly half of approved MAiD requests occur in a private residence may account for the nearly ten-fold increase since 2016. The only variation in access to MAiD appears to be a rural/urban divide, with a larger percentage of MAiD administered in rural settings in Atlantic Canada. However, this rural/urban divide, which caused delays in women accessing abortion as a medical service as TAC tended to be in accredited hospitals in urban settings, has no bearing on accessing MAiD because of its decentralized delivery platform. Greater accessibility to MAiD is also facilitated by the speciality of the health professional that ultimately administers this medical service. More than two-thirds of MAiD procedures were administered by family doctors from 2019 to 2021, followed by palliative medicine (9 percent), nurse practitioners (7.6 percent), anesthesiologists (4.8 percent), and internal medicine (3.5 percent).

The provision of abortion and MAiD are nearly polar opposites in terms of accessibility. With MAiD, we see a decentralized mode of delivery, where the provinces and territories retain much discretion in the provision of this service. Moreover, there is wide-scale support for MAiD by provincial and territorial governments as well as by the colleges that regulate the professional conduct of medical and nurse practitioners. The success of MAiD, in contrast to the accessibility issues facing abortion in many jurisdictions, is remarkable given that its provision is part of a complex implementation chain within each province and territory. Like any medical service, it requires medical and nurse practitioners willing to provide it as the professional colleges that regulate these health professionals provide for conscientious objection.

Another indicator of the success of MAiD, from an implementation perspective, is the yearly increase in the number of medical and nurse practitioners that provide MAiD. In 2019, a total of 1,143 medical and nurse practitioners provided MAiD, and this increased to 1,577 for 2021, which represents a 37.9 percent increase in participating health professionals over the last three years. Nearly 95 percent of MAiD services are provided by medical practitioners in Canada. If there is a downside to the provision of MAiD, it would be that demand for this medical service has far outstripped the supply of medical and nurse practitioners willing to administer this service. While there is a steady increase in the number of health-care professionals providing MAiD, the number of procedures has nearly doubled between 2019 and 2022, requiring those that provide it to increase the frequency of administering MAiD. This increase led Nova Scotia to temporarily pause MAiD referrals in September 2021 for thirty days as unprecedented demand had created a strain on the health-care system.[216]

One of the justifications advanced by the Trudeau government for the restrictive approach to MAiD eligibility in the 2016 *Act on MAiD* was the concern that a permissive approach would normalize death as an end to terminal suffering. The characteristics of those individuals seeking MAiD, however, suggest that this has not borne out and that the procedural safeguards in place ensure that only those with informed consent, enduring grievous and irremediable medical conditions with chronic pain, are being granted MAiD. For instance, the average age of those receiving MAiD between 2019 and 2021 was 75.6 years. Cancer is the most common medical condition of those granted MAiD (67.9 percent), followed by cardiovascular (15.2 percent), respiratory (11.9 percent), and neurological (10.8 percent) diseases.[217] The first year to provide data for non-RFND MAiD was 2021, and the average age of these 219 MAiD recipients (70.1 years) was marginally different from the overall MAiD average of 75.6 years. The main difference is the underlying condition for non-RFND MAiD, which is for those suffering from neurological conditions. The main neurological conditions are multiple sclerosis, Parkinson's disease, and chronic pain due to a combination of medical conditions.[218] These neurological conditions represent nearly half of all non-RFND cases, in which chronic sufferers reported that MAiD was sought as their quality of life had been significantly reduced due to their underlying health conditions.

The media have reported that MAiD has been recommended to military veterans by Veteran Affairs,[219] and stories involving homeless persons seeking MAiD because of their living conditions.[220] Such examples are used to demonstrate that the 2021 *Act on MAiD* and the inclusion of the non-RFND stream for MAiD have brought in a very permissive regime and MAiD on demand. Despite such reports, the reality is that MAiD eligibility for the non-RFND stream introduced by the 2021 *Act on MAiD* is rigorous: it still requires the presence of a "grievous and irremediable" medical condition and, more importantly, an assessment by two medical practitioners that determine that MAiD eligibility has been met and who support the MAiD request. While the 2021 *Act on MAiD* introduced a more permissive MAiD regime, it retains the rigorous procedural safeguards of the 2016 *Act* that question media reporting on the amendments introduced in response to *Truchon*.

Sue Rodriguez, Gloria Taylor, and Kay Carter all suffered from degenerative neurological diseases, and, under the 2016 *Act on MAiD*, only Rodriguez would have been eligible for the medical service that they sought to decriminalize, as only her natural death was reasonably foreseeable. In this respect, the 2021 *Act on MAiD* is a fitting end to the issue of physician-assisted death as it finally included within MAiD eligibility the non-terminal medical conditions that began this judicial-legislative saga for Taylor and Carter. But we should not lose sight of what is required for people with RFND and non-RFND medical conditions to end their suffering with assistance – access to MAiD in the province or territory in which they reside. Despite *Carter* and *Truchon*, provinces and territories determine which services are medically necessary. This is the reality of Canadian federalism that cannot be overcome by a negative rights decision involving section 7 of the *Canadian Charter*. The implementation gap can only be breached by provincial and territorial governments that decide, independent of judicial review, to provide access to a medical service. This is what occurred in the context of MAiD and why policy impact occurred in the shadow of a seminal decision by the Supreme Court of Canada.

Conclusion

Legislating in response to *Carter* and *Truchon* is a clear example of the ability of judicial review to directly shape a government's legislative agenda. Like the Harper government when it responded to *PHS Community Services Society*, the first legislative response to *Carter* was largely determined by the Trudeau government and exhibited another commonality with the government it replaced – an attempt to limit judicial impact by not fully complying with the constitutional parameters established by the Supreme Court of Canada in a unanimous decision. For all the Trudeau government's public statements about respecting the Court and fidelity to the *Canadian Charter*, it acted no differently than the Harper government when faced with a judicial decision it did not fully agree with – it attempted to govern around *Carter* by claiming to govern with the Charter. This distinction would prove more apparent than real once this issue returned to the judicial arena, as the *Truchon* decision laid bare.

The determination that the 2016 *Act on MAiD* was inconsistent with the *Canadian Charter*, as interpreted by the Supreme Court of Canada in *Carter*, is an assessment that was first made by parliamentarians and committee witnesses who considered the Trudeau government's first attempt to legalize assisted death for competent adults suffering grievous and irremediable medical conditions that caused intolerable suffering. However, with a majority government, in which a large majority of Liberal MPs were elected for the first time in 2015, the Trudeau government was able to offset the permissive approach to physician-assisted dying favoured by PDAM, the vast majority of witnesses who appeared before PDAM and JUST, the opposition parties that supported MAiD – the NDP and Bloc Québécois – and the newly independent Senate, which requested that the 2016 *Act on MAiD* comply with *Carter* before giving way to the will of the house. Moreover, it demonstrates the conditions under which a government can engage in legislative disagreement and blunt the impact of judicial review in a salient issue of public policy. *Truchon* also demonstrates that legislative non-compliance can be short-lived, particularly when a government is confronted with the reality of a judicial decision – that the ruling has grown in popularity since the initial judicial decision, which negates the potential for legislative non-compliance in any subsequent amendment.[221] The legislative sleight of hand that allowed the Trudeau government to differentiate *Carter* from the *Canadian Charter* in the 2016 *Act on MAiD*, and, thus, the narrow MAiD eligibility criteria, could not be repeated post-*Truchon*. The Trudeau government accepted this constitutional reality when it decided against appealing *Truchon* and fully complied with *Carter* when it introduced amendments to the *Criminal Code* in the 2021 *Act on MAiD*.

To understand policy impact in a federation requires an acknowledgment that a judicial decision may largely be an exercise in agenda setting. Judicial invalidation may result in legislative changes, but these legislative changes may not require the provision of a service due to federalism. As I have argued in this chapter, overcoming federalism and the implementation gap, which occurred in the context of MAiD, is more accurately an example of collaborative or cooperative federalism than it is of judicially required policy changes. This is not to suggest that the *Carter* decision is unimportant but, simply, that its legislative and policy impacts are separate considerations that respond to different inputs. The *Carter* decision may be one of the most consequential Charter judgments ever delivered by the Supreme Court of Canada. And it may have been one of the most inconsequential, from a policy perspective, if federalism had produced a vast implementation gap. That *Carter* did not suffer the fate of *Morgentaler*, and, to a lesser degree, *PHS Community Services Society*, is the outcome of a provincial-territorial consensus to provide this health service. A negative rights decision, such as occurred in *Carter* and *Truchon*, can only explain so much – the form that a legislative response takes – and, even in this respect, governments determine whether to comply or to engage in non-compliance, as the Trudeau government initially did in regard to paragraph 127 of the *Carter* decision when it passed the 2016 *Act on MAiD*.

If we focus on accessibility aided by a decentralized mode of delivery, MAiD has been a policy success. Some may equate this as evidence of judicial policy impact and that a further round of constitutional review can compel a reluctant government to fully comply with the eligibility criteria established by the Supreme Court in *Carter*. Recognizing that *Carter* is a seminal decision and questioning whether it caused a profound policy shift is not a contradiction. Perhaps it would be in a unitary state or if responsibility for this salient issue of public policy fell solely to one order of government in the Canadian federation. But that is not the reality of this aspect of health-care policy, particularly when the federal government determines under what circumstances assisted dying is legal, and the provincial and territorial governments must decide whether to provide a health service decriminalized by the federal government. That the implementation gap was avoided, and policy impact is observable, is due to a provincial-territorial consensus formed independent of, and not required by, the *Carter* and *Truchon* decisions.

Conclusion
Legislative Disagreements and Policy Implementation in the Charter Era

There is no denying that judicial activism is alive and well in Canada.[1] But should we always equate judicial activism with policy impact? That is the essential question considered in this book. The answer depends on which institution implements a judicial decision, the area of public policy, and the implementation context. Some decisions by the Supreme Court of Canada are implemented by lower courts. The Court has created, and altered, several judicial tests for determining how various constitutional provisions are to be applied throughout the Charter era.[2] The 1989 *Andrews* test, in which the Court outlined how claims of equality rights violations were to be determined, was revised in *Law v Canada*, and again in *Kapp*.[3] The rules governing the exclusion of evidence were established in 1987 – the *Collins* test – and revised in *Stillman* and *Grant*.[4] How to determine whether a trial has been held within a reasonable time (section 11(b)) was established in the 1990 *Askov* case and revised in *Morin* and *Jordan*.[5] And, finally, the Court reworked the *Oakes* test for determining whether a limitation on a right or freedoms within a statutory provisions is a reasonable limit under section 1 in the *Irwin Toy* case.[6] Because lower courts are subordinate to the Supreme Court of Canada and bound by its precedents, we can fully expect that higher court decisions and tests are overwhelmingly implemented and adhered to by lower courts. In these instances, and within this hierarchical relationship, the Supreme Court of Canada's policy impact is direct, measurable, and undeniable.

A more complex relationship exists when the Supreme Court is dependent on Parliament, the provincial legislatures, and the devolved assemblies to implement its rulings. This book has focused on that relationship. It is not hierarchal. And we should not assume that these legislative bodies fully comply with the Court when responding to judicial invalidation, particularly when they disagree with a determination of unconstitutionality in salient issues of public policy.[7] Since the Charter era, the Supreme Court of Canada has played an important role, delivering forceful decisions invalidating statutes as inconsistent with the *Canadian Charter* of Rights and Freedoms (*Canadian Charter*).[8] The sign-law provisions of Bill 101, *Charter of the French Language*, as well as the eligibility requirements for English public instruction in Quebec, were declared unconstitutional.[9] The Court determined that the use of ministerial discretion in regard to supervised consumption sites by the Harper government was unconstitutional. And the Court declared that the *Criminal Code* provisions that prohibited physician-assisted death were also unconstitutional.[10] There are other examples, but these are the ones chosen for analysis.

While important, a judicial decision is simply one part of a large and complex implementation chain when a legislative response to judicial invalidation is imminent. To focus on the most public manifestation of judicial power, which is the invalidation of statutes under section 24(1) of the *Canadian Charter*, overlooks the limited reach of a negative rights instrument. Such an instrument cannot compel government action or require the provision of a government service. It simply prohibits government interference with constitutionally protected rights and freedoms. Negative rights victories in *Morgentaler*, *PHS Community Services Society*, and *Carter* demonstrate that, while the interferences with personal liberty were removed, there were no constitutional requirements placed on the provincial or territorial governments to provide access to abortion services, supervised consumption sites, or medical assistance in dying (MAiD).[11] Judicial activism, while ever present, can only explain so much when it rests on a provision such as section 7 of the *Canadian Charter*.

Mind the Gap

Two factors have been employed to understand the reach of judicial policy impact – the legislative disagreement/agreement dichotomy and the idea that federalism/devolution can create an implementation gap that may reduce the Court's policy impact. Added to this would be the role of private actors and institutions that can be critical for the delivery of, and the demand for, the very public services that motivated the judicialization of a salient area of public policy. This is particularly significant in regard to medical practitioners, who are not required to administer MAiD, to perform abortions, or to monitor the ingestion of illegal narcotics at supervised consumption sites. They retain freedom of conscience over which medical services to administer. In the case of minority language education rights, judicial victories reaffirmed that Quebec had a constitutional obligation to provide access to public English instruction for Canadian citizens. However, the decision by anglophones to send their children to private educational institutions or to the French public system blunted any aspect of judicial activism benefiting the English public system that remained after the introduction of multiple, and forceful, legislative responses by Quebec.

One of the paradoxes of judicial activism is that the very government required to implement a judicial decision is generally the one whose statute has been declared unconstitutional. It is unsurprising that the government in question may not embrace the Court's determination of unconstitutionality. To understand this paradox, I have introduced the idea of legislative disagreement and how an unpopular judicial decision creates the conditions for legislative non-compliance. This dynamic existed in regard to legislative responses to the Court's invalidation of the *Charter of the French Language* by successive Quebec governments, the Harper government's introduction of Bill C-2, *Respect for Communities Act*,[12] and the Trudeau government's first attempt to respond to the *Carter* decision and the eligibility criteria for MAiD in Bill C-14, *An Act on Medical Assistance in Dying* (2016 Act on MAiD).[13] Moreover, we saw how legislative agreement largely explains MAiD's accessibility within the provinces and territories, whereas accessibility issues continue to impact abortion as a medical service and, to a lesser degree, supervised consumption services.

Though a powerful deterrent on judicial power, legislative disagreement is not the default when governments react to judicial invalidation and introduce a legislative response. As most examples of judicial invalidation do not involve significant issues of public policy, we can expect that Parliament and the legislatures will generally comply with a declaration of unconstitutionality and use a court decision as guidance when enacting a legislative response. For Peter Hogg and Allison Bushell, the high frequency of legislative responses was taken as evidence of a robust dialogue between courts and legislatures.[14] What matters is the policy importance of an invalidated statute and not the frequency in which Parliament or the provincial legislatures respond to judicial invalidation. Contending that issue salience is the more pressing consideration, this book has focused on a subset of cases in which legislative disagreements produced the conditions for non-compliance – salient issues of public policy where incumbent governments, regardless of whether they introduced the invalidated statute, disagreed with the Supreme Court of Canada's policy direction and sought to challenge it through a legislative response.

The overarching theme of "constraining the Court" was used to situate these legislative disagreements as a measure of judicial policy impact. To do so, a set of cases in which the Supreme Court of Canada delivered unanimous judgments was used to test the conditions under which legislative non-compliance may emerge. This narrow subset of cases was relied on for a number of reasons. First, I simply could not analyze all instances of judicial invalidation involving salient issues of public policy given that a case study approach was adopted. Other examples that demonstrate the central premise of this book include *Morgentaler* and access to abortion services,[15] *Bedford* and the Harper government's response to the invalidation of the *Criminal Code* provisions regulating sex work,[16] and criminal justice legislative responses to *Seaboyer, Daviault, O'Connor,* and *Mills* that were introduced by the Mulroney and Chrétien governments.[17] Like judicial activism, legislative disagreement is, and has been, an enduring feature of Canadian constitutionalism throughout the Charter era.

A more compelling factor was used to justify the cases and policy issues selected for analysis. Unlike a narrow five-to-four majority decision, in which a dissenting opinion may be used to frame a legislative response that challenges a judicial outcome, the cases chosen for analysis (*Protestant School Boards, Solski, Nguyen, PHS Community Services Society,* and *Carter*) are all unanimous decisions, either authored by a single justice or issued in the name of "The Court."[18] These cases represent the most difficult ones in which to demonstrate how legislative disagreement can lead to non-compliance on the part of Parliament and the legislatures. In short, they are authoritative decisions that provide little or no interpretive discretion to governments that may be required, or desire, to introduce a legislative response when an important statute is declared unconstitutional and "of no force or effect" by the Supreme Court of Canada. What legislative disagreement in the context of salient issues of public policy has revealed is the following – that strong-form judicial decisions, such as unanimous decisions invalidating a statute, may produce an equally forceful strong-form legislative response that mitigates and questions the policy impact of judicial activism.

The legislative agreement/disagreement dichotomy can and does co-exist, creating an implementation gap that further undermines judicial policy impact. Relying on the work of Linda White, this book has explored the importance of federalism and the devolved responsibilities of the territorial governments in the context of judicial policy impact.[19] Although federalism is premised on divided authority, or the "watertight compartment" theory in which governments have clearly defined areas of responsibility without overlap, the functional reality of Canadian federalism is very different. Some issues do conform to the watertight compartment theory of federalism, such as Quebec's *Charter of the French Language*. In this particular instance, Quebec is the only jurisdiction that can respond to judicial invalidation of the *Charter of the French Language*, as it falls under section 92 of the *Constitution Act, 1867*.[20] This book has demonstrated how legislative disagreement and jurisdictional sovereignty have allowed successive Quebec governments to amend the *Charter of the French Language* in a manner that checked judicial activism involving this Charter. In many ways, René Lévesque's quip "to make it as complicated, legitimately, and as difficult as we can for some aspects of that bloody Charter to be applied to Québec"[21] has come to characterize the approach by his successor governments, regardless of party affiliation, to the judicial invalidation of the *Charter of the French Language*.

Some issues, such as health-care policy, function as a concurrent area of responsibility, principally when the federal *Criminal Code* or the *Controlled Drugs and Substances Act (CDSA)*, regulate an aspect of provincial control over health care and, to a lesser degree, that of the territorial assemblies.[22] This dynamic exists in regard to abortion, supervised consumption sites, and MAiD. The concurrent model of federalism can also produce an implementation gap that complicates judicial policy impact, particularly when there is federal-provincial conflict over the judicialization of a shared responsibility. A number of federalism scenarios determine judicial policy impact. The first occurs in the context of legislative disagreement at the federal level, which undermines policy delivery at the provincial or territorial level. This occurred in the context of the Harper government's response to supervised consumption sites. The complexity of the application process introduced by the *Respect for Communities Act* was designed by the Harper government to significantly reduce, if not prevent, the submission of section 56 exemption requests to the federal minister of health by their provincial and territorial counterparts. The principles guiding the use of ministerial discretion, when reviewing section 56 requests, were designed to free the federal minister of health from the constitutional standards established by the Court in *PHS Communities Services Society*. In short, the Harper government did not accept judicial participation in this area of public policy and legislated accordingly. The *Respect for Communities Act* is a clear example of non-compliance that effectively prevented those provinces that advocated for more supervised consumption sites, such as British Columbia, from opening new facilities to address the overdose and opioid crises during the latter part of the Harper era.

The second scenario of federalism and the implementation gap involves the limited reach of a negative rights provision, such as section 7 of the *Canadian Charter* in a functionally concurrent area such as health-care policy. Once the Harper government was replaced by the Trudeau Liberals in 2015, judicial impact on the *CDSA* was direct, measurable, and undeniable. Those parts of the *Respect for Communities Act* that worked against the spirit of the Supreme Court's judgment were rescinded. Bill C-37, *An Act to Amend the Controlled Drugs and Substances Act*, introduced by Minister of Health Jane Philpott, fully aligned the statutory use of ministerial discretion with the five conditions outlined by the Court in paragraph 157 of *PHS Communities Services Society*.[23] The issue of supervised consumption sites moved from non-compliance under the Harper government to full compliance by the Trudeau government. While the Trudeau government closed the legislative gap, this does not fully explain the increase from one supervised consumption site during the Harper years to thirty-nine sites that currently operate in Canada.[24] The manyfold increase occurred because five provinces, with the constitutional authority for health care, agreed with this aspect of harm reduction[25] and supported section 56 applications submitted to Health Canada by local health organizations.

Whereas the Harper and Trudeau governments were bound by a negative rights decision involving supervised consumption sites, the provincial and territorial governments were under no constitutional obligation, emerging out of the decision in *PHS Communities Services Society*, to support section 56 applications. This is because of federalism and the devolved responsibilities of the territorial governments, which are immune from the Court's decision in *PHS Communities Services Society*. What federalism and devolution also show is how the legislative agreement/disagreement dichotomy plays out between the provincial and territorial governments. Given that five provinces and all three territories have yet to submit a section 56 application to the federal minister of health, the absence of a policy consensus by the governments that deliver health care has led to uneven accessibility and stunted policy impact.

The transition from the Notley to the Kenney government in Alberta further illustrates how the switch from agreement to disagreement about supervised consumption sites can occur through a change in government. Under the Notley government, five supervised consumption sites were established, and support for four more applications was provided. These additional sites were never established by the Kenney government as the socio-economic review of these facilities reported against additional facilities in March 2020.[26] Moreover, the Kenney government countered the Trudeau government's changes to the *CDSA* with the *Mental Health Services Protection Act*, the *Mental Health Services Protection Regulation*, and a "recovery-oriented approach" to harm reduction.[27] In short, policy impact in a functionally concurrent area of jurisdiction, such as supervised consumption sites, requires both the legislative gap (Parliament) and the jurisdictional/devolutionary gap (provinces and territories) to be closed or at least closed in some provinces and territories to produce policy change.

The relative success of MAiD, despite its auspicious beginnings with the Trudeau government and the 2016 *Act on MAiD*, represents the third federalism scenario: federal-provincial-territorial consensus that closes the implementation gap and produces widespread policy impact and accessibility to a dimension of health-care policy regulated by the federal *Criminal Code*. The inclusion of restrictive eligibility criteria for MAiD in the 2016 *Act on MAiD*, particularly the reasonable foreseeability of natural death requirement, is an example of non-compliance on the part of the Trudeau government. Legislative disagreement by the Trudeau government was short-lived, and the revised eligibility criteria in Bill C-7, *An Act on Medical Assistance in Dying (2021 Act on MAiD)*, represents the emergence of legislative and judicial agreement between the Supreme Court and the Trudeau government.[28] On their own, compliant statutory amendments involving a negative rights decision, in a functionally concurrent area of jurisdiction, are not enough to produce policy change. What drives policy change, particularly when there is no constitutional, devolutionary, or judicial requirement to provide a service, is widespread support by the governments that provide it as a public good. And, for MAiD, these are the provincial and territorial governments.

Unlike access to abortion, which replicates the uneven pattern evident in supervised consumption sites, this has not been the provincial and territorial response to MAiD. Whereas the implementation gap was left rather wide in the aftermath of *Morgentaler* in 1988, and remains so to this day, provincial-territorial support for MAiD closed the implementation gap. Added to this is the different modes of delivery that exist: a centralized approach in regard to abortion, where a limited number of hospitals in each province provide the service, if at all, whereas MAiD exhibits a more decentralized and accessible mode of delivery. As the yearly reports issued by Health Canada indicate, the large majority of MAiD procedures are administered by family practitioners, occur in the patient's home, and are available in all provinces and territories.[29] Three factors thus account for the widespread policy success, and impact, of MAiD as a judicialized issue of public policy: the Trudeau government's pivot away from legislative disagreement (2016 *Act on MAiD*) to agreement with *Carter* and the eligibility requirements for MAiD (2021 *Act on MAiD*); widespread provincial-territorial consensus to provide MAiD as a medical service in the absence of constitutional or judicial obligations to do so; and, finally, an accessible mode of delivery that avoids the mistakes surrounding the provision of abortion by the provinces and territories.

In this book, a normative position has not been advanced whether legislative non-compliance with a judicial decision is a good or bad thing. I have simply argued that it exists and revealed the conditions under which legislative disagreements manifest and how non-compliance, a negative rights instrument, and federalism/devolution and the implementation context – either the watertight or concurrent model – can require a re-evaluation of judicial activism and the power of the highest courts such as the Supreme Court of Canada. Moreover, it is not confined to one political party in Canada, and it transcends the party-political divide, both federally and provincially. All governments have, at one time or another, governed around the *Canadian Charter*, as interpreted by the Supreme Court of Canada, despite protestations to the contrary.

À la fin – Federalism and the *Canadian Charter*

One objective pursued in this book has been to bring federalism back into the Charter debate but in a different way. The initial scholarship of Alan Cairns, F.L. Morton and Rainer Knopff, Alain Gagnon, and Guy Laforest focused on the danger that the *Canadian Charter* posed to federalism.[30] I referred to this as the "centralization thesis" in one of my earliest publications.[31] The assumption was that the application of the *Canadian Charter* by the Supreme Court of Canada would impose national standards in provincial areas of responsibility. Charter review, it was contended, would undermine provincial autonomy and lead to a standardization of public policy. In response to this initial concern, I argued that redesigned bureaucratic processes could ensure that newly passed statutes survived constitutional review.[32]

Without judicial invalidation, as I suggested, the policy choices of governments would endure because of pre-emptive attempts to design legislation that complied with the *Canadian Charter*.

The focus of this book has added a new dimension to the "Charter and federalism" argument, which largely focused on the agenda-setting and design phases of the legislative cycle. Relying on the work of Matthew Hall, as well as early work by Christopher Manfredi, and echoing Alexander Hamilton in *Federalist no. 78*, I have argued that, in the context of invalidated statutes, the Supreme Court of Canada is an "implementer-dependent" institution.[33] How legislation is implemented (and by whom) in a federal system can, and has, ensured that the centralization thesis has not borne out as we pass the fortieth year of the Charter era. Legislative disagreement, regardless of whether it conforms to the watertight compartment theory or is functionally concurrent, can counter strong-form judicial review when governments are inclined to reassert their authority. This has been the case with the *Charter of the French Language,* supervised consumption sites, and MAiD, though it applies to other salient issues of public policy and legislative disagreements that have not been explored in this book. The notwithstanding clause is the most visible way in which a government can constrain the Court, as section 33 is an overt example of legislative non-compliance. But it is rarely used. As this book demonstrated, when motivated by legislative disagreements, governments are willing to fashion strong-form legislative responses to address strong-form judicial review. A constrained Court, therefore, is more prevalent in our constitutional democracy than the limited use of the notwithstanding clause suggests.

Appendix

Remedial activism, 1982–2022 (Statutes, Ministerial Discretion, and Administrative Decisions)

#	Case	Subject of judicial review	Govt	Remedy	Judgment
1	*Edmonton Journal v Alberta (Attorney General)*, [1989]	*Judicature Act*, RSA 1980, c J-1, s 30	AB	Invalidation	Majority (n = 3)
2	*Black v Law Society of Alberta*, [1989]	*Law Society Act*, RSO 1980, c 233, s 28(c); rules of the Law Society of Alberta, ss 75B, 129, 154	AB	Invalidation	Majority (n = 2)
3	*R v Campbell; R v Ekmecic; R v Wickman*, [1997]	*Provincial Court Judges Act*, SA 1981, c P20.1, s 17(1) – *Payment to Provincial Judges Amendment Regulation*, Alta Reg 116/94	AB	Suspended	Unanimous (n = 1)
4	*Vriend v Alberta*, [1998]	*Individual's Rights Protection Act*, RSA 1980, c I-2, preamble, ss 2(1), 3, 4, 7(1), 8(1), 10, 16(1)	AB	Judicial amendment	Majority (n = 3)
5	*Reference re BC Motor Vehicle Act*, [1985]	*Motor Vehicle Act*, RSBC 1979, c 288, s 94(1)(2)	BC	Invalidation	Unanimous (n = 3)
6	*Andrews v Law Society of British Columbia*, [1989]	*Barristers and Solicitors Act*, RSBC 1979, c 26, s 42	BC	Invalidation	Unanimous (n = 2)
7	*Eldridge v British Columbia (Attorney General)*, [1997]	*Hospital Insurance Act*, RSBC 1979, c 180 (now RSBC 1996, c 204), ss 3(1), 5(1), 9, 10(1), 29(b) – *Medical and Health Care Services Act*, SBC 1992, c 76 (now the *Medicare Protection Act*, RSBC 1996, c 286), ss 1, 4(1)(c), (j), 6, 8	BC	Suspended	Unanimous (n = 1)
8	*UFCW, Local 1518, v KMart Canada Ltd*, [1999]	*Labour Relations Code*, SBC 1992, c 82, ss 1(1), 65, 67	BC	Suspended	Unanimous (n = 1)
9	*Trociuk v British Columbia (Attorney General)*, [2003]	*Vital Statistics Act*, RSBC 1996, c 479, ss 3(1)(b), 3(6)(b), 4(1)(a)	BC	Suspended	Unanimous (n = 1)

10	Health Services and Support – Facilities Subsector Bargaining Assn. v British Columbia, [2007]	Health and Social Services Delivery Improvement Act, SBC 2002, c 2, Part 2, ss 6(2), 6(4), 9	BC	Suspended	Majority (n = 2)
11	Conseil scolaire francophone de la Colombie Britannique v British Columbia, [2020]	nature of remedies under section 24 of the Charter for the realization of section 23 minority language education rights	BC	Judicial amendment	Majority (n = 2)
12	Hunter et al v Southam Inc, [1984]	Combines Investigation Act, RSC 1970, c C-23, ss 10(1), (3)	CA	Invalidation	Unanimous (n = 1)
13	R v Big M Drug Mart Ltd, [1985]	Lord's Day Act, RSC 1970, c L13, s 4	CA	Invalidation	Unanimous (n = 2)
14	Singh v Minister of Employment and Immigration, [1985]	Immigration Act, 1976, RSC 1976–77, c 52, ss 2, 45, 55, 70, 71	CA	Invalidation	Unanimous (n = 2)
15	R v Oakes, [1986]	Narcotic Control Act, RSC 1970, c N1, s 8	CA	Invalidation	Unanimous (n = 2)
16	R v Smith, [1987]	Narcotic Control Act, RSC 1970, c N1, s 5(2)	CA	Invalidation	Majority (n = 5)
17	R v Vaillancourt, [1987]	Criminal Code, RSC 1970, c C34, s 213(d)	CA	Invalidation	Majority (n = 4)
18	R v Morgentaler, [1988]	Criminal Code, RSC 1970, c C-34, s 251	CA	Invalidation	Majority (n = 5)
19	R v Martineau, [1990]	Criminal Code, RSC 1970, c C34, s 213(a), (d)	CA	Invalidation	Majority (n = 3)
20	R v Logan, [1990]	Criminal Code, RSC 1970, c C34, s 21(2)	CA	Judicial amendment	Unanimous (n = 3)
21	R v Hess; R v Nguyen, [1990]	Criminal Code, RSC 1970, c C34, s 146(1)	CA	Invalidation	Majority (n = 3)

#	Case	Subject of judicial review	Govt	Remedy	Judgment
22	R v Swain, [1991]	Criminal Code, RSC 1970, c C34, s 542(2)	CA	Invalidation	Majority (n = 3)
23	R v Seaboyer; R v Gayme, [1991]	Criminal Code, RSC 1985, c C46, s 277	CA	Invalidation	Majority (n = 2)
24	R v Sit, [1991]	Criminal Code, RSC 1970, c C34, s 213(c)	CA	Invalidation	Unanimous (n = 1)
25	Committee for the Commonwealth of Canada v Canada, [1991]	Government Airport Concession Operations Regulations, SOR/79373, s 7(a), (b)	CA	Invalidation	Unanimous (n = 6)
26	Tétreault-Gadoury v Canada (Employment and Immigration Commission), [1991]	Unemployment Insurance Act, 1971, SC 1970–71–72, c 48, s 31(1), (2), (4)	CA	Invalidation	Unanimous (n = 2)
27	R v Bain, [1992]	Criminal Code, RSC 1970, c C34, ss 562(1), (2)	CA	Suspended	Majority (n = 3)
28	R v Généreux, [1992]	National Defence Act, RSC 1985, c N-5, ss 166–70	CA	Suspended	Majority (n = 3)
29	R v Morales, [1992]	Criminal Code, RSC 1985, c X-46, s 515(10)(b)	CA	Invalidation	Unanimous (n = 2)
30	Osborne v Canada (Treasury Board), [1992]	Public Service Employment Act, RSC 1985, c P-33, s 33	CA	Judicial amendment	Majority (n = 3)
31	R v Zundel, [1992]	Criminal Code, RSC 1985, c C-46, s 181	CA	Invalidation	Majority (n = 2)
32	Schachter v Canada, [1992]	Unemployment Insurance Act, 1971, SC 1970/1/2, c 48, s 32	CA	Suspended	Unanimous (n = 2)
33	Baron v Canada; Kourtessi v MNR, [1993]	Income Tax Act, SC 1970/1/2, c 63, s 231.3	CA	Invalidation	Unanimous (n = 1)

34	*Sauvé v Canada (Attorney General)*, [1993]	*Canada Elections Act*, RSC 1985, c E-2, s 51(e)	CA	Invalidation	Unanimous (n = 1)
35	*R v Heywood*, [1994]	*Criminal Code*, RSC 1985, c C-46, s 179(1)(b)	CA	Invalidation	Majority (n = 2)
36	*R v Laba*, [1994]	*Criminal Code*, RSC 1985, c C-46, s 394(1)(b)	CA	Invalidation	Unanimous (n = 3)
37	*RJR-MacDonald Inc v Canada (Attorney General)*, [1995]	*Tobacco Products Control Act*, SC 1988, c 20, ss 3, 4–8, 9, 11–16, 17(f), 18. – *Tobacco Products Control Regulations*, amendment, SOR/93389	CA	Invalidation	Majority (n = 3)
38	*Benner v Canada (Secretary of State)*, [1997]	*Citizenship Act*, RSC 1985, c C-29, ss 3(1), 5(2)(b), 12(3), 19, 20, 22; *Citizenship Regulations*, CRC, c 400, s 20	CA	Suspended	Unanimous (n = 1)
39	*Thomson Newspapers Co v Canada (Attorney General)*, [1998]	*Canada Elections Act*, RSC 1985, c E-2, s 322.1	CA	Invalidation	Majority (n = 2)
40	*R v Lucas*, [1998]	*Criminal Code*, RSC 1985, c C-46, ss 298, 299, 300	CA	Judicial amendment	Majority (n = 4)
41	*Corbiere v Canada (Minister of Indian and Northern Affairs)*, [1999]	*Indian Act*, RSC 1985, c I-5, ss 77(1)	CA	Suspended	Unanimous (n = 2)
42	*United States v Burns*, [2001]	*Extradition Act*, RSC 1985, c E-23, s 25	CA	Invalidation	Unanimous 'The Court'
43	*R v Ruzic*, [2001]	*Criminal Code*, RSC 1985, c C-46, s 17	CA	Invalidation	Unanimous (n = 1)
44	*R v Sharpe*, [2001]	*Criminal Code*, RSC 1985, c C-46, s 164.1(4)	CA	Judicial amendment	Unanimous (n = 2)
45	*R v Hall*, [2002]	*Criminal Code*, RSC 1985, c C-46, s 515(10)(c)	CA	Judicial amendment	Majority (n = 2)

#	Case	Subject of judicial review	Govt	Remedy	Judgment
46	Lavallee, Rackel & Heintz v Canada (Attorney General); White, Ottenheimer & Baker v Canada (Attorney General); R v Fink, [2002]	Criminal Code, RSC 1985, c C-46, s 488.1	CA	Invalidation	Majority (n = 2)
47	Little Sisters Book and Art Emporium v Canada (Minister of Justice), [2002]	Customs Act, RSC 1985, c 1 (2nd Supp.), s 152(3)	CA	Judicial amendment	Majority (n = 2)
48	Ruby v Canada (Solicitor General), [2002]	Privacy Act, RSC 1985, x. P-21, s 51(2)	CA	Judicial amendment	Unanimous (n = 1)
49	Sauvé v Canada (Chief Electoral Officer), [2002]	Canada Elections Act, RSC 1985, c E2, s 51(e)	CA	Invalidation	Majority (n = 2)
50	Figueroa v Canada (Attorney General), [2003]	Canada Elections Act, RSC 1985, c E-2, ss 24(2), 24(3), 28(2)	CA	Suspended	Unanimous (n = 2)
51	R v Demers, [2004]	Criminal Code, RSC 1985, c C-46, ss 672.33, 672.54, 672.81(1)	CA	Suspended	Unanimous (n = 2)
52	Canada (Attorney General) v Hislop, [2007]	Canada Pension Plan, RSC 1985, c C-8, ss 44(1.1), 72	CA	Invalidation	Unanimous (n = 2)
53	Charkaoui v Canada (Citizenship and Immigration), [2007]	Immigration and Refugee Protection Act, SC 2001, c 27, ss 33, 77–85	CA	Suspended	Unanimous (n = 1)
54	R v DB, [2008]	Youth Criminal Justice Act, SC 2002, c 1, ss 62, 63, 64(1), 64(5), 70, 72(1), 72(2), 73(1), 75, 110(2)(b)	CA	Invalidation	Majority (n = 2)
55	Canada (Attorney General) v PHS Community Services Society, [2011]	Controlled Drugs and Substances Act, SC 1996, c 19, ss 4(1), 5(1), 56 (ministerial discretion)	CA	Judicial amendment	Unanimous (n = 1)
56	R v Tse, [2012]	Criminal Code, RSC 1985, c C-46, ss 184.4	CA	Suspended	Unanimous (n = 1)

57	R v St-Onge Lamoureux, [2012]	Criminal Code, RSC 1985, c C-46, ss 258(1)(c), 258(1)(d.01), 258(1)(d.1); Tackling Violent Crime Act, SC 2008, c 6	CA	Judicial amendment	Majority (n = 2)
58	Canada (Attorney General) v Bedford, [2013]	Criminal Code, RSC 1985, c C-46, ss 210, 212(1)(j), 213(1)(c)	CA	Suspended	Unanimous (n = 1)
59	Canada (Attorney General) v Whaling, [2014]	Abolition of Early Parole Act, SC 2011, c 11, s 10(1)	CA	Invalidation	Unanimous (n = 1)
60	Canada (Attorney General) v Federation of Law Societies of Canada, [2015]	Proceeds of Crime (Money Laundering) and Terrorist Financing Act, SC 2000, c 17, ss 5(i), 5(j), 62, 63, 63.1, 64; Proceeds of Crime (Money Laundering) and Terrorist Financing Regulations, SOR/2002–184, ss 11.1, 33.3, 33.4, 33.5, 59.4	CA	Invalidation	Unanimous (n = 2)
61	Canada (Attorney General) v Federation of Law Societies of Canada, [2015]	Proceeds of Crime (Money Laundering) and Terrorist Financing Act, SC 2000, c 17, ss 5(i), 5(j), 62, 63, 63.1, 64; Proceeds of Crime (Money Laundering) and Terrorist Financing Regulations, SOR/2002–184, ss 11.1, 33.3, 33.4, 33.5, 59.4	CA	Judicial amendment	Unanimous (n = 2)
62	Carter v Canada (Attorney General), [2015]	Criminal Code, RSC 1985, c C-46, ss 14, 241(b)	CA	Suspended	Unanimous "The Court"
63	Mounted Police Association of Ontario v Canada (Attorney General), [2015]	Royal Canadian Mounted Police Regulations, 1988, SOR/88–361, (2) s 96; Public Service Labour Relations Act, SC 2003, c 22, s 2(1) "employee" (d)	CA	Suspended	Majority (n = 2)
64	R v Nur, [2015]	Criminal Code, RSC 1985, c C-46, s 95(2)(a)(i), (ii)	CA	Invalidation	Majority (n = 2)
65	R v Smith, [2015]	Controlled Drugs and Substances Act, SC 1996, c 19, ss 4(1), 5(2); Marihuana Medical Access Regulations, SOR/2001–227	CA	Judicial amendment	Unanimous "The Court"
66	Canada (Attorney General) v Chambre des notaires du Québec, [2016]	Income Tax Act, RSC 1985, c 1 (5th Supp.), ss 231.2(1), 231.7, 232(1) "solicitor-client privilege"	CA	Judicial amendment	Unanimous (n = 1)

#	Case	Subject of judicial review	Govt	Remedy	Judgment
67	*R v KRJ*, [2016]	*Criminal Code*, RSC 1985, c C-46, s 161(1)(c)	CA	Judicial amendment	Majority (n = 2)
68	*R v Lloyd*, [2016]	*Controlled Drugs and Substances Act*, SC 1996, c 19, s 5(3)(a)(i)(D)	CA	Invalidation	Majority (n = 2)
69	*R v Safarzadeh-Markhbali*, [2016]	*Criminal Code*, RSC 1985, c C-46, ss 515(9.1), 719(3.1)	CA	Invalidation	Unanimous (n = 2)
70	*R v Boudreault*, [2018]	*Increasing Offenders' Accountability for Victims Act*, SC 2013, c 11; *Criminal Code*, RSC 1985, c C46, s 737	CA	Invalidation	Majority (n = 2)
71	*Frank v Canada (Attorney General)*, [2019]	*Canada Elections Act*, SC 2000, c 9, ss 11(d), 222	CA	Judicial amendment	Majority (n = 3)
72	*R v Morrison*, [2019]	*Criminal Code*, RSC 1985, c C-46, s 172.1(3)	CA	Invalidation	Unanimous (n = 3)
73	*Fraser v Canada*, [2020]	*Royal Canadian Mounted Police Superannuation Act*, RSC 1985, c R-11; *Royal Canadian Mounted Police Superannuation Regulations*, CRC, c 1393	CA	Invalidation	Majority (n = 3)
74	*R v Bissonnette*, [2022]	*Criminal Code*, RSC 1985, c C-46, s 745.51	CA	Invalidation	Unanimous (n = 1)
75	*R v Brown, R v Sullivan*, [2022]	*Criminal Code*, RSC 1985, c C-46, s 33.1	CA	Invalidation	Unanimous (n = 1)
76	*R v Ndhlovu* [2022]	*Criminal Code*, RSC 1985, c C-46, ss 490.012, 490.013(2.1)	CA	Suspended	Majority (n = 2)
77	*Manitoba Provincial Judges Assn v Manitoba (Minister of Justice)*, [1997]	*Public Sector Reduced Work Week and Compensation Management Act*, SM 1993, c 21, s 9(1)	MB	Judicial amendment	Unanimous (n = 1)

78	*Mackin v New Brunswick (Minister of Finance); Rice v New Brunswick,* [2002]	*Act to Amend the Provincial Court Act,* SNB 1995, c 6, preamble	NB	Suspended	Majority (n = 2)
79	*Nova Scotia (Workers' Compensation Board) v Martin; Nova Scotia (Workers' Compensation Board) v Laseur,* [2003]	*Workers' Compensation Act,* SNS 1994–95, c 10, s 10B; *Functional Restoration (Multi-Faceted Pain Services) Program Regulations,* NS Reg 57/96	NS	Suspended	Unanimous (n = 1)
80	*Doucet-Boudreau v Nova Scotia (Minister of Education),* [2003]	Nature of remedies under s 24(1) for the realization of s 23 (minority language education rights)(ministerial discretion)	NS	Judicial amendment	Majority (n = 2)
81	*Rocket v Royal College of Dental Surgeons of Ontario,* [1990]	Regulation 447 of the *Health Disciplines Act,* RRO 1980, ss 37(39), (40)	ON	Invalidation	Unanimous (n = 1)
82	*Miron v Trudel,* [1995]	*Insurance Act,* RSO 1980, c 218, ss 231, 233, Schedule C	ON	Judicial amendment	Majority (n = 3)
83	*M v H,* [1999]	*Family Law Act,* RSO 1990, c F.3, s 29	ON	Suspended	Majority (n = 4)
84	*Dunmore v Ontario (Attorney General),* [2001]	*Labour Relations and Employment Statute Law Amendment Act, 1995,* SO 1995, c 1, s 80; *Labour Relations Act, 1995,* SO 1995, c 1, Sched. A, s 3(b)	ON	Suspended	Majority (n = 3)
85	*Ontario (Attorney General) v G,* [2020]	*Christopher's Law (Sex Offender Registry), 2000,* SO 2000, c 1	ON	Suspended – 12 months + exemption for G	Majority (n = 3)
86	*Reference re Remuneration of Judges of the Provincial Court of Prince Edward Island; Reference re Independence and Impartiality of Judges of the Provincial Court of Prince Edward Island,* [1997]	*Provincial Court Act,* RSPEI 1988, c P25, s 3(3)	PEI	Suspended	Unanimous (n = 1)

#	Case	Subject of judicial review	Govt	Remedy	Judgment
87	Arsenault-Cameron v Prince Edward Island, [2000]	Ministerial decision overturned and school board decision reinstated (ministerial discretion)	PEI	Invalidation	Unanimous (n = 1)
88	AG (Quebec) v Quebec Protestant School Boards, [1984]	Charter of the French Language, RSQ, c C11, s 73	PQ	Invalidation	Unanimous "The Court"
89	Ford v Quebec (Attorney General), [1988]	Charter of the French Language, RSQ, c C11, ss 58, 69	PQ	Invalidation	Unanimous "The Court"
90	Devine v Quebec (Attorney General), [1988]	Charter of the French Language, RSQ, c C11, ss 52, 57, 58, 59, 60, 61, 214; Regulation Respecting the Language of Commerce and Business, RRQ, c C11, r 9	PQ	Invalidation	Unanimous "The Court"
91	Corporation Professionnelle des medecins du Quebec v Thibault, [1988]	Summary Convictions Act, RSQ, c P-15, s 75	PQ	Invalidation	Unanimous (n = 1)
92	Libman v Quebec (Attorney General), [1997]	Referendum Act, RSQ, c C64.1, ss 402, 403, 404, 406, para 3, 413, 414, 416, 417 of Appendix 2	PQ	Invalidation	Unanimous (n = 1)
93	Solski (Tutor of) v Quebec (Attorney General), [2005]	Charter of the French Language, RSQ, c C-11, s 73(2) (ministerial discretion)	PQ	Judicial amendment	Unanimous "The Court"
94	Chaoulli v Quebec (Attorney General), [2005]	Health Insurance Act, RSQ, c A-29, s 15; Hospital Insurance Act, RSQ, c A-28, s 11 (Quebec Charter of Human Rights and Freedoms)	PQ	Suspended	Majority (n = 3)
95	Multani v Commission Scolaire Marguerite-Bourgeoys, [2006]	Reasonable accommodation regarding wearing of kirpan (administrative decision)	PQ	Invalidation	Unanimous (n = 3)
96	Nguyen v Quebec (Education, Recreation and Sports), [2009]	Charter of the French Language, RSQ, c C-11, s 72, paras 2, 3	PQ	Suspended	Unanimous (n = 1)

97	Conférence des juges de paix magistrats du Québec v Québec (Attorney General), [2016]	Act to Amend the Courts of Justice Act and Other Legislative Provisions as Regards the Status of Justices of the Peace, CQLR, c. T-16, ss 27, 30, 32	PQ	Invalidation	Unanimous (n = 1)
98	Quebec (Attorney General) v Alliance du personnel professionnel et technique de la santé et des services sociaux, [2018]	Pay Equity Act, CQLR, c E-12.001, ss 76.3, 76.5, 103.1, para 2	PQ	Invalidation	Majority (n = 2)
99	Loyola High School v Quebec (Attorney General), [2015]	Regulation Respecting the Application of the Act Respecting Private Education, CQLR, c E-9.1, r 1, s 22 (ministerial discretion)	PQ	Judicial amendment	Unanimous (n = 2)
100	Saskatchewan (Human Rights Commission) v Whatcott, [2013]	Saskatchewan Human Rights Code, ss 1979, c S-24.1, s 14(1)(b)	SK	Judicial amendment	Unanimous (n = 2)
101	Saskatchewan Federation of Labour v Saskatchewan, [2015]	Public Service Essential Services Act, ss 2008, c P-42.2	SK	Suspended	Majority (n = 2)

Notes

Acknowledgments

1 Part 1 of the *Constitution Act, 1982,* being Schedule B to the *Canada Act 1982* (UK), 1982, c 11.
2 This is the French translation of Buzz Lightyear's catchphrase from the *Toy Story* franchise: "To infinity ... and beyond!" See Joss Whedon et al., *Toy Story* (Burbank, CA: Disney Pixar, 1995).
3 SQ 1977, s 54. Toys and games, except those referred to in section 52.1, which require the use of a non-French vocabulary for their operation are prohibited on the Quebec market unless a French version of the toy or game is available on the Quebec market on no less favourable terms.
4 *Ford v Quebec (Attorney General),* [1988] 2 SCR 712 [*Ford*]; *Irwin Toy Ltd v Quebec (Attorney General),* [1989] 1 SCR 927.
5 *Ford; Devine v Quebec (Attorney General),* [1988] 2 SCR 790; *Charter of Human Rights and Freedoms,* CQLR, c C-12.
6 James B. Kelly, "Buzz Lightyear and Quebec's Bill 101: Space Ranger or Agent Provocateur?" (Paper presented at Constitutions, Federations, Democracies: A Comparison of the United States, Canada, and Australia, University of Southern California, Los Angeles, February 2013).

Introduction: Constraining the Court

1 *Canadian Charter of Rights and Freedoms,* Part 1 of the *Constitution Act, 1982,* being Schedule B to the *Canada Act 1982* (UK), 1982, c 11 [*Canadian Charter*]. By "activist decisions," I refer to cases in which the Supreme Court of Canada has declared statutes, regulations, and ministerial discretion unconstitutional as a violation of the *Canadian Charter.* Further, those cases in which the Supreme Court of Canada has declared a remedy for a judicially determined Charter breach under section 24(1) of the Charter. The full list of activist decisions from 1982 to 2002 is provided in Appendix 1.

2 Peter W. Hogg and Allison A. Bushell, "The Charter Dialogue between Courts and Legislatures (or Perhaps the Charter of Rights Isn't Such a Bad Thing after All)," *Osgoode Hall Law Journal* 35 (1997): 75–124.
3 SQ 1977, s 54.
4 *Charter of Human Rights and Freedoms*, CQLR, c C-12 [*Quebec Charter*].
5 Emmett Macfarlane, ed., *Policy Change, Courts, and the Canadian Constitution* (Toronto: University of Toronto Press, 2018); Frédéric Bérard, *Charte canadienne et droits linguistiques: pour en finir avec les mythes* (Montreal: Presses de l'Université de Montréal, 2016); Dave Snow and Mark S. Harding, "From Normative Debates to Comparative Methodology: The Three Waves of Post-Charter Supreme Court Scholarship in Canada," *American Review of Canadian Studies* 45, 4 (2015): 456–59; Min Do, "Throughput Legitimacy and the Duty to Consult: The Limits of Law to Produce Quality Interactions in British Columbia's EA Process," *Canadian Journal of Political Science* 53, 3 (2020): 577–95; Dave Snow, "Litigating Parentage: Equality Rights, LGBTQ Mobilization and Ontario's *All Families Are Equal Act*," *Canadian Journal of Law and Society* 32, 3 (2017): 329–48; Larry Savage and Charles W. Smith, *Unions in Court: Organized Labour and the Charter of Rights and Freedoms* (Vancouver: UBC Press, 2017); Danielle McNabb and Dennis Baker, "Ignoring Implementation: Defects in Canada's 'Rape Shield' Policy Cycle," *Canadian Journal of Law and Society* 36, 1 (2021): 23–46.
6 Alan C. Cairns, "The Governments and Societies of Canadian Federalism," *Canadian Journal of Political Science* 10, 4 (1977): 695–725.
7 Bradley C. Canon and Charles A. Johnson, *Judicial Policies: Implementation and Impact* (Washington, DC: CQ Press, 1999), 63–66.
8 Matthew E.K. Hall, *The Nature of Supreme Court Power* (New York: Cambridge University Press, 2010), 15.
9 Linda A. White, "Federalism and Equality Rights Implementation in Canada," *Publius: The Journal of Federalism* 44, 1 (2014): 162–63.
10 *Reference re Senate Reform*, [2014] 1 SCR 704; *Reference re Supreme Court Act, ss 5 and 6*, [2014] 1 SCR 433; *Reference re Securities Act*, [2011] 3 SCR 837.
11 James B. Kelly and Matthew A. Hennigar, "The Canadian Charter of Rights and the Minister of Justice: Weak-Form Review within a Constitutional Charter of Rights," *International Journal of Constitutional Law* 10, 1 (2012): 35–68.
12 Adam M. Dodek, "The Politics of the Senate Reform Reference: Fidelity, Frustration, and Federal Unilateralism," *McGill Law Journal* 60, 4 (2015): 624–72; Emmett Macfarlane, "Unsteady Architecture: Ambiguity, the Senate Reference, and the Future of Constitutional Amendment in Canada," *McGill Law Journal* 60, 4 (2015): 884–903.
13 Hugo Cyr, "The Bungling of Justice Nadon's Appointment to the Supreme Court of Canada," *Supreme Court Law Review* (2d) 67 (2014): 73–109; Carissima Mathen and Michael Plaxton, *The Tenth Justice: Judicial Appointments, Marc Nadon, and the Supreme Court Act Reference* (Vancouver: UBC Press, 2020).
14 For excellent accounts of the use of the reference procedure, see Kate Puddister, *Seeking the Court's Advice: The Politics of the Canadian Reference Power* (Vancouver: UBC Press, 2019); Carissima Mathen, *Courts without Cases: The Law and Politics of Advisory Opinions* (Oxford: Hart, 2019).
15 *Canada (Attorney General) v Bedford*, [2013] 3 SCR 1101 [*Bedford*]; *Criminal Code*, RSC 1985, c C-46.
16 *Canada (Attorney General) v PHS Community Services Society*, [2011] 3 SCR 134 [*PHS Community Services Society*].

17 Emmett Macfarlane, "'You Can't Always Get What You Want': Regime Politics, the Supreme Court of Canada, and the Harper Government," *Canadian Journal of Political Science* 51, 1 (2018): 10–12.
18 *PHS Community Services Society*, para 133.
19 Ibid., para 150.
20 Christopher P. Manfredi, "'Appropriate and Just in the Circumstances': Public Policy and the Enforcement of Rights under the Canadian Charter of Rights and Freedoms," *Canadian Journal of Political Science* 27, 3 (1994): 435–63.
21 Stephen Gardbaum, *The New Commonwealth Model of Constitutionalism: Theory and Practice* (Cambridge, UK: Cambridge University Press, 2013), 121–28; Mark Tushnet, *Weak Courts, Strong Rights: Judicial Review and Social Welfare Rights in Comparative Constitutional Law* (Princeton, NJ: Princeton University Press, 2009), 61–62.
22 Richard Albert explores this question in the context of constitutional amendment. See Richard Albert, "The Most Powerful Court in the World? Judicial Review of Constitutional Amendment in Canada," *Supreme Court Law Review* (2d) 110 (2023): 79–102.
23 Grant Huscroft, "Constitutionalism from the Top Down," *Osgoode Hall Law Journal* 45, 1 (2007): 91–104.
24 Christopher P. Manfredi, *Feminist Activism in the Supreme Court: Legal Mobilization and the Women's Legal Education and Action Fund* (Vancouver: UBC Press, 2005).
25 Christopher P. Manfredi and Antonia Maioni, *Health Care and the Charter: Legal Mobilization and Policy Change in Canada* (Vancouver: UBC Press, 2018).
26 Michael W. McCann, *Rights at Work: Pay Equity Reform and the Politics of Legal Mobilization* (Chicago: University of Chicago Press, 1994), 4.
27 Christopher P. Manfredi, "Conservatives, the Supreme Court of Canada and the Constitution: Judicial-Government Relations, 2006–2015," *Osgoode Hall Law Journal* 52, 3 (2015): 954.
28 *Carter v Canada (Attorney General)*, [2015] 1 SCR 331 [*Carter*].
29 Janet L. Hiebert, "The Charter's Influence on Legislation: Political Strategizing About Risk: Presidential Address to the Canadian Political Science Association, Regina, Saskatchewan, May 31, 2018," *Canadian Journal of Political Science* 51, 4 (2018): 744.
30 SC 2015, c 22; Laura Eggertson, "Legislation Jeopardizes Safe Injection Sites," *Canadian Medical Association Journal* 187, 8 (2015): E225–26; Gloria Galloway, "Harper Government to Throw up Roadblocks for Safe-Injection Sites," *Globe and Mail*, June 6, 2013; "Clement Questions MDs Who Favour Safe Injection Sites," *CBC News*, August 18, 2008.
31 SC 2014, c 25; Andrea Sterling and Emily van der Meulen, "'We Are Not Criminals': Sex Work Clients in Canada and the Constitution of Risk Knowledge," *Canadian Journal of Law and Society* 33, 3 (2018): 291–308; Campbell Clark, "Conservatives Gamble with Tougher Approach to Prostitution," *Globe and Mail*, June 5, 2014.
32 Government of Canada, *Government of Canada Establishes Expert Panel on Options for a Legislative Response to Carter v Canada* (2015).
33 *Truchon c Procureur général du Canada*, 2019 QCCS 3792 [*Truchon*]; Bill C-14 *Act to Amend the Criminal Code and to Make Related Amendments to Other Acts (Medical Assistance in Dying)*, SC 2016, c 3 [2016 *Act on MAiD*].
34 F.L. Morton and Rainer Knopff, *The Charter Revolution and the Court Party* (Toronto: University of Toronto Press, 2000), 58.
35 Christopher P. Manfredi, *Judicial Power and the Charter: Canada and the Paradox of Liberal Constitutionalism*, 2nd ed (Don Mills, ON: Oxford University Press, 2001); Morton and Knopff, *Charter Revolution*.

36 Dennis Baker, *Not Quite Supreme: The Courts and Coordinate Constitutional Interpretation* (Montreal and Kingston: McGill-Queen's University Press, 2010).
37 James B. Kelly and Matthew A. Hennigar, "The Canadian Charter of Rights and the Minister of Justice: Weak-Form Review within a Constitutional Charter of Rights," *International Journal of Constitutional Law* 10, 1 (2012): 35–68.
38 *R v Morgentaler*, [1988] 1 SCR 30.
39 Canada. Office of the Prime Minister, *Minister of Justice and Attorney General of Canada Mandate Letter*, November 11, 2015, 3–4.
40 The vote would become a matter of conscience for the Liberal caucus, as the backbench demanded a free vote on an issue of such importance.
41 Liberal Party of Canada, *Real Change: A New Plan for a Strong Middle Class*, 2015, 30.
42 *Carter*, 335.
43 Laura Stone, "Liberals to Whip the Vote in Favour of the Assisted-Dying Law," *Globe and Mail*, February 11, 2016.
44 Eleni Nicolaides and Matthew A. Hennigar, "Carter Conflicts: The Supreme Court of Canada's Impact on Medical Assistance in Dying Policy," in *Policy Change, Courts, and the Canadian Constitution*, ed. Emmett Macfarlane (Toronto: University of Toronto Press, 2018), 313–35; Hamish Stewart, "Constitutional Aspects of Canada's New Medically-Assisted Dying Law," in *Assisted Death: Legal, Social and Ethical Issues after Carter*, ed. Derek B.M. Ross (Toronto: LexisNexis 2018), 449–55.
45 Dennis Baker, "A Feature, Not a Bug: A Coordinate Moment in Canadian Constitutionalism," in *Constitutional Dialogue: Rights, Democracy, Institutions*, ed. Geoffrey Sigalet, Grégoire Webber, and Rosalind Dixon (Cambridge, UK: Cambridge University Press, 2019), 417–18.
46 Robert Leckey, "Assisted Dying, Suspended Declarations, and Dialogue's Time," *University of Toronto Law Journal* 69, 1 (2019): 75.
47 Carissima Mathen, "A Recent History of Government Responses to Constitutional Litigation," *Constitutional Forum* 25, 3 (2016): 102.
48 2016 *Act on MAiD*; Bill 52, *Act Respecting End-of-Life Care*, RSQ 2014, c S-32.0001.
49 *Truchon*.
50 Daniel LeBlanc, "Ottawa Launches Public Consultations to Meet Court Deadline to Loosen Rules for Medically Assisted Death," *Globe and Mail*, January 13, 2020; Cathy Senay and Sarah Levitt, "Quebec to Expand Law on Medically Assisted Death, Look at Advance Consent," *CBC News*, November 29, 2019.
51 Kent Roach, "Dialogue in Canada and the Dangers of Simplified Comparative Law and Populism," in Sigalet, Webber, and Dixon, *Constitutional Dialogue*, 279–81.
52 Mark Tushnet, *Weak Courts, Strong Rights: Judicial Review and Social Welfare Rights in Comparative Constitutional Law* (Princeton, NJ: Princeton University Press, 2009), 42–43.
53 James B. Kelly, *Governing with the Charter: Legislative and Judicial Activism and Framers' Intent* (Vancouver: UBC Press, 2005), 7–9, 250–54.
54 Bill C-7, *An Act to Amend the Criminal Code (Medical Assistance in Dying)*, SC 2021, c 2 [2021 *Act on MAiD*].
55 *Controlled Drugs and Substances Act*, SC 1996, c 19.
56 George Tsebelis, "Decision Making in Political Systems: Veto Players in Presidentialism, Parliamentarism, Multicameralism and Multipartyism," *British Journal of Political Science* 25, 3 (1995): 301–3.
57 Drew Halfmann, *Doctors and Demonstrators: How Political Institutions Shape Abortion Law in the United States, Britain, and Canada* (Chicago: University of Chicago Press, 2011), 172–80.

58 Andrew Jackson, quoted in Georg Vanberg, "'John Marshall Has Made His Decision': Implementation, Transparency, and Public Support," in *Institutional Games and the U.S. Supreme Court*, ed. James R. Rogers, Roy B. Flemming, and Jon R. Bond (Charlottesville: University of Virginia Press, 2006), 69.
59 Christopher P. Manfredi and James B. Kelly, "Six Degrees of Dialogue: A Response to Hogg and Bushell," *Osgoode Hall Law Journal* 37, 3 (1999): 520–21; Christopher P. Manfredi and James B. Kelly, "Dialogue, Deference and Restraint: Judicial Independence and Trial Procedures," *Saskatchewan Law Review* 64, 3 (2001): 324–30; "Misrepresenting the Supreme Court's Record? A Comment on Sujit Choudhry and Claire E. Hunter, Measuring Judicial Activism on the Supreme Court of Canada," *McGill Law Journal* 49, 4 (2003): 741–64.
60 Emmett Macfarlane, "Dialogue or Compliance? Measuring Legislatures' Policy Responses to Court Rulings on Rights," *International Political Science Review* 34, 1 (2013): 10–11.
61 F.L. Morton, "The Effect of the Charter of Rights on Canadian Federalism," *Publius: The Journal of Federalism* 25, 3 (1995): 176.
62 Peter H. Russell, "The Effect of a Charter of Rights on the Policy-Making Role of Canadian Courts," *Canadian Public Administration* 25, 1 (1982): 22–27.
63 Manfredi, "Conservatives," 954–57.
64 Kent Roach, "The Charter versus the Government's Crime Agenda," *Supreme Court Law Review* (2d) 58 (2012): 2011–14; Don Stuart, "The Charter Balance against Unscrupulous Law and Order Politics," *Supreme Court Law Review* (2d) 57 (2012): 14–16; James B. Kelly and Kate Puddister, "Criminal Justice Policy during the Harper Era: Private Member's Bills, Penal Populism, and the Criminal Code of Canada," *Canadian Journal of Law and Society* 32, 3 (2017): 391–415.
65 Claire L'Heureux-Dubé, "The Dissenting Opinion: Voice of the Future," *Osgoode Hall Law Journal* 38, 3 (2000): 509–12.
66 Carissima Mathen, "Dissent and Judicial Authority in Charter Cases," *University of New Brunswick Law Journal* 52 (2003): 325.
67 Peter H. Russell, *The Judiciary in Canada: The Third Branch of Government* (Toronto: McGraw-Hill Ryerson, 1987), 351.
68 For a comprehensive treatment of the importance and use of anonymous decisions by "The Court," see Peter McCormick and Mark D. Zanoni, *By the Court: Anonymous Judgments at the Supreme Court of Canada* (Vancouver: UBC Press, 2020).
69 *Nguyen v Quebec (Education, Recreation and Sports)*, [2009] 3 SCR 208.
70 *PHS Community Services Society*.
71 *AG (Quebec) v Quebec Protestant School Boards*, [1984] 2 SCR 66 [*Protestant School Boards*]; *Ford v Quebec (Attorney General)*, [1988] 2 SCR 712; *Devine v Quebec (Attorney General)*, [1988] 2 SCR 790; *Libman v Quebec (Attorney General)*, [1997] 3 SCR 569; *Solski (Tutor of) v Quebec (Attorney General)*, [2005] 1 SCR 201 [*Solski*]; *Carter*.
72 *Solski*; *PHS Community Services Society*.
73 Scott Stephenson, *From Dialogue to Disagreement in Comparative Rights Constitutionalism* (Sydney: Federation Press, 2016), 44–47.
74 *Protestant School Boards*; *Solski*; *Nguyen v Quebec (Education, Recreation and Sports)*, [2009] 3 SCR 208.
75 Bill 178, *Charter of the French Language*, RSQ 1988, c 54; Bill 86, *Act to Amend the Charter of the French Language*, RSQ 1993, c 40.
76 Linda A. White, "Federalism and Equality Rights Implementation in Canada," *Publius: The Journal of Federalism* 44, 1 (2014): 162–63. Dennis Baker has explored this in the context of criminal justice policy and the Harper government's response to *Bedford*. See

Dennis Baker, "The Provincial Power to (Not) Prosecute *Criminal Code* Offences," *Ottawa Law Review* 48, 2 (2017): 419–48.
77 Bill C-2, *Respect for Communities Act*, SC 2015, c 22; Bill C-37, *Act to Amend the Controlled Drugs and Substances Act and to Make Related Amendments to Other Acts*, SC 2017, c 7.
78 *Rodriguez v British Columbia (Attorney General)*, [1993] 3 SCR 519.
79 Conservative Party of Canada, *Protect Our Economy: Our Conservative Plan to Protect Our Economy*, 2015, 135.
80 2016 *Act on MAiD*; 2021 *Act on MAiD*.

Chapter 1: Judicial Power and Policy Implementation in the Charter Era
1 Part 1 of the *Constitution Act, 1982*, being Schedule B to the *Canada Act 1982* (UK), 1982, c 11 [*Canadian Charter*].
2 Christopher P. Manfredi, *Judicial Power and the Charter: Canada and the Paradox of Liberal Constitutionalism*, 2nd ed. (Don Mills, ON: Oxford University Press, 2001), 22.
3 Ran Hirschl, *Towards Juristocracy: The Origins and Consequences of the New Constitutionalism* (Cambridge, MA: Harvard University Press, 2009).
4 David Erdos, *Delegating Rights Protection: The Rise of Bills of Rights in the Westminster World* (Oxford: Oxford University Press, 2010).
5 Peter H. Russell, "The Political Purposes of the Canadian Charter of Rights and Freedoms," *Canadian Bar Review* 61, 1 (1983): 30–54.
6 Christopher P. Manfredi, *Feminist Activism in the Supreme Court: Legal Mobilization and the Women's Legal Education and Action Fund* (Vancouver: UBC Press, 2005); Troy Q. Riddell, "The Impact of Legal Mobilization and Judicial Decisions: The Case of Official Minority-Language Education Policy in Canada for Francophones Outside Quebec," *Law & Society Review* 38, 3 (2004): 583–610.
7 Matthew A. Hennigar, "Expanding the 'Dialogue' Debate: Federal Government Responses to Lower Court Charter Decisions," *Canadian Journal of Political Science* 37, 1 (2004): 3–21.
8 James B. Kelly, "Bureaucratic Activism and the Charter of Rights and Freedoms: The Department of Justice and Its Entry into the Centre of Government," *Canadian Public Administration* 42, 4 (1999): 476–511.
9 There are notable exceptions to this statement regarding lack of focus on policy impact. See Emmett Macfarlane, ed., *Policy Change, Courts, and the Canadian Constitution* (Toronto: University of Toronto Press, 2018); Peter H. Russell, "The Effect of a Charter of Rights on the Policy-Making Role of Canadian Courts," *Canadian Public Administration* 25, 1 (1982): 1–33; Janet L. Hiebert, *Charter Conflicts: What Is Parliament's Role?* (Montreal and Kingston: McGill-Queen's University Press, 2002); Miriam Smith, "Social Movements and Judicial Empowerment: Courts, Public Policy, and Lesbian and Gay Organizing in Canada," *Politics & Society* 33, 2 (2005): 327–53.
10 Aileen Kavanagh, "The Lure and the Limits of Dialogue," *University of Toronto Law Journal* 66, 1 (2016): 85.
11 Scott Stephenson, "Constitutional Reengineering: Dialogue's Migration from Canada to Australia," *International Journal of Constitutional Law* 11, 4 (2013): 880–82.
12 Peter W. Hogg and Allison A. Bushell, "The Charter Dialogue between Courts and Legislatures (or Perhaps the Charter of Rights Isn't Such a Bad Thing after All)," *Osgoode Hall Law Journal* 35 (1997): 79.
13 Christopher P. Manfredi and James B. Kelly, "Six Degrees of Dialogue: A Response to Hogg and Bushell," *Osgoode Hall Law Journal* 37, 3 (1999): 519–22.
14 Kelly, "Bureaucratic Activism," 478–79.

15 Peter M. Hogg, Allison A. Bushell Thornton, and Wade K. Wright, "Charter Dialogue Revisited – or 'Much Ado About Metaphors,'" *Osgoode Hall Law Journal* 45, 1 (2007): 2–3.
16 Matthew E.K. Hall, *The Nature of Supreme Court Power* (New York: Cambridge University Press, 2010), 15.
17 Alexander Hamilton, John Jay, and James Madison, *The Federalist: The Gideon Addition* (Indianapolis: Liberty Fund, 2001).
18 Christopher P. Manfredi, "Adjudication, Policy-Making and the Supreme Court of Canada: Lessons from the Experience of the United States," *Canadian Journal of Political Science* 22, 2 (1989): 324.
19 Linda A. White, "Federalism and Equality Rights Implementation in Canada," *Publius: The Journal of Federalism* 44, 1 (2014): 162.
20 Bill 101, *Charter of the French Language*, SQ 1977, s 54.
21 Stephen Gardbaum, *The New Commonwealth Model of Constitutionalism: Theory and Practice* (Cambridge, UK: Cambridge University Press, 2013).
22 Mark Tushnet, *Weak Courts, Strong Rights: Judicial Review and Social Welfare Rights in Comparative Constitutional Law* (Princeton, NJ: Princeton University Press, 2009), 33–36.
23 Ibid., 34.
24 Mark Tushnet, "New Forms of Judicial Review and the Persistence of Rights-and Democracy-Based Worries," *Wake Forest Law Review* 38 (2003): 820–24.
25 James B. Kelly and Matthew Hennigar, "The Canadian Charter of Rights and the Minister of Justice: Weak-Form Review within a Constitutional Charter of Rights," *International Journal of Constitutional Law* 10, 1 (2012): 136–39.
26 Kent Roach, "Dialogue or Defiance: Legislative Reversals of Supreme Court Decisions in Canada and the United States," *International Journal of Constitutional Law* 4, 2 (2006): 363–67; Janet L. Hiebert, *Charter Conflicts: What Is Parliament's Role?* (Montreal and Kingston: McGill-Queen's University Press, 2002), 91–117.
27 *R v Seaboyer; R v Gayme*, [1991] 2 SCR 577; *R v Darrach*, [2000] 2 SCR 443; *R v O'Connor*, [1995] 4 SCR 411; *R v Mills*, [1999] 3 SCR 668.
28 Kelly and Hennigar, "Canadian Charter," 36.
29 Aileen Kavanagh, "What's So Weak About 'Weak-Form Review'? The Case of the UK Human Rights Act 1998," *International Journal of Constitutional Law* 13, 4 (2015): 1009–10.
30 Janet L. Hiebert and James B. Kelly, *Parliamentary Bills of Rights: The Experiences of New Zealand and the United Kingdom* (Cambridge, UK: Cambridge University Press, 2015), 412.
31 Other studies make a similar point regarding the Commonwealth model of constitutionalism. See Claudia Geiringer, "Moving beyond the Constitutionalism/Democracy Dilemma: Commonwealth Model's Scholarship and the Fixation on Legislative Compliance," in *The Unity of Public Law? Doctrinal, Theoretical and Comparative Perspectives*, ed. Mark Elliot, Jason N.E. Varuhas, and Shona Wilson Stark (London: Hart, 2018).
32 James B. Kelly, *Governing with the Charter: Legislative and Judicial Activism and Framers' Intent* (Vancouver: UBC Press, 2005), 23–45.
33 F.L. Morton and Rainer Knopff, *The Charter Revolution and the Court Party* (Toronto: University of Toronto Press, 2000); Hogg and Bushell, "Charter Dialogue."
34 Alison L. Young, *Democratic Dialogue and the Constitution* (Oxford: Oxford University Press, 2017).
35 Geoffrey Palmer, *New Zealand's Constitution in Crisis: Reforming Our Political System* (Dunedin, New Zealand: McIndoe, 1992).

36 George Williams and Daniel Reynolds, *A Charter of Rights for Australia*, 4th ed. (Sydney: University of New South Wales Press, 2017).
37 *Canadian Bill of Rights*, SC 1960, c 44.
38 Morton and Knopff, *Charter Revolution*, 38.
39 Ibid., 23.
40 Charles R. Epp, *The Rights Revolution: Lawyers, Activists, and Supreme Courts in Comparative Perspective* (Chicago: University of Chicago Press, 1998), 17–22, 180–82.
41 Morton and Knopff, *Charter Revolution*, 59–80.
42 Ibid., 95.
43 Ibid., 107–28.
44 Ibid., 129.
45 Marc Galanter, "Why the 'Haves' Come out Ahead: Speculations on the Limits of Legal Change," *Law & Society Review* 9, 1 (1974): 95–160.
46 Manfredi, *Feminist Activism*.
47 Morton and Knopff, *Charter Revolution*, 149.
48 Robert A. Dahl, "Decision-Making in a Democracy: The Supreme Court as a National Policy-Maker," *Journal of Public Law* 6 (1957): 285.
49 Alexander M. Bickel, *The Least Dangerous Branch: The Supreme Court at the Bar of Politics*, 2nd ed. (New Haven, CT: Yale University Press, 1986), 16–33.
50 Cornell W. Clayton and Mitchell Pickerill, "The Politics of Criminal Justice: How the New Right Regime Shaped the Rehnquist Court's Criminal Justice Jurisprudence," *Publius: The Journal of Federalism* 34, 3 (2004): 1391.
51 Emmett Macfarlane, "'You Can't Always Get What You Want': Regime Politics, the Supreme Court of Canada, and the Harper Government," *Canadian Journal of Political Science* 51, 1 (2018): 1–2.
52 Ibid., 2.
53 Ibid., 1.
54 Ibid., 5; Darrell Bricker and John Ibbitson. *The Big Shift: The Seismic Change in Canadian Politics, Business, and Culture and What It Means for Our Future* (Toronto: HarperCollins, 2013).
55 Kent Roach, *The Supreme Court on Trial: Judicial Activism or Democratic Dialogue*, 2nd ed. (Toronto: Irwin Law, 2016), 108.
56 Hogg and Bushell, "Charter Dialogue," 96–99.
57 Ibid., 80–81.
58 Janet L. Hiebert, "Parliamentary Bills of Rights: An Alternative Model?," *Modern Law Review* 69, 1 (2006): 7–28.
59 See, for instance, Scott Stephenson, "Constitutional Reengineering: Dialogue's Migration from Canada to Australia," *International Journal of Constitutional Law* 11, 4 (2013): 870–97; Rosalind Dixon, "Weak-Form Judicial Review and American Exceptionalism," *Oxford Journal of Legal Studies* 32, 3 (2012): 276–300; Alison L. Young, *Democratic Dialogue and the Constitution* (Oxford: Oxford University Press, 2017).
60 James B. Kelly, "Legislative Activism and Parliamentary Bills of Rights: Institutional Lessons for Canada," in *Contested Constitutionalism: Reflections on the Canadian Charter of Rights and Freedoms*, ed. James B. Kelly and Christopher P. Manfredi (Vancouver: UBC Press, 2009), 87–89.
61 James B. Kelly, "A Difficult Dialogue: Statements of Compatibility and the Victorian Charter of Human Rights and Responsibilities Act," *Australian Journal of Political Science* 46, 2 (2011): 257–79; James B. Kelly, "Judicial and Political Review as Limited Insurance:

The Functioning of the New Zealand Bill of Rights Act in 'Hard' Cases," *Commonwealth and Comparative Politics* 49, 3 (2011): 295–317.

62 See, for instance, C.R.G. Murray, "We Need to Talk: Democratic Dialogue and the Ongoing Saga of Prisoner Disenfranchisement," *Northern Ireland Legal Quarterly* 62, 1 (2011): 57–74; Eoin Carolan, "Dialogue Isn't Working: The Case for Collaboration as a Model of Legislative–Judicial Relations," *Legal Studies* 36, 2 (2016): 209–29.

63 Grant Huscroft, "Constitutionalism from the Top Down," *Osgoode Hall Law Journal* 45, 1 (2007): 98–99; Leighton McDonald, "Rights, Dialogue and Democratic Objections to Judicial Review," *Federal Law Review* 32, 1 (2004): 1–28.

64 *RJR-MacDonald Inc. v Canada (Attorney General)*, [1995] 3 SCR 199; *Tobacco Product Control Act*, S.C. 1988.

65 Carissima Mathen, "Dialogue Theory, Judicial Review, and Judicial Supremacy: A Comment on Charter Dialogue Revisited," *Osgoode Hall Law Journal* 45, 1 (2007): 145.

66 Andrew Petter, "Taking Dialogue Theory Much Too Seriously (or Perhaps Charter Dialogue Isn't Such a Good Thing after All)," *Osgoode Hall Law Journal* 45, 1 (2007): 166.

67 Hogg, Thornton, and Wright, "Charter Dialogue Revisited," 31.

68 Ibid., 32.

69 Lorraine Weinrib, "Doug Ford Can't Apply the Notwithstanding Clause Retroactively to Impede Democracy," *Globe and Mail*, September 18, 2018; Bill C-31, *An Act Respecting Cost of Living Relief Measures Related to Dental Care and Rental Housing*, SC 2022, c 14.

70 Alexander Bickel, *The Least Dangerous Branch: The Supreme Court at the Bar of Politics*, 2nd ed. (New Haven, CT: Yale University Press, 1986).

71 Alan C. Cairns, "The Judicial Committee and Its Critics," *Canadian Journal of Political Science* 4, 3 (1971): 319–20.

72 Gerald N. Rosenberg, *The Hollow Hope: Can Courts Bring About Social Change?*, 2nd ed. (Chicago: University of Chicago Press, 2008), 420–22.

73 Ibid., 66; Bradley C. Canon and Charles A. Johnson. *Judicial Policies: Implementation and Impact* (Washington, DC: CQ Press, 1999).

74 Christopher P. Manfredi, "'Appropriate and Just in the Circumstances': Public Policy and the Enforcement of Rights under the Canadian Charter of Rights and Freedoms," *Canadian Journal of Political Science* 27, 3 (1994): 453–54.

75 Alexander Hamilton, John Jay, and James Madison, *The Federalist: The Gideon Addition* (Indianapolis: Liberty Fund, 2001), 402.

76 Hall, *Nature of Supreme Court Power*, 15.

77 Carissima Mathen, "Dialogue Theory, Judicial Review, and Judicial Supremacy: A Comment on Charter Dialogue Revisited," *Osgoode Hall Law Journal* 45, 1 (2007): 125–46; Petter, "Taking Dialogue Theory Much Too Seriously."

78 While lower courts largely adhere to the rulings of superior courts, there are exceptions in the Canadian case such as the exclusion of evidence under section 24(2) and the application of the defence of extreme intoxication immediately after *Daviault* in 1994. *R. v. Daviault* [1994] 3 SCR 63.

79 Tom S. Clark, "The Separation of Powers, Court Curbing, and Judicial Legitimacy," *American Journal of Political Science* 53, 4 (2009): 984–85; Martin J. Sweet, *Merely Judgement: Ignoring, Evading, and Trumping the Supreme Court* (Charlottesville: University of Virginia Press, 2010), 8–9; Alyx Mark and Michael A. Zilis, "Restraining the Court: Assessing Accounts of Congressional Attempts to Limit Supreme Court Authority," *Legislative Studies Quarterly* 43, 1 (2018), 144–47.

80 An excellent overview of the Canadian and comparative approach to judicial remedies can be found in Robert Leckey, *Bills of Rights in the Common Law* (Cambridge, UK: Cambridge University Press, 2015), 92–122.
81 The remedies employed by the Supreme Court of Canada under section 24(1) were altered somewhat in *Ontario (Attorney General) v G*, [2020] SCC 38. As this occurred at the end of this study, which considered decisions between 1982 and 2022, the three-part classification scheme for section 24(1) will be employed.
82 Sujit Choudhry and Kent Roach, "Putting the Past behind Us? Prospective Judicial and Legislative Constitutional Remedies," *Supreme Court Law Review* (2d) (2003): 211–25; Kent Roach, "Remedial Consensus and Dialogue under the Charter: General Declarations and Delayed Declarations of Invalidity," *UBC Law Review* 35 (2001): 211–15.
83 Hogg, Thornton, and Wright, "Charter Dialogue Revisited," 4–5; Kent Roach, *The Supreme Court on Trial: Judicial Activism or Democratic Dialogue*, 2nd ed. (Toronto: Irwin Law, 2016), 197–98.
84 Manfredi and Kelly, "Six Degrees of Dialogue"; Peter W. Hogg and Allison A. Bushell Thornton, "Reply to Six Degrees of Dialogue," *Osgoode Hall Law Journal* 37, 3 (1999): 529–36; Kent Roach, "Sharpening the Dialogue Debate: The Next Decade of Scholarship," *Osgoode Hall Law Journal* 45 (2007):169–91; Emmett Macfarlane, "Dialogue or Compliance? Measuring Legislatures' Policy Responses to Court Rulings on Rights," *International Political Science Review* 34, 1 (2013): 39–56.
85 Roach, *Supreme Court on Trial*, 171.
86 This data set includes all Supreme Court of Canada decisions between 1982 and 2022. Supreme Court of Canada, https://scc-csc.lexum.com/scc-csc/scc-csc/en/nav_date.do. *Canada (Attorney General) v PHS Community Services Society*, [2011] 3 SCR 134.
87 *Chaoulli v Quebec (Attorney General)*, [2005] 1 SCR 791.
88 Morton and Knopff, *Charter Revolution*, 58.
89 Hogg, Thornton, and Wright, "Charter Dialogue Revisited," 10–14.
90 Robert Leckey, "Remedial Practice beyond Constitutional Text," *American Journal of Comparative Law* 64, 1 (2016): 11–13; *Criminal Code*, RSC 1985, c C-46.
91 *R v Logan*, [1987] 2 SCR 731.
92 *Vriend v Alberta*, [1998] 1 SCR 493; *Individual Rights Protection Act*, SA 1972, c 2.
93 *Egan v Canada*, [1995] 2 SCR 513.
94 *Controlled Drugs and Substances Act*, SC 1996, c 19.
95 *Solski (Tutor of) v Quebec (Attorney General)*, [2005] 1 SCR 201.
96 Ibid., paras 39–48.
97 *Arsenault-Cameron v Prince Edward Island*, [2000] 1 SCR 3.
98 White, "Federalism," 175.
99 Thomas Flanagan, "The Staying Power of the Legislative Status Quo: Collective Choice in Canada's Parliament after Morgentaler," *Canadian Journal of Political Science* 30, 1 (1997): 31–53; *R v Morgentaler*, [1988] 1 SCR 30 [*Morgentaler*].
100 Emmett Macfarlane, "The Dilemma of Positive Rights: Access to Health Care and the Canadian Charter of Rights and Freedoms," *Journal of Canadian Studies* 48, 3 (2014): 61–69; Emmett Macfarlane, "Positive Rights and Section 15 of the Charter: Addressing a Dilemma," *National Journal of Constitutional Law* 38, 1 (2018): 153–58; *Carter v Canada (Attorney General)*, [2015] 1 SCR 331.
101 Some academics consider that *Carter* created a positive rights obligation. See, for instance, Matthew Hennigar, "The Most Important Charter Right? The Rise and Future of Section 7," in *Constitutional Crossroads: Reflections on Charter Rights, Reconciliation, and Change*, ed. Kate Puddister and Emmett Macfarlane (Vancouver: UBC Press, 2022),

160–76; Emmett Macfarlane, "Dialogue, Remedies, and Positive Rights: Carter v Canada as a Microcosm for Past and Future Issues under the Charter of Rights and Freedoms," *Ottawa Law Review* 49, 1 (2017): 107–29.
102 White, "Federalism," 161–63.
103 Hall, *Nature of Supreme Court Power*, 18.
104 Matthew E.K. Hall, "The Semiconstrained Court: Public Opinion, the Separation of Powers, and the U.S. Supreme Court's Fear of Nonimplementation," *American Journal of Political Science* 58, 2 (2014): 353–55.
105 Hall, *Nature of Supreme Court Power*, 173–99, Appendix II.
106 Christopher J. Kam, *Party Discipline and Parliamentary Politics* (Cambridge, UK: Cambridge University Press, 2009).
107 Matthew Flinders, *Democratic Drift: Majoritarian Modification and Democratic Anomie in the United Kingdom* (Oxford: Oxford University Press, 2010), 53–56; Donald J. Savoie, *Governing from the Centre: The Concentration of Power in Canadian Politics* (Toronto: University of Toronto Press, 1999), 71–75; Ian Brodie, *At the Centre of Government: The Prime Minister and the Limits on Political Power* (Montreal and Kingston: McGill-Queen's University Press, 2018).
108 The party forming the government in each federal election since 1984 has received the following vote share, with minority governments in italics: 1984 (50.3%); 1988 (43.02%); 1993 (41.24); 1997 (38.46%); 2000 (40.85%); *2004 (36.73%); 2006 (36.27%); 2008 (37.65%);* 2011 (39.62%); 2015 (39.47%); *2019 (33.07%); 2021 (32.6%).*
109 Kelly, *Governing with the Charter*, 253–55; Paul E.J. Thomas and J.P. Lewis, "Executive Creep in Canadian Provincial Legislatures," *Canadian Journal of Political Science* 52, 2 (2019): 366–68.
110 K.D. Ewing, *Bonfire of the Liberties: New Labour, Human Rights, and the Rule of Law* (Oxford: Oxford University Press, 2010), 2; *Human Rights Act 1998* (UK), c 42.
111 Janet L. Hiebert and James B. Kelly, *Parliamentary Bills of Rights: The Experiences of New Zealand and the United Kingdom* (Cambridge, UK: Cambridge University Press, 2015), 248–50.
112 George Tsebelis, "Decision Making in Political Systems: Veto Players in Presidentialism, Parliamentarism, Multicameralism and Multipartyism," *British Journal of Political Science* 25, 3 (1995): 301–3.
113 White, "Federalism," 162.
114 Dennis Baker, "The Provincial Power to (Not) Prosecute *Criminal Code* Offences," *Ottawa Law Review* 48, 2 (2017): 419–48.
115 Alan C. Cairns, *Charter versus Federalism: The Dilemmas of Constitutional Reform* (Montreal and Kingston: McGill-Queen's University Press, 1992), 49–52; see also Donald V. Smiley, "The Case against the Canadian Charter of Human Rights," *Canadian Journal of Political Science* 2, 3 (1969): 277–91.
116 Guy Laforest, *Trudeau and the End of a Canadian Dream* (Montreal and Kingston: McGill-Queen's University Press, 1995), 125–39; F.L. Morton, "The Effect of the Charter of Rights on Canadian Federalism," *Publius: The Journal of Federalism* 25, 3 (1995): 177–83; Troy Q. Riddell and F.L. Morton, "Reasonable Limitations, Distinct Society and the Canada Clause: Interpretive Clauses and the Competition for Constitutional Advantage," *Canadian Journal of Political Science* 31, 3 (1998): 484–92; Peter H. Russell, "The Political Purposes of the Canadian Charter of Rights and Freedoms," *Canadian Bar Review* 61, 1 (1983): 40–43.

117 James B. Kelly, "Reconciling Rights and Federalism during Review of the Charter of Rights and Freedoms: The Supreme Court of Canada and the Centralization Thesis, 1982 to 1999," *Canadian Journal of Political Science* 34, 2 (2001): 324–25.
118 Kelly, *Governing with the Charter*, 215–20.
119 John D. Nugent, *Safeguarding Federalism: How States Protect Their Interests in National Policymaking* (Norman: University of Oklahoma Press, 2012), 55–76.
120 Morton, "Effect of the Charter," 176.
121 White, "Federalism," 162.
122 *Morgentaler*, 59–63.
123 Joanna N. Erdman, "In the Back Alleys of Heath Care: Abortion, Equality, and Community in Canada," *Emory Law Journal* 56 (2006): 1094.
124 Tushnet, *Weak Courts, Strong Rights*, 33–34.
125 Rachael Johnstone, *After Morgentaler: The Politics of Abortion in Canada* (Vancouver: UBC Press, 2017), 81–106.
126 Howard A. Palley, "Canadian Abortion Policy: National Policy and the Impact of Federalism and Political Implementation on Access to Services," *Publius: The Journal of Federalism* 36, 4 (2006): 572–79.
127 Macfarlane, "Dilemma of Positive Rights," 58–59.
128 *Constitution Act, 1867* (UK), 30 & 31 Vict, c 3.
129 *Respect for Communities Act*, SC 2015, c 22.
130 Bill C-37, *Act to Amend the Controlled Drugs and Substances Act and to Make Related Amendments to Other Acts*, SC 2017, c 7.

Chapter 2: Quebec and the *Canadian Charter of Rights and Freedoms*
1 *Canadian Charter of Rights and Freedoms*, Part 1 of the *Constitution Act, 1982*, being Schedule B to the *Canada Act 1982* (UK), 1982, c 11 [*Canadian Charter*].
2 Bill 101, *Charter of the French Language*, SQ 1977, s 54; James B. Kelly, "The Charter of the French Language and the Supreme Court of Canada: Assessing Whether Constitutional Design Can Influence Policy Outcomes," in *Policy Change, Courts, and the Canadian Constitution*, ed. Emmett Macfarlane (Toronto: University of Toronto Press, 2018), 250; Frédéric Bérard, *Charte canadienne et droits linguistiques: pour en finir avec les mythes* (Montreal: Presses de l'Université de Montréal, 2016), 85–86.
3 Although a remedial power does exist under section 93(3) of the *Constitution Act, 1867*, the federal government has never used it. See Peter W. Hogg, *Constitutional Law in Canada* (Toronto: Carswell, 1985), 824–25.
4 Guy Laforest, *Trudeau and the End of a Canadian Dream* (Montreal and Kingston: McGill-Queen's University Press, 1995), 134–35; *Constitution Act, 1867* (UK), 30 & 31 Vict, c 3.
5 Peter H. Russell, "The Political Purposes of the Canadian Charter of Rights and Freedoms," *Canadian Bar Review* 61, 1 (1983): 30–54.
6 *Attorney General (Quebec) v Quebec Protestant School Boards*, [1984] 2 SCR 66 [*Protestant School Boards*].
7 Ibid., 84.
8 *British North America Act, 1867* (UK), 30–31 Vict, c 3; *Constitution Act, 1867* (UK), 30 & 31 Vict, c 3.
9 A total of sixty-five federal and thirty-six provincial statutes or ministerial directives were declared unconstitutional by the Supreme Court of Canada between 1982 and 2022. Provincial statutes and ministerial directives include judicial decisions involving the

Canadian Charter (n = 35) and the Quebec *Charter of Human Rights and Freedoms*, CQLR, c C-12 [*Quebec Charter*] (n = 1).
10 Carissima Mathen, "Dissent and Judicial Authority in Charter Cases," *University of New Brunswick Law Journal* 52 (2003): 325.
11 *Referendum Act*, SC 1992, c 30.
12 F.L. Morton, "The Effect of the Charter of Rights on Canadian Federalism," *Publius: The Journal of Federalism* 25, 3 (1995): 176.
13 *Criminal Code*, RSC 1985, c C-46; see also Troy Q. Riddell and F.L. Morton, "Reasonable Limitations, Distinct Society and the Canada Clause: Interpretive Clauses and the Competition for Constitutional Advantage," *Canadian Journal of Political Science* 31, 3 (1998): 485–87; F.L. Morton, "Judicial Politics Canadian-Style: The Supreme Court's Contribution to the Constitutional Crisis of 1982," in *Constitutional Predicament: Canada after the Referendum of 1982*, ed. Curtis Cook (Montreal and Kingston: McGill-Queen's University Press, 1994), 138–46.
14 Yves de Montigny, "The Impact (Real or Apprehended) of the Canadian Charter of Rights and Freedoms on the Legislative Authority of Quebec," in *Charting the Consequences: The Impact of the Charter of Rights on Canadian Law and Politics*, ed. David Schneiderman and Kate Sutherland (Toronto: University of Toronto Press, 1997), 9–10.
15 Alain G. Gagnon and Raffaele Iacovino, *Federalism, Citizenship and Quebec* (Toronto: University of Toronto Press, 2006), 40–42.
16 Guy Laforest, "The Internal Exile of Quebecers in the Canada of the Charter," in *Contested Constitutionalism: Reflections on the Canadian Charter of Rights and Freedoms*, ed. James B. Kelly and Christopher P. Manfredi (Vancouver: UBC Press, 2009), 253–54.
17 Eugénie Brouillet, *La négation de la nation: l'identité culturelle québécoise et le fédéralisme canadien* (Montreal: Septentrion, 2006), 324.
18 Vanessa J. MacDonnell, "A Theory of Quasi-Constitutional Legislation," *Osgoode Hall Law Journal* 53, 2 (2015): 512–27. Although MacDonnell does not consider either Quebec statute, I would classify, like Emmanuelle Richez, both as quasi-constitutional in nature. See Emmanuelle Richez, "Losing Relevance: Quebec and the Constitutional Politics of Language" *Osgoode Hall Law Journal* 52, 1 (2014): 198.
19 *Ford v Quebec (Attorney General)*, [1988] 2 SCR 712 [*Ford*]; *Devine v Quebec (Attorney General)*, [1988] 2 SCR 790 [*Devine*]; *Libman v Quebec (Attorney General)*, [1997] 3 SCR 569 [*Libman*]; *Solski (Tutor of) v Quebec (Attorney General)*, [2005] 1 SCR 201 [*Solski*]; *Nguyen v Quebec (Education, Recreation and Sports)*, [2009] 3 SCR 208 [*Nguyen*].
20 Eugénie Brouillet, "La Charte de la langue française et la charte canadienne des droits et libertés: la difficile conciliation des logiques majoritaire et minoritaire," in *Légiférer en matière linguistique*, ed. Marcel Martel and Martin Pâquet (Quebec City: Presses de l'Université Laval, 2008), 368–73; Henri Brun, *Les institutions démocratiques du Québec et Canada* (Montreal: Wilson and Lafleur, 2013), 119; Jose Woerhling, "Convergences et divergences entre fédéralisme et protection des droits libertés: l'exemple des États-Unis et du Canada," *McGill Law Journal* 46 (2000): 49–51; Daniel Proulx, "La Loi 101, la clause-Québec et la Charte canadienne devant la Cour suprême: un cas d'espèce?," *Revue générale de droit* 16 (1985): 184–89.
21 A similar conclusion is reached by Frédéric Bérard in his important and recent analysis of Charter invalidation of key provisions of the *Charter of the French Language* by the Supreme Court of Canada. See Bérard, *Charte canadienne*.
22 Ibid., 89–117.

23 Guy Laforest and Rosalie Readman, "More Distress Than Enchantment: The Constitutional Negotiations of November 1981 as Seen from Quebec," in *Patriation and Its Consequences: Constitution Making in Canada*, ed. Lois Harder and Steve Patten (Vancouver: UBC Press, 2016), 173–76.
24 Frédéric Bastien, *La bataille de Londres: dessous, secrets et coulisses du rapatriement constitutionnel* (Montreal: Éditions du Boréal, 2013), 277–307; Donald V. Smiley, "A Dangerous Deed: The Constitution Act, 1982," in *And No One Cheered*, ed. Keith Banting and Richard Simeon (Toronto: Methuen, 1983), 78–80.
25 Gerard Bergeron, "Quebec in Isolation," in Banting and Simeon, *And No One Cheered*.
26 René Lévesque, quoted in Dale Gibson, *The Law of the Charter: General Principles* (Toronto: Carswell, 1983), 90.
27 The *Coalition Avenir Québec* government led by Premier François Legault describes itself as a nationalist and autonomous party as it is a coalition of federalist and former sovereigntist actors that seek to advance Quebec within the Canadian federation.
28 McPierre Foucher, "L'interprétation des droits linguistiques constitutionnels par la Cour suprême du Canada," *Ottawa Law Review* 19, 2 (1987): 386–88.
29 Brun, *Les institutions démocratiques*, 119.
30 Brouillet, *La négation de la nation*, 330; see also Brun, *Les institutions démocratiques*.
31 Kenneth McRoberts, *Misconceiving Canada: The Struggle for National Unity* (Don Mills, ON: Oxford University Press, 1997), 162.
32 *Re: Resolution to Amend the Constitution*, [1981] 1 SCR 753.
33 *Act Respecting the Constitution Act*, SQ 1982, c 21.
34 Lorraine E. Weinrib, "Learning to Live with the Override," *McGill Law Journal* 35 (1990): 544–45; Adam M. Dodek, "The Canadian Override: Constitutional Model or Bête Noire of Constitutional Politics?," *Israel Law Review* 49, 1 (2016): 59–60.
35 *Ford*.
36 *Re: Resolution to Amend the Constitution*.
37 *Re: Objection to a Resolution to Amend the Constitution*, [1982] 2 SCR 793.
38 Peter H. Russell, "The Patriation and Quebec Veto References: The Supreme Court Wrestles with the Political Part of the Constitution," *Supreme Court Law Review* (2d) 54 (2011): 75–76.
39 Lorraine E. Weinrib, "The Canadian Charter's Override Clause: Lessons for Israel," *Israel Law Review* 49, 1 (2016): 82–83.
40 Bill 178, *Charter of the French Language*, RSQ 1988, c 54; *Charter of Human Rights and Freedoms*, CQLR, c C-12 [*Quebec Charter*]; Bill 21, *Act Respecting the Laicity of the State*, RSQ 2019, c 12; Bill 96, *An Act Respecting French, the Official and Common Language of Québec*, RSQ 2022, c 14.
41 Bill 115, *Act Following upon the Court Decision on the Language of Instruction*, RSQ 2010, c 23.
42 The six cases in which the Supreme Court of Canada upheld the constitutionality of Quebec statutes (1982–2022) are: *Irwin Toy Ltd v Quebec (Attorney General)*, [1989] 1 SCR 927; *Ruffo v Conseil de la Magistrature*, [1995] 4 SCR 267; *R v Advance Cutting & Coring Ltd*, [2001] 3 SCR 2009; *Gosselin v Quebec (Attorney General)*, [2002] 4 SCR 429; *Canadian Broadcasting Corp v Canada (Attorney General)*, [2011] 1 SCR 19; *Quebec (Attorney General) v A*, [2013] 1 SCR 61.
43 Peter W. Hogg, Allison A. Bushell Thornton, and Wade K. Wright, "Charter Dialogue Revisited – or 'Much Ado About Metaphors,'" *Osgoode Hall Law Journal* 45, 1 (2007): 51–52.

44 Andrew Petter, "Taking Dialogue Theory Much Too Seriously (or Perhaps Charter Dialogue Isn't Such a Good Thing after All)," *Osgoode Hall Law Journal* 45, 1 (2007): 166.
45 James B. Kelly and Matthew A. Hennigar, "The Canadian Charter of Rights and the Minister of Justice: Weak-Form Review within a Constitutional Charter of Rights," *International Journal of Constitutional Law* 10, 1 (2012): 38–39.
46 Morton, "Effect of the Charter of Rights," 189–94; Laforest, *Trudeau*, 189–94; Laforest, "Internal Exile of Quebecers," 252–54.
47 The examples of non-compliance in salient issues (n = 6) involve the following cases, which, with the exception of *Chaoulli*, involve the *Charter of the French Language*: *Protestant School Boards; Ford; Devine; Solski; Chaoulli v Quebec (Attorney General)*, [2005] 1 SCR 791; *Nguyen*.
48 Despite cross-party condemnation of judicial invalidation of the *Charter of the French Language*, the National Assembly divided on party lines over how to respond to judicial invalidation. The parliamentary votes on legislative amendments to the *Charter of the French Language* in key instances are the following: *Solski* and *Nguyen* (Bill 115): Yeahs (61), Nays (54).
49 *Corp professionnelle des médecins v Thibault*, [1988] 1 SCR 1033; *Summary Convictions Act*, RSQ, c P-15; *Code of Civil Procedure*, RSQ 2019, c-265.01.
50 *Conférence des juges de paix magistrats du Québec v Quebec (Attorney General)*, [2016] 2 SCR 116; *Courts of Justice Act*, CQLR, c T-16; Bill 20, *An Act to Implement Certain Recommendations of the 20 August 2018 Report of the Committee on the Remuneration of Judges and Justices of the Peace for 2016–2019*, RSQ 2019, c 16.
51 *Pay Equity Act*, CQLR, c E-12.001.
52 *Quebec (Attorney General) v Alliance du personnel professionnel et technique de la santé et des services sociaux*, [2018] 1 SCR 464; Bill 10, *An Act to Amend the Pay Equity Act Mainly to Improve the Pay Equity Audit Process*, RSQ 2019, c 4.
53 *Loyola High School v Quebec (Attorney General)*, [2015] 1 SCR 613.
54 Howard Kislowicz, "Loyola High School v Attorney General of Quebec: On Non-Triviality and the Charter Value of Religious Freedom," *Supreme Court Law Review* 71, 2d (2015): 334–35.
55 Bill 115, *Act Respecting Private Education*, RSQ 2010, c E-9.1; *Regulation Respecting the Application of the Act Respecting Private Education*, SQ 1974.
56 *Libman; Multani v Commission Scolaire Marguerite-Bourgeoys*, [2006] 1 SCR 256 [*Multani*].
57 *Multani; Elections Act*, RSQ 1998, c 52.
58 Christopher P. Manfredi and Mark Rush, *Judging Democracy* (Toronto: University of Toronto Press, 2008), 97–99.
59 *Libman*, paras 80–82.
60 Bill 450, *An Act to Amend the Elections Act, the Referendum Act, and other Legislative Provisions*, RSQ 1998, c 52.
61 For an excellent treatment of the Canada-Quebec constitutional saga, see Peter H. Russell, *Constitutional Odyssey: Can Canadians Become a Sovereign People?* (Toronto: University of Toronto Press, 1993).
62 Matthew A. Hennigar, "Unreasonable Disagreement: Judicial-Executive Exchanges About Charter Reasonableness in the Harper Era," *Osgoode Hall Law Journal* 54, 4 (2017): 1248.
63 Peter W. Hogg and Allison A. Bushell, "The Charter Dialogue between Courts and Legislatures (or Perhaps the Charter of Rights Isn't Such a Bad Thing after All)," *Osgoode Hall Law Journal* 35 (1997): 80.
64 Kent Roach, *The Supreme Court on Trial: Judicial Activism or Democratic Dialogue*, 2nd ed. (Toronto: Irwin Law, 2016), 209–11; see also Kent Roach, "Dialogue or Defiance:

Legislative Reversals of Supreme Court Decisions in Canada and the United States," *International Journal of Constitutional Law* 4, 2 (2006): 347–70.
65 Christopher P. Manfredi and James B. Kelly, "Six Degrees of Dialogue: A Response to Hogg and Bushell," *Osgoode Hall Law Journal* 37, 3 (1999): 514–15.
66 *Official Languages Act,* SC 1969, c 54.
67 Manfredi and Kelly, "Six Degrees of Dialogue," 276–79; Bill 22, *Official Language Act,* SQ 1974, c 35.
68 McRoberts, *Misconceiving Canada,* 100–1.
69 *Official Languages Act 1974.*
70 *Charter of the French Language.*
71 McRoberts, *Misconceiving Canada,* 98–103.
72 Québec (Province). Ministre d'État au Développement culturel, *La politique québécoise de la langue française,* Québec, Éditeur officiel de Québec, 1977, présentée à l'Assemblée nationale et au peuple du Québec par Camille Laurin, ministre d'État au Développement culturel, p. 34 et 35.
73 *Charter of the French Language,* s 73.
74 J.R. Mallory, *Social Credit and the Federal Power in Canada* (Toronto: University of Toronto Press, 1954), 8.
75 J.R. Mallory, "Disallowance and the National Interest: The Alberta Social Credit Legislation of 1937," *Canadian Journal of Economics and Political Science* 14, 3 (1948): 349–51.
76 Hogg, *Constitutional Law,* 130.
77 *Supreme Court Act,* RSC 1985, c S-26; Kate Puddister, *Seeking the Court's Advice: The Politics of the Canadian Reference Power* (Vancouver: UBC Press, 2019), 22; Carissima Mathen, *Courts without Cases: The Law and Politics of Advisory Opinions* (Oxford: Hart, 2019), 47.
78 "133. Either the English or the French Language may be used by any Person in the Debates of the Houses of the Parliament of Canada and of the Houses of the Legislature of Quebec; and both those Languages shall be used in the respective Records and Journals of those Houses; and either of those Languages may be used by any Person or in any Pleading or Process in or issuing from any Court of Canada established under this Act, and in or from all or any of the Courts of Quebec. The acts of the Parliament of Canada and of the Legislature of Quebec shall be printed and published in both those Languages."
79 *Devine,* 809.
80 Peter H. Russell, "The Effect of a Charter of Rights on the Policy-Making Role of Canadian Courts," *Canadian Public Administration* 25, 1 (1982): 15–16.
81 Leslie A. Pal, *Interests of State: The Politics of Language, Multiculturalism, and Feminism in Canada* (Montreal and Kingston: McGill-Queen's University Press, 1993), 153–54.
82 Ibid., 171–72.
83 Morton, "Effect of the Charter of Rights," 179–80.
84 *Attorney General of Quebec v Blaikie et al,* [1979] 2 SCR 1016.
85 Morton, "Effect of the Charter of Rights," 181.
86 *Mahe v Alberta,* [1990] 1 SCR 342, 365.
87 Ibid., 366.
88 Ibid., 377.
89 The *Charter of the French Language* does provide other derogations: section 81 allows for exceptions based on learning difficulties, and section 85 allows for English instruction for non-residents staying temporarily in Quebec.

90 Stephen Clarkson and Christina McCall, *Trudeau and Our Times*, vol. 1: *The Magnificent Obsession* (Toronto: McClelland and Stewart, 1990).
91 *Quebec Association of Protestant School Boards v Attorney General of Quebec*, [1982] CS 673.
92 *Quebec Association of Protestant School Boards v Attorney General of Quebec*, [1983] CA 673.
93 Richez, "Losing Relevance," 203–4.

Chapter 3: Minority Language Education Rights and the *Charter of the French Language*

Acknowledgment: Sections of this chapter originally appeared in James B. Kelly, "The *Charter of the French Language* and the Supreme Court of Canada: Assessing Whether Constitutional Design Can Influence Policy Outcomes," in *Policy Change, Courts, and the Canadian Constitution*, ed. Emmett MacFarlane (Toronto: University of Toronto Press, 2018), 250–68. Reprinted with permission of the publisher.

1 *Canadian Charter of Rights and Freedoms*, Part 1 of the *Constitution Act, 1982*, being Schedule B to the *Canada Act 1982* (UK), 1982, c 11 [*Canadian Charter*]; Bill 101, *Charter of the French Language*, SQ 1977, s 54.
2 *Attorney General (Quebec) v Quebec Protestant School Boards*, [1984] 2 SCR 66 [*Protestant School Boards*]; *Solski (Tutor of) v Quebec (Attorney General)*, [2005] 1 SCR 201 [*Solski*]; *Nguyen v Quebec (Education, Recreation and Sports)*, [2009] 3 SCR 208 [*Nguyen*].
3 Bill 86, *Act to Amend the Charter of the French Language*, RSQ 1993, c 40 [1993 *Charter of the French Language Charter*]; *Regulation Defining the Scope of the Expression "Markedly Predominant" for the Purposes of the Charter of the French Language*, RRQ 1993, c C-11; Bill 104, *Act to Amend the Charter of the French Language*, RSQ 2002, c 28; Bill 103, *Act to Amend the Charter of the French Language and Other Amendments*, RSQ 2010, c 11; *Regulation Respecting the Criteria and Weighting Used to Consider Instruction in English Received in a Private Educational Institution Not Accredited for the Purposes of Subsidies*, C-11, r 2.1; *Charter of the French Language*, RSQ 2010, c C-11, s 73.1; Bill 115, *Act Respecting Private Education*, RSQ 2010, c E-9.1; *Regulation Respecting the Application of the Act Respecting Private Education*, E-9.1, r 1.
4 I use the label "anglophone" to refer to any Canadian citizen whose first language is English and resides in Quebec.
5 In 1997, two provinces changed their educational systems to remove the denominational character under section 93 of the *Constitution Act, 1867*, (UK), 30 & 31 Vict, c 3: Newfoundland and Labrador and Quebec. Under the *Constitutional Amendment, 1997 (Quebec)*, SI/97-141, in Quebec, a public-school system organized along linguistic lines – English and French school boards – replaced the Roman Catholic and the Protestant school systems that had existed since 1867.
6 *Protestant School Boards*; 1993 *French Language Charter*; *Solski*; *Nguyen*.
7 James B. Kelly, "Les limites de la mobilisation judiciaire: Alliance Québec, la Charte de la langue française et la Charte canadienne des droits et libertés," in *Le nouvel ordre constitutionnel canadien: du rapatriement de 1982 à nos jours*, ed. François Rocher and Benoît Pelletier (Montreal: Presses de l'Université du Québec, 2013), 205–33.
8 Michael Aguilino, "Qui suis-je?: identité linguistique et exclusion des non-ayants droit par l'article 23 de la Charte," *Ottawa Law Review* 38, 1 (2006): 77–85.
9 James B. Kelly, "Reconciling Rights and Federalism during Review of the Charter of Rights and Freedoms: The Supreme Court of Canada and the Centralization Thesis, 1982 to 1999," *Canadian Journal of Political Science* 34, 2 (2001): 326–28.

10 Frédéric Bérard, *Charte canadienne et droits linguistiques: pour en finir avec les mythes* (Montreal: Presses de l'Université de Montréal, 2016).
11 Stéphanie Chouinard reaches a similar conclusion about the limits of judicial policy-making. See Stéphanie Chouinard, "Section 23 of the Charter and Official-Language Minority Instruction in Canada: The Judiciary's Impact and Limits in Education Policy-making," in *Policy Change, Courts, and the Canadian Constitution*, ed. Emmett Macfarlane, 230–49 (Toronto: University of Toronto Press, 2018).
12 The term "allophone" is used in relation to immigrants to Quebec whose first language is neither French nor English. It is therefore the third linguistic group in the province, where francophones are the largest linguistic group, and anglophones are the smallest linguistic group.
13 *Constitution Act, 1867*.
14 This is referred to as the "St. Andrews principle," which was agreed to at the eighteenth Annual Premiers' Conference, which took place at St. Andrews-by-the-Sea, New Brunswick, on August 18–19, 1977. Text cited from Joseph Eliot Magnet, *Official Languages of Canada: Perspectives from Law, Policy, and the Future* (Cowansville, QC: Editions Yvon Blais, 1995), 145.
15 "Premiers' Communique" (Presented at the Premiers' Conference, Montreal, Quebec, February 23, 1980). Text cited in Magnet, *Official Languages of Canada*.
16 *British North America Act, 1867* (UK), 30–31 Vict, c 3.
17 *The Canadian Charter of Rights and Freedoms Provincial: In the Event That There Is Going to Be Entrenchment*), Doc. 830–84/031, August 28, 1980. The provincial proposal included the following text:

> Official Language and Language Rights
> (*Sections 18–24 and 30 and 31 of the Federal August 22, 1980 Draft would be sections 13–21 if included in this document*)
> Provincial officials have not made a *joint* proposal with respect to these subject matters prior to further discussion by the Minister of Federal Draft Proposals.

18 Committee of Ministers on the Constitution, *Rights and Freedoms within the Canadian Federation, Discussion Draft Tabled by the Delegation of the Government of Canada, July 4*, Doc. 830–81/027, July 8–11, 1980.
19 Ottawa Continuing Committee of Ministers on the Constitution, *The Canadian Charter of Rights and Freedoms, Federal Draft, August 22, 1980*, Doc. 830–84/004, August 26–29, 1980.
20 Federal Provincial First Ministers' Conference, *The Canadian Charter of Rights and Freedoms, Revised Discussion Draft, Federal, September 3, 1980*, Doc. 800–14/064" (September 8–12, 1980).
21 Section 1 of the September 3, 1980, draft reads as follows: "The *Canadian Charter of Rights and Freedoms* recognises the following rights and freedoms subject only to such reasonable limits as are generally accepted in a free and democratic society with a parliamentary system of government." Ibid.
22 James B. Kelly, *Governing with the Charter: Legislative and Judicial Activism and Framers' Intent* (Vancouver: UBC Press, 2005), 65–68. Section 1 of the revised resolution from January 12, 1981, reads as follows: "The *Canadian Charter of Rights and Freedoms* guarantees the rights and freedoms set out in it subject only to such reasonable limits prescribed by law as can be demonstrably justified in a free and democratic society." See also Peter W. Hogg and Annika Wang, "The Special Joint Committee on the Constitution of Canada, 1980–81," *Supreme Court Law Review* (2d) 81 (2017): 10–11.

23 Kelly, *Governing with the Charter*, 58–63.
24 *Canadian Bill of Rights*, SC 1960, c 44.
25 For a detailed discussion of the evolution of the *Canadian Charter* and its various drafts between 1980 and 1981, see Kelly, *Governing with the Charter*, 46–103.
26 Canada, Minister of Justice, *Proposed Resolution for Joint Address to Her Majesty the Queen Respecting the Constitution of Canada, Tabled in the House of Commons and the Senate*, October 6, 1980.
27 Canada, Minister of Justice, *Consolidation of Proposed Resolution and Possible Amendments as Placed before the Special Joint Committee by the Minister of Justice*, January 12, 1981.
28 Canada, Minister of Justice, *Text of the Resolution Respecting the Constitution of Canada, Adopted by the House of Commons on December 2, 1981 and by the Senate*, December 8, 1981.
29 National Assembly of Quebec, *Journal des débats*, 32nd Leg., 3rd session, vol. 26, November 9, 1981, 4 (René Lévesque).
30 Camille Laurin, quoted in *Quebec Association of Protestant School Boards v Procureur Général du Québec*, [1982] CS 673, para 29.
31 Ibid.
32 *Quebec Association of Protestant School Boards v Attorney General of Quebec*, [1983] CA 673.
33 Bill 57, *Charter of the French Language*, RSQ 1984, c 11.
34 Emmanuelle Richez, "Losing Relevance: Quebec and the Constitutional Politics of Language," *Osgoode Hall Law Journal* 52, 1 (2014): 204.
35 Ibid.
36 Ibid.
37 *Charter of the French Language*, s 75.
38 *Solski*.
39 Richez, "Losing Relevance," 204.
40 Ibid., 226.
41 Richez refers to the "exhaustion of legislative counterattacks" and reaches the conclusion that Quebec has been unsuccessful at countering judicial invalidation of the *Charter of the French Language*. Similar to Frédéric Bérard, I reach the opposite conclusion. See Bérard, *Charte canadienne*, 85–165; Frédéric Bérard, "Le phénomène des écoles passerelles: un pont entre la réalité et la fiction," *Revue juridique Thémis* 2–3, 51 (2017): 439–64.
42 Magnet, *Official Languages of Canada*, 147.
43 The first *Canadian Charter* decision delivered by the Supreme Court of Canada was *Law Society of Upper Canada v Skapinker*, [1984] 1 SCR 357. The decision on May 3, 1984, was roughly 2.5 months before the *Protestant School Boards* decision on July 26, 1984).
44 *Protestant School Boards*, 79.
45 Ibid., 86.
46 Notable examples where the Court considered the issue of framers' intent include *Protestant School Boards* as well as *Reference re Senate Reform*, [2014] 1 SCR 704. The concept of originalism receives a comprehensive treatment in Benjamin Oliphant and Léonid Sirota, "Has the Supreme Court of Canada Rejected 'Originalism'?" *Queen's Law Journal* 42, 1 (2016): 107–64.
47 *Protestant School Boards*, 79.
48 Ibid., 86.
49 Ibid., 87.
50 Ibid., 86.
51 Ibid., 88.

52 1993 *Charter of the French Language; Ford v Quebec (Attorney General)*, [1988] 2 SCR 712; *Devine v Quebec (Attorney General)*, [1988] 2 SCR 790.
53 Henri Brun, *Les institutions démocratiques du Québec et Canada* (Montreal: Wilson and Lafleur, 2013), 140; Les Intellectuels pour la souveraineté, *Le projet et loi 103, un projet de loi irrespectueux de la Charte de la langue française*. Présenté à la Commission parlementaire de la culture et de l'éducation de l'*Assemblée Nationale* (2010), 4–5.
54 Bill 63, *An Act to Promote the French Language in Quebec*, RSQ 1969, c 9.
55 Richard Y. Bourhis, "Evaluating the Impact of Bill 101 on the English-Speaking Communities of Quebec," *Language Problems and Language Planning* 43, 2 (2019): 217; Institut de la statistique du Québec, *Effectif scolaire de la formation générale des jeunes, selons diverses variables, années scolaires 2005–2006 à 2021–2022* (Quebec City: Government of Quebec, 2022).
56 Bourhis, "Evaluating the Impact of Bill 101," 217–21.
57 *Official Language Act*, SQ 1974, c 35.
58 Guy Laforest, with the collaboration of Jean-Oliver Roy Laforest, *Un Québec exilé dans la fédération: essai d'histoire intellectuelle et de pensée politique* (Montreal: Québec Amérique, 2014), Chapter 5: "Fondements, complexité et ampleur du déficit fédératif au Canada."
59 André Burelle, *Le mal canadien: essai de diagnostic et esquisse d'une thérapie* (Quebec City: Éditions Fides, 1995), 164.
60 Claude Ryan, "L'impact de la Charte canadienne des droits et libertés sur les droits linguistiques au Québec," *Revue du Barreau* 63 (2003): 565.
61 Bérard, "Le phénomène des écoles passerelles."
62 Giuseppe Valiante, "Quebec's English Private Schools Say Admission Rules Limit Access," *CBC News*, April 3, 2015. The per-year subsidy is based on the 2015–16 academic year,
63 Ministère de l'éducation et de l'énseignement supérieur, *Rapport annuel 2018–2019*, 2019, 3.
64 Ministère de l'éducation, du loisir et du sport, *Indicateurs linguistiques: Secteur de l'éducation*, 2013, 25. The data for Table 3.10 is derived from this document, particularly Tableau 12: Nombre de personnes admissibles à l'enseignement en anglais suivant les raisons invoquées et l'année visée dans la demande, depuis l'entrée en vigueur de la loi 101.
65 Conseil supérieur de la langue française, *Avis sur l'accès à l'école anglaise à la suite du jugement de la Cour suprême du 22 octobre 2009* (2010), 12.
66 Stephen Clarkson and Christina McCall, *Trudeau and Our Times*, vol. 1: *The Magnificent Obsession* (Toronto: McClelland and Stewart, 1990), 9.
67 René Lévesque, quoted in Dale Gibson, *The Law of the Charter: General Principles* (Toronto: Carswell, 1983), 90.

Chapter 4: Bridging Schools and the "Major Part Requirement"
1 Part 1 of the *Constitution Act, 1982*, being Schedule B to the *Canada Act 1982* (UK), 1982, c 11 [*Canadian Charter*]; Bill 57, *Charter of the French Language*, RSQ 1984, C-11 [*1984 Charter of the French Language*]; Bill 101, *Charter of the French Language*, SQ 1977, s 54.
2 Bill 86, *Act to Amend the Charter of the French Language*, RSQ 1993, c 40 [*1993 Charter of the French Language*].
3 *Solski (Tutor of) v Quebec (Attorney General)*, [2005] 1 SCR 201 [*Solski*].
4 Bill 104, *Charter of the French Language*, RSQ 2002, s 73 [*2002 Charter of the French Language*].

5 *Nguyen v Quebec (Education, Recreation and Sports)*, [2009] 3 SCR 208 [*Nguyen*].
6 Bill 115, *An Act Following upon the Court Decision on the Language of Instruction*, RSQ 2010, c 23 [*2010 Charter of the French Language*]; Bill 115, *Act Respecting Private Education*, RSQ 2010, c E-9.1.
7 *Regulation Respecting the Criteria and Weighting Used to Consider Instruction in English Received in a Private Educational Institution Not Accredited for the Purposes of Subsidies*, C-11, r 2.1, c C-11, s 73.1 [*Regulation on Private English Language Instruction*].
8 2002 *Charter of the French Language*, s 73.
9 *JB v Comité de révision sur la langue d'enseignement*, [2002] TAQ 15, para 16 [*JB*].
10 Nadia Duchêne, "Aménagement linguistique, éducation et cohésion sociale en contexte multiculturel," *Language Problems and Language Planning* 36, 3 (2012): 240–42.
11 *Nguyen*, para 42.
12 Ibid., para 6.
13 *JB*, para 17.
14 1993 *Charter of the French Language*.
15 *Solski*, para 25. The Supreme Court of Canada outlined the ministerial directive regarding the administrative approach to assessing the major part requirement (MPR) in *Solski*.
16 Bill 104, *Charter of the French Language*, RSQ 2002, s 83.4.
17 While the MPR would be added to section 73 as part of the 1984 *Charter of the French Language*, a substantive revision of the *Charter of the French Language* occurred in 1993 in response to *Attorney General (Quebec) v Quebec Protestant School Boards*, [1984] 2 SCR 66 [*Protestant School Boards*]. As a result, the *Solski* challenge in 2005 would involve section 73 of the 1993 *Charter of the French Language* and the MPR.
18 *Solski*, para 15.
19 Ibid., para 25.
20 *Arsenault-Cameron v Prince Edward Island*, [2000] 1 SCR 3 [*Arsenault-Cameron*].
21 *Solski*, para 10.
22 1993 *Charter of the French Language*.
23 *Arsenault-Cameron*, para 40.
24 *Solski*, paras 59–60.
25 Ibid., para 27.
26 Ibid., para 25.
27 Ibid., para 28.
28 The ministerial directive regarding the MPR was reproduced in ibid., para 25.
29 Ibid., para 37.
30 Ibid., para 33.
31 2010 *Charter of the French Language*.
32 *Solski*, para 39.
33 Ibid.
34 Ibid., para 41.
35 The data does not include section 73.4 as the MPR is not part of this derogation to section 72 of the *Charter of the French Language*.
36 *Nguyen*.
37 2002 *Charter of the French Language*, s 73.
38 *Nguyen*, para 13.
39 Ibid., para 6.
40 Ibid., para 10.
41 Ibid., para 46.
42 Ibid., para 27.

43 *Protestant School Boards*, 66.
44 *Nguyen*, para 33.
45 Ibid., para 36.
46 Ibid., para 38; *R v Oakes*, [1986] 1 SCR 103.
47 *Nguyen*, para 41.
48 Ibid., para 42.
49 Ibid., para 42.
50 Ibid., para 46.
51 Ibid.
52 Ibid., para 47.
53 Ibid., para 43.
54 Ibid., para 44.
55 Ibid., para 36.
56 Ibid., para 44.
57 *Regulation on Private English Language Instruction*, s 2.1; *Regulation Respecting the Application of the Act Respecting Private Education*, CQLR, c E-9.1, r 1, s 2.1.
58 Ministre de l'éducation de l'enseignement supérieur, "Types des établissements privés non subventionnés (EPNS)," http://www.education.gouv.qc.ca/references/tx-solrtyperecherchepublicationtx-solrpublicationnouveaute/resultats-de-la-recherche/detail/article/categories-des-etablissements-prives-non-subventionnes/.
59 Bill 103, *Act to Amend the Charter of the French Language and Other Amendments*, RSQ 2010, C-11.
60 "Quebec Liberals Push Language Law Through," *CBC News*, October 19, 2010.
61 Peter W. Hogg, Allison A. Bushell Thornton, and Wade K. Wright, "Charter Dialogue Revisited – or 'Much Ado About Metaphors,'" *Osgoode Hall Law Journal* 45, 1 (2007): 874–75; Kent Roach, "Dialogic Remedies," *International Journal of Constitutional Law* 17, 3 (2019): 868–69.
62 Jean-Oliver Roy Laforest, *Un Québec exilé dans la fédération: essai d'histoire intellectuelle et de pensée politique* (Montreal: Québec Amérique, 2014); Eugénie Brouillet, "La Charte de la langue française et la Charte canadienne des droits et libertés: la difficile conciliation des logiques majoritaire et minoritaire," in *Légiférer en matière linguistique*, ed. Marcel Martel and Martin Pâquet (Quebec City: Presses de l'Université Laval, 2008); Guy Laforest, *Trudeau and the End of a Canadian Dream* (Montreal and Kingston: McGill-Queen's University Press, 1995); Henri Brun, *Les institutions démocratiques du Québec et Canada* (Montreal: Wilson and Lafleur, 2013); Jose Woerhling, "De l'effritement à l'érosion," in *Le statut culturel du français au Québec*, ed. Michel Amyot and Gilles Bibeau (Quebec City: Conseil supérieur de la langue française, 1984); Alain G. Gagnon and Guy Laforest, "The Future of Federalism: Lessons from Canada and Quebec," *International Journal* 28, 3 (1993): 470–91; Alain G. Gagnon and Alex Schwartz, "Canadian Federalism since Patriation: Advancing a Federalism of Empowerment," in *Patriation and Its Consequences: Constitution Making in Canada*, ed. Lois Harder and Steve Patten (Vancouver: UBC Press, 2015); Eugénie Brouillet, *La négation de la nation: l'identité culturelle québécoise et le fédéralisme canadien* (Montreal: Septentrion, 2006).
63 Kevin Dougherty, "French Not for Sale, PQ Says of Bill 103," *Montreal Gazette*, September 28, 2010.
64 Dean Ardron, "Amendments to the *Quebec Charter of the French Language* Constitutionally Invalid," *Education and Law Journal* 19, 3 (2010): 247–51.
65 Frédéric Bérard, *Charte canadienne et droits linguistiques: pour en finir avec les mythes* (Montreal: Les Presses de l'Université de Montréal, 2016); Frédéric Bérard, "Le phéno-

mène des écoles passerelles: un pont entre la réalité et la fiction," *Revue juridique Thémis* 2–3, 51 (2017): 249–51.
66 The full list for the 2021–22 school year can be accessed at Ministère de l'éducation de l'énseignement supérieur, "Types des établissements privés."
67 *Solski*, para 47.
68 *Regulation on Private English Language Instruction*, s 3, Division 1: "Schooling."
69 Ibid., Division 1.2 (special mission or purpose).
70 *Solski*, para 33.
71 Ibid.
72 Bill 96, *Act Respecting French, the Official and Common Language of Québec*, RSQ 2022, c 14.
73 All fifteen institutions are located on the Island of Montreal: Kells Academy (seven separate campuses and levels); Miss Edgar's and Miss Cramp's; St-Georges; Selwyn House; Greaves Adventist Academy; Lower Canada College; The Priory School; The Study; Beth Esther Academy.
74 With the exception of OneSchool Global Campus in Montreal, which is located in Baie-D'Urfé in the West Island of Montreal, the rest are in Westmount (St-Georges, The Study, Miss Edgar's and Miss Cramp's) or Notre-Dame-de-Grâce (Lower Canada Canada). Some institutions are considered as two separate schools if English is offered on multiple campuses.
75 *Solski*, para 34.
76 Donald MacPherson, "Bill 103 Is in the Style of Bourassa-Language Law; Charest Government Proposal Reopens English-Education Loophole, but Barely," *Montreal Gazette*, June 3, 2010.
77 Quebec English School Board Association, *Brief to the Commission de la culture de l'éducation*, Brief on Bill 103, October 20, 2010.
78 "OneSchool Global," https://www.oneschoolglobal.com/about-us/#the-plymouth.
79 Dougherty, "French Not for Sale."
80 Office québécois de la langue française, Rapport sur l'évolution de la situation linguistique au Québec, 2002–07, 82, https://www.oqlf.gouv.qc.ca/ressources/sociolinguistique/2008/rapport_complet.pdf.
81 *Regulation on Private English Language Instruction*, s 73.1, Division 3: "Specific situation and overall education."
82 Ibid., s 4.
83 "Bill 103, An Act to Amend the Charter of the French Language and Other Legislative Provisions" (Text of speech by the Quebec ombudsperson before the Committee on Culture and Education, September 8, 2010).
84 "Quebec Liberals Push Language Law Through."
85 Ibid.
86 Lower Canada College and Miss Edgar's and Miss Cramp's were established in 1909, and St. Georges was established in 1930.
87 See, for instance, Ministère de l'éducation, du loisir et du sport, *Indicateurs linguistiques: secteur de l'éducation*, 2013.
88 The figures are derived from Figure 3.6: Certificates of eligibility issued under section 73 of the *Charter of the French Language*, 1977–2013.
89 *Protestant School Boards*, 66.
90 Office québécois de la langue française, Rapport sur l'évolution de la situation linguistique au Québec, April 2019, 38.
91 See, for instance, James B. Kelly, *Governing with the Charter: Legislative and Judicial Activism and Framers' Intent* (Vancouver: UBC Press, 2005).

Chapter 5: Quebec's "Sign Law" and Freedom of Expression

1 Bill 101, *Charter of the French Language*, SQ 1977, s 54.
2 Canada, "Current Affairs: The Speech from the Throne. Following the Address Debate," *House of Commons Debates*, 30th Parliament, 3rd Session, October 19, 1977, 39; Bill 22, *Official Language Act*, SQ 1974, c 35.
3 Pierre Elliott Trudeau, *Memoirs* (Toronto: McClelland and Stewart, 1993), 235.
4 Part 1 of the *Constitution Act, 1982*, being Schedule B to the *Canada Act 1982* (UK), 1982, c 11.
5 René Lévesque, quoted in Michael Mandel, *The Charter of Rights and the Legalization of Politics in Canada* (Toronto: Thompson, 1994), 144.
6 *Ford v Quebec (Attorney General)*, [1988] 2 SCR 712 [*Ford*]; *Devine v Quebec (Attorney General)*, [1988] 2 SCR 790 [*Devine*].
7 *"la survivance"* is a Québécois expression to denote the survival of the French language and culture within the North American context.
8 Peter W. Hogg and Allison A. Bushell, "The Charter Dialogue between Courts and Legislatures (or Perhaps the Charter of Rights Isn't Such a Bad Thing after All)," *Osgoode Hall Law Journal* 35 (1997): 75–124.
9 Samuel v LaSelva, "Re-Imagining Confederation: Moving beyond the Trudeau-Lévesque Debate," *Canadian Journal of Political Science* 26, 4 (1993): 711–12.
10 *Attorney General (Quebec) v Quebec Protestant School Boards*, [1984] 2 SCR 66.
11 *Charter of Human Rights and Freedoms*, CQLR, c C-12.
12 The expression *"visage linguistique"* translates to "linguistic face" and is used in Quebec in the context of public signs and commercial expression.
13 Bill 178, *Charter of the French Language*, RSQ 1988, c 54.
14 Bill 86, *Act to Amend the Charter of the French Language*, RSQ 1993, c 40 [1993 *Charter of the French Language*].
15 *Regulation Respecting the Language of Commerce and Business*, RRQ 1993, C-11, r 9; *Regulation Defining the Scope of the Expression "Markedly Predominant" for the Purposes of the Charter of the French Language*, RRQ 1993, C-11, r 11.
16 Éric Desautels, *Langue de l'affichage public des entreprises de l'île de Montréal, de février à mai 2017* (Montreal: Office québécois de la langue française, 2018), 9.
17 There are exceptions to this requirement. For instance, if a firm name is trademarked in English or if a firm name is established outside of Quebec, then the use of an English-only firm name is permitted.
18 Bill 63, *Act to Promote the French Language in Quebec*, RSQ 1969, c 9.
19 Eugénie Brouillet, *La négation de la nation: l'identité culturelle québécoise et le fédéralisme canadien* (Montreal: Septentrion, 2006), 375.
20 Quebec's linguistic communities are francophones, anglophones, and allophones, with the later referring to new immigrants whose first language is neither French nor English. Since the 1960s, it has been the fastest-growing linguistic group in Quebec and now represents the second largest linguistic group in the province.
21 Pierre Antcil, "The End of the Language Crisis in Quebec: Comparative Implications," in *Canadian Language Policies in Comparative Perspective*, ed. Michael Morris (Montreal and Kingston: McGill-Queen's University Press, 2010), 348–52.
22 William D. Coleman, "From Bill 22 to Bill 101: The Politics of Language under the Parti Quebecois," *Canadian Journal of Political Science* 14, 3 (1981): 460–63.
23 See Gil Rémillard, *Le fédéralisme canadien: la loi constitutionnelle de 1867* (Montreal: Québec Amérique, 1983); *British North America Act, 1867* (UK), 30–31 Vict, c 3.
24 Laforest, *Trudeau*, 4.

25 Alain G. Gagnon and Raffaele Iacovino, *Federalism, Citizenship and Quebec* (Toronto: University of Toronto Press, 2006), 98.
26 William D. Coleman, *The Independence Movement in Quebec 1945–1980* (Toronto: University of Toronto Press, 1984).
27 *Official Languages Act 1969*, S.C. 1969, chapter 0–2.
28 Trudeau, *Memoirs*, 234.
29 Gerard Bergeron, "Quebec in Isolation," in *And No One Cheered*, ed. Keith Banting and Richard Simeon (Toronto: Methuen 1983), 59–60.
30 Peter H. Russell, "Patriation and the Law of Unintended Consequences," in *Patriation and Its Consequences: Constitution Making in Canada*, ed. Lois Harder and Steve Patten (Vancouver: UBC Press, 2015), 234–35.
31 Kenneth McRoberts, *Quebec: Social Change and Political Crisis* (Toronto: McClelland and Stewart, 1993), 295.
32 Frédéric Bérard, *Charte canadienne et droits linguistiques: pour en finir avec les mythes* (Montreal: Presses de l'Université de Montréal, 2016).
33 *Attorney General of Quebec v Blaikie et al*, [1979] 2 SCR 1016.
34 *Charter of the French Language*.
35 The name was changed to Office québécois de la langue française in 2003.
36 *Charter of the French Language*.
37 *Ford*, 722.
38 See Peter McCormick and Mark D. Zanoni, *By the Court: Anonymous Judgments at the Supreme Court of Canada* (Vancouver: UBC Press, 2020).
39 *Ford*, 748–49.
40 Ibid.
41 *Devine*, 813.
42 *Ford*, 754.
43 Ibid., 767.
44 Ibid., 752.
45 Ibid., 767.
46 Richard Moon, *The Constitutional Protection of Freedom of Expression* (Toronto: University of Toronto Press, 2000), 186.
47 Jamie Cameron, "To the Rescue: Antonio Lamer and the Section 2(b) Cases from Quebec," in *The Sacred Fire: The Legacy of Antonio Lamer*, ed. Adam Dodek and Daniel Jutras (Toronto: LexisNexis Canada, 2009), 46, 217.
48 *Ford*, 779–80.
49 Ibid.
50 Patrick J. Monahan, *Meech Lake: The Inside Story* (Toronto: University of Toronto Press, 1991), 156; Robert J. Sharpe and Kent Roach, *Brian Dickson: A Judge's Journey* (Toronto: University of Toronto Press, 2003), 424–25; Ian MacDonald, *From Bourassa to Bourassa: Wilderness to Restoration* (Montreal and Kingston: McGill-Queen's University Press, "2002), 294.
51 Garth Stevenson, *Community Besieged: The Anglophone Minority and the Politics of Quebec* (Montreal and Kingston: McGill-Queen's University Press, 1999), 188.
52 1988 *Charter of the French Language*.
53 Ibid.
54 Ibid., s 58.
55 Ibid., s 58.1.
56 Ibid.

57 National Assembly of Quebec, *Journal des débats*, 33rd Legislature, 2nd Session, vol. 30, December 20, 1988 (Robert Bourassa).
58 Monahan, *Meech Lake*, 295.
59 Stevenson, *Community Besieged*, 194–200.
60 Monahan, *Meech Lake*, 161.
61 Ibid.
62 MacDonald, *From Bourassa to Bourassa*, 295–96; Troy Q. Riddell and F.L. Morton, "Reasonable Limitations, Distinct Society and the Canada Clause: Interpretive Clauses and the Competition for Constitutional Advantage," *Canadian Journal of Political Science* 31, 3 (1998): 85–89, 467.
63 Quoted in Laforest, *Trudeau*, 100.
64 Jamie Cameron, "To the Rescue: Antonio Lamer and the Section 2(b) Cases from Quebec," in *The Scared Fire: The Legacy of Antonio Lamer*, ed. Adam Dodek and Daniel Jutras (Toronto: LexisNexis Canada, 2009), 245.
65 Trudeau, "'Say Goodbye to the Dream' of One Canada," *Toronto Star*, May 27, 1987.
66 Peter H. Russell, *Constitutional Odyssey: Can Canadians Become a Sovereign People?* (Toronto: University of Toronto Press, 1993), 150. Frank McKenna would become a strong supporter of the Meech Lake Accord, and New Brunswick would pass a resolution in support on June 15, 1990, eight days before the three-year ratification period expired.
67 Ronald L. Watts, "Canadian Federalism in the 1990s: Once More in Question," *Publius: The Journal of Federalism* 21, 3 (1991): 176.
68 Russell, *Constitutional Odyssey*, 141–42.
69 Kenneth McRoberts, *Misconceiving Canada: The Struggle for National Unity* (Don Mills, ON: Oxford University Press, 1997), 203.
70 Russell, *Constitutional Odyssey*, 145–46.
71 For a review of the political context, see Cameron, "To the Rescue," 247–48; Sharpe and Roach, *Brian Dickson*, 435–38; Monahan, *Meech Lake*, 159–62.
72 Sharpe and Roach, *Brian Dickson*, 434.
73 Stevenson, *Community Besieged*, 214–16.
74 *Regulation Defining the Scope of the Expression "Markedly Predominant."*
75 *Regulation Respecting the Language of Commerce and Business*, RRQ 1993, c C-11, s 9.
76 *1993 Charter of the French Language*.
77 *Regulation Respecting the Language of Commerce*, s 9.
78 Ibid., s 15.
79 Ibid., s 16.
80 *Entreprises WFH Ltée c Québec (Procureure générale du)*, 2001 QCCA 17598, para 6 [*Entreprises WFH*].
81 Ibid., para 4.
82 Ibid., para 61.
83 Supreme Court of Canada, *Bulletin of October 11, 2002*, https://decisions.scc-csc.ca/scc-csc/bulletins/en/item/314/index.do.
84 *Regulation Defining the Scope of the Expression "Markedly Predominant."*
85 *156158 Canada Inc v Attorney General of Québec*, 2017 QCCA 2055, para 6 [*156158 Canada*].
86 Ibid., para 12.
87 Ibid., para 95.
88 Ibid., para 115.
89 The multinational corporations that challenged the Office québécois de la langue française's interpretation of section 58 of the *Charter of the French Language* and section

25 of the regulation are: Best Buy, Costco Wholesale, Gap Canada, Old Navy Canada, Guess Canada, Toys "R" Us Canada, and Curves International.
90 *Quebec (Attorney General) v Best Buy Stores Ltd,* 2015 QCCA 747, para 33 [*Best Buy Stores*].
91 *Regulation Respecting the Language of Commerce and Business,* RRQ 1993, c C-11, ss 25.1–25.5.
92 *Regulation to Amend the Regulation Respecting the Language of Commerce and Business,* reprinted in *Gazette Officielle du Québec,* vol. 148, November 9, 2016, 45.
93 *Entreprises WFH; 156158 Canada.*
94 *Best Buy Stores.*
95 Ibid.
96 Secrétariat à la politique linguistique, *L'évolution de la situation de l'affichage à Montréal de 1995 à 1997* (Montreal: Office québécois de la langue française, 1997); Desautels, *Langue de l'affichage public.* The Office québécois de la langue française released a similar report in 2012 that considered the language of commercial display on the Island of Montreal in 2010.
97 Secrétariat à la politique linguistique, *L'évolution de la situation.* The yearly breakdown of businesses and messages reviewed are as follows: 1995 (3,000; 26,0000); 1996 (2,000; 17,000); 1997 (2,000; 19,000).
98 Ibid., 5.
99 Ibid., Table 3 (Percentage of businesses with unilingual French signage, Island of Montreal, 1995, 1996, and 1997).
100 Ibid., Table 4 (Percentage of businesses with unilingual English signage, Island of Montreal, 1995, 1996, and 1997).
101 Ibid., Table 9 (Percentage of unilingual French messages by sector and by zone, Island of Montreal, 1995, 1996, and 1997).
102 Desautels, *Langue de l'affichage public,* 17. The Office québécois de la langue française makes a distinction between signs with only French words and those with French and words of an indeterminate nature. Both are classified as "French-only" signs by the Office québécois de la langue française.
103 Ibid., 18.
104 The English translation of this is: "These judicial decisions have thus limited Quebec's ability to legislate to ensure the development of the French language in an environment of singular linguistic difficulty." Translated from Eugénie Brouillet, "Le fédéralisme canadien d'hier à aujourd'hui: quelle reconnaissance de la nation québécoise?," *Iura Vasconiae,* 2010, 420.
105 Matthew Lapierre, "EMSB Officially Closing 3 Schools at the End of the School Year," *CTV News Montreal,* January 20, 2020; Sidhartha Banerjee, "EMSB Announces Legal Action over Transfer of Schools to French Board," *Canadian Press,* September 10, 2019.
106 Richard Y. Bourhis, "Evaluating the Impact of Bill 101 on the English-Speaking Communities of Quebec," *Language Problems and Language Planning* 43, 2 (2019): 217.
107 Alan C. Cairns, "The Judicial Committee and Its Critics," *Canadian Journal of Political Science* 4, 3 (1971): 320–21.

Chapter 6: Supervised Consumption Sites and the *Respect for Communities Act*
Acknowledgment: Sections of this chapter originally appeared in James B. Kelly, "The Charter of Rights and Freedoms, the Supreme Court of Canada, and Public Policy," in *Issues in Canadian Governance,* ed. Jonathan Craft and Amanda Clarke (Toronto: Emond Montgomery, 2018), 91–108. Reprinted with permission of the publisher.

1 *Canada (Attorney General) v PHS Community Services Society*, [2011] 3 SCR 134 [*PHS Community Services Society*]; Dan Small, "Fools Rush in Where Angels Fear to Tread," *International Journal of Drug Policy* 18, 1 (2006): 19.
2 SC 1996, c 19 [*CDSA*].
3 Bill C-2, *Act to Amend the Controlled Drugs and Substances Act*, SC 2015, c 22 [*Respect for Communities Act*].
4 Bill C-37, *Act to Amend the Controlled Drugs and Substances Act and to Make Related Amendments to Other Acts*, SC 2017, c 7.
5 Elaine Hyshka et al., "Harm Reduction in Name, but Not Substance: A Comparative Analysis of Current Canadian Provincial and Territorial Policy Frameworks," *Harm Reduction Journal* 14, 1 (2017): 1–15.
6 *Criminal Code*, RSC 1985, c C-46; *Narcotics Control Act*, RS 1960, c 9.
7 There are some exceptions to this responsibility – the health of inmates within federal penitentiaries is the jurisdictional responsibility of the federal government, as are the First Nations under section 91(24) of the *Constitution Act, 1867* (UK), 30 & 31 Vict, c 3.
8 John Paul Tasker, "Andrew Scheer Slams 'Terrible' Liberal Approach to Safe Injection Sites," *CBC News*, September 24, 2019.
9 For account of social activism and this issue, see Susan Boyd, Donald MacPherson, and Bud Osborn, *Raise Shit! Social Action Saving Lives* (Toronto: Fernwood, 2009).
10 Adam Harmes, "The Political Economy of Open Federalism," *Canadian Journal of Political Science* 40, 2 (2007): 418.
11 J.V. Cain, *Report of the Task Force into Illicit Narcotic Overdose Deaths in British Columbia* (Burnaby, BC: Office of the Chief Coroner, 1994), 5–14.
12 *PHS Community Services Society*, para 4.
13 Health Canada, *Vancouver's Insite Service and Other Supervised Injection Sites: What Has Been Learned from Research? Final Report of the Expert Advisory Committee*, 2008, 14.
14 Travis Lupick, *Fighting for Space: How a Group of Drug Users Transformed One City's Struggle with Addiction* (Vancouver: Arsenal Pulp Press, 2017), 49–53, 135–42.
15 Ibid., 52–55.
16 Cain, *Report of the Task Force*, vii.
17 *PHS Community Services Society v Attorney General of Canada*, [2008] BCSC 661, para 22 [*PHS Community Services Society* 2008].
18 Ibid., para 24.
19 Boyd, MacPherson, and Osborn, *Raise Shit!*, 43.
20 Kathleen Dooling and Michael Rachlis, "Vancouver's Supervised Injection Facility Challenges Canada's Drug Laws," *Canadian Medical Association Journal* 182, 13 (2010): 1440.
21 John S. Millar, *HIV, Hepatitis, and Injection Drug Use in British Columbia: Pay Now or Pay Later?* (Victoria: Office of the Provincial Health Officer, 1998), 15.
22 Alan R. Davidson, "British Columbia's Health Reform: 'New Directions' and Accountability," *Canadian Journal of Public Health* 90, S1 (1999): 35–36.
23 Larry Campbell, Neil Boyd, and Lori Culbert, *A Thousand Dreams: Vancouver's Downtown Eastside and the Fight for Its Future* (Vancouver: Douglas and McIntyre, 2009), 160–61.
24 Thomas Kerr et al., "Supervised Injection Facilities in Canada: Past, Present, and Future," *Harm Reduction Journal* 14, 1 (2017): 2.
25 Vancouver Coastal Health Authority, *Vancouver Community Operational Addictions Plan: A Proposal in Support of the Vancouver Agreement Strategies*, 19 September (Vancouver: Vancouver Coastal Health Authority, 2002).
26 Lupick, *Fighting for Space*, 228.

27 Susan Boyd, Connie I. Carter, and Donald MacPherson, *More Harm Than Good: Drug Policy in Canada* (Winnipeg: Fernwood, 2016), 23. The four pillars of the 1998 National Drug Strategy are education and prevention, treatment and rehabilitation, harm reduction, and enforcement and control.
28 Fred Cutler and J. Scott Matthews, "The Challenge of Municipal Voting: Vancouver 2002," *Canadian Journal of Political Science* 38, 2 (2005): 361.
29 Donald MacPherson, *A Framework for Action: A Four-Pillar Approach to Drug Problems in Vancouver* (Vancouver: City of Vancouver, 2001), 1. The report would be adopted by the City of Vancouver in May 2001.
30 *PHS Community Services Society* 2008, para 39.
31 Cutler and Matthews, "Challenge of Municipal Voting," 362.
32 Health Canada, "Health Canada Approves Vancouver Supervised Injection Pilot Project," news release, June 24, 2003.
33 Campbell, Boyd, and Culbert, *A Thousand Dreams*, 175.
34 Dooling and Rachlis, "Vancouver's Supervised Injection Facility," 1451.
35 Kerr et al., "Supervised Injection Facilities," 2.
36 Evan Wood et al., "The Canadian Government's Treatment of Scientific Process and Evidence: Inside the Evaluation of North America's First Supervised Injecting Facility," *International Journal of Drug Policy* 19, 3 (2008): 221.
37 See David Cameron and Richard Simeon, "Intergovernmental Relations in Canada: The Emergence of Collaborative Federalism," *Publius: The Journal of Federalism* 32, 2 (2002): 49–71.
38 See Boyd, MacPherson, and Osborn, *Raise Shit!*; Campbell, Boyd, and Culbert, *A Thousand Dreams*; Lupick, *Fighting for Space*.
39 See Libby Davies, *Outside In: A Political Memoir* (Toronto: Between the Lines, 2019).
40 See Conservative Party of Canada, *Demanding Better: Conservative Party of Canada, Platform 2004*, 2004, 35–47, "Demand Better Security"; Conservative Party of Canada, *Stand Up for Canada: Conservative Party of Canada Federal Election Platform 2006*, 2006, 21–27, "Stand up for Security"; Conservative Party of Canada, *The True North Strong and Free: Stephen Harper's Plan for Canadians 2008*, 2008, 45–50, "Here for Law-abiding Canadians."
41 "No AIDS Announcement during 'Politicized' Week: Ottawa," *CBC News*, 2006.
42 "Police Group Takes Aim at Vancouver Safe Injection Site," *CBC News*, September 1, 2006, 1403; Wendy Stuek, "RCMP Defends Hiring Experts to Review Insite Research," *Globe and Mail*, October 9, 2008.
43 Evan Wood et al., "Summary of Findings from the Evaluation of a Pilot Medically Supervised Safer Injecting Facility," *Canadian Medical Association Journal* 175, 11 (2006): 1403.
44 Health Canada, "No New Injection Sites for Addicts until Questions Answered Says Minister Clement," news release, September, 1, 2006.
45 *PHS Community Services Society*, para 121.
46 Health Canada, *Vancouver's Insite Service*.
47 Boyd, Carter, and MacPherson, *More Harm Than Good*, 26.
48 The doctrine of inter-jurisdictional immunity has limited application in Canada. In the context of Insite, the PHS Community Services Society argued that the *CDSA*, a valid federal power, interfered with a core provincial responsibility, health care. Based on the doctrine of interjurisdictional immunity, Insite should be exempt from the *CDSA* because it interfered with a core provincial responsibility.

49 Part 1 of the *Constitution Act, 1982*, being Schedule B to the *Canada Act 1982* (UK), 1982, c 11 [*Canadian Charter*].
50 *PHS Community Services Society*, para 5.
51 *PHS Community Services Society* 2008, para 38.
52 *PHS Community Services Society*, para 159.
53 Canada Parliament, House of Commons, Standing Committee on Health, *Minutes of Proceedings and Evidence*, 39th Parliament, 2nd Session, no 32, May 29, 2008, 19.
54 Ibid., 19.
55 Ibid., 24.
56 The party standings following the fortieth federal election, in which the Conservatives would fall twelve seats short of a majority government, were: Conservative (143); Liberal (77); Bloc Québécois (49); NDP (37); Independent (2).
57 "Tony Clement Talks about Insite BC," *YouTube*, https://www.youtube.com/watch?v=xzvkv5tNiqg (transcript on file with author).
58 "Clement Questions MDs Who Favour Safe Injection Sites," *CBC News*, August 18, 2008.
59 Andre Picard, "Supporting Insite Unethical, Clement Tells Doctors," *Globe and Mail*, August 19, 2008.
60 Remshi Nair, "Insite Supporters Try to Crash Harper Speech," *CTV News BC*, October 9, 2008.
61 Matt Kieltyka and Irwin Loy, "Harper Dodges Questions on RCMP's Anti-Insite Research," *The Tyee*, October 9, 2008.
62 *PHS Community Services Society v Canada (Attorney General)*, 2010 BCCA 15, para 193.
63 Ibid., para 193.
64 Canada, Parliament, *Minutes of Proceedings and Evidence*, May 29, 2008, 24.
65 Dwight Newman argues that the Supreme Court of Canada decision is far more activist than either lower court decision because it ignored the importance of the doctrine of inter-jurisdictional immunity to allow a federalism-based resolution of this issue. See Dwight Newman, "The PHS Case and Federalism-Based Alternatives to Charter Activism," *Constitutional Forum* 22 (2013): 85–91.
66 *PHS Community Services Society*, para 66–67.
67 Ibid., para 68.
68 Ibid., para 69.
69 Ibid.
70 Ibid., para 95–96.
71 Ibid., para 114.
72 Ibid., paras 116–17.
73 Ibid., 119.
74 Ibid., para 122.
75 Ibid., para 124.
76 Ibid., paras 129–32.
77 Ibid. para 133.
78 Ibid., para 133.
79 Ibid., para 137.
80 Ibid., para 146.
81 Ibid.
82 Ibid., para 149.
83 Ibid., para 151.
84 Ibid., para 150.

85 Ibid., para 152.
86 Ibid., para 153.
87 Ian Green and Peter McCormick, *Beverley Mclachlin: The Legacy of a Supreme Court Chief Justice* (Toronto: Lorimer, 2019), 116–17.
88 Kent Roach, *The Supreme Court on Trial: Judicial Activism or Democratic Dialogue*, 2nd ed. (Toronto: Irwin Law, 2016), 365.
89 The *Respect for Communities Act*, S.C. 2015, c 22, would be introduced on two occasions by two ministers of health and passed as Bill C-2: Bill C-65, An Act to Amend the Controlled Drugs and Substances Act, in June 2013 and Bill C-2, An Act to Amend the Controlled Drugs and Substances Act, in October 2013.
90 Canada, Parliament, *House of Commons Debates*, 41st Parliament, 1st Session, vol. 146, no 24, September 30, 2011, 1698 (Libby Davies, Vancouver East, NDP).
91 Ibid., 1698 (Leona Aglukkaq, Minister of Health and Minister of the Canadian Northern Economic Development Agency, Conservative).
92 Canada, Parliament, *House of Commons Debates*, 41st Parliament, 1st Session, vol. 146, no 25, October 3, 2011, 1762 (Hedy Fry, Vancouver Center, Liberal).
93 Ibid., 1762 (Leona Aglukkaq, Minister of Health and Minister of the Canadian Northern Economic Development Agency, Conservative).
94 Rainer Knopff et al., "Dialogue: Clarified and Reconsidered," *Osgoode Hall Law Journal* 54, 2 (2017): 633–34.
95 The sequence of the four-yearly extensions of section 56 of the *CDSA* provided to Insite by the Harper government before the passage of the *Respect for Communities Act* are the following: 1) March 2012 to March 2013; 2) March 2013 to March 2014; 3) March 2014 to March 2015; and 4) March 2015 to March 2016.
96 Vancouver Coastal Health, "Insite Receives New, Four-Year Health Canada Exemption," news release, March 17, 2016.
97 Donald MacPherson and Nicholas Klassen, "Vancouver Buyers Club: Safe Injection Sites Save Lives – but Ottawa Still Doesn't Care," *The Walrus*, May 2015.
98 Bill C-65, *Act to Amend the Controlled Drugs and Substances Act* (June 6, 2013).
99 The *Respect for Communities Act* was granted royal assent on June 18, 2015. The Conservative party formed a majority government following the forty-first general election in 2011, winning nearly 54 percent of the seats in the House of Commons (166 of the 308 seats). In the period in which the *Respect for Communities Act* would progress through Parliament (June 2013 to June 2015), the Conservative party seated nearly 60 percent of the Senate (55 of the 92 seats). Although the normal composition of the Senate is 105 members, it averaged ninety-two members during this period due to unfilled vacancies due to resignation or retirement.
100 Bill C-65, *An Act to Amend the Controlled Drugs and Substances Act* (June 6, 2013).
101 Aurora Tejeida, "Conservative Party Starts Petition to 'Keep Heroin out of Our Backyards," *The Hook*, June 7, 2013.
102 Ibid. The text of the online petition is on file with the author.
103 For an overview and history of this legislative technique, see James B. Kelly and Matthew A. Hennigar, "The Canadian Charter of Rights and the Minister of Justice: Weak-Form Review within a Constitutional Charter of Rights," *International Journal of Constitutional Law* 10, 1 (2012): 38–44.
104 *Carter v Canada (Attorney General)*, [2015] 1 SCR 331.
105 Ahmed M. Bayoumi et al., *Report of the Toronto and Ottawa Supervised Consumption Assessment Study, 2012* (Toronto: St. Michael's Hospital and the Dalla Lana School of Public Health, University of Toronto, 2012); Richard Lessard and Carole Morissette,

Toward Supervised Injection Services: Report of a Feasibility Study on the Implementation of Regional Supervised Injection Services in Montréal – Summary Report (Montreal: Agence de la santé et des services sociaux de Montréal, 2011).
106 Elizabeth Church and Verity Stevenson, "Supervised Injection Site Proponents Push on Despite Harper's Opposition," *Globe and Mail,* August 14, 2015.
107 "Denis Coderre Makes Another Push for Montreal Safe Injection Sites," *CBC News,* June 4, 2015
108 Medical Officer of Health, "Supervised Injection Services in Toronto," Memorandum to Board of Health, June 21, 2013, 2, https://www.toronto.ca/legdocs/mmis/2013/hl/bgrd/backgroundfile-59886.pdf.
109 Ibid., 2.
110 Otis Redding, "Respect," *Otis Redding Sings Soul* (Volt Records: September 1965). Aretha Franklin made the song a hit.
111 *PHS Community Services Society,* para 152.
112 *Canada (Attorney General) v Bedford,* [2013] 3 SCR 1101 (the decision was released on December 20, 2013, and determined that the *Criminal Code* provisions regarding prostitution were unconstitutional as a violation of section 7 of the *Canadian Charter*).
113 His Excellency the Right Honourable David Johnson, Governor General of Canada, "Speech from the Throne to Open the Second Session Forty First Parliament of Canada," October 16, 2013, 7–8, https://www.toronto.ca/legdocs/mmis/2013/hl/bgrd/backgroundfile-59886.pdf.
114 Health Canada, "Harper Government Continues to Put Communities First: The Respect for Communities Act Requires Consultations with Local Stakeholders before Supervised Injection Sites Can Be Considered," news release, October 17, 2013.
115 Ibid.
116 Ibid.
117 Canada, Parliament, *House of Commons Debates,* 41st Parliament, 1st Session, vol. 146, no. 268, June 12, 2013, 18257 (Leona Aglukkaq, Minister of Health, Minister of the Canadian Northern Economic Development Agency and Minister for the Arctic Council, Conservative).
118 *Respect for Communities Act.*
119 The eight components of the section 56 application that were only required "if any" evidence or documents were available are: section 56.1(3)(f), (i), (j), (k), (l), (m), (n), and (r).
120 *Respect for Communities Act,* s 56.1(5)
121 Canada, Parliament, *House of Commons Debates,* June 12, 2013, 18256 (Leona Aglukkaq, Minister of Health, Minister of the Canadian Northern Economic Development Agency and Minister for the Arctic Council, Conservative).
122 Ibid., 18256.
123 Canada, Parliament, *House of Commons Debates,* 41st Parliament, 2nd Session, vol. 147, no. 180, February 26, 2015, 11708 (Rona Ambrose, Minister of Health, Conservative).
124 Roach, *Supreme Court on Trial,* 366.
125 Ibid.
126 Ibid., 367.
127 Rainer Knopff et al., "Dialogue: Clarified and Reconsidered," *Osgoode Hall Law Journal* 54, 2 (2017): 630–36.
128 *PHS Community Services Society,* para 152.
129 Canada, Parliament, *House of Commons Debates,* 41st Parliament, 2nd Session, vol. 147, no. 3, October 18, 2013, 98 (Libby Davies, Vancouver East, NDP).

130 Ibid., 115 (Joyce Murray, Vancouver Quadra, Liberal).
131 Canada, Parliament, *House of Commons Debates*, 41st Parliament, 2nd Session, vol. 147, no. 18, November 18, 2013, 959–60 (Megan Leslie, Halifax, NDP).
132 Ibid., 960.
133 Canada, Parliament, House of Commons, Standing Committee on Health, *Minutes of Proceedings and Evidence*, 39th Parliament, 2nd Session, no. 32, May 29, 2008, 19.
134 Canada, Parliament, House of Commons, Standing Committee on Health, Mandate, 41st Parliament, 2nd Session, October 16, 2013 – August 2, 2015, https://www.ourcommons.ca/Committees/en/HESA?parl=41.
135 Bill C-65, *Respect for Communities Act*, was not sent to a standing committee before it was replaced by Bill C-2, *Respect for Communities Act*.
136 Canada, Parliament, House of Commons, Standing Committee on Health, *Mandate*.
137 Canada, Parliament, *House of Commons Debates*, 41st Parliament, 2nd Session, vol. 147, no. 13, November 4, 2013, 678 (Randall Garrison, Esquimalt-Saanich-Sooke, NDP).
138 Canada, Parliament, House of Commons, Standing Committee on Public Safety and National Security, *Minutes of Proceedings and Evidence*, 41st Parliament, 2nd Session, no. 34, October 27, 2014, 2 (Rona Ambrose, Minister of Health, Conservative).
139 Ibid., 6 (Steven Blainey, Minister of Public Safety and Emergency Preparedness, Conservative).
140 Ibid., 13 (Libby Davis, Vancouver East, NDP).
141 Ibid., 13 (Hilary Geller, Assistant Deputy Minister of Health, Healthy Environments and Consumer Safety Branch, Department of Health).
142 Ibid., 13.
143 Ibid., 15.
144 The following appearances were in support of the *Respect for Communities Act:* Canadian Police Association; Drug Prevention Network of Canada; Ottawa Police Association; REAL Women of Canada; Safer Ottawa; Society of Accredited Senior Agents (Real Estate Industry); Toronto Police Association; and Vancouver City Police Department.
145 See, for instance, Canada, Parliament, House of Commons, Standing Committee on Public Safety and National Security, *Minutes of Proceedings and Evidence*, 41st Parliament, 2nd Session, no. 35, October 29, 2014: Matthew Skof (president, Ottawa Police Association); Michael McCormack (president, Toronto Police Association); Bryan Larking (chief of police, Waterloo Regional Police Service, member of the Drug Advisory Committee. Canadian Association of Chiefs of Police, *Minutes of Proceedings and Evidence*, 41st Parliament, 2nd Session, no. 36, November 3, 2014: Scott Thompson (District 1 commander, Operations Division, Vancouver City Police Department); Tom Stamatakis (president, Canadian Police Association).
146 The following appearances were opposed to the *Respect for Communities Act*: Canadian Drug Policy Network; Pivot Legal Society; Toronto Board of Health; and Dean Wilson (Individual).
147 Canada, Parliament, House of Commons, Standing Committee on Public Safety and National Security, *Minutes of Proceedings and Evidence*, 41st Parliament, 2nd Session, no. 35, October 29, 2014, 4 (Dr. David McKeown, Medical Officer of Health, Toronto Board of Health). The following brief was submitted: Toronto Board of Health, *Submission by the Toronto Board of Health to the Standing Committee on Public Safety and National Security*, October 2014.
148 Canada, Parliament, House of Commons, Standing Committee on Public Safety and National Security, *Minutes of Proceedings and Evidence*, October 29, 2014, 5 (Dr. David McKeown, Medical Officer of Health, Toronto Board of Health).

149 Ibid., 5.
150 Ibid., 6.
151 Canada, Parliament, House of Commons, Standing Committee on Public Safety and National Security, *Minutes of Proceedings and Evidence*, October 29, 2014, 15 (Marjolaine Boutin-Sweet, Hochelaga, NDP).
152 Canadian Association of Nurses in HIV/AIDS, *Brief – Bill C-2: Legislation to Amend the Controlled Drugs and Substances Act to Allow Exemptions for Supervised Injection Sites (and Services)*, October 2014, 4.
153 Canadian Bar Association, National Criminal Justice Section, *Bill C-2, Respect for Communities Act*, October 28, 2014, 2.
154 Canadian Medical Association, *Canadian Medical Association Submission to the Standing Committee on Public Safety and National Security, Bill C-2 An Act to Amend the Controlled Drugs and Substances Act (Respect for Communities Act)*, October 28, 2014.
155 Canadian Nurses Association, *Brief for Parliament: Legislation to Amend the Controlled Drugs and Substances Act to Allow Exemptions for Supervised Injection Sites*, November 2013.
156 Canadian Drug Policy Coalition, *An Injection of Reason: Critical Analysis of Bill C-2*, October 2014.
157 Pivot Legal Society, *Pivot Legal Society Submission to the Standing Committee on Public Safety and National Security: Legal Issues with Bill C-2*, November 2013.
158 Canada, Parliament, House of Commons, Standing Committee on Public Safety and National Security, *Minutes of Proceedings and Evidence*, 41st Parliament, 2nd Session, no. 36, November 3, 2014, 11–12 (Adrienne Smith, Health and Drug Policy Staff Lawyer, Pivot Legal Society).
159 Canada, Parliament, *House of Commons Debates*, 41st Parliament, 2nd Session, vol. 147, no. 180, February 26, 2015, 11708 (Rona Ambrose, Minister of Health, Conservative).
160 Opposed to the *Respect for Communities Act* (n = 8); Canadian Association of Nurses in HIV/AIDS Care; Canadian Centre on Substance Abuse; Canadian HIV/AIDS Legal Network; Canadian Medical Association; Criminal Lawyers' Association; Insite; Dean Wilson (Individual); Donna May (Individual). Supportive of *Respect for Communities Act* (n = 4): Canadian Association of Chiefs of Police; Canadian Police Association; Drug Prevention Network of Canada; Safer Ottawa.
161 Canadian Drug Policy Coalition, *An Injection of Reason: Critical Analysis of Bill C-2*, April 2015; Canadian Association of Nurses in HIV/AIDS, *Brief – Bill C-2: Legislation to Amend the Controlled Drugs and Substances Act to Allow Exemptions for Supervised Injection Sites (and Services)*, April 2015; Toronto Board of Health, *Submission by the Toronto Board of Health to the Standing Senate Committee on Legal and Constitutional Affairs*, April 24, 2015; Canadian Bar Association, National Criminal Justice Section, *Bill C-2, Respect for Communities Act*, October 28, 2014; Canadian Medical Association, *Canadian Medical Association Submission to the Standing Senate Committee on Legal and Constitutional Affairs, Bill C-2 An Act to Amend the Controlled Drugs and Substances Act (Respect for Communities Act)*, May 14, 2015; Canadian Nurses Association, *Brief for Standing Senate Committee on Legal and Constitutional Affairs – Bill C-2: An Act to Amend the Controlled Drugs and Substances Act (Respect for Communities Act)*, May 2015; Pivot Legal Society, *Pivot Legal Society Submission to the Standing Senate Committee on Legal and Constitutional Affairs: Legal Issues with Bill C-2*, May 2015; Canadian Union of Public Employees, *Bill C-2: Legislation to Amend the Controlled Drugs and Substances Act to Allow Exemptions for Supervised Injection Sites and Services*, Submission – Standing Senate Committee on Legal and Constitutional Affairs, May 2015.

162 Canada, Parliament, Senate of Canada, *Proceedings of the Standing Senate Committee on Legal and Constitutional Affairs*, 41st Parliament, 2nd Session, no. 30, May 7, 2015, 30:8 (Rona Ambrose, Minister of Health, Conservative).
163 Ibid., 30:11–12 (Steven Blainey, Minister of Public Safety and Emergency Preparedness, Conservative); Bill C-51, *Anti-Terrorism Act*, S.C. 2015, c 20; Bill C-32, *Victims Bill of Rights Act*, S.C. 2015, c 13; Bill C-10, *Safe Streets and Communities Act*, S.C. 2012, c 1.
164 Ibid., at 30:11.
165 Ibid., at 30:12.
166 The following criminal justice bills were granted royal assent alongside Bill C-2, *Respect for Communities Act*: Bill C-12, *Drug-Free Prison Act*, S.C. 2015, c 30; Bill C-26, *Tougher Penalties for Child Predators Act*, S.C. 2015, c 23; Bill C-42, *Common Sense Firearms Licensing Act*, S.C. 2015, c 27; and Bill C-51, *Anti-terrorism Act*, S.C. 2015, c 20.
167 The original version of section 56 of the *CDSA* that permitted the minister of health to grant exemptions to operate a safe injection site totalled seventy-one words: "56. The Minister may, on such terms and conditions as the Minister deems necessary, exempt any person or class of persons or any controlled substance or precursor or any class thereof from the application of all or any of the provisions of this Act or the regulations if, in the opinion of the Minister, the exemption is necessary for a medical or scientific purpose or is otherwise in the public interest."
168 Andrew Jackson, quoted in Georg Vanberg, "'John Marshall Has Made His Decision': Implementation, Transparency, and Public Support," in *Institutional Games and the U.S. Supreme Court*, ed. James R. Rogers, Roy B. Flemming, and Jon R. Bond (Charlottesville: University of Virginia Press, 2006), 69; *Worcester v Georgia*, 31 US 515 (1832).
169 Bill C-37, *An Act to Amend the Controlled Drugs and Substances Act and to Make Related Amendments to Other Acts*, SC 2017, c 7.

Chapter 7: The Opioid Crisis and Canadian Federalism
1 Elizabeth Church and Verity Stevenson, "Supervised Injection Site Proponents Push on Despite Harper's Opposition," *Globe and Mail*, August 14, 2015.
2 To legally operate a safe consumption site under the *Controlled Drugs and Substances Act*, a provider must be granted a section 56 exemption by the federal minister of health. Bill C-2, *Act to Amend the Controlled Drugs and Substances Act*, SC 2015, c 22 [*Respect for Communities Act*]; *Controlled Drugs and Substances Act*, SC 1996, c 19 [*CDSA*].
3 Canada, Office of the Prime Minister, "Minister of Justice and Attorney General Mandate Letter," news release, November 12, 2015.
4 The mandate letters issued to the first Trudeau ministry on November 12, 2015, are available at Office of the Prime Minister, "Archived Mandate Letters," https://www.pm.gc.ca/en/all-archived-mandate-letters.
5 Bill C-37, *An Act to Amend the Controlled Drugs and Substances Act and to Make Related Amendments to Other Acts*, SC 2017, c 7 [*Act to Amend the CDSA*].
6 Part 1 of the *Constitution Act, 1982*, being Schedule B to the *Canada Act 1982* (UK), 1982, c 11 [*Canadian Charter*].
7 Laura Stone, "Liberals to Whip the Vote in Favour of Assisted-Dying Law," *Globe and Mail*, February 11, 2016. The Liberal house leader was quoted as saying: "At the end of the day, the Supreme Court has defined a right around the issue of assisted dying, and we will be always voting to uphold Charter rights."
8 Evidence for legislative non-compliance on the part of the Harper government includes medical assistance in dying in response to *Carter v Canada (Attorney General)*, [2015] 1

SCR 331 [*Carter*], and reform of the *Criminal Code* provisions regulating prostitution/sex work in response to *Canada (Attorney General) v Bedford*, [2013] 3 SCR 1101 [*Bedford*].
9 Canada, Office of the Prime Minister, "Minister of Justice and Attorney General Mandate Letter," news release, November 12, 2015.
10 *Canada (Attorney General) v PHS Community Services Society*, [2011] 3 SCR 134 [*PHS Community Services Society*].
11 At the time of writing (February 2023), there are a total of thirty-nine facilities in Canada: Insite in the Downtown Eastside of Vancouver (DTES), which opened in 2008, and thirty-eight facilities that have been approved by the Trudeau government since 2017. There are also nine open applications currently being reviewed by Health Canada. See Health Canada, "Supervised Consumption Sites: Status of Applications," https://www.canada.ca/en/health-canada/services/substance-use/supervised-consumption-sites/status-application.html.
12 Monica Muise, "Liberals Stick with Existing Rules to Approve Safe-Injection Sites, for Now," *Global News*, March 14, 2016; Roshini Nair and Jon Hernandez, "Liberal Government's Refusal to Repeal Bill C-2 'Disappointing,' Supervised Injection Site Advocate Says," *CBC News*, August 24, 2016.
13 Kent Roach, "A Charter Reality Check: How Relevant Is the Charter to the Justness of Our Criminal Justice System?," *Supreme Court Law Review* (2d) 40 (2008), 719.
14 Ontario Ministry of Health and Long Term Care, "Applications Now Open for Overdose Prevention Sites. Temporary Locations to Offer Life-Saving Harm Reduction Services," news release, January 11, 2018.
15 Supervised safe consumption sites are only available in five provincial jurisdictions, as of January 2023: Alberta, British Columbia, Ontario, Quebec, and Saskatchewan. Grande Prairie, Alberta, is the most northern facility and Montreal is the most eastern in Canada. Yukon has announced its intention to open a supervised consumption site in Whitehorse as part of the "supply and confidence" agreement between the territorial Liberal and NDP parties but has yet to submit an application to Health Canada for a section 56 exemption under the *CDSA*.
16 For a discussion of federalism and the "implementation gap," see Linda A. White, "Federalism and Equality Rights Implementation in Canada," *Publius: The Journal of Federalism* 44, 1 (2014): 160–63. Dennis Baker explores this in the context of criminal justice policy. See Dennis Baker, "The Provincial Power to (Not) Prosecute *Criminal Code* Offences," *Ottawa Law Review* 48, 2 (2017): 419–48; Dennis Baker, "The Temptation of Provincial Criminal Law," *Canadian Public Administration* 57, 2 (2014): 275–94.
17 Elaine Hyshka et al., "Harm Reduction in Name, but Not Substance: A Comparative Analysis of Current Canadian Provincial and Territorial Policy Frameworks," *Harm Reduction Journal* 14, 1 (2017): 2.
18 White, "Federalism," 158–59.
19 Richard J. Schultz, *Federalism, Bureaucracy, and Public Policy* (Montreal and Kingston: McGill-Queen's University Press, 1980), 147–68.
20 For an overview, see Hyshka et al., "Harm Reduction."
21 The following five jurisdictions represent 100 percent of the thirty-nine supervised consumption sites that operate under section 56 of the *CDSA*: Ontario (n = 24); British Columbia (n = 5); Alberta (n = 5); Quebec (n = 4); and Saskatchewan (n = 1). The following provinces have open applications (n = 9): Quebec (n = 4); Ontario (n = 3); British Columbia (n = 2).
22 Benjamin Perrin, "Alberta's War against Safe Injection Sites," *Maclean's*, March 12, 2020.

23 Darryl Dyck, "Ontario to Review Safe Injection, Overdose Prevention Sites, Health Minister Says," *Canadian Press*, July 24, 2018.
24 For a discussion of "complex intergovernmental problems" in the Canadian federation, see Mireille Paquet and Robert Schertzer, "Covid-19 as a Complex Intergovernmental Problem," *Canadian Journal of Political Science* 53, 4 (2020): 343–44.
25 The use of the phrase "evidence-based policy" was repeatedly used by the Trudeau government during its first mandate in an attempt to differentiate it from its predecessor, the Harper government.
26 Alan C. Cairns, "The Judicial Committee and Its Critics," *Canadian Journal of Political Science* 4, 3 (1971): 319–30.
27 Alan C. Cairns, "The Governments and Societies of Canadian Federalism," *Canadian Journal of Political Science* 10, 4 (1977): 695–725.
28 Vancouver Police Department, *The Opioid Crisis: The Need for Treatment on Demand*, May 2017, 7–8.
29 Ibid., 5.
30 Ibid., 7; Benjamin Perrin, *Overdose: Heartbreak and Hope in Canada's Opioid Crisis* (Toronto: Penguin Canada, 2020), 17–18.
31 Vancouver Police Department, *Opioid Crisis*, 8.
32 Ibid., 7.
33 Perrin, *Overdose*, 18.
34 Vancouver Police Department, *Opioid Crisis*, 8. A microgram is 1/1,000 of a milligram.
35 Perrin, *Overdose*, 18.
36 Vancouver Police Department, *Opioid Crisis*, 8.
37 Public Health Agency of Canada, *Opioid and Stimulant-Related Harms in Canada* (Ottawa: Public Health Agency of Canada, 2021), 5.
38 *Public Health Act*, SC 2006, c 5; Joint Task Force on Overdose Prevention and Response, *Progress Update on B.C.'s Response to the Opioid Overdose Public Health Emergency*, 5th progress update (2017), 2. The number of deaths related to the opioid crisis in British Columbia are the following: 2014 (n = 369); 2015 (n = 529); 2016 (n = 992); 2017 (n = 1,492); and 2018 (n = 1,548).
39 Health Canada, "Notice: Prescription Drug List (Pdl): Naloxone," news release, March 22, 2016.
40 College of Pharmacists of British Columbia, "Naloxone Now Available in BC without a Prescription," news release, March 24, 2016.
41 Canadian Centre on Substance Abuse, "The Availability of Take-Home Naloxone in Canada," news release, March 2016.
42 College of Pharmacists of British Columbia, "Naloxone Now Available." *BC Drugs Schedule Regulations*, B.C. Reg 9/98.
43 Ibid.
44 Health Canada, "Interim Order Respecting Naloxone Hydrochloride Nasal Spray," news release, July 6, 2016.
45 Health Canada, "Authorized Canadian Naloxone Nasal Spray (Narcan) Coming to Market," news release, June 30, 2017.
46 College of Pharmacists of British Columbia, "Non-Prescription Naloxone Now Available Outside of Pharmacies," news release, September 21, 2016.
47 BC Centre for Disease Control, "Administration of Naloxone," news release, December 2016; *Health Professionals Act*, RSBC 1996, c 183 *Emergencies Health Services Act*, RSBC 1996, c 182.

48 Paquet and Schertzer, "Covid-19," 344.
49 Government of Canada, "Statement from the Minister of Health: Health Canada Authorizes Dr. Peter Centre to Operate Second Supervised Consumption Site in Canada," news release, January 15, 2016.
50 Mike Hager, "Injection Site Supporters Say Tories Are Heel Dragging," *Globe and Mail*, January 13, 2015.
51 "Federal Government Approves Three Supervised Injection Sites in Montreal," *Canadian Press*, February 6, 2017. The Montreal facilities were not operational until February 2017.
52 "Insite Receives New, Four-Year Health Canada Exemption," *Vancouver Coastal Public Health*, March 17, 2016.
53 Canadian Pharmacists Association, "CPHA Applauds Announcement of Opioid Summit," news release, July 26, 2016.
54 Heath Canada, "Health Canada to Propose Regulatory Change to Enable Consideration of Applications under the Special Access Program to Facilitate Treatment of Chronic Relapsing Opioid Dependence," news release, May 13, 2016. The regulations were in force as of September 7, 2016.
55 Muise, "Liberals Stick with Existing Rules"; Nair and Hernandez, "Liberal Government's Refusal."
56 Kyle Duggan, "Philpott Expects More Applications for Safe Injection Sites," *iPolitics*, February 10, 2016.
57 For accounts of how community activism has driven responses to harm reduction, see Travis Lupick, *Fighting for Space: How a Group of Drug Users Transformed One City's Struggle with Addiction* (Vancouver: Arsenal Pulp Press, 2017); Susan Boyd, Donald MacPherson, and Bud Osborn, *Raise Shit! Social Action Saving Lives* (Toronto: Fernwood, 2009); Larry Campbell, Neil Boyd, and Lori Culbert, *A Thousand Dreams: Vancouver's Downtown Eastside and the Fight for Its Future* (Vancouver: Douglas and McIntyre, 2009).
58 Kyle Duggan, "NDP MPs Call on Government to Make It Easier to Set up Harm-Reduction Sites," *iPolitics*, March 2, 2016.
59 City of Vancouver, "Letter to Minister of Health Jane Philpott Regarding Safe Injection Sites," news release, August 30, 2016. The letter was also signed by the executive director of the Dr. Peter AIDS Foundation and three notable academics from the University of British Columbia.
60 New Democratic Party of Canada, "NDP Secure Emergency Study of Opioid Crisis," news release, September 22, 2016. The Health Committee studied this issued between October 4 and December 8, 2015. The report was released December 12, 2016.
61 Canada, Parliament, House of Commons, Standing Committee on Health, *Report and Recommendations on the Opioid Crisis in Canada: Report of the Standing Committee on Health*, 2016.
62 Government of Canada, "Joint Statement of Action to Address the Opioid Crisis," news release, November 19, 2016.
63 Travis Lupick, "Health Minister Says a Change to Harper's Anti-Insite Law Likely Needed to Meet Rising Overdose Deaths," *Georgia Straight*, November 10, 2016.
64 Canada, Parliament, House of Commons, Standing Committee on Health, *Interim Report and Recommendations on the Opioid Crisis in Canada: Report of the Standing Committee on Health*, 2016.
65 Bruce Wallace, Flora Pagan, and Bernadette Pauly, "The Implementation of Overdose Prevention Sites as a Novel and Nimble Response during an Illegal Drug Overdose Public Health Emergency," *International Journal of Drug Policy* 66 (2019): 5.

66 Alexandra B. Collins et al., "Harnessing the Language of Overdose Prevention to Advance Evidence-Based Responses to the Opioid Crisis," *International Journal of Drug Policy* 55 (2018): 7.
67 Lupick, *Fighting for Space* (for a detailed discussion, see Chapter 21 "The Hair Salon").
68 British Columbia, Office of the Premier, "Joint Task Force Mobilized to Scale up Overdose Response," news release, July 27, 2016.
69 Joint Task Force on Overdose Prevention and Response, *B.C.'s Public Health Emergency Update on B.C.'s Response to the Opioid Overdose Crisis: Third Progress Report*, 2017, 5–6; Andrea Woo, "British Columbia Opens Drug Injection Sites Amid Opioid Crisis," *Globe and Mail*, December 8, 2016.
70 Province of British Columbia, Order of the Minister of Health, Ministerial Order no. M488, "Emergency Services Act," December 9, 2016, https://www.bclaws.gov.bc.ca/civix/document/id/mo/hmo/m0488_2016.
71 Joint Task Force on Overdose Prevention and Response, *B.C.'s Public Health Emergency Update*, 5–6.
72 Travis Lupick, "Dodging Drug Laws, B.C. Unveils Plans to Immediately Offer Supervised-Injection Services in Vancouver and Other Cities," *Georgia Straight*, December 8, 2016.
73 Health Canada, "Supervised Consumption Sites and Services: Explained," https://www.canada.ca/en/health-canada/services/substance-use/supervised-consumption-sites/explained.html.
74 BC Overdose Prevention, "Overdose Prevention Sites, Supervised Consumption Service and Drug Checking," https://www2.gov.bc.ca/gov/content/overdose/what-you-need-to-know/overdose-prevention.
75 Woo, "British Columbia"; Lupick, "Dodging Drug Laws."
76 Terry Lake, quoted in Andrea Woo, "Sidestepping Federal Law, B.C. Social-Housing Providers Offer Spaces for Drug Use," *Globe and Mail*, January 24, 2017.
77 Ontario Ministry of Health and Long-Term Care, "Applications Now Open," 5. The provincial and territorial governments refer to these facilities as overdose prevention sites.
78 Health Canada, "Government of Canada Highlights Support for Safer Drug Supply Projects in Ontario," news release, September 18, 2020.
79 Standing Committee on Health, *Government Response to the Report of the Standing Committee on Health Entitled Report and Recommendations on the Opioid Crisis in Canada*, 2016, 16.
80 Government of Canada, "The New Canadian Drugs and Substances Strategy," news release, December 12, 2016.
81 Ibid. The four pillars are prevention, treatment, enforcement, and harm reduction.
82 Government of Canada, "Government of Canada Announces New Comprehensive Drug Strategy Supported by Proposed Legislative Changes," news release, December 12, 2016.
83 Government of Canada, "Streamlining Applications for Supervised Consumption Sites," news release, December 12, 2016; Peter Zimonjic and Matthew Kupfer, "Philpott, Goodale Announce Changes to Laws to Make Safe Injection Sites Easier to Open," *Globe and Mail*, December 12, 2016.
84 Government of Canada, "Action to Reduce the Supply of Illicit Opioids and Other Drugs," news release, December 12, 2016.
85 Government of Canada, "Joint Statement of Action."
86 Canada, Parliament, *House of Commons Debates*, 42nd Parliament, 1st Session, vol. 148, no. 130, January 31, 2017, 8203 (Jane Philpott, Markham-Stouffville, Liberal).

87 Ibid., 8205.
88 Canada, Parliament, *House of Commons Debates*, 42nd Parliament, 1st Session, vol. 148, no. 141, February 15, 2017, 8978 (Jane Philpott, Markham-Stouffville, Liberal).
89 *Customs Act*, RSC 1985, c 1.
90 Government of Canada, "Modernizing Legislation to Reduce the Risk of Diversion of Controlled Substances," news release, December 12, 2016.
91 Health Canada, "Backgrounder: Royal Assent of Bill C-37 – an Act to Amend the Controlled Drugs and Substances Act and to Make Related Amendments to Other Act," news release, May 18, 2017.
92 Ibid.
93 Rainer Knopff et al., "Dialogue: Clarified and Reconsidered," *Osgoode Hall Law Journal* 54, 2 (2017): 632–35.
94 Canada, Parliament, *House of Commons Debates*, 42nd Parliament, 1st Session, vol. 148, no. 130, January 31, 2017, 8205 (Jane Philpott, Markham-Stouffville, Liberal).
95 *Act to Amend the CDSA*.
96 Canada, Parliament, Senate, Senate Standing Committee on Legal and Constitutional Affairs, *Proceedings*, 42nd Parliament, 1st Session, no. 25, March 30, 2017, 25:8 (Jane Philpott, Markham-Stouffville, Liberal).
97 Government of Canada, "Streamlining Applications."
98 Canada, Parliament, *House of Commons Debates*, January 31, 2017, 8204 (Jane Philpott, Markham-Stouffville, Liberal).
99 Government of Canada, "Streamlining Applications."
100 Canada, Parliament, *House of Commons Debates*, January 31, 2017, 8205 (Jane Philpott, Markham-Stouffville, Liberal).
101 *Act to Amend the CDSA*.
102 Canada, Parliament, *House of Commons Debates*, January 31, 2017, 8205 (Jane Philpott, Markham-Stouffville, Liberal).
103 Government of Canada, "Supervised Consumption Site: Guidance for Application Form," news release, May 26, 2017.
104 *Respect for Communities Act*.
105 *PHS Community Services Society*, para 152.
106 Government of Canada, "Streamlining Applications."
107 Ibid.
108 Ibid.
109 Matthew Kupfer, "NDP Tries to Fast-Track Bill to Make Supervised Injection Sites Easier to Open," *CBC News*, December 13, 2016.
110 The combined Independent Senate Group and Senate Liberal Caucus majority voting bloc was fifty-three of ninety-nine. The Senate standings in February to May 2017 were the following: Conservative Party (n = 39), Independent Senate Group (n = 35), Senate Liberal Caucus (n = 18), Non-affiliated (n = 7), Vacancies (n = 6).
111 Emmett Macfarlane, *Constitutional Pariah: Reference Re Senate Reform and the Future of Parliament* (Vancouver: UBC Press, 2021); Jason Robert VandenBeukel, Christopher Cochrane, and Jean-François Godbout, "Birds of a Feather? Loyalty and Partisanship in the Reformed Canadian Senate," *Canadian Journal of Political Science* 54, 4 (2021): 840–42.
112 Jean-François Godbout, *Lost on Division: Party Unity in the Canadian Parliament* (Toronto: University of Toronto Press, 2020), Chapter 9: "Partisanship in the Senate."
113 *PHS Community Services Society v Canada (Attorney General)*, [2010] BCCA 15.
114 Bill C-65, *An Act to Amend the Controlled Drugs and Substances* (June 6, 2013).

115 *Bedford*.
116 *Carter*; *Criminal Code*, RSC 1985, c C-46.
117 White, "Federalism," 158.
118 In the two case studies – same-sex marriage and abortion access – White, "Federalism," focuses on the implementation gap that occurs when individual provincial governments fail to provide access to a service that Parliament has either legalized (same-sex marriage) or a service that is permitted in the absence of federal regulation (abortion). As I argue, the implementation gap can occur when Parliament legislates in opposition to the provision of a service, as the Harper government did in relation to safe consumption sites.
119 *Constitution Act, 1867* (UK), 30 & 31 Vict, c 3, s 91(24): "Indians, and lands reserved for the Indians. This provision extends to the Inuit living on lands where no provincial or territorial services are accessible."
120 Yukon Liberal Caucus, "2021 Confidence and Supply Agreement between the Yukon Liberal Caucus and the Yukon NDP Caucus," press release, 2021, 6, https://yukonliberalcaucus.ca/wp-content/uploads/2021/04/2021-CASA-Yukon-Liberals-Yukon-NDP.pdf.
121 Colleen M. Flood, Carolyn Tuohy, and Mark Stabile, "What Is In and Out of Medicare? Who Decides?," in *Just Medicare: What's In, What's Out, How We Decide*, ed. Colleen M. Flood (Toronto: University of Toronto Press, 2006), 26–27.
122 Safe consumption sites exist in two forms: a fixed location or a mobile unit. The four provinces that account for thirty-eight of the thirty-nine facilities are Ontario (n = 24), British Columbia (n = 5), Alberta (n = 5), and Quebec (n = 4).
123 Rachael Johnstone, *After Morgentaler: The Politics of Abortion in Canada* (Vancouver: UBC Press, 2017), 128–35.
124 *Auton (Guardian of) v British Columbia (Attorney General)*, [2004] 3 SCR 657, 696; *Canada Health Act*, RSC 1985, c C-6.
125 The Quebec City application was submitted to Health Canada in November 2020. The confidence and supply agreement in which Yukon NDP supports the minority Yukon Liberal government calls for the establishment of a facility in Whitehorse by August 31, 2021. As of January 7, 2022, an application has yet to be submitted by a health organization in Yukon.
126 As of 2022, there have been four ministers of health in the Trudeau ministry: Jane Philpott (November 4, 2015 to August 28, 2017); Ginette Petipas Taylor (August 28, 2017 to November 20, 2019); Patty Hadju (November 20, 2019 to October 26, 2021); and Jean-Yves Duclos (October 26, 2021 to the present).
127 Hyshka et al., "Harm Reduction."
128 White, "Federalism."
129 Paul Chiasson, "Mayor Coderre Pledges Safe Injection Sites in Montreal Even without Federal Approval," *Canadian Press*, September 3, 2015; "Denis Coderre Makes Another Push for Montreal Safe Injection Sites," *CBC News*, June 4, 2015. Montreal currently has three safe consumption sites and one mobile site.
130 "Quebec to Invest $12m in Safe Injection Sites," *CBC News*, September 28, 2016.
131 Virgo Planning and Evaluation Consultants, *Improving Access and Coordination of Mental Health and Addiction Services: A Provincial Strategy for All Manitobans: Final Report*, 2018.
132 Ibid.; "Manitoba Government on Hot Seat after Safe Injection Site Recommendation Cut from Report," *CBC News*, May 14, 2018; Chaviva Manson-Singer and Sara Allin, "Understanding the Policy Context and Conditions Necessary for the Establishment of Supervised Consumption Sites in Canada: A Comparative Analysis of Alberta and Manitoba," *Health Reform Observer* 8, 2 (2020): 10–11.

133 Jason Kenney was replaced by Daniella Smith as leader of the United Conservative Party (UPC), and Alberta premier, in October 2022. The UPC approach to harm reduction remains the same under Premier Smith.
134 James B. Kelly, "Reconciling Rights and Federalism during Review of the Charter of Rights and Freedoms: The Supreme Court of Canada and the Centralization Thesis, 1982 to 1999," *Canadian Journal of Political Science* 34, 2 (2001): 324–26. Although I published this more than twenty years ago, the critique of the "centralization thesis" associated with the *Canadian Charter* and its interpretation by the Supreme Court of Canada still remains an accurate understanding of the judicialization of politics in the Canadian federation. If anything, my conclusions have become more robust since 2001, particularly when salient issues of public policy are judicialized and the policy response is analyzed.
135 Ahmed M. Bayoumi et al., *Report of the Toronto and Ottawa Supervised Consumption Assessment Study, 2012* (Toronto: St. Michael's Hospital and the Dalla Lana School of Public Health, University of Toronto, 2012), 14.
136 Toronto Board of Health, *Supervised Injection Services in Toronto (HL 23.1)*, July 10, 2013.
137 Dalton McGinty was premier of Ontario from 2003 to 2013 and was succeeded by Kathleen Wynne from 2013 to 2018.
138 Daniel Dale, "Ontario Rejects Toronto's Call for Supervised Drug Injection Site," *Toronto Star*, July 10, 2013.
139 Tom Blackwell and Natalie Alcoba, "Ontario Rejects Safe Injection Sites," *National Post*, April 11, 2012.
140 Christine Chubb, "On Safe-Injection Sites, Wynne Says Society Has a Responsibility to Reduce Harm," *Canadian Press*, March 16, 2016.
141 Jennifer Pagliaro, "Mayor John Tory to Back Supervised Injection Sites," *Toronto Star*, June 24, 2016.
142 Toronto Board of Health, *Implementing Supervised Injection Services in Toronto (HL 13.2)*, 2016.
143 "Toronto City Councillors Vote in Favour of Safe Injection Sites," *CBC News Toronto*, July 14, 2016.
144 Andrew Duffy, "Ottawa Must Decide Whether It Wants a Safe Injection Site: Provincial Health Minister," *Ottawa Citizen*, April 8, 2016.
145 Jon Willing, "Council Politics Taken Out of Ottawa Supervised Injection Site Debate after Letter by Mayor," *Ottawa Citizen*, January 4, 2017.
146 Ontario Ministry of Health and Long-Term Care, "Statement from the Minister of Health and Long-Term Care on Supervised Injection Services," news release, January 9, 2017.
147 Ontario Ministry of Finance, *2017 Ontario Budget: A Stronger, Healthier Ontario. The Hon. Charles Sousa, Minister of Finance*, April 27, 2017, 117.
148 The Canadian Press, "Doug Ford Says He's 'Dead against' Supervised Injection Sites," *Canadian Press*, April 20, 2018.
149 Collin Butler, "Doug Ford Won't Say If He'd Support Supervised Consumption Site for London," *CBC News*, May 18, 2018.
150 Dyck, "Ontario to Review Safe Injection."
151 Ontario Ministry of Health and Long-Term Care, *Backgrounder: Review of Supervised Consumption Services and Overdose Prevention Sites – Key Findings*, October 22, 2018.
152 Carly Weeks and Jeff Gray, "Ontario Cuts Funding to Three Supervised Drug-Use Sites," *Globe and Mail*, March 29, 2019.
153 Cayley Russell et al., "'Small Communities, Large Oversight': The Impact of Recent Legislative Changes Concerning Supervised Consumption Services on Small Communities

in Ontario, Canada," *International Journal of Drug Policy* 82 (2020): 3; Bianca R. Ziegler, Alexander J.D. Wray, and Isaac Luginaah, "The Ever-Changing Narrative: Supervised Injection Site Policy Making in Ontario, Canada," *International Journal of Drug Policy* 74 (2019): 3.

154 Ontario Ministry of Health and Long-Term Care, *Consumption and Treatment Services: Application Guide*, October 2018, 11.
155 Ibid., 3.
156 Ibid., 10.
157 Ibid.
158 Ibid., 11.
159 Ontario's motto on its Coat of Arms, *Ut Incepit Fidelis Sic Permanet*, translates as "Loyal She Began, Thus She Remains."
160 Greg Davis, "Ontario Commits $1.35 M Annually for Peterborough Safe Consumption and Treatment Site," *Global News*, February 25, 2022.
161 Lieutenant Governor of Alberta, *2017 Speech from the Throne: Third Session of the Twenty-Ninth Legislature*, March 2, 2017).
162 Government of Alberta, "Calgary Supervised Consumption Site Approved," news release, October 27, 2017. The following six applications were approved in October 2017: Edmonton (n = 4), Calgary (n = 1), and Lethbridge (n = 1). The seventh facility was approved for Grande Prairie in 2018.
163 Andrew Jeffrey, "New Mobile Supervised Drug Consumption Site Announced for Forest Lawn," *Toronto Star*, May 2, 2019.
164 *There and Back Again* is the alternate title to J.R.R. Tolkien's *The Hobbit*. See J.R.R. Tolkien, *The Hobbit or There and Back Again* (London: George Allen and Unwin, 1937).
165 Reid Southwick, "UCP Leader Jason Kenney Draws Fire for Saying Safe Consumption Sites Help Addicts 'Inject Poison,'" *CBC Calgary*, March 2, 2018.
166 "Tony Clement Talks about Insite BC," *YouTube*, https://www.youtube.com/watch?v=xzvkv5tNiqg (transcript on file with author).
167 Jason Kenney, Facebook, March 2, 2018; Jason Kenney, Twitter, March 2, 2018.
168 Ibid.
169 Ibid.
170 United Conservative Party of Alberta, *Alberta Strong and Free: Getting Alberta Back to Work*, 2019, 54.
171 Ibid.
172 Ibid.
173 Ibid.
174 In the 2019 Alberta election, the UCP led by Jason Kenney won sixty-three out of eighty-seven seats (or 72.4 percent) in the Legislative Assembly on a popular vote of 54.88 percent. The remaining twenty-four seats were won by the Alberta NDP led by Rachel Notley.
175 Stephen Hunt, "Funding for New Safe Injection Sites Frozen by Alberta Government until Further Notice," *CBC Calgary*, June 1, 2019.
176 Alberta, Parliament, *Alberta Hansard*, 30th Legislature, 1st Session, June 3, 2019, 294 (Rachel Notley, Edmonton-Strathcona, NDP).
177 Alberta, Parliament, *Alberta Hansard*, June 3, 2019, 294 (Jason Kenney, Calgary-Lougheed, UCP).
178 "Edmonton Safe Injection Sites Set to Face Legal Challenge," *CBC Edmonton*, November 22, 2018.

179 Alexandra Zabjek, "Downtown Edmonton Business Group Loses Legal Fight against Supervised Injection Sites," *CBC News*, February 28, 2019.
180 Government of Alberta, *Supervised Consumption Review*, 2019.
181 Submitted to the Government of Alberta by the Supervised Consumption Services Review Committee, *Impact: A Socio-Economic Review of Supervised Consumption Sites in Alberta*, 2020.
182 Ibid.; Government of Alberta, "Supervised Consumption Services Review: An Expert Committee Reviewed the Social and Economic Impacts of Current and Proposed Supervised Consumption Services," news release, March 5, 2020. Town Halls occurred in 2019: Medicine Hat (September 3), Lethbridge (September 5), Red Deer (September 10), Calgary (September 11–12), Grande Prairie (September 16), and Edmonton (September 18–19).
183 Supervised Consumption Services Review Committee, *Impact*, 8–23.
184 Ibid., 34.
185 Ibid., 37. There are additional recommendations made in the report, but these are the main ones.
186 Ibid., 38.
187 Alanna Smith, "Academics Question Methodology of UCP Approved Supervised Consumption Sites Report," *Calgary Herald*, March 8, 2020.
188 Canadian Drug Policy Coalition, "Open Letter: Calling on the Alberta Government to Retract Supervised Consumption Report – Poor Methodological Quality, Lack of Transparency, and Biased Presentation of Results," news release, March 18, 2020.
189 Canadian HIV/AIDS Legal Network, "Open Letter: Rejection the Socio-Economic 'Review' of Supervised Consumption Sites in Alberta," news release, March 23, 2020.
190 James D. Livingston, "Supervised Consumption Sites and Crime: Scrutinizing the Methodological Weaknesses and Aberrant Results of a Government Report in Alberta, Canada," *Harm Reduction Journal* 18, 4 (2021): 3.
191 Health Canada, *Vancouver's Insite Service and Other Supervised Injection Sites: What Has Been Learned from Research? Final Report of the Expert Advisory Committee*, 2008.
192 Government of Canada, "Expert Panel Report on Supervised Injection Site Released," news release, April 11, 2008.
193 Jason Luan, quoted in Hannah Kost, "'A System of Chaos': Supervised Consumption Services Review Committee Releases Findings," *CBC News*, March 5, 2020.
194 Jason Kenney, quoted in ibid.
195 Kevin Maimann, "This Government Is Defunding One of North America's Busiest Safe Injection Sites," *Vice News*, August 14, 2020; Jason Herring, "Harm Reduction Advocates Send Open Letter to Province Protesting Lethbridge Scs Closure," *Calgary Herald*, August 31, 2020.
196 Sammy Hudes, "UCP Pulls Funding to Lethbridge Supervised Consumption Site Following Audit," *Calgary Herald*, July 16, 2020.
197 Alanna Smith, "Lethbridge Police Investigation of Arches Finds Records for 'Unaccounted Funds;'" *Calgary Herald*, December 22, 2020.
198 Lieutenant Governor of Alberta, *Speech from the Throne*, 13th Parliament, 2nd Session, February 25, 2020.
199 Perrin, "Alberta's War."
200 Alberta Health, "Psychoactive Substance Use," Doc. HCS-33, November 6, 2020, https://extranet.ahsnet.ca/teams/policydocuments/1/clp-harm-reduction-for-psychoactive-substance-use-policy.pdf; *Mental Health Services Protection Act*, RSA 2020, c M-13.2.

201 Alberta Health, *Recovery-Oriented Overdose Prevention Services Guide*, April 2021; *Mental Health Services Protection Regulation*, Alta. Regulation 114/2021.
202 Kashmala Fida Mohatarem, "Boyle Street Supervised Consumption Site Closing Permanently," *CBC Edmonton*, April 28, 2021.
203 The likely approval of the Calgary mobile site and the fixed location site in Medicine Hat is based on the fact that the Trudeau government, to date (February 2022), has only approved section 56.1 applications submitted to Health Canada and has never ruled against an application.
204 The five supervised consumption sites by location, as of January 2023, are Edmonton (n = 3), Calgary (n = 1), and Grande Prairie (n = 1).
205 Alberta Health, "Psychoactive Substance Use."
206 Janet French, "Advocates Worry Health Policy Change Another Government Dismissal of Harm Reduction," *CBC Edmonton*, March 8, 2021.
207 Lieutenant Governor of Alberta, *Speech from the Throne*, 7.
208 Alberta, Parliament, *Alberta Hansard*, 30th Legislature, 2nd Session, March 5, 2020, 132 (Tyler Shandro, Calgary-Acadia, UCP).
209 Alberta Health, *Recovery-Oriented Overdose*, 5.
210 F.L. Morton, "The Effect of the Charter of Rights on Canadian Federalism," *Publius: The Journal of Federalism* 25, 3 (1995): 176.
211 Kelly, "Reconciling Rights."
212 *Mental Health Services Protection Act*.
213 Ontario Ministry of Health and Long-Term Care, *Consumption and Treatment Services*.
214 Supervised Consumption Services Review Committee, *Impact*, 1.
215 Government of Canada, "Streamlining Applications."
216 *Mental Health Services Protection Act*, s 4, Schedule – Requirements Respecting Residential Addiction Treatment Service Providers and Services.
217 The five letters required as part of a section 56 application under the *Respect for Communities Act* were: the provincial or territorial minister of health; the local government in which the site was to be located; the head of the local police force; the lead provincial/territorial health official; and the provincial/territorial minister responsible for public safety.
218 Alberta Health, *Recovery-oriented Overdose*, 18.
219 Canada, Parliament, *House of Commons Debates*, 42nd Parliament, 1st Session, vol. 148, no. 131, February 1, 2017, 8343 (Cathy McLeod, Kamloops-Thompson-Cariboo, CPC); Canada, Parliament, *House of Commons Debates*, 42nd Parliament, 1st Session, vol. 148, no. 140, February 14, 2017, 8900–01 (Mark Strahl, Chilliwack-Hope, CPC); Canada, Parliament, *House of Commons Debates*, 42nd Parliament, 1st Session, vol. 148, no. 142, February 15, 2017) at 8991–92 (Michael Cooper, St. Albert – Edmonton, CPC).
220 Alberta, Parliament, *Alberta Hansard*, 30th Parliament, 1st Session, June 3, 2019, 294 (Jason Kenney, Calgary-Lougheed, UCP).
221 Alberta Health, *Recovery-oriented Overdose*, 6.
222 Ibid.
223 Ibid., 18.
224 Ibid.
225 *Mental Health Services Protection Regulation*, s 4(a).
226 Alberta Health, *Recovery-oriented Overdose*, 7–13, s 4, Site operational requirements.
227 Ibid., 12.
228 Janet French, "ID Requirements at Alberta Supervised Consumption Sites Delayed, Advocates Say," *CBC News Edmonton*, September 7, 2021.

229 *Moms Stop the Harm Society v Alberta*, 2022 ABQB 24; *Moms Stop the Harm Society v Alberta*, 2022 ABCA 35.
230 *Moms Stop the Harm Society* ABQB, para 67.
231 Ibid., para 68.
232 *Moms Stop the Harm Society* ABCA, paras 34–35.
233 Elaine Hyshka et al., *Risk Behaviours and Service Needs of Marginalized People Who Use Drugs in Edmonton's Inner City: Results from the Edmonton Drug Use and Health Survey* (Edmonton: University of Alberta School of Pubic Health, January 7, 2016), 43–44.
234 *PHS Community Services Society v Attorney General of Canada*, [2008] BCSC 661.

Chapter 8: Physician-assisted Suicide to Medical Assistance in Dying

1 *Carter v Canada (Attorney General)*, [2015] 1 SCR 331 [*Carter*]; *Rodriguez v British Columbia (Attorney General)*, [1993] 3 SCR 519 [*Rodriguez*].
2 *Criminal Code*, RSC 1985, c C-46.
3 Bill C-14, *An Act to Amend the Criminal Code and to Make Related Amendments to Other Acts (Medical Assistance in Dying)*, SC 2016, c 3 [2016 *Act on MAiD*]. The term "second look case" occurs when the Supreme Court of Canada reviews the constitutionality of a legislative amendment in response to judicial invalidation on Charter grounds. For a discussion, see Kent Roach, "Sharpening the Dialogue Debate: The Next Decade of Scholarship," *Osgoode Hall Law Journal* 45 (2007): 174–76. Although the Supreme Court of Canada did not review the constitutionality of the 2016 *Act on MAiD*, as it was a lower court invalidation, it does satisfy the criteria of a "second look" case in regard to medical assistance in dying (MAiD).
4 *Truchon c Procureur Général du Canada*, 2019 QCCS 3792 [*Truchon*]. The Superior Court also invalidated parts of Quebec's Bill 52, *Act Respecting End-of-Life Care*, RSQ 2014, c S-32.0001, and the Legault government also decided against appealing the ruling.
5 Bill C-7, *An Act to Amend the Criminal Code (Medical Assistance in Dying)*, SC 2021, c 2 [2021 *Act on MAiD*].
6 For a discussion of the parliamentary dialogue on MAiD, see Thomas J. Bateman and Matthew LeBlanc, "Charter Dialogue and the Constitutionality of Canada's Maid Legislation," in *Assisted Death: Legal, Social and Ethical Issues*, ed. Derek B.M. Ross (Toronto: LexisNexis, 2018), 387–426; Kent Roach, *The Supreme Court on Trial: Judicial Activism or Democratic Dialogue*, 2nd ed. (Toronto: Irwin Law, 2016), 367–71. For a critique of MAiD as dialogue, see Emmett Macfarlane, "Dialogue, Remedies, and Positive Rights: *Carter v Canada* as a Microcosm for Past and Future Issues under the Charter of Rights and Freedoms," *Ottawa Law Review* 49, 1 (2017): 112–16.
7 Government of Canada, *Government of Canada Establishes Expert Panel on Options for a Legislative Response to Carter v Canada*, 2015.
8 "Federal Government Releases Report of the External Panel on Options for a Legislative Response to Carter v Canada," news release, January 18, 2016; External Panel on Options for a Legislative Response to Carter v Canada (External Panel), *Consultations on Physician-Assisted Dying: Summary of Results and Key Findings*, 2015.
9 Canada, Department of Justice, "Statement by the Attorney General of Canada on Timelines for a Government Response on Physician-Assisted Dying," news release, January 15, 2016.
10 *Carter v Canada (Attorney General)*, [2016] 1 SCR 13, para 2 [*Carter II*].
11 Canada Department of Justice, "Statement by the Minister of Justice and Attorney General of Canada and Minister of Health on Medical Assistance in Dying Legislation," news release, June 17, 2016.

12 Part 1 of the *Constitution Act, 1982*, being Schedule B to the *Canada Act 1982* (UK), 1982, c 11; Dennis Baker, "A Feature, Not a Bug: A Coordinate Moment in Canadian Constitutionalism," in *Constitutional Dialogue: Rights, Democracy, Institutions*, ed. Geoffrey Sigalet, Grégoire Webber, and Rosalind Dixon (Cambridge, UK: Cambridge University Press, 2019), 399–403; Matthew A. Hennigar, "The Most Important Charter Right? The Rise and Future of Section 7," in *Constitutional Crossroads: Reflections on Charter Rights, Reconciliation, and Change*, ed. Kate Puddister and Emmett Macfarlane (Vancouver: UBC Press, 2022), 166–67; Eleni Nicolaides and Matthew A. Hennigar, "Carter Conflicts: The Supreme Court of Canada's Impact on Medical Assistance in Dying Policy," in *Policy Change, Courts, and the Canadian Constitution*, ed. Emmett Macfarlane (Toronto: University of Toronto Press, 2018), 323–24.
13 For a discussion of *Carter* as creating a positive right, see Matthew A. Hennigar, "The Most Important Charter Right? The Rise and Future of Section 7," in Puddister and Macfarlane, *Constitutional Crossroads*, 166–67.
14 I agree with the assessment of Nicolaides and Hennigar that the 2016 *Act on MAiD* is an example of legislative non-compliance by the Trudeau government. See Nicolaides and Hennigar, "Carter Conflicts," 326.
15 Linda A. White, "Federalism and Equality Rights Implementation in Canada," *Publius: The Journal of Federalism* 44, 1 (2014): 158–60.
16 Health Canada, *Third Annual Report on Medical Assistance in Dying Canada 2021*, July 2022, 19.
17 Bill 52, *Act Respecting End-of-Life Care*, RSQ 2014, c S-32.0001. For a discussion of the enactment of the *Act Respecting End-of-Life Care*, see Robert Leckey, "Assisted Dying, Suspended Declarations, and Dialogue's Time," *University of Toronto Law Journal* 69, 1 (2019): 69–73.
18 Matthew E.K. Hall, *The Nature of Supreme Court Power* (New York: Cambridge University Press, 2010), 15–18, 97–102.
19 Christopher P. Manfredi, "'Appropriate and Just in the Circumstances': Public Policy and the Enforcement of Rights under the Canadian Charter of Rights and Freedoms," *Canadian Journal of Political Science* 27, 3 (1994): 447–53.
20 *R v Morgentaler*, [1988] 1 SCR 30.
21 For a discussion of legislative disagreement limiting the impact of *Morgentaler*, see Rachael Johnstone, *After Morgentaler: The Politics of Abortion in Canada* (Vancouver: UBC Press, 2017).
22 Ontario Ministry of Health and Long-Term Care, "Provincial-Territorial Expert Advisory Group Completes Report on Physician-Assisted Dying," news release, December 14, 2015.
23 Dave Snow and Kate Puddister, "Closing a Door but Opening a Policy Window: Legislating Assisted Dying in Canada," in Macfarlane, *Policy Change*, 45–46.
24 Bateman and LeBlanc, "Charter Dialogue," 423.
25 Special Joint Committee on Physician-Assisted Dying (PDAM), *Medical Assistance in Dying: A Patient-Centred Approach*, 42nd Parliament, 1st Session, February 2016, 13–16.
26 Ian MacLeod, "Parts of Assisted-Death Bill 'Not Good Enough,' Liberal MP Who Co-Chaired Committee Says," *Ottawa Citizen*, April 15, 2016.
27 Joan Bryden, "Senators Balk at Limiting Assisted Dying to Canadians near Death," *Maclean's*, June 7, 2016; John Paul Tasker, "Physician-Assisted Dying Bill Passes Senate 64–12, Send Back to House: Justice Minister Jody Wilson-Raybould Has Already Thrown Cold Water on a Major Amendment," *CBC News*, June 15, 2016.

28 Marie-Danielle Smith, "Tory, Liberal Senate Leaders Call Assisted Suicide Bill 'Unconstitutional' as Deadline Nears," *National Post*, May 30, 2016.
29 Laura Stone, "Jane Philpott 'Concerned' About Senate Changes to Assisted-Dying Bill," *Globe and Mail*, June 9, 2016.
30 Marie-Danielle Smith, "A Transformative Day': Senate Concedes to Government's Will, Sending Assisted Dying Law to Royal Assent," *National Post*, June 17, 2016.
31 For a critical discussion of *Rodriguez*, see Jocelyn Grant Downie, *Dying Justice: A Case for Decriminalizing Euthanasia and Assisted Suicide in Canada* (Toronto: University of Toronto Press, 2004), 132–34.
32 *Rodriguez*, 520.
33 *Canadian Charter*, s 241(b), cited in ibid., 532.
34 *Rodriguez*, 589.
35 Ibid.
36 Ibid., 601–2.
37 Ibid., 608.
38 Ibid., 620.
39 Ibid., 624.
40 Ibid., 627–28.
41 Snow and Puddister, "Closing a Door," 44–45.
42 *Death with Dignity Act*, ORS, ss 127.800 to 127–897, 1997.
43 Trudo Lemmens, "Charter Scrutiny of Canada's Medical Assistance in Dying Law and the Shifting Landscape of Belgian and Dutch Euthanasia Practice," in Ross, *Assisted Death*, 468–73; Jocelyn Downie, "Permitting Voluntary Euthanasia and Assisted Suicide: Law Reform Pathways for Common Law Jurisdictions," *QUT Law Review* 16, 1 (2016): 90.
44 Leckey, "Assisted Dying," 69–70.
45 Michelle Giroux, "Informing the Future of End-of-Life Care in Canada: Lessons from the Quebec Legislative Experience," *Dalhousie Law Journal* 39 (2016): 436.
46 Royal Society of Canada, *End-of-Life Decision Making*, November 2011, 9.
47 Bill 52, *An Act Respecting End-of-Life Care*, RSQ 2014, c S-32.0001; Leckey, "Assisted Dying," 71–72.
48 Forum Research, "Support for Assisted Suicide Increases," news release, June 15, 2014.
49 "Three Quarters Approve of Supreme Court Ruling on Assisted Death," news release, February 11, 2015.
50 Angus Reid, "Quebecers Overwhelmingly Call for Assisted Suicide Guidelines," news release, February 14, 2013.
51 Canadian Medical Association, *End-of-Life Care: A National Dialogue*, June 2014.
52 Canadian Medical Association policy cited in *Factum of the Intervener: the Canadian Medical Association, in the Supreme Court of Canada (on Appeal from the Court of Appeal for British Columbia) between Lee Carter, Hollis Johnson, Dr. William Shoichet, the British Columbia Civil Liberties Association, and Gloria Taylor (Appellants) and Attorney General of Canada and Attorney General of British Columbia (Respondents)*, June 27, 2014.
53 Liberal Party of Canada, *Policy Resolution 165: Death with Dignity – Legalizing Medically-Assisted Death*, February 20–23, 2014.
54 *Carter*, paras 11–12.
55 Ibid., para 17.
56 *Carter v Canada (Attorney General)*, 2012 BCSC 886, 887.
57 Ibid., 83, para 1378.
58 *Carter v Canada (Attorney General)*, 2013 BCCA 435, paras 8–9.

59 Section 14 reads as follows: "No person is entitled to have death inflicted on him, and such consent does not affect the criminal responsibility of any person by whom death may be inflicted on the person by whom consent is given."
60 *Carter*, para 44.
61 Ibid., para 47.
62 *Canada (Attorney General) v Bedford*, [2013] 3 SCR 1101.
63 *Carter*, para 83–89.
64 *Canada (Attorney General) v PHS Community Services Society*, [2011] 3 SCR 134.
65 *Carter*, para 53.
66 Ibid., para 66.
67 Ibid., para 84.
68 Ibid., para 86.
69 Ibid., paras 116–17.
70 Ibid., para 119.
71 See Snow and Puddister, "Closing a Door."
72 *Carter*, para 127.
73 External Panel, *Consultations on Physician-Assisted Dying*, 57.
74 *Carter*, para 126.
75 Ibid., para 127.
76 Jocelyn Downie, "Bouquets and Brickbats for the Proposed Assisted Dying Legislation," *Policy Options*, 2016.
77 Hamish Stewart concluded that the eligibility criteria for MAiD in the 2016 *Act on MAiD* were most likely unconstitutional. See Hamish Stewart, "Constitutional Aspects of Canada's New Medically-Assisted Dying Law," in Ross, *Assisted Death*, 453–55. A counter-argument is provided by Thomas McMorrow, "MAiD in Canada?: Debating the Constitutionality of Canada's New Medical Assistance in Dying Law," *Dalhousie Law Journal* 44, 1 (2018): 96–98.
78 *Carter*, para 132.
79 Ibid.
80 Ibid.
81 Ibid., para 128.
82 Canada, Department of Justice, "Statement by the Minister of Justice Regarding the Supreme Court of Canada Ruling in Carter et al v Attorney General of Canada," news release, February 6, 2015.
83 Stephanie Levitz, "Government Unlikely to Invoke Notwithstanding Clause over Assisted Suicide Ruling: Peter Mackay," *National Post*, February 10, 2015.
84 Mike Blanchfield and Joan Bryden, "Don't Expect Law on Doctor-Assisted Death before Election, Mackay Says," *Globe and Mail*, April 27, 2015.
85 External Panel, *Consultations on Physician-Assisted Dying*, iv.
86 The membership of the External Panel was the following: Harvey Max Chochinov, Catherine Frazee, and Benoît Pelletier.
87 Canada, Department of Justice, "Letter from Minister Wilson-Raybould and Minister Philpott to the External Panel on Options for a Legislative Response to Carter v Canada," news release, November 14, 2015.
88 External Panel, *Consultations on Physician-Assisted Dying*, 57.
89 Ibid., 133.
90 Mark Kennedy, "Deadline on Doctor-Assisted Suicide Law Could Be Delayed," *Ottawa Citizen*, November 16, 2015.

91 Canada, Department of Justice, "Statement by the Attorney General of Canada on Timelines."
92 *Carter II*.
93 Canada, Department of Justice, "Statement by the Minister of Justice and Attorney General of Canada and Minister of Health on Establishing a Special Joint Committee on Physician-Assisted Dying," news release, December 15, 2015.
94 *Carter II*, paras 2–4; *Act Respecting End-of-Life Care*.
95 The majority on issues 2 and 3 were Abella, Karakatsanis, Wagner, Gascon, and Côte JJ. The minority were McLachlin, Cromwell, Moldaver, and Brown JJ.
96 *Carter II*, para 2.
97 Ibid., para 6.
98 For instance, the Liberal government of Pierre Elliott Trudeau had a majority on the Special Joint Committee on the Constitution of Canada in 1980–81.
99 Janet L. Hiebert and James B. Kelly, *Parliamentary Bills of Rights: The Experiences of New Zealand and the United Kingdom* (Cambridge, UK: Cambridge University Press, 2015), 291–92.
100 PDAM, *Medical Assistance in Dying*, 35–38.
101 Ibid., 12.
102 Ibid., 51–56.
103 2016 *Act on MAiD*, s 241.1(3).
104 Stewart, "Constitutional Aspects," 55–58, 443–44.
105 Bateman and LeBlanc, "Charter Dialogue."
106 Canada, Parliament, *House of Commons Debates*, 42nd Parliament, 1st Session, vol. 148, no. 62, May 31, 2016, 3796–97 (Jody Wilson-Raybould, Minister of Justice and Attorney General of Canada, Liberal). The dialogue metaphor was also employed by Jeannette Ettel, a Department of Justice official that appeared before PDAM. Canada, Parliament, House of Commons, PDAM, *Minutes of Proceedings and Evidence*, 42nd Parliament, 1st Session, no. 2, January 18, 2016, 9–10. For an earlier discussion of dialogue as non-compliance, see James B. Kelly and Matthew A. Hennigar, "The Canadian Charter of Rights and the Minister of Justice: Weak-Form Review within a Constitutional Charter of Rights," *International Journal of Constitutional Law* 10, 1 (2012): 38–44.
107 2016 *Act on MAiD*, s 241.2(2).
108 Dianne Pothier, "Doctor-Assisted Death Bill Falls Well within Top Court's Ruling," *Policy Options*, 2016; Lemmens, "Charter Scrutiny."
109 Jocelyn Downie and Kate Scallion, "Foreseeably Unclear: The Meaning of the 'Reasonably Foreseeable' Criterion for Access to Medical Assistance in Dying in Canada," *Dalhousie Law Journal* 41, 1 (2018): 23–57; Nicolaides and Hennigar, "Carter Conflicts."
110 *Truchon*.
111 Canada, Department of Justice, "Legislative Background: Medical Assistance in Dying (Bill C-14) – Addendum," June 13, 2016.
112 Canada, Department of Justice, "Charter Statements (22 April 2016): Bill C-14 (Medical Assistance in Dying)," https://www.justice.gc.ca/eng/rp-pr/other-autre/adra-amsr/toc-tdm.html.
113 Canada, Parliament, House of Commons, PDAM, *Minutes of Proceedings and Evidence*, 42nd Parliament, 1st Session, no. 2, January 18, 2016, 9 (Joanne Klineberg, Senior Counsel, Criminal Law Policy Section, Department of Justice).
114 *R v O'Connor*, [1995] 4 SCR 411 [*O'Connor*]; *R v Mills*, 1999] 3 SCR 668 [*Mills*].
115 *O'Connor*.

116 Bill C-46, *Act to Amend Criminal Code (Production of Records in Sexual Offence Proceedings)*, SC 1997, c 30.
117 Kelly and Hennigar, "Canadian Charter of Rights," 41–42.
118 *Mills*.
119 Canada, Parliament, House of Commons, PDAM, *Minutes of Proceedings and Evidence*, January 18, 2016, 9 (Jeanette Ettel Klineberg, Senior Counsel, Human Rights Law Section, Department of Justice).
120 *R v Oakes*, [1986] 1 SCR 103.
121 Canada, Parliament, *House of Commons Debates*, 42nd Parliament, 1st Session, no. 45, April 22, 2016, 2581 (Jody Wilson-Raybould, Minister of Justice and Attorney General of Canada).
122 Ibid.; Canada, Parliament, *House of Commons Debates*, 42nd Parliament, 1st Session, no. 62, May 31, 2016 (Jody Wilson-Raybould, Minister of Justice and Attorney General of Canada); Canada, Parliament, *House of Commons Debates*, 42nd Parliament, 1st Session, no. 74, June 16, 2016 (Jody Wilson-Raybould, Minister of Justice and Attorney General of Canada).
123 Canada, Parliament, House of Commons, Standing Committee on Justice and Human Rights, *Minutes of Proceedings and Evidence*, 42nd Parliament, 1st Session, no. 10, May 2, 2016, 1–4 (Jody Wilson-Raybould, Minister of Justice and Attorney General of Canada).
124 Canada, Parliament, *Proceedings of the Standing Senate Committee on Legal and Constitutional Affairs*, 42nd Parliament, 1st Session, no. 8, May 5, 2016), 10–62 (Jody Wilson-Raybould, Minister of Justice and Attorney General of Canada).
125 See Eleni Nicolaides, "Carter Compliance: Litigating for Access to Medical Assistance in Dying in Canada," in Puddister and Macfarlane, *Constitutional Crossroads*, 202–4.
126 Bill C-37, *An Act to Amend the Controlled Drugs and Substances Act and to Make Related Amendments to Other Acts*, SC 2017, c 7 [*Act to Amend the CDSA*].
127 Christopher P. Manfredi, *Judicial Power and the Charter: Canada and the Paradox of Liberal Constitutionalism*, 2nd ed. (Don Mills, ON: Oxford University Press, 2001), 180–83.
128 Ibid., 180.
129 Canada. Parliament, *Proceedings of the Standing Senate Committee on Legal and Constitutional Affairs*, 42nd Parliament, 1st Session, no. 8, May 6, 2016, 83 (Joseph J. Arvay).
130 Joseph J. Arvay, *Written Submissions of Joseph J. Arvay, Q.C. Lead Counsel in Carter v Canada to the Standing Committee on Justice and Human Rights. In View of Its Study on Bill C-14, an Act to Amend the Criminal Code and to Make Related Amendments to Other Acts (Medical Assistance in Dying)*, May 5, 2016, 1–2. Emphasis in original text.
131 Canada, Parliament, *Proceedings of the Standing Senate Committee on Legal and Constitutional Affairs*, May 6, 2016, 83 (Joseph J. Arvay).
132 Ibid., 80 (Jocelyn Downie, Dalhousie University).
133 Canada, Parliament, House of Commons Standing Committee on Justice and Human Rights, *Minutes of Proceedings and Evidence*, 42nd Parliament, 1st Session, no. 14, May 5, 2016, 11–12 (Josh Paterson, BC Civil Liberties Association).
134 Canadian Medical Association, *CMA Submission: Supporting the Enactment of Bill C-14, Medical Assistance in Dying. Submission to the House of Commons Standing Committee on Justice and Human Rights*, May 2, 2016.
135 Canadian Civil Liberties Association, *Submission to the Standing Committee on Justice and Human Rights. Bill C-14: Medical Assistance in Dying*, 2016; Canadian Bar Association, *Re: Bill C-14 – Medical Assistance in Dying*, 2016; British Columbia Civil Liberties Association, *BCCLA Brief on Bill C-14 (Medical Assistance in Dying)*, 2016; Barreau du Québec, *Brief from the Barreau du Québec: Bill C-14 – An Act to Amend the Criminal Code*

and to Make Related Amendments to Other Acts (Medical Assistance in Dying). Submitted to the House of Commons Standing Committee on Justice and Human Rights, 2016; College of Family Physicians of Canada, *Written Submission to the Standing Committee on Justice and Human Rights*, 2016; Dying with Dignity Canada, *Dying with Dignity Canada's Submission to the House of Commons Standing Committee on Justice and Human Rights – Brief on Bill C-14*, 2016.

136 Canada, Parliament, *Proceedings of the Standing Senate Committee on Legal and Constitutional Affairs*, May 6, 2016, 19, 34 (Senator Serge Joyal, Kennebec, Senate, Liberal).
137 Canada, Parliament, *Proceedings of the Standing Senate Committee on Legal and Constitutional Affairs*, 42nd Parliament, 1st Session, no. 10, June 9, 2016, 75 (Peter Hogg).
138 Canada, Parliament, *Proceedings of the Standing Senate Committee on Legal and Constitutional Affairs*, May 6, 2016, 16 (Senator James Cowan, Nova Scotia, Senate, Liberal).
139 Smith, "Tory, Liberal Senate Leaders."
140 There were additional amendments adopted by the Senate on Bill C-14, but they largely focused on procedural changes to the administrative safeguards for MAiD. The removal of the requirement that natural death be reasonably foreseeable by the Senate was a substantive change to Bill C-14.
141 Canada, Parliament, *Debates of the Senate*, 42nd Parliament, 1st Session, vol. 150, no. 45, June 8, 2016, 938 (Senator Serge Joyal).
142 Canada, Parliament, *Debates of the Senate*, 42nd Parliament, 1st Session, vol. 150, no. 50, June 15, 2016, 1167–68.
143 *Canada (Attorney General) v EF*, 2016 ABCA 155 [*EF*].
144 *Carter II*, para 7.
145 *EF*, para 9.
146 Ibid., para 41.
147 Ibid., para 59.
148 *J(I) v Canada (Attorney General)*, 2016 ONSC 3380, para 19.
149 Canada, Parliament, *Proceedings of the Standing Senate Committee on Legal and Constitutional Affairs*, 42nd Parliament, 1st Session, no. 8, May 5, 2016, 20 (Jody Wilson-Raybould, Minister of Justice and Attorney General of Canada); Ibid., 36 (William F. Pentney, Deputy Minister of Justice).
150 Ibid., 36 (William F. Pentney, Deputy Minister of Justice).
151 Arvay, *Written Submissions*, 2. Emphasis in original text.
152 The definition provided by Joseph Arvay to the Department of Justice during the judicial proceedings for "grievous and irremediably ill" is the following:

   1. A person is "grievously and irremediably ill" when he or she has a serious medical condition that has been diagnosed as such by a medical practitioner and which:
      a. is without remedy, as determined by reference to treatment options acceptable to the person; and
      b. causes the person enduring physical, psychological or psychosocial suffering that:
         i. is intolerable to that person; and
         ii. cannot be alleviated by any medical treatment acceptable to that person.
   2. A "medical condition" means an illness, disease or disability, and includes a disability arising from traumatic injury.

153 Arvay, *Written Submissions*, 2.
154 Ibid., 3.

155 *Carter*, paras 58, 66, 90, 121.
156 Canada, Parliament, *Proceedings of the Standing Senate Committee on Legal and Constitutional Affairs*, 42nd Parliament, 1st Session, no. 10, June 2, 2016, 17 (William F. Pentney, Deputy Minister of Justice).
157 Canada, Parliament, *Proceedings of the Standing Senate Committee on Legal and Constitutional Affairs*, 42nd Parliament, 1st Session, no. 8, May 5, 2016, 95–96 (Joseph J. Arvay).
158 Ibid., 90.
159 David Lametti, Facebook, May 31, 2016, https://www.facebook.com/plugins/post.php?href=https%3A%2F%2Fwww.facebook.com%2Fdavidlamettilev%2Fposts%2Fpfbid02-w3NfpzXr6bsFCsq54YN5QfHd3sNxp9MWMhtJ2ffdzCXuA3EJES5byaqyr2tZCotHl (on file with author).
160 In addition to David Lametti, the following Liberal members of parliament voted against Bill C-14: Rob Oliphant, Nathaniel Erskine-Smith, and Robert-Falcon Ouellette.
161 2021 *Act on MAiD*.
162 Laura Stone, "Assisted-Death Bill Back to Senate after Key Proposal Rejected," *Globe and Mail*, June 16, 2016.
163 PDAM, *Medical Assistance in Dying*, 12–13.
164 Provincial-Territorial Expert Advisory Group on Physician-Assisted Dying, *Final Report*, 2015, 7. The Quebec government did not participate, and British Columbia's participation was limited to that of an observer.
165 Canada, Parliament, *House of Commons Debates*, 42nd Parliament, 1st Session, no. 74, June 16, 2016, 4602 (Jody Wilson-Raybould, Minister of Justice and Attorney General of Canada).
166 Ibid., 4603.
167 Ibid., 4603.
168 Ibid., 4605 (Luc Thériault, Montcalm, Bloc Québécois).
169 *Bedford*, para 113.
170 Ibid., para 121. Emphasis appears in *Bedford* decision.
171 Canada, Parliament, *House of Commons Debates*, June 16, 2016, 4643 (Jody Wilson-Raybould, Minister of Justice and Attorney General of Canada).
172 Canada, Department of Justice, "Legislative Background: Medical Assistance in Dying (Bill C-14) – Addendum," June 13, 2016.
173 Ibid., 20–21.
174 Canada, Parliament, *House of Commons Debates*, June 16, 2016, 4643–44.
175 Canada, Parliament, *Debates of the Senate*, 42nd Parliament, 1st Session, vol. 150, no. 52, June 17, 2016, 1209.
176 Ibid., 1210 (Senator Peter Harder); 1233 (Senator Frances Lankin); 1234 (Senator Art Eggleton); 1235 (Senator Bob Runciman); 1235 (Senator David Tkachuk); 1236 (Senator Victor Oh).
177 Canada, Department of Justice, *Statement by the Minister of Justice and Attorney General of Canada and Minister of Health on Medical Assistance in Dying Legislation*, June 17, 2017.
178 2016 *Act on MAiD*, 1–2.
179 Canada, Parliament, House of Commons, PDAM, *Minutes of Proceedings and Evidence*, 42nd Parliament, 1st Session, no. 2, January 18, 2016, 4 (Joanne Klineberg, Senior Counsel, Criminal Law Policy Section, Department of Justice).
180 Canada, Parliament, *Proceedings of the Standing Senate Committee on Legal and Constitutional Affairs*, May 6, 2016, 68–69 (William F. Pentney, Deputy Minister of Justice).
181 To date, only Manitoba has protected the right to conscience objection to MAiD by medical and nurse practitioners in legislation. *Medical Assistance in Dying (Protection for*

Health Professionals and Others) Act, SM 2017, c 38 [*Medical Assistance in Dying*]. In every other jurisdiction, this is provided by the professional guidelines of the colleges of physicians and surgeons or equivalent organizations.

182 Canada, Parliament, House of Commons, PDAM, *Minutes of Proceedings and Evidence*, 42nd Parliament, 1st Session, no. 5, January 26, 2016, 3, 7 (Benoît Pelletier).
183 Canada, Parliament, House of Commons Standing Committee on Justice and Human Rights, *Minutes of Proceedings and Evidence*, 42nd Parliament, 1st Session, no. 10, May 2, 2016, 5–9 (Jane Philpott, Minister of Health).
184 *Canada Health Act*, RSC 1985, c C-6. The five principles of the Canada Health Act are public administration, comprehensiveness, universality, portability, and accessibility.
185 Katherine Fierlbeck, *Health Care in Canada: A Citizen's Guide to Policy and Politics* (Toronto: University of Toronto Press, 2011), 7–8.
186 *Auton (Guardian of) v British Columbia (Attorney General)*, [2004] 3 SCR 657. ABA/IBI (Applied Behavioural Analysis/Intensive Behavioural Intervention).
187 Ibid., para 35–36; see also Christopher P. Manfredi and Antonia Maioni, *Health Care and the Charter: Legal Mobilization and Policy Change in Canada* (Vancouver: UBC Press, 2018), 77–78.
188 Canada, Parliament, House of Commons, PDAM, *Minutes of Proceedings and Evidence*, 42nd Parliament, 1st Session, no. 3, January 25, 2016, 5 (Abby Hoffman, Assistant Deputy Minister, Strategic Policy, Department of Health).
189 Ibid., 5.
190 White, "Federalism," 62–63, 159–60.
191 *Lamb v Canada (Attorney General)*, 2017 BCSC 1802; *Truchon*.
192 Jocelyn Downie, "From Prohibition to Permission: The Winding Road of Medical Assistance in Dying in Canada," *HEC Forum*, June 20, 2022, 16–17.
193 *Truchon*, para 574.
194 2021 *Act on MAiD*.
195 Unlike the 2016 *Act on MAiD*, which requires two independent witnesses to verify a written request for MAiD, the 2021 *Act on MAiD* only requires one witness.
196 Heath Canada, *Third Annual Report on Medical Assistance in Dying in Canada 2021*, 2021, 13.
197 2021 *Act on MAiD*, s 241.2(3.1)(i).
198 Erin Anderssen, "Ottawa Seeking to Delay Expansion of MAiD for Mental Disorders," *Globe and Mail*, December 15, 2022.
199 Hall, *Nature of Supreme Court Power*, 16–18, 26–27.
200 Bill 101, *Charter of the French Language*, SQ 1977, s 54.
201 Support for MAiD has been high since the *Carter* decision in 2015. Forum Research found that 75 percent of Canadians supported the *Carter* decision in the period immediately after the Court released its judgment. See "Three Quarters Approve of Supreme Court Ruling on Assisted Death," *Forum Research*, February 11, 2015.
202 IPSOS, *Support for Medically-Assisted Dying in Canada*, February 2021.
203 IPSOS, *Support for Medically-Assisted Dying in Canada*, January 2021.
204 Johnstone, *After Morgentaler*, 81–82; Kate McKenna, *No Choice: The 30-Year Fight for Abortion in Prince Edward Island* (Halifax: Fernwood Press, 2018).
205 Katie DeRosa, "Woman with Terminal Cancer Forced to Transfer from St. Paul's Hospital for Assisted Dying," *Vancouver Sun*, June 23, 2023.
206 At the present time, Nunavut does not compile data on MAiD-related deaths in the territory.

207 Andrea Frolic and Allyson Oliphant, "Introducing Medical Assistance in Dying in Canada: Lessons on Pragmatic Ethics and the Implementation of a Morally Contested Practice," *HEC Forum*, August 4, 2022, 3.
208 Health Canada, *First Annual Report on Medical Assistance in Dying in Canada 2019*, 2019, 13.
209 College of Physicians and Surgeons of Newfoundland and Labrador, *Standard of Practice: Medical Assistance in Dying*, 2022, s 1.1(e); College of Physicians and Surgeons of Prince Edward Island, *Policy on Medical Assistance in Dying*, 2019, 3; College of Physicians and Surgeons of New Brunswick, *Guidelines – Moral Factors and Medical Care*, 2017; College of Physicians and Surgeons of Nova Scotia, *Professional Standard Regarding Medical Assistance in Dying*, 2017, s 2.1.4; College of Physicians and Surgeons of Ontario, *Medical Assistance in Dying: Advice to the Profession*, 2016, s 12; College of Physicians and Surgeons of Manitoba, *Standard of Practice: Medical Assistance in Dying (MAID)*, 2019, s 1; College of Physicians and Surgeons of Saskatchewan, *Policy – Medical Assistance in Dying*, 2016, 3; College of Physicians and Surgeons of Alberta, *Standards of Practice: Medical Assistance in Dying (MAID)*, 2016; College of Physicians and Surgeons of British Columbia, *Practice Standard: Medical Assistance in Dying*, 2016, 2–3; Yukon Medical Council, *Standard of Practice – Medical Assistance in Dying (MAID)*, 2016, 4; Government of Northwest Territories, *Medical Assistance in Dying – Interim Guidelines for the Northwest Territories*, 2016, 3;
210 Barbara Pesut et al., "Medical Assistance in Dying: A Review of Canadian Nursing Regulatory Documents," *Policy, Politics, and Nursing Practice* 20, 3 (2019): 115.
211 *Medical Assistance in Dying*, s 2.
212 Ontario passed an omnibus bill to clarify certain provincial responsibilities regarding MAiD – Bill 84, *Act to Amend various Acts with Respect to Medical Assistance in Dying*, SO 2017, c 7. This act amended the *Excellent Care for All Act*, SO 2010, c 14, to provide immunity for medical and nurse practitioners that administered MAiD (section 13.8(1)).
213 College of Physicians and Surgeons of Manitoba, *Standard of Practice*, s 1(1.2)(1.2.3).
214 All of the MAiD statistics provided in the remainder of this chapter are derived from the yearly figures contained within the following reports issued by Health Canada: Health Canada, *First Annual Report on Medical Assistance in Dying in Canada*, 2019; Health Canada, *Second Annual Report on Medical Assistance in Dying in Canada*, 2020; Health Canada, *Third Annual Report on Medical Assistance in Dying Canada*, 2021.
215 Health Canada, *Third Annual Report*, 5. Nunavut does not report MAiD-related deaths.
216 Michael MacDonald, "Nova Scotia's Medically Assisted Dying Program Paused Amid 'Unprecedented' Demand," *Canadian Press*, September 30, 2021.
217 The total exceeds 100 percent as medical and nurse practitioners are permitted to list multiple medical conditions as satisfying the eligibility criteria for MAiD.
218 Health Canada, *Third Annual Report*, 28–29.
219 Lee Berthiaume, "Veterans' Case Raise Fresh Concerns About Expanding Assisted Dying Law," *Globe and Mail*, December 4, 2022.
220 "Are Canadians Being Driven to Assisted Suicide by Poverty or Health Care Crisis?," *The Guardian*, May 11, 2022.
221 Nicolaides, "Carter Compliance," 202–4.

Conclusion: Legislative Disagreements and Policy Implementation in the Charter Era

1 Richard Albert, "The Most Powerful Court in the World? Judicial Review of Constitutional Amendment in Canada," *Supreme Court Law Review* (2d) 110 (2023): 79–102;

Tristin Hopper, "Why Canada Has the Most Activist Supreme Court in the World – And How It Has Changed the Country," *National Post*, January 3, 2022.
2 *Canadian Charter of Rights and Freedoms*, Part 1 of the *Constitution Act, 1982*, being Schedule B to the *Canada Act 1982* (UK), 1982, c 11 [*Canadian Charter*].
3 *Andrews v Law Society of British Columbia*, [1989] 1 SCR 143; *Law v Canada (Minister of Employment and Immigration)*, [1999] 1 SCR 497; *R v Kapp*, [2008] 2 SCR 483.
4 *R v Collins*, [1987] 1 SCR 265; *R v Stillman*, [1997] 1 SCR 607; *R v Grant*, [2009] 2 SCR 353.
5 *R v Askov*, [1990] 2 SCR 1199; *R v Morin*, [1992] 1 SCR 771; *R v Jordan*, [2016] 1 SCR 631.
6 *R v Oakes*, [1986] 1 SCR 103; *Irwin Toy Ltd. v Quebec (Attorney General)*, [1989] 1 SCR 927.
7 Matthew E. K. Hall, *The Nature of Supreme Court Power* (New York: Cambridge University Press, 2010).
8 *Canadian Charter*.
9 Bill 101, *Charter of the French Language*, SQ 1977, s 54.
10 *Criminal Code*, RSC 1985, c C-46.
11 *R v Morgentaler*, [1988] 1 SCR 30; *Canada (Attorney General) v PHS Community Services Society*, [2011] 3 SCR 134; *Carter v Canada (Attorney General)*, [2015] 1 SCR 331.
12 Bill C-2, *Act to Amend the Controlled Drugs and Substances Act*, SC 2015, c 22.
13 Bill C-14, *An Act to Amend the Criminal Code and to Make Related Amendments to Other Acts (Medical Assistance in Dying)*, SC 2016, c 3 [*2016 Act on MAiD*].
14 Peter W. Hogg and Allison A. Bushell, "The Charter Dialogue between Courts and Legislatures (or Perhaps the Charter of Rights Isn't Such a Bad Thing after All)," *Osgoode Hall Law Journal* 35 (1997): 96–99.
15 Rachael Johnstone, *After Morgentaler: The Politics of Abortion in Canada* (Vancouver: UBC Press, 2017).
16 *Canada (Attorney General) v Bedford*, [2013] 3 SCR 1101; Hamish Stewart, "The Constitutionality of the New Sex Work Law," *Alberta Law Review* 54, 1 (2016): 80–87.
17 *R v Seaboyer; R v Gayme*, [1991] 2 SCR 577; *R. v. Daviault* 3 SCR 63; *R v O'Connor*, [1995] 4 SCR 411; *R v Mills*, 1999] 3 SCR 668; James B. Kelly and Matthew A. Hennigar, "The Canadian Charter of Rights and the Minister of Justice: Weak-Form Review within a Constitutional Charter of Rights," *International Journal of Constitutional Law* 10, 1 (2012): 38–44.
18 *Attorney General (Quebec) v Quebec Protestant School Boards*, [1984] 2 SCR 66; *Solski (Tutor of) v Quebec (Attorney General)*, [2005] 1 SCR 201; *Nguyen v Quebec (Education, Recreation and Sports)*, [2009] 3 SCR 208.
19 See Linda A. White, "Federalism and Equality Rights Implementation in Canada," *Publius: The Journal of Federalism* 44, 1 (2014): 161–63.
20 *Constitution Act, 1867* (UK), 30 & 31 Vict, c 3.
21 René Lévesque, quoted in Dale Gibson, *The Law of the Charter: General Principles* (Toronto: Carswell, 1983), 90.
22 *Controlled Drugs and Substances Act*, SC 1996, c 19.
23 Bill C-37, *An Act to Amend the Controlled Drugs and Substances Act and to Make Related Amendments to Other Acts*, SC 2017, c 7.
24 As of February 2023.
25 The subset of jurisdictions where federal-provincial agreement on supervised consumption currently exists is British Columbia, Alberta, Saskatchewan, Quebec, and Ontario.
26 Submitted to the Government of Alberta by the Supervised Consumption Services Review Committee, *Impact: A Socio-Economic Review of Supervised Consumption Sites in Alberta*, 2020.

27 *Mental Health Services Protection Act*, RSA 2020, c M-13.2; *Mental Health Services Protection Regulation*, Alberta Regulation 114/2021, s 4(a); Alberta Health, *Recovery-Oriented Overdose Prevention Services Guide*, April 2021, 7–13 (4. Site operational requirements).
28 Bill C-7, *An Act to Amend the Criminal Code (Medical Assistance in Dying)*, SC 2021, c 2.
29 Heath Canada, *Third Annual Report on Medical Assistance in Dying in Canada 2021*, 2021.
30 Alan C. Cairns, *Charter versus Federalism: The Dilemmas of Constitutional Reform* (Montreal and Kingston: McGill-Queen's University Press, 1992); F. L Morton and Rainer Knopff, *The Charter Revolution and the Court Party* (Toronto: University of Toronto Press, 2000); Alain G. Gagnon and Guy Laforest, "The Future of Federalism: Lessons from Canada and Quebec," *International Journal* 28, 3 (1993): 470–91; Guy Laforest, *Trudeau and the End of a Canadian Dream* (Montreal and Kingston: McGill-Queen's University Press, 1995).
31 James B. Kelly, "Reconciling Rights and Federalism during Review of the Charter of Rights and Freedoms: The Supreme Court of Canada and the Centralization Thesis, 1982 to 1999," *Canadian Journal of Political Science* 34, 2 (2001): 321–55.
32 James B. Kelly, "Bureaucratic Activism and the Charter of Rights and Freedoms: The Department of Justice and Its Entry into the Centre of Government," *Canadian Public Administration* 42, 4 (1999): 476–511; James B. Kelly, *Governing with the Charter: Legislative and Judicial Activism and Framers' Intent* (Vancouver: UBC Press, 2005).
33 Hall, *Nature of Supreme Court Power;* Christopher P. Manfredi, "'Appropriate and Just in the Circumstances': Public Policy and the Enforcement of Rights under the Canadian Charter of Rights and Freedoms," *Canadian Journal of Political Science* 27, 3 (1994): 435–63; Alexander Hamilton, John Jay, and James Madison, *The Federalist: The Gideon Addition* (Indianapolis: Liberty Fund, 2001), 401.

Bibliography

Cases Cited
156158 Canada Inc. v Attorney General of Quebec, 2017 QCCA 2055
AG (Quebec) v Quebec Protestant School Boards, [1984] 2 SCR 66
Andrews v Law Society of British Columbia, [1989] 1 SCR 143
Arsenault-Cameron v Prince Edward Island, [2004] 1 SCR 3
Attorney General v Arthur William Taylor, [2018] NZSC 104
Attorney General of Quebec v Blaikie et al., [1979] 2 SCR 1016
Auton (Guardian of) v British Columbia (Attorney General), [2004] 3 SCR 657
Canada (Attorney General) v Bedford, [2013] 3 SCR 1101
Canada (Attorney General) v E.F., 2016 ABCA 155
Canada (Attorney General) v PHS Community Services Society, [2011] 3 SCR 134
Canadian Broadcasting Corp. v Canada (Attorney General), [2011] 1 SCR 19
Carter v Canada (Attorney General), 2012 BCSC 886
Carter v Canada (Attorney General), 2013 BCCA 435
Carter v Canada (Attorney General), [2015] 1 SCR 331
Carter v Canada (Attorney General), [2016] 1 SCR 13
Chaoulli v Quebec (Attorney General), [2005] 1 SCR 791
City of Toronto et al. v Ontario (Attorney General), 2018 ONSC 5151
Conférence des juges de paix magistrats du Québec v Quebec (Attorney General), [2016] 2 SCR 116
Corporation professionnelle des médecins v Thibault, [1988] 1 SCR 1033
Devine v Quebec (Attorney General), [1988] 2 SCR 790
Doucet-Boudreau v Nova Scotia (Minister of Education), [2003] 3 SCR 3
Dunmore v Ontario (Attorney General), [2001] 3 SCR 1016
Egan v Canada, [1995] 2 SCR 513
Eldridge v British Columbia (Attorney General), [1997] 3 SCR 624
Entreprises WFH Ltée. c Québec (Procureure Générale du), 2001 QCCA 17598

Ford v Quebec (Attorney General), [1988] 2 SCR 712
Good Spirit School Division v Christ the Teacher School Division and the Government of Saskatchewan, 2017 SKQB 109
Gosselin v Quebec (Attorney General), [2002] 4 SCR 429
Hak c Procureur Général du Québec, 2021 QCCS 1466
Health Services and Support – Facilities Subsector Bargaining Assn. v British Columbia, [2007] 2 SCR 391
Irwin Toy Ltd. v Quebec (Attorney General), [1989] 1 SCR 927
J.B. v Comité de révision sur la langue d'enseignement, [2002] TAQ 15
J.(I.) v Canada (Attorney General), 2016 ONSC 3380
Lamb v Canada (Attorney General), 2017 BCSC 1802
Law v Canada (Minister of Employment and Immigration), [1999] 1 SCR 497
Law Society of Upper Canada v Skapinker, [1984] 1 SCR 357
Libman v Quebec (Attorney General), [1997] 3 SCR 569)
Loyola High School v Quebec (Attorney General), [2015] 1 SCR 613
M. v H., [1999] 2 SCR 3
Mahe v Alberta, [1990] 1 SCR 342
Miron v Trudel, [1995] 2 SCR 418
Mitchell c Procureur général du Québec, 2022 QCCS 2983
Moms Stop the Harm Society v Alberta, 2022 ABQB 24
Moms Stop the Harm Society v Alberta, 2022 ABCA 35
Mounted Police Association of Ontario v Canada (Attorney General), [2015] 1 SCR 3
Multani v Commission scolaire Marguerite-Bourgeoys, [2006] 1 SCR 256
Nguyen v Quebec (Education, Recreation and Sports), [2009] 3 SCR 208
PHS Community Services Society v Attorney General of Canada, 2008 BCSC 661
PHS Community Services Society v Canada (Attorney General), 2010 BCCA 15
Quebec (Attorney General) v A., [2013] 1 SCR 61
Quebec (Attorney General) v Alliance du personnel professionnel et technique de la santé et des services sociaux, [2018] 1 SCR 464
Quebec (Attorney General) v Best Buy Stores Ltd., 2015 QCCA 747
Quebec Association of Protestant School Boards v Attorney General of Quebec, [1982] CS 673
Quebec Association of Protestant School Boards v Attorney General of Quebec, [1983] CA 77
R. v Advance Cutting & Coring Ltd., [2001] 3 SCR 209
R. v Askov, [1990] 2 SCR 1199
R. v Big M Drug Mart Ltd., [1985] 1 SCR 295
R. v Collins, [1987] 1 SCR 265
R. v Darrach, [2000] 2 SCR 443
R. v Grant, [2009] 2 SCR 353
R. v Hall, [2002] 3 SCR 309
R. v Jordan, [2016] 1 SCR 631
R. v Kapp, [2008] 2 SCR 483
R. v Logan, [1987] 2 SCR 731
R. v Mills, [1999] 3 SCR 668
R. v Morales, [1992] 3 SCR 711
R. v Morin, [1992] 1 SCR 771
R. v Morgentaler, [1988] 1 SCR 30
R. v Nur, [2015] 1 SCR 773
R. v O'Connor, [1995] 4 SCR 411
R. v Seaboyer; R. v Gayme, [1991] 2 SCR 577

R. v Sharpe, [2001] 1 SCR 45
R. v Stillman, [1997] 1 SCR 607
R. v Oakes, [1986] 1 SCR 103
Re: Objection to a Resolution to Amend the Constitution, [1982] 2 SCR 793
Re: Resolution to Amend the Constitution, [1981] 1 SCR 753
Reference re the Power of the Governor General in Council to Disallow Provincial Legislation and the Power of Reservation of a Lieutenant-Governor of a Province, [1938] SCR 71
Reference re Remuneration of Judges of the Provincial Court of Prince Edward Island; Reference re Independence and Impartiality of Judges of the Provincial Court of Prince Edward Island; R v Campbell, R v Ekmecic, R v Wickman; Manitoba Provincial Judges Assn. v Manitoba (Minister of Justice), [1997] 3 SCR 3
Reference re Senate Reform, [2014] 1 SCR 704
RJR-MacDonald Inc. v Canada (Attorney General), [1995] 3 SCR 199
Rodriguez v British Columbia (Attorney General), [1993] 3 SCR 519
Ruffo v Conseil de la magistrature, [1995] 4 SCR 267
Saskatchewan Federation of Labour v Saskatchewan, [2015] 1 SCR 245
Solski (Tutor of) v Quebec (Attorney General), [2005] 1 SCR 201
Toronto (City) v Ontario (Attorney General), 2018 ONCA 761
Truchon c. Procureur général du Canada, 2019 QCCS 3792
UFCW, Local 1518, v Kmart Canada Ltd, [1999] 2 SCR 1083
Vriend v Alberta, [1998] 1 SCR 493
Working Families Ontario v Ontario, [2021] ONSC 4076

Acts and Regulations

Legislative Assembly of Alberta. *Bill 1 (Alberta Sovereignty within a United Canada Act)*, RSA 2022
–. *Mental Health Services Protection Act*, RSA 2020, c M-13.2
–. *Mental Health Services Protection Regulation*, Alberta Regulation 114/2021
Legislative Assembly of Manitoba. *Medical Assistance in Dying (Protection for Health Professionals and Others) Act*, SM 2017
Legislative Assembly of New Brunswick. Bill 11, *Act Respecting Proof of Immunization*
Legislative Assembly of Ontario. Bill 5, *Act to Amend the City of Toronto Act, 2006, the Municipal Act, 2001 and the Municipal Elections Act, 1996*, SO 2019. C 11
–. Bill 28, *Act to Resolve Labour Disputes Involving School Board Employees Represented by the Canadian Union of Public Employees*, SO 2022, c 19
–. Bill 31, *Act to Amend the City of Toronto Act, 2006, the Municipal Act, 2001, the Municipal Elections Act, 1996 and the Education Act and to Revoke Two Regulations*
–. Bill 84, *An Act to Amend Various Acts with Respect to Medical Assistance in Dying*, SO 2017, c 7
–. Bill 35, *Act to Repeal the Keeping Students in Class Act*, SO 2022, c 20
–. Bill 254, *Act to Amend Various Acts with Respect to Elections and Members of the Assembly*, SO 2021, c 5
–. Bill 307, *Act to Amend the Elections Finance Act*, SO 2021, c 31
Legislative Assembly of Saskatchewan. Bill 88, *Act to Assert Saskatchewan's Exclusive Legislative Jurisdiction and to Confirm the Autonomy of Saskatchewan*, SS 2023, c 9
–. Bill 89, *School Choice Protection Act*, SS 2018, c 39
National Assembly of Quebec. Bill 4, *Act to Recognize the Oath Provided in the Act Respecting the National Assembly as the Sole Oath Required in Order to Sit in the Assembly*, RSQ 2022, c 30

–. Bill 10, *Act to Amend the Pay Equity Act Mainly to Improve the Pay Equity Audit Process*, SQ 2019, c 4
–. Bill 20, *Act to Implement Certain Recommendations of the 20 August 2018 Report of the Committee on the Remuneration of Judges and Justices of the Peace for 2016–2019*, SQ 2019, c 16
–. Bill 21, *Act Respecting the Laicity of the State*, RSQ 2019, L-03
–. Bill 22, *Official Languages Act*, SQ 1974, c 35
–. Bill 33, *Act to Amend the Act Respecting Health Services and Social Services and Other Legislative Provisions*, RSQ 2006, c 43
–. Bill 52, *Act Respecting End-of-Life Care*, RSQ 2014, c S-32.0001
–. Bill 62, *Act Respecting the Constitution Act*, SQ 1982, c 21
–. Bill 63, *An Act to Promote the French Language in Quebec*, RSQ 1969, c 9
–. Bill 86, *Act to Amend the Charter of the French Language*, RSQ 1993, c 40
–. Bill 96, *Act Respecting French, the Official and Common Language of Québec*, RSQ 2022, c 14
–. Bill 101, *Charter of the French Language*, RSQ 1977, c 54
–. Bill 103, *Act to Amend the Charter of the French Language and Other Amendments*, RSQ 2010, c 14
–. Bill 104, *Charter of the French Language*, RSQ 2002, c 73
–. Bill 115, *Act Respecting Private Education*, RSQ 2010, c E-9.1
–. Bill 178, *Charter of the French Language*, RSQ 1988, c 54
–. *Regulation Respecting the Application of the Act Respecting Private Education*, CQLR, c E-9.1, r 1
–. *Regulation Defining the Scope of the Expression "Markedly Predominant" for the Purposes of the Charter of the French Language*, RRQ 1993, c C-11, r 11
–. *Regulation Respecting the Language of Commerce and Business*, RRQ 1993, C-11, r 9
–. *Regulation Respecting the Criteria and Weighting Used to Consider Instruction in English Received in a Private Educational Institution Not Accredited for the Purposes of Subsidies, Charter of the French Language*, RRQ 2010, C-11, 2.1
Parliament of Australia. *Human Rights (Parliamentary Scrutiny) Act 2011*, no. 186
Parliament of Canada. Bill C-2, *Act to Amend the Controlled Drugs and Substances Act*, SC 2015, c-22
–. Bill C-7, *Act to Amend the Public Service Labour Relations Act, the Public Service Labour Relations and Employment Board Act and Other Acts and to Provide for Certain Other Measures*, SC 2017, c 2
–. Bill C-14, *Act to Amend the Criminal Code and to Make Related Amendments to Other Acts (Medical Assistance in Dying)*, SC 2016, c 3
–. Bill C-16, *Act to Amend the Canada Elections Act*, SC 2007, c 31
–. Bill C-23, *Act to Modernize the Statutes of Canada in Relation to Benefits and Obligations*, SC 2000, c 12
–. Bill C-36, *Act to Amend the Criminal Code in Response to the Supreme Court of Canada Decision in Attorney General of Canada v Bedford and to Make Consequential Amendments to Other Acts*, SC 2014, c 25
–. Bill C-37, *Act to Amend the Controlled Drugs and Substances Act and to Make Related Amendments to Other Acts*, SC 2017, c 7
–. Bill C-46, *An Act to Amend Criminal Code (Production of Records in Sexual Offence Proceedings*, SC 1997, c 30
–. Bill C-69, *Act to Amend the Criminal Code in Response to the Supreme Court of Canada Decision in R v Nur*

–. Bill C-89, *Act to Provide for the Resumption and Continuation of Postal Services*, SC 2018, c 25

Government and Parliamentary Documents

Alberta. Parliament. *Alberta Hansard*, 30th Parliament, 1st Session. June 3, 2019 (Rachel Notley, Edmonton–Strathcona, NDP).
Alberta Health. *Recovery-oriented Overdose Prevention Services Guide*. April 2021.
Alberta Health Services. *Psychoactive Substance Use*. Doc. HCS-33. November 6, 2020.
–. Supervised Consumption Services Service Provider Licence Application. https://www.alberta.ca/supervised-consumption-service-provider-licensing.
Arvay, Joseph J. *Written Submissions of Joseph J. Arvay, Q.C. Lead Counsel in Carter v Canada to the Standing Committee on Justice and Human Rights. In view of its study on Bill C-14, An Act to Amend the Criminal Code and to Make Related Amendments to Other Acts (Medical Assistance in Dying)*. 2016.
–. Canada, Parliament. *Proceedings of the Standing Senate Committee on Legal and Constitutional Affairs*, 42nd Parliament, 1st Session, no. 8. May 6, 2016.
–. Canada, Parliament. *Proceedings of the Standing Senate Committee on Legal and Constitutional Affairs*, 42nd Parliament, 1st Session, no. 8. May 5, 2016.
Barreau du Quebec. *Brief from the Barreau du Québec. Bill C-14: An Act to Amend the Criminal Code and to Make Related Amendments to Other Acts (Medical Assistance in Dying). Submitted to the House of Commons Standing Committee on Justice and Human Rights*. 2016.
British Columbia. Office of the Premier. "Joint Task Force Mobilized to Scale Up Overdose Response." News release. July 27, 2016.
British Columbia Centre for Disease Control. "Administration of Naloxone." News release. December 2016.
British Columbia Civil Liberties Association. *BCCLA Brief on Bill C-14 (Medical Assistance in Dying)*. 2016.
Canada. Department of Justice. "Charter Statements (22 April 2016): Bill C-14 (Medical Assistance in Dying)." https://www.justice.gc.ca/eng/rp-pr/other-autre/adra-amsr/toc-tdm.html.
–. "Legislative Background: Medical Assistance in Dying (Bill C-14) – Addendum." June 13, 2016.
–. "Letter from Minister Wilson-Raybould and Minister Philpott to the External Panel on Options for a Legislative Response to Carter v Canada." News release. November 14, 2015.
–. "Statement by the Attorney General of Canada on Timelines for a Government Response on Physician-assisted Dying." News release. January 15, 2016.
–. "Statement by the Minister of Justice and Attorney General of Canada and Minister of Health on Establishing a Special Joint Committee on Physician-Assisted Dying." News release. December 15, 2015.
–. "Statement by the Minister of Justice and Attorney General of Canada and Minister of Health on Medical Assistance in Dying Legislation." News release. June 17, 2016.
–. "Statement by the Minister of Justice Regarding the Supreme Court of Canada Ruling in Carter et al v Attorney General of Canada." News release. February 6, 2015.
Canada. Minister of Justice. *Consolidation of Proposed Resolution and Possible Amendments as Placed Before the Special Joint Committee by the Minister of Justice*. January 12, 1981.
–. *Proposed Resolution for Joint Address to Her Majesty the Queen Respecting the Constitution of Canada, Tabled in the House of Commons and the Senate*. October 6, 1980.

–. *Text of the Resolution Respecting the Constitution of Canada Adopted by the House of Commons on December 2, 1981 and by the Senate.* December 8, 1981.

Canada. Office of the Prime Minister. "Minister of Justice and Attorney General Mandate Letter." News release. November 12, 2015.

Canada. Parliament. *Debates of the Senate*, 42nd Parliament, 1st Session, vol. 150, no. 52. June 17, 2016.

–. *Debates of the Senate*, 42nd Parliament, 1st Session, vol. 150, no. 50. June 15, 2016.

–. House of Commons. Special Joint Committee on Physician-Assisted Dying. *Medical Assistance in Dying: A Patient-Centred Approach*, 42nd Parliament, 1st Session. February 2016.

–. House of Commons. Special Joint Committee on Physician-Assisted Dying, *Minutes of Proceedings and Evidence*, 42nd Parliament, 1st Session, no. 2. January 18, 2016 (Jeannette Ettel, Department of Justice).

–. House of Commons. Special Joint Committee on Physician-Assisted Dying. *Minutes of Proceedings and Evidence*, 42nd Parliament, 1st Session, no. 2. January 18, 2016.

–. House of Commons. Special Joint Committee on Physician-Assisted Dying, *Minutes of Proceedings and Evidence*, 42nd Parliament, 1st Session, no. 2. January 18, 2016 (Joanne Klineberg, Senior Counsel, Criminal Law Policy Section, Department of Justice).

–. House of Commons. Special Joint Committee on Physician-Assisted Dying, *Minutes of Proceedings and Evidence*, 42nd Parliament, 1st Session, no. 3. January 25, 2016 (Abby Hoffman, Assistant Deputy Minister, Strategic Policy, Department of Health).

–. House of Commons. Special Joint Committee on Physician-Assisted Dying, *Minutes of Proceedings and Evidence*, 42nd Parliament, 1st Session, no. 5. January 26, 2016 (Benoît Pelletier).

–. House of Commons. Standing Committee on Health. *Government Response to the Report of the Standing Committee on Health Entitled Report and Recommendations on the Opioid Crisis in Canada*. 2016.

–. House of Commons. Standing Committee on Health. *Interim Report and Recommendations on the Opioid Crisis in Canada: Report of the Standing Committee on Health*. 2016.

–. House of Commons. Standing Committee on Health. *Mandate*, 41st Parliament, 2nd Session. October 16, 2013 – August 2, 2015. https://www.ourcommons.ca/Committees/en/HESA?parl=41.

–. House of Commons. Standing Committee on Health. *Minutes of Proceedings and Evidence*, 39th Parliament, 2nd Session, no. 32, May 29, 2008.

–. House of Commons. Standing Committee on Health. *Report and Recommendations on the Opioid Crisis in Canada. Report of the Standing Committee on Health*. 2016.

–. House of Commons. Standing Committee on Justice and Human Rights. *Minutes of Proceedings and Evidence*, 42nd Parliament, 1st Session, no. 10. May 2, 2016 (Jane Philpott, Minister of Health).

–. House of Commons. Standing Committee on Justice and Human Rights. *Minutes of Proceedings and Evidence*, 42nd Parliament, 1st Session, no. 10. May 2, 2016 (Jody Wilson-Raybould, Minister of Justice and Attorney General of Canada).

–. House of Commons. Standing Committee on Justice and Human Rights, *Minutes of Proceedings and Evidence*, 42nd Parliament, 1st Session, no. 14. May 5, 2016 (Josh Paterson, BCCLA).

–. House of Commons. Standing Committee on Public Safety and National Security. *Minutes of Proceedings and Evidence*, 41st Parliament, 2nd Session, no. 34. October 27, 2014.

–. House of Commons. Standing Committee on Public Safety and National Security. *Minutes of Proceedings and Evidence*, 41st Parliament, 2nd Session, no. 35. October 29, 2014.
–. *House of Commons Debates*, 41st Parliament, 1st Session, vol. 146, no. 24. September 30, 2011.
–. *House of Commons Debates*, 41st Parliament, 1st Session, vol. 146, no. 25. October 3, 2011.
–. *House of Commons Debates*, 42nd Parliament, 1st Session, no. 74. June 16, 2016 (Jody Wilson-Raybould, Minister of Justice and Attorney General of Canada).
–. *House of Commons Debates*, 42nd Parliament, 1st Session, vol. 148, no. 62. May 31, 2016 (Jody Wilson-Raybould, Minister of Justice and Attorney General of Canada).
–. *House of Commons Debates*, 42nd Parliament, 1st Session, no. 45. April 22, 2016 (Jody Wilson-Raybould, Minister of Justice and Attorney General of Canada).
–. *House of Commons Debates*, 42nd Parliament, 1st Session, no. 74. June 16, 2016.
–. *Proceedings of the Standing Senate Committee on Legal and Constitutional Affairs*, 42nd Parliament, 1st Session, no. 8. May 5, 2016 (Jody Wilson-Raybould, Minister of Justice and Attorney General of Canada).
–. *Proceedings of the Standing Senate Committee on Legal and Constitutional Affairs*, 42nd Parliament, 1st Session, no. 8. May 6, 2016.
–. *Proceedings of the Standing Senate Committee on Legal and Constitutional Affairs*, 42nd Parliament, 1st Session, no. 8. May 6, 2016 (Jocelyn Downie, Dalhousie University).
–. *Proceedings of the Standing Senate Committee on Legal and Constitutional Affairs*, 42nd Parliament, 1st Session, no. 8. May 6, 2016 (Senator James Cowan, Nova Scotia).
–. *Proceedings of the Standing Senate Committee on Legal and Constitutional Affairs*, 42nd Parliament, 1st Session, no. 8. May 6, 2016 (Senator Serge Joyal, Kennebec).
–. *Proceedings of the Standing Senate Committee on Legal and Constitutional Affairs*, 42nd Parliament, 1st Session, no. 10. June 2, 2016 (William F. Pentney, Deputy Minister of Justice).
–. *Proceedings of the Standing Senate Committee on Legal and Constitutional Affairs*, 42nd Parliament, 1st Session, no. 10. June 9, 2016 (Peter Hogg).
–. Senate of Canada, *Proceedings of the Standing Senate Committee on Legal and Constitutional Affairs*, 41st Parliament, 2nd Session, no. 30. May 7, 2015 (Rona Ambrose, Minister of Health, Conservative).
–. Senate of Canada, *Proceedings of the Standing Senate Committee on Legal and Constitutional Affairs*, 41st Parliament, 2nd Session, no. 30. May 7, 2015 (Steven Blainey, Minister of Public Safety and Emergency Preparedness, Conservative).
Canadian Association of Nurses in HIV/AIDS. *Brief – Bill C-2: Legislation to Amend the Controlled Drugs and Substances Act to Allow Exemptions for Supervised Injection Sites (and Services)*. April 2015.
Canadian Bar Association. *Re: Bill C-14 – Medical Assistance in Dying*. 2016.
–. National Criminal Justice Section. *Bill C-2, Respect for Communities Act*. October 28, 2014.
Canadian Centre on Substance Abuse. "The Availability of Take-Home Naloxone in Canada." News release. March 2016.
The Canadian Charter of Rights and Freedoms Provincial: In the Event That There Is Going to Be Entrenchment), Doc. 830–84/031. August 28, 1980.
Canadian Civil Liberties Association. *Submission to the Standing Committee on Justice and Human Rights. Bill C-14: Medical Assistance in Dying*. 2016.

Canadian Drug Policy Coalition. "Open Letter: Calling on the Alberta Government to Retract Supervised Consumption Report – Poor Methodological Quality, Lack of Transparency, and Biased Presentation of Results." News release. March 18, 2020.

–. *An Injection of Reason: Critical Analysis of Bill C-2*. April 2015.

–. *An Injection of Reason: Critical Analysis of Bill C-2*. October 2014.

Canadian HIV/AIDS Legal Network. "Open Letter: Rejection the Socio-Economic 'Review' of Supervised Consumption Sites in Alberta." News release. March 23, 2020.

Canadian Medical Association. *CMA Submission: Supporting the Enactment of Bill C-14, Medical Assistance in Dying. Submission to the House of Commons Standing Committee on Justice and Human Rights*. 2016.

–. *Canadian Medical Association Submission to the Standing Senate Committee on Legal and Constitutional Affairs, Bill C-2 An Act to Amend the Controlled Drugs and Substances Act (Respect for Communities Act)*. May 14, 2015.

–. *Canadian Medical Association Submission to the Standing Committee on Public Safety and National Security, Bill C-2 An Act to Amend the Controlled Drugs and Substances Act (Respect for Communities Act)*. October 28, 2014.

–. *End-of-Life Care: A National Dialogue*. June 2014.

–. *Factum of the Intervener: the Canadian Medical Association, in the Supreme Court of Canada (on Appeal from the Court of Appeal for British Columbia) between Lee Carter, Hollis Johnson, Dr. William Shoichet, the British Columbia Civil Liberties Association, and Gloria Taylor (Appellants) and Attorney General of Canada and Attorney General of British Columbia (Respondents)*. June 27, 2014.

Canadian Nurses Association. *Brief for Parliament – Legislation to Amend the Controlled Drugs and Substances Act to Allow Exemptions for Supervised Injection Sites*. November 2013.

–. *Brief for Standing Senate Committee on Legal and Constitutional Affairs – Bill C-2: An Act to Amend the Controlled Drugs and Substances Act (Respect for Communities Act)*. May 2015.

Canadian Pharmacists Association. "CPhA Applauds Announcement of Opioid Summit." News release. July 26, 2016.

Canadian Union of Public Employees, *Bill C-2: Legislation to Amend the Controlled Drugs and Substances Act to Allow Exemptions for Supervised Injection Sites and Services*. Submission – Standing Senate Committee on Legal and Constitutional Affairs. May 2015.

City of Vancouver. "Letter to Minister of Health Jane Philpott Regarding Safe Injection Sites." News release. August 30, 2016.

College of Family Physicians of Canada. *Written Submission to the Standing Committee on Justice and Human Rights*. 2016.

College of Pharmacists of British Columbia. "Naloxone Now Available in BC without a Prescription." News release. March 24, 2016.

–. "Non-Prescription Naloxone Now Available Outside of Pharmacies." News release. September 21, 2016.

College of Physicians and Surgeons of Alberta. *Standards of Practice: Medical Assistance in Dying (MAID)*. 2016.

College of Physicians and Surgeons of British Columbia. *Practice Standard: Medical Assistance in Dying*. 2016.

College of Physicians and Surgeons of Manitoba. *Standard of Practice: Medical Assistance in Dying (MAID)*. 2019.

College of Physicians and Surgeons of Newfoundland and Labrador. *Standard of Practice: Medical Assistance in Dying*. 2022.

College of Physicians and Surgeons of New Brunswick. *Guidelines – Moral Factors and Medical Care.* 2017.
College of Physicians and Surgeons of Nova Scotia. *Professional Standard Regarding Medical Assistance in Dying.* 2017.
College of Physicians and Surgeons of Ontario. *Medical Assistance in Dying: Advice to the Profession.* 2016.
College of Physicians and Surgeons of Prince Edward Island. *Policy on Medical Assistance in Dying.* 2019.
College of Physicians and Surgeons of Saskatchewan. *Policy – Medical Assistance in Dying.* 2016.
Committee of Ministers on the Constitution. *The Canadian Charter of Rights and Freedoms, Federal Draft, August 22, 1980.* Doc. 830–84/004. August 26–29, 1980.
–. *Rights and Freedoms within the Canadian Federation, Discussion Draft Tabled by the Delegation of the Government of Canada, July 4,* Doc. 830–81/027. July 8–11, 1980.
Conseil supérieur de la langue française. *Avis sur l'accès à l'école anglaise à la suite du jugement de la Cour suprême du 22 octobre 2009.* 2010.
Conservative Party of Canada. *Demanding Better: Conservative Party of Canada.* Platform 2004.
–. *Policy Declaration – as Amended by the Delegates to the National Convention.* August 25, 2018.
–. *Protect Our Economy: Our Conservative Plan to Protect Our Economy.* 2015.
–. *Stand Up for Canada: Conservative Party of Canada Federal Election.* Platform 2006.
–. *The True North Strong and Free: Stephen Harper's Plan for Canadians.* 2008.
Dying with Dignity Canada. *Dying with Dignity Canada's Submission to the House of Commons Standing Committee on Justice and Human Rights – Brief on Bill C-14.* 2016.
External Panel on Options for a Legislative Response to Carter v Canada. *Consultations on Physician-Assisted Dying: Summary of Results and Key Findings.* 2015.
Federal Provincial First Ministers' Conference. *The Canadian Charter of Rights and Freedoms, Revised Discussion Draft, Federal, September 3, 1980.* Doc. 800–14/064. September 8–12, 1980.
Government of Alberta. "Calgary Supervised Consumption Site Approved." News release. October 27, 2017.
–. *Supervised Consumption Review.* 2019.
–. "Supervised Consumption Services Review: An Expert Committee Reviewed the Social and Economic Impacts of Current and Proposed Supervised Consumption Services." News release. March 5, 2020.
Government of Canada. "Action to Reduce the Supply of Illicit Opioids and Other Drugs." News release. December 12, 2016.
–. "Expert Panel Report on Supervised Injection Site Released." News release. April 11, 2008.
–. "Federal Government Releases Report of the External Panel on Options for a Legislative Response to Carter v Canada." News release. January 18, 2016.
–. "Government of Canada Announces New Comprehensive Drug Strategy Supported by Proposed Legislative Changes." News release. December 12, 2016.
–. "Government of Canada Establishes Expert Panel on Options for a Legislative Response to Carter v Canada." 2015. –. "Joint Statement of Action to Address the Opioid Crisis." News release. November 19, 2016.
–. *Legislative Background: Medical Assistance in Dying (Bill C-14).* 2016.

–. "Modernizing Legislation to Reduce the Risk of Diversion of Controlled Substances." News release. December 12, 2016.
–. "The New Canadian Drugs and Substances Strategy." News release. December 12, 2016.
–. "Statement from the Minister of Health: Health Canada Authorizes Dr. Peter Centre to Operate Second Supervised Consumption Site in Canada." News release. January 15, 2016.
–. "Streamlining Applications for Supervised Consumption Sites." News release. December 12, 2016.
–. "Supervised Consumption Site: Guidance for Application Form." News release. May 26, 2017.
Government of Northwest Territories, *Medical Assistance in Dying – Interim Guidelines for the Northwest Territories.* 2016.
Health Canada. "Authorized Canadian Naloxone Nasal Spray (NARCAN) Coming to Market." News release. June 30, 2017.
–. "Backgrounder: Royal Assent of Bill C-37 – An Act to Amend the Controlled Drugs and Substances Act and to Make Related Amendments to Other Act." News release. May 18, 2017.
–. *First Annual Report on Medical Assistance in Dying in Canada.* 2019.
–. "Government of Canada Highlights Support for Safer Drug Supply Projects in Ontario." News release. September 18, 2020.
–. "Harper Government Continues to Put Communities First: The Respect for Communities Act Requires Consultations with Local Stakeholders before Supervised Injection Sites Can Be Considered." News release. October 17, 2013.
–. "Health Canada Approves Vancouver Supervised Injection Pilot Project." News release. June 24, 2003.
–. "Health Canada to Propose Regulatory Change to Enable Consideration of Applications under the Special Access Program to Facilitate Treatment of Chronic Relapsing Opioid Dependence." News release. May 13, 2016.
–. "Interim Order Respecting Naloxone Hydrochloride Nasal Spray." News release. July 6, 2016.
–. "No New Injection Sites for Addicts until Questions Answered Says Minister Clement." News release. September 1, 2006.
–. "Notice: Prescription Drug List (PDL): Naloxone." News release. March 22, 2016.
–. *Second Annual Report on Medical Assistance in Dying in Canada 2020.* June 2021.
–. *Third Annual Report on Medical Assistance in Dying Canada 2021.* July 2022.
–. *Vancouver's INSITE Service and Other Supervised Injection Sites: What Has Been Learned from Research? Final Report of the Expert Advisory Committee.* 2008.
His Excellency the Right Honourable David Johnson, Governor General of Canada. *Speech from the Throne to Open the Second Session Forty First Parliament of Canada.* October 16, 2013.
Institut de la statistique du Québec. *Effectif scolaire de la formation générale des jeunes, selons diverses variables, années scolaires 2005–2006 à 2021–2022, Québec.* Quebec City: Government of Quebec, 2022.
Intellectuels pour la souveraineté. *Le projet et loi 103, un projet de loi irrespectueux de la Charte de la langue française. À la Commission parlementaire de la culture et de l'éducation de l'Assemblée nationale.* 2010.
Joint Task Force on Overdose Prevention and Response. *BC's Public Health Emergency Update on BC's Response to the Opioid Overdose Crisis: Third Progress Report.* 2017.

–. *Progress Update on BC's Response to the Opioid Overdose Public Health Emergency: Fifth Progress Update.* 2017.

Kenney, Jason. *Facebook,* March 2, 2018. Twitter, March 2, 2018.

Lametti, David. *Facebook,* May 31, 2016. https://www.facebook.com/plugins/post.php?href=https%3A%2F%2Fwww.facebook.com%2Fdavidlamettilev%2Fposts%2Fpfbid02w3NfpzXr6bsFCsq54YN5QfHd3sNxp9MWMhtJ2ffdzCXuA3EJES5byaqyr2tZCotHl (on file with author).

Lessard, Richard, and Carole Morissette. "Toward Supervised Injection Services: Report of a Feasibility Study on the Implementation of Regional Supervised Injection Services In Montréal: Summary Report." Ed. Agence de la santé et des services sociaux de Montréal. 2011.

Liberal Party of Canada. *Policy Resolution 165. Death with Dignity: Legalizing Medically-Assisted Death.* February 20–23, 2014.

–. *Real Change: A New Plan for a Strong Middle Class.* 2015.

Lieutenant Governor of Alberta. *2020 Speech from the Throne.* 30th Parliament, 2nd Session. February 25, 2020.

–. *2017 Speech from the Throne.* 29th Parliament, 3rd Session. March 2, 2017.

Millar, John S. *HIV, Hepatitis, and Injection Drug Use in British Columbia: Pay Now or Pay Later?* Victoria: Office of the Provincial Health Officer, 1998.

Ministère de l'éducation, du loisir et du sport. *Indicateurs linguistiques: Secteur de l'éducation.* 2013.

Ministère de l'éducation et de l'enseignement supérieur. *Catégories des établissements privés non subventionnés.* 2010–23.

–. *Rapport annuel 2018–2019.* 2019.

–. "Types des établissements privés non subventionnés (EPNS)." http://www.education.gouv.qc.ca/references/tx-solrtyperecherchepublicationtx-solrpublicationnouveaute/resultats-de-la-recherche/detail/article/categories-des-etablissements-prives-non-subventionnes/.

New Democratic Party of Canada. "NDP Secure Emergency Study of Opioid Crisis." News release. September 22, 2016.

Office québécois de la langue française. *Rapport sur l'évolution de la situation linguistique au Québec, 2002–2007.* April 2019.

Ontario Ministry of Finance. *2017 Ontario Budget: A Stronger, Healthier Ontario. The Hon. Charles Sousa, Minister of Finance.* April 11, 2017.

Ontario Ministry of Health and Long-Term Care. "Applications Now Open for Overdose Prevention Sites. Temporary Locations to Offer Life-Saving Harm Reduction Services." News release. January 11, 2018.

–. *Backgrounder: Review of Supervised Consumption Services and Overdose Prevention Sites: Key Findings.* 2018.

–. *Consumption and Treatment Services: Application Guide.* October 2018.

–. "Provincial-Territorial Expert Advisory Group Completes Report on Physician-Assisted Dying." News release. December 14, 2015.

–. "Statement from the Minister of Health and Long-Term Care on Supervised Injection Services." News release. January 9, 2017.

Pivot Legal Society. *Pivot Legal Society Submission to the Standing Committee on Public Safety and National Security: Legal Issues with Bill C-2.* November 2013.

–. *Pivot Legal Society Submission to the Standing Senate Committee on Legal and Constitutional Affairs: Legal Issues with Bill C-2.* May 2015.

Provincial-Territorial Expert Advisory Group on Physician-Assisted Dying. *Final Report.* 2015.

Public Health Agency of Canada. *Opioid and Stimulant-related Harms in Canada.* Ottawa: Public Health Agency of Canada, 2021.

Quebec English School Board Association. *Brief to the Commission de la culture de l'éducation.* Brief on Bill 103. October 20, 2010.

Royal Society of Canada. *End-of-Life Decision Making.* November 2011.

Secrétariat à la politique linguistique. *L'évolution de la situation de l'affichage à Montréal de 1995 à 1997.* Montreal: Office québécois de la langue française, 1997.

Statistics Canada. *Interprovincial Migration between Quebec and Other Provinces and Territories for the Population with English as a Mother Tongue, 1971 to 2016.* 2021.

–. *Immigrants to Canada, by Province or Territory.* Table 17–10–0011–01. 2007.

Supervised Consumption Services Review Committee. *Impact: A Socio-Economic Review of Supervised Consumption Sites in Alberta.* March 5, 2020.

Thériault, Luc (Montcalm, BQ). Canada, Parliament, *House of Commons Debates,* 42nd Parliament, 1st Session, no. 74, June 16, 2016.

Toronto Board of Health. *Implementing Supervised Injection Services in Toronto (HL 13.2).* 2016.

–. *Submission by the Toronto Board of Health to the Standing Committee on Public Safety and National Security.* October 2014.

–. *Submission by the Toronto Board of Health to the Standing Senate Committee on Legal and Constitutional Affairs.* April 24, 2015.

–. *Supervised Injection Services in Toronto (HL 23.1).* 2013.

United Conservative Party of Alberta. *Alberta Strong and Free: Getting Alberta Back to Work.* 2019.

Vancouver Coastal Health. "Insite Receives New, Four-Year Health Canada Exemption." News release. March 17, 2016.

Vancouver Police Department. *The Opioid Crisis: The Need for Treatment on Demand.* May 2017.

Virgo Planning and Evaluation Consultants. *Improving Access and Coordination of Mental Health and Addiction Services: A Provincial Strategy for all Manitobans: Final Report.* 2018.

Yukon Liberal Caucus. *2021 Confidence and Supply Agreement between the Yukon Liberal Caucus and the Yukon NDP Caucus.* February 28, 2021.

Yukon Medical Council. *Standard of Practice: Medical Assistance in Dying (MAID).* 2016.

Newspaper Articles

"Alberta NDP Continues to Lead UCP in Voter Support: Angus Reid Poll." *CTV News Calgary,* January 20, 2022. https://calgary.ctvnews.ca/alberta-ndp-continues-to-lead-ucp-in-voter-support-angus-reid-poll-1.5748115.

Alphonso, Caroline, Jeff Gray, and Dustin Cook. "CUPE to End Education Protests in Ontario after Doug Ford Says He Will Repeal Legislation Banning Strike," *Globe and Mail,* November 4, 2022. https://www.theglobeandmail.com/canada/article-doug-ford-announcement-cupe/.

"Alta. Safe Injection Sites Not on Radar, Health Minister Says." *CBC News,* June 5, 2011. https://www.cbc.ca/news/canada/edmonton/alta-safe-injection-sites-not-on-radar-health-minister-says-1.1067917.

Anderssen, Erin. "Ottawa Seeking to Delay Expansion of MAiD for Mental Disorders." *Globe and Mail,* December 15, 2022. https://www.theglobeandmail.com/canada/article-maid-expansion-delay-mental-disorders/.

"Are Canadians Being Driven to Assisted Suicide by Poverty or Health Care Crisis?" *The Guardian*, May 11, 2022. https://www.theguardian.com/world/2022/may/11/canada-cases-right-to-die-laws.

Banerjee, Sidhartha. "EMSB Announces Legal Action over Transfer of Schools to French Board." *Canadian Press*, September 10, 2019.

Bélair-Cirino, Marco. "La CAQ dépose son projet de loi sur la laïcité à l'Assemblée nationale." *Le Devoir*, March 28, 2019. https://www.ledevoir.com/politique/quebec/550869/depot-projet-de-loi?

Bellavance, Joël-Denis. "Trudeau envisage de se tourner vers la Cour suprême." *La Presse*, January 23, 2023. https://www.lapresse.ca/actualites/politique/2023-01-21/disposition-de-derogation/trudeau-envisage-de-se-tourner-vers-la-cour-supreme.php.

Berthiaume, Lee. "Veterans' Case Raise Fresh Concerns About Expanding Assisted Dying Law." *Globe and Mail*, December 4, 2022. https://www.theglobeandmail.com/canada/article-veterans-cases-raise-fresh-concerns-about-expanding-assisted-dying-law-2/.

Blackwell, Tom, and Natalie Alcoba. "Ontario Rejects Safe Injection Sites." *National Post*, April 11, 2012. https://nationalpost.com/news/canada/ontario-rejects-safe-injection-sites.

Blanchfield, Mike, and Joan Bryden. "Don't Expect Law on Doctor-Assisted Death before Election, Mackay Says." *Globe and Mail*, April 27, 2015. https://www.theglobeandmail.com/news/national/dont-expect-law-on-doctor-assisted-suicide-before-election-mackay-says/article24147566/.

Bryden, Joan. "Near-death Provision in Assisted-Dying Bill Is Non Negotiable: Ministers." *Maclean's*, June 16, 2016.

–. "Senators Balk at Limiting Assisted Dying to Canadians Near Death." *Maclean's*, June 7, 2016.

Butler, Collin. "Doug Ford Won't Say If He'd Support Supervised Consumption Site for London." *CBC News*, May 18, 2018. https://www.cbc.ca/news/canada/london/london-ontario-doug-ford-healthcare-1.4669079.

"Canada: Quebec Makes Oath to King Optional for Politicians." *BBC News*, December 9, 2022. https://www.bbc.com/news/world-us-canada-63924746.

Chase, Stephen. "Conservatives Vote to End Official Opposition to Gay Marriage." *Globe and Mail*, May 28, 2016. https://www.theglobeandmail.com/news/politics/conservatives-end-official-opposition-to-gay-marriage/article30197721/.

Chiasson, Paul. "Mayor Coderre Pledges Safe Injection Sites in Montreal Even Without Federal Approval." *Canadian Press*, September 3, 2015. https://montrealgazette.com/news/local-news/mayor-coderre-pledges-safe-injection-sites-in-montreal-even-without-federal-approval.

"Chrétien, Romanow and McMurtry Attack Ford's Use of the Notwithstanding Clause." *Maclean's*, September 14, 2018.

Church, Elizabeth, and Andrea Woo. "Insite Gets Stamp of Approval from Canada's Health Minister." *Globe and Mail*, January 21, 2016. https://www.theglobeandmail.com/news/british-columbia/insite-gets-stamp-of-approval-from-canadas-health-minister/article28332223/.

Church, Elizabeth, and Verity Stevenson. "Supervised Injection Site Proponents Push on Despite Harper's Opposition." *Globe and Mail*, August 14, 2015. https://www.theglobeandmail.com/news/national/safe-injection-site-proponents-push-on-despite-harpers-opposition/article25967472/.

Clark, Campbell. "Conservatives Gamble with Tougher Approach to Prostitution." *Globe and Mail*, June 5, 2014. https://www.theglobeandmail.com/news/politics/globe-politics-insider/conservatives-gamble-with-tougher-approach-to-prostitution/article 18996262/.

"Clement Questions MDs Who Favour Safe Injection Sites." *CBC News*, August 18, 2008.

Coyne, Andrew. "Are We Going to Do Anything to Protect Quebec's Minorities?" *National Post*, March 30, 2019. https://nationalpost.com/opinion/andrew-coyne-are-we-going-to-do-anything-to-protect-quebecs-minorities.

—. "In Canada, the Rule of Law Is Giving Away to the Rule of Will." *Globe and Mail*, October 13, 2021. https://www.theglobeandmail.com/opinion/article-in-canada-the-rule-of-law-is-giving-way-to-the-rule-of-will/.

Dale, Daniel. "Ontario Rejects Toronto's Call for Supervised Drug Injection Site." *Toronto Star*, July 10, 2013. https://www.thestar.com/news/gta/ontario-rejects-toronto-s-call-for-supervised-drug-injection-site/article_5b0f4001-b87b-5af6-90f3-c33625122aa1.html.

Davis, Greg. "Ontario Commits $1.35 M Annually for Peterborough Safe Consumption and Treatment Site." *Global News*, February 25, 2022. https://globalnews.ca/news/8645659/ontario-funding-peterborough-safe-consumption-treatment-site/.

"Denis Coderre Makes Another Push for Montreal Safe Injection Sites." *CBC News*, June 4, 2015. https://www.cbc.ca/news/canada/montreal/safe-injection-sites-supervised-trudeau-canada-government-quebec-1.3319725.

DeSosa, Katie. "Woman with Terminal Cancer Forced to Transfer from St. Paul's Hospital for Assisted Dying." *Vancouver Sun*, June 23, 2023. https://vancouversun.com/news/local-news/woman-with-terminal-cancer-forced-to-family-upset-by-st-pauls-hospital-maid-policy.

"Doug Ford Says He's 'Dead Against' Supervised Injection Sites." *Canadian Press*, April 20, 2018. https://www.cbc.ca/news/canada/windsor/doug-ford-says-he-s-dead-against-supervised-injection-sites-1.4628547.

Dougherty, Kevin. "French Not for Sale, PQ Says of Bill 103." *Montreal Gazette*, September 28, 2010.

Duffy, Andrew. "Ottawa Must Decide Whether It Wants a Safe Injection Site: Provincial Health Minister." *Ottawa Citizen*, April 8, 2016. https://ottawacitizen.com/news/local-news/ottawa-must-decide-whether-it-wants-a-safe-injection-site-provincial-health-minister.

Duggan, Kyle. "NDP MPs Call on Government to Make It Easier to Set Up Harm-Reduction Sites." *iPolitics*, March 2, 2016. https://www.ipolitics.ca/news/ndp-mps-call-on-government-to-make-it-easier-to-set-up-harm-reduction-sites.

—. "Philpott Expects More Applications for Safe Injection Sites." *iPolitics*, February 10, 2016. https://www.ipolitics.ca/news/philpott-expects-more-applications-for-safe-injection-sites.

Dunfield, Allison. "Alliance Launches Motion on Same-Sex Marriage." *Globe and Mail*, September 16, 2003. https://www.theglobeandmail.com/amp/news/national/alliance-launches-motion-onsame-sex-marriage/article1166777/.

Dyck, Darryl. "Ontario to Review Safe Injection, Overdose Prevention Sites, Health Minister Says." *Canadian Press*, July 24, 2018. https://www.cbc.ca/news/canada/toronto/ontario-safe-injection-sites-limbo-1.4760002.

"Edmonton Safe Injection Sites Set to Face Legal Challenge." *CBC Edmonton*, November 22, 2018. https://www.cbc.ca/news/canada/edmonton/legal-challenge-chinatown-business-association-safe-injection-sites-1.4917539.

"Federal Government Approves Three Supervised Injection Sites in Montreal." *Canadian Press*, February 6, 2017. https://www.ctvnews.ca/health/federal-government-approves-three-supervised-injection-sites-in-montreal-1.3273222.

Fine, Sean. "More Provinces Offer Assisted-Dying Clarity in Absence of Federal Law." *Globe and Mail*, June 8, 2016. https://www.theglobeandmail.com/news/national/more-provinces-offer-assisted-dying-clarity-in-response-to-absence-of-federal-law/article30363285/.

French, Janet. "Advocates Worry Health Policy Change Another Government Dismissal of Harm Reduction." *CBC Edmonton*, March 8, 2021. https://www.cbc.ca/news/canada/edmonton/advocates-worry-health-policy-change-another-government-dismissal-of-harm-reduction-1.5939394.

—. "ID Requirements at Alberta Supervised Consumption Sites Delayed, Advocates Say." *CBC News Edmonton*, September 7, 2021. https://www.cbc.ca/news/canada/edmonton/alberta-court-says-supervised-consumption-sites-can-ask-for-health-id-numbers-1.6311502.

Galloway, Gloria. "Harper Government to Throw Up Roadblocks For Safe-Injection Sites." *Globe and Mail*, June 6 2013. https://www.theglobeandmail.com/news/politics/harper-government-to-throw-up-roadblocks-for-safe-injection-sites/article12378472/.

Gerster, Jane. "Opposition MLAs Grill Tories over Report's Deleted 'Safe Injection Site' Recommendation." *Winnipeg Free Press*, May 15, 2018. https://www.winnipegfreepress.com/breakingnews/2018/05/14/mental-health-addictions-care-in-manitoba-inadequate-in-need-of-major-overhaul-long-awaited-report-says.

Hager, Mike. "Injection Site Supporters Say Tories Are Heel Dragging." *Globe and Mail*, January 13, 2015. https://www.theglobeandmail.com/news/british-columbia/injection-site-supporters-say-tories-are-heel-dragging/article22407729/.

Herring, Jason. "Harm Reduction Advocates Send Open Letter to Province Protesting Lethbridge SCS Closure." *Calgary Herald*, August 31, 2020. https://calgaryherald.com/news/local-news/harm-reduction-advocates-send-open-letter-to-province-protesting-lethbridge-scs-closure.

Hébert, Chantal. "The Provinces Are Chipping Away at Canada's Constitution. Why Won't Justin Trudeau Say Anything?" *Toronto Star*, October 17, 2021. https://www.thestar.com/politics/political-opinion/the-provinces-are-chipping-away-at-canada-s-constitution-why-won-t-justin-trudeau-say/article_cbd84c85-f9b2-5203-b332-5a01df623ce7.html?.

Hopper, Tristin. "Why Canada Has the Most Activist Supreme Court in the World – and How It Has Changed the Country." *National Post*, January 3, 2022. https://nationalpost.com/news/canada/canada-most-activist-supreme-court-world.

Howell, Mike. "Vancouver Coastal Health Considers More Drug Injection Sites – VCH Awaits Nod from Health Canada on Current 'Illegal' Injection Facility." *Vancouver Courier*, March 30, 2015. https://www.vancouverisawesome.com/courier-archive/news/vancouver-coastal-health-considers-more-drug-injection-sites-2996344.

Hudes, Sammy. "UCP Pulls Funding to Lethbridge Supervised Consumption Site Following Audit." *Calgary Herald*, July 16, 2020. https://calgaryherald.com/news/politics/ucp-pulls-funding-to-lethbridge-supervised-consumption-site-following-audit.

Hunt, Stephen. "Funding for New Safe Injection Sites Frozen by Alberta Government Until Further Notice." *CBC Calgary*, June 1, 2019. https://www.cbc.ca/news/canada/calgary/safe-injection-site-funding-frozen-by-ucp-1.5158975.

Hutchins, Aaron. "Why Doug Ford Went Straight to the 'Nuclear Option' on Toronto City Council." *Maclean's*, September 10, 2018. https://macleans.ca/politics/why-doug-ford-went-straight-to-the-nuclear-option-on-toronto-city-council/.

Jeffrey, Andrew. "New Mobile Supervised Drug Consumption Site Announced for Forest Lawn." *Toronto Star*, May 2, 2019. https://www.thestar.com/calgary/new-mobile

-supervised-drug-consumption-site-announced-for-forest-lawn/article_49fc1eaa-b175-5fe7-9b6f-2973f267ba05.html.
"Judge Suspends Two Articles of Quebec's Bill 96 Regarding Legal Translations." *CTV News Montreal*, August 12, 2022. https://montreal.ctvnews.ca/judge-suspends-two-articles-of-quebec-s-bill-96-regarding-legal-translations-1.6025156.
Keele, Jeff. "Pallister against Safe Injection Sites for Manitoba." *CTV News*, December 18, 2018. https://winnipeg.ctvnews.ca/pallister-against-safe-injection-sites-for-manitoba-1.4222955.
Kennedy, Mark. "Deadline on Doctor-Assisted Suicide Law Could Be Delayed." *Ottawa Citizen*, November 16, 2015.
Kieltyka, Matt, and Irwin Loy. "Harper Dodges Questions on RCMP's Anti-Insite Research." *The Tyee*, October 9, 2008. https://thetyee.ca/Blogs/TheHook/Health/2008/10/09/HarperDodgesInsiteQuestions/.
Kirkup, Kristy. "Justice Minister Troubled by Senate Change to Assisted Dying Bill." *Canadian Press*, June 10, 2016. https://www.ctvnews.ca/mobile/canada/justice-minister-troubled-by-senate-change-to-assisted-dying-bill-1.2940999?cache=yesclipId10406200text/html;charset=utf-80404/7.258454/7.656680/7.622985.
Kost, Hannah. "'A System of Chaos': Supervised Consumption Services Review Committee Releases Findings." *CBC News*, March 5, 2020. https://www.cbc.ca/news/canada/calgary/ucp-supervised-consumption-site-review-committee-announcement-findings-1.5486579.
Kupfer, Matthew. "NDP Tries to Fast-Track Bill to Make Supervised Injection Sites Easier to Open." *CBC News*, December 13, 2016. https://www.cbc.ca/news/politics/opioid-crisis-committee-1.3894504.
Lapierre, Matthew. "EMSB Officially Closing 3 Schools at the End of the School Year." *CTV News*, January 20, 2020. https://montreal.ctvnews.ca/emsb-officially-closing-3-schools-at-the-end-of-the-school-year-1.4776064.
Larin, Vincent. "Le PLQ critique la position de la CAQ." *La Presse*, January 23, 2023. https://www.lapresse.ca/actualites/politique/2023-01-22/disposition-de-derogation/le-plq-critique-la-position-de-la-caq.php.
Leblanc, Daniel. "Ottawa Launches Public Consultations to Meet Court Deadline to Loosen Rules for Medically Assisted Death." *Globe and Mail*, January 13, 2020. https://www.theglobeandmail.com/politics/article-ottawa-launches-public-consultations-to-meet-court-deadline-to-loosen/.
Levitz, Stephanie. "Government Unlikely to Invoke Notwithstanding Clause over Assisted Suicide Ruling: Peter Mackay." *National Post*, February 10, 2015. https://nationalpost.com/news/politics/government-not-likely-to-invoke-notwithstanding-clause-over-assisted-suicide-ruling-peter-mackay.
Lowrie, Morgan. "Legault Defends Quebec's Religious-Symbol Bill, Calls Notwithstanding Clause 'Legitimate Tool.'" *Globe and Mail*, March 31, 2019. https://www.theglobeandmail.com/canada/article-legault-defends-quebecs-religious-symbols-bill-calls-notwithstanding/.
Lupick, Travis. "Dodging Drug Laws, B.C. Unveils Plans to Immediately Offer Supervised-Injection Services in Vancouver and Other Cities." *Georgia Straight*, December 8, 2016. https://www.straight.com/news/843146/dodging-drug-laws-bc-unveils-plans-immediately-offer-supervised-injection-services.
–. "Health Minister Says a Change to Harper's Anti-Insite Law Likely Needed to Meet Rising Overdose Deaths." *Georgia Straight*, November 10, 2016. https://www.straight.

com/news/826771/health-minister-says-change-harpers-anti-insite-law-likely-needed-meet-rising-overdose.

MacDonald, Michael. "Nova Scotia's Medically Assisted Dying Program Paused Amid 'Unprecedented' Demand." *Canadian Press*, September 30, 2021. https://www.cbc.ca/news/canada/nova-scotia/nova-scotia-s-medically-assisted-dying-program-paused-amid-unprecedented-demand-1.6195412.

Macleod, Ian. "Parts of Assisted-Death Bill 'Not Good Enough,'" Liberal MP Who Co-Chaired Committee Says." *Ottawa Citizen*, April 15, 2016. https://nationalpost.com/news/politics/parts-of-assisted-death-bill-not-good-enough-liberal-mp-who-co-chaired-committee-says.

Macpherson, Donald. "Bill 103 Is in the Style of Bourassa-Language Law; Charest Government Proposal Reopens English-Education Loophole, But Barely." *Montreal Gazette*, June 3, 2010.

Macpherson, Donald, and Nicholas Klassen. "Vancouver Buyers Club: Safe Injection Sites Save Lives – But Ottawa Still Doesn't Care." *The Walrus*, May 2015. https://thewalrus.ca/vancouver-buyers-club/.

Maimann, Kevin. "This Government Is Defunding One of North America's Busiest Safe Injection Sites." *VICE News*, August 14, 2020. https://www.vice.com/en/article/xg8mkq/alberta-government-is-defunding-arches-one-of-north-americas-busiest-safe-injection-sites.

"Manitoba Government on Hot Seat After Safe Injection Site Recommendation Cut from Report." *CBC News*, May 14, 2018. https://www.cbc.ca/news/canada/manitoba/manitoba-addiction-mental-health-virgo-report-1.4661795.

Markusoff, Jason. "Jason Kenney Is Sinking. How It All Went Wrong for Him." *Maclean's*, November 1, 2021. https://macleans.ca/longforms/jason-kenney-is-sinking-how-it-all-went-wrong-for-him/.

Martin, Lawrence. "The Supreme Court Is Harper's Real Opposition." *Globe and Mail*, July 1, 2014. https://www.theglobeandmail.com/opinion/the-supreme-court-is-harpers-real-opposition/article19395285/.

Mckenna, Kate. "Quebec Seeks to Change Canadian Constitution, Make Sweeping Changes to Language Laws With New Bill." *CBC News*, May 13, 2021. https://www.cbc.ca/news/canada/montreal/quebec-bill-101-language-revamp-1.6023532.

Mohatarem, Kashmala Fida. "Boyle Street Supervised Consumption Site Closing Permanently." *CBC News Edmonton*, April 28, 2021. https://www.cbc.ca/news/canada/edmonton/edmonton-boyle-street-supervised-consumption-1.6005939.

Montpetit, Jonathan, and Benjamin Shingler. "Quebec Superior Court Upholds Most of Religious Symbols Ban, But English-Language Schools Exempt." *CBC News*, April 20, 2021. https://www.cbc.ca/news/canada/montreal/bill-21-religious-symbols-ban-quebec-court-ruling-1.5993431.

Muise, Monica. "Liberals Stick With Existing Rules to Approve Safe-Injection Sites, for Now." *Global News*, March 14, 2016. https://globalnews.ca/news/2577356/liberals-stick-with-existing-rules-to-approve-safe-injection-sites-for-now/.

"N.B. Invokes Notwithstanding Clause in Bill Making Vaccination Mandatory." *Canadian Press*, November 22, 2019. https://atlantic.ctvnews.ca/n-b-invokes-notwithstanding-clause-in-bill-making-vaccination-mandatory-1.4698400.

Nair, Remshi. "Insite Supporters Try to Crash Harper Speech." *CTV News*, October 9, 2008.

Nair, Roshini, and Jon Hernandez. "Liberal Government's Refusal to Repeal Bill C-2 'Disappointing,' Supervised Injection Site Advocate Says." *CBC News*, August 24, 2016.

"New Brunswick Legislators Defeat Controversial Mandatory Vaccination Bill." *Canadian Press*, June 18, 2020. https://atlantic.ctvnews.ca/new-brunswick-legislators-defeat-controversial-mandatory-vaccination-bill-1.4990085.

"No AIDS Announcement During 'Politicized' Week: Ottawa." *CBC News*, August 17, 2006. https://www.cbc.ca/news/canada/no-aids-announcement-during-politicized-week-ottawa-1.573667.

"On Safe-Injection Sites, Wynne Says Society Has a Responsibility to Reduce Harm." *Canadian Press*, March 16, 2016. https://toronto.citynews.ca/2016/03/16/on-safe-injection-sites-wynne-says-society-has-a-responsibility-to-reduce-harm/.

"Ontario Government Backs Supervised Injection Sites in Toronto." *Canadian Press*, January 9, 2017. https://www.cbc.ca/news/canada/toronto/ontario-backs-toronto-injection-sites-1.3927679.

"Ontario Pauses Opening Three Overdose-Prevention Sites As It Conducts Review." *Canadian Press*, August 13, 2018. https://toronto.citynews.ca/2018/08/13/ontario-pauses-opening-three-overdose-prevention-sites-as-it-conducts-review/.

"Ontario Rejects Safe Injection Sites." *National Post*, April 11, 2012. https://nationalpost.com/news/canada/ontario-rejects-safe-injection-sites.

Pagliaro, Jennifer. "Mayor John Tory to Back Supervised Injection Sites." *Toronto Star*, June 24, 2016. https://www.thestar.com/news/gta/city-hall/mayor-john-tory-to-back-supervised-injection-sites/article_ab42f7eb-0c2b-5c00-a6e7-f05125e2e5c3.html.

Perreaux, Les. "Legault to Use Notwithstanding Clause to Ban Religious Symbols for Civil Servants." *Globe and Mail*, October 2, 2018. https://www.theglobeandmail.com/canada/article-francois-legault-to-invoke-notwithstanding-clause-to-ban-quebec-public/.

–. "Quebec Tables Legislation on Religious-Symbols Ban, Includes Provisions for Notwithstanding Clause." *Globe and Mail*, March 28, 2019. https://www.theglobeandmail.com/canada/article-quebec-tables-legislation-on-religious-symbols-ban-includes/.

Perrin, Benjamin. "Alberta's War against Safe Injection Sites." *Maclean's*, March 12, 2020. https://macleans.ca/opinion/albertas-war-against-safe-injection-sites/.

Picard, André. "Clement's Insite Attack Leaves WHO Red-Faced." *Globe and Mail*, August 6, 2008. https://www.theglobeandmail.com/life/clements-insite-attack-leaves-who-red-faced/article1058485/.

–. "Supporting Insite Unethical, Clement Tells Doctors." *Globe and Mail*, August 19, 2008. https://www.theglobeandmail.com/news/national/supporting-insite-unethical-clement-tells-doctors/article17969869/.

"Police Group Takes Aim at Vancouver Safe Injection Site." *CBC News*, September 1, 2006. https://www.cbc.ca/news/canada/british-columbia/police-group-takes-aim-at-vancouver-safe-injection-site-1.609861.

Poitras, Jacques. "New Brunswick Uses Notwithstanding Clause in 2nd Bid to Pass Vaccination Bill," *CBC News*, November 29, 2019. https://www.cbc.ca/news/canada/new-brunswick/cardy-notwithstanding-clause-mandatory-vaccination-bill-1.5369965.

Pratt, André. "Under Legault, Quebec's Separatists Are Winning By Stealth." *National Post*, June 17, 2022. https://nationalpost.com/opinion/andre-pratte-under-legault-quebecs-separatists-are-winning-by-stealth.

"Quebec to Invest $12M in Safe Injection Sites." *CBC News*, September 28, 2016. https://www.cbc.ca/news/canada/montreal/quebec-to-invest-12m-in-safe-injection-sites-1.3783424.

"Quebec Liberals Push Language Law Through." *CBC News*, October 19, 2010. https://www.cbc.ca/news/canada/montreal/quebec-liberals-push-language-law-through-1.969976.

"Quebec Oks Bid for Montreal Safe-Injection Sites." *Canadian Press*, April 30, 2015. https://www.thespec.com/news/quebec-oks-montreal-safe-injection-sites/article_ad1a9997-fb92-596a-9828-531a8164ec53.html.

Senay, Cathy, and Sarah Levatt." Quebec to Expand Law on Medically Assisted Death, Look at Advance Consent." *CBC News*, November 29, 2019. https://www.cbc.ca/news/canada/montreal/medical-assistance-in-death-report-1.5377890.

"Serge Joyal Urges Provinces to Test Constitutionality of Assisted Dying Law." *Maclean's*, June 18, 2016. https://macleans.ca/news/canada/serge-joyal-urges-provinces-to-test-constitutionality-of-assisted-dying-law/.

Smith, Alanna. "Academics Question Methodology of UCP Approved Supervised Consumption Sites Report." *Calgary Herald*, March 8, 2020. https://calgaryherald.com/news/local-news/academics-question-methodology-of-ucp-approved-supervised-consumption-sites-report.

—. "Lethbridge Police Investigation of ARCHES Finds Records for 'Unaccounted Funds.'" *Calgary Herald*, December 22, 2020. https://calgaryherald.com/news/local-news/lethbridge-police-investigation-into-arches-finds-records-for-unaccounted-funds.

Smith, Marie-Danielle. "Jane Philpott 'Concerned' About Senate Changes to Assisted-Dying Bill." *Globe and Mail*, June 9, 2016. https://www.theglobeandmail.com/news/politics/jane-philpott-concerned-about-senate-changes-to-assisted-dying-bill/article30387436/.

—. "Liberals to Whip the Vote in Favour of Assisted-Dying Law." *Globe and Mail*, February 11, 2016. https://www.theglobeandmail.com/news/politics/liberals-to-whip-the-vote-in-favour-of-assisted-dying-law/article28734747/.

—. "Tory, Liberal Senate Leaders Call Assisted Suicide Bill 'Unconstitutional' As Deadline Nears." *National Post*, May 30, 2016. https://nationalpost.com/news/politics/tory-liberal-senate-leaders-call-assisted-suicide-bill-unconstitutional-as-deadline-nears.

—. "A Transformative Day': Senate Concedes to Government's Will, Sending Assisted Dying Law to Royal Assent." *National Post*, June 17, 2016.

Southwick, Reid. "UCP Leader Jason Kenney Draws Fire for Saying Safe Consumption Sites Help Addicts 'Inject Poison.'" *CBC Calgary*, March 2, 2018. https://www.cbc.ca/news/canada/calgary/jason-kenney-safe-consumption-lethbridge-1.4559556.

Stone, Laura. "Liberals to Whip the Vote in Favour of Assisted-Dying Law." *Globe and Mail*, February 11, 2016. https://www.theglobeandmail.com/news/politics/liberals-to-whip-the-vote-in-favour-of-assisted-dying-law/article28734747/.

Stuek, Wendy. "RCMP Defends Hiring Experts to Review Insite Research." *Globe and Mail*, October 9, 2008. https://www.theglobeandmail.com/news/national/rcmp-defends-hiring-experts-to-review-insite-research/article1063395/.

Subramaniam, Vanmala. "Dough Ford's Use of the Notwithstanding Clause Had the Unintended Effect of Bringing Canada's Largest Unions Together." *Globe and Mail*, November 9, 2022. https://www.theglobeandmail.com/business/article-ford-cupe-notwithstanding-canadian-unions/.

Tasker, John Paul. "Andrew Scheer Slams 'Terrible' Liberal Approach to Safe Injection Sites." *CBC News*, September 24, 2019. https://www.cbc.ca/news/politics/scheer-injection-sites-terrible-1.5294321.

—. "Physician-Assisted Dying Bill Passes Senate 64–12, Send Back to House: Justice Minister Jody Wilson-Raybould Has Already Thrown Cold Water on a Major Amendment." *CBC News*, June 15, 2016. https://www.cbc.ca/news/politics/senate-amendments-c14-1.3636488.

Tejeida, Aurora. "Conservative Party Starts Petition to 'Keep Heroin Out of Our Backyards." *The Hook*, June 7, 2013. https://thetyee.ca/Blogs/TheHook/2013/06/07/CPP-Petition/.

"Toronto City Councillors Vote in Favour of Safe Injection Sites." *CBC News Toronto*, July 14, 2016.

"Trudeau Says Ottawa Not Interested in 'Fighting' With Alberta After Sovereignty Act Passes." *CBC News*, December 9, 2022.

Valiante, Giuseppe. "Quebec's English Private Schools Say Admission Rules Limit Access." *CBC News*, April 30, 2015. https://www.cbc.ca/news/canada/montreal/quebec-s-english-private-schools-say-admission-rules-limit-access-1.3055101.

Weeks, Carly. "What Access to Abortion Looks Like Across Canada." *Globe and Mail*, May 3, 2022. https://www.theglobeandmail.com/canada/article-abortion-access-laws-canada/.

Weeks, Carly, and Jeff Gray. "Ontario Cuts Funding to Three Supervised Drug-Use Sites." *Globe and Mail*, March 29, 2019. https://www.theglobeandmail.com/canada/article-ontario-to-close-three-supervised-drug-use-sites/.

Weinrib, Lorraine. "Doug Ford Can't Apply the Notwithstanding Clause Retroactively to Impede Democracy." *Globe and Mail*, September 18, 2018. https://www.theglobeandmail.com/opinion/article-doug-ford-cant-apply-the-notwithstanding-clause-retroactively-to/.

Willing, Jon. "Council Politics Taken Out of Ottawa Supervised Injection Site Debate After Letter By Mayor." *Ottawa Citizen*, January 4, 2017. https://ottawacitizen.com/news/local-news/council-politics-taken-out-of-ottawa-supervised-injection-site-debate-after-letter-by-mayor.

Woo, Andrea. "British Columbia Opens Drug Injection Sites amid Opioid Crisis." *Globe and Mail*, December 8, 2016. https://www.theglobeandmail.com/news/british-columbia/opioid-crisis-prompts-bc-to-open-more-overdose-prevention-sites/article33276659/.

—. "Ottawa Approves Second Supervised Injection Site." *Globe and Mail*, January 15, 2016. https://www.theglobeandmail.com/news/british-columbia/vancouver-facility-becomes-canadas-second-approved-supervised-injection-site/article28216557/.

—. "Sidestepping Federal Law, BC Social-Housing Providers Offer Spaces for Drug Use." *Globe and Mail*, January 24, 2017. https://www.theglobeandmail.com/news/british-columbia/bc-cant-wait-for-feds-approval-during-drug-crisis-terry-lake/article33731436/.

Zabjek, Alexandra. "Downtown Edmonton Business Group Loses Legal Fight against Supervised Injection Sites." *CBC News*, February 28, 2019. https://www.cbc.ca/news/canada/edmonton/chinatown-business-loses-challenge-injection-site-1.5037158.

Zimonjic, Peter, and Matthew Kupfer. "Philpott, Goodale Announce Changes to Laws to Make Safe Injection Sites Easier to Open." *CBC News*, December 12, 2016.

Secondary Sources

Aguilino, Michael. "Qui suis-je: identité linguistique et exclusion des non-ayants droit par l'Article 23 de la Charte." *Ottawa Law Review* 38, 1 (2006): 67–93.

Albert, Richard. "The Most Powerful Court in the World? Judicial Review of Constitutional Amendment in Canada," *Supreme Court Law Review* (2d) 110 (2023): 79-102.
Angus Reid. "Quebecers Overwhelmingly Call for Assisted Suicide Guidelines." News release. February 14, 2013.
Antcil, Pierre. "The End of the Language Crisis in Quebec: Comparative Implications." In *Canadian Language Policies in Comparative Perspective*, ed. Michael A. Morris, 344–68. Montreal and Kingston: McGill-Queen's University Press, 2010.
Ardron, Dean. "Amendments to the Quebec Charter of the French Language Constitutionally Invalid." *Education & Law Journal* 19, 3 (2010): 247–51.
Bakan, Joel. *Just Words: Constitutional Rights and Social Wrongs*. Toronto: University of Toronto Press, 1997.
Baker, Dennis. "A Feature, Not a Bug: A Coordinate Moment in Canadian Constitutionalism." In *Constitutional Dialogue: Rights, Democracy, Institutions*, ed. Geoffrey Sigalet, Grégoire Webber, and Rosalind Dixon, 397–420. Cambridge, UK: Cambridge University Press, 2019.
–. *Not Quite Supreme: The Courts and Coordinate Constitutional Interpretation*. Montreal and Kingston: McGill-Queen's University Press, 2010.
–. "The Provincial Power to (Not) Prosecute *Criminal Code* Offences," *Ottawa Law Review* 48, 2 (2017): 419–48.
–. "The Temptation of Provincial Criminal Law," *Canadian Public Administration* 57, 2 (2014): 275–94.
Bakht, Natasha. *In Your Face: Law, Justice, and Niqab-wearing Women in Canada*. Toronto: Delve Books, 2020.
Barker, Paul, and John Church. "Revisiting Health Regionalization in Canada: More Bark Than Bite?" *International Journal of Health Services* 47, 2 (2017): 333–51.
Bastien, Frédéric. *La bataille de Londres: dessous, secrets et coulisses du rapatriement constitutionnel*. Montreal: Éditions du Boréal, 2013.
Bateman, Thomas J., and Matthew LeBlanc. "Charter Dialogue and the Constitutionality of Canada's MAiD Legislation." In *Assisted Death: Legal, Social and Ethical Issues*, ed. Derek B.M. Ross, 387–433. Toronto: LexisNexis, 2018.
Bayoumi, Ahmed M., Carol Strike, Naushaba Degani, Benedikt Fischer, Richard Glazier, Shaun Hopkins, Lynne Leonard, et al. *Report of the Toronto and Ottawa Supervised Consumption Assessment Study, 2012*. Toronto: St. Michael's Hospital and the Dalla Lana School of Public Health, University of Toronto, 2012.
Behiels, Michael D. *Prelude to Quebec's Quiet Revolution: Liberalism versus Neo-Nationalism, 1945–60*. Montreal and Kingston: McGill-Queen's University Press, 1985.
Bérard, Frédéric. *Charte canadienne et droits linguistiques: pour en finir avec les mythes*. Montreal: Presses de l'Université de Montréal, 2016.
–. "Le phénomène des écoles passerelles : un pont entre la réalité et la fiction." *Revue juridique Thémis* 2–3, 51 (2017): 439–64.
Bergeron, Gerard. "Quebec in Isolation." In *And No One Cheered*, ed. Keith Banting and Richard Simeon, 59–73. Toronto: Methuen, 1983.
Bickel, Alexander M. *The Least Dangerous Branch: The Supreme Court at the Bar of Politics*. 2nd ed. New Haven, CT: Yale University Press, 1986.
Bourhis, Richard Y. "Evaluating the Impact of Bill 101 on the English-Speaking Communities of Quebec." *Language Problems and Language Planning* 43, 2 (2019): 198–229.
Boyd, Susan, Connie I. Carter, and Donald MacPherson. *More Harm Than Good: Drug Policy in Canada*. Winnipeg: Fernwood, 2016.

Boyd, Susan, Donald MacPherson, and Bud Osborn. *Raise Shit! Social Action Saving Lives.* Toronto: Fernwood, 2009.

Bricker, Darrell, and John Ibbitson. *The Big Shift: The Seismic Change in Canadian Politics, Business, and Culture and What It Means for Our Future.* Toronto: HarperCollins, 2013.

Brodie, Ian. *At the Centre of Government: The Prime Minister and the Limits on Political Power.* Montreal and Kingston: McGill-Queen's University Press, 2018.

Brouillet, Eugénie. "La Charte de la langue française et la Charte canadienne des droits et libertés: la difficile conciliation des logiques majoritaire et minoritaire." In *Légiférer en matière linguistique,* ed. Marcel Martel and Martin Pâquet, 359–88. Quebec City: Presses de l'Université Laval, 2008.

–. "Le fédéralisme canadien d'hier à aujourd'hui: quelle reconnaissance de la nation québécoise?" *Iura Vasconiae* 7 (2010): 407–27.

–. *La négation de la nation: l'identité culturelle québécoise et le fédéralisme canadien.* Montreal: Septentrion, 2006.

Brun, Henri. *Les institutions démocratiques du Québec et Canada.* Montreal: Wilson and Lafleur, 2013.

Burelle, André. *Le mal canadien: essai de diagnostic et esquisse d'une thérapie.* Quebec City: Éditions Fides, 1995.

Bzdera, André. "Comparative Analysis of Federal High Courts: A Political Theory of Judicial Review." *Canadian Journal of Political Science* 26, 1 (1993): 3–29.

Cain, J. *Report of the Task Force Into Illicit Narcotic Overdose Deaths in British Columbia.* Burnaby, ON: Office of the Chief Coroner, 1994.

Cairns, Alan C. *Charter versus Federalism: The Dilemmas of Constitutional Reform.* Montreal and Kingston: McGill-Queen's University Press, 1992.

–. "The Governments and Societies of Canadian Federalism." *Canadian Journal of Political Science* 10, 4 (1977): 695–725.

–. "The Judicial Committee and Its Critics." *Canadian Journal of Political Science* 4, 3 (1971): 301–45.

Cameron, David, and Richard Simeon. "Intergovernmental Relations in Canada: The Emergence of Collaborative Federalism." *Publius: The Journal of Federalism* 32, 2 (2002): 49–72.

Cameron, Jamie. "To the Rescue: Antonio Lamer and the Section 2(b) Cases from Quebec." In *The Sacred Fire: The Legacy of Antonio Lamer,* ed. Adam Dodek and Daniel Jutras, 237–62. Toronto: LexisNexis Canada, 2009.

Campbell, Larry, Neil Boyd, and Lori Culbert. *A Thousand Dreams: Vancouver's Downtown Eastside and the Fight for Its Future.* Vancouver: Douglas and McIntyre, 2009.

Canon, Bradley C. "The Supreme Court and Policy Reform: The Hollow Hope Revisited." In *Leveraging the Law: Using the Courts to Achieve Social Change,* ed. David A. Schultz, 215–49. New York: Peter Lang, 1998.

Canon, Bradley C., and Charles A. Johnson. *Judicial Policies: Implementation and Impact.* Washington, DC: CQ Press, 1999.

Carolan, Eoin. "Dialogue Isn't Working: The Case for Collaboration as a Model of Legislative–Judicial Relations." *Legal Studies* 36, 2 (2016): 209–29.

Choudhry, Sujit, and Kent Roach. "Putting the Past Behind Us? Prospective Judicial and Legislative Constitutional Remedies." *Supreme Court Law Review* (2d) 21 (2003): 205–66.

Chouinard, Stéphanie. "Section 23 of the Charter and Official-Language Minority Instruction in Canada: The Judiciary's Impact and Limits in Education Policymaking."

In *Policy Change, Courts, and the Canadian Constitution*, ed. Emmett Macfarlane, 230–49. Toronto: University of Toronto Press, 2018.

Clark, Tom S. *The Limits of Judicial Independence*. New York: Cambridge University Press, 2011.

Clarke, Harold D., Allan Kornberg, Thomas Scotto, and Joe Twyman. "Flawless Campaign, Fragile Victory: Voting in Canada's 2006 Federal Election." *Political Science and Politics* 39, 4 (2006): 815–19.

Clarkson, Stephen, and Christina McCall. *Trudeau and Our Times*. Vol. 1: *The Magnificent Obsession*. Toronto: McClelland and Stewart, 1990.

Clayton, Cornell W., and J. Mitchell Pickerill. "The Politics of Criminal Justice: How the New Right Regime Shaped the Rehnquist Court's Criminal Justice Jurisprudence." *Georgetown Law Journal* 94 (2005): 1385–1425.

Coleman, William D. "From Bill 22 to Bill 101: The Politics of Language under the Parti Quebecois." *Canadian Journal of Political Science* 14, 3 (1981): 459–85.

–. *The Independence Movement in Quebec 1945–1980*. Toronto: University of Toronto Press, 1984.

Collins, Alexandra B., Ricky N. Bluthenthal, Jade Boyd, and Ryan McNeil. "Harnessing the Language of Overdose Prevention to Advance Evidence-Based Responses to the Opioid Crisis." *International Journal of Drug Policy* 55 (2018): 77–79.

Cossman, Brenda. "Same-Sex Marriage beyond Charter Dialogue: Charter Cases and Contestation within Government." *University of Toronto Law Journal* 69, 2 (2019): 183–210.

Cutler, Fred, and J. Scott Matthews. "The Challenge of Municipal Voting: Vancouver 2002." *Canadian Journal of Political Science* 38, 2 (2005): 359–82.

Cyr, Hugo. "The Bungling of Justice Nadon's Appointment to the Supreme Court of Canada." *Supreme Court Law Review* (2d) 67 (2014): 73–109.

Dahl, Robert A. "Decision-making in a Democracy: The Supreme Court as a National Policy-maker." *Journal of Public Law* 6 (1957): 279–95.

Davidson, Alan R. "British Columbia's Health Reform: 'New Directions' and Accountability." *Canadian Journal of Public Health* 90, S1 (1999): 35–38.

Davies, Libby. *Outside In: A Political Memoir*. Toronto: Between the Lines, 2019.

Desautels, Éric. *Langue de l'affichage public des entreprises de l'île de Montréal, de février à mai 2017*. Montreal: Office québécois de la langue française, 2018.

Dixon, Rosalind. "An Australian (Partial) Bill of Rights." *International Journal of Constitutional Law* 14, 1 (2016): 80–98.

–. "Weak-form Judicial Review and American Exceptionalism." *Oxford Journal of Legal Studies* 32, 3 (2012): 487–506.

Do, Min. "Throughput Legitimacy and the Duty to Consult: The Limits of Law to Produce Quality Interactions in British Columbia's EA Process," *Canadian Journal of Political Science* 53, 3 (2020): 577–95.

Dodek, Adam M. "The Canadian Override: Constitutional Model or Bête Noire of Constitutional Politics?" *Israel Law Review* 49, 1 (2016): 45–65.

–. "The Politics of the Senate Reform Reference: Fidelity, Frustration, and Federal Unilateralism." *McGill Law Journal* 60, 4 (2015): 623–72.

Dooling, Kathleen, and Michael Rachlis. "Vancouver's Supervised Injection Facility Challenges Canada's Drug Laws." *Canadian Medical Association Journal* 182, 13 (2010): 1440–44.

Downie, Jocelyn. "Bouquets and Brickbats for the Proposed Assisted Dying Legislation." *Policy Options*, April 20, 2016.

–. *Dying Justice: A Case for Decriminalizing Euthanasia & Assisted Suicide in Canada.* Toronto: University of Toronto Press, 2004.

–. "Permitting Voluntary Euthanasia and Assisted Suicide: Law Reform Pathways for Common Law Jurisdictions." *QUT Law Review* 16, 1 (2016): 84–112.

–. "From Prohibition to Permission: The Winding Road of Medical Assistance in Dying in Canada." *HEC Forum*, 2022.

Downie, Jocelyn, and Kate Scallion. "Foreseeably Unclear: The Meaning of the 'Reasonably Foreseeable' Criterion for Access to Medical Assistance in Dying in Canada." *Dalhousie Law Journal* 41, 1 (2018): 23–57.

Duchêne, Nadia. "Aménagement linguistique, éducation et cohésion sociale en contexte multiculturel." *Language Problems and Language Planning* 36, 3 (2012): 237–51.

Duclos, Nitya, and Kent Roach. "Constitutional Remedies as Constitutional Hints: A Comment on R v Schachter." *McGill Law Journal* 36 (1990): 1–38.

Eggertson, Laura. "Legislation Jeopardizes Safe Injection Sites." *Canadian Medical Association Journal* 187, 8 (2015): 225–26.

Epp, Charles R. *The Rights Revolution: Lawyers, Activists, and Supreme Courts in Comparative Perspective.* Chicago: University of Chicago Press, 1998.

Erdman, Joanna N. "In the Back Alleys of Heath Care: Abortion, Equality, and Community in Canada." *Emory Law Journal* 56 (2006): 1093–1155.

–. "A Constitutional Future for Abortion Rights in Canada." *Alberta Law Review* 54, 3 (2016): 727–51.

–. "Constitutionalizing Abortion Rights in Canada." *Ottawa Law Review* 49, 1 (2017): 221–61.

Erdos, David. "Aversive Constitutionalism in the Westminster World: The Genesis of the New Zealand Bill of Rights Act (1990)." *International Journal of Constitutional Law* 5, 2 (2007): 343–69.

–. *Delegating Rights Protection: The Rise of Bills of Rights in the Westminster World.* Oxford: Oxford University Press, 2010.

Ewing, K.D. *Bonfire of the Liberties: New Labour, Human Rights, and the Rule of Law.* Oxford: Oxford University Press, 2010.

Fierlbeck, Katherine. *Health Care in Canada: A Citizen's Guide to Policy and Politics.* Toronto: University of Toronto Press, 2011.

Flanagan, Thomas. "The Staying Power of the Legislative Status Quo: Collective Choice in Canada's Parliament after Morgentaler." *Canadian Journal of Political Science* 30, 1 (1997): 31–53.

Flood, Colleen, M., Carolyn Tuohy, and Mark Stabile. "What Is In and Out of Medicare? Who Decides?" In *Just Medicare: What's In, What's Out, How We Decide,* ed. Colleen M. Flood, 15–41. Toronto: University of Toronto Press, 2006.

Forum Research. "Support for Assisted Suicide Increases." News release. June 15, 2014.

–. "Three Quarters Approve of Supreme Court Ruling on Assisted Death." News release. February 11, 2015.

Foucher, McPierre. "L'interprétation des droits linguistiques constitutionnels par la Cour suprême du Canada." *Ottawa Law Review* 19, 2 (1987): 381–411.

Frolic, Andrea, and Allyson Oliphant. "Introducing Medical Assistance in Dying in Canada: Lessons on Pragmatic Ethics and the Implementation of a Morally Contested Practice." *HEC Forum*, August 4, 2022.

Gagnon, Alain G., and Alex Schwartz. "Canadian Federalism since Patriation: Advancing a Federalism of Empowerment." In *Patriation and Its Consequences: Constitution*

Making in Canada, ed. Lois Harder and Steve Patten, 244–66. Vancouver: UBC Press, 2015.

Gagnon, Alain G., and Guy Lachapelle. "Québec Confronts Canada: Two Competing Societal Projects Searching for Legitimacy." *Publius: The Journal of Federalism* 26, 3 (1996): 177–91.

Gagnon, Alain G., and Guy Laforest. "The Future of Federalism: Lessons from Canada and Quebec." *International Journal* 28, 3 (1993): 470–91.

Gagnon, Alain-G., and Raffaele Iacovino. *Federalism, Citizenship and Quebec*. Toronto: University of Toronto Press, 2006.

Galanter, Marc. "Why the 'Haves' Come out Ahead: Speculations on the Limits of Legal Change." *Law & Society Review* 9, 1 (1974): 95–160.

Garcea, Joseph. "The Immigration Clause in the Meech Lake Accord." *Manitoba Law Journal* 21, 2 (1992): 274–300.

Gardbaum, Stephen. *The New Commonwealth Model of Constitutionalism: Theory and Practice*. Cambridge, UK: Cambridge University Press, 2013.

–. "Reassessing the New Commonwealth Model of Constitutionalism." *International Journal of Constitutional Law* 8, 2 (2010): 167–206.

Geiringer, Claudia. "Moving beyond the Constitutionalism/Democracy Dilemma: 'Commonwealth Model's Scholarship and the Fixation on Legislative Compliance." In *The Unity of Public Law? Doctrinal, Theoretical and Comparative Perspectives*, ed. Mark Elliot, Jason N.E. Varuhas, and Shona Wilson Stark, 301–26. London: Hart, 2018.

–. "What's the Story? The Instability of the Australasian Bills of Rights." *International Journal of Constitutional Law* 14, 1 (2016): 156–74.

Gibson, Dale. *The Law of the Charter: General Principles*. Toronto: Carswell, 1983.

Ginsburg, Tom. *Judicial Review in New Democracies: Constitutional Courts in Asian Cases*. New York: Cambridge University Press, 2003.

Giroux, Michelle. "Informing the Future of End-of-Life Care in Canada: Lessons from the Quebec Legislative Experience." *Dalhousie Law Journal* 39 (2016): 431–54.

Glover, Kate. "Structure, Substance and Spirit: Lessons in Constitutional Architecture from the Senate Reform Reference." *Supreme Court Law Review* (2d) 67 (2014): 221–55.

Godbout, Jean-François. *Lost on Division: Party Unity in the Canadian Parliament*. Toronto: University of Toronto Press, 2020.

Green, Ian, and Peter McCormick. *Beverley McLachlin: The Legacy of a Supreme Court Chief Justice*. Toronto: Lorimer, 2019.

Green, William. "Schools, Signs, and Separation: Quebec Anglophones, Canadian Constitutional Politics, and International Language Rights." *Denver International Journal of International Law and Policy* 27, 3 (1999): 449–81.

Halfmann, Drew. *Doctors and Demonstrators: How Political Institutions Shape Abortion Law in the United States, Britain, and Canada*. Chicago: University of Chicago Press, 2011.

Hall, Matthew E.K. *The Nature of Supreme Court Power*. New York: Cambridge University Press, 2010.

–. "The Semiconstrained Court: Public Opinion, the Separation of Powers, and the U.S. Supreme Court's Fear of Nonimplementation." *American Journal of Political Science* 58, 2 (2014): 352–66.

Hamilton, Alexander, John Jay, and James Madison. *The Federalist: The Gideon Addition*. Indianapolis: Liberty Fund, 2001.

Harmes, Adam. "The Political Economy of Open Federalism." *Canadian Journal of Political Science* 40, 2 (2007): 417–37.

Hennigar, Matthew A. "Expanding the 'Dialogue' Debate: Federal Government Responses to Lower Court Charter Decisions." *Canadian Journal of Political Science* 37, 1 (2004): 3–21.
–. "Exploring Complex Judicial-Executive Interaction: Federal Government Concessions in Charter of Rights Cases." *Canadian Journal of Political Science* 43, 4 (2010): 821–42.
"The Most Important Charter Right? The Rise and Future of Section 7." In *Constitutional Crossroads: Reflections on Charter Rights, Reconciliation, and Change*, ed. Kate Puddister and Emmett Macfarlane, 160–76. Vancouver: UBC Press, 2022.
–. "Reference Re Same-Sex Marriage: Making Sense of the Government's Litigation Strategy." In *Contested Constitutionalism: Reflections on the Canadian Charter of Rights and Freedoms*, ed. James B. Kelly and Christopher P. Manfredi, 209–30. Vancouver: UBC Press, 2009.
–. "Unreasonable Disagreement: Judicial-Executive Exchanges About Charter Reasonableness in the Harper Era." *Osgoode Hall Law Journal* 54, 4 (2017): 1245–74.
Hiebert, Janet L. *Charter Conflicts: What Is Parliament's Role?* Montreal and Kingston: McGill-Queen's University Press, 2002.
–. "The Charter's Influence on Legislation: Political Strategizing about Risk: Presidential Address to the Canadian Political Science Association, Regina, Saskatchewan, May 31, 2018." *Canadian Journal of Political Science* 51, 4 (2018): 727–47.
–. "Compromise and the Notwithstanding Clause: Why the Dominant Narrative Distorts Our Understanding." In *Contested Constitutionalism: Reflections on the Canadian Charter of Rights and Freedoms*, ed. James B. Kelly and Christopher P. Manfredi. Vancouver: UBC Press, 2009.
–. "Interpreting a Bill of Rights: The Importance of Legislative Rights Review." *British Journal of Political Science* 35, 2 (2005): 235–55.
–. "The Notwithstanding Clause and Charter Compliance: Why Infrequent Use Should Not Be Equated with Charter Compliance." In *Oxford Handbook of the Canadian Constitution*, ed. Peter Oliver, Patrick Macklem, and Nathalie Des Rosiers. Oxford: Oxford University Press, 2017.
–. "Parliamentary Bills of Rights: An Alternative Model?" *Modern Law Review* 69, 1 (2006): 7–28.
Hiebert, Janet L., and James B. Kelly. *Parliamentary Bills of Rights: The Experiences of New Zealand and the United Kingdom*. Cambridge, UK: Cambridge University Press, 2015.
Hirschl, Ran. *Towards Juristocracy: The Origins and Consequences of the New Constitutionalism*. Cambridge, MA: Harvard University Press, 2009.
Hogg, Peter W. *Constitutional Law in Canada*. Toronto: Carswell, 2008.
Hogg, Peter W., and Allison A. Bushell. "The Charter Dialogue between Courts and Legislatures (Or Perhaps the Charter of Rights Isn't Such a Bad Thing after All)." *Osgoode Hall Law Journal* 35 (1997): 75–124.
Hogg, Peter W., and Allison A. Bushell Thornton. "Reply to Six Degrees of Dialogue." *Osgoode Hall Law Journal* 37, 3 (1999): 529–36.
Hogg, Peter W., Allison A. Bushell Thornton, and Wade K. Wright. "Charter Dialogue Revisited – or 'Much Ado About Metaphors.'" *Osgoode Hall Law Journal* 45, 1 (2007): 1–65.
Hogg, Peter W., and Annika Wang. "The Special Joint Committee on the Constitution of Canada, 1980–81." *Supreme Court Law Review* (2d) 81 (2017): 1–23.

Huscroft, Grant. "Constitutionalism from the Top Down." *Osgoode Hall Law Journal* 45, 1 (2007): 91–104.
–. "'Thank God We're Here': Judicial Exclusivity in Charter Interpretation and Its Consequences." *Supreme Court Law Review* (2d) 25 (2004): 241–67.
Hyshka, Elaine, Jalene Anderson, Zing-Wae Wong, and T. Cameron Wild. *Risk Behaviours and Service Needs of Marginalized People Who Use Drugs in Edmonton's Inner City: Results from the Edmonton Drug Use and Health Survey*. Edmonton: University of Alberta School of Pubic Health, January 7, 2016.
Hyshka, Elaine, Jalene Anderson-Baron, Kamagaju Karekezi, Lynne Belle-Isle, Richard Elliott, Bernie Pauly, Carol Strike, et al. "Harm Reduction in Name, But Not Substance: A Comparative Analysis of Current Canadian Provincial and Territorial Policy Frameworks." *Harm Reduction Journal* 14, 1 (2017): 1–15.
IPSOS. *Support for Medically-Assisted Dying in Canada*. January 2021.
–. *Support for Medically-Assisted Dying in Canada*. February 2021.
Johnstone, Rachael. "Canadian Abortion Policy and the Limitations of Litigation." In *Policy Change, Courts, and the Canadian Constitution*, ed. Emmett Macfarlane, 336–55. Toronto: University of Toronto Press, 2018.
–. *After Morgentaler: The Politics of Abortion in Canada*. Vancouver: UBC Press, 2017.
Kam, Christopher J. *Party Discipline and Parliamentary Politics*. Cambridge, UK: Cambridge University Press, 2009.
Kavanagh, Aileen. "A Hard Look at the Last Word." *Oxford Journal of Legal Studies* 35, 4 (2015): 825–47.
–. "The Lure and the Limits of Dialogue." *University of Toronto Law Journal* 66, 1 (2016): 83–120.
–. "What's So Weak About "Weak-Form Review"? The Case of the UK Human Rights Act 1998." *International Journal of Constitutional Law* 13, 4 (2015): 1008–39.
Kelly, James B. "Bureaucratic Activism and the Charter of Rights and Freedoms: The Department of Justice and Its Entry into the Centre of Government." *Canadian Public Administration* 42, 4 (1999): 476–511.
–. "Buzz Lightyear and Quebec's Bill 101: Space Ranger or Agent Provocateur?" Presented at Constitutions, Federations, Democracies: A Comparative Assessment of the United States, Canada, and Australia, University of Southern California, Los Angeles. February 28, 2013.
–. "The Charter of the French Language and the Supreme Court of Canada: Assessing Whether Constitutional Design Can Influence Policy Outcomes." In *Policy Change, Courts, and the Canadian Constitution*, ed. Emmett Macfarlane, 250–68. Toronto: University of Toronto Press, 2018.
–. "A Difficult Dialogue: Statements of Compatibility and the Victorian Charter of Human Rights and Responsibilities Act." *Australian Journal of Political Science* 46, 2 (2011): 257–79.
–. *Governing with the Charter: Legislative and Judicial Activism and Framers' Intent*. Vancouver: UBC Press, 2005.
–. "Judicial and Political Review as Limited Insurance: The Functioning of the New Zealand Bill of Rights Act in 'Hard' Cases." *Commonwealth and Comparative Politics* 49, 3 (2011): 295–317.
–. "Legislative Activism and Parliamentary Bills of Rights: Institutional Lessons for Canada." In *Contested Constitutionalism: Reflections on the Canadian Charter of Rights*

and Freedoms, ed. James B. Kelly and Christopher P. Manfredi, 86–106. Vancouver: UBC Press, 2009.

–. "Les limites de la mobilisation judiciaire: Alliance Québec, la Charte de la langue française et la Charte canadienne des droits et libertés." In *Le nouvel ordre constitutionnel canadien: du rapatriement de 1982 à nos jours*, ed. François Rocher and Benoît Pelletier, 205–33. Montreal: Presses de l'Université du Québec, 2013.

–. "Reconciling Rights and Federalism during Review of the Charter of Rights and Freedoms: The Supreme Court of Canada and the Centralization Thesis, 1982 to 1999." *Canadian Journal of Political Science* 34, 2 (2001): 321–55.

Kelly, James B., and Kate Puddister. "Criminal Justice Policy during the Harper Era: Private Member's Bills, Penal Populism, and the Criminal Code of Canada." *Canadian Journal of Law and Society* 32, 3 (2017): 391–415.

Kelly, James B., and Matthew A. Hennigar. "The *Canadian Charter* of Rights and the Minister of Justice: Weak-Form Review within a Constitutional Charter of Rights." *International Journal of Constitutional Law* 10, 1 (2012): 35–68.

Kelly, James B., and Michael Murphy. "Shaping the Constitutional Dialogue on Federalism: Canada's Supreme Court as Meta-Political Actor," *Publius: The Journal of Federalism* 35, 2 (2005): 217–43.

Kerr, Thomas, Sanjana Mitra, Mary Clare Kennedy, and Ryan McNeil. "Supervised Injection Facilities in Canada: Past, Present, and Future." *Harm Reduction Journal* 14, 1 (2017): 1–9.

Kislowicz, Howard. "Loyola High School v Attorney General of Quebec: On Non-Triviality and the Charter Value of Religious Freedom." *Supreme Court Law Review* (2d) 71 (2015): 331–51.

Knopff, Rainer, Rhonda Evans, Dennis Baker, and Dave Snow. "Dialogue: Clarified and Reconsidered." *Osgoode Hall Law Journal* 54, 2 (2017): 609–44.

L'Heureux-Dubé, Claire. "The Dissenting Opinion: Voice of the Future." *Osgoode Hall Law Journal* 38, 3 (2000): 495–517.

Laforest, Guy. "The Internal Exile of Quebecers in the Canada of the Charter." In *Contested Constitutionalism: Reflections on the Canadian Charter of Rights and Freedoms*, ed. James B. Kelly and Christopher P. Manfredi, 251–62. Vancouver: UBC Press, 2009.

–. "Interpreting the Political Heritage of André Laurendeau." In *After Meech Lake: Lessons for the Future*, ed. David E. Smith, Peter MacKinnon, and John C. Courtney, 99–107. Saskatoon: Fifth House, 1991.

–. *Trudeau and the End of a Canadian Dream*. Montreal and Kingston: McGill-Queen's University Press, 1995.

Laforest, Guy, avec la collaboration de Jean-Oliver Roy. *Un Québec exilé dans la fédération: essais d'histoire intellectuelle et de pensée politique*. Montreal: Québec Amérique, 2014.

Laforest, Guy, and Rosalie Readman. "More Distress Than Enchantment: The Constitutional Negotiations of November 1981 as Seen from Quebec." In *Patriation and Its Consequences: Constitution Making in Canada*, ed. Lois Harder and Steve Patten, 159–79. Vancouver: UBC Press, 2016.

LaSelva, Samuel V. "Re-imagining Confederation: Moving Beyond the Trudeau-Lévesque Debate." *Canadian Journal of Political Science* 26, 4 (1999): 699–720.

Leckey, Robert. "Assisted Dying, Suspended Declarations, and Dialogue's Time." *University of Toronto Law Journal* 69, 1 (2019): 64–83.

–. *Bills of Rights in the Common Law*. Cambridge, UK: Cambridge University Press, 2016.

–. "Remedial Practice Beyond Constitutional Text." *American Journal of Comparative Law* 64, 1 (2016): 1–35.

Lemmens, Trudo. "Charter Scrutiny of Canada's Medical Assistance in Dying Law and the Shifting Landscape of Belgian and Dutch Euthanasia Practice." In *Assisted Death: Legal, Social and Ethical Issues*, ed. Derek B.M. Ross, 459–544. Toronto: LexisNexis, 2018.

Leslie, Peter. "Canada: The Supreme Court Sets Rules for the Secession of Quebec." *Publius: The Journal of Federalism* 29, 2 (1999): 135–51.

Livingston, James D. "Supervised Consumption Sites and Crime: Scrutinizing the Methodological Weaknesses and Aberrant Results of a Government Report in Alberta, Canada." *Harm Reduction Journal* 18, 4 (2021): 1–5.

Lupick, Travis. *Fighting for Space: How a Group of Drug Users Transformed One City's Struggle with Addiction*. Vancouver: Arsenal Pulp Press, 2017.

MacDonald, Ian. *From Bourassa to Bourassa: Wilderness to Restoration*. Montreal and Kingston: McGill-Queen's University Press, 2002.

MacDonnell, Vanessa J. "A Theory of Quasi-Constitutional Legislation." *Osgoode Hall Law Journal* 53, 2 (2015): 508–39.

Macfarlane, Emmett. *Constitutional Pariah: Reference re Senate Reform and the Future of Parliament*. Vancouver: UBC Press, 2021.

–. "Dialogue, Remedies, and Positive Rights: Carter v Canada as a Microcosm for Past and Future Issues under the Charter of Rights and Freedoms." *Ottawa Law Review* 49, 1 (2017): 107–29.

–. "Dialogue or Compliance? Measuring Legislatures' Policy Responses to Court Rulings on Rights." *International Political Science Review* 34, 1 (2013): 39–56.

–. "The Dilemma of Positive Rights: Access to Health Care and the *Canadian Charter of Rights and Freedoms*." *Journal of Canadian Studies* 48, 3 (2014): 49–78.

–. "Introduction: Judicial Policy Impact in Canada." In *Policy Change, Courts, and the Canadian Constitution*, ed. Emmett Macfarlane, 3–18. Toronto: University of Toronto Press, 2018.

–. "Positive Rights and Section 15 of the Charter: Addressing a Dilemma." *National Journal of Constitutional Law* 38, 1 (2018): 147–68.

–. "Provincial Constitutions, the Amending Formula, and Unilateral Amendments to the Constitution of Canada: An Analysis of Quebec's Bill 96." *Osgoode Hall Law Journal* (forthcoming).

–. "Unsteady Architecture: Ambiguity, the Senate Reference, and the Future of Constitutional Amendment in Canada." *McGill Law Journal* 60, 4 (2015): 883–903.

–. "'You Can't Always Get What You Want': Regime Politics, the Supreme Court of Canada, and the Harper Government." *Canadian Journal of Political Science* 51, 1 (2018): 1–21.

MacPherson, Donald. *A Framework for Action: A Four-Pillar Approach to Drug Problems in Vancouver*. Vancouver: City of Vancouver, 2001.

Magnet, Joseph Eliot. *Official Languages of Canada: Perspectives from Law, Policy, and the Future*. Cowansville, QC: Editions Yvon Blais, 1995.

Mallory, J.R. "Disallowance and the National Interest: The Alberta Social Credit Legislation of 1937." *Canadian Journal of Economics and Political Science* 14, 3 (1948): 342–57.

–. *Social Credit and the Federal Power in Canada*. Toronto: University of Toronto Press, 1954.

Mandel, Michael. *The Charter of Rights and the Legalization of Politics in Canada.* Toronto: Thompson, 1994.

Manfredi, Christopher P. "Adjudication, Policy-Making and the Supreme Court of Canada: Lessons from the Experience of the United States." *Canadian Journal of Political Science* 22, 2 (1989): 313–35.

–. "'Appropriate and Just in the Circumstances': Public Policy and the Enforcement of Rights under the *Canadian Charter* of Rights and Freedoms." *Canadian Journal of Political Science* 27, 3 (1994): 435–63.

–. "Conservatives, the Supreme Court of Canada and the Constitution: Judicial-Government Relations, 2006–2015." *Osgoode Hall Law Journal* 52, 3 (2015): 951–84.

–. *Feminist Activism in the Supreme Court: Legal Mobilization and the Women's Legal Education and Action Fund.* Vancouver: UBC Press, 2005.

–. *Judicial Power and the Charter: Canada and the Paradox of Liberal Constitutionalism.* 2nd ed. Don Mills, ON: Oxford University Press, 2001.

–. "Judicial Power and the Charter: Three Myths and a Political Analysis." *Supreme Court Law Review* (2d) 14 (2001): 331–39.

Manfredi, Christopher P., and James B. Kelly. "Dialogue, Deference and Restraint: Judicial Independence and Trial Procedures." *Saskatchewan Law Review* 64, 3 (2001): 323–46.

–. "Misrepresenting the Supreme Court's Record? A Comment on Sujit Choudhry and Claire E. Hunter, Measuring Judicial Activism on the Supreme Court of Canada." *McGill Law Journal* 49, 4 (2003): 741–64.

–. "Six Degrees of Dialogue: A Response to Hogg and Bushell." *Osgoode Hall Law Journal* 37, 3 (1999): 513–27.

Manfredi, Christopher P., and Antonia Maioni. *Health Care and the Charter: Legal Mobilization and Policy Change in Canada.* Vancouver: UBC Press, 2018.

Manson-Singer, Chaviva, and Sara Allin. "Understanding the Policy Context and Conditions Necessary for the Establishment of Supervised Consumption Sites in Canada: A Comparative Analysis of Alberta and Manitoba." *Health Reform Observer* 8, 2 (2020): 1–22.

Mathen, Carissima. *Courts without Cases: The Law and Politics of Advisory Opinions.* Oxford: Hart, 2019.

–. "Dialogue Theory, Judicial Review, and Judicial Supremacy: A Comment on Charter Dialogue Revisited." *Osgoode Hall Law Journal* 45, 1 (2007): 125–46.

–. "Dissent and Judicial Authority in Charter Cases." *University of New Brunswick Law Journal* 52 (2003): 321–32.

–. "A Recent History of Government Responses to Constitutional Litigation." *Constitutional Forum* 25, 3 (2016): 101–8.

–. "The Shadow of Absurdity and the Challenge of Easy Cases: Looking Back on the Supreme Court Act Reference." *Supreme Court Law Review* (2d) 71 (2016): 161–89.

Mathen, Carissima, and Michael Plaxton. *The Tenth Justice: Judicial Appointments, Marc Nadon, and the Supreme Court Act Reference.* Vancouver: UBC Press, 2020.

McAllister, Debra M. "Charter Remedies and Jurisdiction to Grant Them: The Evolution of Section 24 (1) and Section 52 (1)." *Supreme Court Law Review* (2d) 25 (2004): 1–76.

McCormick, Peter J. "The Choral Court: Separate Concurrence and the McLachlin Court, 2000–2004." *Ottawa Law Review* 37, 1 (2005): 1–33.

McCormick, Peter J., and Mark D. Zanoni. *By the Court: Anonymous Judgments at the Supreme Court of Canada.* Vancouver: UBC Press, 2020.

McDonald, Leighton. "Rights, Dialogue and Democratic Objections to Judicial Review." *Federal Law Review* 32, 1 (2004): 1–28.

McDonald, Terry. "The Québec Provincial Election of 1998 plus c'est la même chose, plus ça change!" *Representation* 36, 1 (1999): 85–96.

McKenna, Kate. *No Choice: the 30-year Fight for Abortion in Prince Edward Island*. Halifax: Fernwood Press, 2018.

McLeod Arnopoulos, Sheila, and Dominique Clift. *The English Fact in Quebec*. 2nd ed. Montreal and Kingston: McGill-Queen's University Press, 1984.

McMorrow, Thomas "MAID in Canada?: Debating the Constitutionality of Canada's New Medical Assistance in Dying Law." *Dalhousie Law Journal* 44, 1 (2018): 69–120.

McNabb, Danielle, and Dennis Baker, "Ignoring Implementation: Defects in Canada's 'Rape Shield' Policy Cycle." *Canadian Journal of Law and Society* 36, 1 (2021): 23–46.

McRoberts, Kenneth. *Misconceiving Canada: The Struggle for National Unity*. Don Mills, ON: Oxford University Press, 1997.

–. *Quebec: Social Change and Political Crisis*. Toronto: McClelland and Stewart, 1993.

Meadwell, Hudson. "The Future of Quebec." *Scottish Affairs* 37, 2 (2014): 54–64.

Monahan, Patrick J. *Meech Lake: The Inside Story*. Toronto: University of Toronto Press, 1991.

Montigny, Yves de. "The Impact (Real or Apprehended) of the *Canadian Charter* of Rights and Freedoms on the Legislative Authority of Quebec." In *Charting the Consequences: The Impact of the Charter of Rights on Canadian Law and Politics*, ed. David Schneiderman and Kate Sutherland, 3–33. Toronto: University of Toronto Press, 1997.

Moon, Richard. *The Constitutional Protection of Freedom of Expression*. Toronto: University of Toronto Press, 2000.

Morton, F.L. "The Effect of the Charter of Rights on Canadian Federalism." *Publius: The Journal of Federalism* 25, 3 (1995): 173–88.

–. "Judicial Politics Canadian-Style: The Supreme Court's Contribution to the Constitutional Crisis of 1982." In *Constitutional Predicament: Canada after the Referendum of 1982*, edited by Curtis Cook, 132–48. Montreal and Kingston: McGill-Queen's University Press, 1994.

Morton, F.L., and Rainer Knopff. *The Charter Revolution and the Court Party*. Toronto: University of Toronto Press, 2000.

Murray, C.R.G. "We Need to Talk: Democratic Dialogue and the Ongoing Saga of Prisoner Disenfranchisement." *Northern Ireland Legal Quarterly* 62, 1 (2011): 57–74.

Newman, Dwight. "The PHS Case and Federalism-Based Alternatives to Charter Activism." *Constitutional Forum* 22 (2013): 85.

Newman, Warren J. "Putting One's Faith in a Higher Power: Supreme Law, the Senate Reform Reference, Legislative Authority and the Amending Procedures." *National Journal of Constitutional Law* 34, 2 (2015): 99–120.

Nicolaides, Eleni. "Carter Compliance: Litigating for Access to Medical Assistance in Dying in Canada." In *Constitutional Crossroads: Reflections on Charter Rights, Reconciliation, and Change*, ed. Kate Puddister and Emmett Macfarlane, 193–213. Vancouver: UBC Press, 2022.

Nicolaides, Eleni, and Matthew A. Hennigar. "Carter Conflicts: The Supreme Court of Canada's Impact on Medical Assistance in Dying Policy." In *Policy Change, Courts, and the Canadian Constitution*, ed. Emmett Macfarlane, 313–35. Toronto: University of Toronto Press, 2018.

Nugent, John D. *Safeguarding Federalism: How States Protect Their Interests in National Policymaking*. Norman: University of Oklahoma Press, 2012.

Oliphant, Benjamin, and Léonid Sirota, "Has the Supreme Court of Canada Rejected 'Originalism'?" *Queen's Law Journal* 42, 1 (2016): 107–64.

Orwell, George. *Politics and the English Language.* London: Horizon, 1946.

Pal, Leslie A. *Interests of State: The Politics of Language, Multiculturalism, and Feminism in Canada.* Montreal and Kingston: McGill-Queen's University Press, 1993.

Palley, Howard A. "Canadian Abortion Policy: National Policy and the Impact of Federalism and Political Implementation on Access to Services." *Publius: The Journal of Federalism* 36, 4 (2006): 565–86.

Palmer, Geoffrey. *New Zealand's Constitution in Crisis: Reforming our Political System.* Dunedin, New Zealand: McIndoe, 1992.

Paquet, Mireille, and Robert Schertzer. "COVID-19 as a Complex Intergovernmental Problem." *Canadian Journal of Political Science* 53, 4 (2020): 343–47.

Pelletier, Benoît. "The Notwithstanding Clause Is at the Very Heart of Federalism." *Policy Options*, November 18, 2022.

Perrin, Benjamin. *Overdose: Heartbreak and Hope in Canada's Opioid Crisis* Toronto: Penguin Canada, 2020.

Pesut, Barbara, Sally Thorne, Catherine J. Schiller, Christine Penney, Carolyn Hoffman, Madeleine Greig, and Josette Roussel. "Medical Assistance in Dying: A Review of Canadian Nursing Regulatory Documents." *Policy, Politics, and Nursing Practice* 20, 3 (2019): 113–30.

Petter, Andrew. "Taking Dialogue Theory Much Too Seriously (Or Perhaps Charter Dialogue Isn't Such a Good Thing after All)." *Osgoode Hall Law Journal* 45, 2 (2007): 147–67.

Plaxton, Michael, and Carissima Mathen. "Purposive Interpretation, Quebec, and the Supreme Court Act." *Constitutional Forum* 22, 3 (2013): 15–25.

Pothier, Dianne. "Doctor-assisted Death Bill Falls Well within Top Court's Ruling." *Policy Options*, April 29, 2016.

Proulx, Daniel. "Loi 101, la clause-Québec et la Charte canadienne devant la Cour suprême: un cas d'espèce?" *Revue générale de droit* 16 (1985): 167–93.

Puddister, Kate. *Seeking the Court's Advice: The Politics of the Canadian Reference Power.* Vancouver: UBC Press, 2019.

Quinn, Herbert F. *The Union Nationale: Quebec Nationalism from Duplessis to Lévesque.* Toronto: University of Toronto Press, 1979.

Rémillard, Gil. *Le fédéralisme canadien: la Loi constitutionnelle de 1867.* Montreal: Québec Amérique, 1983.

Richez, Emmanuelle. "Losing Relevance: Quebec and the Constitutional Politics of Language." *Osgoode Hall Law Journal* 52, 1 (2014): 191–233.

Riddell, Troy Q. "The Impact of Legal Mobilization and Judicial Decisions: The Case of Official Minority-Language Education Policy in Canada for Francophones outside Quebec." *Law and Society Review* 38, 3 (2004): 583–610.

Riddell, Troy Q., and F.L. Morton. "Reasonable Limitations, Distinct Society and the Canada Clause: Interpretive Clauses and the Competition for Constitutional Advantage." *Canadian Journal of Political Science* 31, 3 (1998): 467–93.

Roach, Kent. "The Charter versus the Government's Crime Agenda." *Supreme Court Law Review* (2d) 58 (2012): 211–43.

–. "A Charter Reality Check: How Relevant Is the Charter to the Justness of Our Criminal Justice System?" *Supreme Court Law Review* (2d) 40 (2008): 717–59.

–. "Dialogue in Canada and the Dangers of Simplified Comparative Law and Populism" In *Constitutional Dialogue: Rights, Democracy, Institutions*, ed. Geoffrey Sigalet, Grégoire

Webber, and Rosalind Dixon, 267–307. Cambridge, UK: Cambridge University Press, 2019.
–. "Dialogue or Defiance: Legislative Reversals of Supreme Court Decisions in Canada and the United States." *International Journal of Constitutional Law* 4, 2 (2006): 347–70.
–. "Dialogic Remedies." *International Journal of Constitutional Law* 17, 3 (2019): 860–83.
–. "Principled Remedial Discretion under the Charter." *Supreme Court Law Review* (2d) 25 (2004): 101–50.
–. "Remedial Consensus and Dialogue under the Charter: General Declarations and Delayed Declarations of Invalidity." *UBC Law Review* 35, 2 (2001): 211–69.
–. "Sharpening the Dialogue Debate: The Next Decade of Scholarship." *Osgoode Hall Law Journal* 45 (2007): 169.
–. *The Supreme Court on Trial: Judicial Activism or Democratic Dialogue*. 2nd ed. Toronto: Irwin Law, 2016.
Rosenberg, Gerald N. *The Hollow Hope: Can Courts Bring About Social Change?* 2nd ed. Chicago: University of Chicago Press, 2008.
Rouleau, Paul S., and Linsey Sherman. "*Doucet-Boudreau*, Dialogue and Judicial Activism: Tempest in a Teapot?" *Ottawa Law Review* 41, 2 (2009): 171–206.
Roznai, Yaniv. "Internally Imposed Constitutions." In *The Law and Legitimacy of Imposed Constitutions*, ed. Richard Albert, Xenophon Contiades, and Alkmene Fotiadous, 45–59. New York: Routledge, 2018.
Russell, Cayley, Sameer Imtiaz, Farihah Ali, Tara Elton-Marshall, and Jürgen Rehm. "'Small Communities, Large Oversight': The Impact of Recent Legislative Changes Concerning Supervised Consumption Services on Small Communities in Ontario, Canada." *International Journal of Drug Policy* 82 (2020): 102822.
Russell, Peter H. "Can the Canadians Be a Sovereign People?" *Canadian Journal of Political Science* 24, 4 (1991): 691–709.
–. "Canadian Constraints on Judicialization from Without." *International Political Science Review* 15, 2 (1994): 165–75.
–. "The Charter and Canadian Democracy." In *Contested Constitutionalism: Reflections on the Canadian Charter of Rights and Freedoms*, ed. James B. Kelly and Christopher P. Manfredi, 287–306. Vancouver: UBC Press, 2009.
–. *Constitutional Odyssey: Can Canadians Become a Sovereign People?* Toronto: University of Toronto Press, 1993.
–. "The Effect of a Charter of Rights on the Policy-Making Role of Canadian Courts." *Canadian Public Administration* 25, 1 (1982): 1–33.
–. *The Judiciary in Canada: The Third Branch of Government*. Toronto: McGraw-Hill Ryerson, 1987.
–. "Patriation and the Law of Unintended Consequences." In *Patriation and Its Consequences: Constitution Making in Canada*, ed. Lois Harder and Steve Patten, 229–43. Vancouver: UBC Press, 2015.
–. "The Patriation and Quebec Veto References: The Supreme Court Wrestles with the Political Part of the Constitution." *Supreme Court Law Review* (2d) 54 (2011): 69–76.
–. "The Political Purposes of the *Canadian Charter* of Rights and Freedoms." *Canadian Bar Review* 61, 1 (1983): 30–54.
–. "The Supreme Court and Federal-Provincial Relations: The Political Use of Legal Resources." *Canadian Public Policy* 11, 2 (1985): 161–70.
–. "The Supreme Court Proposals in the Meech Lake Accord." *Canadian Public Policy* 14, S1 (1988): 93–106.

Ryan, Claude. "L'impact de la Charte canadienne des droits et libertés sur les droits linguistiques au Québec." *Revue du Barreau* 63 (2003): 543–606.

Savage, Larry, and Charles W. Smith. *Unions in Court: Organized Labour and the Charter of Rights and Freedoms.* Vancouver: UBC Press, 2017.

Savoie, Donald J. *Governing from the Centre: The Concentration of Power in Canadian Politics.* Toronto: University of Toronto Press, 1999.

Schneiderman, David. "Dual (Ling) Charters: The Harmonics of Rights in Canada and Quebec." *Ottawa Law Review* 24, 1 (1992): 235–63.

Schultz, David A., and Stephen E. Gottlieb. "Legal Functionalism and Social Change: A Reassessment of Rosenberg's The Hollow Hope." In *Leveraging the Law: Using the Courts to Achieve Social Change*, ed. David A. Schultz, 169–213. New York: Peter Lang, 1998.

Schultz, Richard J. *Federalism, Bureaucracy, and Public Policy.* Montreal and Kingston: McGill-Queen's University Press, 1980.

Sharpe, Robert J., and Kent Roach. *Brian Dickson: A Judge's Journey.* Toronto: University of Toronto Press, 2003.

Simeon, Richard. "Meech Lake and Shifting Conceptions of Canadian Federalism." *Canadian Public Policy* 14, S1 (1988): 7–24.

Small, Dan. "Fools Rush in Where Angels Fear to Tread." *International Journal of Drug Policy* 18, 1 (2006): 18–26.

Smiley, Donald V. "The Case against the *Canadian Charter* of Human Rights." *Canadian Journal of Political Science* 2, 3 (1969): 277–91.

–. "A Dangerous Deed: The Constitution Act, 1982." In *And No One Cheered*, ed. Keith Banting and Richard Simeon, 74–95. Toronto: Methuen, 1982.

Smith, Miriam. *Political Institutions and Lesbian and Gay Rights in the United States and Canada.* New York: Routledge, 2008.

Snow, Dave, and Kate Puddister. "Closing a Door but Opening a Policy Window: Legislating Assisted Dying in Canada." In *Policy Change, Courts, and the Canadian Constitution*, ed. Emmett Macfarlane, 40–60. Toronto: University of Toronto Press, 2018.

Snow, Dave, and Mark S. Harding. "From Normative Debates to Comparative Methodology: The Three Waves of Post-Charter Supreme Court Scholarship in Canada." *American Review of Canadian Studies* 45, 4 (201): 451–66.

Sossin, Lorne. *The Boundaries of Judicial Review: The Law of Justiciability in Canada.* 2nd ed. Toronto: Thomas Reuters, 2012.

–. "Harper's Petard? The Relationship between the Courts and the Executive under the Conservative Government." In *The Harper Decade*, 2015. http://www.theharperdecade.com/blog/2015/4/20/harpers-petard-the-relationship-between-the-courts-and-the-executive-under-the-conservative-government.

Stephenson, Scott. "Constitutional Reengineering: Dialogue's Migration from Canada to Australia." *International Journal of Constitutional Law* 11, 4 (2013): 870–97.

–. *From Dialogue to Disagreement in Comparative Rights Constitutionalism.* Sydney: Federation Press, 2016.

–. "Is the Commonwealth's Approach to Rights Constitutionalism Exportable?" *International Journal of Constitutional Law* 17, 3 (2019): 884–903.

Sterling, Andrea, and Emily van der Meulen. "'We Are Not Criminals': Sex Work Clients in Canada and the Constitution of Risk Knowledge." *Canadian Journal of Law and Society* 33, 3 (2018): 291–308.

Stevenson, Garth. *Community Besieged: The Anglophone Minority and the Politics of Quebec.* Montreal and Kingston: McGill-Queen's University Press, 1999.

Stewart, Hamish. "Constitutional Aspects of Canada's New Medically-Assisted Dying Law." In *Assisted Death: Legal, Social and Ethical Issues after Carter*, ed. Derek B.M. Ross, 438–58. Toronto: LexisNexis 2018.

–. "The Constitutionality of the New Sex Work Law." *Alberta Law Review* 54, 1 (2016): 69–88.

Stone, Bruce, and Nicholas Barry. "Constitutional Design and Australian Exceptionalism in the Adoption of National Bills of Rights." *Canadian Journal of Political Science* 47, 4 (2014): 767–85.

Strayer, Barry L. "Life under the *Canadian Charter*: Adjusting the Balance between Legislatures and Courts." *Public Law* 3 (1988): 347–69.

Stuart, Don. "The Charter Balance against Unscrupulous Law and Order Politics." *Supreme Court Law Review* (2d) 57 (2012): 13–38.

Sweet, Martin J. *Merely Judgment: Ignoring, Evading, and Trumping the Supreme Court*. Charlottesville: University of Virginia Press, 2010.

Tetley, William. "Language and Education Rights in Quebec and Canada (a Legislative History and Personal Political Diary)." *Law and Contemporary Problems* 45, 4 (1982): 177–219.

Thomas, Paul E.J., and J.P. Lewis. "Executive Creep in Canadian Provincial Legislatures." *Canadian Journal of Political Science* 52, 2 (2019): 363–83.

Tolkien, J.R.R. *The Hobbit or There and Back Again*. London: George Allen and Unwin, 1937.

Trudeau, Pierre Elliott. *Memoirs*. Toronto: McClelland and Stewart, 1993.

Tsebelis, George. "Decision Making in Political Systems: Veto Players in Presidentialism, Parliamentarism, Multicameralism and Multipartyism." *British Journal of Political Science* 25, 3 (1995): 289–325.

Turgeon, Luc, Antoine Bilodeau, Stephen E. White, and Ailsa Henderson. "A Tale of Two Liberalisms? Attitudes toward Minority Religious Symbols in Quebec and Canada." *Canadian Journal of Political Science* 52, 2 (2019): 247–65.

Tushnet, Mark. "Judicial Activism or Restraint in a Section 33 World." *University of Toronto Law Journal* 53, 1 (2003): 89–100.

–. "New Forms of Judicial Review and the Persistence of Rights and Democracy-Based Worries." *Wake Forest Law Review* 38 (2003): 813–38.

–. *Weak Courts, Strong Rights: Judicial Review and Social Welfare Rights in Comparative Constitutional Law*. Princeton, NJ: Princeton University Press, 2009.

–. "Weak-form Judicial Review: Its Implications for Legislatures." *New Zealand Journal of Public and International Law* 2, 1 (2004): 7–23.

Vanberg, Georg. "'John Marshall Has Made His Decision': Implementation, Transparency, and Public Support." In *Institutional Games and the US Supreme Court*, ed. James R. Rogers, Roy B. Flemming, and Jon R. Bond, 69–96. Charlottesville: University of Virginia Press, 2006.

VandenBeukel, Jason Robert, Christopher Cochrane, and Jean-François Godbout. "Birds of a Feather? Loyalty and Partisanship in the Reformed Canadian Senate." *Canadian Journal of Political Science* 54, 4 (2021): 830–49.

Vipond, Robert C. "Constitutional Politics and the Legacy of the Provincial Rights Movement in Canada." *Canadian Journal of Political Science* 18, 2 (1985): 267–94.

Wallace, Bruce, Flora Pagan, and Bernadette Pauly. "The Implementation of Overdose Prevention Sites as a Novel and Nimble Response during an Illegal Drug Overdose Public Health Emergency." *International Journal of Drug Policy* 66 (2019): 64–72.

Webber, Grégoire, Eric Mendelsohn, and Robert Leckey. "The Faulty Received Wisdom around the Notwithstanding Clause." *Policy Options*, 2019.

Webber, Jeremy. *Reimagining Canada: Language, Culture, Community, and the Canadian Constitution*. Montreal and Kingston: McGill-Queen's University Press, 1994.

Weinrib, Lorraine. "The *Canadian Charter*'s Override Clause: Lessons for Israel." *Israel Law Review* 49, 1 (2016): 67–102.

–. "Learning to Live with the Override." *McGill Law Journal* 35 (1990): 541–75.

White, Linda A. "Federalism and Equality Rights Implementation in Canada." *Publius: The Journal of Federalism* 44, 1 (2014): 157–82.

Williams, George, and Daniel Reynolds. *A Charter of Rights for Australia*. 4th ed. Sydney: University of New South Wales Press, 2017.

Woerhling, Jose. "Convergences et divergences entre fédéralisme et protection des droits et libertés: l'exemple des États-Unis et du Canada." *McGill Law Journal* 46 (2000): 21–68.

–. "De l'effritement à l'érosion." In *Le statut culturel du français au Québec*, ed. Michel Amyot and Gilles Bibeau, 47–75. Quebec City: Conseil supérieur de la langue française, 1984.

–. "La Reconnaissance du Québec comme société distincte et la dualité linguistique du Canada: conséquences juridiques et constitutionnelles." *Canadian Public Policy* 14, S1 (1988): 43–62.

Wood, Evan, Mark W. Tyndall, Julio S. Montaner, and Thomas Kerr. "Summary of Findings from Evaluation of a Pilot Medically Supervised Safer Injecting Facility." *Canadian Medical Association Journal* 175, 11 (2006): 1399–1404.

Wood, Evan, Thomas Kerr, Mark W. Tyndall, and Julio S.G. Montaner. "The Canadian Government's Treatment of Scientific Process and Evidence: Inside the Evaluation of North America's First Supervised Injecting Facility." *International Journal of Drug Policy* 19, 3 (2008): 220–25.

Young, Alison L. *Democratic Dialogue and the Constitution*. Oxford: Oxford University Press, 2017.

Ziegler, Bianca R., Alexander J.D. Wray, and Isaac Luginaah. "The Ever-Changing Narrative: Supervised Injection Site Policy Making in Ontario, Canada." *International Journal of Drug Policy* 74 (2019): 98–111.

Index

Note: Page numbers followed by "(f)" indicate a figure; page numbers followed by "(t)" indicate a table

abortion services: access to, 13, 42–43, 250–51, 287–88, 299; concurrent federalism, 297; equality rights (*CCRF*, s 15), 40–41, 352*n*118; failure of legislative response, 37; implementation context, 8, 13, 15, 22, 37, 40–43, 46, 250, 251, 288, 294–95, 297, 352*n*118; judicial policy impact, 294, 296; life, liberty, and security (*CCRF*, s 7), 42; *Morgentaler* (1988), 8, 13, 37, 38, 42–43, 46, 251, 284, 294, 303(t); negative rights, 38, 43, 46, 284, 294; private actors, 22, 295; settings for access, 286–88, 299–300; therapeutic abortion committee (TAC), 286–87

academic studies. *See* judicial politics scholarship; judicial politics scholarship: theories

An Act to Amend the CDSA (2013, Bill C-65), 188–93, 225, 342*n*89, 344*n*135

An Act to Amend the CDSA (2017, Bill C-37): availability by province, 47, 227, 229–33; comparison of Bill C-2 and Bill C-37, 220–26, 222(t); implementation, 43, 46–47, 208–11, 226–27, 229–33, 241, 246–47, 298; incomplete applications, 208, 213, 222(t), 223; judicial policy impact, 43, 46–47, 207–11, 220–27, 222(t), 246–47 298–299; ministerial discretion criteria, 222(t), 224; new exemptions and renewals, 222(t), 224, 226–27, 229; opioid provisions, 214, 219–20, 225; overview, 218–27, 222(t), 246–47, 298; preamble, 223; public consultations, 221, 222(t); replacement for Bill C-2, 46–47, 206–7; Senate passage, 224–25, 351*n*110; statistics, 227, 246–47, 298, 347*n*11; time frame, 225–26; transparency, 222(t), 224. *See also* Alberta, drug problem and policies

An Act Following upon the Court Decision on the Language of Instruction (Quebec, 2010, Bill 115), 56, 103

An Act on Medical Assistance in Dying (2016, Bill C-14): dialogue theory, 252–53, 264, 266–68, 276, 357*n*6, 361*n*106; equality rights (*CCRF*, s 15), 281;

extensions on remedies, 249; judicial policy impact, 8–10, 251–52, 279–80, 286, 290–92; JUST, 252–53, 267, 270–71, 273–74, 279–80, 291, 363n152; LCJC, 267, 271, 279; Liberals against, 275, 283, 364n160; life, liberty, and security (*CCRF*, s 7), 10, 253–54, 277, 281–82; limitations (*CCRF*, s 1), 263, 266–67, 270–71, 273–75, 278; non-compliance with decision, 149–50, 263–70, 358n14, 360n77; overbreadth, 282; PDAM, 19, 249, 252–53, 261–66, 276, 279–80, 291, 361n106; overview, 8–10, 248–52, 262–68; preamble, 279–80, 285; P/T Expert Advisory Group (2015), 251, 253, 276, 364n164; safeguards, 263–64, 270–71, 276–77, 282–83, 289–90, 363n140, 365n195; "second look cases," 30, 48, 248, 357n3; Senate's amendments, 9, 252–53, 275–78, 363n140; statistics on use (2016–21), 251, 286–89, 286(f), 287(f); Wilson-Raybould as minister, 8, 252–53, 263–70, 273–78, 282–83, 289–90, 361n106. *See also* Trudeau, Justin: medical assistance in dying (MAiD)
– eligibility criteria: consent, 263; *E.F.* (2016), 272–73; "grievous and irremediable" conditions, 258–60, 264, 270, 272–74, 277, 363n152; justification for RFND, 265–70; *Lamb* (2017), 281; mental illness criteria, 262, 271, 272–73, 283, 284; non-compliance with decision, 263–70, 358n14, 360n77; overview, 262–75; RFND (reasonable foreseeability of natural death), 265–84; Senate's removal of RFND, 9, 252–53, 271–76, 278, 363n140; *Truchon* (2019) overview, 281–82. *See also Truchon c Procureur général du Canada* (2019)
– implementation context: conscientious objection, 255, 279–80, 285–86, 364n181, 366n209, 366n212; federalism, 278–81, 284, 290–92; implementation chain, 265; judicial policy impact, 8–10, 265, 284, 290–92; medical professionals, 279–81, 285–86, 366n209, 366n212; overview, 278–81, 285–92;

preamble on, 279; provincial-territorial agreement, 279–81; settings for access, 279, 286–88, 287(f); statistics on use (2016–21), 251, 286–89, 286(f), 287(f)

An Act on Medical Assistance in Dying (2021, Bill C-7): access to, 285–92, 286(f), 287(f), 299–300; dialogue theory, 252; eligibility (RFND and non-RFND), 282, 286, 286(f), 289–90, 299; extensions on remedies, 249, 282, 283; federalism, 290–92, 299–300; implementation context, 284–92; judicial policy impact, 150, 283–84, 286, 290–92; Lametti as minister, 275, 282–84; medical professionals, 279–80, 285–86, 288–89, 364n181, 366n209, 366n212; mental illness criteria, 283, 284; overview, 248–50, 282–92, 299–300; political context, 282–84; preamble, 283; public opinion, 284, 365n201; response to *Truchon*, 275, 282–83; safeguards, 282–83, 289, 365n195; settings for access, 279, 286–88, 287(f), 299–300; statistics on use (2016–21), 251, 286–89, 286(f), 287(f). *See also* Trudeau, Justin: medical assistance in dying (MAiD)

An Act on the Production of Records in Sexual Offence Proceedings (1997, Bill C-46), 266, 268–70

An Act to Promote the French Language in Quebec (1969, Bill 63), 92–93, 146

An Act Respecting End-of-Life Care (Quebec, 2014, Bill 52), 10, 251, 255, 261, 281–82, 357n4, 358n17, 361n95

An Act Respecting Private Education (Quebec, 2010, Bill 115), 59(t), 60(t), 62, 70(t), 103, 115, 117(t), 137, 311(t)

activism, remedial. *See* Supreme Court of Canada: remedies (*CCRF*, s 24(1))

actors, private: abortion services, 22, 295; Court Challenges Program (CCP), 26, 67–68, 87; as implementation agents, 13, 18, 22, 36–37, 40–41, 145–46, 295; MAiD services, 295; overview, 36–37, 295; Quebec anglophones, 67, 76, 87, 110, 135, 295; Quebec signs and firm names, 18, 145–46, 158; Quebec unsubsidized private schools (UPS),

97–99, 98(f), 101, 104–5; supervised consumption sites, 295
administrative appeals (ATQ), Quebec, 105, 106, 111
agenda setting, 22, 53, 140, 142, 251–52, 291, 301. *See also* Supreme Court of Canada (SCC)
Aglukkaq, Leona, 186, 193, 196
agreement with decisions. *See* legislative responses, agreement/disagreement
Alberta: E.F. (2016), 272–73, 276; *Individual Rights Protection Act (IRPA)*, 36, 302(t); *Mahe* (1990), 68; Meech Lake Accord, 156; SCC invalidation by decision type, 51–52, 52(t); SCC remedial activism, 34–36, 35(t), 302(t); *Vriend* (1998), 36, 302(t). *See also* Kenney, Jason, Alberta UCP government
– drug problem and policies: closure of supervised consumption sites, 239–40; D. Smith's support for Harper-like policies, 234, 245–46, 353n133; exemptions under Kenney, 235, 237, 240–44, 299; exemptions under Notley, 233, 240, 299; judicial policy impact, 241–47, 299; Kenney's support for Harper-like policies, 233–47, 237(t), 299, 353n133; law-and-order approach, 234–39; *Mental Health Services Protection Act*, 239, 241–45, 299; Notley's support for sites, 210, 233, 235–38, 240, 243, 245–46, 299, 354n174; opioid crisis, 211–12, 245; OPS (overdose prevention sites), 235; overview, 210, 230, 233–47, 299; provincial regulation, 237–45, 299; public consultation, 235–36, 243–44; "recovery-oriented approach," 237, 239–40, 244–45, 299; review committee report (*Impact*), 236–39, 237(t), 242, 299; supervised consumption sites, 47, 233, 246–47, 299, 347n21, 352n122, 354n162, 356nn203–4. *See also* Kenney, Jason, Alberta UCP government
Alliance du personnel professionnel et technique de la santé, Quebec v (2018), 60(t), 62–63, 311(t)
Alliance Quebec, 67
allophones: CEGEP system, 125–26; choice of language instruction, 65–66,

93–94, 94(f), 135, 146; demographics, 146, 329n12; *Nguyen* (2009), 111, 122; *Protestant School Boards* (1984), 91–92, 94, 97–99, 98(f); *Solski* (2005), 105–6; terminology, 329n12, 335n20; universities, 126; unsubsidized private schools (UPS), 97–99, 98(f), 101, 104–5, 111–13, 119–22. *See also* Quebec: immigration; Quebec: language policy
allophones, defined, 329n12
Ambrose, Rona, 186, 190, 192–93, 196, 202–3, 213, 219
anglophones, defined, 328n4. *See also* Quebec: anglophones
Arsenault-Cameron v Prince Edward Island (2004), 36, 106, 310(t)
Attorney General (Que) v Quebec Protestant School Boards. *See Protestant School Boards* (1984)
Arvay, Joseph, 270, 273–75, 363n152
Auton v British Columbia (2004), 228, 280

Baker, Dennis, 7, 249, 316n76, 347n16
Barrette, Gaetan, 255
Bateman, Thomas, 252, 264
Baudouin, Christine, 282
Bedford, Canada v (2013): Harper's non-compliance, 5, 6, 15, 192, 226, 296, 316n76, 346n8; SCC decision, 226, 277, 307(t), 343n112
Bérard, Frédéric, 77, 148, 324n21, 330n41
Best Buy Stores Ltd., Quebec v (2015), 165–66, 338n89
Bickel, Alexander, 27, 31
Bill 52. *See An Act Respecting End-of-Life Care* (Quebec, 2014, Bill 52)
Bill 57. *See Charter of the French Language (CFL)* (1984, Bill 57)
Bill 63. *See An Act to Promote the French Language in Quebec* (1969, Bill 63)
Bill 86. *See Charter of the French Language (CFL)* (1993, Bill 86)
Bill 101. *See Charter of the French Language (CFL)* (1977, Bill 101)
Bill 104. *See Charter of the French Language (CFL)* (2002, Bill 104)
Bill 115. *See Charter of the French Language (CFL)* (2010, Bill 115)

Bill 178. *See Charter of the French Language (CFL)* (1988, Bill 178)
Bill C-2. *See Respect for Communities Act* (2015, Bill C-2)
Bill C-7. *See An Act on Medical Assistance in Dying* (2021, Bill C-7)
Bill C-14. *See An Act on Medical Assistance in Dying* (2016, Bill C-14)
Bill C-37. *See An Act to Amend the CDSA* (2017, Bill C-37)
Bill C-46. *See An Act on the Production of Records in Sexual Offence Proceedings* (1997, Bill C-46)
Bill C-65 (*An Act to Amend the CDSA*) (2013), 188–93, 225, 342*n*89, 344*n*135
bills of rights, parliamentary, 23–25, 29, 31, 47
Blaikie et al, Quebec v (1979), 67–68, 149
Blainey, Steven, 192–93, 203–4
Bloc Québécois, 283, 284, 291, 341*n*56
BNA Act. See Constitution Act (1867) (*BNA Act*)
Bourassa, Robert, Quebec Liberal government: on collective rights vs individual freedom, 153; election platform (1985), 151–53; language of instruction, 89; notwithstanding clause (*CCRF*, s 33), 56, 145, 152–53, 156–58, 163–64; *Official Language Act* (1974, Bill 22), 64–65, 93–94, 142, 147–48; signs and firm names, 145, 151–53, 154(t)–155(t)
Bourhis, Richard, 93, 93(f), 94(f), 95(f)
Bricker, Darrell, 27
"bridging schools," 112–15, 132, 137, 140. *See also Charter of the French Language (CFL)* (2010, Bill 115): education
British Columbia: *Auton* (2004), 228, 280; *Lamb* (2017), 281; SCC invalidation by decision type, 51–52, 52(t); SCC remedial activism, 34–36, 35(t), 302(t)–303(t). *See also Rodriguez v British Columbia* (1993)
– drug problem and policies: drug policy and health care, 175–76; naloxone (Narcan), 212, 216–17; opioid crisis, 210–12, 215–16, 348*n*38; OPS (overdose prevention sites), 215–18; supervised consumption sites, 47, 229, 347*n*21, 352*n*122. *See also PHS Community Services Society, Canada v* (2011); Vancouver, Downtown Eastside of Vancouver (DTES); Vancouver, Insite safe injection facility
British North America Act. See Constitution Act (1867) (*BNA Act*)
Brouillet, Eugénie, 53, 55, 120, 168, 338*n*104
Brun, Henri, 54–55, 120
Burelle, André, 95
Bushell, Allison, 21, 25, 29–30, 35, 63, 120, 295

Cairns, Alan, 31–32, 41, 169, 211, 300
Cameron, Jamie, 156
"Canada clause" (*CCRF* s 23), 77, 81–87, 82(t)–83(t). *See also* minority language rights (*CCRF*): Quebec (*CCRF*, s 23)
Canada Health Act (CHA): *Auton* (2004), 228, 280; core and non-core services, 182, 228–29, 247, 280–81; five principles, 280, 365*n*184; MAiD, 280–81; overview, 228, 280–81; supervised consumption sites, 228
Canadian Bill of Rights: court party thesis, 25–26, 31–32, 48
Canadian Charter of Rights and Freedoms (CCRF): centralizing effects of judicial review, 41, 77, 148, 300–1, 324*n*21, 330*n*41, 353*n*134; constitutional document, 24, 89; framers' intent, 51, 88–89, 100, 112–13, 138, 330*n*46; nation-building instrument, 53, 120; negative rights instrument, 11–12, 32, 38, 46, 68, 74–75, 145–46, 208, 294; strong-form vs weak-form judicial review, 23–25, 296, 301
– Quebec: decision types in invalidation, 51–52, 52(t); implementation context, 53–54; as nation-building instrument, 53; opposition to patriation, 53–55, 142–43; overview, 17–18, 50–51; Quebec as unlike other provinces, 51–54, 52(t); rationale for research focus on Quebec, 50–51, 53, 56; SCC invalidation by decision type, 51–52, 52(t); SCC invalidation of statutes and administrative decisions, 57–61, 58(t)–

60(t); unpopularity of SCC decisions, 53–54, 57, 284. *See also* education, Quebec: minority language rights; minority language rights (*CCRF*): Quebec (*CCRF*, s 23)
– by section: section 1 (*see* limitations clause [*CCRF*, s 1]); section 2 (*see* freedom of expression [*CCRF*, s 2(b)]); section 7 (*see* life, liberty, and security of person [*CCRF*, s 7]); section 15 (*see* equality rights [*CCRF*, s 15]); sections 16–23 (*see* minority language rights [*CCRF*]); section 23 (*see* minority language rights [*CCRF*]: Quebec [*CCRF*, s 23]); section 24 (*see* Supreme Court of Canada: remedies [*CCRF*, s 24(1)]); section 33 (*see* notwithstanding clause [*CCRF*, s 33])
Canadian Medical Association: conscientious objection, 260, 364n181; MAiD, 254, 255, 260, 271; supervised consumption sites, 180
Canon, Bradley, 32–33
CAQ. *See* Coalition Avenir Québec (CAQ). *See also* Legault, François, Quebec CAQ government
Carignan, Claude, 271
Carter, Kay, 255–56, 275, 290
Carter, Lee, 256
Carter II. See Carter v Canada (2016) (*Carter II*)
Carter v Canada (2015): assisted suicide in other democracies, 254–55, 257; BC Court of Appeal (2013), 256; BC Supreme Court (2011), 256, 258, 273–74, 363n152; *CC* (ss 14 and 241(b)), 10, 253, 256–60; dialogue theory, 249; eligibility criteria, 259–61, 276; equality rights (*CCRF*, s 15), 256; extensions on remedies, 249, 260–61; federalism, 43, 46; fundamental justice principles, 254, 256–58, 260, 263, 277; "grievous and irremediable" condition, 273–74, 363n152; gross disproportionality, 257, 258, 277; groups vs individuals, 275; Harper's response, 6–7, 19, 226, 260–61; implementation context, 258, 261, 290–92; inter-jurisdictional immunity, 257–58; judicial policy impact, 8–10,
150, 290–92, 299–300; life, liberty, and security (*CCRF*, s 7), 38, 43, 46, 256–60, 267, 277–78, 290, 294, 298; limitations (*CCRF*, s 1), 256, 258–60, 273–75; negative rights, 46, 150, 259–60, 290, 291, 294, 321n101; overbreadth, 257, 258, 260, 277; overview, 43, 45(t), 46, 248–49, 251; public opinion, 255, 284, 365n201; *Rodriguez* (1993), 256–59; safeguards, 259, 276; SCC judgment, 256–61, 269–71, 276
Carter v Canada (2016) (*Carter II*): interim process for approvals, 261–62, 272–73; Quebec's *Act Respecting End-of-Life Care,* 261, 361n95; RFND not required, 273; SCC judgment, 261–62, 278, 361n95
CCP. *See* Court Challenges Program (CCP)
CCRF. *See Canadian Charter of Rights and Freedoms (CCRF)*
CDSA. *See Controlled Drugs and Substances Act (CDSA)*
centralization thesis, 41, 77, 148, 300–1, 324n21, 330n41, 353n134
certificates of eligibility. *See Charter of the French Language (CFL)* (1984, Bill 57), education: certificates of eligibility
CHA. *See Canada Health Act (CHA)*
Chaoulli v Quebec (2005), 59(t), 310(t), 326n47
Charest, Jean, Quebec Liberal government: notwithstanding clause (*CCRF*, s 33), 56; overview, 103–4, 115–22; *Solski* (2005) and *Nguyen* (2009) legislative responses, 13, 103–4, 115–22, 116(t)–117(t), 131–32, 134, 140
Charlottetown Accord, 87, 156
Charter of the French Language (CFL) (1977, Bill 101): anglophones, 92–93, 100–1; appearance of compliance ("sleight of hand"), 54, 56, 76–77, 143–44; *Blaikie* (1979), 67–68, 149; *CCRF* framers' intent, 88–89, 100, 138; centralizing effects of judicial review, 41, 77, 148, 300–1, 324n21, 330n41, 353n134; comparison of language of instruction (*CCRF, CFL* 1977, *CFL*

1984), 69–72, 70(t)–71(t); comparison of Quebec and Canada clauses (*CCRF*, and *CFL* 1977 and 1984), 81–87, 82(t)–83(t); cultural identity, 146, 150; dialogue theory, 63–64, 143–44; earlier version (1977), 69; education enrollment (1971–2022), 92–93, 93(f), 94(f), 100–1; freedom of expression, xiii, 145; French as official language (s 1), 64, 67–68, 146–49; implementation context, 57, 61–64, 145–48; judicial policy impact, 143–45, 166–69; judicial review as strategy against, 65, 67–68; legislative disagreement, 14–15, 61, 73, 143–45; *Official Language Act* (1974, Bill 22) as basis, 64–65, 93–94, 146–48; overview, 17–18, 50, 64–73, 70(t)–71(t), 77–78, 138–45; political context, 7, 14–15; political purpose to invalidate, 17–18, 50–51, 68–69, 77; preamble, 150; *Protestant School Boards* (1984), 85–86, 144; provincial jurisdiction, 50, 67, 78; Quebec's opposition to patriation, 17, 53–55, 69, 142–43, 148; text of (ss 72 and 73), 70(t)–71(t); unpopularity of SCC decisions, 52–54, 57, 284; *visage linguistique*, 150–51, 164, 166–69, 335*n*12
- signs and firm names: enforcement and penalties, 149, 336*n*35; federalism, 144, 146–47; firm names, 145, 149, 152–56, 154(t)–55(t), 335*n*17; freedom of expression, 44(t), 145, 149–53, 157; implementation context, 18, 145–48; judicial policy impact, 18, 143–48, 166–69; legislative disagreement, 43–47, 44(t)–45(t), 143–46; negative rights, 145–46; overview, 18, 64–67, 142–46, 149–63; private actors, 18, 145–46, 158; research studies, 166–68, 335*n*17, 336*n*35, 338*n*102, 338*nn*96–97

Charter of the French Language (CFL) (1984, Bill 57), education: allophones, 65–66; comparison of language of instruction (*CCRF, CFL* 1977, *CFL* 1984), 69–72, 70(t)–71(t); comparison of Quebec and Canada clauses (*CCRF*, and *CFL* 1977 and 1984), 81–87, 82(t)–83(t); criteria for access to English education, 81–87, 82(t)–83(t); federal constitutional challenges, 66–67; judicial policy impact, 148; *Nguyen* (2009), 69; objectives, 65–66; overview, 72–73, 81–84, 82(t)–83(t), 138–45; *Protestant School Boards* (1984), 72–73; text of (ss 72 and 73), 70(t)–71(t). *See also* education, Quebec: minority language rights
- certificates of eligibility: criteria for access to English education, 81–87, 82(t)–83(t), 97–99, 98(f); decline in requests for, 77, 120; key questions, 75–76, 110; ministerial directives, 85, 105–6; *Nguyen* (2009), 105–6, 111, 114; overview, 75–77, 84–87, 91, 97–99, 98(f); *Protestant School Boards* (1984), 90(t), 91; *Solski* (2005), 105–8; statistics on certificates (1977–2013), 97–99, 98(f), 104, 109, 113, 137; unnecessary for private schools, 97; unsubsidized private schools (UPS), 97–99, 98(f), 101, 104–5
- major part requirement (MPR): administrative appeals, 105, 106; allophones, 91–92, 97–99, 98(f); comparison of *CCRF* (s 23) with *CFL* (1993), 89–91, 90(t); comparison of *CFL* (ss 72 and 73) and *CCRF* (s 23), 69–73, 70(t)–71(t); comparison of Quebec and Canada clauses (*CCRF*, and *CFL* 1977 and 1984), 81–87, 82(t)–83(t); ministerial directive, 36, 102, 105–6; overview, 69–73, 70(t)–71(t), 81–84, 82(t)–83(t), 84–87, 100–4, 138–41; *Protestant School Boards* (1984), 85–86, 90(t), 100–1; *Solski* (2005), 36, 105–8; text of, 70(t)–71(t), 82(t)–83(t); unsubsidized private schools (UPS), 97–99, 98(f), 101–5

Charter of the French Language (CFL) (1988, Bill 178): dialogue theory, 163; freedom of expression, 152–53, 157; notwithstanding clause, 56, 145, 152–53, 154(t)–155(t), 157; overview, 18, 151–56, 154(t)–55(t); political context, 146–48, 151–53, 156–58
- signs and firm names: comparison of *CFL* (1983 and 1988), 154(t)–155(t);

comparison of *CFL* (1988 and 1993), 145, 160(t)–162(t); *Devine* (1988) and *Ford* (1988), 58(t), 149–59, 154(t)–155(t), 163–69; firm names, 152–56, 154(t)–155(t), 159, 160(t)–162(t); inside/outside rule, 152–56, 154(t)–155(t), 158, 160(t)–161(t); "marked predominance" of French, 58(t), 151, 153, 154(t)–155(t), 157–59, 160(t)–161(t), 163–64

Charter of the French Language (CFL) (1993, Bill 86): *Blaikie* (1979), 67–68, 149; comparison of *CCRF* (s 23) with *CFL* (1993), 89–91, 90(t); MPR requirements, 89–105, 90(t), 98(f), 138–41; overview, 143–45

– signs and firm names: *Best Buy* (2015), 165–66, 338n89; comparison of *CFL* (1988 and 1993), 145, 160(t)–162(t); *Devine* (1988) and *Ford* (1988), 58(t), 149–59, 163–69; enforcement and penalties, 164–65; *Entreprises WFH* (2001), 163–64, 337n80; firm names, 158–59, 160(t)–162(t), 163–66; freedom of expression, 156, 163–64; inside/outside rule, 158; judicial policy impact, 18, 143–46, 158, 166–69; limitations (*CCRF*, s 1), 165–66; "marked predominance" of French, 145–46, 158–64, 160(t)–162(t); notwithstanding clauses, 145, 152–53, 156–59, 163–64; Office québécois de la langue française, 149, 164–68, 336n35, 338n89, 338n102, 338nn96–97; overview, 18, 58(t), 89, 152–53, 158–69, 160(t)–162(t); political context, 146–48, 156–58; private actors, 18, 158; recent cases, 163–66; regulations, 159–66, 160(t)–62(t); regulatory responses, 58(t)

Charter of the French Language (CFL) (2002, Bill 104): ban on unsubsidized private schools for MPR, 102–6, 110–13, 132; criteria for access to English education, 110–13; judicial policy impact, 148; ministerial directive, 105–6, 119; *Nguyen* (2009), 110; overview, 104–6, 110–15, 138–45, 168–69; passed unanimously, 115

Charter of the French Language (CFL) (2010, Bill 115): appearance of compliance ("sleight of hand"), 120–22, 143–44; dialogue theory, 115, 119–20, 143–44; implementation context, 137–41; judicial policy impact, 120, 138–41, 148; overview, 103, 115–22, 116(t)–118(t), 137–45, 168–69; passed with party-political vote, 115, 326n48

– education: "bridging schools," 112–15, 132, 137, 140; criteria for access to English education, 82(t)–83(t), 119–22; *Loyola High School* (2015), 60(t); ministerial directives, 119, 120, 136; MPR requirements, 108, 119–20, 125–26, 128–29, 136; *Nguyen* (2009), 103, 119–21; ombudsperson's criticisms, 136; overview, 103, 115–22, 116(t)–118(t), 137–45, 168–69; siblings' school attendance, 128–31, 130(t), 136; *Solski* (2005), 59(t), 103, 108, 115, 119–21, 123, 128, 139; tuition fees, 133(t), 134–35; types of schools, 122–37, 124(t)–125(t), 127(t), 130(t); unsubsidized private schools (UPS), 103, 115, 120–22

– education regulations: attendance at French language schools, 129(t), 130(t); "authenticity" requirements, 135–36; "bridging schools," 132, 137, 140; certificates of eligibility, 122–23, 135–39, 138(f); elite anglophone schools in Montreal, 122, 126, 132–36, 133(t), 334nn73–74; exempt schools, 126; overview, 119–43, 124(t)–125(t), 127(t)

Charter of Human Rights and Freedoms. See *Canadian Charter of Rights and Freedoms (CCRF)*

Charter of Human Rights and Freedoms (Quebec Charter): *Chaoulli* (2005), 35, 59(t), 310(t); *Devine* (1988) and *Ford* (1988), 149–53; freedom of expression (s 3), xiii, 145, 149–53; limitations (s 9.1), 150–52; notwithstanding clause, 56, 153; overview, 3–4, 17; signs and firm names (s 3), xiii, 145, 149–51; statistics on SCC decisions, 35, 323n9

Chrétien, Jean, 79, 175, 177, 182, 215, 296

Clarkson, Stephen, 99

Clayton, Cornell, 27

Clement, Tony, 173, 178–82, 186, 198, 234, 238

Coalition Avenir Québec (CAQ), 325*n*27. *See also* Legault, François, Quebec CAQ government
complex intergovernmental problems, 210–14, 217, 348*n*24
Conférence des juges de paix magistrats du Québec v Quebec (Attorney General) (2016), 60(t), 61–63, 311(t)
Conservative Party of Canada: similarity of legislative responses, 7, 14–15. *See also* Harper, Stephen, Conservative government
Constitution Act (1867) *(BNA Act)*: cabinet review of Quebec language legislation (s 90), 66; disallowance powers (s 56), 66; education jurisdiction (ss 92 and 93), 46, 50, 67, 78, 146–47, 328*n*5; federal jurisdiction for Indigenous peoples and inmates (s 91), 227, 339*n*7, 352*n*119; federal remedial powers (s 93(3)), 323*n*3; parliamentary and court proceedings in English or French (s 133), 67–68, 327*n*78
Constitution Act (1982): Meech Lake Accord, 87, 143, 150, 156–57, 168, 337*n*66; patriation, 78–81, 110, 361*n*98; Quebec's opposition to patriation, 17, 53–55, 69, 81, 142–43, 148. *See also Canadian Charter of Rights and Freedoms (CCRF); Canadian Charter of Rights and Freedoms (CCRF): by section; Canadian Charter of Rights and Freedoms (CCRF): Quebec*
Controlled Drugs and Substances Act (CDSA): dual purpose of public safety and public health, 183, 185, 187–88, 191–93, 192(f), 197–202, 220; federal jurisdiction, 171, 226–27; fundamental justice, 182–83; implementation, 43, 46–47, 226–27; life, liberty, and security (*CCRF*, s 7) in *PHS*, 178–79, 181–82; OPS outside exemption process, 215–16; overview, 43, 46–47, 170–71, 178–79; shift to/from public safety and public health purposes, 207–11, 220; specific narcotics (s 4(1)), 178–79, 181–82; text (s 56), 346*n*167; trafficking (s 5(1)), 178–79, 181–82. *See also An Act to Amend the CDSA* (2017, Bill C-37);

drug problem and policies; *PHS Community Services Society, Canada v* (2011); *Respect for Communities Act* (2015, Bill C-2); supervised consumption sites (SCS); Vancouver, Insite safe injection facility; Vancouver, Insite safe injection facility: exemptions for *CDSA*
Court Challenges Program (CCP), 26, 67–68, 87
court party thesis, 25–26, 31–32, 48
COVID-19, 212, 217, 348*n*24
Cowan, James, 271
Criminal Code (CC): federal jurisdiction, 171, 197; implementation gap, 41–43; judicial remedies, 35–36. *See also* medical assistance in dying (MAiD)
Customs Act, 220

Dahl, Robert, 27–29
Darrach, R v (2000), 24
Davies, Don, 214–15, 224–25
Davies, Libby, 177, 186, 197, 199–200
decisions of Supreme Court of Canada. *See* Quebec: Supreme Court of Canada decisions; Supreme Court of Canada (SCC): decisions
Devine v Quebec (1988): appearance of compliance ("sleight of hand"), 54, 143–44; *BNA Act* provincial jurisdiction (s 92), 67; *CFL* signs and firm names (1988, Bill 178), 58(t), 152–58, 154(t)–155(t); *CFL* signs and firm names (1993, Bill 86), 58(t), 152, 157, 158–66, 160(t)–162(t); dialogue theory, 143–44, 163; freedom of expression, 44(t), 149–53; implementation context, 144–46; judicial policy impact, 143, 166–69; limitations clauses, 150–51; "marked predominance" of French, 145–46, 151; negative rights, 145–46; notwithstanding clause (*CCRF*, s 33), 56, 145, 152, 153, 156–58; overview, 18, 44(t), 58(t), 143, 149–56; political context, 143, 149–50; SCC unanimous judgment, 145, 149–51, 296; *visage linguistique* (public face) after, 145, 149–51, 164, 166–69
dialogue theory: benefits for public policy, 48–49, 143; clarification dialogue,

186–87, 188–89, 191, 196; counter-majoritarian difficulties, 20–21, 27, 31, 34, 47–48; criticisms of, 21, 29–30, 61, 63–64, 143–44, 252–53; focus on act vs substance of response, 21, 32, 48–49, 61, 63–64, 252; lateral vs vertical issues, 33, 37, 39; MAiD, 249, 252, 266–67, 357n6, 361n106; metaphor vs theory, 49, 266–67; notwithstanding clause (*CCRF*, s 33), 21; overview, 3–4, 21, 25–26, 29–32, 48–49, 143; parliamentary and judicial supremacy, 29–31; Quebec legislative responses, 61, 63–64, 143–44, 163; salient issues, 61, 63–64, 295–96; SCC as implementer-dependent institution, 48–49, 63–64; "second look cases," 30, 48, 248, 357n3; supervised consumption sites, 186–87, 188–89, 191, 196. *See also* judicial politics scholarship: theories

Dion, Léon, 156

disagreement with decisions. *See* legislative responses, agreement/disagreement

Downie, Jocelyn, 272

Dr. Peter Centre, Vancouver, 190, 204–5, 213

drug problem and policies: community activism, 173–78, 214–15, 349n57; federalism, 172, 175–77, 210–11, 226–27, 246–47, 298–99; four-pillars approach, 175–81, 223, 339n27; harm reduction, 174–76, 178, 179, 181, 187, 203, 208, 210, 215, 217–18, 223, 229–30; HIV-AIDS crisis, 173, 174, 201, 216, 238; law-and-order approach, 175, 177–78; National Drug Strategy, 175, 178, 339n27; opioid crisis overview, 211–18, 246–47; OPS (overdose prevention sites), 208–10, 215–18, 246, 350n77; overview, 172, 173–77, 210–11. *See also* Alberta: drug problem and policies; British Columbia: drug problem and policies; Quebec: drug problem and policies

– opioid crisis: community activism, 214–15; complex intergovernmental problem, 210–14, 217, 348n24; drug traffickers, 211, 220; fentanyl, 211, 213, 216–17, 220; harm reduction, 210, 215, 217–18, 229–30; HESA report, 214–15, 217; J. Trudeau's Bill C-37 provisions, 214, 219–20, 225; naloxone (Narcan), 212, 216–17; OPS (overdose prevention sites), 208–10, 215–18, 235, 246, 350n77; overview, 210–19, 246–47; as policy driver, 210–18; statistics, 211, 348n38

DTES. *See* Vancouver, Downtown Eastside of Vancouver (DTES)

EAC. *See* Expert Advisory Committee (EAC)

education, Quebec: appearance of compliance ("sleight of hand"), 54, 76–77, 120–22, 143–44; CEGEP system, 125–26; elite anglophone schools in Montreal, 122, 126, 132–36, 133(t), 334nn73–74; implementation context, 76–77, 169; judicial policy impact, 74–77, 89, 138–41, 168–69; Office québécois de la langue française, 135, 138–39; overview, 74–77, 100–1, 125–26, 168–69; private actors, 169, 295; private schools, 97; universities, 125–26; unsubsidized private schools (UPS), 97–99, 98(f), 101–5, 119–22. *See also* minority language rights (*CCRF*): Quebec (*CCRF*, s 23); *and entries beginning with* Charter of the French Language

– English school boards: enrollment decline, 92–96, 93(f), 94(f), 95(f), 141; judicial policy impact, 138–41, 168–69; key questions, 75–76; overview, 75–77, 92–96, 93(f), 94(f), 100–1; rights beneficiaries, 75; services "where numbers warrant," 11, 68–72, 70(t)–71(t), 74–75, 78, 80, 84–85, 87, 91; statistics, 75, 97

– minority language rights: constitutional patriation, 78–81, 87, 110; Court Challenges Program (CCP), 26, 67–68, 87; dialogue theory, 63–64; implementation context, 76–77; key questions, 75–76; overview, 63–64, 69–77, 70(t)–71(t), 87; pan-Canadian impacts, 91–93, 92(f), 96; positive rights, 11, 74–75, 93; salient issues, 63–64

E.F., Canada v (2016), 272–73, 276
Egan v Canada (1995), 36
emergency overdose prevention sites. See OPS (overdose prevention sites)
end-of-life medical services. See medical assistance in dying (MAiD)
Entreprises WFH Ltée c Québec (2001), 163–64, 337n80
Epp, Charles, 26
Equality Party, 156, 158
equality rights (CCRF, s 15): abortion access, 40–41, 352n118; federalism and implementation gap, 37, 40–41, 226–27, 297, 352n118; MAiD, 256, 281; same-sex marriage, 40–41, 352n118; sexual orientation, 36; tests, 293; Vriend (1998), 36, 302(t)
Erdman, Joanna, 42–43
ethical and moral issues: health care, 43, 46, 295, 364n181; overview, 43, 47; supervised consumption services, 19, 295
Ewing, K.D., 40
Expert Advisory Committee (EAC), safe injection facilities, 178, 183, 238

federal government: majority/minority governments, 27, 37, 39–40, 264, 267, 322n108; reference questions to SCC, 66–67; SCC invalidation and decision type, 51–52, 52(t); SCC remedial activism, cases, 34–36, 35(t), 303(t)–308(t); vote share (1984–2021), 39–40, 322n108. See also federalism; political parties; Senate; and names of prime ministers
federalism: complex intergovernmental problems, 210–14, 217, 348n24; constraints on judicial policy impact, 4–5, 21–23, 49, 144, 296; jurisdiction and judicial policy impact, 209–10, 250, 296–300; key questions, 38; overview, 12–13, 22–23, 49, 209–10, 296–301; two founding peoples, 146–47
– implementation context: appearance of compliance ("sleight of hand"), 54, 56, 76–77, 120–22, 143–44, 291; co-existence of legislative agreement/disagreement, 46–47; coordinated and voluntary relations of levels, 43, 46, 209–10; devolution to other levels of government, 12–13; implementation gap, 22–23, 40–43, 297–98; implementation spectrum, 250; inter-jurisdictional immunity, 178, 181–82, 187, 257–58, 340n48, 341n65; key questions, 38; legislative disagreement, 12–16, 144, 296–300; overview, 12–13, 17, 40–41, 171, 209–10, 250, 296–301; public and private actors, 4–5, 22–23, 32, 146, 294–95; salient issues, 12–14, 49; watertight federalism, 43, 144, 297. See also legislative responses, agreement/disagreement
firm names and signs. See Charter of the French Language (CFL) (1977, Bill 101): signs and firm names; Charter of the French Language (CFL) (1988, Bill 178): signs and firm names; Charter of the French Language (CFL) (1993, Bill 86): signs and firm names
Flood, Colleen, 227–28
Ford, Doug, 31, 210, 230–33, 241
Ford v Quebec (1988): appearance of compliance ("sleight of hand"), 54, 143–44; CFL signs and firm names (1988, Bill 178), 58(t), 152–58, 154(t)–155(t); CFL signs and firm names (1993, Bill 86), 58(t), 158–66, 160(t)–162(t); dialogue theory, 143–44, 163; freedom of expression, 44(t), 149–53; implementation context, 145–46; judicial policy impact, 143, 166–69; limitations clauses, 150–51, 157–58; "marked predominance" of French, 145–46, 151; negative rights, 145–46; notwithstanding clause (CCRF, s 33), 55–56, 145, 152, 153, 156–58; overview, 18, 44(t), 58(t), 143, 149–56; political context, 143, 149–50; regulatory responses as non-compliance, 58(t); SCC unanimous judgment, 145, 149–51, 296; visage linguistique (public face) after, 145, 149–51, 164, 166–69
freedom of expression (CCRF, s 2(b)): author's experience, xii–xiii; constitutional patriation, 142; Devine (1988) and Ford (1988), 44(t), 149–53; election

expenses, 62–63; *Libman* (1997), 58(t), 62–63; limitations (*CCRF*, s 1), xiii, 150–51; minority language rights, 142; negative right, 44(t), 145–46; overview, 145, 149–53; signs and firm names, 44(t), 145, 149–53, 157, 163–64
freedom of expression (*Quebec Charter*, s 3), xiii, 145, 149–53
Fry, Hedy, 186, 200
fundamental justice principles, 182–83, 254, 256–58, 263, 277

Gagnon, Alain, 120, 147, 300
Galanter, Marc, 26
Gardbaum, Stephen, 23–25
Garrison, Randall, 199
Godbout, Jean-François, 225
Gosselin v Quebec (2002), 112–13
government. *See* federal government; federalism; federalism: implementation context; political parties; provincial and territorial governments
gross disproportionality, 183, 191, 258, 277

Hall, Matthew, 21, 32–33, 37–39, 251, 284, 301
Hamilton, Alexander, 21, 32–33, 301
Harper, Stephen, Conservative government: election (2006), minority, 172, 177–78; election (2008), minority, 180–81, 341*n*56; election (2011), majority, 172, 188, 342*n*99; election (2015), defeat, 19, 170, 188, 190, 249, 260; law-and-order agenda, 5, 15, 170–71, 177–78, 181, 198–99, 203, 346*n*166; legislative responses, 6–7, 46–47, 171; majority/minority governments and vote share (1984–2021), 39–40, 322*n*108; overview, 5–7; prostitution regulation (*Bedford*), 5, 6, 192, 316*n*76; regime politics approach (RPA), 27–29
– medical assistance in dying (MAiD): dialogue theory, 249; External Panel, 249, 253, 261–62, 279, 360*n*86; notwithstanding clause not used, 261; response to *Carter* (2015), 6–7, 19, 260–61
– supervised consumption sites: delay after *PHS* (2011), 19, 172, 188–90, 225– 26; EAC report, 178, 183, 238; health ministers, 186; lack of new facility approvals, 19, 172, 178, 187–88; law-and-order approach, 170–71, 177–81, 191–93, 198–99, 203–5, 234, 346*n*166; legislative responses to *PHS* (2011), 6–7, 46–47, 170–72, 187–91, 196–97, 204–5, 225–26, 240–41; majority government, 172, 188; ministerial discretion on exemptions, 5, 182–88, 197–200, 218, 297–98, 346*n*167; National Anti-Drug Strategy, 178–80, 186, 203, 217–18; online petition, 189; opposition to, 6–7, 46–47, 177–81, 185, 187–90, 197–205, 240–41; overview, 6–7, 170–73, 177–81, 204–5, 297–98; transfer to minister of public safety, 178, 192–93, 203–4, 218. *See also Respect for Communities Act* (2015, Bill C-2)
health care: access provided by devolved assemblies, 22, 41–42; co-existence of legislative agreement/disagreement, 46–47, 228; concurrent federalism, 297; *Criminal Code* regulation, 37; implementation context, 10, 22, 43–47, 294–95, 297–98; inter-jurisdictional immunity, 178, 181–82, 187, 257–58, 340*n*48, 341*n*65; as moral issues, 43, 46, 295; negative rights cases, 38, 43, 46, 298; overview, 22–23, 37, 41–44, 294–98; private actors for implementation, 22, 37, 295. *See also* abortion services; medical assistance in dying (MAiD); supervised consumption sites (SCS)
Hennigar, Matthew, 7, 24, 63, 249, 358*n*14
HESA. *See* Standing Committee on Health (HESA)
Hiebert, Janet, 24–25
HIV-AIDS, 173, 174, 201
Hivon, Véronique, 255
Hogg, Peter, 21, 29–31, 35, 63, 120, 271, 295
human rights charters. *See Canadian Bill of Rights; Canadian Charter of Rights and Freedoms (CCRF); Charter of Human Rights and Freedoms (Quebec Charter)*
Huscroft, Grant, 29

Iacovino, Raffaele, 147
Ibbitson, John, 27
immigration, Quebec. *See* allophones; Quebec: immigration
impact of judicial decisions. *See* judicial policy impact; research project on judicial policy impact
implementation context: Alexander Hamilton on, 21, 32–33, 301; case studies, by chapter, 43–47, 44(t)–45(t); co-existence of legislative agreement/disagreement, 46–47; complex intergovernmental problems, 210–14, 217, 348*n*24; complex vs simple, 13; constraints in, 21–23; coordinated and voluntary, 43, 46; federalism, 13, 17, 296–301; implementation chain, 4–5, 43–47, 44(t)–45(t), 49; implementation gap, 40–43, 297–98; jurisdictional structure, 43–47; key questions, 38; lateral vs vertical issues, 33, 37, 39; overview, 4–5, 8, 13, 17, 22–23, 32–33, 293–95; public and private actors, 4–5, 12, 22, 146, 294–95; salient issues and legislative disagreements, 12–14, 43–47, 44(t)–45(t), 49, 144, 295–96; veto players, 43–47, 44(t)–45(t); watertight federalism, 43, 144, 297. *See also* federalism; federalism: implementation context; judicial policy impact; legislative responses, agreement/disagreement; popularity of judicial decisions
Individual Rights Protection Act (IRPA) (Alberta), 36, 302(t)
injection sites. *See* supervised consumption sites (SCS)
Insite. *See PHS Community Services Society, Canada v* (2011); Vancouver, Insite safe injection facility
inter-culturalism, 147–48
interest groups. *See* actors, private
inter-jurisdictional immunity, 178, 181–82, 187, 257–58, 340*n*48, 341*n*65
invalidation. *See* Supreme Court of Canada: remedies (*CCRF*, s 24(1))
IRPA. *See Individual Rights Protection Act (IRPA)* (Alberta)
issues, salient. *See* salient issues

Jackson, Andrew, on enforcement, 13, 205, 207
Johnson, Charles A., 32–33
Johnson, Hollis, 256
Johnstone, Rachael, 43
Joyal, Serge, 271–74, 276, 278
Judicial Committee of the Privy Council, 31–32
judicial policy impact: agenda setting, 22, 53, 140, 142, 251–52, 291, 301; constraints on the Court, 4–5, 21–23, 49, 144, 296; court hierarchies, 293; federalism, 296–301; implementation chain, 21–22, 32; implementation gap, 40–43, 226–27, 250, 281, 297; implementation spectrum, 250; judicial activism, 293; legislative delay, 188–90, 226; overview, 4, 16–17, 20–23, 293–301; popularity of decision, 12–13; research project, 16–19. *See also* implementation context; legislative responses, agreement/disagreement; popularity of judicial decisions; research project on judicial policy impact
judicial politics scholarship: key questions, 3, 13–14, 38, 47–48; neglected areas, 31–32; overview, 4, 13–14, 47–49, 300–1. *See also* research project on judicial policy impact
– theories: centralization thesis, 41, 77, 148, 300–1, 324*n*21, 330*n*41, 353*n*134; counter-majoritarian difficulties, 20–21, 27, 31, 34, 47; court as implementer-dependent institution, 31–36, 48–49, 56, 251, 301; court party thesis, 25–26, 31–32, 48; legal mobilization, 16; overview, 16–17, 23–36, 300–1; regime politics approach (RPA), 27–29; remedies (*CCRF*, s 24(1)), 33–36, 35(t); theory assumptions, 16–17, 31–32; watertight federalism, 43, 144, 297. *See also* dialogue theory; research project on judicial policy impact
judicial review: centralizing effects of, 41, 77, 148, 300–1, 324*n*21, 330*n*41, 353*n*134; overview, 3–10; "second look cases," 30, 48, 248, 357*n*3; strong-form vs weak-form, 10, 16, 23–25, 185, 257,

296, 301. *See also* Supreme Court of Canada (SCC)
judicial-legislature relationships. *See* dialogue theory; federalism; judicial policy impact; judicial politics scholarship; judicial review; *and entries beginning with* Supreme Court of Canada (SCC)
JUST. *See* Standing Committee on Justice and Human Rights (JUST)

Kavanagh, Aileen, 21, 25
Kelly, James B. *See* research project on judicial policy impact
Kenney, Jason, Alberta UCP government: applications for *CDSA* exemptions, 235, 237, 240–44; in office, 353*n*133, 354*n*174; support for Harper-like drug policies, 233–47, 237(t), 299, 353*n*133. *See also* Alberta: drug problem and policies
Knight, Wade, 120
Knopff, Rainer, 7, 25–26, 31–32, 48, 186–87, 188–89, 191, 196, 300

Laforest, Guy, 61, 95, 120, 147, 300
Lamb v Canada (2017), 281
Lametti, David, 275, 282–84
Landry, Bernard, 104
language policy: language of instruction, 17, 72; official bilingualism, 64–65, 142, 147–48. *See also* minority language rights (*CCRF*): Quebec (*CCRF*, s 23); Quebec: language policy; *and entries beginning with* Charter of the French Language
Laurendeau, André, 156
Laurin, Camille, 65, 81, 85
LCJC. *See* Standing Senate Committee on Legal and Constitutional Affairs (LCJC)
LeBlanc, Dominic, 8–9, 206–7
LeBlanc, Matthew, 252, 264
Legault, François, Quebec CAQ government, 7–8, 56, 126, 325*n*27
legislative responses, agreement/disagreement: appearance of compliance ("sleight of hand"), 54, 56, 76–77, 120–22, 143–44, 291; case studies, by chapter, 43–47, 44(t)–45(t); co-existence of legislative agreement/disagreement, 46–47; coordinated construction, 249; delay as defiance, 188–90, 226; failure to respond, 37; federalism, 296–301; implementation context, 10–11, 20–21; implementation gap, 40–43, 226–27, 294–95, 297; judicial policy impact, 142, 294–95, 297; jurisdictional structures, 43, 46–47; key questions, 38; lack of partisan response differences, 7; lateral vs vertical issues, 33, 37, 39; negative and positive rights overview, 11–12, 38, 46, 68, 73–75, 294, 298; overview, 4–8, 10–11, 14–16, 43–49, 294–301; parliamentary systems, 24, 39–40; popularity of judicial opinions, 33, 38–40, 284; salient issues, 12–14, 49, 295–96; strong-form government vs strong-form judicial review, 25, 296, 301. *See also* Quebec: legislative responses
Leslie, Megan, 197–98
Lévesque, René, Quebec PQ government: independence/sovereignty association politics, 69, 146–47; interprovincial migration of anglophones, 92, 92(f); legislative response to invalidation of *CFL*, 73, 85–89, 297; notwithstanding clause (*CCRF*, s 33), 55–56; opposition to constitutional patriation, 17, 53–55, 69, 81, 100, 142–43, 148; overview, 64–65, 73, 142–43, 297; politicization of language, 50, 64, 66–67, 69, 72, 99–100, 142–43; referendum, 66, 92
Liberal Party of Canada: judicial policy impact, 7–10; similarity of legislative responses, 7, 14–15. *See also* Chrétien, Jean; Trudeau, Justin, Liberal government; Trudeau, Pierre, Liberal government
Liberal Party of Quebec. *See* Parti Liberal du Québec
Libman v Quebec (Attorney General) (1997), 57, 58(t), 62–63, 310(t)
life, liberty, and security of person (*CCRF*, s 7): *Bedford* (2013), 277, 343*n*112; *Carter* (2015), 38, 43, 46, 256–60, 267, 277–78, 290, 294, 298; gross

disproportionality, 277; judicial policy impact, 250; *Morgentaler* (1988), 42; negative rights, 11, 45(t), 208, 250, 260, 290, 298; *PHS* (2011), 178–79, 181–82; *Rodriguez* (1993), 253–54, 258; *Truchon* (2019), 10, 265, 281–82

limitations clause (*CCRF*, s 1): constitutional patriation, 79–80; minority language rights, 79–80, 87–89, 113; *Nguyen* (2009), 111, 113; *Oakes* test, 113, 267, 278, 293; overview, 30, 113; *Protestant School Boards* (1984), 87–89; signs and firm names, 150–51, 157–58, 165–66

limitations clause (*Quebec Charter*, s 9.1), 150–52

Livingston, James, 238

Logan, R v (1990), 36

Loyola High School v Quebec (2015), 60(t), 62–63, 311(t)

Macfarlane, Emmett, 14, 27–28, 38

Mahe v Alberta (1990), 68

MAiD. *See* medical assistance in dying (MAiD)

Maioni, Antonia, 6

major part requirement (MPR). *See Charter of the French Language (CFL)* (1984, Bill 57), education: major part requirement (MPR)

Manfredi, Christopher, 6–7, 14, 20, 21–22, 25–26, 32, 251, 268–69, 301

Manitoba: MAiD conscience rights, 364n181; Meech Lake Accord, 157; SCC invalidation by decision type, 51–52, 52(t); SCC remedial activism, 34–36, 35(t), 308(t); supervised consumption sites, 229–30

Mathen, Carissima, 9–10, 15, 30

McCall, Christina, 99

McGuinty, Dalton, Ontario Liberal government, 231, 353n137

McKenna, Frank, 157, 337n66

McKeown, David, 201

McLachlin, Beverley, decisions: *Carter* (2015), 248, 254, 256–58, 263; *Mills* (1999), 269, 280; *PHS* (2011), 5, 170–71, 182–85, 187–88, 190–91, 196–97, 202, 204, 220–21, 224, 240; *Rodriguez* (1993), 254, 256–57

medical assistance in dying (MAiD): access, 284–92, 286(f), 287(f); *CC* provisions, 10, 253–54, 256–60, 265; concurrent federalism, 297; conscientious objection, 255, 260, 279–80, 285–86, 364n181, 366n209, 366n212; dialogue theory, 249, 252, 266–67, 357n6, 361n106; federalism, 250–51, 266, 284, 290–92, 299–301; implementation context, 10–11, 41–42, 250–53, 285–92, 294, 297, 299–300; judicial policy impact, 8–10, 250–52, 290–92, 299–300; legislative agreement, 285–90, 299–300; legislative disagreements, 14–16, 37, 251, 290–92, 299–300; medical associations and access, 253, 267, 285–86, 366n209, 366n212; as moral issue, 248; negative rights, 46, 250, 284, 290, 291–92, 294, 300; in other democracies, 254–55, 257; overview, 45(t), 248–53, 297, 299–300; PDAM hearings, 19, 249, 252–53, 261–66, 276, 279–80, 291, 361n106; popularity of decisions, 284, 291, 365n201; preamble to act (2021), 283; private actors for implementation, 22, 253, 295; public opinion, 253, 255, 284, 365n201; *Rodriguez* (1993), 253–54; settings for access, 279, 286–88, 287(f), 299–300; statistics on use (2016–21), 251, 286–89, 286(f), 287(f). *See also An Act on Medical Assistance in Dying* (2016, Bill C-14); *An Act on Medical Assistance in Dying* (2021, Bill C-7); *Carter v Canada* (2015); Harper, Stephen: medical assistance in dying (MAiD); Quebec: medical assistance in dying (MAiD); *Truchon c Procureur général du Canada* (2019); Trudeau, Justin: medical assistance in dying (MAiD)

Meech Lake Accord, 87, 143, 150, 156–57, 168, 337n66

Mills, R v (1999), 15, 24, 266–70, 296

minority language rights (*CCRF*): constitutional patriation, 78–81, 110; Court Challenges Program (CCP), 26, 67–68, 87; criteria to receive services, 87; overview, 78–81, 87, 110; positive rights, 11, 87; provincial jurisdiction, 78–80;

services "where numbers warrant," 78, 80. *See also* education, Quebec: minority language rights
– Quebec (*CCRF*, s 23): *CCRF* framers' intent, 17, 88–89, 100, 138; choices of rights bearers, 18, 77, 87, 93–94, 94(f), 100–1; comparison of *CCRF* (s 23) with *CFL* (1993), 89–91, 90(t); comparison of *CFL* (ss 72 and 73) and *CCRF* (s 23), 69–73, 70(t)–71(t); comparison of Quebec and Canada clauses (*CCRF*, and *CFL* 1977 and 1984), 81–87, 82(t)–83(t); constitutional patriation, 78–81, 110, 142; decline in English public instruction, 18, 92–96, 93(f), 94(f), 95(f), 100–1, 120, 141, 168–69; dual remedy (s 23(3) and s 24(1)), 69, 72; implementation context, 74, 92–93, 100–1, 137–41, 144; judicial decisions invalidating Quebec statutes, 50–53, 52(t); judicial policy impact, 74–77, 89, 99–101, 138–41, 144; key questions, 75–76; notwithstanding clause (*CCRF*, s 33) unavailable, 50–51, 69, 86; overview, 50–54, 68–73, 80–84, 85, 110, 138–44, 146–47; political purpose to invalidate *CFL*, 50–51, 68–69, 74, 77; positive rights, 11, 68–69, 74–75, 93; provincial jurisdiction, 50, 80; rationale for research focus on Quebec, 50–51, 53, 56; rights beneficiaries, 74–75; services "where numbers warrant," 11, 68–72, 70(t)–71(t), 74–75, 78, 80, 84–85, 87, 91; special status (s 23(1)(a)), 87; text of, 70(t)–71(t), 82(t)–83(t), 85; unanimous decisions invalidating Bill 101 (*CFL*), 50–51
Monahan, Patrick, 156
Montreal: elite anglophone private schools, 122, 126, 132–36, 133(t), 334*nn*73–74; safe consumption sites, 190, 205, 213, 219, 349*n*51, 352*n*129; signs and firm names, 145, 166–68, 338*n*102, 338*nn*96–97
Moon, Richard, 150
moral issues. *See* ethical and moral issues
Morgentaler, R v (1988), 8, 13, 37, 38, 42–43, 46, 251, 284, 294, 303(t). *See also* abortion services

Morton, F.L., 7, 14, 25–26, 31–32, 41, 48, 53, 61, 68, 72, 240, 300
MPR. *See Charter of the French Language (CFL)* (1984, Bill 57), education: major part requirement (MPR)
Mulroney, Brian, Progressive Conservative government, 15, 175, 296
Multani v Commission Scolaire Marguerite-Bourgeoys (2006), 59(t), 62, 310
multiculturalism, 147
Murray, Joyce, 197

negative rights. *See* rights, negative and positive
New Brunswick: Meech Lake Accord, 157, 337*n*66; minority language services, 11; SCC invalidation by decision type, 51–52, 52(t); SCC remedial activism, 34–36, 35(t), 309(t)
New Democratic Party (NDP): election (2008), 341*n*56; MAiD, 262, 280, 283, 284, 291; opioid crisis, 349*n*60; supervised consumption sites, 177, 186, 197, 199, 214–15, 224–25
New Zealand, 25
Newman, Dwight, 341*n*65
Nguyen v Quebec (2009): allophones, 111, 122; appeals (ATQ), 111; "bridging" school vs unsubsidized school, 112–14, 137, 140; criteria for access to English education, 110–14, 121–22; framers' intent, 112–13, 138; *Gosselin* (2002), 112–13; implementation context, 59(t), 103–5, 120–21; judicial policy impact, 76–77, 103–4, 119–21, 138–41; limitations (*CCRF*, s 1), 111, 113; ministerial directive, 105–6, 119–20; MPR requirement, 105, 110–13, 121; overview, 17–18, 44(t), 59(t), 76–77, 102, 110–22, 138–41; regulations, 59(t), 120–22, 136; SCC unanimous judgment (LeBel), 59(t), 76–77, 101–3, 111–14, 121, 296; *Solski* (2005), 112–15; suspension (1 year), 59(t), 111, 114–15, 119; unsubsidized private schools, 59(t), 97, 101–5, 110–13, 119–22, 132
Nicolaides, Eleni, 249, 358*n*14
non-RFND (non-reasonable foreseeability of natural death), 282, 286, 286(f),

289–90. *See also An Act on Medical Assistance in Dying* (2021, Bill C-7)

Notley, Rachel: supervised consumption sites, 210, 233, 235–38, 240, 243, 245–46, 299, 354*n*174

notwithstanding clause (*CCRF,* s 33): blanket use, 55–56; Bourassa's use, 55–56, 145, 152–53, 156–58, 164; dialogue theory, 21; overview, 55–56, 301; signs and firm names, 56, 145, 152–53, 154(t)–155(t), 157–59, 164; unused for MAiD, 261; unused for minority language education rights, 50–51, 69, 86; weak-form judicial review, 24

notwithstanding clause (*Quebec Charter*), 56, 153

Nova Scotia: MAiD use, 289; SCC invalidation by decision type, 51–52, 52(t); SCC remedial activism, 34–36, 35(t), 309(t)

Nunavut: lack of MAiD statistics, 365*n*206

Oakes test, 113, 267, 278, 293. *See also* limitations clause (*CCRF,* s 1)

O'Connor, R v (1995), 15, 24, 266–69, 296

official languages. *See* language policy; Quebec: language policy

Official Languages Act (1969), 64, 147–48

Official Language Act (Quebec, 1974, Bill 22), 64–65, 93–94, 142, 146

Oliphant, Rob, 252

Ontario: MAiD conscience rights, 285–86, 366*n*212; McGuinty government, 231, 353*n*137; SCC invalidation by decision type, 51–52, 52(t); SCC remedial activism, 34–36, 35(t), 309(t); supervised consumption sites, 47, 190, 201, 210, 227, 229–33, 241, 347*n*21, 352*n*122; Toronto supervised consumption sites, 190, 201, 231; Wynne government, 210, 230–31, 233, 353*n*137

opioid crisis. *See* drug problem and policies: opioid crisis

OPS. *See* overdose prevention sites (OPS)

overdose prevention sites (OPS), 208–10, 215–18, 235, 246, 350*n*77

Owen, Philip, 175–76

Parti Liberal du Québec: legislative responses, 7–8. *See also* Bourassa, Robert, Quebec Liberal government; Charest, Jean, Quebec Liberal government

Parti Québécois (PQ), 7, 69, 146–47. *See also* Lévesque, René, Quebec PQ government

Pay Equity Act (Quebec), 60(t), 61–62, 311(t)

PDAM (Special Joint Committee on Physician-Assisted Dying), 19, 249, 252–53, 261–66, 276, 279–80, 291, 361*n*106

Pelletier, Benoît, 279, 360*n*86

Petter, Andrew, 30, 61

Philpott, Jane: External Panel's report (2015), 261–62; MAiD policies, 252–53, 261, 268, 279–80; supervised consumption sites, 171, 187, 206, 208, 213–15, 217–24, 222(t), 298, 349*n*59

PHS. *See* Portland Hotel Society (PHS)

PHS Community Services Society, Canada v (2011): BC Court of Appeal (2010), 170, 180–82, 198; BC Superior Court (2008), 170, 174, 178–79, 182; comparison of Bill C-2 and Bill C-37, 220–24, 222(t); dialogue theory, 186–87, 188–89, 191, 196; fundamental justice, 182–83, 191; Harper's non-compliance, 46–47, 170–72, 188–91, 196–97, 202, 209–10; implementation, 43, 45(t), 46–47, 208–11, 246–47, 298; inter-jurisdictional immunity, 178, 181–82, 187, 257–58, 340*n*48, 341*n*65; J. Trudeau's compliance, 208–11, 298; judicial policy impact, 46–47, 171, 185, 196, 204–11, 220–26, 222(t), 246–47, 298; jurisdictional structure, 43, 45(t), 46–47, 182, 298; life, liberty, and security (*CCRF,* s 7), 178–79, 181–82; ministerial discretion, 5, 36, 182–90, 197–200, 218, 224; negative rights, 38, 46–47, 171, 208, 227–28, 294, 298; overview, 43, 45(t), 46–47, 170–73, 178–79, 204–5, 298; political context, 175–81, 188–90; remedies, 170, 184–87, 226, 228; SCC judgment criteria to "generally grant" an exemption, 191, 197–98, 202, 224; SCC reading-in of ministerial guidelines, 5, 36, 47, 170, 185–88; SCC unanimous judgment, 5, 36, 45(t), 170, 181–87, 294, 296. *See also* supervised consumption sites (SCS); Vancouver, Downtown Eastside of Vancouver (DTES); Vancouver, Insite safe injection facility

physician-assisted death, 248, 255. *See also* medical assistance in dying (MAiD)

Pickerill, Mitchell, 27

policy congruence, 40. *See also* popularity of judicial decisions

policy impact. *See* judicial policy impact; research project on judicial policy impact

political parties: popularity of judicial decisions, 39; regime politics approach (RPA), 27–29; similarity of legislative responses, 7, 14–15, 300. *See also* Bloc Québécois; Conservative Party of Canada; Liberal Party of Canada; New Democratic Party (NDP); Progressive Conservative Party (PC)

political parties, Quebec. *See* Bloc Québécois; Coalition Avenir Québec (CAQ); Parti Liberal du Québec; Parti Québécois (PQ)

popularity of judicial decisions: implementation context, 22–23, 33; judicial policy impact, 12–13; lateral vs vertical issues, 33, 37, 39; majority/minority governments, 39–40, 264; McLachlin on, 185; overview, 12–13, 33, 38–40, 284; parliamentary systems, 38–40; public opinion surveys, 39. *See also* legislative responses, agreement/disagreement; salient issues

pop-up overdose prevention. *See* overdose prevention sites (OPS)

Portland Hotel Society (PHS), Vancouver, 173. *See also PHS Community Services Society, Canada v* (2011)

positive rights. *See* rights, negative and positive

PQ. *See* Parti Québécois (PQ)

Prince Edward Island: abortion services, 288; *Arsenault-Cameron* (2004), 36, 106, 310(t); SCC invalidation by decision type, 51–52, 52(t); SCC remedial activism, 34–36, 35(t), 309(t)–310(t)

Progressive Conservative Party (PC), 15, 28. *See also* Mulroney, Brian, Progressive Conservative government

prostitution. *See Bedford, Canada v* (2013)

Protestant School Boards (1984): allophones, 91–92, 94, 97–99, 98(f); anglophones, 58(t), 91–97, 92(f); comparison of CCRF (s 23) with CFL (1993), 89–91, 90(t), 101; framers' intent, 51, 88–89, 100, 138, 330n46; implementation context, 44(t), 91–95, 95(f), 100–1; judicial policy impact, 76–77, 85–89, 91–101, 138–41, 144; limitations (CCRF, s 1), 87–89; overview, 17–18, 44(t), 58(t), 72–73, 76–77, 87–91, 90(t), 99–101, 138–41, 144; Quebec Court of Appeal, 72–73, 81; Quebec Superior Court, 72–73, 81; SCC unanimous judgment, 44(t), 51, 58(t), 76–77, 87–89, 94–95, 99–100, 296; watertight federalism, 43, 144, 297

provincial and territorial governments: access to federally regulated services, 40–43; co-existence of legislative agreement/disagreement, 46–47; coordinated and voluntary compliance, 43, 46; implementation gap, 40–43, 226–27, 297–98; popularity of judicial decisions, 40; SCC invalidation and decision type, by province, 51–52, 52(t); SCC remedial activism, by province, 34–36, 35(t); sovereignty impacts of judicial review, 41; watertight federalism, 43, 144, 297–98. *See also* federalism; *and specific provinces and territories*
– drug problem and policies: harm reduction, 229–30; overview, 210, 227–30; supervised consumption sites, by province, 47, 227–30. *See also* Alberta: drug problem and policies; British Columbia: drug problem and policies; drug problem and policies; Quebec: drug problem and policies

public opinion. *See* popularity of judicial decisions

Puddister, Kate, 259

Quebec: collective identity, 147, 153; constitutional patriation, 17, 53–55, 69,

78–81, 110, 142–43, 148; election (1989), 153, 156, 158; inter-culturalism, 147–48; judicial policy impact, 50–54, 56, 89, 99–101, 138–41; *la question nationale*, 144, 146–48; Meech Lake Accord, 156–57; opioid crisis, 211; overview, 50–54, 146–48; politicization of language, 64, 146; Quiet Revolution, 61, 64, 147; rationale for research focus on, 50–51, 53, 56; referenda (1980 and 1995), 92, 147; *la survivance*, 143, 147, 335n7; as unlike other provinces, 51–54. *See also* Montreal

– anglophones: demographic declines, 77, 91–96, 92(f), 93(f), 94(f), 141, 168–69; dialogue theory, 110; elite anglophone schools in Montreal, 122, 126, 132–36, 133(t), 334nn73–74; enrollment trends, 93–96, 93(f), 94(f), 95(f); Equality Party (1989 election), 156, 158; interprovincial migration (1971–2016), 91–93, 92(f), 96; overview, 75–78, 91–97, 92(f), 100–1, 110; as private actors, 67, 76, 87, 110, 135, 295; unsubsidized private schools (UPS), 97–99, 98(f), 101, 120–22. *See also* education, Quebec: English school boards

– *Canadian Charter of Rights and Freedom. See Canadian Charter of Rights and Freedoms (CCRF)*: Quebec

– Charter. *See Charter of Human Rights and Freedoms (Quebec Charter)*

– drug problem and policies: opioid crisis, 211; supervised consumption sites, 47, 213, 219, 229, 347n21, 349n51, 352n122, 352n125. *See also* drug problem and policies

– immigration: allophones, 65–66, 91–92, 94, 97–99, 98(f), 146, 335n20; collective identity, 147; inter-culturalism, 147–48; interprovincial migration and immigration (1971–2018), 96–97, 96(f), 101; language policy, 146–48; overview, 146–48; patterns, 75. *See also* allophones

– language policy: *Blaikie* (1979), 67–68, 149; federalism, 144; French as official language, 64–65, 67, 142, 147–49; immigration dilemma, 146–47; implementation context, 53–54, 139–42, 145–48; inter-culturalism, 147–48; judicial policy impact, 148, 166–69; language as cultural identity, 150; Office québécois de la langue française, 149, 164–68, 336n35, 338n89, 338n102, 338nn96–97; *Official Language Act* (1974, Bill 22), 64–65, 93–94, 142, 146; overview, 142–43, 146–48; politicization of, 142–43, 146–48; *visage linguistique*, 145, 149–51, 164, 166–69, 335n12. *See* education, Quebec: minority language rights; minority language rights (*CCRF*): Quebec (*CCRF*, s 23); *and entries beginning with* Charter of the French Language

– legislative responses: appearance of compliance ("sleight of hand"), 54, 56, 76–77, 120–22, 143–44; dialogue theory, 61, 63–64, 143–44, 163; implementation context, 53–54; jurisdictional sovereignty (*BNA Act*, s 92), 146–47; overview, 7–8, 53–56, 57–64, 58(t)–60(t); salient issues, 57–64, 295–96; similarity of political parties, 7, 14–15; statutes and administrative decisions, 57–64, 58(t)–60(t); unpopularity of SCC decisions, 53–54, 57, 61–62, 284. *See also* notwithstanding clause (*CCRF*, s 33); *and entries beginning with* Charter of the French Language

– medical assistance in dying (MAiD): *An Act Respecting End-of-Life Care* (2014, Bill 52), 10, 251, 255, 261, 281–82, 357n4, 358n17, 361n95; public opinion, 255, 284; Select Committee on Dying with Dignity (2009), 255. *See also Carter v Canada* (2016) (*Carter II*); medical assistance in dying (MAiD); *Truchon c Procureur général du Canada* (2019)

– political parties. *See* Bloc Québécois; Coalition Avenir Québec (CAQ); Parti Liberal du Québec; Parti Québécois (PQ)

– signs and firm names. *See Charter of the French Language (CFL)* (1977, Bill 101): signs and firm names; *Charter of the French Language (CFL)* (1988, Bill 178): signs and firm names; *Charter of the French Language (CFL)* (1993, Bill 86): signs and firm names

– Supreme Court of Canada decisions: agenda setting, 46, 53–54, 57, 140, 148, 301; appearance of compliance ("sleight of hand"), 143–44; decision types in invalidation, 51–52, 52(t); invalidated statutes and administrative decisions, 57–64, 58(t)–60(t); overview, 57–61, 58(t)–60(t); remedial activism, 34–36, 35(t), 310(t)–311(t), 312n1; salient issues, 17–18, 57–64, 58(t)–60(t); statistics, 52, 52(t), 57. *See also* Supreme Court of Canada (SCC): decisions

"Quebec clause" (*CFL* s 73), 77, 81–87, 82(t)–83(t)

Quebec Protestant School Boards, A.G. (Que) v (1984). *See Protestant School Boards* (1984)

Rankin, Murray, 214, 280
reasonable foreseeability of natural death (RFND). *See An Act on Medical Assistance in Dying* (2016, Bill C-14); *An Act on Medical Assistance in Dying* (2021, Bill C-7); eligibility criteria
reasonable limits. *See* limitations clause (*CCRF*, s 1)
Referendum Act (Quebec), 52, 58(t), 62, 310(t)
regime politics approach (RPA), 27–29
remedies. *See* Supreme Court of Canada: remedies (*CCRF*, s 24(1))
reproductive choice. *See* abortion services
research project on judicial policy impact: case studies, by chapter, 43–47, 44(t)–45(t); constraints on the Court, 4–5, 21–23, 49, 144, 296; documents, 16; judicial policy impact tests, 48; key questions, 38, 75–76; lack of normative position, 300; legislative response factors, 38; overview, 16–19, 296–97; pattern of discussions, 16; rationale for Quebec focus, 50–51, 53, 56; salience of issues, 49, 296. *See also* judicial politics scholarship: theories
Respect for Communities Act (2015, Bill C-2): alternatives to legislation, 187–88, 226; Bill C-65 replaced by, 188–93, 342n89, 344n135; comparison of Bill C-2 and Bill C-37, 220–26, 222(t); delay after *PHS* (2011), 19, 172, 188–90, 225–26; dialogue theory, 186–87, 188–89, 191, 196; gross disproportionality, 191; hearings (HESA, SECU, LCJC), 179, 181, 198–204, 215, 221, 342n99, 344nn144–47; judicial policy impact, 46–47, 189, 196, 204–8, 220–27, 222(t), 246–47, 297–98; law-and-order approach, 170–71, 177–78, 198–99, 203–5; non-compliance with *PHS* (2011), 6–7, 46–47, 170–72, 188–91, 196–97, 202, 204–5; organizations in support or opposed, 200–3; political context, 170–72, 188–90, 204–5, 210–11, 342n99; overview, 6–7, 46–47, 171–72, 204–5, 218–27, 222(t), 297–98; preamble, 191, 192(f); replacement (Bill C-37), 46–47, 206–7, 214; Senate hearings, 202–3, 342n99; time frame, 225–26

– new exemptions and renewals: application criteria in *PHS* (2011), 5, 185–88, 190, 196–98, 202, 204, 220–24, 222(t); application process, 46, 193–98, 356n217; assessment principles (6), 195, 222(t), 223–24; comparison of Bill C-2 and Bill C-37, 220–24, 222(t); delay after *PHS* (2011), 19, 172, 189–90; exemption (s 56) only in "exceptional circumstances," 191, 195, 197–200, 224; Harper's opposition to, 6–7, 187–91; incomplete applications under Harper, 195–97, 199, 201; incomplete applications under J. Trudeau, 208, 213, 222(t), 223; J. Trudeau's approvals, 208, 213–14; lack of approvals, 172, 204–5, 219; lack of transparency, 195–96, 199–201, 219, 222(t), 224; ministerial discretion under Harper, 5, 182–91, 197–201, 218; ministerial discretion under J. Trudeau, 213–14; obstacles to approvals, 46–47, 190–91, 200–5, 214, 219; overview, 6–7, 46–47, 172, 187–98, 204–5, 219, 220–24, 222(t); police background checks, 201, 220, 221, 242; public consultations, 193–97, 199, 201, 221; renewals, 194–95, 200, 213, 224; time frame, 172, 196, 219

RFND. *See* reasonable foreseeability of natural death (RFND)

Richez, Emmanuelle, 84, 86–87, 324*n*18, 330*n*41
rights, charters of. *See Canadian Bill of Rights; Canadian Charter of Rights and Freedoms (CCRF); Charter of Human Rights and Freedoms (Quebec Charter)*
rights, negative and positive: case studies, by chapter, 43–47, 44(t)–45(t); *CCRF* as largely negative rights, 11–12, 46, 68, 145–46; implementation context overview, 43–47, 44(t)–45(t); judicial policy impact, 4–5, 208, 250, 294; negative rights as prohibition on interference, 11–12, 38, 46, 68, 294, 298; negative rights of Quebec sign laws, 145–46; overview, 11–12, 38, 68, 74–75, 294, 298; positive rights as access to services, 11–12, 38; positive rights of minority language education, 11, 68–69, 72–75, 93, 109
RJR-Macdonald Inc. v Canada (1995), 29, 305(t)
Roach, Kent, 10, 24, 27–28, 34–35, 64, 120, 157–58, 185, 196, 208
Rodriguez, Sue, 253, 290
Rodriguez v British Columbia (1993): approaches in other democracies, 254–55; case on one person, 275; *CC* (s 241(b)), 253–54, 258; decriminalizing euthanasia, 359*n*31; foreseeable death, 290; life, liberty, and security (*CCRF*, s 7), 253–54, 258; limitations (*CCRF*, s 1), 254; overview, 253–59; as precedent for *Carter*, 256–59; SCC narrow judgment, 248, 253–54, 257
Rosenberg, Gerald, 32–33
Russell, Peter H., 14, 55, 157
Ryan, Claude, 158

safe injection sites. *See* supervised consumption sites (SCS); Vancouver, Insite safe injection facility
salient issues: case studies, by chapter, 43–47, 44(t)–45(t); compliance on minor issues, 57–58, 295–96; dialogue theory, 61, 63–64, 295–96; implementation context, 12–13, 43–47, 44(t)–45(t), 57; judicial policy impact, 48–49; legislative disagreement with courts, 12–13; overview, 12–14, 48–49, 57–58, 295–96; popularity of decision, 12–13, 22–23, 57; Quebec overview, 17–18, 57–64, 58(t)–60(t); strong-form responses to strong-form judicial review, 12–13, 24, 296, 301. *See also* popularity of judicial decisions
Santé Montréal, 190, 205, 352*n*129
Saskatchewan: Meech Lake Accord, 156; SCC invalidation by decision type, 51–52, 52(t); SCC remedial activism, 34–36, 35(t), 311(t); supervised consumption sites, 47, 227, 347*n*21
SCC. *See* Supreme Court of Canada (SCC)
Schultz, Richard, 209
SCS. *See* supervised consumption sites (SCS)
Seaboyer, R v (1991), 24, 296, 304
"second look cases," 30, 48, 248, 357*n*3
SECU. *See* Standing Committee on Public Safety and National Security (SECU)
security of person. *See* life, liberty, and security of person (*CCRF*, s 7)
Senate: Harper's reference (2014), 330*n*46; Independent Senate Group, 225; J. Trudeau's reforms, 40; judicial policy impact, 40, 252–53; LCJC hearings, 202–4, 221, 267, 271, 279, 342*n*99; MAiD requirement for RFND, 9, 252–53, 271–76, 278, 291, 363*n*140, 364*n*176; supervised injection sites, 202–3, 221, 224–25, 342*n*99, 351*n*110
sex work. *See Bedford, Canada v* (2013)
sexual orientation: equality rights (*CCRF*, s 15), 36; same-sex marriage, 40–41, 352*n*118; *Vriend* (1998), 36, 302(t)
Sharpe, Robert, 157–58
significance of policies. *See* salient issues
signs and firm names. *See Charter of the French Language (CFL)* (1977, Bill 101): signs and firm names; *Charter of the French Language (CFL)* (1988, Bill 178): signs and firm names; *Charter of the French Language (CFL)* (1993, Bill 86): signs and firm names
Smith, Adrienne, 202

Smith, Danielle, 230, 234, 245–46, 353n133
Snow, Dave, 259
Solski v Quebec (2005): administrative appeals (ATQ), 105, 106; *Arsenault-Cameron* (2004), 36, 106, 310(t); certificates of eligibility, 106–9, 109(f); dialogue theory, 110; implementation context, 59(t), 103–5, 108–9, 120–21; judicial policy impact, 76–77, 103–4, 108–10, 119–21, 138–41; legislative response, 56, 59(t), 73, 76–77, 115, 120–22; ministerial directive, 36, 59(t), 102, 105–10, 109(f), 119–20, 332n15; MPR requirement, 59(t), 105–10, 332n17, 332n28, 332n35; overview, 17–18, 44(t), 59(t), 73, 76–77, 105–10, 109(f), 120–22, 138–41; positive rights, 109; regulations, 59(t), 120–22, 139; SCC reading in of MPR test, 36, 107–10; SCC unanimous judgment, 44(t), 59(t), 76–77, 101–3, 106–10, 128, 296; unsubsidized private schools, 59(t), 101–5, 106–10, 119–22, 128
Special Joint Committee on Physician-Assisted Dying (PDAM), 19, 249, 252–53, 261–66, 276, 279–80, 291, 361n106
Stabile, Mark, 227–28
Standing Committee on Health (HESA), 179, 181, 198–99, 214–17
Standing Committee on Justice and Human Rights (JUST), 252–53, 267, 270–71, 273–74, 279–80, 291
Standing Committee on Public Safety and National Security (SECU), 198–202
Standing Senate Committee on Legal and Constitutional Affairs (LCJC), 202–4, 221, 267, 271, 279, 342n99
Stewart, Hamish, 263, 360n77
strong-form vs weak-form judicial review, 23–25, 185, 190, 296, 301
supervised consumption sites (SCS): availability by province, 47, 227, 347n15, 347n21; community activism, 173–78, 214–15, 349n57; concurrent federalism, 297–98; definition by Health Canada, 216; dialogue theory, 186–87, 188–89, 191, 196; Harper's disagreement with *PHS* (2011), 46–47, 172, 204–5, 209–10; health benefits, 223; identity documents, 244–45; judicial policy impact, 46–47, 185, 196, 204–11, 220–28, 222(t), 246–47; medical-quality heroin, 213; mobile and fixed units, 352n122; negative rights, 38, 46–47, 171, 208, 227–28, 284, 294, 298; as non-core health services, 228–29, 247; overview, 45(t), 46–47, 170–73, 204–11, 216–18; police background checks, 201, 220, 221, 242; political context, 210–11; private actors, 295; urban centres, 204, 228; variation in operation, 46–47, 171, 209, 247. *See also* Harper, Stephen: supervised consumption sites; *PHS Community Services Society, Canada v* (2011); Trudeau, Justin: supervised consumption sites; Vancouver, Insite safe injection facility
– implementation context: coordinated and voluntary, 43, 45(t), 46–47, 209; federal/provincial jurisdiction, 171, 209–11, 226–29, 246–47; implementation context, 13, 46–47, 171, 294; implementation gap, 41–42, 226–27, 229, 297–98; implementation spectrum, 250; negative rights, 46–47, 208, 227–28, 298; overview, 208–11, 216, 228–33, 246–47, 297–98; provincial jurisdiction for operation, 171; statistics on, 209, 210, 231, 246–47, 298, 347n11, 347n21
Supreme Court of Canada (SCC): agenda setting, 22, 53, 140, 251–52, 291, 301; appointment processes, 27, 54–55; court party thesis, 25–26, 31–32, 48; delay as defiance, 188–90, 226; fundamental justice, 182–83, 254, 256–58; implementer-dependent institution, 17, 21–23, 31–36, 48–49, 56, 63–64, 251, 301; lateral vs vertical issues, 33, 37, 39, 293; overview, 3–10, 31–36, 296; as powerful court, 5–6, 20–21, 26; precedents, 257; reference cases, 66–67; remedial activism, 34–36, 312n1; remedial activism, cases, 302(t)–311(t), 312n1; "second look cases," 30, 48, 248, 357n3; tests, 293. *See also* judicial policy impact

– decisions: A. Hamilton on implementation, 21, 32–33, 301; compliance, 15–17; dialogue theory, 48–49, 63–64; divided decisions, 15, 51–52; lateral vs vertical issues, 33, 37, 39, 293; legislative responses to types, 52; majority decisions, 51–52; minority decisions, 15–16; statistics, 34–35, 35(t), 51–52, 52(t), 323*n*9; types of decisions, 51–52, 52(t); unanimous single or concurring opinions, 15–16, 51–52, 296. *See also* implementation context; judicial policy impact; Quebec, Supreme Court of Canada decisions; Supreme Court of Canada: remedies (*CCRF*, s 24(1))

– remedies (*CCRF*, s 24(1)): amendment and reading-in, 16, 34–36, 35(t), 302(t)–311(t); appearance of compliance ("sleight of hand"), 143–44; by decision type, 51–52, 52(t); dual remedy (s 23(3) and s 24(1)), 69, 72; interpretation as expansive, 5–6; invalidation, 34–36, 35(t), 302(t)–311(t); invalidation by decision type, 51–52, 52(t); ministerial discretion, 36; negative and positive rights overview, 11–12, 38, 68, 74–75, 298; *Ontario v G.* (2020), 321*n*81; overview, 5–7, 24, 33–38, 35(t), 60(t); remedial activism, 34–36, 35(t), 312*n*1; remedial activism, cases, 302(t)–311(t), 312*n*1; statistics, 34–36, 35(t); strong-form vs weak-form judicial review, 23–25, 185, 190, 296, 301; suspended declarations, 34–36, 35(t), 310(t)–311(t). *See also* rights, negative and positive

Taylor, Gloria, 255–56, 258, 275, 290
theory. *See* judicial politics scholarship: theories
Thériault, Luc, 277
Thibault, Corporation Professionnelle des medecins du Quebec v (1988), 58(t), 61, 310(t)
Thornton, Alison A. Bushell, 21, 25, 29–31, 35, 63, 120, 295
Tobacco Product Control Act, 29, 305(t)
Truchon c Procureur général du Canada (2019): appeals process not used, 10, 249, 267, 282; *CC* (s 241.2), 10, 265; dialogue theory, 249; judicial policy impact, 10, 249, 290–92; legislative response, 249, 275; life, liberty, and security (*CCRF*, s 7), 10, 265, 281–82; limitations (*CCRF*, s 1), 10, 267, 282; negative rights, 291–92; overview, 10–11, 281–84, 289–92; political context, 282–84; popularity of decision, 284, 291, 365*n*201; Quebec Superior Court, 10, 248, 265, 267; "second look case," 30, 48, 248, 357*n*3; suspension and extensions, 10, 282

Trudeau, Justin, Liberal government: election (2015), majority, 164, 206, 249, 267, 291; election (2019), minority, 282–84; "evidence-based policy," 211, 214, 348*n*25; health ministers, 352*n*126; majority/minority governments and vote share (1984–2021), 39–40, 322*n*108; mandate letter on Charter compliance, 8–9, 206–7; Senate appointment reform, 40; whipped votes, 8–9

– medical assistance in dying (MAiD): appeals process not used, 10, 249, 267; compliance with *Truchon*, 149–50, 290–92; dialogue theory, 249–50, 267–68, 276, 357*n*6, 361*n*106; election (2015), majority, 291; election (2019), minority, 282–84; judicial policy impact, 8–10, 250–52, 290–92, 299–300; Lametti as minister, 275, 282–84; non-compliance with *Carter*, 263–70, 290–92, 358*n*14; overview, 8–10, 248–50, 290–92, 299–300; PDAM hearings, 19, 249, 252–53, 261–66, 276, 279–80, 291, 361*n*106; Philpott as minister, 252–53, 261, 268, 279–80; Wilson-Raybould as minister, 252–53, 263–70, 273–78, 282–83, 289–90, 361*n*106. *See also An Act on Medical Assistance in Dying* (2016, Bill C-14); *An Act on Medical Assistance in Dying* (2021, Bill C-7); medical assistance in dying (MAiD)

– supervised consumption sites: community activism, 214–15; complex intergovernmental problems, 210–14, 217, 348*n*24; coordinated federalism,

209–11, 246–47, 297–98; drugs and substance strategy, 218; exemption approvals, 187, 208, 213–14, 356*n*203; harm reduction, 171, 208, 210, 215, 217–18; judicial policy impact, 208–11, 220–24, 222(t), 246–47, 298; legislative response, 225–26; mandate letter on Charter compliance, 8–9, 206–7, 346*n*4; overdose prevention sites (OPS), 208–10, 215–18, 246, 350*n*77; overview, 46–47, 206–11, 298; Philpott as minister, 171, 187, 206, 208, 213–14, 217–19, 298, 349*n*59; *PHS* (2011) compliance, 208–11, 298; statistics, 227, 246–47, 347*n*11. *See also An Act to Amend the CDSA* (2017, Bill C-37); supervised consumption sites (SCS)

Trudeau, Pierre, Liberal government: bilingual vision, 64–65, 147–48; constitutional patriation, 17, 53–55, 69, 79–81, 87, 100, 148; Court Challenges Program (CCP), 26, 67–68, 87; Meech Lake, 87, 143, 156; *Official Languages Act* (1969), 64, 147–48; opposition to CFL, 66–72, 99–100, 142–43, 147–48; overview, 64–73, 99–101

Tsebelis, George, 40

Tuohy, Carolyn, 227–28

Tushnet, Mark, 10, 23–25

UCP. *See* United Conservative Party (UCP)

United Conservative Party (UCP). *See* Kenney, Jason, Alberta UCP government

United Kingdom: bills of rights, 25, 40; judicial policy impact, 25, 31–32, 40

United States: bipartisanship, 29; A. Hamilton on implementation context, 21, 32–33, 301; judicial policy impact, 32, 37, 39–40, 227–28; MAiD approaches, 254–55; popularity of judicial decisions, 39–40; regime politics approach (RPA), 28–29; "safeguarding federalism" response to judicial decisions, 41; strong-form judicial review, 24, 29

unpopular decisions. *See* popularity of judicial decisions

Vancouver, Downtown Eastside of Vancouver (DTES): demographics, 173, 174; Dr. Peter Centre supervised injection site, 190, 204–5, 213; drug policy consensus, 175–77, 181; Non-Partisan Association (NPA), 175–77; opioid crisis, 211–15; OPS (overdose prevention sites), 215–18; overview, 173–77. *See also PHS Community Services Society, Canada v* (2011)

Vancouver, Insite safe injection facility: collaborative federalism, 176–77; community activism, 173–78, 214–15; EAC report, 178, 183, 238; harm reduction, 174–76, 179, 181; Harper's opposition to, 5, 179–80, 187–88, 194–95; J. Trudeau's support, 213–14; overview, 5, 174–79, 215–16; political context, 175–81, 187–88; research studies, 176. *See also PHS Community Services Society, Canada v* (2011)

– exemptions for *CDSA*: first exemption (2003), 176–77, 215; Harper's exemptions, 5, 174, 177–78, 179–80, 187–88, 194–95, 342*n*95; J. Trudeau's exemptions, 187, 213; judicial decisions, 5, 45(t), 170, 178–80, 182–88; judicial remedies, 184–87; overview, 187–88, 222(t)

Vancouver Area Network of Drug Users (VANDU), 174, 215

Vancouver Coastal Health Authority (VCHA), 175–76, 178, 183

Vancouver Police Department (VPD), 172, 176–77, 211

VANDU. *See* Vancouver Area Network of Drug Users (VANDU)

VCHA. *See* Vancouver Coastal Health Authority (VCHA)

vertical vs lateral issues, 33, 37, 39

VPD. *See* Vancouver Police Department (VPD)

Warawa, Mark, 265–66

weak-form vs strong-form judicial review, 23–25, 185, 190, 296, 301

Weinrib, Lorraine, 31

White, Linda, 18, 22–23, 37, 40–43, 226–27, 229, 281, 297–98, 352*n*118
Wilson-Raybould, Jody: expulsion from caucus, 283–84; External Panel's report (2015), 261–62; MAiD (Bill C-14), 252–53, 263–70, 273–78, 282–83, 289–90, 361*n*106; mandate letter on Charter, 8–9, 206–7

Woerhling, Jose, 120
Worcester v Georgia (1832, US), 13, 205
Wright, Wade K., 29–31
Wynne, Kathleen, Ontario Liberal government, 210, 230–31, 233, 353*n*137

Yukon: supervised consumption sites, 227, 229, 352*n*125

Printed and bound in Canada by Friesens

Set in Myriad and Sabon by Artegraphica Design Co. Ltd.

Copy editor: Stacy Belden

Proofreader: Sophie Pouyanne

Indexer: Judy Dunlop

Cover designer: Setareh Ashrafologhalai

Cover images: "The Peace Tower of Parliament Hill is seen past the Statue of Justice at the Supreme Court of Canada in Ottawa," November 14, 2019. The Canadian Press/Sean Kilpatrick